IDEOLOGY AND POWER IN THE MIDDLE EAST

■

IDEOLOGY AND POWER IN THE MIDDLE EAST

Studies in Honor of George Lenczowski

■

Edited by Peter J. Chelkowski
and Robert J. Pranger

■

Duke University Press
Durham and London 1988

Printed in the United States of America
on acid-free paper ∞

Library of Congress Cataloging-in-Publication Data
Ideology and power in the Middle East.
Studies in honor of George Lenczowski.
Bibliography: p.
Includes index.
1. Middle East—Politics and government—1945–
2. Lenczowski, George. I. Chelkowski, Peter J.
II. Pranger, Robert J. III. Lenczowski, George.
DS63.1.I28 1988 956′.04 87–30371
ISBN 0–8223–0781–2
ISBN 0–8223–0788–X (pbk.)

CONTENTS

■

FOREWORD

■

David Pierpont Gardner

The Middle East is one of the most fascinating areas on the globe, the focus of many of the world's greatest hopes and deepest fears. It is an area whose variety and complexity demand first-rate scholarship, and fortunately George Lenczowski has been contributing such scholarship for some forty years. The quality and scope of his contributions to a better understanding of the Middle East, and particularly a better understanding of its international relations, its revolutions, and the crucial role of oil, have earned him the compliment of this volume of essays by leading scholars in the field from the United States, Canada, Europe, and the Middle East.

I first made Professor Lenczowski's acquaintance more than twenty-five years ago at the University of California's Berkeley campus. Already the author of the first major work on Middle Eastern politics, he organized and served as the first chairman of Berkeley's Committee on Middle Eastern Studies during the 1960s and labored diligently to expand the university's offerings in that critical field of study. Over the years my admiration has grown for the skill, intelligence, and effective commitment he brings to every endeavor he undertakes—and his energy is as considerable as his talents. Teacher, scholar, consultant, author—to each of these roles he has brought remarkable gifts that have made him internationally recognized and respected. I am delighted to add my voice to those of his colleagues and admirers who have assembled this volume in the belief that his forty years of accomplishment merit this extraordinary tribute.

David Pierpont Gardner
President
University of California

PREFACE

■

To a colleague whose career in various professional capacities has been directed by his commitment to the contemporary Middle East, it seems fitting to pay tribute with a volume similarly dedicated. Thus, the following work is not a *Festschrift* in the traditional sense of what the French call a *mélange*, an often eclectic pastiche of articles loosely bound by a general subject heading. We present, rather, a collection of studies unified by the theme "ideology and power." Just as George Lenczowski has devoted his life to the Middle East by way of many professional roads—as scholar, writer, educator, and consultant to the federal government and U.S. corporations—so this book concerns itself with the many manifestations of this theme in the dynamics of contemporary Middle Eastern politics.

George Lenczowski's forty years of productive scholarship have witnessed the adoption of many of his writings by both academic and nonacademic institutions in the United States and overseas as standard works. Many of his students hold important positions both at home and overseas in academia, business, and government. Several of the contributors to this volume were themselves students of Lenczowski's. It is a credit to him that they perpetuate his legacy of dedication and energy through their active participation in research on Middle Eastern affairs.

The transliteration of Middle Eastern names and terms has been a nightmare for all associated with the field since the advent of Western interest in it. Obtaining consistency in the chapters written by twenty individuals has hardly left us dreaming about sugarplum fairies either. The editors have tried to employ those transliterations most commonly used in the leading American newspapers and in *Webster's New Collegiate Dictionary,* not because these publications offer the most profound and erudite system but because they represent common and contemporary parlance. So, for example, we use Shiite instead of Shi'i or Shi'ia; Hussein instead of Hoseyn or Husayn; Koran instead of Qur'an; and sheikh instead of shaykh. The exception is made in the chapters dealing with Islam and the state: the nature of these chapters calls for a careful transliteration of certain terms and derivates. In the ensuing chapters we have retained the transliterations preferred by individual authors for names of infrequently mentioned political figures and institutions and the titles of Arabic publications and their authors.

This publication has been made possible thanks to the generosity of Exxon, Mobil, the Foundation for Iranian Studies, and S. D. Bechtel and AI International Corporation.

We would like to thank John O'Malley and Lee Radovich for their comments. Special thanks are extended to Jennifer Thayer for her help in the final stages of editing and assembling the manuscript.

Peter J. Chelkowski
Robert J. Pranger

THE LIFE AND WORK OF GEORGE LENCZOWSKI

■

Peter J. Chelkowski

George Lenczowski was born in 1915 in St. Petersburg, Russia, of Polish parents. His landowning family, with traditions of military and church service in Poland, traces its origins back to 1343.

His formative years were spent in independent Poland between the two world wars in an atmosphere of dedication to public service. He attended an eminent secondary school, the Adam Mickiewicz Gimnazium in Warsaw. His university studies centered on law and political science. Having received an LL.M. degree from the University of Warsaw and a diploma in civil law from the University of Paris, he studied for his doctorate under Professors Jean-Pierre Niboyet and Henri Mazeaud in France. In 1937 he obtained a J.S.D. degree from the University of Lille. The subject of his dissertation, published in Paris in 1938, was contracts in private international law.

During his university days he cofounded a literary society, Club S, and served as secretary-general and, later, delegate for France of the Polish Students' Association for International Cooperation, "Liga." Fluent in German, he was also the chief spokesman for the Polish students' delegation that toured German university centers in 1935. He traveled extensively in Western Europe and the Balkan and Danubian countries.

George Lenczowski's goal was to combine an academic career with foreign service. Early in 1938 he was appointed to the Polish

Foreign Service, and his first assignment was in British-mandated Palestine. After twenty months there, on September 1, 1939, he was transferred to the Polish Ministry of Foreign Affairs in Warsaw, just as World War II was breaking out. Leaving Poland again on the day of the Soviet invasion, September 17, he returned to the Middle East, where he joined the Polish Carpathian Brigade, established within the British Middle East Command. He participated in the Libyan campaign, including the defense of Tobruk (1941–42), and, following officer-candidate training in Alexandria, Egypt, and Gaza, Palestine, rose in rank from private to second lieutenant.

In November 1942, while stationed in the Kirkuk-Mosul region of Iraq, he was called back into the Polish Foreign Service and appointed press attaché at the Polish Embassy in Tehran, Iran, where he served for three years. It was in Iran that he met his future wife, who, following a forced sojourn in Soviet Russia, was employed by the Polish London government's Labor and Welfare Office in Tehran. They were married in 1943. In 1945, following the Yalta agreement, the Lenczowskis decided they would not serve the new communist government in Poland and left for the United States, becoming citizens in 1951.

George Lenczowski's academic career in the United States began with his appointment in 1945 as research fellow at the School of Advanced Studies (SAIS, later Johns Hopkins-affiliated) in Washington, D.C. Between 1946 and 1952 he taught at Hamilton College in Clinton, New York, advancing from instructor to associate professor. It was there that he wrote his first two books on the Middle East: *Russia and the West in Iran* (1949) and *The Middle East in World Affairs* (1952). In 1952 he began his long association with the University of California at Berkeley, first as associate professor, then advancing to full professorship. In the mid-sixties he served as vice-chairman of the political science department there, and as chairman of the committee on Middle Eastern studies on the Berkeley campus.

While teaching at Berkeley, he also received various visiting academic appointments, including one at St. Antony's College, Oxford, in 1958 and one at the University of Michigan, Ann Arbor, in the sixties. He frequently gave guest lectures at both American and foreign universities, in Tehran, Baghdad, Beirut, London,

Jerusalem, Geneva, and Toronto, and read numerous papers at international scholarly meetings, from the Orientalistic Congress in New Delhi to political science and energy conferences in Libyan Tripoli, Geneva, Turin, Oxford, Toronto, and Bellagio.

During his three decades at Berkeley, Lenczowski also published extensively—books, contributions to anthologies, articles. His standard work, *The Middle East in World Affairs*, went through four editions and was translated into Arabic, Persian, and Chinese. *Oil and State in the Middle East* (1960) was also published in Arabic and Persian.

In addition to his academic work Lenczowski performed consultative services for various governmental and private institutions, among them the National War College, the Army War College, the National Security Council, the U.S. Information Agency, the Chase Manhattan Bank, Radio Free Europe, and corporations in the oil and steel industries. In the fifties he was awarded a research fellowship from the Ford Foundation, and in the sixties one from the Rockefeller Foundation.

Between 1968 and 1975 Lenczowski served as director of the Middle East Research Project of the American Enterprise Institute for Public Policy Research (AEI) in Washington, D.C. In this capacity he supervised the publication of eleven studies in a series entitled "U.S. Interests in the Middle East." In 1975 he was appointed senior research fellow and chairman of the Middle East Committee at the Hoover Institution.

Over the years Lenczowski has also served on various academic and educational boards, including the board of governors of the Middle East Institute in Washington, D.C.; the governing board of the American Research Institute in Turkey; the board of trustees of the College Preparatory School at Berkeley; the academic advisory board of the American Enterprise Institute; the advisory council of the Lawrence Hall of Science at Berkeley; and the editorial boards of the *Journal of Politics* and the *Western Political Quarterly*. He was also coeditor of the University of California publications in political science.

Both his academic pursuits and his consultative services have necessitated much travel. From 1955 he has spent six to ten weeks a year overseas, invariably in the Middle East and in Europe, with research-oriented visits to Egypt, Saudi Arabia, the Gulf states,

Iran, Iraq, Syria, Lebanon, Jordan, Israel, Libya, Morocco, Germany, Switzerland, France, Italy, and England. Many of Lenczowski's students have attained high positions in governmental, academic, or business fields. These include American ambassadorships in Caracas and Damascus, an assistant secretaryship of state, a university presidency in Tehran, two cabinet memberships in Iraq, ambassadorial and deputy foreign minister's positions in Saudi Arabia, and chairmanships of major corporations in the United States, Kuwait, and Saudi Arabia.

The Lenczowskis have two sons: John, a foreign policy specialist, and Hubert, an attorney, both born in the United States.

A BIBLIOGRAPHY OF THE PUBLICATIONS AND LECTURES OF GEORGE LENCZOWSKI

■

Peter J. Chelkowski

Books and Monographs

Contribution à l'étude des obligations contractuelles en droit international privé. Paris: Domat-Montchrestien, 1938. 152 pp.

Russia and the West in Iran, 1918–1948: A Study in Big-Power Rivalry. Ithaca, N.Y.: Cornell University Press, 1949. 383 pp. Reprint. New York: Greenwood Press, 1968.

The Middle East in World Affairs. Ithaca, N.Y.: Cornell University Press, 1952. 479 pp.

Supplement to Russia and the West in Iran. Ithaca, N.Y.: Cornell University Press, 1954. 44 pp.

The Middle East in World Affairs. 2d ed., rev. and enlarged. Ithaca, N.Y.: Cornell University Press, 1956. 576 pp.

Tarikh Khavar Mianeh. Persian translation of *The Middle East in World Affairs.* Tehran: Eqbal, 1958. Sponsored by Franklin Publications, Inc., New York.

Oil and State in the Middle East. Ithaca, N.Y.: Cornell University Press, 1960. 379 pp.

Naft ve Daulat dar Khavar Mianeh. Persian translation of *Oil and State in the Middle East.* Tehran: Eqbal, n.d. Sponsored by Franklin Publications, Inc., New York.

Al-Petrol wa'l Daulah fi'l Sharq al-Awsat. Arabic translation of *Oil and State in the Middle East.* Beirut: Al-Maktab al-Tijari li'l Taba'ah wa'l Tauzi' wa'l Nashr, 1961.

The Middle East in World Affairs. 3d ed. Ithaca, N.Y.: Cornell University Press, 1962. 723 pp.

Al-Sharq al-Awsat fi'l Shu'un al-Alamiyah. 2 vols. Arabic translation of *The Middle East in World Affairs*. Vol. 1, Baghdad: Dar al-Kashaf, 1962; vol. 2, Baghdad: Dar al-Mutanabbi, 1965. Sponsored by Franklin Publications, Inc., New York.

Shih-chieh chü-shih chung-chih chung-tung. 2 vols. Chinese translation of *The Middle East in World Affairs*. Translated by Wang Chao-Ch'üan. Taipei: Commercial Press, 1970. Sponsored by Dr. Sun Yat-Sen Foundation.

Soviet Advances in the Middle East. Washington, D.C.: American Enterprise Institute, 1971. 176 pp.

Middle East Oil in a Revolutionary Age. Washington, D.C.: American Enterprise Institute, 1976. 36 pp.

The Middle East in World Affairs. 4th ed. Ithaca, N.Y.: Cornell University Press, 1980. 862 pp.

Books Edited

United States Interests in the Middle East. Washington, D.C.: American Enterprise Institute, 1968. 129 pp.

The Political Awakening in the Middle East. Englewood Cliffs, N.J.: Prentice-Hall, 1970. 180 pp.

Political Elites in the Middle East. Washington, D.C.: American Enterprise Institute, 1975. 227 pp.

Iran under the Pahlavis. Stanford, Calif.: Hoover Institution Press, 1978. 550 pp.

Contributions to Collective Works

"Political Institutions," in Ruth N. Anshen, ed., *Mid-East: World Center*. New York: Harper, 1956.

"The Objects and Methods of Nasserism," in J. H. Thompson and R. D. Reischauer, eds., *Modernization of the Arab World*. Princeton: Van Nostrand, 1966.

"Democracy, Development, and Political Integration in the Arab World: A Search for a Comprehensive Formula," in Carl Leiden, ed., *The Conflict of Traditionalism and Modernism in the Muslim Middle East*. Austin: University of Texas Press, 1966.

"Conditions and Prospects for Tranquility in the Middle East," in

G. Lenczowski, ed., *United States Interests in the Middle East*. Washington, D.C.: American Enterprise Institute, 1968.
"Evolution of American Policy in the Middle East," in Paul Seabury and Aaron Wildavsky, eds., *U.S. Foreign Policy: Perspectives and Proposals for the 1970s*. New York: McGraw-Hill, 1969.
"The Arab Cold War," in Willard A. Beling, ed., *The Middle East: Quest for an American Policy*. Albany: State University of New York Press, 1973.
"The Politics of World Oil," in Edward J. Mitchell, ed., *Dialogue on World Oil*. Washington, D.C.: American Enterprise Institute, 1974.
"The Middle East: Politics and the Energy Crisis," in John Duke Anthony, ed., *The Middle East: Oil, Politics, and Development*. Washington, D.C.: American Enterprise Institute, 1975.
"Socialism in Syria," in Helen Desfosses and Jacques Levesque, eds., *Socialism in the Third World*. New York: Praeger, 1975.
"The Oil Producing Countries," in Raymond Vernon, ed., *The Oil Crisis*. New York: Norton, 1976.
"U.S. Policy towards Iran," in Abbas Amirie and Hamilton A. Twitchell, eds., *Iran in the 1980s*. Tehran: Institute for International Political and Economic Studies, 1978. Sponsored by Stanford Research Institute, SRI International.
"From Assertion of Independence to the White Revolution" and "Political Process and Institutions in Iran: The Second Pahlavi Kingship," in G. Lenczowski, ed., *Iran under the Pahlavis*. Stanford, Calif.: Hoover Institution Press, 1978.
"The Arc of Crisis: Its Central Sector," in Waris Shere, ed., *In Search of Peace*. Hauppauge, N.Y.: Exposition Press, 1980.
"The Middle East: Local Constraints on U.S. Policy Options," in *The 1980s: Decade of Confrontation*. Proceedings of the Eighth National Security Affairs Conference, 1981. Washington, D.C.: National Defense University Press, 1981.
"New Dimensions of Big-Power Rivalry in the Middle East," in Carl F. Pinkele and Adamantia Pollis, eds., *The Contemporary Mediterranean World*. New York: Praeger, 1983.
"U.S. Policy in the Middle East: Problems and Prospects," in Dennis Bark, ed., *To Promote Peace: U.S. Foreign Policy in the Mid-1980s*. Stanford, Calif.: Hoover Institution Press, 1984.

"Preface," in John Amos, Robert Darius, and Ralph Magnus, eds., *Gulf Security into the 1980s: Perceptual and Strategic Dimensions*. Stanford, Calif: Hoover Institution Press, 1984.

"Foreign Powers' Intervention in Iran during World War I," in Edmund Bosworth and Carole Hillenbrand, eds., *Qajar Iran, 1800–1925: Political, Social, and Cultural Change*. In honor of Professor L. P. Elwell-Sutton. Edinburgh: University of Edinburgh Press, 1984.

Articles, Book Reviews, Interviews

"The Communist Movement in Iran." *Middle East Journal* 1, no. 1 (January 1947).

Review: *Zeitenwende in Iran*, by Wipert Von Blucher. *Middle East Journal* 4, no. 4 (October 1950).

Review: *The Persian Corridor and Aid to Russia*, by T. H. Vail Motter. *Middle East Journal* 6, no. 4 (Autumn 1952).

"Iran's Deepening Crisis." *Current History*, April 1953.

Review: *Fleckender Halbmond: Hintergrund der Islamischen Unruhe*, by Friedrich Wilhelm Fernau. *Middle East Journal* 8, no. 1 (Winter 1954).

Review: *Frühot in Iran*, by Schulze-Holthus. *Middle East Journal* 8, no. 1 (Winter 1954).

"Soviet Policy in the Middle East: A Summary of Developments since 1945." *Journal of International Affairs* 8, no. 1 (1954).

"Literature on the Clandestine Activities of the Great Powers in the Middle East." *Middle East Journal* 8, no. 2 (Spring 1954).

Review: *The Middle East: Problem Area in World Politics*, by Halford L. Hoskins (1954). *American Political Science Review* 49, no. 1 (March 1955).

Review: *Oil Diplomacy: Powderkeg in Iran*, by Nasrollah Saifpour Fatemi. *Middle East Journal* 9, no. 1 (Winter 1955).

Review: *The Middle East, Oil, and the Great Powers*, by Benjamin Shwadran. *Middle East Journal* 10, no. 2 (Spring 1956).

"Middle East in Crisis." *California Monthly* 67, no. 8 (April 1957).

Review: *Die Sowietunion und Iran*, by Dietrich Geyer, and *U.S.-Persian Diplomatic Relations, 1883–1921*, by Abraham Yeselson. *Middle East Journal* 11, no. 2 (Spring 1957).

"Evolution of Soviet Policy toward the Middle East." *Journal of Politics* 20, no. 1 (February 1958).
Review: *Tensions in the Middle East*, edited by Ph. W. Thayer (1958). *American Political Science Review*, March 1959.
Review: *The Near East: A Modern History*, by William Yale. *Middle East Journal* 13, no. 4 (Autumn 1959).
"The Social Cost of Middle East Economic Progress." Interview with George Lenczowski. *Land Reborn* 11, no. 1 (April–May 1960).
"Oil in the Middle East." *Current History*, May 1960.
Review: *Arab Oil: A Plan for the Future*, by Ashraf Lutfi. *Middle East Journal* 15, no. 4 (Autumn 1961).
"Syria: A Crisis in Arab Unity." *Current History*, May 1962.
"The Objects and Methods of Nasserism." *Journal of International Affairs* 19, no. 1 (1965).
"Iraq: Seven Years of Revolution." *Current History*, May 1965.
"Changing Patterns of Political Organization in the Twentieth-Century Middle East." *Western Political Quarterly* 18, no. 3 (September 1965).
"Radical Regimes in Egypt, Syria, and Iraq: Some Comparative Observations on Ideologies and Practices." *Journal of Politics* 28, no. 1 (1966).
"Democracy, Development, and Political Integration in the Arab World: A Search for a Comprehensive Formula." *The Texas Quarterly* 9, no. 2 (Summer 1966).
"United Arab Republic." *The 1966 World Book.*
Review: *The Ideological Revolution in the Middle East*, by Leonard Binder (1966) and *The League of Arab States*, by Robert W. Macdonald (1965). *American Political Science Review* 60, no. 3 (September 1966).
"The Middle East." *World Topics Year Book*, 1966.
"Tradition and Reform in Saudi Arabia." *Current History*, February 1967.
Review: *Crisis in Lebanon: 1958*, by M. S. Agwani. *The Review of Politics* 29, no. 2 (April 1967).
"The Contribution of the Oil Companies to Iranian Development." *Iranian-American Economic Survey*, 1967.
"Arab Bloc Realignments." *Current History*, December 1967.

"Soviet Policy in the Middle East." *Current History*, November 1968.

"Islam and the West in the Middle East." *Current History*, March 1969.

"Rozwój Polityki Amerykańskiej na Środkowym Wschodzie." *Tematy* (New York/London), Fall–Winter 1969.

"Multinational Oil Companies: A Factor in the Middle East International Relations." *California Management Review* 13, no. 2 (Winter 1970).

"Arab Radicalism: Problems and Prospects." *Current History* 60, no. 353 (January 1971).

"Foreword," in James B. Mayfield, *Rural Politics in Nasser's Egypt*. Austin: University of Texas Press, 1971.

"United States Support for Iran's Independence and Integrity, 1945–1959." *Annals of the American Academy of Political and Social Science* 401 (May 1972). Special issue: *America and the Middle East.*

Review: *Republican Iraq: A Study of Iraqi Politics since the Revolution of 1958*, by Majid Khadduri. *Middle East Journal* 26, no. 3 (Summer 1972).

"Egypt and the Soviet Exodus." *Current History*, January 1973.

"Popular Revolution in Libya." *Current History*, February 1974.

"Middle East Politics and the Energy Crisis: Probing the Arab Motivations." *International Perspectives* (Ottawa), March–April 1974.

"Israel in 1973." *World Book Year Book*, 1974.

"The Oil-Producing Countries." *Daedalus* 104, no. 4 (Fall 1975).

"The Middle East: A Political-Economic Dimension." *The Columbia Journal of World Business* 12, no. 2 (Summer 1977).

"The Middle East in Soviet Strategy." *Problems of Communism* 27 (November–December 1978). Book review article.

"The Arc of Crises: Its Central Sector." *Foreign Affairs*, Spring 1979.

"Iran, the Awful Truth: Behind the Shah's Fall and the Mullah's Rise." *The American Spectator* 12 (December 1979).

"The Persian Gulf Crisis and Global Oil." *Current History* 80, no. 462 (January 1981).

"The Soviet Union and the Persian Gulf: An Encircling Strategy." *International Journal* (Toronto) 37, no. 2 (Spring 1982).

Selected Papers and Lectures Delivered at Conferences and Scholarly Meetings

"Arab Nationalism—Diagnosis and Prognosis." Western Political Science Association, February 22, 1957, Los Angeles.

"The Truman and Eisenhower Doctrines in U.S. Foreign Policy." Lecture delivered at St. Antony's College, Oxford University, June 1958.

"Soviet Policy in the Middle East." Lecture delivered at the Royal Institute of International Affairs, Chatham House, London, June 1958.

"Major Concerns of Middle Eastern Students: Dominant Characteristics of Principal Ethnic Groups in the Middle East." Cowell Hospital Psychiatric Group, University of California, Berkeley, November 6, 1963.

"Changing Patterns of Political Organization in the Twentieth-Century Middle East." 26th Congress of Orientalists, New Delhi, January 4–11, 1964, and Institut de Hautes Etudes Internationales, University of Geneva, January 16, 1964.

"Change and Revolution in the Middle East: Their Nature and Direction." Mid-America Conference of American Assembly, University of Oklahoma, Stillwater, May 7, 1964.

"Unity and Disunity in the Arab World." Lecture at the Institute of Oriental Studies, Hebrew University, Jerusalem, 1965.

"Poland's Western Legacy." Keynote Speech, Observance Committee of Northern California to commemorate the Millennium of Poland's Christianity, Mark Hopkins Hotel, San Francisco, May 28, 1966.

Memo on Khartoum Conference for Council on Foreign Relations, New York, December 14, 1968.

"The Tasks and Challenges Facing the Arab Youth." Paper read at the conference held at the Libyan University, Tripoli, June 1968.

"The Soviet Union and Iraq." Conference on Russia and the Middle East, Stanford University, November 7–8, 1969.

"The Northern Tier." National War College, Washington, D.C., March 17, 1971.

"The Polish Question: A Memorandum Concerning the Boundaries and the Likely Attitudes during the Forthcoming Elections." American Enterprise Institute, Washington, D.C., April 1972.

"National and International Policies Regarding World Energy Shortage." Conference on Energy, Ditchley Foundation, Oxford, 1973.

"The U.S. and the Soviet Union in World Politics." Foreign Ministry Club, Tehran, August 22, 1973.

"The Middle East: Politics and the Enegry Crisis." Conference on Oil and the Middle East, University of Toronto, January 25, 1974.

"United States Policy toward the Middle East in the 1970s." Read at Western Political Science Association meeting, Denver, April 1974.

"Oil and the Middle East: Lessons of October." Bohemian Grove, California, June 8, 1974.

"Intellectuals and U.S. Business Community." 79th Congress of National Association of Manufacturers, Waldorf-Astoria Hotel, New York City, December 5–6, 1974.

"Policies of Oil-Producing Countries: Perceptions, Strategies, Behavior." Conference on Oil Crisis, Turin, Italy, January 15–18, 1975.

"Nationalism and Modernization in the Middle East." University of Toronto, October 1976. Keynote Address, Conference on the World of Islam.

"Middle East: A Turning Point." Commonwealth Club, San Francisco, January 21, 1977.

"The Arab Boycott and U.S. Legislation: Legal, Political, and Economic Issues." Conference, Probe International and Middle East Institute, Sheraton Hotel, San Francisco, April 1, 1977.

"America: The Promise and the Price." Lecture to new citizens, Alameda Superior Court, Oakland, Calif., January 20, 1978.

"The Middle East Oil Supplies in the 1980s." Columbia University Energy Forum, Arden House, Harriman, New York, March 1978.

"Comparative Analysis of Middle Eastern Coups d'Etat: Common Denominators and Differences." American Historical Association, Saint Francis Hotel, San Francisco, December 29, 1978.

"Iran's Revolution and the Issues It Generates." Columbia University Energy Forum, Arden House, Harriman, New York, March 1979.

"Ideology, Politics, and Foreign Alignments in the Arab World." Aspen Institute for Humanities Studies, Amman, Jordan, April 1979.

"Iran's Revolution: Causes and Consequences." Washington State University, Pullman, April 23, 1979.

"New Dimensions of Big-Power Rivalry in the Middle East." International Conference on the Mediterranean, Bellagio, Italy, Villa Serbelloni, August 1981.

"The Middle East—Challenges to U.S. Policy." U.S. Business Council, Hot Springs, Virginia, October 10, 1981.

"Comments on the U.S. Bishops' Draft Pastoral Letter on Nuclear Weapons." To Bishop John S. Cummins, Oakland, Calif., December 6, 1982.

INTRODUCTION

Ideology and Power in the Middle East

■

Robert J. Pranger

The essays in this volume have been collected with a view toward introducing students of the Middle East to key ideologies in the region and the relationship between them and the two major forms of political power—regimes and movements. In other words, the governments and politics of the Middle East have been organized here according to ideological groupings. This has been done in frank recognition that the exercise of power in modern politics has become heavily dependent on organized political ideas and beliefs—ideologies—for developing and maintaining authority and legitimacy. Even where governmental institutions operate on the basis of ancient custom and usage, as in Great Britain, one discovers the importance of ideology in the field of political action for purposes of mobilizing mass electorates and delineating party differences. Indeed, it is fair to say that Prime Minister Margaret Thatcher is as militant an ideological conservative as the Ayatollah Khomeini is a militant Shiite fundamentalist, the disparity being that Mrs. Thatcher operates within a constitutional democratic tradition and Khomeini in an autocratic one. While the latter difference makes the two leaders individually distinctive in their exercise of political power, it does not obviate a need both of them have to sharpen the focus of their rule by ideological means for mobilizing mass sentiment behind their policies.

It is necessary to recognize the universal importance of ideologies in modern politics in order to avoid easy generalizations about the Middle East which, on closer inspection, could as easily be made about political life in Great Britain or the United States. That even highly educated electorates are ignorant and inattentive about political realities should come as no surprise to political leadership in London and Washington any more than in Cairo; surely the level of literacy or formal education in a country does not make an electorate either more or less likely to be swayed by the often simplistic beliefs found in ideologies. In fact, the German electorate of the early 1930s moved with solidarity behind Hitler's bizarre ideology in a way that would have made President Nasser envious in his efforts to mobilize his own public for much more benign purposes. One of the truly frightening political phenomena of the twentieth century has been the tendency of highly educated publics to be caught up in mass delirium by magicians weaving their spell through politicized half-truths parading as serious ideas. Ideologies in the Middle East have found origins and counterparts in the West.

The universality of political ideology means that one must approach the subject of power and ideology in the Middle East with a relativistic attitude free of stereotypes. There is no special propensity of Middle Easterners to display political emotion or even irrationality based on exotic ideologies. Indeed, in the area of left-wing ideologies, the Middle East has probably shown more skepticism than any other region in the world. In other words, ideology and power in the Middle East, while exhibiting some special characteristics obvious in this book, may be treated as part of a much more universal phenomenon today and not as a matter "typically" Middle Eastern.

General Linkages between Ideology and Power

As handmaiden to power, ideology was politically irrelevant until "new regimes" emerged from revolutionary movements organized to destroy "old regimes" in the course of modern European history. Critical to understanding the connection between ideology and power are two central forms of modern politics, the "regime" and the "movement." Historically speaking, the importance of ideology in politics can be almost precisely dated: the French Revolution of 1789 with its destruction of l'ancien régime and its creation of a *democratic* movement determined to build a *revolutionary* regime. In fact, the revolution was to encompass not only a violent change of regime, but an equally traumatic shift of national ideology in which no one was spared, aristocrat or commoner.[1]

In the nineteenth and twentieth centuries the "ideologist" appears as a practitioner of doctrinaire political beliefs and as an "unmasker" of the true motivations of ruling elites hiding behind the cloak of religious and other ideals.[2] At the same time, for their own radical purposes revolutionaries correctly saw the paramount importance of a politics that would intervene not only in the harsh realities of everyday life, but in matters of so-called public virtue as well. More mundane questions of "interest" (the idea of interest was very important in the founding of the American republic but not the French) would now be judged not in pragmatic but in normative terms, based on the new regime's revolutionary—often ersatz—concepts of political virtue. Now ideology would become artificially linked to power and not appear in the traditionalist guise that Marxist-Leninists—in the spirit of the French Revolution and of Hegel, who greatly admired the results in 1789 in bringing the "march of ideas in history" into full historical concreteness—have called "false consciousness."[3]

Politics was no longer statecraft in a technical sense only, but an activity directed to the heart and mind as well: not only the regime but individual citizens were to be radically transformed. Hence, "ideology" assumed two related meanings: on the one hand, the ideational screen behind which "real" and "unvirtuous" interests lurked; and on the other hand, a more explicit articulation of the relations between "correct" personal belief and political reality in a campaign of reeducation. Virtuous ideology, rather than false consciousness, would create a "new man" and a "new politics." Political ideas would henceforth generate a highly voluntaristic politics; language must act as a hammer beating on the anvil of the human brain, wrote the nineteenth-century Frenchman Pierre-Joseph Proudhon.[4] No important revolution since 1789—whether radical or conservative in origins—has neglected the strong connection between politics and belief; only now secular regimes and movements would take the place formerly occupied by the medieval church in this linkage. Khomeini's Iran is the one great exception to this rule of secularization of the spirit, but its occurrence has been so recent that it is still difficult to draw important conclusions about the future from it.

"Regime" represents settled authority and established political values against which the revolutionary "movement" battles with its own futuristic and voluntaristic vision of authority and value in politics. If successful, the movement will build its own regime in turn, often with traumatic impact on the movement and with results that lead not to stability but further instability. Within the tradition of the French Revolution, a movement that wishes to establish itself in power often resorts to violence and terror in order to eliminate its own raison d'être, which is impermanence and change. The momentous battle between Stalin and Trotsky after the Russian Revolution was, perhaps, the most dramatic evidence in the twentieth century of the struggle between forces within a movement over the future character of a revolutionary regime, but in a more contemporary context, tensions of this sort are still unresolved in China.

In the terror that aims at building a permanent and "virtuous" regime on an impermanent movement, ideology plays a crucial role, as events in China continue to demonstrate. The models for this transition from movement to regime are impressive in their dedication to the linkage between ideology and power: the French, the Soviet, and the Chinese on the left, and the Nazi on the right. There are many others somewhere between these extremes; the so-called "totalitarian" examples are not the only movements to work, once in power, for realization of their special version of a "virtuous republic."

Until the Islamic Revolution became victorious in Iran during 1979, no linkage between ideology and power in the Middle East approached the great models of modern times. It is clear from the essays in this volume that not even the Afghani and South Yemeni victories for communism come as close to "model behavior" as does the Khomeini regime. Roger Savory's analysis of Islamic fundamentalism, in Part 5 of this volume, notes uncomfortable parallels between the Iranian Shiite and Soviet revolutions—notably the phenomenon of totalitarian rule—that cannot be found even in Soviet-occupied Afghanistan or the socialist potpourri of the People's Democratic Republic of Yemen.

Is it not possible to talk of a kind of ideology even where political ideas are not used by a movement or regime in any deliberately systematic sense to enforce beliefs, but where, instead, the linkage between ideas and power comes of some underlying assumptions or prescriptions by which citizens live? One author has said that ideologies are "incorporations of the supreme values held by influential segments of society or, in a much rarer contingency, by society as a whole. . . . They impel their adherents to action for their realization . . . the 'spirit' of the political dynamism of a particular state society."[5] For example, Part 4 deals with "democracy" in Israel, Lebanon, and Turkey. It is correct to use "ideology" in this more ambiguous sense, but it should be noted that modern Israel and Turkey were founded on much more explicit ideological precepts than they follow today, while Lebanon's pluralism actually encouraged narrowly ideological movements whose activities have undermined the kind of accommodation for which Lebanon was noted before the mid-1970s.[6] In fact, democracy in the Third World has almost invariably originated within more narrowly ideological movements, most notably nationalistic ones, and has had great trouble stabilizing democratic regimes along Western lines. And even within Western democracies there are persistent tendencies among various participants to redefine agencies of toleration according to narrower ideological lines where politics becomes divided into "true" and "false" beliefs (or "consciousness" in the Marx-Lenin "scientific" formulation). Parallels between Protestant and Shiite fundamentalism are noted by Roger Savory in Part 5.

Whether ideology provides a systematic or more generalized structure of belief for politics, there is little doubt that it strengthens political power in its efforts to establish its authority and legitimacy in society. By using the "incantatory effects" of words and symbols, ideologies invite citizens, in Kenneth Burke's words, "to make themselves over in the image of their imagery."[7] This capability of symbols to create their own "image-worlds" and to produce their own reality, in politics as elsewhere in culture, is fundamental to understanding power based on ideology and the power of ideology. Such power may be called "political symbolization."[8]

At the base of the linkage between ideology and power, then, is an even profounder political process than the activities of regimes and movements in their objective aspects, the operation of subjective political culture where leaders and led are involved in interactions based on what may be shared "figments of imagination" drawn not only from language in its more positivistic sense but from myth and even magic.[9] The great ideologies of the West—capitalism, socialism, nationalism, racism, and others—build their political strength on unconscious as well as conscious images in both active and passive political symbolization. No one is allowed by these ideologies to adopt total passivity, but is required, through indoctrination and possible pain of punishment, to engage in both private and public behavior that exemplifies political virtues central to these ideologies.

The most fundamental linkage between ideology and power is a dramaturgy of political morals that fuses conscious and unconscious image-worlds in such a way as to empower these images with spiritual as well as secular authority. Rather than being created in the image of God, men now make themselves over in "the image of their imagery" that divides "us" from "them," "true" from "false." The twentieth-century experience, in the words of William Butler Yeats, is that our "ladders are gone,"[10] and modern ideologies that have secularized the spiritual and spiritualized the temporal not only exemplify this experience but have accentuated it. The most important critique of this ideological temperament, that of Albert Camus, has explored secularist, not religious, ways to reestablish traditional distinctions between spiritual and temporal dimensions of experience in the absence of Yeats's "ladders."[11]

It could be argued, of course, that the rise of political ideology as the ascendant force it has become for the last two centuries is simply a reflection of the need secularized authority has for transcendental sanction, but this would underestimate what has been referred to earlier as power based on ideology and the power of ideology. What ideologists discovered in the French Revolution was not politics but *politicization,* wherein virtue itself was transformed into a deliberately fabricated—ersatz—political idea as both critique of the old regime and foundation for the new. Few aspects of society or corners of personal conscience could any longer escape what one author has called "totalitarian democracy."[12] Distinctions between "private" and "public" prove unimportant in ideological politics, because whether one is a partisan of the "private" or the "public," this partisanship is judged to have political consequences. The idea of "privacy" itself has important implications for modern politics, and every important Western ideology seeks to make political everything from the most to the least personal.

Ideology in the Middle East has seldom approximated the totalitarian tendencies implicit in the so-called "war of ideas" in the West, even though Middle Eastern ideologies have drawn heavily on this ideological struggle. Something in the Western consciousness—and perhaps in the West's advanced political sophistication—has made its linkage between power and ideology more violent and intrusive, more given to what some would term "zero-sum" political conflict, than one finds in the Middle East, where this linkage has been mediated by certain indigenous and apolitical sensibilities.[13] Only in the Khomeini case is it possible to discern an authentically Middle East ideology approaching the ideological Manicheanism found in the struggle between capitalism and communism, and Khomeini has dramatically phrased his own ideology in starkly anti-Western terms as if to intimate that even Shiite fundamentalism would scarcely be possible today without the West's penetration—and corruption—of the Middle East.

The power of ideology is found in its politicization of not only normal areas of public life, such as legislative activity, but also in the way individual citizens think about private as well as public affairs. In other words, ideology uses what was earlier called the "incantatory effects" of words and symbols to invite citizens "to make *themselves* over in the image of their imagery." Through the power of this political symbolization a political culture is created where leaders and led share "figments of imagination" drawn not only from objective language itself but from myth and even magic. In the depths of Europe's despair in the first half of this century the psychologist C. G. Jung pointed to a revival of Wotanism in European politics,[14] and Thomas Mann centered one of his most important novels upon Satan himself.[15] Both connected such mythic and magical themes to the ideological fanaticism of Europe in the interwar period, a form of political evil not previously experienced in human history. To understand the magnitude of ideology's power over private as well as public life, attention must be paid to the importance of political culture.

Political Culture

Culture is that part of the environment created by human beings. Political culture is the area of human artifice devoted to power and participation in common undertakings to meet and resolve authoritatively social conflict with a minimum of violence. There are two dimensions to political culture, one objective and the other subjective.[16]

Objective political culture involves those aspects of politics that demand attention from citizens and their leaders. Found in this culture are political actors, actions, settings (geographic boundaries, political vocabularies, economic systems, institutions, and the like), and interests. The field of political science has traditionally, though not exclusively, concentrated a good deal of its analysis on this dimension of political culture. Increasingly, however, social scientists have come to recognize the importance of what Walter Lippmann called "the pictures in people's heads" when it comes to understanding politics, the dimension of subjective political culture and the domain where ideology exercises its power.[17]

Subjective political culture directs, rather than demands, the attention of citizens and leaders. This part of political culture involves "insider" or "member" status in a realm of shared experiences and meanings for citizens, and helps define "us" as opposed to "them." What differentiates an "American" from a "Frenchman" or "Russian" will be largely mediated by a subjective culture that comprises political communications, socialization and education, and role-playing, as well as feedback to objective political culture.

Like all forms of culture, politics involves highly symbolic relationships among people, in both objective and subjective forms of experience. The process by which political culture is built in the minds of citizens is called political symbolization, and it is through this process that ideology makes its impact in politics. This symbolization comprises the active appropriation of both objective and subjective political environments by individuals and groups who derive meanings relevant to themselves in what Susanne Langer called "symbolic transformation."[18] She noted that the human mind operates more like a very complex transformer than a switchboard. Ideologies, as systems of political belief, function as agents of this transformation by supplying necessary image-worlds where political meanings can be both shared and differentiated according to the special needs of individuals and groups. Symbolic transformation suggests, of course, that symbols such as "democracy" can be converted in various ways into even their opposites, as in George Orwell's *1984*, a novel written to dramatize the symbolic power of modern ideology.

Some ideologies, such as communism, are more oriented toward sharing than differentiation, while others, such as capitalism, stress individual differentiation rather than commonality. This difference in ideological emphasis, however, should not be mistaken for a way of distinguishing an ideology's power: Capitalism's emphasis on individual decision does not make it any less powerful an ideology than communism. An ideology's power is measured totally in terms of the degree to which citizens "make themselves over in the image of their imagery," thereby establishing a solidarity of interest and meaning in a regime or movement: the evidence is that capitalism, in this respect, is as powerful in the United States as communism is in the Soviet Union. In both countries there is little room for sharp deviance from basic ideological norms, even though constraints on eccentricity may be less obvious in one nation than in the other.

Neither objective nor subjective political culture should be seen as somehow the same as what can be called "personal perception" in politics: ideology, whether explicitly systematic or more inchoate, is designed to penetrate such perception and shape it in ways that will prevent perception from becoming critical of ideology itself. This moves the analysis of ideology and power into the difficult area of "the phenomenology of perception," as the French philosopher Maurice Merleau-Ponty has called it, where both objective and subjective forces in the environment are present as "givens" for individuals, but where individual consciousness itself is, to some undefined extent, preexistent as well.[19] The interaction or even collision between individual and culture, then, creates a tremendous challenge for the authority and legitimacy of any political movement or regime which must "aggregate" these individuals into a common political entity, an identity made all the more difficult because it is not a primary identification such as is found in the family. An interesting aspect of modern ideologies has been their attempt to convert politics into something more closely identified with basic human needs fulfilled by intimate communities such as the family, either by closely identifying political institutions with such primary groups or by developing a political imagery that suggests that politics is itself something like a family.[20] Every movement and regime, of course, takes great interest in the socialization of young individuals as "good citizens," but there is always tension between self and collectivity.

Ideologies, then, are artificial belief systems promoted by movements and regimes to penetrate individual consciousness with the objective of creating personal commitment. From an ideological standpoint, every future adult citizen should, early in life, be "educated" in public virtue as defined by a given movement or regime, an inculcation—or even indoctrination—of "values" that will initiate individuals into full membership status in his or her society. Anathema to political ideologies of every coloration is the idea that individuals might "hold out" or "have reservations" about ideology. There is no educational system in the modern world that explains to every young citizen—in advance of or during formative "civics" training—the role of political ideology in buttressing power or the power of ideology in directing personal allegiance. By the time this power may become apparent for the few who study it, they are already socialized into seeing a world that appears to be quite naturally divided, politically speaking, between "us" and "them." The mind has been "scratched," so to speak.[21]

It is through the agency of political symbolization that ideology moves individuals into conformity with a movement or regime. Langer's argument that the mind is a transformer not switchboard is well understood in modern politics: all successful ideologies adopt what might be called a "carrot and stick" approach to individuals in a socialization process which is conceived by all contemporary movements and regimes to be lifelong. Ideological conformity can produce important dividends, while deviance may be punished. Quite naturally there is a range of politics in terms of how much emphasis is placed on carrots rather than sticks, but no form of modern political life is without its penalty system for ideological nonconformity. Of course the idea that deviance might be a reflection of a normal, preexistent tension between self and society—an "asymptotic" relationship between citizen and state with citizenship a more creative role than is normally thought—is not actively encouraged anywhere as a starting point for civic education.[22] Where it may be tolerated, as in the United States, it is generally a subject for those interested in "participatory politics," often seen as poor cousin to the "real political world" of "power politics."[23]

The capability of humans "to make themselves over in the image of their imagery," which operates to ensure the highest of achievements, including political ones, also opens the door for the most base and anticivilized activity. By first understanding the importance of ideology in power and the power of ideology in all political movements and regimes, from the most democratic to the most totalitarian, one can then raise questions about the *relative* merits of one ideology vis-à-vis another, and the *relative* importance of ideology in a region like the Middle East. No ideology aims to free individuals from political obligations; in one way or another, political belief aims at socialization in order to create personal commitment to prevailing views of power in movements and regimes. By the nature of its function, every ideology is both exclusive and inclusive.

The first problem for students of ideology is to disengage themselves enough from all ideologies, even those to which they owe allegiance, in order to understand the key distinctions between political *ideology* on the one hand, and political *thought* on the other, the latter achieved through thinking about politics rather than through politicized thinking.[24] Through careful political analysis the intricate connections between ideology and power that exist everywhere in modern politics can be discovered and some understanding of the symbolic power of ideology achieved.

The Middle East, penetrated greatly by Western influence and yet resilient enough to maintain a flourishing indigenous politics as well, provides an important and comprehensive laboratory for the study of the relations between ideology and power. Its politics are, for Westerners, similar to their own and yet also different enough to allow for some relatively disengaged understanding of the positive and negative features of modern political ideologies.

The Middle East

In any study of the Middle East, most of all one that aims, as this volume does, to explore the linkages between ideology and power in the region, extreme care must be taken in order not to fall into the conceptual trap so capably analyzed by Edward Said. This trap, which Said calls "Orientalism," involves the strategic importance of the Middle East in world affairs for great powers, such as the United States, whose "interests" in the region are vital enough that they have extended their imperium into this troubled area of the world.[25] In order to gain "better understanding" of the movements and regimes operating there, American scholarship finds itself studying problems of interest to policy in ways that will enable this understanding to become an important tool for protecting vital interests. This scholarship may or may not be explicitly directed toward this end, but the important point is that the research agenda itself has been conditioned by the undeniable fact that the Middle East is "vital" for American interests in certain important respects.

In subsequent study of the Middle East it may seem mandatory that research be both objective and meaningful to American scholars already involved in the ambiance of "vital interests," even if they choose to explicitly deny that their research has direct relevance to such interests. Objectivity and meaning for Americans in the study of the Middle East, however, leads into the Orientalist trap: the region must be made meaningful not to Middle Easterners but to other Americans, which means that inevitably language and methodology will be employed that dramatizes the distinctness of the Middle East as a place where vital interests are challenged. Through the "poetics of space" an effort is made to create spatial distance between Western observer and Middle Easterner and to do so in such a way that Americans can understand the region *on their terms*, not from the perspective of those living there.[26]

When it comes to approaching the Middle East in terms of ideology and power, therefore, a temptation exists for some Americans and others to employ categories that both "make sense of the region in ways we can understand" and yet "retain the uniqueness of the Middle East." A gap is created between "us" and "them," the latter exotic in some sense and only relevant to our interests in the Middle East rather than to how we might govern our lives in this country. Contemporary terminology for this kind of distancing project, which nonetheless also creates a kind of specious familiarity with the Middle East, is readily available in both journalistic and academic treatment of the region: terrorism, fundamentalism, radicalism, and moderation, to name a few examples.

The present volume has organized the subject of ideology and power in the Middle East in ways comprehensible to Middle Easterners as well as Westerners: royalist authoritarianism; radical and reformist military regimes; Marxist movements and governments;

democratic practices and principles; Islamic fundamentalism; liberation movements; and problems in strategy and security. For example, virtually no one in the Middle East, except the Israelis, sees the PLO, in its full organizational outlines, as a "terrorist" organization, but rather as a "liberation movement." We have adopted the latter designation of the PLO and have included it in Part 6 of this volume, not to avoid problems most surely associated with the PLO, but to provide its proper context in the field of ideology and power in the Middle East.

What the Orientalist approach to the Middle East undermines is a truly comparative approach to the region whereby problems common to Western nations and Middle Eastern states, such as the relationships between ideology and power, can be discussed with some attention to the region as a promising laboratory for discovering certain more general truths about these problems. In this comparative work it is more important to have an analytical vocabulary common to the Middle East and the West, instead of a special language for analysis that emphasizes differences. Even theories of comparative politics often develop vocabularies that distance the Middle East from Western experience, even though the intent is to build a comprehensive "framework" for analysis. This was very noticeable in the school of the "politics of the developing areas" in American political science, where distinctions were made between fully developed and developing nations, with the latter presumably moving toward "full development" along Western lines.

From the standpoint of linkages between ideology and power, the Middle East is a bit like the Galápagos and, at the same time, similar to certain developments in Western Europe and the United States as well. On the one hand, monarchy—analyzed in Part 1—has more power today in the Middle East, even absent the shah of Iran, than in any other region of the world, and this monarchy has demonstrated a flair for modernization that is quite astonishing. Similarly, another medieval relic seems alive and well in the region, Islamic fundamentalism—Khomeini's regime in Part 5—again demonstrating a good deal of sophistication about matters such as modern warfare against an avowedly avant garde, secular, socialist state, Iraq. In other words, like certain species on the Galápagos, contemporary politics in the Middle East gives political Darwinists a rare opportunity to study firsthand a broader sweep of historical evolution than available elsewhere: monarchies and theocracies in the region are no mere semblances of their former selves; they are as strong today in certain parts of the Middle East as they were at the founding of Islam.

At the same time, however, the Middle East contains some unusual variants of modern regimes and movements, all the more interesting because they seem atypical for this region. Part 3 deals with Marxist movements and regimes and Part 4 with challenges to democratic practices and principles. Both Marxism and democracy have been judged, by some, to be out of place in the Middle East, alien presences in a highly uncongenial environment. Yet survival is possible and the methods for this survival are very interesting for understanding some of the more general strengths and weaknesses of Marxism and democracy as ideologies and forms of political power. For both, the Middle East is a kind of experiment in desert agronomy where special conditions and hybrids are important if certain forms of agriculture are to flourish.

A central category of ideology and power in the Middle East, especially in the Arab world, has been the realm of radical and reformist military regimes, covered in Part 2 of this volume. In fact the most important of Arab powers, other than Saudi Arabia, all belong to this group: Egypt, Iraq, and Syria. Yet each exhibits significant differences, even though Iraq and Syria are Ba'thist regimes. When North Yemen is added to this group, there emerges a picture of a serious effort to build state institutions that will outlast military rule itself. Here students will become aware of the complexity underlying any generalization about military rule and instability in the Middle East.

Every one of the forms of ideology and power in the Middle East has serious implications for international as well as regional security. Increasingly it is recognized by specialists in international relations that the internal working of movements and regimes, constantly changing as events interact with actors and institutions, have important effects on conflict within the wider international order. Important here are the main sources of this conflict in domestic, regional, and international politics: security, ideology, ethnicity, and political economy.

The linkages between power and ideology in the Middle East interact with conflicts in the security sphere to create difficult problems in foreign policy for countries such as the United States, problems compounded by American domestic politics. In other words, by its very internal diversity the Middle East provides an excellent laboratory for new approaches to international security that emphasize the vital role of domestic politics and intraregional factors in shaping the security field in which nations such as the United States attempt to protect their vital interests.

Part 7 of this volume approaches security problems with multiple dimensions in view: international, regional, and domestic. Again it is clear that on some key issues the most relevant foreign policy interaction between the United States and certain Middle Eastern states may be domestic, not international, bringing with it ethnic, ideological, and political-economic conflicts rather than the classical political-military conflicts of sovereign nations. In managing regional and international conflict in the Middle East, different methods are required depending on the type and level of conflict involved, and, once more, the region provides an excellent laboratory for innovative foreign policy.

This volume, therefore, approaches ideology and power as a linkage important for every nation today, with the Middle East, where there is an abundance of political movements and regimes unequaled for their diversity by any other region, as a kind of laboratory for studying this relationship. States in the Middle East exist in ancient, medieval, and modern forms today, all of them fully capable of using the technology of the twenty-first century and employing political techniques comparable to those available for the 1988 American presidential elections. This richness of political resources has never been given the same prominence as that of the region's most noteworthy natural resource, oil. Yet from the standpoint of students of ideology and power, the Middle East's amazing variety of political forms makes it a region of immense intellectual profit and, one hopes, of important policy relevance to nations elsewhere, including the United States, who must constantly relate the ideologies of movements and regimes to the requirements of power, while at the same time preserving a margin of freedom from the more extreme tendencies of ideological politics.

PART 1

Royalist Authoritarianism

■

IRAN

The Nature of the Pahlavi Monarchy

■

Gholam Reza Afkhami

The Pahlavi era began in Iran with the coup d'état of 1921, when Reza Khan, the first of the Pahlavis, moved into Tehran at the head of his Cossak forces. The king, Ahmad Shah Qajar, honored him with the title of "Sarda Sepah," commander of the armed forces, and after some negotiations named his political partner, Sayyid Zia al-Din Tabataba'i, as the new prime minister. Sayyid Zia al-Din had to resign his office and leave the country after three months. Reza Khan, however, became the minister of war in two months, prime minister in three years, the only candidate for the presidency of a briefly contemplated Iranian republic in four years, and, in less than five years, the first king of a new dynasty.[1]

By the time Reza Khan assumed the title of shah on December 15, 1925, he was already acknowledged as the most powerful man in Iran. During the years that had elapsed between the coup d'état and his ascent to the throne, he had assured the integrity of the nation and established internal security by quelling a number of tribal revolts and revolutionary uprisings in various parts of the country. During the next sixteen years, before he was forced to leave Iran in 1941 under pressure from the Allied Occupation Forces, he not only reigned but also ruled over the country with an iron hand. The paraphernalia of constitutional government remained intact, but no one doubted that supreme power lay with the king. He used this power to initiate the construction of an infrastructure that would support Iran's subsequent progress toward modernization and socioeconomic development. He introduced new concepts in the management of Iranian society by modernizing the educational, legal, and administrative systems. He pioneered fundamental changes in communication by building roads, railways, postal services, and telephone, telegraphic, and wireless networks. He paved the way for the eventual admission of half of Iran's population into the country's social, economic, and cultural life by unveiling women. And he established the supremacy of the central government by building a modern army and extending its power over Iran's entire national territory.[2]

Yet despite the qualitative importance of the changes Reza Shah initiated, their actual influence on Iranian society remained relatively limited during his reign. In 1941, when he abdicated his throne in favor of his son, over three-fourths of Iran's population still lived in the countryside, where traditional landlord-peasant and/or tribal relations prevailed, with all their economic, social, cultural, and political implications; no more than 10 percent of the population was literate; annual per capita income did not exceed $85; and the clergy retained its traditional sway over the great majority of Iranians. Iran, in short, was still predominantly a rural society whose interrelationships were basically affective and filial, dominated by a worldview that was a cross between Shiite Islamic universalism and local subnational parochialism.

Reza Shah's heir, Crown Prince Muhammad Reza, took the oath of office on September 1, 1941, in extremely precarious political conditions. His father's abdication had created a political vacuum, into which were now released a host of frustrated forces, previously held under his control. Traditional power groups—landlords, tribal khans, clerics, and bazaar leaders—and the few, but increasingly vociferous, representatives of modernism—intellectuals, professionals, bureaucrats, technocrats—began to compete for power in a political arena wanting in institutional capability. Men of stature in the pre-Reza Shah period, such as Zaka al-Mulk Furoughi, Ahmad Ghavam (Ghavam al-Saltaneh), Sayyid Zia al-Din Tabataba'i, Sayyid Hassan Taqizadeh, and Dr. Muhammad Musaddeq, as well as some younger men, mostly products of Reza Shah's bureaucratic and educational reforms, surfaced to take the helm and lead the country through the turbulent years of World War II and after.

In these years of conflict, power tended to gravitate to those whose bases were either traditionally sanctioned (crown, clergy), organizationally efficient (army, Tudeh), or socioeconomically commanding (landlords, tribal chiefs, bazaar leaders). Religious groups, led by Ayatollah Kashani, and political movements reflecting the full range of the ideological spectrum, from the extreme left to the extreme right—Tudeh, Third Force, Iran, Workers and Toilers, Democrat, National Will, as well as ultranationalist and pseudo-fascist parties—clashed in urban arenas in the hope of achieving political power. None emerged totally triumphant.[3]

By 1963, the year of the White Revolution, Muhammad Reza Shah had emerged as the nation's supreme leader. The White Revolution was the springboard that launched Iran's economic and social development. In fifteen years it transformed the character of Iranian society. In the countryside, its basic objective was to liberate the peasant by transforming the legal and traditional rules that governed his relationship to the land and the landlord.[4] On the labor front, it proposed to allow labor to share in the profits resulting from increasing industrial productivity (based on the development of modern technology) as well as to provide labor with new incentives for the promotion of productivity.[5] In the area of women's rights, suffrage became the basis for a widespread and concerted effort to transform the archetypal image of woman as man's mother, wife, and sexual companion to that of a citizen with equal rights and privileges.[6]

Between 1963 and 1976 Iran's average annual industrial growth exceeded 20 percent, while the number of industrial plants and the size of the industrial work force doubled. The GNP increased thirteen times, from $4 billion in 1961/1962 to $53 billion in 1975/1976. Annual per capita income went up eight times in the same period, from about $195 to about $1,600.[7] By 1978 it reached $2,000. Comparing Iran's overall economic picture in 1976 with what it was at the beginning of the Pahlavi dynasty's ascent to power, we see that by 1976 the GNP had grown 700 times, per capita income 200 times, domestic capital formation 3,400 times, and imports almost 1,000 times.[8] It is clear that by the time of the Khomeini assault most economic and social indicators had shown appreciable progress, from education to labor, from production to consumption, from infrastructure to social welfare.

Both Pahlavis were obviously modernizing kings. The father and son, however, were considerably different in terms of their personal backgrounds, temperaments, and vision. Reza Shah was a rough soldier who had fought his way up through the ranks and become the master of the country by the sheer force of his personality. He had lived a lower-middle-class life and could not help but know the basic characteristics of his countrymen simply by looking inward into his own soul and mind. Except for one trip to Turkey, he had never set foot outside Iran, had no firsthand experience of other cultures, and had no vision of a future drastically different from what he and his countrymen already knew.

He realized, however, that in some respects Iran had to change, and that those changes would entail not only the adoption of new techniques, but possibly new ways of thinking. He knew instinctively that a progressive future was unimaginable unless the country was freed from superstition and the forces that fed on superstition and ignorance;[9] hence, his efforts to break the clergy's hold on society by initiating the modernization of the educational and judicial systems, unveiling women, and limiting the use of clerical garb to bona fide clerics.[10]

Muhammad Reza Shah's background was quite different. By the time he was born in 1919, his father, under whose shadow he would grow up, was already well-placed in the military hierarchy, ready to plunge into the coup d'état. Early in life the son was introduced to democratic precepts as a student in Le Rosey in Switzerland. Unlike Reza Shah, he was by nature mild-mannered and relatively shy. Growing up in the shelter of the palace, he was physically separated from the ordinary people. Even more important, his lifestyle, his education, and his travels separated him culturally from the majority of his countrymen. As his familiarity with the world far exceeded that of his father's, so also did his vision of Iran's future. Reza Shah was a nationalist reformer whose model was Ataturk's Turkey. Muhammad Reza Shah fancied himself as a nationalist revolutionary, and dreamed of a "great civilization," a remarkable facsimile of a modern, Westernized, socialistically inclined welfare state, to be reached by the implementation of the principles he called collectively the "White Revolution."[11]

In spite of its tremendous achievements, the Pahlavi regime proved politically fragile and vulnerable. Both shahs met with tragic ends. Reza Shah fell in the face of the obviously superior power of the British and Soviet forces. Muhammad Reza Shah, however, succumbed to a series of events that could, at least with the benefit of hindsight, have been averted and/or overcome if the Iranian political system had been structurally better conceived and organized.

Muhammad Reza Shah was forced to leave Iran on January 16, 1979, under the pressure of one of the most extraordinary revolutionary upheavals in the history of the Third World. In one year's time, between 1977 and 1978, power, so palpably apparent in the shah's person, imploded, as it were, creating a vacuum that was filled, step-by-step, by the ferocious intensity of a group of passionate, vengeful mullahs. The Pahlavi regime, which had fathered the most phenomenal period of transition in Iranian history, yielded to what is conceivably the most backward of possible alternatives: a theocracy, a milder prototype of which the country had already rejected more than seventy years before in its days of poverty and superstition.

To understand the nature of the Pahlavi monarchy, we must look at the contradictions behind the mission the two Pahlavi shahs undertook—namely, the transformation and modernization of Iranian society. Discussion of the following questions may shed some light on the reasons for the phenomenal progress of Iranian society under the Pahlavis and the weakness of the political system the Pahlavi regime represented: (1) What were the institutional characteristics of Iranian kingship? (2) What have the effects of historical forces on political power and political leadership been in modern Iran? (3) What were the contradictions involved in the role of the king as political leader in modern Iran? (4) Was it possible or not to resolve the contradictions under the Pahlavi monarchy?

By the time the Iranian monarchy passed to the Pahlavis, it had become the repository of three general conceptual trends. Of these, the first was essentially of a metaphysical nature and derived from the ancient idea of *khvarnah*, which bound not only the king and the priesthood but all Iranians of Zoroastrian faith to the benevolence of their God Ahura Mazda, and charged them with the responsibility of waging war on behalf of the Ahuran light against the forces of evil.[12] In that the Ahuran conception of the universe foresaw periodic ascendance of the "Ahriman," the evil principle, implicit in it were also the notions of renewal and regeneration. Therefore, as Pio Fillipani-Ranconi suggests, "the essence of the Iranian kingship was not mere enhancement of the human function on earth, but rather supernatural power aiming at *'renewing' the world after a celestial pattern.*" "We have seen that such a renewal, religiously expressed by the adverb *frash*—apparently derived from the stem *fra-ank* 'proceeding forward,'—'advancing to completion,'—is a recreation that, in the case of the king's work, does not abide in the realm of abstraction; rather, it must appear as embedded in a physically visible mold."[13]

According to the mythology of ancient Iran, a king was bestowed with divine glory as long as he followed the Ahura's path by working for the betterment of society. Jamshid, the most glorious of the *Shahnameh*'s mythical kings, was so blessed until he strayed from the right path, as a result of which the country plunged into Zahak's millennium of the rule of darkness.

The special relationship between the king's divine *farr* (glory) and the nation's felicity remained an essential pillar of the Iranian political culture during the Achaemenid (559–330 B.C.) and Sasanian (A.D. 224–651) periods. But it was also carried over into the Islamic era and was regenerated anew with the Safavid dynasty. Isma'il, the first of the Safavid kings, was considered by his followers, mainly the *qizilbash*, tribes of Turkish origin, as being divinely ordained. He was called *Vali Allah*, the vicar of God, a title that in Shiism has been traditionally reserved for the first imam, Ali. As both shah and *murshid-i kamil*, or perfect spiritual director, he combined in his person the functions of both the temporal and the spiritual leader.[14] The idea was handed down, albeit in the more nebulous concept of *Zill Allah* (God's shadow), through the Safavids' successor dynasties, particularly the Afshars and Qajars, which, as constituent tribes of the *qizilbash*, were the main pillars of Safavid power.

The sacral connotations of Iranian kingship were a basic reason why the doctrinal contradiction between religious and secular concepts of legitimate authority in Shiism did not affect the institution of kingship but were in fact reconciled in it, until the Pahlavi era, when the king personally became the embodiment of the thrust toward secularism and modernization.

This point is particularly germane to our discussion. In the universes of Ahuran and Islamic thought, the world and the law were, and are, essentially given. In Zoroastrian Iran, they were seen as embodied in the accepted traditions of society, in its division of classes and division of labor. Justice was doing that which was the accepted norm. History was seen as cyclical in its movement, and regeneration meant essentially beginning the cycle anew. Thus, Khosrow Anushiravan, one of the most powerful Sasanian kings, would remain the epitome of justice even though he slaughtered the Mazdakis by resorting to what by modern standards are patently dishonorable methods. He had brought the cycle of history back onto the right path by ridding the world of nefarious and antitraditional influences.[15] In Islam also, the word, the law, and indeed the world, are given in the Koran.[16] In Shiism in particular, *bid'at*, or newfangledness in matters pertaining to religion, has been traditionally considered a sin, the work of the devil. And as Islam encompasses nearly every dimension of social and moral existence, the implications are clear: authority is not justified in approving, let alone spearheading, structural change. If the world moves off the path ordained by the word, it must be set aright. Thus, as long as the crown operates within the framework accepted by the religious authority, its sanctity is respected. If it sides with the world, it becomes practically profane, and falls into conflict with the religious concept of legitimacy.

The conflict between the Pahlavis and religious authority in Iran was inevitable. Reza Shah came to power and ascended the throne when the conflict between the religious and secular concepts of legitimacy had already been exacerbated as a result of changes brought about inside the country by prevailing international conditions. The crown as an institution was already torn between the forces of the future and of the past. And the only way Reza Shah could have come to power was to side with the forces of the future, for the past had already been preempted by the reigning Qajar dynasty. Indeed, by the early 1920s, under the influence of the Turkish events, certain modernizing forces in Iran, which Reza Khan also represented, were seriously entertaining the idea of a republic.[17] The crown was retained, however, because the Shiite establishment believed that it was still the best guarantor of traditionalism.

A second characteristic of Iranian kingship, in addition to its sacral quality, resulted from the exigencies of power. Iranian tradition always placed a premium on valor. The Shahnameh's heroes, among other things, were men of *razm* and *bazm*, valiant in battle and in feasting.[18] In practice the tribal origin of Iranian dynasties meant that both the achievement and preservation of the throne required the ability to wage war against enemies outside and to use cunning against enemies at home. Most of the Iranian dynasties came to power as a result of victory on the battlefield, and they also lost their thrones in wars. From Cyrus to Reza Shah, glory had belonged to the strong and warlike. Justice and power were seen as the two edges of the king's sword. If nothing more, the king had to be strong enough to prevent his servants from plundering the country.

The crown was thus both the repository of power and the dispenser of justice. A just king had to be powerful even though, obviously, not all powerful kings were just. But the expectation remained, even when the king in fact could no longer wield power. He would still be blamed for the country's disarray and the calamities that befell the people. The king had to be a leader in every sense of the word. He had to be able to mobilize armies, to defeat aggressors, to see that justice was meted out and that the norms of the society were not violated. Thus Shah Sultan Hussein (1694–1722), the last of the reigning Safavid kings, a weakling by all counts but personally not a bad man, was held in contempt, while his immediate successor, Nadir Shah of the Afshars, renowned for his taste for bloodshed and plunder, went down in history as a great king because he was a genius on the battlefield. In the same vein, Ahmad Shah (1909–25), the last of the Qajars, a decent man but one who did not have the stomach for battle, had to yield power to a stronger personality who would be able to unify the country, largely by means of force.

The third characteristic of the institution of monarchy under the Pahlavis resulted from the establishment of the constitution of 1906. Limitations of space do not permit an in-depth analysis of the constitutional movement in Iran. It was essentially a response to a vaguely understood experience of colonialism—vaguely because most of the people who participated in the constitutional revolution did not quite understand its meaning either in terms of the legal properties of the document itself or of its correspondence to cultural and socioeconomic conditions in Iran.[19] In the course of time most of them came to believe in the constitution as a panacea for all the ills of society. When, under internal and external pressure, social conditions deteriorated, many of them naturally became disillusioned, which led to further fragmentation of society, threatening the country's already fragile basis of independence and national integrity.

The constitution was meant as an instrumental response to the need for the rationalization of political power. The original document—ratified in 1906 by a constituent assembly that later reconstituted itself as the first majlis, the National Consultative Assembly—envisaged a parliament composed of the representatives of six classes of people charged with the power and the responsibility to legislate state revenues and oversee their expenditure. A year later, in 1907, a supplement was added that contained a bill of rights and defined the powers and responsibilities of the executive and judicial branches of the government, the prerogatives of the crown and of the religious establishment, and the powers and manner of formulation of local councils, as well as a number of other points concerning the army, the flag, and other matters pertaining to the state's symbols.[20]

The constitution's main objective was to assert the popular sovereignty of Iranians, but at the same time it had to take into account the realities of Iranian history and culture. While it was essentially borrowed from French and Belgian prototypes, it also represented the two basic Iranian institutions, the monarchy and Shiism. The shah remained the head of state, and was also recognized as commander in chief of the armed forces, head of the executive branch, and a partner in legislation. As head of state and symbol of the majesty of the nation, his person was pronounced inviolate and inviolable. Executive responsibility was assigned to the ministers, who consequently were pronounced individually and collectively answerable before the majlis. On the other hand, Article 2 of the Supplementary Fundamental Law stipulated that laws passed by the majlis had to conform to the tenets and rules of the shari'a, for which purpose a body of five knowledgeable *mujtahids* (learned '*ulama*) selected by the Shiite hierarchy was to pass judgment on the admissibility of the laws. Thus the crown and the clergy each achieved a veto power over legislation. The crown's power in theory was less extensive, in that insofar as money matters were concerned, it could be overruled by a parliamentary majority. The clergy's prerogative, however, was both absolute and permanent, for it was stipulated that the article that defined it could not be amended and would remain perpetually in force until the reappearance of the Twelfth Imam, at the end of historical time.

The constitution thus incorporated ideas both of the future and of the past, of modernity and of traditionalism. Unconsciously, the framers of the constitution imbued the document with a dialectical logic that reflected the contradictions that had just begun to emerge in Iranian society. The future was represented by the notion of popular sovereignty on which the bulk of the constitution was based. But popular sovereignty could not be realized as long as popular culture rejected it. The Shiite creed that defined the worldview of the majority of Iranians divided the population into two groups: the *mujtahids*, who were versed in the shari'a and therefore were, or potentially could be, *marja' taqlid*, or a "source of emulation," and the bulk of the population, who were not so trained and therefore had to be *muqallids*, or "emulators of the mujtahids." As Shiism does not recognize distinctions between religious and nonreligious spheres of life, politics could not be separated from the religious domain. Thus, within the confines of Shiite orthodoxy, popular sovereignty could have no meaning other than the sovereignty of the *faqih*—namely, the *mujtahid* learned in Shiite jurisprudence.[21]

On the other side of the scale, the crown was conceived of as having its origin in a will beyond the realm of social determination. From a practical point of view, of course, the Safavid era had established the political necessity for the king to be a Shiite, and as such he was henceforth considered to be the shadow of God on earth, the Zill Allah. To bridge the gap between popular sovereignty and the divine qualities of kingship, the constitution referred to the crown as a divine gift bestowed on the person of the shah through the intermediary of the people.[22]

The apparent contradictions in the constitutional document were perhaps the main reason for its relative longevity. During the seventy-two years of existence, 1907 to 1979, they made it possible for different factions to interpret the document according to their own interests. The shahs, the clergy, and the liberals all found in it what they needed to base their arguments on. Controversies tended to revolve around the manner of interpreting the document, never around the document itself. As a result, the constitution, which, unlike monarchy and Shiism, was originally only of instrumental value, achieved in the course of time an institutional dimension as well, in spite of the fact that political power remained the final arbiter. It was only in the latter part of 1978 that the document itself became a matter of contention.

Iran regained its national consciousness in the latter part of the nineteenth century, in a world dominated by colonialism. Colonialism was largely responsible for establishing the framework that would define the manner and direction of Iran's economic, social, cultural, and political development. It was this framework also that would limit the choices available to Iran's leaders.

The colonial experience led initially to a cultural dichotomization and later to a cultural fragmentation of Iranian society. Extensive poverty, paucity of means of communication, widespread illiteracy, social hierarchy, class barriers, and general insulation of the bulk of the rural and a majority of the urban population did not allow for a uniform exposure to, much less a uniform assimilation of, Western values. Only a small minority of Iranians, mostly belonging to the upper and middle classes, came into contact with Western culture, at first merely emulating its more superficial social characteristics, but gradually achieving the necessary consciousness to derive models for political action from it. In time, they influenced a much larger number of their countrymen, many of whom possessed little or no knowledge of the bases of these new values, and enticed them to rise against the archaic Qajar political system and replace it with the Western bourgeoisie's paraphernalia of governance.

The first stage of consciousness corresponded to a feeling of admiration for the sociopolitical characteristics of the colonial powers. The constitutional revolution of 1906 reflected this feeling not only in its almost wholesale adoption of the principles of the Belgian and French constitutions, but also in a pervasive belief that the resulting document would be a panacea for the nation's problems. Naively, the constitutionalists thought that by emulating the political paraphernalia of the Western societies and by introducing Western concepts of legality, they would automatically usher in desired economic, social, and cultural changes as well.[23]

This expectation did not, of course, materialize. Not because the constitutional process was vitiated, but rather because it could not possibly have led to the socioeconomic consequences the constitutionalists desired. The essence of Western constitutionalism, from the very first, was the primacy of the society over the polity. The quest for political freedom was governed by the objective reality of the power of the middle class. The bourgeoisie demanded and got a political organization that would respond to its need for freedom of choice and action. As it was historically the most progressive sector of the society, its power meant, in effect, the elimination of artificial barriers to socioeconomic progress. Responding to this fact, major Western ideological models—Lockean liberalism, Burkean conservatism, Marxian socialism—all assumed the primacy of the society over the polity. Indeed, so strong and in many ways definitive was the power of the middle class that socialism in Western Europe had to adapt itself to the bourgeoisie's social and economic conditions in order to be admitted as a serious partner in the political game.

In the absence of a strong and developed middle class, constitutionalism in the Iran of 1906, as in other comparable Third World countries, was likely to lead to a conservatism of a most reactionary order. The reason was clear, even though it was not clearly understood. The aim of Western constitutionalism was not only to limit the state's power, but also to allow the existing socioeconomic groups to participate, according to their relative capabilities, in the determination of the affairs of the state. In Iran, however, the influential socioeconomic groups—aristocratic landlords, tribal chiefs, bazaaris, and others—all had vested interests in the preservation of the status quo. And the status quo was what the constitutional revolution presumably had hoped to change. The result was fourteen years of political paralysis and socioeconomic chaos, at the end of which most of the original constitutionalists came to support the rule of Reza Shah, fully aware that it presaged the end of "constitutionalism" in government.

Thus, Reza Shah came to power only in part because he commanded the Iranian armed forces, but mainly because a majority of the Iranian political and social elites had reluctantly come to realize and accept as hopeless the democratic experiment. In the constituent assembly of 1925 that elected Reza Khan to the throne, Musaddeq spoke halfheartedly against the measure, arguing, correctly, that it would turn the crown into an instrument of despotic rule.[24] But he also spoke with great admiration of Reza Khan, the man, as an agent of power who had brought substantial peace, order, and tranquillity to the country, and he went along with the final decision. The assembly chose Reza Khan with only three abstentions, cast as a matter of principle by the three socialist delegates headed by Suleiman Mirza Eskandari, the Qajar prince who was elected first secretary general of the Tudeh party immediately after its establishment in 1941.[25]

When Reza Shah assumed the throne, Iran had already begun to enter the second stage of colonial consciousness. Many in the Iranian elite had come to believe that the essence of colonalism was the disparity in the economic and technological conditions of the Western and the colonized countries. To truly face itself, therefore, Iran had to adopt policies that would lead to the development of its economy through modern technology. Much of this, of course, had social and cultural overtones, insofar as it required not only the acceptance of Western techniques but also the assimilation of facts and values that constituted the intellectual bases of modern technology.

The development process, however, could not be initiated through consensus, as it entailed the adoption of policies that would necessarily come into conflict with the objective and/or subjective interests of the traditional power groups in Iranian society. On the other hand, the political system, which was now to be charged not only with the performance of the traditional functions of the state—namely, the assurance of national independence and the preservation of internal security—but also with preparing the way for the socioeconomic transformation of society, required a corresponding system-management capability. At the very minimum, such capability meant a capacity to mobilize the human and material resources necessary for the formulation and implementation of the system's goals. To the extent that the goals of modernization entailed the transformation of the society's basic interrelationships and could not be formulated through a consensus reached by democratic means, they either had to be abandoned or reached by various forms of coercion. The progressive evolution of the understanding of colonialism as based on foreign economic and technological superiority blocked, in principle, the option to abandon such goals. As the state came to be progressively seen as the main lever of change, polity assumed primacy over society.

The reversal of the traditional relationship between state and society was accelerated by another factor. In the absence of a pervasive and sufficiently developed middle class, modernization and development had to be spearheaded by social groups whose power derived essentially from their special kinds of knowledge—professionals, technocrats, bureaucrats, intellectuals. Their know-how, however, in contradistinction to that of the scribes and clerics who in the past had traditionally supported the status quo, was to be used ostensibly for the transformation of conditions that historically had brought about and assured the bases of traditional power.

These groups, ideologically alienated from specific class affiliations, became attached to the state, and their power and prestige waxed and waned with it. Their position, however, as they proposed to perform for Iran the functions historically assigned in the West to the middle class, was inherently contradictory: most of them subjectively adopted the ideology of the middle class without enjoying the objective power base that was its distinguishing characteristic. Thus, they favored democracy, but they could not accept the results of democratic politics in an essentially feudal and traditional society.[26] As a result, they remained generally bewildered by the contradiction underlying their political position. Many of them worked in the government and in government-related organizations and were instrumental in the building of the whole edifice of state power under Reza Shah. Yet they remained cynical and resentful of Reza Shah's power, ready to explode into the political void once it had been removed.

A generation later, the same type of individuals, with far greater technological ability, became the architects of Iran's phenomenal transformation during the last fifteen years of Muhammad Reza Shah's rule.[27] Yet as the nation made progress in the economic and social fields, these progressive agents also exhibited palpable signs of disaffection. They were dissatisfied with the prevailing political conditions, but remained ambivalent concerning the system they sought. The alternative they seemed to desire was democracy, but the form of democracy they understood (i.e., the same form that had led to the adoption of the French and Belgian portions of the constitution) appeared out of reach, initially because of the socioeconomic characteristics of the society, but finally also because so much power had already accumulated in the crown, and in the civil and military bureaucracies. The result was an unhappy consciousness pervading the entire structure of the political system, including its bureaucratic backbone. In the end, in response to forces with which they had nothing in common, the skilled, progressive elements of Iranian society attacked the system from within, and destroyed it beyond recognition by repudiating almost all that they themselves had achieved.[28]

As the contradictions between the requirements of progress and Shiite values were for the most part deemed to be unresolvable, the Reza Shah regime proposed, in effect, to extricate Iranian nationalism from the retardative proclivities of the socially dominant Shiite worldview. Supported by the new elite,[29] it tried to build an intellectual and emotional bridge to pre-Islamic Iran, over some fourteen centuries of Islamic experience, by extolling and propagating the virtues of the Achaemenid and Sasanian periods as the proper basis for the expression of Iranian identity, while disparaging or ignoring the reality of contemporary Iranian culture, expressed largely in Shiite ideology. However, as the distant past could not really be reappropriated, and the future was no longer to be based on the reality of the present, nationalism and modernization in Iran tended to assume a culturally vacuous quality, a condition that led to recurrent difficulties in achieving a link between action and meaning.

Nevertheless, Reza Shah did have considerable success with his policy of de-Islamization of Iranian nationalism, as evidenced by the characteristics of nationalist expression among the intellectuals, professionals, students, and others during the politically open decade of the 1940s. A majority in each of these groups shunned religious slogans, adopting a variety of secular ideologies in the general anticolonial struggles of the period.[30]

Iranian nationalism, however, both in its negative antiforeign proclivities and in its positive developmental manifestations, remained essentially devoid of cultural meaning. Its xenophobic dimensions, expressed by the National Front leader, Dr. Muhammad Musaddeq, could elicit great passion, but scarcely addressed the nation's developmental requirements; the developmental dimension, expressed by the shah, changed the nature of Iranian society over some twenty-five years, but was scarcely capable of eliciting political zeal and enthusiasm.[31] Thus, the first twelve years of Muhammad Reza Shah's reign, between 1941 and 1953, were marked by volatile and highly enthusiastic expressions of anti-Soviet and anti-British feelings. The period ended in the defeat of Dr. Muhammad Musaddeq, the recognized leader of the Iranian nationalist movement and easily the most charismatic of all the secular leaders in recent Iranian history, because of a series of internal and external impasses from which he could not extricate himself. The resolution of the contradictions that led to Musaddeq's fall, on the other hand, required the adoption of policies that could not satisfy the national urge for self-assertion, which, under the prevailing colonial circumstances, could be realized only against an external symbol. The post-Musaddeq regime had to accept the legitimacy of compromise, which meant accepting something less than what Musaddeq had adamantly demanded (and failed to receive).[32]

The preceding pages have shown that, as in other Third World countries, power has demonstrated a proclivity toward centralization and concentration in Iran. Since the existing dominant social, economic, and cultural powers favored the status quo, and the fragmentation of political culture prevented the evolution of a historically meaningful consensus on political substance and procedure, proponents of social change had to rely fundamentally on force, whether of arms (Reza Shah), mobs (Musaddeq), various ideological organizations of minorities (Tudeh), or ephemeral majorities (Ghavam, Musaddeq, Khomeini).

In the absence of viable political institutions, the tendency of political power toward concentration and centralization favored personal styles of leadership. Reza Shah's rise to power paralleled those of Chiang Kai-shek in China and Mustafa Kemal in Turkey before World War II. Musaddeq's rise foreshadowed the rise, after the war, of Third World leaders such as Nasser, Nkrumah, and Sukarno. Iran's situation, however, differed in two basic respects:

first, Musaddeq was an aristocrat of traditional sensibilities, not quite in tune with the evolving characteristics of postwar Third World politics; and secondly, the Iranian crown possessed a far greater institutional capability than existed in some of the other countries. Quite possibly, had a man of different intellectual and temperamental endowments achieved Musaddeq's popularity—for example, General Razm Ara—the crown might not have survived. In the event, however, the crown became the repository of political power, and the shah emerged, of necessity, as political leader.

All through the Third World the rise of personal power coincided with the salience of organizations and procedures that were particularly responsive to the requirements of command. In most cases, the military, the bureaucracy, and the single political party, the latter in either unique or dominant forms, emerged, in some combination, as the main instruments for the exercise of leadership and political control. The leaders themselves, however, were generally unencumbered by the institutional requirements of their office.

Muhammad Reza Shah's power depended largely on the military and bureaucracy. In fact, both were admirably suited to the crown's requirements. For one thing, these organizations were constitutionally under the shah's ultimate command in his capacity as head of state, head of the executive power, and commander in chief of the armed forces. Moreover, the shah, in his historical role as God's shadow on earth and as the symbolic father of his people, brought a degree of legitimacy to national leadership that the bureaucracy and army lacked. The decisions worked out by the experts in the civil and military bureaucracies could always receive the sanction of legitimacy by being made and implemented in the name of the crown. Theoretically, a happy combination could evolve if the instrumental capabilities of the bureaucracy were adequate to the intended task of development. This is precisely what happened in the first decade of the White Revolution, 1963–71. Major decisions were made and implemented by the bureaucracy in the name of the Revolution of the Shah and the People. The people's participation was at best vicarious, but the process proved highly effective, as the government succeeded in bypassing all the traditional forces that had in the past blocked the path of socioeconomic modernization. As most of the measures corresponded to the demands made by liberal and leftist interests, whether in the areas of landlord-peasant relations, labor management relations, women's rights, the nationalization of forests, pastures, underground waters, and the like, the shah also largely succeeded in co-opting whatever political space these interests may have wished to occupy.

In deference to Western practice, Reza Shah had toyed with the idea of establishing two political parties. Time and chance did not allow him to implement the design, but clearly, had parties been established, they would have fared even worse under him than those under his son did. Reza Shah's rule, therefore, remained purely bureaucratic.

When the crown emerged anew as the respository of power in 1953, political parties once more became for all intents and purposes irrelevant. However, the shah did experiment: initially with a two-party system composed of the majority "Melliyun" and minority "Mardom" in the fifties; then with a one-party dominant system composed of thc Iran Novin and Mardom between 1964 and 1975; and finally with a one-party system, the "Rastakhiz," or Resurrection Party of the Iranian People, in 1975.

The Iran Novin came closest to being a real political party, because for a time it harnessed the élan created by the White Revolution. Its strength was presumably based on the support of the newly emancipated sectors of Iranian society—peasants, workers, women, and retailers—and the governing elite, who together constituted the bulk of the population. But even in its heyday, in the late sixties and early seventies, the party's membership was basically made up of the official organizations representing the regime's new progressive programs: various types of rural cooperatives, labor unions, guilds, and other service-oriented government organizations. In short, it was the political manifestation of the bureaucracy. Therefore, as long as the capabilities of the civil administration were adequate to the political requirements of development, the party also appeared briskly efficient, in spite of the grumblings of a few intellectuals and fewer dissidents.

Even then, however, a basic contradiction was palpably present. The Iran Novin party, like all parties, could become politically significant only if it could also become a meaningful bridge giving its membership access to political power. Power, however, belonged to the crown and the bureaucracy, both of which were supposed to be nonpartisan. Thus, if the Iran Novin was to remain in the political limelight, it had to present itself as the party that was uniquely related to both the shah and the bureaucracy. In fact, under Prime Minister Hoveida's leadership (1965–75), it succeeded in doing both, thereby checkmating both the shah and the opposition Mardom party. The government's program became the shah's program, with the curious, but logical, result that whenever the loyal opposition was called upon to criticize the government, it ended up by seeming to criticize the shah. The shah, however, was constitutionally above criticism, for he not only represented the majesty of the state but also was pronounced above and beyond responsibility by the constitution. Hence, neither the Mardom party nor, by the same token, the Iran Novin party, could have become full-fledged carriers of political power unless the shah had been prepared to retire from a significant sphere of political decision making.[33]

The shah, of course, was not prepared to curtail his own involvement in political affairs. Indeed, such a move would have required an extraordinary measure of philosophical wisdom and strength of character, for he would simultaneously have had to withstand the human will to power and the objective and subjective political forces that pushed him increasingly into the fray. The phenomenal progress the country was making was presumed to depend on his person and the encompassing qualities of the crown; and those who made the decisions with him infinitely preferred to respond to what he represented than to a melee of forces the effects of which could never be certain.

By the early 1970s, however, it had become reasonably clear that the bureaucracy was beginning to bend under the political and administrative pressures it was called upon to sustain. The nation's progress appeared to be outstripping the evolution of the political system's capability. Two basic ideas, administrative decentralization and political participation, began to be discussed in the cabinet, the court, and various ministries, and in fact, by 1975, were pronounced the official policies of the state. The system, however, was never able to implement them. In the meantime, the Iran Novin party became progressively more ossified, and the political system became increasingly less adequate to the demands of its domestic and international environments.

It bears emphasis here that the general tendency of political power in the Third World toward centralization, concentration, and personalization appears to gather momentum under environmental pressure. This is borne out by the evidence of history (ancient hydraulic societies, socialist and/or fascist interwar movements in Europe, the New Deal in the depression-ridden United States, Third World politics under colonial conditions, etc.), as well as by the findings of comparative studies of contemporary large-scale organizations.[34]

By the early 1970s attacks on the shah in the Western media, particularly by left-leaning liberals in Europe and the United States, had increased demonstrably. (The shah interpreted this as indicating a behind-the-scenes Soviet presence engaged in the dissemination of disinformation.) By 1974 the cordial understanding between the shah and the Nixon administration, an understanding that had previously been a boon to the shah's domestic and international prestige and power, was becoming a liability, inasmuch as President Nixon was being ignominiously forced out of office under the dual pressures of Vietnam and Watergate. Periodic guerrilla attacks in Iran and elsewhere were also a reminder of the dangers to which the shah, his system, and his policies were exposed. Furthermore, the shah's clerical opponents continued to use every opportunity to criticize the galloping pace of modernization (albeit cautiously, within the bounds of political propriety). On the other hand, the quadrupling of oil prices in 1973–74 brought hitherto unimaginable wealth, and with it a sense of opportunity and adventure to the country. In addition to all this, there was the shah's illness, the effect of which on subsequent decisions remains a source of conjecture.

Here a short theoretical digression may be in order. Historically, it may be hypothesized, the tenacity of political systems has depended largely on their ability to respond adequately to the requirements of their environment. This truism has important implications for a rudimentary theory of political development. According to Marxist theory, for example, the French Revolution was the result of the contradiction between the bourgeoisie's economic power and an ossified political system geared to an aristocratic style of governance but devoid of aristocratic political power and socioeconomic efficiency. The deterministic dimensions of Marxist theory presuppose a teleological process leading to a "stateless" world composed of "classless" societies. Both the scientific and prophetic dimensions of the theory make it inapplicable to our point. What is applicable is the implicit notion of systemic efficiency.

Historically, in countries that have moved toward successful socioeconomic development political participation has expanded. Such participation, however, has assumed two distinct patterns. Where socioeconomic development occurred naturally, propelled by the society's inner dynamic, as in Western Europe and North America, the primacy of the society was preserved, and the polity, limited in scope, content, and procedure, responded to new environmental demands as these demands took shape and were communicated to the political system through a series of evolving channels for interest articulation and interest aggregation. In such cases political participation was extensive, less structured, sometimes chaotic, often decentralized, and generally free.

On the other hand, where socioeconomic development was taken up as conscious policy of the state in response to either an explicit ideology (Leninism) or unstated objective forces (colonialism), political participation often assumed totalitarian proclivities, i.e., it became essentially concentrated in relatively few and small elites who, based on a combination of ideological injunction and personal leadership, were charged with guiding and transforming the society along ideologically preordained paths.

At the center of totalitarianism lies a notion of single truth whose source and reality are outside the sphere of give and take of the political marketplace. Truth may lie in history, in God, in *volk*, or in power, but it is, by definition, not something that could issue from a freely reached consensus. As a result, totalitarianism becomes the imposition of a particular will, based on a contrived value system, on a diversified society containing different social types, each with its own basket of mores and values. Consequently, it must adopt alienated concepts—proletariat cum masses; *volk* cum archetypal individual representing past, present, and future; *Mustaz'af* cum *naas*. In the end, of course, abstract concepts must be reflected in tangible political agents. And here Lenin's most cunning contribution to totalitarianism comes into play—namely, the elite party. The genius of the elite party is that it does not belong to anyone, or any one group of social types; rather, it belongs primarily to the ideology. Hence, the efficiency of a given totalitarian system depends largely on the degree of correspondence between the ideology and the characteristics of the cultural, social, economic, and political structures that both normatively and existentially constitute the referents of the ideology.

The point that is germane to our discussion is that once the economic conditions in a society change beyond certain levels, unless ways are found to translate the new socioeconomic power into systemic political capability by engaging the evolving socioeconomic forces in the political process, through either open and democratic or closed and totalitarian patterns of political participation, the political system will tend to become fragile, increasingly underdeveloped relative to its socioeconomic environment, and therefore vulnerable. Thus, Hobbesian models—i.e., nonparticipative political systems that demand right of way but leave their subjects relatively free in the economic, social, and cultural domains—cannot endure in the face of socioeconomic change. However, two caveats may be in order. The point of change which the process of political underdevelopment sets in varies with the characteristics of the prevailing political culture. Secondly, systemic fragility renders the system vulnerable to attack, but does not necessarily produce the attack. Many vulnerable systems may last for quite some time under different protective umbrellas—for example, other powers, geographic seclusion, or general cultural passivity.

In Iran in 1975 the shah opted for the totalitarian alternative without either an ideological or a structural support basis. In a surprise move, he announced the establishment of the Rastakhiz, the Resurrection Party of the Iranian People. By accepting the leadership of the party, he formalized his own partisan role, a step he would later regret. On the other hand, by assuming the leadership of the Rastakhiz he also condemned the party to failure, because the institutional properties of Iranian kingship could not accommodate totalitarian politics.

As a historical institution, kingship in Iran belonged to the whole of society, in all its manifestations. The shah, as the crown's symbol, could not disassociate himself from any group of Iranian people, either sociologically (workers, peasants, toilers, capitalists, landowners, upper classes, merchants, etc.), or ideologically (communists, liberals, conservatives, fundamentalists, etc.). As a result, the party of which the shah became the leader had to encompass the entire population in all of its sociological and ideological diversity. The Rastakhiz became such a party, coextensive with the political society, which is the same as saying that it never was, nor could it have ever been developed into, a real party under the monarchical system. The only germane idea to which the Rastakhiz could possibly have corresponded was that of a movement from whose interstices genuine political parties might emerge. This tendency was recurrently demonstrated by the operations of the party wings, factions based on majlis coalitions, dubbed the thought basins of the party. But the wings were never allowed to develop and the party became an additional deadweight on the shoulders of bureaucracy.

As a result, the political system became further debilitated. Increasingly it lost what capacity it had to translate the socioeconomic vitality of the society into political capability. While the budget years 1975 and 1976 saw increases in GNP of approximately 38 and 18 percentage points, respectively,[35] the shah's government remained politically petrified, demanding more of a bureaucracy that could no longer deliver. By the end of 1976, the system had already embarked upon a series of policy choices that, in retrospect, could not but lead to its destruction.[36] At the end, everyone looked to the shah—the *image* of power—to handle the revolutionary beast that had suddenly been unleashed, but the shah was in fact helpless, as the conditions that had previously propelled him to the pinnacle of leadership no longer existed. The shah was now politically powerless because the totalitarian option had depoliticized the system's political support. The alternative was the use of ruthless force, a decision that was also left to the shah; it was an option he rejected from the very beginning.

The Pahlavi monarchy was at once the repository of the Iranian crown's institutional characteristics and the creature of a set of historical conditions that determined the properties and proclivities of political power in Iran, as they did in all Third World countries. The interaction between the two sets of conditions produced a dialectic of progress and transformation that led on the one hand to periodic bursts of vigorous movement and on the other to periods of stasis and fragility. After a certain point, however, the historical conditions became the determining factor to which the monarchical institution needed to adjust, while Muhammad Reza Shah and his advisers remained unconscious of the resilience and institutional requirements of Iranian kingship, and thus of how much careful effort such adjustment would take. The shah acted like any other Third World leader. For a period of time, the agreement between the crown's properties and the requirements of development produced a happy combination that led to the extraordinary socioeconomic takeoff of the 1960s and early 1970s. The reason was that the bureaucratic capability legitimized by the crown's authority was not only adequate to the development requirements of the period, but was, perhaps, ideally suited to it.

The resulting change, however, was unprecedented. By mid-1975 the quantitative explosions in the economic, social, and cultural domains had led to a qualitative change in the objective bases of the demands made on the political system: demands for more goods and services were transformed into demands for participation in the allocative decisions. This change appeared to be historically mandated partly because it was inherent in the Iranian national ethos as represented in the ideals of constitutionalism and political freedom, and also, more important, because without such transformation the political system would no longer be able to respond efficaciously to the requirements of its domestic and international environments.

The Iranian political system responded to the evolving strains in typical Third World fashion, by opting for concentrated and centrally directed political participation. By the time the system began to liberalize itself, it was too late. While in 1975 the shah would have been acting from a position of strength, relinquishing power essentially to friends, by 1978 the devolution of power became a process of appeasement, strengthening enemies and weakening the regime.

It should be clear that the suggestion that the shah's government should have moved in the direction of political participation and administrative decentralization does not mean that it could or should have opted from the start for a Western type of democracy. If the shah had not accepted the role of leader, the alternative would most probably have been another leader-dominated regime, not a liberal democracy. On the other hand, a deliberate policy of liberalization in 1974–75 would have brought into the political process elements that were largely supportive of the existing system and of the shah's policies. The shah was not faced in those years with a Frankenstein's monster, but rather with an evolving energy that required room for collective (political) expression. Under the monarchical system, the only way this space could have been provided was through decentralization and deconcentration of power.

The following two points may be suggested in conclusion. First, the fact that the Iranian political system under the monarchical constitution had become fragile did not by itself presage the fall of the regime. Had the shah resorted to the use of force, the regime most probably would not have fallen. If the Reagan administration had come to power four years sooner, or if the shah's system had lasted another two years (assuming that the Reagan administration would have followed Carter's), the shah's system would most probably have survived. But the dialectical dilemma would have remained: the system needed to decentralize and share power if it was to achieve the required balance between the evolving socioeconomic conditions and the responsive capabilities of the political system.

Secondly, monarchies may be conceived of as forms of insurance against totalitarianism, since their survival seems to depend on the system's ability to move toward liberalization of political power once the society adopts a course of rapid socioeconomic development. The fact that all developed monarchical societies belong to the most democratic genres of polities may not be historically fortuitous; rather, it may be the result of historically correct responses to the evolving requirements of socioeconomic change.

SAUDI ARABIA

Traditionalism versus Modernism—

A Royal Dilemma?

■

Hermann Frederick Eilts

In June 1982, following the death of King Khalid ibn 'Abd al-'Aziz, Crown Prince Fahd ascended the Saudi Arabian throne. The sixty-two-year-old Fahd was the fourth successive ruler of the Banu 'Abd al-'Aziz, as the thirty-seven male progeny of the late King 'Abd al-'Aziz ibn 'Abd al-Rahman Al Saud, the founder of the third Saudi state, are generally designated. ("Al," capitalized, signifies "family of," e.g., Al Saud, Al Fahd, Al Shaykh; when not captalized and hyphenated to the succeeding word, denotes the definitive article, e.g., al-Hijaz, al-Hasa.) Fahd is the senior member of the largest and most powerful "sibling cluster." The term refers to subgroups of half brothers, sired by the same father, but from separate mothers.[1] Generally known as the Al Fahd, or sometimes as the Sudayri Seven, a designation derived from their maternal side and their number, this group of princes controls the armed forces of the kingdom, its police and frontier guards (through the Ministry of Interior), and civil aviation.

Because of the concentration of power in the hands of Al Fahd, its members are resented somewhat by smaller, less influential groups of half brothers. Such resentment should not be overstated, however, since the members of Al Saud, with rare exceptions, are keenly aware of the need to project a public image of cohesion if the family's status in the kingdom is to be maintained. Given the extended nature of Al Saud—the late King Faisal (1964–75) once told the author that he estimated there were about five thousand family members—it is only natural that there should be divergent views among the senior members on domestic and foreign issues. Such differences tend to be argued out in closed family councils of a score or so of senior family members until some kind of consensus is reached. It is indeed extraordinary how little is known outside of Al Saud of intrafamily disagreements. Nevertheless, rumors of their existence cannot be quashed. They inevitably give rise to speculation that deep divisive schisms exist within Al Saud.

Before assuming the throne, Fahd had served, first, as director general of education and, subsequently, as minister of education under his elder half brother, King Saud ibn 'Abd al-'Aziz (1953–64). When Faisal ascended the throne in 1964, Fahd was elevated to minister of the interior. Moreover, in 1967, at the suggestion of then Crown Prince Khalid, and after two elder half brothers, Princes Nasir and Sa'd, had waived their seniority rights, he was also designated by Faisal as second vice-president of the Council of Ministers. Although a supporter of Faisal in the protracted power struggle with Saud, he was seldom close to Faisal as monarch. Unlike his younger full brother, Prince Sultan ibn 'Abd al-'Aziz, the dynamic minister of defense and civil aviation, Fahd rarely went through the ritual of "sitting" with the king.[2] His newly added function meant, however, that he henceforth presided over most Saudi cabinet sessions. For personal and temperamental reasons, Khalid considered this duty distasteful, and only titularly continued to hold the position of first vice-president of the Council of Ministers. Fahd's new designation, in the eyes of Al Saud and of the Saudi public, moved him a step closer to eventual accession to the throne.

Already as minister of education, Fahd had acquired a reputation as forward looking. Under his stewardship significant growth of schools in Saudi Arabia had taken place. He was also an early advocate of women's primary and secondary education at a time when the majority of conservative Saudis still looked askance upon such notions. In subsequent years, partly because of his coterie of Lebanese and Palestinian associates, whose putative influence upon him sometimes worried Faisal, Fahd came to be viewed in Saudi Arabia as one of the more "progressive" members of the royal family.[3] To be sure, his "progressivism" remained well within the boundaries of the prevailing sociopolitical system. As such, it both contrasted and overlapped with some of the views of the so-called "free" princes—Talal, Abd al-Muhsin, and Nawwaf—who defected to Nasser's Egypt in 1962 in order to protest the slow pace of change in Saudi Arabia, only to recant two years later and contritely return to the family fold. Fahd's admirers, who included numerous younger Saudis educated abroad, did not hold this against him. Although Nasserism had its adherents in Saudi Arabia, Fahd's supporters cerdited him with perceptively analyzing the weaknesses of the Nasser regime and recognizing that domestic reform in Saudi Arabia, although needed, could not ape the Egyptian Arab socialist model.

In the fifties and especially in the sixties, Fahd spoke to all who would listen, the author among them, of the need for accelerated sociopolitical reform in the kingdom. Such a need had already come to be felt during the reign of King Saud ibn 'Abd al-'Aziz, whose profligacy had created a massive internal and external debt for the state and whose sons were intent on monopolizing power. Members of the royal family, led by Crown Prince Faisal (who later, when prime minister, managed, through an austerity program, to eliminate the debt), as well as Saudi commoners had become persuaded that structural change in the kingdom was required. With changing times the authoritarian governmental system that had been tolerable under 'Abd al-'Aziz had become less so under the often erratic and weak Saud and required modification. Among the Banu 'Abd al-'Aziz, consensus, meaning greater royal family involvement in decision making, was sought; Saudi commoners, for their part, began to voice—as yet mutedly—demands for a greater participatory role in the affairs of government.

Two developments, one originating in the area, the other outside it, bolstered those seeking reform. The first was the overthrow of the monarchy in Egypt in 1952 by a group of military officers led by Gamal Abdul Nasser, and Nasser's increasing stature as the symbol of Arab nationalism. This gradually generated the concomitant suggestion that the Saudi monarchy might also be anachronistic and in need of structural and policy alterations if it was to endure. The second came from the United States, especially after the inauguration in 1961 of President John F. Kennedy, who pressed the Saudi regime to liberalize as the price for continued

U.S. support. On one occasion, when in response to instructions from Washington, the American ambassador to Saudi Arabia urged the cause of reform on King Faisal, the latter angrily retorted, "Do you want the kingdom to become another Berkeley campus?" With Kennedy's death, Secretary of State Dean Rusk wisely took the position that the Saudi leadership was competent to decide where its own best interests lay, and such pressure was discontinued.

Faisal had himself, in 1962, when still crown prince, proposed a ten-point reform program. It called for a strengthened *majlis ash-shura*, or consultative assembly, for provincial assemblies, for a ministry of justice, and for broadened social welfare programs. Once on the throne, however, Faisal procrastinated in implementing these promised reform measures. It was a case of recognizing in principle the need for some structural change as a "safety valve" in order to meet internal and external pressures, yet fearing that once the Pandora's box of change was even slightly opened it would be difficult to prevent wholesale political transformation of the state.

Fahd, in his capacity of minister of interior, argued in effect for more expeditious implementation of the reforms that Faisal had earlier promised. Specifically, Fahd spoke of a Basic Law for the Kingdom, which would supplement rather than replace the Koran as the constitution of the realm; endorsed the concept of a strengthened *majlis ash-shura* and a ministry of justice; and, in rather vague terms, called for provincial assemblies. Fahd's frequent public espousal of these ideas troubled Faisal, who suspected his half brother might be utilizing a reform platform as a means of garnering public support for personal ambitions.

Most of Faisal's promised reforms remained unimplemented or only partially implemented during his almost eleven-year reign. The principal exception was the establishment of a ministry of justice, in late 1970, under the respected *gadhi*, or judge, of Jidda, Muhammad al-Harakan, and a three-tiered *shari'a* appellate court system. Several years later, however, pressure from Al Shaykh, the descendants of the founder of Islamic unitarianism, resulted in the ministerial position going to a member of that distinguished religious family, which continues to hold it to this day.[4]

Faisal's own cautious nature and the conservative counsel of his close advisers inside and outside the royal family kept most of the promised reform measures in limbo. In most other Middle Eastern states neither Faisal's nor Fahd's reform proposals would have been viewed as constituting significant political progress. In the rigidly structured Saudi state, however, they were unquestionably forward looking. Perhaps more importantly, had they been implemented, they were seen as a means of catalyzing future, broader reforms. Faisal's apparent foot dragging on the issue of reform meant that those favoring it turned to the outspoken Fahd as the harbinger of future change. Once Fahd became monarch, his admirers confidently asserted, Saudi Arabia would be on the road to accelerated political and social reform.

The accession of Khalid to the Saudi throne, in the wake of Faisal's assassination in March 1975, initially raised hopes that a new era of reform had dawned in Saudi Arabia. True, Khalid personally was staunchly conservative, but knowledgeable Saudis recalled that even as first vice-president of the Council of Ministers he had rarely shown much interest in participating in policy decisions and had been content to be kept informed. This lack of interest, it was assumed, would surely carry over and would allow Fahd, who now became crown prince and first vice-president of the Council of Ministers, to govern in effect while Khalid reigned titularly. One sensed from Fahd that he, too, may initially have shared that expectation, but it was not to be.

While Fahd did indeed manage most of the routine and even the less routine affairs of the kingdom, Khalid frequently intervened on matters of particular interest to him in response to pressures from elements of the extended Saud family, restive with Al Fahd's perceived preeminence. Sometimes Khalid's interventions simply resulted in indefinite deferral of decisions, leaving issues hanging. Foreign visitors who met Khalid, with Fahd in attendance, former president Jimmy Carter among them, were often struck by Fahd's obvious deference to his elder half brother and sovereign. He seldom said much on such occasions. When not in the presence of Khalid, Fahd was more animated and spoke more freely. Had such foreign visitors known more of traditional Arab family protocol, they might have been less surprised.[5]

During Khalid's almost seven-year reign, with the exception of impressive, expansive, and costly welfare programs for the Saudi public, social and political reform in the kingdom remained largely static. Fahd's admirers attributed this to the fact that he did not have the free scope necessary to put into effect his more forward-looking ideas because of Khalid's sporadic interventions, usually in the interests of conservatism. Once Fahd assumed the throne in his own right, they argued, some changes would surely take place in the sociopolitical fabric of the state.

Fahd has now been monarch for a half decade. While social and political movement is intrinsically glacial in pace in the kingdom (except for madcap driving on Saudi roads), three preliminary judgments are being heard on his performance to date.

One, articulated with some disappointment, suggests that he is deferring too much to the ultraconservative unitarian *'ulama,* who dissuade him from translating some of his previously expressed reform ideas into action. A second, expressed with slightly jaded optimism, contends that the king needs more time to implement his reform ideas and that this must be a slow, step-by-step process. The obstacles—the unsettled Middle East situation, coupled with forces inside and outside the royal family which oppose sociopolitical reform—can be overcome only gradually and subtly. A third view, voiced by Saudi cynics with an "I told you so" smugness, suggests that any belief that Fahd might have more modern attitudes was misplaced from the outset, and that no member of Al Saud can be expected to champion meaningful sociopolitical reform. The summary dismissal of the respected and liberal Dr. Ghazi al-Qusaybi from his position as minister of health in April 1984 because of his published poetic lament that the king was excessively heeding conservative and self-serving advisers is pointed to as evidence of alleged current lack of interest in reform.[6]

Any definitive judgment of Fahd's commitment to reform is still premature, but an assessment of the problems that confront him in undertaking substantial change in the eighties may be useful. Is he indeed faced with a personal and official dilemma as to how to proceed in implementing his long-avowed ideas, as some contend? The question also needs to be considered against the backdrop of the extensive transformation that has taken place in Saudi Arabia in the past forty years.

Modernization of Saudi Arabia

Saudi leaders regard the kingdom as a Third-World, nominally nonaligned, Arab state, whose political and social structures are not reactionary, as Nasser charged, but rather traditional in form. The latter description derives from the sternly orthodox Islamic unitarian configuration of the state, Al Saud's leadership role, the kingdom's responsibility to the world Muslim community as guardian of the sacred cities of Mecca and Medina, and the essentially conservative outlook of much of its population. To be sure, its enormous oil-derived wealth and petroleum reserves have given Saudi Arabia the means to modernize the country's physical façade within a relatively short span of time. But these natural endowments have also given rise to a nagging sense of national insecurity, caused by the perceived covetousness of various less well-endowed neighbors. Although the kingdom's territory is sizable, its long land and sea frontiers are vulnerable, and its indigenous population of five million rattle around in it. First-time observers of Saudi Arabia are usually struck by these aspects of the Saudi environment and sometimes conclude that the state is out of place in the twentieth-century world.

They are wrong; the kingdom has more resiliency than ill wishers and other skeptics believe. The sometimes mooted parallel with prerevolutionary Iran is misleading. Such similarities as do exist between the two countries are more superficial than real: Al Saud, whatever its shortcomings, is not like the Pahlavi family; Sunni and Shiite religio-political doctrines, as practiced in Saudi Arabia and Iran, respectively, vary greatly; Saudi development programs have been devised with considerable thought to public sensitivities; there are no Savak-like abuses in Saudi Arabia; and the kingdom's leadership, while authoritarian, is esssentially benevolent in nature. Moreover, Saudi Arabia has made considerable strides in the past forty years on the road to infrastructural modernization. Anyone who knew the kingdom in the forties, again in the sixties, and who revisits the country today cannot help but be struck by the immensity of some of the changes that have taken place in these intervals.

In the late forties, for example, Jidda, the country's principal seaport for Muslim pilgrims and imports, was a small, still partially walled community. Potable water had to be brought from wells some ten miles distant and carried up to storage tanks on roofs. Riyadh, the country's capital, was a desert oasis, whose so-called palaces and private buildings were constructed of wattle and mud brick in proximity to the palm groves of the Wadi Hanifa, the agricultural valley that traverses much of central Arabia. Foreigners who visited the capital were required to don Arab robes and headgear and were not allowed to smoke in the streets. While the Dhahran and Abqaiq oil districts of the Eastern Province (al-Hasa) had already been partially modernized through the activities of the Arabian American Oil Company (ARAMCO), the towns of Hofuf, 'Anayza, Burayda, Hayil, Tabuk, Khaybar, and Abha were no more than desert oases. They were governed by royally appointed *amirs*, who, together with similarly appointed *gadhis*, dispensed justice in accordance with the *shari'a* (Islamic law) and *'urf* (extralegal traditional tribal law). Mecca and Medina were ill-prepared to accommodate the hundreds of thousands of pilgrims who arrived during the annual *hajj* to the holy cities of Islam and invariably faced serious health, food, water, and accommodation problems.

Apart from the oil areas of the Eastern Province, no Saudi town—and that was all they were—had electricity (except for a few privately owned generators) and kerosene lanterns remained the primary source of illumination. Telephones were virtually nonexistent, and the few that could be found were archaic. Schools and dispensaries were few in number. The national currency consisted of Saudi silver *riyals* and half *riyals* (first minted in Birmingham and later in Philadelphia), small *qursh* pieces (minted locally), and imported British gold sovereigns. As regularly as such gold sovereigns and silver riyals were brought into the country, they were smuggled out to the bullion centers of India, Greece, and the Far East, where their gold and silver content fetched higher prices. Banking was rudimentary and largely in the hands of established money changer families. At the Netherlands Trading Society building in Jidda, the government banker, customers frequently had to climb over a large pile of gold sovereigns, newly received as oil royalties and dumped onto the lobby floor, which were being sorted by a Saudi equivalent of coolie labor into two heaps of "kings" and "queens." Saudi society regularly valued those with Queen Victoria's head on the obverse at several riyals less than the King Edward or George types. Never did the Dutch bank experience any theft in this totally unguarded process.

Even though some of their number had been decisively defeated by 'Abd al-'Aziz in the 1928–30 *ikhwan* rebellion, the large bedouin tribes still roamed their *dirahs*, or proprietary grazing grounds, and remained a force to be reckoned with.[7] One could observe tribal sheikhs periodically coming to the *Bayt al-Mal*, or treasury, in Riyadh to receive their subsidy payments from the government in the form of sacks of silver riyals. Payment was based upon lists of paramilitary levies each such sheikh might muster, if called upon to do so.

Only two strips of two-lane asphalted road existed in the kingdom, one the forty-mile stretch connecting Jidda and Mecca, the other the fifty-mile stretch between Dhahran and Abqaiq. In the rest of the country tracks over sand and gravel desert had to be used by the few trucks and automobiles in the kingdom, and drivers and passengers could count upon laborious efforts to extract vehicles mired in desert sand. It took three days of hard driving to get from Jidda to Riyadh and another day and a half to get from Riyadh to Dhahran. Although a modern, American-built airfield existed at Dhahran, other locales, Riyadh and Jidda included, had no more than landing strips of hard-packed earth, with wind socks as their only landing aid. Large, bare Quonset huts, stifling in the heat, housed airport and custom officials. For a time, in the late forties, the director of the Jidda airport kept a "pet" hyena tied up in the hut. Dirty, mangy, and untamed, it was hardly an inspiring welcome to the few arriving air passengers! A telegraph of sorts connected Jidda, Mecca, Riyadh, and Dhahran, but was often out of operation and seldom reliable.

Western expatriates were relatively few. They consisted of several hundred ARAMCO-employed Americans and their dependents, resident in the company's Dhahran and Abqaiq compounds; a few American contractor personnel; a handful of American airmen manning the Dhahran airfield; some Italian ex-prisoners of war working for ARAMCO; and a small foreign diplomatic community of no more than thirty in Jidda.

Twenty years later, by the 1960s, the Saudi landscape had altered dramatically. Jidda's wall had been razed and the city had expanded seven miles north of its earlier limits. Riyadh, that erstwhile palm oasis, had become a thriving metropolis with large palaces and government buildings. Al-Khobar, the port of Dhahran, and nearby Dammam were tolerably busy seaports. A transpeninsular paved highway, linking Jidda, Riyadh, and the Eastern Province, was completed in 1966. A part of that highway, connecting Mecca and Tayif, was an engineering masterpiece, spiraling its way up the precipitous Jabal Qara. Paved roads were beginning to be built to Medina, the Qasim in central Arabia, and, in the Western Province, northward to the Jordanian border. The Tapline road traversed northern Saudi Arabia.

Hayil (in the northern Jabal Shammar) and Abha (in the southwestern 'Asir Province) still remained isolated and neglected, except for air travel. The latter had been facilitated by the construction of small airports throughout the country. Saudi Airlines had grown from its initial four DC-3s, piloted by Americans, to become the largest commercial air fleet in the Middle East. It included Boeing 707s, Douglas DC-9s, and other modern planes, with Saudi pilots sharing cockpit responsibilities with Americans. An improved telephone system connected most points in the country. Apart from small villages in the north and south, where electricity was still generated by decrepit generators and distributed through helter-skelter wiring, most Saudi towns now had electricity and some measure of sanitation.

Medical services, while perhaps still lacking in quality, existed in the main cities, staffed by Pakistani doctors and male nurses and some Lebanese and Syrian physicians. Pakistani paramedical personnel had been engaged for village dispensaries in the provinces. Schools, including two secular universities and two Islamic religious colleges, had been opened. Women were beginning to attend higher-level institutions, admittedly on a segregated basis. No longer was the national currency solely gold and silver specie. Despite the earlier predictions of Saudi and non-Saudi "experts" that the public would never accept anything but silver and gold coinage, paper money had been introduced with scarcely a ripple. This was first accomplished in the early fifties through the medium of paper hajj receipts, issued by the Saudi Arabian Monetary Agency (SAMA) to Muslim pilgrims who, upon arrival, deposited expense monies. These receipts were then used as script in payment for local services and goods. From this, it was but a short step to SAMA-issued bank notes.[8] Though banking had been modernized, usury was proscribed in accordance with Islamic practice.

Bedouin life had also changed. Alongside the black goat-hair tents of the nomads, which took a long time to make, one saw more and more frequently white canvas tents imported from the West, bought in local *suqs*, or markets. Flatbed and tanker trucks, used to bring water *to* the nomads' sheep and goats or to haul their camels to distant markets, were commonplace in tribal encampments. And, when bedouin were asked to whose domain an area belonged, the response was now *Dirat as-Sa'ud*, rather than the traditional tribal ascription. Dramatic evidence of government control over the nomads could be seen at Turayf, on the Tapline road, where thousands of camels, bearing the *wasm*, or brand, of different tribes, were now watered in the dry summer months with hardly an incident. Bedouin settlement was also being pursued, although Faisal insisted that age-old enmities still made it desirable to separate tribal groups when establishing such settlements. Tribal levies had been replaced by the Saudi Arabian National Guard, still drawn from the tribes, but in fixed encampments and centrally commanded.

By the 1960s, over one million foreigners lived in Saudi Arabia. Most of them were Yemenis and Hadhramis, with a few Palestinians, but there were also some seven thousand Americans, a thousand or so Britons, several thousand Pakistanis, and members of various other nationalities. In contrast to the logistical and medical problems that had in earlier years plagued the annual hajj, the pilgrimage had become a generally well-managed affair. The Saudi Arabian authorities took their responsibilities to the Muslim world seriously and spent much time and effort in improving pilgrimage facilities. Oil income had increased tenfold, and national development planning was being revitalized. And, in the security field, the beginnings of a modern army and air force, separate from the National Guard, had been organized.

Politically, the succession issue had been peacefully resolved in 1964 with Saud's enforced abdication, at the insistence of the Saudi royal family, and Faisal's designation to succeed him.[9] The changeover was legitimized by a *fatwa*, or advisory opinion, issued by the ulama. The precedent thus established offered promise that future successions, in contrast to some in the eighteenth century, could be handled without civil conflict—a significant political achievement in a traditional polity.

Yet another ten years later, with the advent of substantially greater petroleum revenues resulting from the price increases imposed in 1973, and with the implementation of two ambitious five-year development plans, observable changes in Saudi Arabia became even more dramatic. Indeed, physical change in the country had run amok. Jidda, Riyadh, the Dammam-Dhahran-Khobar triangle, Mecca, and Medina had become megapoli, each with over half a million people. The more remote cities, including Hayil and Abha, had been largely rebuilt and supplied with water and electricity. Power grids extended even to small villages. Vast industrial complexes were being built at Jubayl on the Persian Gulf and at Yanbu al-Bahr, on the Red Sea. Television had been introduced on Faisal's orders, and had proliferated throughout the country, although programming still tended to be heavily religious. In some more conservative areas, especially in the Qasimi town of Burayda, known for the dourness of its inhabitants, efforts on the part of ultraconservative elements to prevent the installation of TV stations had had to be countered with force. Education at all levels was available to more and more people, although male and female students were still segregated. Medical facilities throughout the country now included the latest state-of-the-art equipment, sometimes beyond the capability of Pakistani, Lebanese, and newly imported Egyptian doctors to operate. American and European doctors and nurses now staff the better Saudi hospitals.

A network of paved highways crisscrosses the kingdom from east to west and from north to south. No longer is any area of Saudi Arabia isolated from others, as was the case only a generation earlier. A new Saudi telephone network is the envy of many more extensively developed countries and allows foreign numbers to be dialed and connected within seconds. Housing throughout the kingdom has increasingly been modernized, as the Saudi Arabian government provides aspiring house owners with land and interest-free capital to construct their homes. A kind of welfare state has evolved. New airports have been built in Jidda and Riyadh; the one in Jidda, it is boasted, is almost as large as the entire settled area of Bahrain! The annual pilgrimage is managed with exemplary efficiency and minimum hardship for pilgrims, even in the hot summer season.

In short, the process of physical change in Saudi Arabia, which has largely taken the form of the creation of all kinds of infrastructure, has been nothing short of astounding. Mistakes were inevitable in any such accelerated, telescoped process (e.g., high rises in Jidda and Riyadh that no one wants to live in), but the overall achievement is commendable, even awesome. Few who have known Saudi Arabia over these past four decades can fail to appreciate the magnitude of the Saudi accomplishment.

Implicit in so vast a development effort is the notion of a "boom" economy. The kingdom's first three five-year development programs, beginning in 1970, lubricated the national economy, provided some measure of wealth to old and new Saudi entrepreneurs, and in general created a welfare pattern of society from which every citizen of the state benefits in one way or another. With cars, TV, radio, and appliances of all sorts, life for today's Saudi national is a far cry from the largely subsistence economy endured by his parents. Indeed, the expansive nature of the Saudi economy has created attitudinal problems among many Saudis, who today are reluctant to undertake manual labor—taxi driving and heavy and light equipment operation excepted—and believe this should be left to foreign workers. For Saudis, their country is engaged in a service economy with its inevitable deemphasizing of individual productivity. The present petroleum glut situation, which has resulted in decreased oil production and reduced oil income, has not yet seriously affected the Saudi citizen, although wiser Saudis are wondering if present-day Saudi society, accustomed as it has become to relative affluence, would be able to cope with serious financial and economic stringencies, should these recur. Moreover, the concept of individual and family "honor," so powerful a force in traditional Arab culture, while not yet dead, shows signs of fraying as a value in present-day, increasingly materialistic Saudi society, although "face" remains important to the individual Saudi.

Dramatic as the aforementioned physical and economic transformation of the kingdom has been, social and political change has lagged far behind. The modernization process in Saudi Arabia has been skewed, and contradictions are everywhere apparent. Among the most notable are the lack of any participatory role for the Saudi citizen in the affairs of government; the continued second-class status of women; and the continued ban on public entertainment and motion pictures, although private video sets abound. Similarly, a ban exists on the consumption of alcohol, although, in what many decry as hypocrisy, some drinking does take place among members of the Saudi elite in private homes. Some observers predict that the failure to institute social and political reform, commensurate at least in some degree with the physical and economic modernization that has taken place, could ultimately adversely affect future political stability in the country.

Fahd, though not a product of any Western educational system, has long been aware of competing pressures within the kingdom for and against rapid social and political change. He must weigh the forces at work on both sides of the sociopolitical modernization ledger and arrive at a reasonable balance between the two. It is tempting for outsiders to contend that if he really means what he previously talked about, he should simply institute needed reform by royal edict. In fact, the process is anything but simple, and his assessment of the relative strength of the forces at work will have to take into account a complex of competing internal and external considerations.

Stimuli for Sociopolitical Change

As already suggested, alongside the enormous physical and infrastructural changes that have taken place in Saudi Arabia during the past four decades, and influenced by them, there has also been a modicum of social change. To be sure, the latter has not kept pace with the galloping physical reconfiguration of the kingdom. To the uninitiated outsider, such social change as has taken place is often unrecognized (for example, education for women) or, when pointed out, is dismissed as tokenism or as something to be expected. It used to be said during the late King Faisal's reign that social change in Saudi Arabia was a "two steps forward, one step backward" process. To the extent that this was true, it nevertheless indicated a slow but steady movement forward. Various recent observers of Saudi Arabia believe that in the past several years the process may have stagnated, even retrogressed, and hope that it will before long be resumed. Clearly, stimuli for sociopolitical change exist in the kingdom, and they cannot be contained permanently.

These stimuli for change are present in the very nature of present-day Saudi society. First, Saudi Arabia's traditional geographical and political isolation has steadily been eroded. The kingdom is an active participant in Arab, Third World, and nonaligned congeries of states. Its past constructive and exceedingly difficult role in seeking to arrange an acceptable Lebanese settlement was a case in point. Moreover, its membership in the United Nations and in the latter's specialized agencies, including the International Bank for Reconstruction and Development and the International Monetary Fund, bring it into regular contact with the international community. While such international associations may have only limited effect upon the domestic structure of Saudi society, it nevertheless means that the country's leadership cannot be blind to changes taking place in the world at large.

Second, as already noted, Saudi Arabia has become the affluent society par excellence. The reduced petroleum income resulting from the current oil glut does not appreciably alter the nation's intrinsic affluence. Its reserve coffers and foreign investments remain high. In any case, the expectation exists that the present oil glut will be reversed in the next few years and that the kingdom will once again be assured of a sizable annual income. Despite inequities in the distribution of Saudi Arabia's oil-derived wealth, the welfare-state concept, from which virtually all Saudis benefit to some degree, persists. Indeed, Saudi society, in its entirety, has become accustomed to massive imports of commodities, including luxury items, all financed through the allocation of petroleum revenues. True, there have been frequent complaints from members of older business firms that government contracts, upon which a large part of the economy depends, have been unequally apportioned; that there is favoritism and corruption among many members of the Saudi elite; and that newer business firms are intruding on the commercial turf of older merchants. Creditors also complain about long delays in payments due them by the Saudi government. But such developments, inevitable in the mushrooming economy that has characterized Saudi development over the past decade, do not appreciably alter the fact that the kingdom remains relatively well-off in contrast to many of its neighbors.

An affluent society inevitably gives rise to greater leisure, which in turn leads the quest for human satisfactions to seek broader outlets. Saudis, both the rich and the less well-off, have increasingly sought to breach the mores of a rigid socioreligious system. Education, freely available to all Saudis, has meant that not only men but more and more women enroll in the nation's burgeoning university system. While a substantial core of Islamic studies is still required in Saudi Arabia's secular universities, higher educational curricula now also include nonreligious subject matter. Women, although still studying in separate classrooms, often with closed-circuit TV and microphones to allow them to question the distant male lecturer, have in frequent instances surpassed their male counterparts in academic achievement.

One increasingly hears of women graduates, while insisting upon respect for Islamic and family values, wanting to use their education and skills in employment outside the home. Fewer and fewer Saudi women are today wholly content with the traditional role of their mothers as homemakers and rearers of children. Feminism in Saudi Arabia has not reached the point of rejecting such responsibilities, but many women clearly aspire to more intellectually satisfying complementary outlets.

Long-time observers of Saudi Arabia note that veils, while still worn, are more transparent than they were twenty years ago. In many instances, Saudi women traveling to Europe or elsewhere quickly shed their long black *abayas* upon arriving at their foreign destination. There they don the most fashionable dresses and clearly enjoy the social freedoms available in Europe. Were Saudi Arabia not the strong male-dominated society that it is, they would doubtless seek to exercise their freedoms to an even greater extent than they currently do.

To be sure, there is an inconsistency to the process of women's liberation in the kingdom. Some retrogression has occurred in the past five years, for example, because of recent government decrees enjoining conservative female dress, the heightened vigilance of the detested committees of public morality, and the enforced removal of women from employment in foreign firms—all actions prompted by male concern that Saudi women's aspirations may be getting out of hand. Yet, however long this may persist, it cannot permanently stay the subtle, yet irresistible, dynamism of women's progress. The kingdom is in desperate need of more indigenous labor to perform the multitudinous tasks arising from rapid economic development. Sooner or later, the as yet untapped reservoir of Saudi women, capable of performing a much broader variety of functions than is currently assigned them, will have to be recognized as the national asset that it is and be more effectively utilized in the economic development of the state.

A third important stimulus to social change in Saudi Arabia is the fact that, as a function of affluence, more and more Saudis—men and women alike—have the means to travel abroad. Their exposure to the cities of Europe and America is frequent and constant. Those with means often spend the hot summer months outside the kingdom. While abroad, they experience the freedoms of modern societies. For some, this more or less regularized experience is a kind of safety valve that makes life tolerable for the rest of the year in more rigid social conditions. Others, it must be acknowledged, are repulsed by what they perceive to be the excessively materialistic style of Western life and its attendant erosion of religion and family values. Saudis in both categories, however, return home with the desire that at least some aspects of Western sociopolitical practices be introduced into the kingdom, even if wrapped in stricter Islamic garb. A similar reaction can be observed among many of the fifteen thousand or more Saudi students currently studying in American and European universities and who eventually return to their native land. Most have little difficulty in reverting, at least publicly, to the strictures of their native social system; privately, however, one hears many yearn for accelerated, even if modest, sociopolitical change.

A fourth stimulus to change, often overlooked, is the influence of more secularized Arab societies—Egyptian, Syrian, Lebanese, Iraqi, and Palestinian. A fair number of Saudi men, including a good many princes of the royal family, are married to women from other Arab countries. The latter have in many instances been brought up in far freer social conditions. Though they may indeed have to conform to more rigid Saudi social codes while in the kingdom, and some have no difficulty in doing so, the subtle influence of such foreign wives on their husbands, urging social liberation, is persistent. Peer pressure in Saudi Arabia may still limit the effect of such influences in public, including segregation and veiling, but in private one finds greater social contact among younger Saudis, including mixed couples. The home remains the sanctuary of Saudi society, and what transpires within its walls is beyond the purview—at least nominally—of the ubiquitous committees of public morality. In any event, meddlesome *mutawa'iin*, as the religious police are called, can usually be appeased with a gratuity.

Still another stimulus to social change is the spillover effect of the large number of foreigners, especially Americans and Europeans, who work in Saudi Arabia as part of the kingdom's massive five-year development programs. There are now some two and a half million such expatriates in the country, or about 33 percent of the total population. Admittedly, in order to minimize the cultural and social influence of foreigners on Saudi society, many of them are required to reside in special compounds or in separate quarters of the larger cities, and are isolated in other ways from Saudi society. But the system is not foolproof. There is increasing contact between Saudis and Westerners, not only in the workplace but also at home and occasionally on the sports field. Conversely, many Saudis have come to resent the pervasive Western presence.

In the case of expatriates from the Far East—Koreans, Japanese, and Filipinos—many come without families and thus have no particular interest in associating with Saudi society. Nevertheless, the overall effect of such large numbers of foreigners from differing cultures and broader social systems must inevitably have some impact. Recognition of this fact has prompted concern on the part of Saudi traditionalists, and the current five-year development plan calls for a reduction in the number of non-Arab residents in order to reduce the risk of cultural "taint" on Saudi society. Such efforts can have only limited effect. In the years ahead, Saudi Arabia will still require large numbers of foreign experts to implement its development programs, which will entail the omnipresent risk of exposing Saudi society to broader social concepts.

Finally, improved communication systems acquaint Saudis in every part of the kingdom with political, social, and cultural developments abroad. The national television network can be controlled by the Saudi Arabian authorities, but foreign films shown on television—even after censorship—must inevitably instill into Saudi viewers new ideas about the optimal functioning of society. So do smuggled video tapes, foreign radio programs, and so on.

In the strictly political sphere, stimuli for reform are more indirect. While Saudi newspaper editors usually prudently mute their comments on national political issues, and instead focus complaints upon local and municipal problems, there are occasional guarded calls by more venturesome journalists for greater public participation in national decision making. This is particularly true since Fahd became king. Paradoxically, some of these journalists themselves remain traditionalists in their insistence upon women's segregation. Although they tend to be dubbed radical by the Saudi elite, they are so only in relative terms. Their discreet prodding is unquestionably indicative of a greater desire on the part of the Saudi intelligentsia for a voice in the nation's affairs.

Many young Saudi bureaucrats and technocrats, trained in American, European, and Egyptian universities, consider themselves better qualified for responsible government positions than are some members of the royal family. They aspire to responsibilities commensurate with their university degrees and their self-perceived talents. They chafe under the prevailing system, where their high-sounding bureaucratic titles often bear little relationship to the responsibilities allotted them. When commoners have attained ministerial rank—and some serve with conspicuous distinction—they have been largely in technical or nonsensitive policy ministries.

The possibility of augmenting and contributing to governmental income by extracurricular business activities eases some of the frustrations and pent-up pressures of Saudi technocrats and bureaucrats, but it is no permanent substitute for their aspirations to greater policy-making roles. Unfortunately, the need to find senior positions in government for members of the various branches of Al Saud, in the interest of maintaining royal family consensus and harmony, reduces the number of senior positions available to Saudi commoners and creates an undercurrent of restiveness. The perception that exists among some younger, Western-trained Saudis that the kingdom is primarily a Saud family fiefdom and that their prospects are limited as long as it remains such is a potential source of political discontent. At the same time it should be emphasized that the Saudi royal family has a great many well-trained, able, and dedicated members, who contribute materially to the well-being of the nation. The image of idle, effete princes, mainly interested in personal gain, which some elements of the American media like to draw, is unfair, misleading, and off the mark. There are such individuals, but there are far more outstanding Saudi princes, who, through sheer competence, would make their mark in any society.

Constraints on Sociopolitical Reform

From the days of 'Abd al-'Aziz to the present, Saudi monarchs have faced significant obstacles to their efforts to bring about change in the country's social and political structures. They have had to be conscious of the danger, in an orthodox Islamic society, of being charged with *bida'*, or innovation, and have often had to resort to devious measures to counter such charges. Some Saudi leaders have been more adept at doing so than others; all have had to contend with the problem. Fahd is no exception to the rule.

No Saudi leader can ignore the religious traditionalism in which the Saudi polity is steeped. The central Arabian Najdi provenance of the state, in contrast to its more cosmopolitan Hijazi and Hasawi accretions, bespeaks an orthodox, narrow, even xenophobic weltanschauung. The historic alliance between Al Saud and Al Shaykh, beginning with the first Saudi empire in the mid-eighteenth century and still maintained through intermarriage, remains a significant determinant of the socioreligious policies of the state. Since politics in Islam are inextricably interwoven with religion, it likewise affects national political policies, especially on the domestic front. Indeed, the political legitimacy of Al Saud is rooted in its strict adherence to advocacy of rigid unitarian doctrine.

No Saudi ruler, whatever his personal inclinations, can stray far from Islamic religious precepts in devising policy without risking ulama censure and a consequent erosion of domestic political legitimacy. However antiquated the idea may be, the raison d'être of the Saudi state is perceived by the ulama to be the promotion of rigid unitarian values. Such environmental modernization as has taken place only spurs ulama resolve to protect what they perceive to be their society's endangered spiritual values from outside secular and cultural pollution.

The Saudi ulama, especially the senior members of Al Shaykh and the blind éminence grise, Shaykh 'Abd al-'Aziz al-Baz, see themselves as guardians of the conduct of the community of believers. They are quick to condemn anything novel as innovation, hence contrary to divine ordinance. Consistent with a practice followed since 'Abd al-'Aziz's day, the ulama meet frequently with the monarch. In those sessions they vent their concerns about what they perceive to be the de-Islamization of Saudi society because of pernicious Western or other non-Muslim influences. Al-Baz has even railed against foreign travel as a polluting influence. Moreover, the hope that existed a decade ago that a younger and more internationally traveled group of ulama would gradually come into being, whose social outlook would be broadened by foreign exposure, has not thus far materialized.

One wonders what the effect upon the conservative, ulama-dominated society of Riyadh will be now that the entire diplomatic corps has moved there from Jidda, as mandated by the Saudi authorities. Diplomats can, if necessary, do without alcoholic libations, but reasonably free socializing will almost certainly be demanded. So will the right to Christian worship, without this having to be exercised in a Saudi equivalent of Roman catacombs. It is regrettable that the influence of the ulama led the Saudi leadership to expel a number of Christian lay leaders in 1984.

The influence of the ulama is enhanced by the fact that senior members of "sibling clusters," resentful of the Al Fahd, are prepared to use them against the king, should he appear to be introducing measures they consider deleterious to their own or to the family's overall interests. While Fahd is the titular head of the family, he must contend with factionalism in Al Saud. The late King Faisal once told the author that one of his greatest problems was managing the extended and often fractious royal family; the task is doubtless even more difficult for Fahd. In order to prevent family members from seeking to use the ulama against him, and thereby challenging his political legitimacy, it is incumbent upon Fahd to go out of his way to solicit the support of the religious savants, even if it often means propitiating them. The need to do so inevitably works against sociopolitical reform.

There is in any case little enthusiasm in Al Saud, with a few exceptions, for accelerated reform measures. Although a few younger members of the family profess to favor broader participation by commoners in policy-making councils, the bulk of the royal family fears that any extensive restructuring of the state will inevitably erode its privileged status. They are right; it probably would, although one could conceive of a greater sharing of decision-making authority with nonroyal Saudis without seriously damaging the family's present preeminent role. Yet, most family members are tepid about any such suggestion, or at most give it lip service.

Nor does the concept of decentralization—that is, provincial assemblies—evoke much enthusiasm. Many Saudis contend that such provincial assemblies would at best mean a marginally greater participatory role in government. The likely members of such assemblies, they point out, would be the traditional tribal and town leaders of the provinces. These would hardly be representative. Still other Saudis dismiss provincial assemblies as running counter to the difficult and sometimes politically painful efforts made by the late King Faisal to try to fuse the disparate geographical elements of the country into some kind of a cohesive nationality after their enforced unification by his father.

Some five years ago, younger princes of Al Saud were designated to the governorates of the Northern (Jabal Shammar) and Southern ('Asir) provinces. Royal family members already governed the Western (Hijaz) and Central (Najd) provinces. This meant that only the Eastern (al-Hasa) province, where the collateral Jiluwi branch of the family governed, was outside the immediate control of the main branch of the royal family.[10] In early March 1985 Amir Muhammad ibn Fahd, a son of the monarch, assumed the governorate of the Eastern Province, replacing the Jiluwi *amir*. Thus, all five major provinces are now directly in royal family hands. There is some value to such arrangements. These princely governors can appeal to the central authorities in Riyadh for needed financial and personnel support. Although they, too, find themselves strapped for funds as a result of declining oil exports and reduced prices, their access to the highest national authorities places them in a favorable position to obtain at least some funding for public projects. Their ability to do so has resulted in substantial development efforts in the previously neglected Northern and Southern provinces. In each case, too, they have proved themselves in their handling of the governor's daily public *majlis*, or petition-receiving session, by dispensing equitable and expeditious administrative judgments.[11]

It is frankly doubtful that any Saud family *amir* in the provinces would be particularly anxious to have a potentially assertive provincial assembly share his governorship. A strictly consultative role would be acceptable, but sharing of decision making would not be. Provincial assemblies may eventually be established, but their powers are certain to be limited.

The seizure of the *masjid al-haram* in Mecca, on November 20, 1979, by fanatical Saudi millenarians, led by and consisting mainly of 'Utayba tribesmen and assisted by some fundamentalist Muslim expatriates—including two American black Muslims who were studying at the Islamic shari'a college in Medina—has also had at least a temporarily negative impact on sociopolitical reform. Although the incident was an aberration, it was a searing experience for the Saudi leadership, not only because it happened, but also because of the difficulty experienced in forcibly recapturing the sacred shrine. It inevitably raised questions in the broader Muslim world—to whom the Saudi leadership is responsible for the guardianship of the Islamic *Haramayn*—about the security of the holy places. The incident was widely criticized by devout Saudis and other Muslims throughout the world, and by critics of Al Saud, as having violated the prescribed sanctity of the holiest shrine of Islam. Moreover, some of the charges leveled by the insurgent leaders against the irreligiousness of members of Al Saud hit home.

Although some Saudis, men and women alike, voiced the view immediately after the incident that it would impel an "opening" of Saudi society, largely in the belief that the ulama and the forces of ultraconservative Islam had been discredited in the public eye, subsequent events proved this was wishful thinking. Rather than liberalize, the authorities deemed it prudent once again to backtrack on such modest social development as had evolved. The already mentioned dress codes were rigidified, the committees of public morality were enjoined to greater vigilance, and there was a general clamping down on activities criticized by the ulama as contrary to Islam. Saudi customs and immigration authorities throughout the kingdom became more difficult and, in the name of Islam, security was tightened everywhere. The ensuing rigidification has now lasted seven years, a longer time than any such past cyclical Saudi patterns.

The protracted nature of the current social retrogression is also attributable to concern on the part of the Saudi leadership over sporadic media attacks by the Ayatollah Khomeini's Iranian Islamic Republic on the Saudi regime as irreligious, corrupt, and contrary to Islam. Khomeini's belated conclusion that "kingship" is inconsistent with Islam is a charge to which Al Saud—and especially the reigning monarch, Fahd—must be sensitive. He must bear in mind that the unitarian ulama have never been comfortable with "kingship" and insist that sovereignty can be vested only in God.

Aggravating this is the fact that the Iranian Islamic Republic's proclaimed "revolution for export" has as one of its prime objectives the overthrow of the Saudi monarchy. Various reasons exist for Iran's implacable enmity toward a sister Islamic state. Historically, and in Iranian eyes today, the Sunni unitarian regime of Saudi Arabia has discriminated against and persecuted their fellow sectarians, the Saudi Imami Shiite minority, resident mainly in the Eastern Province, and in the late twenties forced many to flee to Bahrain. Then, too, the Saudi Arabian government had correct, even if not always cordial, relations with the late shah of Iran. Today, because of Saudi financial assistance and free transit facilities accorded Iraq, the kingdom is condemned as aiding the enemies of the Iranian Islamic Republic. Moreover, Saudi Arabia's close relations with the United States make the kingdom, in Iranian eyes, an associate of the "great satan." In fact, "Establishment Islam" in Saudi Arabia—rigidly orthodox though unitarianism is—is castigated by Iranians as *Islami al-Amerika*, or "American Islam." There can be no greater slur or more effective way of wounding Saudi sensitivities, however spurious the charge may be. Finally, the two states compete, as they have in the past, for political and military preeminence in the Arabian/Persian Gulf.

Although the Saudi Arabian authorities, consistent with the security policies of Saudi regimes from the time of 'Abd al-'Aziz, have looked to the United States to offer some vague kind of defense commitment against Iran and other putative external threats—not overly enthusiastically, to be sure, considering American-Saudi differences over Arab-Israeli issues—whatever protection Washington might be willing or able to offer is of little use in coping with the insidious and indirect appeal implicit in the success of the Iranian Islamic revolution. Like Muslims elsewhere, Saudis, while wanting a better quality of life, have long chafed at what they perceive to be materialistic Western modernization models, largely introduced by Americans. Some barely conceal their displeasure with Al Saud's heavy dependence upon the United States. Frustrated, some even talk of using the "oil weapon" against the United States if it does not pursue more equitable policies on Arab-Israeli issues. This may not be realistic, but it reflects a growing anti-American public mood.

If for Asiatics the lesson of Vietnam was that an Eastern people could successfully challenge an industrialized Western society, Khomeini's revolution represents an Eastern Islamic society's parallel and comparable success. Many Saudis are convinced they can do the same, and would like to remove the widely perceived stigma of their nation allegedly being an American surrogate. The prolonged inability of the United States, under President Carter, to obtain the release of the American diplomatic hostages in Iran, coupled with the abortive Tabes rescue operation, conjured in the minds of many Muslims—including Saudis—an exaggerated image of the potential strength of resurgent Islamic determination and of a corresponding weakness of the West.

Few educated Saudis wish to emulate the Iranian model of government that has evolved. Even traditionalists among them have their own conceptual models, most of which are only vaguely articulated, but which stress justice and equity for all believers and a protected client status for indigenous non-Muslim minorities. In fact, the dissident millenarians involved in the Mecca incident included in their litany of complaints alleged official Saudi coddling of the nation's Shiite minority. Yet this in no way dims the image of a successful Islamic revolution, as projected by the Iranian example, encouraging Muslim resurgence elsewhere against both established authority and Western associations. Iranian broadcasts directed at Saudi Arabia, as well as regular propagandizing done by annual Iranian pilgrimage contingents, serve to fan such latent sentiments.

To a point, the Saudi authorities can manage this by close surveillance, police measures, and expulsions, but these are not enough. Living in an atmosphere of recurrent Iranian charges of perfidy, dissoluteness, and pro-Americanism makes it incumbent upon the senior Saudi princes, and especially upon Fahd as monarch, to adhere as closely as their temperaments permit to orthodox unitarian practices in order to avoid alienating the conservative elements of the Saudi public. Whatever Fahd's own preferences may be, the present moment is hardly propitious for him to be boldly innovative and to attempt to liberalize the nation's sociopolitical structure. Some contend that doing so would, in fact, redound to his domestic political benefit, but taking that risk now is simply too dangerous, even if Fahd were actively interested in doing so.

Various sociopolitical reform measures continue to be promised by the Saudi regime to its public; most are simply said to be "under study." Even the draft of the new Basic Law has been in limbo for five years, allegedly being scrutinized by a committee headed by Prince Nayif ibn 'Abd al-'Aziz, one of the monarch's brothers. One cannot escape the conclusion that senior members of Al Saud currently feel no urgency about introducing long-promised political reforms. Nor, it must be admitted, does one detect at present any unmanageable public undercurrent demanding accelerated action on proposed reform. While occasional mutterings of dissatisfaction with the slow pace of reform are heard, and expatriate Saudi dissident organizations publicly pillory the regime, often with little regard to truth, there are no effective means of translating reformist views into action.

As long as the Saudi military remains passive on the issue of sociopolitical reform—and all signs point to its being largely disinterested so long as modern weaponry and personal perquisites are provided to the officer corps—putative reformers must simply bide their time. A few in the military may plot in private, and one sometimes hears of arrests or cashiering of officers suspected of disloyalty. Partly to guard against this, and partly because of individual princes' genuine professional interest in the military, members of Al Saud have undergone military training and have been placed in strategic command positions, where they can monitor any disaffection that may develop in the armed services. Pakistani mercenaries have also been introduced to bolster external defense.

Murky Crystal Gazing

The ability of any Saudi monarch to juggle the aforementioned countervailing stimuli and constraints to sociopolitical reform in a fashion such that some forward movement ensues is a function of several interacting factors: his personal temperament, the depth of his conviction of the need for reform, his reputation within and outside the family, the domestic power assets he controls, and his personal leadership skills. Whoever the monarch may be, gradualism rather than any sharp break with past practice is likely to remain the order of the day.

Much, too, will depend upon the length of the monarch's rule. It takes time to institute change in Saudi Arabia. Fahd had first to establish his authority over the family and the contending elements favoring and opposing reform. Kingship in Saudi Arabia cannot be arbitrary as far as Al Saud is concerned; it is a primus inter pares situation, requiring constant concessions to one or another "sibling cluster." Above all, the king must have the requisite Islamic religious knowledge to be able to demonstrate, at least publicly, that proposed reform measures are not inconsistent with—the double negative is deliberate—Muslim canonical practice.

In theory, Hanbalism, the root school of unitarianism, allows certain canonical flexibility. Thus, for example, *takhayyur*, or legal borrowing from other Sunni schools, is permitted. So is *ijtihad*, or independent reasoning. But the exercise of these two approved procedural devices to foster a broadening of the canonically permissible depends, in the final analysis, upon the willingness of the ulama to make use of them in a positive and innovative manner. Here, the power and influence of the minister of justice of Saudi Arabia, the ultimate arbiter of shari'a legal opinions since the abolition of the grand *mufti* position, are crucial. The minister comes from Al Shaykh, and there has long been muted grumbling among younger Saudis that his training, experience, and mind-set are such that he invariably opts for rigid rather than creative canonical interpretations.

The king, it must be remembered, is no longer the *imam*, or supreme religious leader, as was the case with his grandfather and, nominally, with his father.[12] Were he still that, he could intervene in canonical disputation. The Saudi imamate fell into desuetude with the death of 'Abd al-'Aziz. Saud was hardly qualified for it; Faisal was, by virtue of his early training, but never claimed it; neither Khalid nor Fahd have done so.

To be sure, through the use of such procedures as *takhsis al-qada*, or special ordinancial authority, various ordinances (*nizam*) have been issued over the years, in the form of royal decrees, for areas inadequately covered by the shari'a, such as labor, minerals, commerce, and so forth. These have often established extralegal, arbitral tribunals to handle cases involving Saudis and foreign contractors. They represent efforts to complement the shari'a rather than instruments to promulgate significant sociopolitical change. Such ordinances are invariably drafted with ulama participation so that the latter are assured that they do not intrude upon what they perceive to be the prerogatives of the religious establishment. There are reports that some such proposed ordinances are opposed by the religious savants, allegedly for trespassing on the shari'a, and are therefore either dropped, long delayed, or emasculated before eventual issuance. Moreover, unless compliance with such extralegal arbitral judgments is voluntary, no effective enforcement mechanism exists, as the current line of unpaid foreign creditors attests. Indeed, the sudden "religiosity" of some Saudi businessmen defaulters, in order to have complaints against them heard by more sympathetic shari'a courts rather than extralegal tribunals, represent efforts to change legal contractual ground rules to their advantage.

The Islamic doctrine of *'ijma*, or consensus, which could theoretically be used in support of social reforms in Saudi Arabia, is also subject to ulama-imposed restrictions, hence sharply constrains change in the system. In these circumstances, imagination, infinite patience, deftness, and persistence on the part of the ruler are critical to achieve any reform objectives, however modest they may be.

King 'Abd al-'Aziz was able to persuade the reluctant ulama to accept the telephone as a harmless facilitator of the conversations of the faithful and, subsequently, radio as a carrier of Koranic recitations. He could then argue that anything that conveyed the word of God could hardly be irreligious, novel though these instruments were in Saudi society. Such successful royal suasion did not, however, transpire in a single act; the author recalls 'Abd al-'Aziz once relating that inducing the skeptical ulama, including his aging and rigidly orthodox father, in the case of the telephone, to accept such technological innovations took considerable time and effort. Saud was less venturesome on this score. Faisal, partly because of his maternal Al Shaykh origins, partly because of his acute sensitivity to ulama concerns, and partly because of his undisputed leadership of Al Saud and the nation, had more success. Yet even he was sometimes described as moving forward backward. Khalid, respected though he was by all, was conservative in temperament and essentially uninterested in extensive sociopolitical reform. Fahd, his own inclinations aside, needs to take into account the experience of his four predecessors in this regard and to proceed with caution.

The personality and leadership style of the monarch are clearly critical elements in any process of change. While there are those who disbelieve Fahd's commitment to sociopolitical reform, others who have known him for a long time—among them the present author—believe he is sincere in wanting some modest kind of reform. Perhaps more than most of his siblings and nephews, Fahd realizes that the Saudi state cannot indefinitely endure without trying to meet the sociopolitical aspirations of its people.

Fahd is a man of considerable sagacity, but is also somewhat shy. His five-year reign, concurrent as it has been with a highly roiled Middle East situation, has been too short to date to enable him to establish and to exercise undisputed authority. On controversial issues, both in the domestic and foreign spheres, he still needs to forge and to maintain family consensus. He must conciliate the sometimes divergent views on policy issues of his powerful half brother Crown Prince 'Abd Allah and also of the other leading members of the extended Al Saud. For Fahd, seeking such consensus demands greater compromise than was the case, for example, with either 'Abd al-'Aziz or Faisal. This does not suggest weakness, as some claim, but simply reflects the realities of the current situation. Fahd can still have what he wants, if he insists upon it, but prudence dictates not invoking arbitrary royal command authority too often with members of the family and showing sensitivity to sibling concerns. In the past two years he has reportedly withdrawn to a considerable extent from his brothers, rarely visits Riyadh, prefers to live in Jidda, and relies heavily on his Ibrahimi family in-laws and his sons for counsel, much to the distress of his siblings.

In seeking to assert a leadership role, Fahd has a number of vulnerabilities. For example, some elements of the Saudi public and some members of the royal family, including Crown Prince 'Abd Allah, regard him as too pro-American in outlook. Fahd believes strongly that the future of the kingdom must be tied to a close relationship with the United States, however much he shares the wider Saudi view that American policy in the Middle East is flaccid, ineffective, and biased against Arab interests. Despite widespread advice that the kingdom loosen its ties to America—few responsible Saudis would argue that they be entirely eliminated—he has been steadfast in insisting that the "special relationship" between the two countries be maintained. Indeed, the recently disclosed Saudi contribution to the Nicaraguan "contras" reflects Fahd's personal desire to pander to the Reagan administration.

Fahd's pro-American orientation elicits some criticism of his domestic policies as well—for example, past excessive oil production at the behest of the United States. This in turn militates, albeit indirectly, against vigorous efforts on his part to promote broader sociopolitical reforms. His ability to push through the latter would be considerably enhanced if an active and balanced American Middle East peace initiative, one felt by the Arabs in general to be fair to them as well as to Israel, were in train. His reliance upon the

United States would then be seen as producing positive political results and, in consequence, give him freer scope elsewhere. This is not likely to be the case in the foreseeable future.

Fahd's second vulnerability is his past reputation for being something of a playboy. There are still Saudis who recall the large sums of money that he allegedly lost at European gaming tables. He is not the first Saudi ruler to have enjoyed the fleshpots of Europe before becoming king—Faisal and others, in their youth, also did so—but Fahd must still, in the eyes of the ulama, live this down. He may be king, but they insist upon prescribing proper Islamic conduct for the ruler. In this context, the assertion from across the Gulf that "kingship" is un-Islamic becomes especially dangerous and can be countered only by a visible deference to the counsel of the ulama, however archaic their views may at times be. To demonstrate his unitarian humility, Fahd, in 1986, publicly discarded the royal "majesty" trapping and replaced it with "servant (*khadim*) of the holy places." Some Saudis greeted the change with wry smiles; others appreciated it.

Nor has the behavior of some of Fahd's offspring helped him. Charges of excessively high commissions levied by one of his sons on business transactions some years ago are still heard. From all indications, Fahd has curbed some such practices by his privileged sons, but Saudi memories are long, and royal favoritism toward his sons remains a source of criticism. At a minimum, it will take time for Fahd to build at home an image of true devoutness, incorruptibility, and strong leadership.

Much will depend upon Fahd's health. He has suffered in the past from back problems, which have given him considerable pain, from a diabetic condition, and from overweight. Only he knows the extent to which these ailments sap his energies, and energy and drive are critical elements that any Saudi monarch needs in order to reconfigure existing sociopolitical patterns. The king's working habits are reportedly somewhat sporadic: he will totally engross himself in his work for several days, then will often be unavailable for many days. He enjoys trips abroad, usually on official missions or for health or rest purposes, and sometimes tends to stay away longer than expected. In such instances, the nation's affairs are in the hands of caretakers who lack the authority to make definitive policy decisions.

But even when he is in the kingdom, Fahd must make a judgment on priorities: whether to concentrate on internal or external issues. Since ascending the Saudi throne, he has had to cope with serious problems in close proximity to the nation's borders: the Iraqi-Iranian war, a putative Iranian threat to Saudi Arabia itself, a possible Syrian threat to Jordan, and the Lebanese quagmire. The United States has persistently urged that Saudi Arabia play an active role in seeking to find solutions to these issues. Indeed, American urgings for proposed Saudi actions have sometimes been beyond the political capabilities of the kingdom. To Fahd's credit, he has usually tried to play as constructive a role as the kingdom's limited influence allows—although some Saudis contend that the kingdom, at American behests, may be unwisely exposing itself on some of these issues.

Recent Iranian military successes in Iraq are worrisome in terms of a putative spillover threat to Saudi territory. In Saudi eyes, whatever the financial burden may be, Iraq needs to be supported to be able to defend itself, even if doing so incurs the militant ire of the Iranians. Should the latter happen, either in the form of an Iranian air attack on Saudi territory or an Iranian effort to close the Straits of Hormuz, Fahd must hope for U.S. military assistance in order to preserve the political independence and territorial integrity of the Saudi state. While there is considerable Saudi enthusiasm for the Gulf Cooperation Council, few Saudis—and certainly no one as realistic as Fahd—seriously believe that its member states can effectively defend the Gulf against Iranian military attacks. At the same time, given Saudi uncertainty about United States reliability and the obvious limitation of GCC security posture, the Saudi leadership is quietly seeking to propitiate Iran. It is an unenviable dilemma for Fahd.

Understandably, therefore, Fahd has given priority to trying to cope with these external issues. One might wish that the kingdom could concurrently deal with the issue of domestic reform, but for reasons already discussed, it is simply not structured to do so. There is no great sense of urgency about sociopolitical reform, and those anxious to defer it use the nation's current preoccupation with external and economic matters as a pretext.

Occasionally, elements in the Saudi leadership announce that before long the draft of a new Basic Law will be reported out of committee. As part of this, or separately, the *majlis ash-shura* may be restructured to allow for a phased introduction of elected members to sit alongside royally appointed ones. Even if this eventually transpires, it will be little more than a palliative to the Saudi public. The emphasis will still be on gradualism and form rather than active encouragement of a wider public participatory role in governance. Meanwhile, the ulama are propitiated, the committees for public morality make a nuisance of themselves, and the existing social and political systems show scant signs of change. Whatever the king's long-term objective in instituting reforms may be, he is not currently in a position to push the cause of innovation. It is doubtful, in this author's judgment, that this poses any real dilemma for him, since existing domestic pressures for change are still only vaguely articulated. They will not remain so indefinitely, however. Sooner or later the Saudi leadership will have to come to grips with instituting needed sociopolitical progress. Fahd, in his earlier position, seemed to carry the banner for such reform. One may hope that, as ruler, he will before long give it the attention that his earlier pronouncements suggested he believes it deserves.

If Fahd rules for ten years, and if the current troubled Middle East situation subsides, he may yet turn more actively to this unfulfilled aspect of his avowed mission. One purely human factor needs nevertheless be borne in mind. In any political system, it is one thing for a leader to call for reform when not in office; it is quite another matter for that same leader, once in office, actually to institute reform, with all of the risks inherent in consciously circumscribing his future powers and those of the elite that he represents. Fahd is precisely in that position. Pushing through reforms, however modest they may be, will have to be in ways acceptable to Al Saud and the ulama. The task, if and when attempted, will tax Fahd's political skills to the utmost. The outcome is at best uncertain, but such an effort will have to be made at some point. Upon it, and its success, may depend the future stability of the Saudi state.

The winds of change do not yet gust in Saudi Arabia, but waft they already do. They will become stronger. The test of Saudi leadership in the years ahead will be furthering constructive sociopolitical reform, including wider public participation in the affairs of government and enabling women to use their talents more broadly in the service of the nation. The wisdom of its leaders and the good sense of the Saudi people gives promise that this can be achieved in orderly, phased fashion and without significantly compromising the praiseworthy twin regulators of Saudi social conduct: belief in God and family values.

JORDAN

Balancing Pluralism and Authoritarianism

■

Peter Gubser

In May 1953 Hussein ibn Talal ibn Abdullah took the constitutional oath as king of the Hashemite kingdom of Jordan, making him by 1987 the longest ruling monarch and the second longest ruling head of state in the world. To achieve this enviable record, the king and his advisers have at times deemed it necessary to deal harshly with significant elements of Jordan's population. At other times, his regime has allowed and promoted notable measures of economic, social, and personal freedom. Through extensive governmental and private efforts, and despite the lack of natural resources, Jordan has attained respective levels of social and economic development. From the political standpoint, however, while more pluralistic groups and movements have been permitted in recent years and some have actually been encouraged, this trend is still restrained at the highest levels of decision making. Even though broad consultation takes place, it appears that major national decisions and ultimate authority rest with the royal court. The recall in 1984 of the previously suspended elected parliament does mitigate this pattern, as does the fact that many lesser political decisions are easily and readily made by other institutions, such as the cabinet, ministries, councils, and municipalities. In short, as the title to this chapter suggests, King Hussein's Jordan is indeed an example of balancing pluralism and authoritarianism.

Social Groups

In Jordan the most important of social groups are: the bedouin; rural tribes; the Palestinians; Muslims in general; and other religious and ethnic groupings. These groups are not static; on the contrary, they are highly influenced by the forces of socioeconomic change in the country.

The Bedouin

At the beginning of the twentieth century nearly half of the population of what was to become Transjordan was bedouin. Today the proportion is about 5 percent, but their influence is distinctly felt throughout the country for two principal reasons: their role in the military and the idealization of their traditional life-style.

The bedouin of today, for the most part, live differently from their ancestors. In previous generations they were nomadic, living in tents and moving periodically, usually within a recognized territory. Their economy was based on raising animals (camels, sheep, goats, horses) and trading them and their products with their settled neighbors for metal tools and weapons, cloth, and grain. (Even though they frequently traded for grain, they usually cultivated catch crops of wheat and barley in desert areas where it had recently rained.) Another mainstay was transportation: their camels were truly the proverbial ships of the desert. Socially and politically the bedouin were organized in tribes, some of which numbered in the thousands. The tribal leader (sheikh), usually chosen from a recognized notable family, was the first among equals. He was an important dispute settler and a leader of caravans and bedouin raids, but he possessed very little additional power or material with which to influence his fellow tribesmen.

Today only a small proportion of the people who still consider themselves bedouin practice the nomadic way of life. Most are settled in permanent housing—stone or mud-brick homes—in settlement schemes or around wells or other sources of water. Over a third of the able-bodied men serve in the military or other security forces, where they are considered very loyal to the crown. The balance of the labor force depends on other forms of government service, farming irrigated plots, animal husbandry, and, with their diminishing number of camels, occasionally smuggling.

The loyalty of the bedouin to the Hashemites was not gained without effort. Initially, Transjordanian officials took a confrontational posture vis-à-vis the group. In the early 1920s the British head of the Transjordan armed services, Colonel Frederich Peake, viewed them as an unruly segment of the population that needed to be controlled. This policy was reversed in 1930, about ten years after the founding of the amirate (princedom) of Transjordan, with the arrival of Captain John Glubb, who started recruiting a special force based on bedouin enlistees. This new policy had two major effects. First, it quickly quelled the very disruptive bedouin raiding of neighboring nomadic and settled tribes, which had become endemic. Second, the new regime in Amman gave the bedouin an interest in internal order, and over time they came to be among the most loyal servants and defenders of the Hashemite regime. To ensure this loyalty, Amir (Prince) Abdullah, the leader of Transjordan, and later King Hussein purposely paid close attention to the material needs and politics of the bedouin, meeting frequently with their sheikhs and with ordinary tribesmen.

As the kingdom gained additional fiscal resources after World War II, it made certain that a disproportionately large share reached its bedouin supporters. In the 1960s, for example, a few irrigation and settlement schemes were provided, as was some health care through the military. With even greater resources available in the 1970s, the government directly and through other agencies made certain that the bedouin received, or were slated to receive, many rural services: schools, clinics, potable water, welfare assistance, and, quite important, economic infrastructure projects designed primarily to assist agriculture.

Tribes of the Rural Areas

The people of Jordan's villages and small towns have changed their economy and mode of life in parallel with the bedouin. In the middle of the nineteenth century the majority of villagers lived in tents, from which they tended their crops and animals. They termed themselves *fallahs* (tillers of the soil, peasants), as distinct from bedouin. The crucial difference is that the latter kept camels, lived in the desert, and moved frequently, while the former lived in parts of the country where rain-fed agriculture was practiced, and thus they moved infrequently or just short distances. By early in the twentieth century, as the region came to enjoy greater civil order, the fallahs built homes on fixed sites, which are their villages today. Prior to the rapid economic change that began in the 1950s, their livelihood was largely based on agriculture. During the present decade this pattern has radically shifted, with less than 40 percent of the rural population dependent on agriculture for their income—and over half of a village's population, seeking work outside the village in trades, commerce, industry, government, and military.[1]

These rural fallahs, who currently constitute about 30 percent of Jordan's population, are, like their bedouin cousins, organized along tribal lines. Their tribes tend to be smaller than those of the bedouin, and are also smaller in the north than in the south. In addition, sociopolitical relationships are comparatively more static because the villages are tied to the land and in this century the people live in nonmovable housing. As the bedouin settle, these forces influence their social patterns as well.

Tribal loyalty, for the villagers and the bedouin alike, has historically been very important. All members of a tribe are considered to be related by blood—whether it be in fact or fiction. In consequence, an individual or group of individuals is automatically required to support in word or action the rest of the group and/or an individual member of the group.

This tribal loyalty was and is of crucial significance for the patterns of loyalty to the country's leadership. Both Amir Abdullah and King Hussein carefully cultivated this loyalty by showing their great interest in the welfare of the tribes and by paying close attention to their internal developments. Through such efforts each monarch established a very personalistic leadership relationship with the tribes, which was reciprocated in turn with tribal loyalty to the two leaders. Thus the ordinary tribesman, whether in the desert or on the farm or in the military, gave his automatic loyalty to the monarchs. Abdullah and Hussein thereby enjoyed an executive freedom to make policy and undertake actions without worrying about the immediate reaction of the population.[2]

In the 1980s this relationship is shifting. The older generation perhaps retains this loyalty pattern, but the younger generation has been influenced in other ways. It is more educated and affluent; tribal loyalties are weaker, but loyalties to the state, to a sort of

Jordanian entity, are greater, and religion, once a part of the old and new loyalty, is being influenced by novel, potentially disruptive forces from other parts of the Middle East. Thus King Hussein today has relatively less executive freedom: he must pay closer attention to the people's potential reaction to his actions because his people have changed and changes continue. Nevertheless, while the king's executive freedom has been truncated, he does retain a significant measure of control because of tribal lines of loyalty among the older generation and among some of the younger tribesmen as well. This gradual shift is not an unwanted development for King Hussein. Like Amir Abdullah, he has consciously sought to modernize his country. These leaders' interest in and ability to deliver on social and economic development have contributed greatly to their legitimacy as Jordanian monarchs.

Palestinians

The separate identity of the Palestinians vis-à-vis East Jordanians is the most fundamental split within the country and, along with the current waves of religious fervor, is the most challenging to the nation. Simply put, as defined by the East Jordanians and the Palestinians, the East Jordanians are those people who were living in Jordan prior to 1948, primarily the bedouin and rural tribes. Palestinians, on the other hand, are those people who originate from Palestine—that is, the land that lies to the west of the Jordan River, the Dead Sea, and the Wadi al-Arabah. The East Jordanians view Jordan as their home, tend to have considerable loyalty to the Hashemites, and in their national vision combine the interest and development of Jordan with a certain loyalty to Arab nationalism. Regaining Palestine, while it may be of varying degrees of importance to some, is not their foremost, fundamental interest. For the Palestinians, on the other hand, regaining the West Bank and Gaza Strip and/or the rest of Palestine is the foremost national goal, and it significantly defines their identity. Many view their Jordanian citizenship as a temporary convenience while awaiting a different future.

The Palestinians arrived in Jordan in two major waves (in 1948 and 1967) and numerous minor flows. In 1948, with the establishment of Israel, Jordan occupied, then annexed, the West Bank.

During this time Jordan's population was more than doubled by the indigenous population of the West Bank and the hundreds of thousands of Palestinian refugees from Israel who took up residence on the west and east banks of the Jordan.

Not only did these groups have fundamentally different national identities, but there were also significant socioeconomic differences between them. The Palestinians were more educated, had higher standards of health (as measured by the doctor-to-population ratio and infant mortality rates), had more access to the media, and were somewhat more urban. As such, many Palestinians had a feeling of superiority vis-à-vis their new fellow citizens and they resented the fact that the East Jordanians dominated the politics of the day.

The division between the peoples of the east and west banks was not absolute, however. Links had long existed between the two neighboring regions. For example, the town of Karak on the East Bank had close trade and social ties (including those of marriage) with Hebron on the West Bank, as did Es Salt with Nablus. In addition, both banks of the Jordan shared the broader Arab nationalist identity, and in both the large majority of the population practiced the same Sunni Muslim religion. With the passage of time many of the earlier differences, especially the socioeconomic ones, have disappeared or been altered: Palestinians and East Jordanians live within the same infrastructure; many attend the same schools; some join together in business; they work in the same bureaucracies, serve in the same army, and contract marriages with each other.

But this pattern of merging can only be taken so far. The two groups do identify separately. Jordan is not Palestine; Palestinians do not claim Jordan as their country. Because some questions have been raised about this very point, it is worth exploring further. First, most important, the Palestinians identify themselves as Palestinian, and with the land west of the Jordan River. To deny a group's self identity is offensive to free choice. Second, there is a clear historical separation between the two regional entities. At the end of World War I Transjordan and Palestine initially fell under the rule of King Faisal in Damascus as part of Greater Syria. European imperial powers, however, decided differently. Operating on the principles laid out in the Sykes-Picot Agreement, France extended its control over Syria and Lebanon and ousted King Faisal in

1920. Britain picked up the mandate for Palestine and Transjordan. The two territories' separateness was formally recognized in 1922. In the papers Britain submitted to the League of Nations in accordance with its mandate responsibilities, Transjordan was defined as an entity distinct from Palestine and was explicitly excluded from all provisions of the Balfour Declaration. Additionally, Transjordan was administered indirectly through the government of Amir Abdullah, not directly through a British colonial governor, as in Palestine. In short, the Palestinians have long lived in Palestine and have closely identified with it, even though in recent decades some have been forced to live east of the Jordan River while awaiting the determination of their future—all of which is crucial to their identity and patterns of behavior in and toward Jordan.

The foregoing discussion addresses the Palestinians as a whole, but this is not to say that they constitute a homogeneous group. They can be divided into five subgroups, based on the date of their moving to Jordan and their living conditions: first, a few Palestinian families settled in East Jordan prior to 1948. They tend to identify strongly as Jordanians, are for the most part prosperous, and usually give considerable allegiance to the Hashemites.

Second, the Palestinians who fled to East Jordan in 1948 or during the following few years and who do not live in the refugee camps may be characterized as the least disgruntled, and perhaps a kind of silent majority. Taking advantage of their superior skills, sophistication, and often capital, they prospered in Jordan's free-market economy. Some have risen to positions of responsibility in the government and the military, as well as in the private sector. While they, like their other Palestinian brothers, long to see part or all of Palestine regained for the Palestinians, for the most part they would not give up their present homes in Amman or elsewhere in Jordan and jeopardize their jobs, positions, or property.

The third group is made up of those who fled to the East Bank in 1967 and do not live in camps. They were forced or caused to move more recently than their brothers of 1948, and perhaps feel their nationalism more intensely than do the latter. Some were the frontline fighters in the Palestinian civil war against Jordan in 1970. Today, however, most members of this group have already found jobs or entered businesses. Enjoying various levels of success, they are no longer the challenge to the regime they once were.

The refugees of 1948 and 1967 who live in refugee camps constitute the fourth Palestinian group. Largely laborers, living in crowded camps, dependent on the United Nations for essential services, under the eyes of Jordanian police posts, they are the least settled of the Palestinian subgroups and certainly the most disgruntled. They served, it is reported, as the backbone of the 1970 resistance, and many were forced to flee Jordan upon their defeat. Given their refugee-camp status (about 10 percent of East Jordan's population lives in refugee camps) and lack of a stake in the country, it is judged that many of this group would return to some part of Palestine given the opportunity.

The fifth group is more anomalous; they are the Palestinians of the West Bank. When we speak of the 2.6 million people of Jordan, that number excludes the 850,000 Palestinians who enjoy Jordanian citizenship but reside on the Israeli-occupied West Bank. This exclusion is not a political statement by the writer but an objective recognition of their very separate status. The Jordanian census of 1979 also did not enumerate this group as part of the total population. These Palestinians have Jordanian passports; they travel frequently to Amman and ofter have relatives, businesses, or property there. Their political loyalty is to the broad concept of the PLO (Palestine Liberation Organization) as it represents their sense of Palestinian nationalism. This loyalty does not entirely eschew King Hussein, however. An important and outspoken minority (perhaps 20 percent) do strongly criticize and reject the Hashemites, especially for the direct Jordanian rule on the West Bank during the 1948–67 period, but the balance express various levels of acceptance; many or most would like to see strong and active PLO cooperation with King Hussein. In this context, it should be remembered that 70 percent of the West Bank population is rural. The rural West Bankers for the most part did not have a difficult time under Hashemite rule. Notably, in comparison to their fate under the present Israeli military government, they did not lose their land or water rights, two crucial aspects of rural life.

Muslims

About 95 percent of Jordan's population is Sunni Muslim, making the state remarkably homogeneous in religious terms. As a consequence, some would conclude that religion would not be a political factor in Jordan. This, however, is not the case.

As many have observed, religion in the Middle East heavily influences the entire society. Accordingly, in order to look after its relationship with the population (and, most observers believe, out of conviction), the Jordanian regime pays close attention to religious concerns and symbols. The Hashemites' relationship to the Prophet Muhammad is a part of the king's identity. Similarly, unlike the shah of Iran, King Hussein has not sought to challenge religious leaders and religious feeling; rather, his regime has sought to co-opt them. For example, despite the banning of political parties, Muslim Brotherhood activities have long been permitted (and the group has responded by giving considerable loyalty to King Hussein). Islamic rules are publicly obeyed, considerable radio and television time is devoted to religious programs, mosque-building has long been supported, and Islamic symbols are consciously used to reinforce loyalty in the military. Until recent years this program successfully co-opted and contained religious political activism. The potentially disruptive or regime-threatening aspects of religious fervor were thereby redirected so as to be expressed in ways that would not undermine the regime.

By the mid 1980s, however, the winds of Islamic fundamentalism were blowing strongly in the Middle East, and Jordan has not entirely escaped them. Lying behind this fundamentalist surge within Jordan are three important forces: (1) rapid socioeconomic change, which is disrupting the society and causing some to seek a known belief with which they can identify as they face the unknown; (2) political frustration deriving from, on the one hand, lack of access to political decision making and, on the other hand, from the notable lack of success at addressing the Palestinian problem and the Arab-Israeli conflict; and (3) the success of the Ayatollah Khomeini, not as a direct manipulator in Jordanian affairs but as an example of what can be done in the name of and through the force of Islam.

The people who feel and react to this religious fervor are both organized and unorganized. About half are members of small groups with identifiable leadership; the rest are unaffiliated and simply meet in mosques and elsewhere to exchange thoughts and feelings. These various groups and individuals were strong enough to dominate the 1984 (but not subsequent) parliamentary by-elections. The Muslim fundamentalists, it should be underlined, come from all groups and strata. They are both East Jordanian and Palestinian, urban and rural, camp dwellers and well-educated professionals, merchants, and laborers.

As of this writing, most observers believe that Islamic fundamentalism is not capable of undermining the Hashemite regime. However, if political frustration were to increase significantly, or if an important Arab country came under the direct influence of fundamentalism (e.g., if Iran were to defeat Iraq at war), fundamentalism could easily become a direct threat to the Jordanian royal court and current establishment.

Other Religious and Ethnic Groups

Religious divisions in Jordan do not have the great importance they have in other Middle East countries such as Lebanon, Syria, Iraq, or Israel. The small Jordanian Christian community, perhaps 5 percent of the population, is successful and well integrated, quite prominent in business and banking. While Christians have held important government posts, often related to the economy or development, they do not aspire to the prime ministership; nor, some judge, would a Christian be allowed to hold the position. With the current emphasis on Islamic fundamentalism and the public expressions thereof, some Christians clearly feel pressured in ways they were not a decade earlier.

Circassians and Shishanis are Sunni Muslims like most of the Arab Jordanians, but they are of a different linguistic and ethnic group, which migrated from the Caucasus to Jordan in the 1870s and 1880s. Amir Abdullah's palace guards were recruited from this small minority; they have held a disproportionately great number of positions in government; and, financially, they have fared well, partly because they owned great tracts of land in the Amman area, which escalated in value after 1948.

Institutions

In a country caught between authoritarianism and pluralism one finds only a limited number of institutions with real political importance. The salient ones in Jordan are the monarchy, the military, the cabinet, parliament, and municipal councils, professional organizations, and cooperatives.

The Monarchy

Crucial to the institution of the monarchy, as personified by the reigning and ruling king, are the attributes that give him legitimacy in the eyes of Jordanians. First, the Hashemites have a special claim on the origins of Arab nationalism. King Hussein's great-grandfather and his three sons (Sherif Hussein, Amir Faisal, Amir Abdullah, and Amir Ali, respectively) were the founders and leaders of the great Arab Revolt against the Ottomans that, with the assistance of the British, helped free Arab lands from Ottoman control in World War I (only for them to fall under European imperial control shortly afterward). After the war Amir Abdullah of Transjordan continued to seek an Arab unity greater than then existed. After about a quarter of a century, he realized an increment of greater Arab nationalism with the occupation of the West Bank, then its annexation, by vote of joint parliament, to Transjordan (1948–50). King Hussein has clearly inherited the mantle of Arab nationalism. However, he has not sought to realize the ever-illusive goal of Arab political unity. Rather he judges Arab nationalism to be a mutually beneficial cultural, social, economic, and occasionally strategic relationship among the Arab states and peoples that makes the whole greater than the sum of its parts.

King Hussein and his forefathers can also claim legitimacy because of their special relationship to Islam: they are the direct descendants of the Hashemite family of the Prophet Muhammad. This religious relationship and the kings' assiduous attention to religious issues and leaders hold special meaning for many of the more traditional and religious Jordanians.

A third attribute that helps build the monarchy's legitimacy is the interest it has shown and the success it has achieved in socioeconomic development. Few would deny the king's and his brother's (Crown Prince Hassan's) roles in helping create a favorable environment for such efforts, which, in turn, have become a frequent subject of discussion and action in conferences, at ceremonial meetings, and on radio and television. Hussein and his brother are perceived to be genuinely concerned for the welfare of all Jordanians, and equally important, it is widely recognized that they have been able to deliver on many development projects, often irrespective of the political currents of the day in the Middle East.

A fourth attribute of Jordanian rule that reflects well on the king is the relatively high degree of personal freedom enjoyed by Jordan's citizens and the level of civil order—especially as compared to most other Arab countries in the Middle East. Thus, when a Jordanian, whether an East Banker or a Palestinian, compares his personal situation to that of his neighbors, he readily chooses Jordan. There are qualifications, however: the Hashemites have not allowed great degrees of political freedom, and at times the security forces are notably strict. From another standpoint, the third and fourth attributes, taken together, are more meaningful for some elements of the population than for others. The urban poor and some of the refugee-camp residents appreciate or feel the economic advancement and personal freedom the least (but even they enjoy some trickle-down benefits).

Fifth, the Hashemites' and especially King Hussein's longevity in the face of adversity and regime-challenges creates respect. Success of a popular leader breeds success. Finally, the king is personally attractive, speaks beautiful Arabic, is courageous, and has a personable and active family. Equally, many Jordanians appreciate seeing their leader—the leader of a small, not inherently wealthy state—dealing as an equal and on their behalf with the leaders of the Arab Middle East and the world.

The Military

In Jordan the military is both less and more important than in other Arab countries. On the one hand, there have been no successful coups d'état. The military does not rule and has not ruled, as it has in so many other states of the region. Furthermore, it has a long tradition of loyalty to the Hashemite regime. On the other hand, the military at various times has been crucial in a number of aspects of Jordanian national life. It has been fundamental for internal and external security, has acted as modernizer and educator for the Jordanian people, and has provided technical and security assistance to neighbors, in turn gaining monetary and security benefits for Jordan.

The Arab Legion, the forerunner of the Jordan Arab Army (JAA) was founded in 1921. Because Captain F. Peake, who headed the embryonic Arab Legion, numbering perhaps 1,300, perceived the bedouin of Jordan to be the primary threat to order, he established a policy of recruiting from the sedentary population so that the bedouin would have little influence in the affairs of the country. This Transjordanian armed force quickly performed two major functions in support of the fledgling emirate. First, it quelled a few town revolts—largely local actions against the collection of taxes and the projection of state power from the capital, Amman. Second, in 1922 and 1924, in cooperation with the British Royal Air Force, it successfully confronted and drove back Saudi-based Wahhabi armed incursions. Both actions helped demonstrate the power of and need for the military, as well as the power (and authority) of the central government.

In 1930 Major John Bagot Glubb was transferred from Britain's Iraqi to its Transjordanian mandate. Ostensibly subordinate to Peake, he followed quite an independent course, proceeding to form a desert unit of the Arab Legion from a considerably different political position. He specifically set out to recruit the force from among the bedouin in order to take advantage of their desert skills and give them a stake in the state, as previously described. Eventually Glubb Pasha, as he came to be known, formally replaced Peake as head of the Arab Legion.

In the post–World War II period the JAA has played a vital role in the country and undergone gradual evolution. In 1948 the commander was still General Glubb, and a number of senior officers were British. By the late 1950s the army had been Arabized (Glubb was dismissed in 1956). In 1948 army personnel were largely drawn from the bedouin and the settled tribes. By 1970 its makeup was 45 percent Palestinian, a population group not part of Jordan before 1948. Of significance is the fact that for the most part the Palestinians in the army remained loyal during the 1970 civil war. In 1976 national conscription was introduced. By the mid-1980s 25 percent of the 100,000-man army was made up of draftees, about half with university degrees. Not unexpectedly this has caused a few social problems.

The Cabinet and Parliament

The Jordanian cabinet is appointed by, and serves at the pleasure of, the king. It is required, however, to submit its program to the parliament, which may dismiss the cabinet via a vote of no confidence.

The Hashemites have always had an uneasy relationship with elected bodies. In the early 1920s urban Jordanians pressed for the establishment of some sort of representative body. Finally, in 1928, a new Organic Law allowed for an indirectly elected legislative council. It was quickly dissolved, however, when it failed to pass part of the Arab Legion's budget. Subsequent councils were more compliant.

The present parliament operates under the constitution promulgated in 1952. The 1952 constitution replaced that of 1946, which was put in place upon Jordan's independence from the British mandate. Each allowed for the direct election of a chamber of deputies, but each curtailed its power. There is also a house of notables in the Jordanian bicameral parliament, which is appointed by the king and which enjoys less legislative authority than the lower house. As noted, parliaments can bring down governments, but the king has the stronger hand, being vested with both legislative and executive powers. Also, he convenes, adjourns, dissolves, and recalls parliament, as well as calling for or postponing elections.

Historically, direct elections in Jordan have enjoyed only circumscribed freedom. Traditionally controls were used whereby some candidates were prevented from running, or voting was simply rigged. In the 1960s parties were banned and remain so, but observers note that in stark contrast to the 1961 election those of 1962 and 1967 were comparatively free. The by-elections of 1984 and afterward also enjoyed relative freedom, but political parties were still not allowed.

The 1967 Arab-Israeli war and the attendant loss of the West Bank seriously influenced the role of the Jordanian parliament. The first problem was the impossibility of holding elections on the occupied West Bank, from which half the members of each chamber hail. Because an election was held shortly before the 1967 war, the issue did not arise until 1971, the expiration date of the parliament. The dilemma was dealt with by simply extending the terms of all members. The second major problem arose in 1974, when the Arab summit at Rabat declared the PLO to be the sole representative of the Palestinian people, and King Hussein felt compelled to accept the resolution. As a result, a new cabinet was appointed with decidedly fewer West Bank Palestinians serving, and the parliament was dissolved so as to remove Palestinian representation.

After the dismissal of parliament, there shortly emerged a demand for a national deliberative body. The negative attitude toward Palestinians having changed somewhat, it was decided that holding elections without allowing the Jordanian citizens of the West Bank to vote was unacceptable. As a temporary solution the king appointed a national consultative council (NCC). This body of sixty men and women was drawn from citizens living on the East Bank, but a substantial number were of Palestinian origin. The NCC sat from 1978 to 1983. Although it did not have the power to legislate or vote no-confidence motions against the cabinet, the cabinet did present its programs to it for review and did not promulgate any new law not also approved by vote of the NCC.

This nonelected body did not, however, completely or democratically answer the call for a popularly based national deliberative institution. Bowing to popular pressure, but also to generate greater legitimacy for potential national decisions of fundamental importance to the country, King Hussein recalled the parliament in early 1984. To fill seats vacated due to death and illness, by-elections were held on the East Bank. Because it was still impossible to hold elections on the West Bank, a constitutional amendment was adopted allowing the sitting members of the lower chamber to fill the seats allotted to that territory. Elections for the full chamber had been scheduled for 1988 but were postponed for two years by King Hussein in the fall of 1987.

Demographic shifts have also affected the relationship between both banks and the distribution of deputies. In 1967, each bank had approximately the same population and they were equally represented in parliament. By 1987, 2.6 million people lived on the East Bank and about 850,000 on the West Bank, but the equal proportions of deputies remained. Somewhat ameliorating this imbalance, West Bankers residing on the East Bank were occasionally being elected to the chamber.

Debates in the newly constituted Chamber of Deputies have

been lively, but decorous. Quite sensitive issues, such as the way the government handles security measures, have been the subject of thorough debate. The newly elected Muslim fundamentalists have formed a sort of loyal opposition. While part of the chamber and apparently accepting its rules, they have strongly criticized the government, especially with respect to issues relating to the release of political prisoners and the eradication of corruption in government. This level of criticism, to date, has been tolerated by the regime. More problematic perhaps will be the debate on when and if Jordan (and perhaps the PLO) should seek negotiations with Israel. It is not known if the fundamentalists will continue to abide by the "rules," especially given their harsh rhetoric on the subject, including explicit calls for retribution against "Zionist injustice."

Other Institutions

Because Jordan has a free economy, and Amman does not attempt to control numerous aspects of life from the center, many decisions and actions with a political content are made at a nonnational level or by nonnational institutions. It is here that the greatest degree of plurarism is realized in Jordan: in municipal councils, cooperatives, village councils, chambers of commerce and industry, professional associations (of doctors, lawyers, engineers, journalists, and the like), and in charitable societies, and clubs. I shall describe the first two briefly.

The municipal council has had a history of mixed success in Jordan. In essence, it was a foreign import, artificially installed in the region in the latter part of the nineteenth century. Initially, it only distorted the natural politics of the time by formalizing and hardening relationships among the affected tribes. Additionally, it commanded material resources, and thus power, in a manner that had not previously existed. Briefly, the new institution was either dominated by one man and his group to the exclusion of others, or it would fall into deadlock and consequently not perform the basic services for which it was needed, such as water delivery and trash collection. Then the central government would be forced to intervene via the local governor and temporarily usurp the duties and authority of the council. During the past decade the municipal councils have become integrated into the local structure and reportedly are operating adequately. Since the mid-1970s, two series of nationwide elections for municipalities have taken place. Young technocrats, some of them former members of the banned political parties, have been frequent winners, along with some Muslim fundamentalists and a few who base their positions on traditional tribal ties alone. Many candidates with technical and/or religious attributes also benefit from tribal affiliation. These newly emerging trends have been either encouraged or tolerated by the regime. In sum, the artificially adopted institution has been adequately adapted to local constraints and conditions, but local society has also changed sufficiently to be able to take further advantage of such an institution.

The cooperative movement has had a similar experience. It was established in the early 1950s but experienced slow growth and enjoyed little central government support for the subsequent two decades. In many cases, it is reported, individual cooperatives operated in a manner contrary to the overall intent of the cooperative movement: a few rich people would come to dominate them, depriving the ordinary member of fair benefits. In the mid-1970s, however, the regime clearly made a decision to help the cooperatives grow. The Jordan Cooperative Organization's (JCO) budget was doubled (and has been solidly supported and increased ever since), and a dynamic director was appointed. These rural (agricultural) and urban (consumer and savings) cooperatives are now run by their full membership through elected executive committees, often assisted by managers subsidized by the JCO.

The councils, cooperatives, associations, chambers, and societies, as well as many informal groups, participate in the national decision-making process:

> The issues debated by such groups are the normal ones, such as import tariffs, salary levels, direction or emphasis of development planning and projects, and in times of crisis, national honor and direction. Some of the groups have actual "nonpolitical" formal organizations, such as the syndicates or various clubs; others have no formal organizations but a kind of natural leadership. Each group's leaders, in the appropriate forum, advocate positions beneficial to their respective groups.[3]

Recent History

The Hashemites are proud of their moderation or centrism in a Middle East setting beset by radicalism.[4] This emphasis recurs time and again in their recent history. The political pattern of the 1950s reflected attempts by the young King Hussein to respond to popular and pluralistic demands, and his inability to do so because these demands outstripped the potential of the young and fragile system.

The period of the early 1950s in Jordan was shaped and affected by five conditions.[5] The first was the inclusion of the Palestinians, many of whom criticized the Hashemites as the "servants" of the imperialist British. Quite vocal in the opposition, they readily joined political parties challenging the authorities.

A second condition was the mushrooming influence of Arab nationalism, which tends to legitimize one Arab state's interference in another Arab state's affairs on grounds of their both being Arab. A case in point is King Abdullah's claim to neighboring areas throughout his reign, and his actual occupation of the West Bank during the first war against Israel. When criticized for leading his army into Palestine in May 1948, his response was, "I am an Arab king; I shall do as I please!" In the 1950s the tables were turned: bigger countries, with more powerful governments and fewer internal problems than Jordan (by then, refugees made up a third of Jordan's population) readily penetrated Jordan's politics via radio, newspapers, paid agents, and political parties. Egypt, then led by Gamal Abdul Nasser, was very active in this regard. Starting in the 1950s, the pan-Arab political parties, supplemented by pan-Islamic parties, were another manifestation of Arab nationalism. Those active in Jordan were the Ba'th party, the Arab Nationalist movement, the Muslim Brotherhood, and the Islamic Party of Liberation.

A third condition of the 1950s was the decline of British power in the region and the rise of American influence. For a small country heavily dependent on Britain for financial aid, military assistance, and political advice, this quasi exchange of roles, or at least alteration of roles, was of considerable importance.

The existence of a new neighbor to the west was the fourth new condition. The Arab world considered itself to be at war with this state, and Jordan had the longest border, bar none, with it. Israel was also the cause of the refugee problem, the considerable burden of which was borne by Jordan, as well as by Syria and Lebanon. It was a Palestinian who assassinated King Abdullah in 1951, ostensibly out of anger over the king's secret peace negotiations with Israel. Another equally unsettling aspect of this situation was the Israeli policy of punitive raids on Palestinian villages. The Jordanian authorities, noting their weakness vis-à-vis the Israeli army and desiring to maintain a quiet border, undertook to prevent Palestinians from crossing the armistice line. However, villagers did occasionally cross to harvest crops in their fields, to attempt to retrieve belongings from their lost homes, and at times for revenge. The Israelis responded with military retaliation and organized counterraids. Such raids provoked incensed reactions from the Palestinians, who insisted on effective defense and retaliation by the Jordanian army, all of which was decidedly unsettling for the kingdom.

The fifth condition was the sorry state of the economy. Most writers during the 1950s considered Jordan an economic basket case. It was a poor country with an artificially large population, of which fully one-third were refugees. Jordan had at best a rudimentary economic infrastructure, characterized by unemployment and underemployment. On the positive side, some Palestinian refugees brought with them capital and know-how. The United Nations Relief and Works Agency for Palestine Refugees contributed considerably to the refugees' welfare and education. The British, later supplanted by the Americans, contributed budgetary and economic-development support, as did UN agencies, bilateral aid agencies, and private groups such as the Ford Foundation. Thus, despite the very low level of development in the early 1950s, Jordan steadily progressed, but not without considerable problems, many of which were engendered by the political tumult.

In the summer of 1956 Nasser nationalized the Suez Canal, and in October the British, French, and Israelis invaded Egypt's Sinai Peninsula. Given the power of Arab nationalism and the anti-imperialist feeling, popular reaction was marked. In this unsettled atmosphere, Jordan held elections that were markedly freer than previous ones, and King Hussein invited the leader of the party with the greatest plurality, Sulayman Nabulsi of the National Socialist party, a Jordanian group with a radical, nationalist platform, to form a government. Nabulsi's government, consisting of left-wing and strongly Arab-nationalist members of parliament, quickly turned to challenging the royal court on basic issues, even putting forth statements questioning the existence of a separate Jordanian state. Also, it soon drew closer to the Egyptian and Syrian governments.

Given his recent partial termination of ties with Britain, Hussein reacted by moving closer to the United States. In early January 1957 President Eisenhower had promulgated the Eisenhower Doctrine, which inter alia proffered American assistance if and when a country in the Middle East faced internal or external communist subversion. Although the king did not directly endorse or accept the doctrine, it can be argued that he operated under its protection, as he established close diplomatic and assistance ties with the United States.

In April 1957 the king faced a more serious threat, but one that proved to be a watershed for internal Jordanian political developments. Apparently the Nabulsi cabinet, in league with a small group of Jordanian army officers, including Ali Abu Nuwar, the chief of staff, attempted to overthrow the Hashemite regime. Hearing of the cabal from loyal army officers, Hussein, in an important show of personal courage, started out for the major Zirqa army base, east of Amman, in the company of Ali Abu Nuwar. En route they met loyal troops coming to assist the young monarch. They at once feted Hussein and almost ended Abu Nuwar's life.

The effects of the episode were manifold and still influence Jordanian political relations. Most important, the king established his personal role and high respect in the army. By his actions he started to assume the stature of his grandfather and to become the supreme sheikh of the bedouin and the tribes from which the loyal cadres of the army are recruited. The 1956–57 period was also the last time a prime minister was chosen from among nonloyal Jordanian citizens. Henceforth, only men such as the Rifais, Badran, Sharaf, Mufti, and Obeidat would accede to that post. In a parallel manner, the regime commenced exerting much greater control over parliament. Members were either replaced or quieted. The next election, that of 1961, was controlled to such an extent that it was an embarrassment. The following election, called quickly in 1962, was freer, but political parties were outlawed and thoroughly suppressed.

In brief, the 1950s were marked in Jordan by the curtailment of pluralism and an attempt to contain radical Arab nationalism and interference from other Arab countries. On another level, slow but steady socioeconomic development continued to progress, despite the absence of basic natural resources.

In 1964 an Arab summit was held to respond to Israel's intention to divert a share of the headwaters of the Jordan River larger than allowed under the American-sponsored Johnston Plan. Three decisions were made at the summit: a portion of the headwaters of the Jordan River in Lebanon and Syria was to be diverted; a united Arab military command was established under Egyptian leadership; and the Palestine Liberation Organization was created. Ahmad Shukairy, chosen by Egypt, set up the PLO in Jerusalem. (In 1963 Yasser Arafat had founded the guerrilla organization Fatah, which took control of the PLO after the 1967 Arab-Israeli war.) The three decisions taken by the Arab League and the Israeli action to which they were a reaction played a role in initiating the train of events that culminated in the 1967 war. They also helped set the stage for future Jordanian-Palestinian relations.

The border between the West Bank and Israel, never exceptionally quiet, flared up frequently in the post-1964 period. Palestinians would cross it, and Israelis would counterattack. Even though the regime realized that it would be unpopular if it undertook to stop these Palestinian raids and to rid the country of the PLO, an organization neither of its making nor under its control, it eventually ordered it banned in 1966.

Expelling the PLO did not end problems arising from PLO actions. For example, in 1966 Fatah undertook a series of small military actions against Israel, emanating from Lebanese and Syrian territory. In a major reprisal, not against positions in those two countries but inexplicably against Jordan, the Israeli army attacked the West Bank village of Samu', destroying many houses and killing dozens of people. Popular demonstrations ensued throughout the West Bank. The Hashemite regime was attacked for not providing an adequate defense and for not taking a sufficiently militant stand against Israel.

The 1967 Arab-Israeli war, as most students of the Middle East are aware, still affects the region today, and Jordan is no exception. For Hussein's kingdom it was nothing less than cataclysmic. Jordan lost the West Bank, which, although only a small percentage of its land, contained half its population, constituted about half the economy, and included all the religious shrines of Jerusalem and Bethlehem.

The war also taught the Palestinians an important lesson. Previously they had relied variously on Arab states, Arab or Muslim parties, the "revolution," or a combination thereof to regain Palestine. The 1967 Arab defeat caused them to turn inward and realize they had to rely more on their own people, their own strength. A consequence was the rapid growth of the guerrilla movements (including Fatah), which quickly gained a foothold among the Palestinians in Jordan.

In the time immediately after the 1967 war, the guerrilla groups attempted to attack Israel. Unsuccessful, and sustaining considerable damage, some decided to refocus their efforts and concentrate on Jordan before addressing Israeli forces. By 1970 the PLO and the guerrillas had created a state within a state in the kingdom, and clashes with the government security apparatus escalated.

During September 1970 the situation came to a head, and King Hussein's regime emerged victorious. Actually, Jordan faced major challenges from two directions: a civil war with the PLO and a simultaneous Syrian invasion, with two hundred tanks, across Jordan's northern frontier. Fearing defeat on the Syrian front while he was facing Palestinian guerrillas in Amman, King Hussein requested U.S. intervention in the form of air strikes against the invading tanks on September 20.

> Over the next two tumultuous days, the king was to send mixed signals about what he wanted and from whom he wanted it. Initially, it appeared that Nixon wanted to use only U.S. forces in support of Jordan, but he eventually came around to the Kissinger position that the Israelis were better suited and positioned to help. As the Israelis were mobilizing on the Golan Heights, they contended that air and ground attacks would be necessary. The Jordanian king, however, was quite averse to having Israeli ground forces aid him (it would certainly have crossed his mind that it might be very difficult to rid his soil of

these forces once they entered) and ambivalent about Israeli air support, preferring that of the United States.[6]

Within a couple of days, however, the king laid these questions to rest. His own air force took to the air (and was not met by the superior Syrian air force) and decisively defeated the invading tank force, which returned to Syrian territory.

Meanwhile on the ground in Amman, after seeming initial vacillation, Hussein also took decisive action. He appointed a general to the prime ministership, and a loyal East Jordanian, General Habis al-Majali, was made commander of the Jordan Arab Army. After heavy fighting, resulting in considerable physical destruction and death, the Palestinian guerrillas were defeated. Mopping-up exercises continued until the spring of 1971, and Jordan faced extensive security problems from the remnants of these guerrilla forces, as well as from individuals seeking revenge, through the middle of the decade.

In the post-1970 period security concerns and the legacy of the 1970 fighting provoked a strong reaction from the regime: little if any dissent was allowed. Thus while Jordan tried to accommodate, at least temporarily, Palestinian expressions of nationhood and desire for a part or all of their homeland, both in 1964 and again following the 1967 war the government nevertheless felt constrained to curtail Palestinian groups. The defeat of the Palestinians and the restrictions on their activities are only one aspect of Jordanian-Palestinian relations, however. It is highly significant that even during these troubled times the large majority of the Palestinians in the JAA remained loyal. Also, while certainly many (but not all) of the Palestinians in the PLO fighting Jordan were Jordanian citizens, Jordan's Palestinian citizenry as a whole did not rise up against the regime. Perhaps very disgruntled and not soon forgiving of the regime, they remained silent.

In 1972 King Hussein presented a new proposal for future Jordanian-Palestinian relations. Recognizing the claim of the Palestinians, especially those of the West Bank, to a separate status vis-à-vis the Jordanians—and, in a manner, somewhat denying the seamless unity of the Arabs—King Hussein proposed the establishment of the United Arab Kingdom, whereby the West Bank and

East Bank would share one army and one foreign policy, but have two capitals with authority over local and territorial matters. The plan is strikingly similar to President Reagan's Middle East peace initiative of September 1982. The 1972 plan was quickly rejected by the defeated PLO leaders and by some leaders on the West Bank, as well as by Golda Meir, the prime minister of Israel, who was quoted as saying: "How can the king give away something he does not have?"

A nadir in Palestinian-Jordanian relations was struck at the Rabat Arab summit of 1974. Owing to successful politicking by Yasser Arafat, the summit unanimously declared the PLO to be the sole legitimate representative of the Palestinian people. Given the tenor of the day, King Hussein had no option but to accept the resolution. The repercussions back in Amman were strongly felt. As noted earlier, the parliament, a body in which half the members were Palestinians from the West Bank, was dissolved. Also, a new cabinet was formed on which few Palestinians sat. More traditionally balanced cabinets ensued with the next change, in 1976, but the regime decidedly avoided larger Palestinian issues until once again presented with them in the Camp David period.

Jordan can be justifiably proud of its economic and social progress, although this has not been matched by equivalent political advances. Working from an infrastructure significantly built up in the 1950s and 1960s, Jordan's economy expanded greatly in the post-1974 period, partly aided by funds from petroleum-producing Arab countries. Per capita income, to use one gross indicator, exceeded $2,000 by the early 1980s. Starting from a very rudimentary base, Jordan has sustained a yearly GDP growth rate of 8 percent (with the exception of a short period following the 1967 war). The oil-producing countries of Saudi Arabia and the Persian Gulf have provided numerous grants and concessional loans, as did Iraq in the early days of its war with Iran. United Nations agencies and other bilateral funders have also participated. Also, perhaps 400,000 Jordanian citizens live and work in the Arabian Peninsula and send back remittances. The planners in Jordan as well as the entrepreneurs have been able to sustain a 40 to 50 percent gross domestic capital formation rate since the mid 1970s as compared to a 15 to 20 percent rate in the 1950s and 1960s. It should be underlined, though, that this national dependence on external sources for capital formation and Jordan's unusually large defense expenditures (needed to face perceived threats from Syria and Israel and assist its conservative neighbors in security matters) contribute to Jordan's political vulnerability. Because of this high dependence, Jordan feels especially constrained to subordinate many of its policies to the desires of its rich neighbors. In addition, Jordan is vulnerable to cycles in its neighbors' economies.

Despite Jordan's admirable record, its economy does face a number of structural problems. The service sector still dominates the economy from the standpoint of both production and employment. According to analysts, the trade gap is uncomfortably high (in 1982 Jordan had a $2.5 billion trade imbalance), and the difference is largely made up by the financial transfers noted above. Linked to rapid economic development, and fueled indirectly by the oil-producing countries, are inflation (now under control), housing shortages (in the 1970s), high rates of urbanization, speculation, and some conspicuous consumption.[7]

Turning to political considerations, however, it must be said that, with the exception of the recall of parliament in 1984, there has been little progress in Jordan to alleviate the imbalance between political and economic development. Given the relatively stagnant political climate, cabinets have remained comparatively stable.

The renewed parliament was discussed in the previous section. The regime's reasons for recalling it illuminate the Jordanian political process. First, many Jordanians had pressed the royal court to do so, citing the great need for a responsible national deliberative body. Second, Jordan is facing a number of difficult economic decisions related to the decline in assistance from its neighbors and necessary adjustments in some sectors. Involving a popularly elected chamber of deputies would help legitimize any troublesome economic changes the government may have to make in the coming years. Third, decisions and actions may have to be taken with respect to the Palestinian problem, and again the government would want as broad a legitimacy as can be garnered. Some have suggested that parliament, half its members being Palestinian, could give Jordan an alternative to the PLO. This argument, while perhaps ultimately true, seems to be undermined by King Hussein's extensive negotiations with PLO Chairman Yasser Arafat and their February 1985 mutually agreed framework for peace. (By 1987 both parties had suspended the framework.)

King Hussein would like to regain the West Bank so that he will not go down in history as the Arab king who lost Jerusalem. In the meantime, however, he wishes to contain the Palestinian conflict in a West Bank–Gaza Strip context. He does not want it moved to the East Bank (as suggested by some Israeli leaders), where it would seriously threaten his throne. The king must nonetheless pay attention to his Palestinian constituency on both the east and west banks. Jordan cannot enter into negotiations with Israel without the participation of leading Palestinians who have the blessing of the PLO. If Jordan were to act alone, it would be highly criticized and probably punished by some of its neighbors. It should be remembered that Jordan is a small country that must be responsive to the stronger Arab states and is dependent partially on the largest of its richer neighbors for its relative prosperity. Accordingly, it feels compelled to have the agreement of Egypt, Iraq, and Saudi Arabia before it embarks on negotiations, and some form of agreement with Syria is also a virtual prerequisite.

What is the balance in Jordan between pluralism and authoritarianism in 1987? On the side of pluralism there is the vigorous, but decorous, debate in the recalled parliament; the growth of numerous lower-level institutions that help build the fabric of a stronger society, but also are the nexus around which certain decisions are made; the sustenance of economic and personal freedom; and the decline (but not disappearance) of the king's executive freedom. On the side of authoritarianism there are the realities that ultimate power and decisions on national questions remain with a relatively narrow group centered in the palace; that political parties are still banned; that a certain degree of censorship is current; and, because of the challenges to the regime from within and without, that security concerns and measures take a forward position. The sum of the above is a position somewhere toward the middle of the continuum between the two extremes.

LABOR POLITICS, ECONOMIC CHANGE, AND THE MODERNIZATION OF AUTOCRACY IN CONTEMPORARY BAHRAIN

■

Fred Lawson

Bahrain provides a striking case of an autocratic, tribally oriented regime confronting the challenges of a well-organized industrial labor movement in the context of regional instability and rapidly diminishing oil reserves. Developments in this country may thus presage future trends in other Gulf oil-producing countries. As George Lenczowski observed in 1956, the patriarchal regimes of the Gulf region are confronted with a political situation that "can be compared to the advent of the Atomic Age in the Western world."[1] In present-day Bahrain the crisis stage of this new age appears to be imminent.

Three fundamental dynamics lie at the heart of contemporary Bahraini politics. The first is the continual expansion of the country's state administration. During the past thirty years or so Bahrain's governmental bureaucracy has grown markedly both in size and in scope. This administrative system now bears little if any resemblance to the "primitiveness of the state apparatus" that characterized the smaller Persian Gulf countries in the mid-1950s.[2] The second dynamic is the substantial level of industrial and financial development that has taken place in the country since the mid-1960s. Bahrain's domestic economy can no longer be reduced to oil production and local refining operations without seriously distorting not only the shape of the country's internal economic affairs but also the economic role that Bahrain plays in the Gulf region as a whole.[3] In the past twenty-five years or so the country's shrinking petroleum sector has been substantially augmented, if not actually supplanted, by the creation of both a profitable heavy industrial sector and a prosperous financial sector. The third dynamic is Bahrain's labor movement, which has retained its ability to disrupt industrial and commercial operations throughout the country despite a concerted effort by the regime to break up workers' organizations and insulate local laborers from the appeals of Arab socialism and other radical ideologies.

How these three dynamics relate to one another constitutes the most significant theoretical issue in present-day Bahraini politics. On one hand, economic growth may both necessitate greater administrative capabilities and increase the level of social instability within the country. From this point of view an expanding bureaucracy and escalating demands by workers would be the direct consequences of changes in the scale and organization of production.[4] Alternatively, the primary interest of Bahrain's ruling class—which is to maintain its dominant position within Bahraini society—may lead its members to implement development projects that simultaneously increase the amount of economic profit under their own control and enhance their power relative to that of the country's other social groups. In this view, a program of heavy industrialization and financial development, in conjunction with measures designed to suppress political activity by the labor movement, would represent efforts by the dominant social coalition in Bahrain, the forces with intimate ties to the governmental bureaucracy, to reinforce the existing social order. What these two very different perspectives share is a basic assumption that over the past thirty years or so the state has been pursuing a set of strategies intended to foster within Bahrain the social and political requisites for an expanding capitalist economy. That assumption is open to serious question on both conceptual and empirical grounds.

Political Dynamics in Contemporary Bahrain

Most of the studies that have been done of Bahraini politics in recent years have taken one particularly salient aspect of the country's political affairs and dealt with that feature more or less on its own.[5] What is generally lacking in this literature is a more comprehensive perspective on Bahrain's political and economic affairs. This essay will try to lay the groundwork for such a perspective. But before this can be done, the most significant findings of the specialized literature on Bahrain need to be summarized.

State Administrative Expansion

Bahrain's governmental structure in the mid-1950s differed very little from that which existed in 1920, a year that has been called "a base year—a zero point of development" in the country's political and economic apparatus.[6] At that time the ruler (or amir) governed the archipelago as an absolute monarch, although in most circumstances central authority was narrowly circumscribed by the tribal structure of Bahraini society and did not reach outside the court in any regularized fashion.[7] Financial and commercial matters were dealt with in a largely ad hoc manner. Furthermore, the ruler relied upon the British political officer and his staff for advice regarding petroleum and foreign affairs.

It was only in the mid-1950s that formal administrative agencies were first established in Bahrain. In April of 1955 the ruler, Sheikh Sulman bin Hammad al-Khalifah, appointed a nine-member Labor Ordinance Advisory Committee to formulate a basic labor law for the country. This committee was chaired by one of the ruler's cousins, Sheikh 'Ali bin Muhammad al-Khalifah, and included another member of the ruling family, a British adviser, three representatives of the local oil industry, and three representatives of the country's workers. It was provided with a small staff of its own to deal with legal technicalities and functioned as an advisory body for both the ruler and his British political officer, Sir Charles Belgrave.[8] The following spring a considerably more important administrative body—the Administrative Council—was created, also by royal decree. This body included seven members: the chair and three others drawn from the ruling Al Khalifah family, the British adviser who had served on the Labor Ordinance Advisory Committee, and two well-to-do commoners. It was charged with discussing and carrying out a limited range of public business, not including financial and foreign affairs.[9] The bureaucratic structure that grew up around this council during the following fourteen years came to include twenty-one separate departments, ranging from a department of police to a department for minors. These departments were not organized hierarchically. Instead, "all of the 21 departments were placed at the same level; and the head of each reported directly to the ruler."[10] The most important of these agencies was probably the Department of Labor and Social Affairs, since it was given responsibility for licensing any proposed labor organizations in the country according to the terms of the revised Labor Ordinance of November 1957, as well as all social clubs and societies in the islands, according to a law promulgated in 1959.[11]

Along with these bureaucratic changes came two significant administrative directives. The first was a law establishing municipal agencies in the country's larger urban centers. The second imposed a "state of emergency" throughout the country. Put into effect by the ruler's decree of December 28, 1956, this directive "gave the ruler the right to arrest, detain, or interrogate anyone suspected of disturbing internal security."[12] It was subsequently reinforced by three *amiri* orders of April 22, 1965, that are collectively known as the Law of Public Security, which empowered the ruler to maintain a state of emergency indefinitely, to "issue any orders which he deems essential for the public good, safety and security," and to detain anyone "if in the opinion of the Ruler the detention of [that] person is in the interest of public security."[13] At the end of July these ordinances were supplemented by a comprehensive press law that both required the licensing of newspapers by the Department of Information and regulated the content of the reports published in these newspapers.[14]

In 1968 the present ruler, Sheikh 'Isa bin Sulman, announced that the government was setting up a national guard under the command of his son, Sheikh Hamad.[15] The formation of this military force was followed in January 1969 by the creation of the Department of Foreign Affairs under the direction of the ruler's first cousin, Sheikh Muhammad bin Mubarak.[16]

In the years after 1970, Bahrain's state administration began playing an increasingly greater role in the country's political and economic affairs. This trend was facilitated by a major overhauling of the organizational structure of the government, announced by the ruler on January 19, 1970. The measures adopted at that time replaced the existing administrative council with a thirteen-member Council of State.[17]

The 1970s were a decade of substantial growth in the scale of government intervention in the country's political and economic affairs. In March 1972 Bahrain was chosen by the Organization of Arab Petroleum Exporting Countries as the site for a modern shipyard able to service and repair very large oil tankers and other cargo vessels. This project involved the Bahraini government in an 18.84 percent share of the investment in, operating costs for, and equity in the completed facility. A member of the Al Khalifah was appointed to the directorship of the managing firm, the Arab Shipbuilding and Repair Yards.[18] In April the minister of labor and social affairs proposed establishing a network of workers' committees in the country's larger industrial concerns. Elections to determine the membership of these committees were to be supervised by officials from this ministry. Negotiations between these committees and management were to be carried out under the ministry's auspices. And any necessary arbitration was to be done by this department's employees.[19] Workers' committees of this sort were subsequently set up at both Aluminum Bahrain (ALBA) and the Bahrain Petroleum Company (BAPCO), but they accomplished little in the way of redressing workers' grievances at these two plants.

Two measures adopted in August and September of 1974 signaled a marked acceleration in the growth of Bahrain's state bureaucracy. The first was the introduction of government subsidies to moderate the prices of rice, sugar, flour, and meat on local markets.[20] This represented a sharp reversal in the government's longstanding opposition to state regulation of Bahrain's economic affairs. The second was the government's acquisition of a 60 percent share in BAPCO from its American owners, the Standard Oil Company of California and Texaco. Under the terms of the agreement reached by these three parties, the government's takeover was made effective retroactively to January 1, 1974, and included all of BAPCO's assets except the refinery complex at Awali/Sitrah.[21]

In late May of 1975 the government announced that it would take over "full operational control" of the country's domestic and international telecommunications services during the following twelve months.[22] This was accompanied by a concerted effort by the state to acquire a majority holding in ALBA, a goal that was achieved in early June, when the government acquired a 52.4 percent interest in the firm.[23] The following January the state purchased the shares of two more of its foreign partners in this enterprise, giving it a 77.9 percent stake in the company. In announcing this purchase, the government reiterated publicly its interest in buying out the shares of any of its remaining private partners.[24] A month later Sheikh 'Isa issued a decree capitalizing the Bahrain National Oil Company (BANACO) as the operator of the government's 60 percent interest in BAPCO; the minister of development and industry was subsequently appointed its first director.[25] Later that spring the Ministry of Development and Industry announced the government's intention to develop a state-owned aluminum extrusion plant that would prepare ALBA-produced materials for use in Bahrain's construction industry.[26]

A comprehensive labor law was adopted in July 1975, which prohibited strikes and unionization within the country and instead mandated the arbitration procedures proposed by the minister of labor and social affairs in 1972. A week after this law was promulgated, Sheikh 'Isa ordered the creation of a Supreme Manpower Council. Among its responsibilities was the coordination of efforts by the ministries of health, commerce, education, and development and industry to provide "centralized social projects" for Bahrain's work force.[27]

In conjunction with the government's decision to dissolve Bahrain's national assembly, the ruler significantly increased the power of the Council of State and its component ministries in 1975. On August 24 Sheikh 'Isa asked Sheikh Khalifah to put together a new cabinet that would have "full legislative powers." This cabinet included four new ministries: Transport; Housing; Public Works, Electricity and Water; and Commerce and Agriculture. It also reorganized the existing Ministry of Development and Engineering into the Ministry of Development and Industry.[28] In the area of regulatory legislation, 1975 ended with the promulgation of a new commercial code that required all trading companies operating in Bahrain to have majority Bahraini ownership and register with the Ministry of Commerce.[29]

Finally, at the end of 1976, having consolidated its position in the country's industrial, commercial, and labor affairs, the state became directly involved in Bahrain's rapidly growing financial sector as well. Sheikh 'Isa officially opened the offices of the Gulf International Bank in Manama on December 15. This institution was owned in equal parts by the governments of Bahrain, Qatar, and the United Arab Emirates.[30]

Subsequent to this flurry of governmental activity, Bahrain's state administration has expanded only marginally. A joint government-business committee was formed in early September of 1977 to discuss ways of dealing with the country's economic situation at that time.[31] Six months later the cabinet approved a plan proposed by the Ministry of Development and Industry to acquire 100 percent ownership of BAPCO's local production and marketing operations.[32] A contraction in the operations of the country's central bureaucracy was indicated, however, by the announcement on February 8, 1979, that Saudi Arabia intended to purchase a 20 percent holding in ALBA from the Bahraini government.[33]

Six significant trends are evident in all this. Bahrain's state administration grew substantially during 1955–56, albeit from an extremely rudimentary level. This period of bureaucratic expansion was followed by a considerably longer period in which the structure of the country's governmental apparatus changed little if at all. A second jump in the level of bureaucratic development took place in the years between 1964 and 1970, but this trend fell off from the second quarter of 1970 to the second quarter of 1972. Administrative expansion increased much more gradually beginning in mid-1972 than it had in 1964–65 and reached an apex of sorts around 1975–76. The size and scope of governmental operations in Bahrain have gone through a period of relative contraction since about 1978. Bureaucratization has thus been neither inexorable nor constant in the recent political history of this Gulf state. On the contrary, pronounced discontinuities have been present in the growth of centralized administration within Bahraini society since the mid-1950s.

Industrial and Financial Development

Bahrain's first wave of industrial expansion subsequent to the establishment of the local oil industry in the early 1930s occurred between 1966 and the end of 1968. It was inaugurated by the formation of the Bahrain Fishing Company, a consortium that included the Ross Group of Grimsby (with a 40 percent interest) and a number of local shareholders. The company's primary operations involved the processing and export of shrimp for markets in Europe,

Japan, and the United States.[34] It also operated a fleet of eight shrimping boats in Gulf waters. On March 15, 1967, this firm opened a modern processing factory designed to freeze prawns for shipping overseas.[35] In January of the following year the British telecommunications firm Marconi announced plans to construct an earth station for receiving satellite transmissions at Abu Jarjur. This project was part of a £2.1 million contract between Marconi and the local firm Cable and Wireless, which effectively made the latter part of a global network of telecommunications operations.[36] As these plans were being drawn up, Bahrain's ruler and the director of customs and ports were discussing with Saudi officials the possibility of building a causeway to link the two countries. Such a causeway would be almost nineteen kilometers long and was projected to cost approximately $27 million.[37]

But by far the most ambitious of these industrial projects was unveiled in London on October 1, 1968. Called "the largest industrial project to be undertaken in Bahrain since the construction of the refinery almost 30 years [earlier]," it proposed the building of a £20 million aluminum smelter on the island. ALBA, the smelter's operating company, was at the start a joint venture by the Bahraini government and a number of foreign firms, and Bahrain's directors of finance and oil affairs were founding members of ALBA's board of directors.[38] Work was begun on the project in early January 1969, when it was announced that the facility's original capacity would be substantially increased. At the time construction started, the firm's management expected virtually all of its product to be marketed outside Bahrain itself.[39] To close out this wave of industrial expansion, the Bahraini government awarded a contract worth almost $1 million to the British firm of Thomas Robinson and Sons for the construction of a modern flour mill with the capacity to produce one hundred tons of flour per day.[40]

Industrial development in Bahrain from 1968 until the spring of 1972 was confined to the completion and bringing on line of these four plants. Then began a second, and markedly shorter, period of major industrial expansion. This upswing was the result of OAPEC's choosing, in March 1972, to finance construction of a $60 million shipyard on the site of the former British naval yard in Bahrain. This facility—named the Arab Shipbuilding and Repair Yard (ASRY)—was to be the first in the Gulf area designed to handle vessels larger than 400,000 d.w.t. Building such a shipyard was expected to require almost twice the number of workers employed to build the ALBA plant. And operating it was expected to require almost the same number of workers as at ALBA.[41]

More than two years elapsed between the initiation of ASRY and the next period of industrial expansion in Bahrain. In early October 1974 BAPCO announced that it was going to invest $120 million in enlarging its operations. The country's Ministry of Transport awarded a contract worth almost $5.5 million for enlarging the main air terminal at Muharraq later that same month. In mid-November work was started on six new berths at the port of Mina Sulman and extensive dredging was carried out to deepen the port's main channel.[42]

Economic affairs in Bahrain entered a new phase of development with the government's decision in October 1975 to permit the establishment of offshore banking units (OBUS). This decision was a response to the substantial rise in foreign banking activity that had begun in the spring of that year.[43] But the growth of the country's financial sector following the creation of the OBUS was nothing short of phenomenal. "Within four months, 32 applications had been approved, all from banks with the highest possible standing. By November 1978, 48 banks had been licensed, and [by September 1979] this number had reacher 53."[44] Accompanying this rush of activity in the country's financial sector, the Ministry of Finance authorized ALBA to raise $10 million for the construction of a factory that would press section lengths of aluminum out of ingots produced at its existing plant.[45] The following year, 1976, the Ministry of Development and Industry initiated work on the aluminum extrusion plant in an effort to expand Bahrain's building industry.[46] At about the same time private interests began to build a $10-million aluminum cable factory as a further spin-off from ALBA's operations.[47]

On the whole, however, 1975–76 represented the last great rush of industrial and financial development in Bahrain to this time. Banking continued to grow during the later years of the decade, but at a less frantic rate than in 1975–76. A similar pattern is evident with regard to major industrial projects. In February 1978 Japan Gas Corporation was awarded a contract by BANACO for the construction of a plant to extract and treat natural gas. Later that same year Bahrain, Qatar, and the United Arab Emirates announced plans to lay a seabed cable to provide reliable and economical telecommunications among themselves.[48] During 1979 and 1980 ALBA added new equipment that enhanced its capacity to generate electrical power and thereby boosted total output by more than one-third.[49]

In short, diversification of Bahrain's economy away from oil production and refining has occurred in three major waves since the 1950s. The first of these occurred in 1966–68 with the consolidation of the country's fishing industry into one major company, the construction of Bahrain's first modern telecommunications facility, and the beginning of work on ALBA's main plant. The second wave began in the spring of 1972 with the building of ASRY. The third took shape in the late fall of 1974 and continued into 1976. This wave included a marked increase in the size and number of large-scale operations in the heavy industrial sector of Bahrain's economy and also incorporated the sharp rise in banking activities that resulted from the creation of OBUS.

Labor Movement Activity

Bahrain's workers have a long history of organized and violent political protest. Fuad Khuri remarks that "since the twenties, protests and rebellions have become expected features of Bahraini polity, as if they were seasonally ongoing processes."[50] Between September 1953 and June 1954, rioting broke out at least twice at the BAPCO refinery. These disturbances consisted primarily of clashes between Sunni and Shiite workers at the facility and appear to have raised no clearly defined class-related demands.[51] It was not until September 1954 that a measure of organization and politicization came to characterize demonstrations on the islands. Those involved in the demonstrations demanded some measure of popular participation in government, the formulation of a uniform civil and criminal code, and the right of working people to organize trade unions. At a public meeting outside Manama on October 13, 1954, striking workers created their own political organization and elected a governing council to direct it.[52] This organization, called the Higher Executive Committee, carried out a series of negotiations with the Al Khalifah during the next two years. These negotiations took place within the context of continuing popular disorder, centered particularly in Manama and Muharraq.[53] Only the arrest of the majority of the HEC's members in November 1956 succeeded in suppressing this first phase of organized labor militance.

Bahrain's second period of widespread labor protest was precipitated by a strike against BAPCO that broke out on March 9, 1965. This strike was a response to a series of dismissals of experienced workers at the refinery that resulted from the firm's attempts to automate production.[54] The strikers' demands centered primarily on the issue of ending layoffs at the refinery. But they also included recognition of the right to unionize, the lifting of the state of emergency that had been declared in 1956, an end to police harassment, and other matters.[55] Police and military units were once again used to break up the strike (during the summer of 1965), and the leaders of the striking workers and of the students who had joined them were imprisoned or exiled.

Smaller, less well-organized protests occurred periodically over the next seven years in Bahrain. Emile Nakhleh reports that electrical workers walked off their jobs in early 1968 demanding the right to form a trade union, improved working conditions, and salary increases proportional to the rising cost of living.[56] A more significant series of strikes occurred between May and November 1970. The demands voiced by these workers were virtually identical to those expressed by the electrical workers two years earlier.[57]

In March 1972 a significantly more important series of strikes broke out across the country. Workers at Gulf Aviation, the Sulmaniyyah Hospital, the port of Mina Sulman, and ALBA walked off their jobs, demanding, among other things, improved safety procedures on the job, increased wages, and the right to unionize.[58] By all accounts this uprising ranks with those of 1954–56 and of March 1965 as the most serious of the country's recurrent labor disputes.

Although workers militance in Bahrain had diminished somewhat in scale and intensity since 1972, it has not disappeared completely. ALBA employees carried on a series of walkouts and other demonstrations at the company's main complex during the summer of 1974. The primary demands appear to have been for higher wages and the reinstatement of dismissed colleagues.[59] A more widespread industrial action in the country was reported by Kuwaiti sources in April 1976. According to these reports, transportation, shipyard, and hospital workers walked out in protest against a proposed regulation prohibiting them from joining a union "until they had worked within an organization for five years."[60] Strikes were also reported in May 1976. They appear to have been an attempt to force the country's employers to come up with pay raises that would offset the rising cost of living on the islands.[61] But none of these more recent actions has been as threatening to the Bahraini regime as the general strikes of 1954–56, 1965, and 1972.

Conventional Accounts of the Political Economy of Bahrain

Those who have written about the political economy of modern Bahrain have limited their attention to the relationship between the state and industrial-financial development. Their arguments can for the most part be placed into two broad categories. The first sees the state as encouraging new industrial and financial ventures as a way of ensuring the maximum rate of return on the country's declining oil revenues. Thus J. S. Birks and C. A. Sinclair argue that "the development of the *entrepot* trade, an aluminum industry, a commercial centre, and now a dry dock are attempts to create a source of income and employment unrelated to oil."[62] Michael Field sees this as a more general trend among the Gulf oil-producing countries. In his view, "The producers' awareness of the diminishing nature of their asset has meant that after an early flush of wild spending, all governments have conceived the major long term economic ambition of developing supplementary sources of income. . . . The main emphases seem to have been in heavy process plant industry, light industry, the development of associated and unassociated gas, banking and foreign investment services (mainly in Kuwait and Bahrain) and, in Bahrain, the development of a role as a regional communications, leisure and service center in which many of the foreign companies operating in the Gulf have established their bases."[63] Finally, A. S. Gerakis and O. Roncesvalles observe that Bahrain "was first in its geographical area to produce oil but is also likely to be among the first where production will run out—indeed, in the not too distant future. That is why the Bahrainis have attached considerable importance to a policy of diversifying their economy. The establishment of the OBUS should be seen in this perspective."[64]

This way of conceptualizing the connection between state policy and changes in Bahrain's economic affairs shares a number of features with what has been called the state-derivation (or "form-derivation") school of current political economy. Writers in this school argue that changes in government policy—as well as in the size, scope, and organization of state institutions—can be traced directly to (or "derived from") the requirements of an expanding capitalist economy.[65]

State-derivation theorists can point to a number of features of politics in contemporary Bahrain that substantiate their argument. Periods of the greatest expansion in the country's administrative apparatus came not during the early years of petroleum production, when the government had unprecedented amounts of revenue at its disposal, but rather during the mid-1970s, when current and future resources were becoming increasingly scarce. The growth of the Bahraini state can be seen as the concrete expression of the need for rational planning and the coordination of economic activity that has accompanied the islands' steady decline as a major oil producer. State intervention in the country's domestic market and state participation in heavy industrial and financial projects have in fact begun to reverse the drop in the aggregate rate of profit attributable to the oil sector of the country's economy. Consequently, the rate of expansion of the Bahraini administration has also diminished in recent years. Only in the oil industry—the sector in which the labor movement is most firmly established—and in the construction of workers' townships has the government continued to play an active administrative role.

Others who write about the political economy of contemporary Bahrain place less emphasis on "economic" trends as determinants of Bahraini state policy. Instead, they see recent efforts to diversify the country's economy primarily as a result of trends in the domestic political arena. More specifically, they point out that over the past thirty-five years the regime has used the creation of new industrial and financial ventures as a way of co-opting or buying off powerful social forces whose existence predates the rise of the petroleum economy. Thus Arnold Hottinger argues that "Bahrain has been the first oil state to face the transition from an oil to a post-oil economy. But this transition has been relatively easy for the island state. Because the oil revenues were always reasonably limited, a non-oil economy had always been maintained and was added to over the years."[66] Avi Plascov claims that the regime's administrative and economic programs have had a more specific political objective. In his view,

> apart from attempting to keep its house in order and to attend promptly to any grievances, each dynasty [in the Gulf] has sought to widen its base of power by broadening the foundations of government. . . . The Al Khalifa ruling family, which began to face opposition as early as the mid-1950s, has followed the Iraqi pattern, in an attempt to defuse sectarian strife from tearing Bahrain apart. In 1975 five Shi'i ministers were brought in to head the less important offices in the Sunni-dominated seventeen-member cabinet. Today over half of the Ministers and most Heads of Government Departments are non-royal.[67]

Similarly, Plascov sees the government's support for large-scale industrial projects and housing construction as representing efforts "to placate Shiites."[68]

This second way of conceptualizing the link between state policy and economic change in Bahrain closely resembles the theory advanced by a second major school of contemporary political economy. Writers in this school argue that the most important aspects of state activity can be explained in terms not only of conflicts among the dominant forces that are present in any particular society, but also in terms of conflicts between these dominant forces and powerful subordinate classes in that society. Under these circumstances, the primary role of the state is to "maintain the political conditions necessary for the reproduction of the (dominant) mode of production" by "managing class contradictions and thereby securing cohesion" among contending social forces.[69]

Those who emphasize the hegemonic character of the capitalist state can also find aspects of Bahraini politics that support their position. Periods of substantial expansion in the country's central bureaucracy have on the whole occurred as a response to widespread labor disorders that have disrupted normal economic relations on the islands. These waves of administrative expansion in turn created conditions in which relatively advanced forms of capitalist economic enterprises—such as modern factories and international banks—could take root and flourish. But because of the strength of the country's labor movement, this latter process did not occur until relatively late in Bahrain's economic history. Even since the mid-1970s, moreover, Bahrain's economic development has required the support of powerful capitalist institutions centered outside the country's own borders. Consequently, there is today a paradoxical combination of demands for further "Bahrainization" of the work force on the one hand and growing dependence on foreign capital, both Western and Saudi, on the other.[70]

It is tempting to try to construct a critical experiment that might indicate which of these two ways of conceptualizing the country's politics is more credible. Recent work by Arthur Stinchcombe illustrates the potential of this sort of exercise.[71] But there are serious difficulties with both the state-derivation and the hegemonic approaches to the poltical economy of contemporary Bahrain that make it impossible to accept either of these accounts as they are presently formulated. Both approaches assume a degree of rationality and attention to long-term consequences that Bahrain's rulers have only partially realized.

According to the state-derivation perspective, Bahrain's administration should be pursuing an economic program that provides the most profitable alternatives to the income now being derived from the country's rapidly disappearing oil reserves. Such a program could include a wide variety of industrial and commercial projects. Which particular projects are actually implemented is, according to this view, a function of the relative surplus that each can contribute to capital accumulation. How profitable any of these projects turns out to be is in turn determined by a wide range of class-related factors, such as the availability of relatively inexpensive skilled labor. What would bring this theoretical perspective into question would be the state's implementing an economic program that failed to maximize the level of capital accumulation in society. During the mid-1970s, Bahrain's government carried out just this sort of suboptimal economic program.

ALBA's success in operating at a profit made this enterprise virtually unique among the industrial diversification projects undertaken in the Arab Gulf countries in the 1970s. The Bahraini government's decision to encourage the project is therefore considered a major achievement in its effort to wean the country's economy away from its overwhelming reliance on revenues derived from the petroleum sector. From a state-derivation point of view, one would have expected the regime to consolidate its success by encouraging the development of a heavy industrial sector on the islands that would be tied to aluminum production. But instead of pursuing such a course, in the fall of 1975 Bahrain's government adopted measures to expand the financial-services sector of the country's economy. This move represented a clear step away from sectors "which in revenue supplement terms could make a much bigger contribution than financial services."[72] The economic implications of this change in policy were not lost on local observers. On November 13, 1975, the weekly newspaper *Al-Adwa* criticized the state's support for the OBUS, observing that "offices here and investments elsewhere is a matter which we cannot encourage to continue." Although the paper expressed its support for the government's general effort to pull foreign capital into the Bahraini market, it commented that "the capital we need is that which builds factories."[73]

More important, in state-derivation terms, Bahrain's program of heavy industrialization continues to rely on various forms of petroleum production, not only as a source of revenues to cover construction and start-up costs, but also as a major input into the manufacturing process itself. By 1976 almost 10 percent of the country's oil production was being consumed locally.[74] Moreover, ALBA makes use of a significant proportion of the natural gas produced on the islands in its smelting plant. And the country's heavy industrial sector continues to require greater levels of petroleum products even at a time when shipments of oil from Saudi Arabia are becoming increasingly vital in maintaining an efficient level of operations at the islands' refinery complex and other manufacturing firms. From a state-derivation perspective, it is hard to explain why the government has encouraged this sort of industrial expansion as a way of "replacing" oil revenues instead of sponsoring a wider range of commercial ventures that would have fewer ties to the petroleum sector and its products.

Those who emphasize the hegemonic character of the Bahraini state expect the state to carry out an economic program that increases the level of political and ideological cohesion among all the forces that constitute Bahraini society. What specific kinds of projects end up being authorized is explained in terms of conflicts both within the dominant political coalition and between this bloc and subordinate classes. Since the primary function of the administration is to diffuse or ameliorate these conflicts, it would be contradictory for the state to carry out projects that substantially reduce the level of domestic social cohesion. Yet it was just this sort of economic program that the Bahraini state adopted during the 1970s.

Perhaps the most explosive domestic political issue in the Gulf involves the role of expatriate labor in the local economy. This issue, along with that of the right of workers to unionize, has provided the most important rallying point for Bahrain's labor movement over the past thirty years.[75] As a way of diffusing this volatile issue, the government made a concerted effort during the late 1960s and early 1970s to reduce the number of immigrant laborers in the islands. The success of this effort was apparent by 1975, when the total number of foreigners in Bahrain dropped to 26,089 from an already reduced figure of 37,885 in 1971.[76] This trend, however, was not evident across all sectors of the country's economy, and has not continued. Foreigners had succeeded in gaining a greater share in the areas of construction, agriculture and fishing, and wholesale and retail trade by 1976 than they had occupied in 1970, and the expansion of the financial sector after 1975 further increased the number of non-Bahrainis working the country.[77] Moreover, J. S. Birks and C. A. Sinclair estimated in 1980 that the number of migrant workers employed in Bahrain would show a substantial rise between 1975 and 1978.[78] Thus whatever else the state may have accomplished in the way of enhancing cohesion among Bahrain's social forces, it has not only largely failed to remove one of the basic catalysts to radical political action on the islands, but is actually allowing it to reemerge.

Hegemonic-state theorists also include among the primary functions of the capitalist state its role in ensuring the security of domestic economic activities. Policies that jeopardize the ability of local capitalists to carry on with their business exacerbate class conflict and for this reason are to be avoided. How, then, are we to explain the Bahraini regime's shift from industry-led to finance-led development? A. S. Gerakis and O. Roncesvalles listed a number of ways in which this decision has increased the level of interstate tension in the Gulf region.[79] Furthermore, it seems clear that even under the best of circumstances international financial activities are a relatively insecure means of promoting national economic growth, since financial affairs are subject to the control of sovereign countries that issue and regulate currency in their own interests. This basic feature of international economics was brought home to the Bahraini OBUS in July 1979, when the Kuwaiti government adopted liquidity restrictions that forced Kuwaiti banks operating in Bahrain to return a significant portion of their deposits to their home offices.[80]

Social Conflict and Political Economy in Contemporary Bahrain

It is clear from the evidence presented above that developments such as state administrative expansion or the creation of new economic enterprises are the results of a number of powerful social forces. Seeing these outcomes as the result of conscious intent on the part of any single social force entails not only serious conceptual problems but significant empirical difficulties as well. On the other hand, arguing that the growth of Bahrain's administrative apparatus or the formation of ALBA represented an attempt to enhance the level of class cohesion or increase the scale of capital accumulation in the country ignores the ways in which efforts by any one social actor to achieve its own interests become derailed by the presence of other actors. As Scott Lash and John Urry have concluded in a similar context, "the existence of other social entities . . . mean[s] that whatever the collective agents intend, these [intentions] cannot be necessarily realized and must produce some *transmutation* of the explicit objectives."[81] In other words, what government officials say they are doing in carrying out any given policy—or what purpose outside observers detect in that policy—is by itself an inadequate focus for political analysis. Bahrain's shift from industry- to finance-based development, for example, was a consequence of several simultaneous conflicts within Bahraini society during the mid-1970s. It was not the result of deliberate choice on the part of the country's most powerful interests.

This point can be made in empirical terms as well. If any one of the three political dynamics discussed in this paper were solely responsible for changes in the other two, a much greater degree of congruence would be present among them. As it is, these indicators—administrative expansion, economic change, and labor movement activity—show quite dissimilar patterns of relationship across time. Consequently, the relationship among the three must be more complex than existing theories of the capitalist state suggest. This complexity can only be disentangled if one first recognizes that the three dynamics represent the unintended consequences of a number of different struggles occurring in Bahraini society over the past thirty-five years. It is the most important task of further scholarship to uncover the bases and contours of these interdependent struggles.

Second, this study implies that an adequate explanation for political change in Bahrain will have to concern itself with other social forces besides government officials, captains of industry and finance, and industrial workers. Fuad I. Khuri has shown that the social relations associated with agriculture and fishing on the islands during the early twentieth century played a major role in determining not only the scope and extent of Al Khalifah authority but also the scale and direction of the opposition to this authority.[82] Bahraini society is no less heterogeneous at the present time than it was during the 1920s. Important changes occurred in the 1970s in the agricultural and commercial sectors of the country's economy. Small-scale farming appears to have reasserted itself during this decade at the expense of operations using large numbers of wage laborers. At the same time, the size of the paid labor force in trade and tourism has grown dramatically, even as the number of self-employed merchants and vendors in the country rose by almost 13 percent.[83] Work has not even begun on mapping the course of these trends in the less salient sectors of the Bahraini economy.[84]

Political outcomes should be seen as the unintended consequences of strategic interaction among the forces that make up Bahraini society. Conflicts in all sectors of the country's economy—and not just in its most obvious ones—should be seen as affecting the course of political change on the islands. Only thus will we be able to overcome the inadequacies of current theorizing about the political economy of the Gulf states; and only then will we have the tools with which "to probe further to discover which capitalists constitute the governing group [in countries such as Bahrain] and on what their supremacy is based."[85]

PART 2

Radical and Reformist Military Regimes

■

APPROACHES TO THE UNDERSTANDING OF EGYPT

■

Robert Springborg

Because of its preeminence in the Arab world, its role as barometer of change likely to occur elsewhere in the region, and its comparative accessibility, Egypt has been closely scrutinized by political scientists. As a result, one can speak accurately of various and fairly well elaborated schools of thought about Egyptian politics.

The manner in which a political system is analyzed is of more than abstract interest. It directly influences how we understand a country's real political choices and possibly how we predict those of the future. What might be called the Pharaonic interpretation of Egyptian politics, for example, assigns to the ruler virtually sole responsibility for decision making. Hence it is to his political psyche that one must turn for an understanding of events. One recent work in this vein has determined that it was Sadat's Nasser complex that propelled him, and therefore Egypt, down the path that was followed from 1970 to 1981.[1] Another close observer of Sadat has assessed him as a megalomaniac, not because of the years spent in Nasser's shadow, but because of feelings of personal inadequacy stemming from his supposedly negroid features.[2]

For others the leader is a representative, captive, or arbiter of dominant groups or classes pursuing their interests; it is, therefore, to class structure and the political economy more generally that one must turn for an appreciation of the causes of specific political outcomes. In this view Sadat liberalized the economy and polity because it was in the interest of the class upon which his power was based. He went to Jerusalem because that class was seeking an accommodation with Western capital.

The concept of Egypt as a "praetorian state" or military society has preoccupied several writers,[3] and the bureaucracy has also been nominated for the role of dominant institution. Infrastructure on the input side of the political process has likewise occasionally been credited with paramount importance. During the Nasser period, for example, the Arab Socialist Union was identified as the chief vehicle of change.

There are at least two other macropolitical conceptualizations within the mainstream of scholarship on Egypt, although neither is as systematically elaborated as those mentioned above. The first is a broader interpretation of Egyptian civilization than that offered by those who speak of a military or bureaucratic polity. With this approach the task of analysis amounts to a psycho-cultural explanation of contemporary events. Fouad Ajami characterized the battle between Sadat and his detractors in the wake of Camp David as "the struggle for Egypt's soul,"[4] believing that the party that better appreciated the world-weary, inherently conservative "soul" of Egypt was the one likely to emerge victorious. Jacques Berque casts the country as one of many protagonists in a worldwide decolonization struggle that caused in Egypt, as in other former colonies, a fundamental assessment of "one's own self."[5] Whether focusing on the interplay of geopolitical, social, and historical conditions, or on the compelling centrality of a single shared experience, this type of approach is akin to Gestalt psychology, in which the wholeness of the subject of study is emphasized.

Another interpretation of politics and political change in Egypt is a neo-Khaldunian cyclical theory of the state. A new and dedicated ruler, such as Muhammad Ali (1805–48) or Gamal Abdal Nasser (1952–70), sweeps away parasitic elements that have been exploiting the masses and siphoning off potential state revenues. In their stead more efficient administrators under strict governmental supervision are charged with the tasks of extraction and regulation. But the zenith of state power is quickly reached, and decline ensues, enabling servants of the state to convert public into private wealth and allowing entrepreneurial elements once again to begin the process of capturing resources at the expense of both the state and the exploited masses.

The dynamic driving the state in these endless cycles is seen by some analysts to lie outside Egypt. The growth of state power in the Nile Valley leads inevitably to expansionist tendencies, which in the modern period have been checked by extraregional states, sometimes working through local agents. So Muhammad Ali met his Waterloo at the hands of the Great Powers in Syria, while Nasser eventually fell to America's surrogate, Israel.

In this view the upswing of the pendulum, the consolidation of state power, has historically been a more or less natural occurrence, given Egypt's strategic position on the Nile and the relative resource impoverishment of her neighbors. Left to its own devices and free from external constraints, the Egyptian state would remain static—powerful, centralized, and preeminent in the region.[6]

In addition to the Pharaonic explanation mentioned above, there is another approach to Egyptian politics that emphasizes individuals and relations between them. Based largely on Max Weber's analysis of bureaucracy and authority, this approach views Egyptian politics as patrimonial, sultanic, and/or based on interaction within and between small groups, including those founded on kinship. Accordingly, large institutions, including the military, the bureaucracy, and political input structures, are seen not as cohesive political actors but as arenas within which patrons and clients, colleagues, cohorts, and kin pursue their own interests.

Frameworks that assign to Egyptian politics the status of dependent variable and to external factors that of independent variable tend to view the latter in specific geographical terms—either the global or the regional system is seen as crucial in determining Egypt's fate. The interpretation that stresses the global perspective takes two forms: one emphasizes the politico-military dimension and the hostility of the Great Powers to Egyptian regional hegemony, while the second, which is more frequently encountered, places more weight on economic considerations, arguing that Egypt must be seen for what, above all else, it is—a poor, overpopulated, Third World country. Its consequent economic dependence on real and potential donor states is thus the major constraint, indeed the determinant of its foreign and domestic policies, for the first priority inevitably must be to feed the ever increasing millions. With its range of choices severely circumscribed, Egypt can do little more than barter her strategic location for food, capital, and consumer goods, all the while walking a tightrope between foreign-inspired financial orthodoxy and domestic political rebellion. In this, it is claimed, Egypt differs little from other poor, overpopulated, dependent states, except insofar as her unique geopolitical situation allows greater leverage.

At the regional level it is also the economic rather than the military dimension that is increasingly seen as exerting the greatest influence on Egyptian decision making. Its role as dominant Middle East power now eclipsed, Egypt, like other Arab states, is being drawn inexorably into the rapidly specializing regional economy. For Egypt this is occurring on unfavorable terms. With the Arab center of economic gravity now in the Gulf, Egypt's allotted role is that of labor exporter, not industrial power. Faced with a desperate need for Arab economic resources, but aware that acceptance of them implies perpetual regional dependency, Egypt is left with a Hobson's choice. According to this logic, the regional imperative is of greater political moment than the global one because of the immediate involvement of so many expatriate Egyptians living in neighboring states and because of the unique salience of regional politics for regime legitimacy in the Arab world. In sum, regional imperatives of a political, economic, and military nature have imposed a straitjacket on Egypt, one that constrains not only regional but also domestic choices. Policies of a radical political and economic nature are simply not compatible with Egypt's role in the Middle East, or so the argument goes.

The regionalist perspective did not simply emerge with these recent developments in the Middle East and the Arab world. During the Nasser period the relative underdevelopment of other states in the region and the challenges of Arab radicalism were also seen as primary determinants of Egypt's aggressive foreign and radical domestic policies. There was a vacuum, and Egypt, led by Nasser, filled it. Now the context has changed, but it is still primarily at the regional level, according to this view, that state policies are determined.

There are, no doubt, other ways of categorizing approaches to the understanding of Egyptian politics, just as there are other approaches. Emphasis will be placed here on explanations that rely on domestic factors rather than external ones, limiting the discussion to the conditions unique to Egypt. Finally, aspects of these approaches will be used to structure some comments and speculations on the Mubarak era.

Social Aggregate Analysis

The simplest form of interpretation assigning a dominant role to social aggregates is that which postulates the seizure of power by a single class. During the Nasser era, for example, the lower middle class, the upper middle class, and the rural middle class were alternately identified as the dominant class. A variant of this position stresses the relative autonomy of the state, leaving open the possibility that a new class may emerge from within the (bureaucratic-authoritarian) state to become the paramount force in the political system. These and other class-based conceptualizations contend that political outcomes reflect the relative power of contending social classes. Some, particularly Egyptian Marxists and neo-Marxists, see considerable power residing with the masses, whose demands and political strength placed significant constraints on even Nasser's options.[7] Others contend that the most severe limitation on his freedom to maneuver was the residual strength of the bourgeoisie,[8] or in a variation on the argument, the consumerist orientation of the very class on which he depended for power, the amalgam of officers and technocrats labeled the new class.[9]

The most novel role analysis of large social aggregates assigns to one key group an intermediary position, a brokerage role between the ruler and ruled. Leonard Binder sees the rural middle class as this crucial element, the second stratum that "does not rule but is the stratum without which the rulers cannot rule."[10] Two students of Egyptian professionals see their subjects of study as modern-day *ulama,* who act as interlocutors between ruler and ruled. For Clement Henry Moore, *ulama,* like contemporary Egyptian engineers, "had traditionally been co-opted into the ruling establishment, in exchange for the legitimacy they might bestow."[11] Donald M. Reid ascribes a similar function to lawyers.[12] But both Moore and Reid concede that modern secular professional "middlemen" are not the political equals of their religious forerunners because of the mass appeal, hence mobilizational capabilities, of the latter.

Problems with class analyses lie both in the conceptualization of what is offered as the key social aggregate and in the determination of the political role that aggregate is said to play. Enough has already been written on the heterogeneity of the new middle class that that point need not be belabored here.[13] Not only was that aggregate inappropriately constituted from markedly dissimilar social categories, but its political role was also inaccurately ascribed. Manfred Halpern contended that his professionals, intellectuals, technocrats, and others of the new middle class would modernize Egyptian political life just as education had modernized the country's vocational structure.[14] In fact, however, as Moore and Reid contend, in the drama of Egyptian politics, civilian members of the new class play the roles of middlemen or brokers—in short, of contemporary *ulama*, rather than of politicians in a Western parliamentary sense. As for the hypothetical military wing of the new middle class, Amos Perlmutter erred in considering the military to be a cohesive institution, rather than a heterogeneous collection of individuals only semi-socialized into a military ethos.[15]

Problems of formulating definitions of other allegedly crucial social aggregates have been equally problematic and frustrating. The interminable wrangle over defining exploiters and exploited in the countryside is one example.[16] Are the former all those who employ labor, hence almost all landowners, or should the line be drawn below the middle group, those owning, say, ten feddans (1.038 acres)? Or are the exploiters only the wealthy landowners, who own in excess of twenty, fifty, or more feddans? A more compelling question than that of operationalization, but one that has received less attention, is what political role these groups, however categorized, actually play. It must at the very least be established that political relations in the countryside are actually of consequence at the political center. If rural Egypt is politically nothing more than the recipient and interpreter of policies that emanate from Cairo, it merits scant attention.

Investigations of rural-urban linkages have taken different forms. One has been to focus on prominent individuals and analyze the connections established between them in their home provinces and subsequently utilized in national politics.[17] From this data it is apparent that rural-based connections are useful, but not crucial, sources of influence at the national level, even for those closely identified with the countryside. Another approach, as yet insufficiently employed, is the analysis of policy.[18] Despite occasional successes by the rural sector, the bulk of evidence suggests that policy toward nonurban Egypt is made primarily with the country's cities in mind.

The most extensively argued case for strong rural-urban linkages turns on the question of recruitment of national political elites. Because the rural middle class has been so heavily represented in the elite, the interests of that class, it is argued, must have been protected. Deficiencies in this proposition again turn on the specification of the aggregate itself and its hypothesized role. Whereas Binder sees one million Egyptians as members of his second stratum, John Waterbury cannot conceive of this group's exceeding 125,000.[19] But in what sense is the rural middle class a coherent, cohesive social class in any case? Rural origins, especially those of a father or grandfather, are unlikely to be an overriding determinant of contemporary political outlook. Unless evidence is presented to the contrary, there is no reason to attribute to this aggregate more cohesion or homogeneity than to Halpern's urban-centered new middle class. As far as political continuity, prominence, and role are concerned, the case is also far from impressive. Binder's own data trace the political decline of this group over the period he analyzes, even though he concludes the opposite,[20] while other evidence suggests both a significant political turnover rate in rural politics and the erosion of the rural base of urbanized elements of the rural middle class.[21]

The inability of the rural middle class to prevent the Nasserite-inspired shift in urban-rural terms of trade calls into question the general proposition that Egyptian regimes depend on specific classes. Why, for example, did Nasser stop at a fifty-feddan maximum for landholdings? The argument that he could not lower the ceiling further because of landowner opposition is not convincing, although to be sure it would have been difficult for him to do so when his political fortunes were at a low ebb. In fact, restraint was largely self-imposed and resulted from Nasser's increasingly skeptical attitude toward large, public enterprises in the agricultural sector, coupled with an awareness of the debilitating consequences of fragmentation of landholdings.

But the argument that leadership is unconstrained can be pushed too far. Waterbury's contention, for example, that Nasser's unwillingness to squeeze the present generation economically for the sake of the next was the result of a personal preference, not of political choice, is overstated.[22] In the wake of the 1967 war, Nasser partially opened the doors to consumerism because he needed to shore up his weakened political position. He could buy off the urban lower middle class by making accessible such mundane, but previously almost unobtainable, commodities as toothpaste, while for the comparatively wealthy the price was a television set or an automobile. Consumerism may be a sign of a regime's weakness, but it is not necessarily an indication of the strength of the middle and upper classes.

This leaves unanswered the question of what political force constrains the choices made by Egypt's ruler. If it is not the rural middle class or privileged classes more generally, except in very vague terms, what is it? The so-called new class, composed of politicians and bureaucrats and strategically located in the state apparatus, is an obvious candidate.

The problem with this concept is not in its operationalization, for unlike other classes seen as being crucial, the "new class" consists of officeholders; hence their numbers can be tallied, and have been.[23] But can it be established that the few thousand high-ranking civil servants, public-sector managers, and top-level advisers act as a constraint on leadership, or that it enhances our understanding to reconceptualize administrators as a class? Clearly they have been divided amongst themselves on key policy issues. With the educational explosion their skills are no longer in short supply—as individuals they are replaceable. Educational expansion, combined with regime change, has moreover had a leveling effect. Since the onset of the Nasser era, the social background of members of the "new class" has become increasingly mixed, although recruitment is still disproportionately from the privileged strata.[24] The "new class" does not engage in collective political action. Professional syndicates are at best proto-political. The extent of their intervention in political decision making is determined more by the access of their patrons than by the force of their collective wills.[25]

Individually, in small groups, and in patron-client networks, members of the hypothetical "new class" impose constraints on the ruler, who in turn balances off contending forces, divides and rules, and in general acts to secure his position against challengers within the patrimonial hierarchy. While he may be threatened by an individual and his supporters, as Nasser was by Field Marshal Amer, he does not confront a unified class capable of withdrawing its support en masse. This is so even when he chooses to move against the objective interests of this class, for its members do not constitute a self-conscious collectivity.

There is, in short, no identifiable social class that can reasonably be said to subordinate Egypt's ruler to its will. The most that can be argued is that particular social aggregates possess occasional veto power over specific initiatives. Over the long haul, however, resources at the disposal of the ruler are sufficient to overcome intermittent setbacks.

The weakness of the link between social class and political organization is further illustrated by the political role of radical Islam. The social center of gravity of some sections of the Muslim Brotherhood and of various shadowy Islamic political associations that have emerged since the early 1970s is said to be the lower middle class or, more specifically, young, relatively well-educated social marginals, who are so by virtue of their father's occupation and/or their recent urbanization.[26] But the range of variation in members' backgrounds is obviously considerable, not only between radical Islamic organizations but within them. The Muslim Brotherhood, or at least significant sections of its factionalized leadership, are more representative of the middle or upper than the lower middle class. The *Takfir wal Hijra*, that bane of the government's existence, consisted at its organizational apex of an agricultural engineer, two military officers, and the owner of a bookstore, while further down in the ranks educational and vocational backgrounds were less illustrious.[27] The ambiguity of Egyptian Islamic revivalism on economic matters, paralleled by the struggle over economic policy in contemporary Iran, suggests that the doctrinal ambivalence of Islam on economics is not so much a handicap as a convenience that enables disparate social groupings to coalesce. The crunch comes only if power is seized, or closely approached, and slogans have to be turned into concrete policy, thereby favoring some class interests at the expense of others.

The strength of Islamic revivalism is, therefore, simultaneously its weakness. A protest movement, it rallies under its banner those of diverse class backgrounds. Cohesive organization within the framework of Islamic resurgence is thus not possible across the movement as a whole, but only within compartmentalized segments, such as the *Jund Allah*, *Takfir wal Hijra*, and so on. The groups are too small to pose mortal threats to the political order. Fissures in larger organizations provide the astute patrimonial leader and his security services with considerable opportunity to divide and rule. Since the days of King Farouk's courtly games with the Muslim Brotherhood, this has been a standard tactic of Egypt's rulers.

Nevertheless, Islamic revivalism does pose a threat to the government of Egypt. The ranks of the movement are swelling as a result of the inability of the economic system to adequately absorb members of the younger generations, whose numbers, given Egypt's population explosion, are truly prodigious. To the degree that the economy is unable to respond and foreign policy is frozen by a condition of near-dependency, the mounting pressure has to be contained by the use of counter forces, such as the secular left. Sadat devoted insufficient attention to these tactics and brought the system to a perilous state. Mubarak has proven capable of distinguishing between system-challenging opposition and those who simply want more say in political matters, and has dealt with each accordingly. The emergency laws, for example, directed primarily against Islamic extremism, have annually been renewed, while political parties, which cater primarily to the secularized middle class, have been permitted increased latitude of operations. Yet Egypt's fundamental economic and social problems continue to mount, raising the question of the ultimate success of any containment strategy, even one as comparatively well executed as Mubarak's.

In summary, conceptualizations of Egyptian politics in class terms overstate the cohesiveness of large social aggregates and correspondingly underemphasize the importance of leaders and their choices. The Ali Sabry, Sami Sharaf, and Sharawy Goma' troika, for example, came perilously close to edging Sadat out of power in 1971. Had they done so it is difficult to imagine that Egypt in the 1970s would have followed the course Sadat actually pursued. Such speculation in turn casts doubt on the argument that the resurgence of the middle class in the wake of the 1967 war left Nasser and his successor no choice but to opt for conservative policy packages. More generally it suggests that the absence of cohesive, class-based political organizations provides ample room within which Egypt's rulers can maneuver.

Institutional Analysis: The Military

A major theme of the literature following Nasser's 1952 coup d'état against King Farouk was the military's domination of politics, although there was never agreement on precisely what that meant. Class analysts had to reconceptualize the military to fit within their framework. Halpern, for example, saw the military as the tool of the new middle class, while Hassan Riad considered it as a political manifestation of the haute bourgeoisie.[28] For Anouar Abdel-Malek, the army became a defender of class privilege and the instrument used to preempt more radical change, which he alleged was in the offing in 1952.[29] Another approach viewed the political role of the Egyptian army as a manifestation of the praetorianism inherent in Islamic and Egyptian political theory and practice.[30] Many writers simply categorized Egypt with other new nations in which coups d'état occurred because colonial rule had prevented the emergence of institutions of government other than the military and the bureaucracy.[31]

However, empirical and theoretical reevalution of the role of the Egyptian military in politics suggests that it was less profound than previously thought. The progressive demilitarization of the cabinet, which began slowly and erratically under Nasser, gathered pace under Sadat and Mubarak. It has met with little response from the military itself, which suggests that officers as a corporate group have been unable or unwilling to maintain positions of political power.[32] This in turn raises the question of whether the military ever dominated Egypt's political elite as thoroughly as Abdel-Malek, Perlmutter, and others contend. Nazih Ayubi, for example, concludes his review of the relevant data by observing that former Egyptian officers have not been notably more successful in penetrating the civil service and public sector than have their British counterparts.[33]

Egypt's presidents have all been former officers, as have many, but by no means all, of their top advisers and confidants. But this is not conclusive evidence of the military's preeminence. One of the three leaders, Sadat, spent comparatively little of his adult life in the army, as he was for all intents and purposes a full-time revolutionary nationalist. That other countries, including Western democracies, have had former officers as presidents is not taken to indicate that their civilian political institutions are secondary. For the military to be dominant, officer members of the elite must be bound together by corporate solidarities. This has not been the case in Egypt. Primary units of loyalty have been graduating classes from officer schools and various informal groupings that are not military per se. As Shahrough Akhavi has observed, "The notion of praetorian solidarities binding a military elite together is simply not an accurate description of the Egyptian political system."[34]

Institutional Analysis: The Bureaucracy

That Egypt is first and foremost a bureaucratic polity is a recurrent theme in the literature on Egypt.[35] It is an idea, moreover, that has been put forward by observers from various quarters, including those schooled in the Marxist tradition,[36] traditional public administration,[37] and contemporary political science.[38] Furthermore, numerous analysts have concentrated on the role of the bureaucracy in administering and even mobilizing sectors of Egyptian society, thereby implying the central role of that institution in political and governmental processes.[39] Ayubi identifies the bureaucracy as a key element in a cyclic model, with the comparative power and wealth of the bureaucracy's members varying in inverse proportion to that of the political elite.[40]

At macro-historical and comparative levels, however, the durability, continuity, and uniqueness of Egypt's bureaucratic polity are debatable. The origins of the contemporary bureaucracy can be traced to Muhammad Ali and to the colonial period, not to the Mamlukes, Ayubids, Fatimids, or Pharaohs as is implied in some conceptualizations. The existence of a large, centralized bureaucracy is not uniquely Egyptian, nor has it been established that Egypt's bureaucracy, in proportion to its population, is quantitatively, to say nothing of qualitatively, different from the bureaucracies of other Arab states. They are, in fact, depressingly alike.

Empirical and theoretical shortcomings of the bureaucratic polity model are further apparent when one looks closely at Egypt itself today. There is little to suggest that the bureaucracy is a cohesive, united, or effective actor in Egyptian politics. On the contrary, there is evidence pointing to its fragmentation, to penetration by informal networks, and to inefficiency. This in turn suggests the bureaucracy is only one of several arenas in which political networks operate. This interpretation is consistent with behavioral reality as described in Moore's analysis of the domestic policy-making process in Egypt.[41] It is, moreover, consonant with the performance of the bureaucracy in the countryside, as revealed in a detailed study of the daily life of a contemporary Egyptian peasant; with the exception of his ordeal in marketing sugarcane through a governmental instrumentality, the peasant has no discernible dealings with any branch of the bureaucracy.[42] Can it be that the numerous descriptions of the government's leading role in the countryside is a Cairo-centered view colored by the predisposition to accept governmental claims of administrative capability? While the life and times of one peasant are certainly not conclusive, other evidence likewise suggests that the bureaucracy's prevalence may have been overestimated, both in the countryside and in urban areas.[43]

The bureaucracy has also failed to defend itself adequately. During the Nasser period it was manhandled by the president and his colleagues, who first tried to invigorate it, then, when that failed, developed institutions parallel to it, and finally converted the whole into satrapies for competing would-be "sultans."[44] During the Sadat era the assault came from another direction—that of privatization of the economy. Politically manipulated, financially deprived, and suffering from declining social status, bureaucrats, actual and potential, deserted the civil service and public sector for the flourishing private economy.

Yet, despite its factionalization, absence of corporatism, inefficiency, and comparative weakness, the bureaucracy is an important base of support for the regime, as is evidenced by the magnitude of planned corruption within its ranks (the political elite would not have to give it a share of the spoils if it were completely without power);[45] by the utilization of administrative organs during elections;[46] by its role as an agent of repression;[47] and simply because it has converted millions of Egyptians into wards of the state. But undisputed political significance does not justify claims for paramount importance, or support contentions that Egypt's bureaucracy is unique.

Additionally, the bureaucracy's loyalty cannot be taken for granted. It is now a prime source of recruitment into dissident organizations, especially those of an Islamic revivalist character.[48] Political defection is stimulated by the declining status and remuneration of bureaucrats, whose corporate loyalties are not sufficiently binding to overcome feelings of disaffection. Egypt's recent rulers, having sought to anchor their regimes in a broadened bureaucratic base, may have spread the rewards too thinly for the strategy to continue to be effective.

Institutional Analysis: Political Input and Conversion Structures

While Nasser's "pioneering experiment" with the National Assembly captured the imagination of some analysts,[49] the Arab Socialist Union has received more attention. The thrust of this commentary is that the ASU was designed primarily as an instrument with which Nasser intended to mobilize and transform the political system.[50] When, with the benefit of hindsight, it became apparent that Nasser's experiment with this and two previous proto-parties had not significantly altered his authoritarian rule, the alleged failure was generally ascribed not to intent, which was not adequately investigated, but to faulty implementation. Anthony Nutting, for example, saw the fatal flaw as being Nasser's suspicious nature, which undermined his efforts to create viable political institutions.[51] Various structural explanations were also offered, ranging from the president's ultimate dependence on particular social formations[52] to a cyclical pattern of economic and political decay inherent in Third World state capitalist systems[53] and the domestic impact of regional and/or global factors.[54] That the ASU was originally conceived by Nasser essentially and primarily as an instrument of authority and as a check on some of his rivals' ambitions, and as such was relatively successful, was not an interpretation given sufficient credence.

Institutions performing input and conversion functions in Sadat's Egypt have also been conceptualized as agents of radical change. The People's Assembly, the press, professional syndicates, and the emerging multiparty system are seen as instruments through which the new leader sought a partial democratization. That this failed to occur is again frequently explained by reference to factors at the individual level.

To some observers Sadat had a loss of will. Originally he had sought to liberalize the polity, but his ineptness in reading the mood of the public and channeling its demands for participation led to frustration on both sides, then to hostility, and finally to cancellation of the democratic experiment and a return to authoritarian rule. Liberalization, a real possibility, had simply been mismanaged.[55] Other analysts look more deeply into Sadat's character for an explanation of the failure. They identify ego weaknesses that prevented Sadat from liberalizing: he was simply not the sort of man who would willingly share the limelight.[56]

There are, however, convincing structural interpretations that view Sadat's liberalization as a tactical move rather than a manifestation of a fundamental political commitment. Because he sought to base his regime on a coalition of the new and old upper classes, for example, he had to satisfy some of their demands for participation. That economic liberalization required political democratization has also been hypothesized. Sadat's strategy of seeking U.S. support is seen by some as stimulating the need to liberalize, while others regard regional politics as being more relevant. According to this latter view, Sadat sought to demonstrate his comparative popularity to other Arab rulers, who could not afford even these limited reforms.

What concerns us here is not determining for the historical record whether Nasser ever intended a mass mobilization or whether Sadat had a significant commitment to democracy. Instead, we want to know if Nasser and Sadat, in introducing these reforms, were responding to temporary political circumstances or to more fundamental, long-term developments. Could it be that social mobilization has led to significant demands for political participation, demands that in turn are providing the bases on which political input institutions can be strengthened which will gradually circumscribe heretofore arbitrary authority? Might it not further be argued that the increasingly widely articulated critique of Arab regimes as having failed to adopt and implement successful domestic and foreign policies because they are undemocratic is something other than a temporary intellectual fad? The call for democracy, it is claimed, is the inevitable consequence of education, urbanization, and other aspects of social mobilization that have raised the political consciousness of Arab peoples. In this view, we are witnessing not the epiphenomenon of an ideology articulated by isolated and alienated intellectuals, but the tip of a veritable iceberg of pent-up demands for political participation among the masses of the population.[57] Accordingly, Hosni Mubarak's room for maneuver is less than his predecessors' and bound to be further encroached on by political institutions infused with ever more strength and vitality as the consequences of social mobilization work their way progressively downward in the social structure.

Contemporary demands for democratization of Arab regimes, however, have been occasioned by inadequate performance rather than by dissatisfaction with political processes per se. Failure to share petro-dollars adequately and to invest them wisely, coupled with inability to handle unwanted intrusions into the Arab world, have been linked to authoritarian rule in Egypt as elsewhere. But assessing the value of a form of government by its performance alone could also undercut the appeal of liberalization. Under Nasser, for example, the intellectuals' approval of his goals led them to accept the means by which he sought to achieve them. Like him they were impatient with the democracy they had known during the ancien régime and saw it largely as an impediment to progress. The proof of the pudding is a system that works, and if that system is nondemocratic, so be it. There is little reason to believe that the accommodation Egyptian intellectuals reached with authoritarian Nasserism could not occur on a wide scale once again, assuming of course that an authoritarian ruler could convince the public that their basic demands were being dealt with effectively. Moreover, the trade-off between performance and participation need not be an all-or-nothing proposition. Presumably, some measure of success in foreign and domestic policies could be coupled with a partial liberalization to achieve a stable, legitimate regime. It is precisely this sort of balance, in fact, that Mubarak appears intent on establishing.

The relative ease with which Nasser, Sadat, and Mubarak have manipulated political organizations also casts doubt on the proposition that political participation is being increasingly institutionalized. Nasser, for example, encouraged debate and political participation following the 1961 Syrian secession from the United Arab Republic and after the disaster of the 1967 war with Israel. In 1972 Sadat permitted vigorous parliamentary activity and freewheeling discussions in the ASU and professional syndicates because he had as yet to consolidate his hold on power and because he was manipulating that debate to discredit his opponents. When the danger had passed, both presidents then reined in debate and the institutions in which it had formerly been encouraged. In short, one leadership tactic is to play out line when under stress, and then to reel it in quickly once the crisis has passed. Another is straight-out repression, which Sadat increasingly relied upon toward the end of his life. Still another is encouraging debilitating competition between institutions, as Nasser did between the military and the ASU from 1962 to 1967, and Sadat with the ASU and parliament between 1972 and 1976. Mubarak may be playing a similar game, encouraging the various political parties, even including the Wafd, resurrected from the ancien régime, and the leftist Progressive Unionists, to function as counterweights to Islamic extremists. This is, after all, just the reverse of King Farouk's tactic, which was to encourage the Muslim Brotherhood to counterbalance the Wafd.

It would be hard to contend, in fact, that Egypt's rulers have been progressively more restricted by the country's political institutions. The direction of influence still flows clearly from the former to the latter. The temporary ascendancy of a particular political organization is as likely to result from its transitory utility to the ruler as it is from factors inherent in the organization itself. Predictions of a qualitative change in the structuring of Egyptian political participation could well be based on an erroneous assumption—namely, that political demands must necessarily be expressed and processed through corporate political organizations. The lack of organizational cohesion characteristic of Egypt's administrative institutions, civilian and military, seems also to be an abiding feature of its political parties, interests groups, and its parliament.

As far as parties are concerned, those created by incumbent regimes since 1952, including the Liberation Rally, National Union, Arab Socialist Union, Egyptian Socialist party, and National Democratic party, have all been grafts onto the administrative trunk of the state. As such, they have not had a separate existence, and so have passed immediately into history when that administrative support has been withdrawn. Those parties that have enjoyed a semi or completely autonomous existence, such as the Socialist Liberal party, Socialist Labor party, Progressive Unionist party, or the new Wafd party, are more complex. The Socialist Liberals, created to serve as the establishment opposition, are little different from the National Democrats. Ibrahim Shukry's Socialist Labor party, whose fate was intended by Sadat to be the same as that of the Socialist Liberals, carved out a unique role for itself owing mainly to the sagacity and extensive political experience of Shukry himself. That party, however, despite its sometimes courageous criticism of the regime, is no more than Shukry himself and some of his old cronies from Misr al Fatat (Young Egypt), along with some new admirers and the party newspaper, *Al Shaab*. Khaled Muhyi al Din's Unionist Progressive party is a similar enterprise further to the left. Although organizationally more impressive than the Socialist Labor party, the Unionist Progressives would still be hard pressed to outlive the departure of their founder-president. This leaves the Wafd, which has the greatest mobilization potential of all secular organizations in Egypt, but has yet to demonstrate that in its new form it is fundamentally different from the corrupt patronage machine that fell apart so readily when Nasser seized power. Whether the uneasy coalition of former party loyalists and other ancien régime political activists, together with various products of Nasserite and post-Nasserite politics, can weld together a unified Wafd party remains to be seen. Even the Muslim Brotherhood, the organization in modern Egyptian political life that comes closest to resembling a true mass party, appears to be a coalition of patrons and their networks of clients.

In sum, political parties are of three types, none of which is likely to serve as the organizational backbone for integrating effective, wide-scale political participation. Those of the regime are administrative structures assigned political tasks, and as such are inherently limited as instruments of mobilization. The smaller parties are based on loyalties to a man or a small group of leaders and therefore unlikely to broaden their appeal sufficiently. Potentially large party organizations, such as the Wafd and the Muslim Brotherhood, are susceptible to fragmentation into competitive patron-client networks. As a whole, the party system since 1952, having traced a path from single party, to one party dominant, to a potentially multiparty system under Mubarak, has remained an appendage to presidential rule. Those occasions on which parties have appeared to be assuming significant roles in the Egyptian political process have been the result of the president's personal power requirements, not the consequences of institutionalized mass political participation that has become so strong it can no longer be denied.

What is true of political parties is likewise true of parliament and interest groups. The 1972 session of the People's Assembly, for example, was the most active parliamentary session of the Nasser and Sadat eras,[58] despite the fact that Sadat's political liberalization was not to be declared until after the October 1973 war. That parliamentarians were so active in interrogating ministers and proposing legislation was owing in some measure to Sadat's desire to make political capital out of the reaction to Nasser's tight controls, and in larger measure to his tactic of using the assembly to undermine the left-leaning government of Prime Minister Sidqy. The upsurge of activity in professional syndicates at that time is similarly explained.[59] In both institutions outspoken members were protected by the president's political need for criticism of his opponents and through personal connections to powerful members of the elite, not by virtue of organizational legitimacy or cohesion.

Political Cycles and Civilization as Metaphors

Analyses of contemporary Egyptian politics in neo-Khaldunian cyclical terms are, like the original, metaphorical in that they compare the state to organisms and their life cycles.[60] That analogy can be challenged on several grounds. The state, after all, is not one but a multitude of organisms, all at different stages in their respective life cycles. And what evidence is there that states wax and wane in predictable cycles? Moreover, the cyclical approach ignores linear developments, such as the massive population growth Egypt has experienced, the nation's integration into the global economy, and development of various of its capabilities as a result of technological advancement.

As we do not know what causes the wheel to turn, or even if that is an appropriate metaphor, there is little more than illustrative value in attempting to place the regimes of Nasser, Sadat, and Mubarak in their appropriate locations. Presumably, the Egyptian state has been on a downward trajectory since Nasser's consolidation of authority, so it may be just about to begin a new phase of reassertion of power. The most obvious candidate for the role of *asabiya,* the force hypothesized as propelling the change, is resurgent Islam, despite the absence of an identifiable standard bearer. But this mechanistic formulation simply ignores politics. Mubarak may after all be a more adept leader than his predecessor and succeed in gathering into his hands much of the power that Sadat dissipated. Those attempting to mobilize opposition around the banner of Islam may, on the other hand, be singularly incompetent as revolutionaries and as politicians.

The hypothesis that Egypt is a distinctive political civilization proves, on closer inspection, to be no more helpful than the theory of cycles. The sheer range of variation in interpreting its alleged essence is indicative of the absence of clear-cut and agreed upon guidelines by which the Egyptian political system may be characterized. In examining Egypt's struggle for independence, Jacques Berque, for example, found a nation eagerly and creatively searching for its national character, and therefore its future foreign role and internal structure. P. J. Vatikiotis, on the other hand, analyzing the same period, saw a collapse of cultural and intellectual standards that made possible the emergence of a populist, authoritarian ruler and an undifferentiated, undiscerning mass public.[61] Fuad Ajami is impressed by the inherent conservatism of the Egyptians and by their cynical, world-weary nature, manifested in a comparative detachment from slogans and causes.[62] Gabriel Baer has discerned a long tradition of peasant radicalism and rebellion,[63] while Anouar Abdel-Malek and Hassan Riad detect revolutionary tendencies at various levels of society. There is, in short, considerable disagreement on what constitutes the essence of the Egyptian political character or community.

Patrimonialism, Political Clientelism, and Kinship

Given the historical background of the Egyptian state, Max Weber's conceptualizations of authority have naturally been used to explain Egyptian political processes.[64] One of the key notions underlying Weber's understanding of patrimonialism is that it is based on face-to-face interactions. With regard to Egypt, a variety of networks of personal interactions have been determined to exist within the political elite. Their importance, moreover, is not static but varies both in linear and cyclical fashions. Modernization, for example, has eroded rural patron-client networks as important elements in Egyptian politics, presumably once and for all. Family connections, on the other hand, have varied in importance with the strength and preferences of the ruler.[65] Nasser, suspicious of families and powerful enough not to have to concede much political leeway to them, constructed his system of authority on networks of clients extending downward from his hand-picked assistants. Sadat encouraged the resurgence of family-based networks within the elite, in part to control and counterbalance the political apparatus

Nasser had bequeathed him. These and other changes in the means through which state power is exercised both reflect more broad-based changes and contribute to them.

Peripheral political formations, whose structural characteristics are the antithesis of the structure of the state, are likewise generally based on personal networks. Heikal's account of Takfir wal Hijra provides evidence of this phenomenon in small opposition groups, as does Moore's account of the politics of the engineering profession.[66]

Weberian analysis may also be used to shed some light on what has loosely been referred to as the crisis confronting the New Arab Order, which, among other things, is said to consist of fundamental changes in the social and economic structures of the countries of the region. As a consequence of these changes, Arab political systems are confronting the challenge posed by the second major wave of social dislocation in the past one hundred years. The first, chronicled by Hanna Batatu for Iraq and Gabriel Baer for Egypt, was the erosion of traditional institutions, roles, and economic formations, such as tribes, guilds, sufi orders, urban quarters, village *umad* (mayors), and so on, primarily as a result of imperialist penetration.[67] Batatu among others sees this pulverization of the traditional society and economy as having led to an Arab mass society with inadequate social bases to generate political groupings to constrain arbitrary, capricious, and potentially unstable governments.

But other observers, and especially those concerned with Egypt, have seen the emergence of modern professional, political, and administrative institutions, coupled with the adaptation of traditional loyalties to new structures and settings, as having provided limited bases for relatively stable, not altogether arbitrary, political systems. But now, it is argued, the destruction of these relatively fragile modern institutions as a result of rapid socioeconomic change and political repression, combined with the erosion of the effectiveness of informal personal connections, will bring about the condition of mass society that the first wave of change did not quite achieve. In Egypt the primary cause of this social decay, and hence of political disruption, is above all else the population explosion. Egypt produced over half a million university graduates during the 1970s, about double the number it had produced throughout its history prior to that time.[68]

With rising expectations matched only by frustration, Egypt's youth, it is feared, will desert the established order, thereby paving the way for chaos and revolutionary change.

Conclusion

There can be no doubt that Egypt is undergoing rapid social changes, which have significant consequences for politics. But that these socioeconomic changes are completely deterministic, that their consequences for politics are unambiguous and inescapable, is untrue. On the other hand, conceptualizing the political system as a smorgasbord of choices from which the president, unconstrained by domestic or external factors, selects a few favorites, is likewise erroneous, as it misrepresents the degree of freedom enjoyed by Egypt's leader. Neither a prisoner of circumstances nor a free agent, he consciously or unconsciously elaborates a political strategy designed to deal with a great variety of factors at the national, regional, and global levels. Whether he succeeds in shaping those factors or remains in a completely reactive position depends on circumstances and on his own skills. Hosni Mubarak, having inherited difficult internal and external conditions, has shown considerable ability in responding to them.

Mubarak's political style is akin to that of a military tactician. He identifies specific threats and tailors countermeasures to confront them. In the sphere of domestic politics, for example, he has dealt cleverly with several potentially very antagonistic groupings. He has kept the Sadat entourage on the defensive, gradually easing such luminaries as Sayed Marei, Nabawy Ismail, Ashraf Marwan, Mustafa Khalil, and Jihan Sadat herself out of the limelight. Not being attacked tooth and nail, they have had neither cause nor opportunity to mobilize their considerable resources against Sadat's successor.

Mubarak has been careful not to offer Islamic extremists a clear target to attack. At the personal level he preserves a comparatively austere life-style and keeps his wife at home. He has allowed the courts to wrestle with the thorny problems of Coptic militancy, including Pope Shenouda's attempt to regain his patriarchy. The thrust toward Islamization of the legal system has been deflected, but Mubarak has ensured that he is not seen as the main roadblock.

Another aspect of his strategy has been to divide political militants from possible allies. Thus while the mainstream, conservative element of the Muslim Brotherhood continues to function, the emergency laws designed at the end of the Sadat regime to deal with subversive political activities remain in effect. Several thousand militant activists, the target of those laws, are under detention. Lest there be a wall-to-wall coalition of the opposition, including secularists, Mubarak has simultaneously granted considerable freedoms to political parties. In so doing he is clearly trying to head off the coalition of secular and semi-secular middle classes and Islamic radicals that the shah of Iran fell victim to.

Mubarak's assessment of the politically active secular and semi-secular middle and upper classes is that they do not pose a significant threat to him. He can afford to indulge them by granting rights of expression in the form of newspapers, political parties, elections, and so on, for not only are their demands limited, but the expression of them is almost as important as their fulfillment. For the small price he pays in granting such political activists limited influence on decision making, he obtains their consent to his rule and their support in his campaign to isolate radical extremists.

Lest Mubarak be open to the charge that he is insufficiently nationalist or remiss in support of Arabism, he has worked assiduously at redefining Egypt's role in the area and at modifying the Egyptian-American relationship. Whether consciously imitating the Saudis or not, his policy of reconciling acceptability in Arab circles with an American alliance is very similar to Riyadh's. The tactics of lecturing Americans in Washington about their disregard of Arab, particularly Palestinian, interests, combined with a rejection in the Middle East of radical Arabism and aggressive Zionism, has established for Egypt a clear role as a champion of moderation. Moreover, connections in Washington, Jerusalem, European and Arab capitals, and even in the Communist bloc, enhance Egypt's standing as a key middleman. Mubarak has, in a relatively short time, converted many of Sadat's foreign policy liabilities into net assets. While he has not yet converted this foreign policy capital into a significant legitimating factor at the domestic level, it seems likely that he will be able to do so in the not so distant future.

BA'THIST ETHICS AND THE SPIRIT OF STATE CAPITALISM

Patronage and the Party in Contemporary Syria

■

Yahya M. Sadowski

Does the Ba'th party still matter in Syrian politics? This question has plagued Syrians and foreign observers alike for the past decade. The prevailing view has been that the Ba'th is no longer an effective political force, in fact that it has become a carapace, a lifeless shell barely cloaking an Alawi cabal that holds the true reins of power. This view became especially popular after 1970, when Hafez al-Assad, himself an Alawi, took command of the party and sponsored a rapid promotion of officers and religious minorities into its inner circles. Party members purged during this period complained that the Ba'th's new recruits were largely opportunists and careerists with little commitment to its ideals or programs.[1] Fear that this new elite would use its authority to pursue personal ambitions or sectarian interests prompted rising opposition to the regime, culminating in a full-scale civil war during 1979 and 1980. The ruthless manner in which this opposition was suppressed, including the killing of 10,000 civilians during a February 1982 insurrection at Hama, convinced many that the Ba'th was a far less important base for the Assad regime than was the coercive apparatus of the state.

A minority, however, have insisted that the Ba'th remains Syria's foremost political institution and point to an array of activities in which it appears to have real influence. The party does shape the vocabulary of Syrian politics through its supervision of the press and telecommunications, its control of intellectual life, and the mandatory instruction of its principles in public school curricula. It maintains offices in most villages and urban neighborhoods and employs thousands of people as military personnel, officials, and functionaries. Its members dominate diverse public bodies, including student groups, women's associations, and sports clubs; they supply the leadership for the country's trade unions and peasant federations; and they form solid majorities in both the cabinet and the People's Council (the national parliament). Some scholars have gone so far as to describe the Ba'thist political apparatus as a "quasi-Leninist system."[2]

In fact, the Ba'th is neither a mere façade erected to help legitimize the regime nor a classic "mass party" deriving its strength from ideology and organizational skills. It is a political machine of a type that has no precise analogues in the industrialized world, East or West. Certainly some of the party's slogans are only pious frauds (including its commitment to "Unity, Liberty, and Socialism"), but others express a genuine program which is being translated into national policy. The party's hold over its membership is not rooted in its representation of popular demands or generation of totalitarian devotion, yet it retains the capacity to discipline its rank and file into an effective political force. While control of the state apparatus gives President Assad considerable autonomy from the party, his regime is still respectful of—and ultimately responsible to—the Ba'th. Not only is the party a real power in Syria, but there are reasons to believe its influence is still growing.

Confessionalism and Patronage

Estimates of how much power the Ba'th commands vary partly because observers differ over the importance they assign to religion in Syrian politics. Those who belittle the party's influence commonly assert that the real centers of power in Syria are religious cliques and that the government of President Assad is, in effect, an Alawi regime that only uses Ba'thism to disguise its sectarian objectives.[3] Conversely, those who believe the Ba'th's powers are more substantial tend to stress its secularist ideology or the prominence of Sunnis in the leadership of both party and regime. There is some truth in both of these perspectives, but either taken separately gives a one-sided distortion of the interplay between religion and politics.

On the other hand, it is clear that religion is an important issue both within the Ba'th and in its relationship to society at large. When the Ba'th split into *gawmi* (pan-Arabist) and *qutri* (Syrian-regional) factions in the 1960s, members of the former accused their opponents of appealing to sectarian sentiments and courting tribes and clans at the expense of party principles. Similar accusations have persisted ever since the regional wing of the party triumphed through a bloody coup in February 1966.[4] The Muslim Brotherhood, the largest underground opposition party, denounced the first Ba'thist governments for atheism, but later revised its critique, claiming that neo-Ba'thist governments formed after 1966 were purely puppets of the Alawis.[5] While this claim may have been self-serving, it accurately reflected the evolution of popular perceptions. Particularly after Assad's coup of November 1970, Alawis and other minorities rose rapidly into positions of power. By 1976 Alawis, who formed 12 percent of the total population, held 20 percent of the seats in the Ba'th's highest organ, the Regional Command. Promotions of "politically reliable" officers resulted in Alawis commanding half of all army divisions by 1980. Indeed, several military units, including the Third Armored Division and the Air Force Officer Corps, drew most of their recruits from the province of Ladhiqiya—a heavily Alawi district and home to the Assad family.[6]

On the other hand, this proliferation of Alawis did not in fact mean that their sect had come to control the Ba'th and its program. Most Ba'thist cadres, Alawis and others, remained sincere secularists. The party's membership stayed broadly interconfessional, with a strong following among both Sunnis (who formed 60 percent of the total population) and minorities (including Christians, Druze, and Ismailis as well as Alawis). Assad's own political associations belied the image of a sectarian regime. His most intimate supporters, and after him the most powerful figures in the party, were largely Sunni—such as 'Abd al-Halim Khaddam (the foreign minister), Mustafa al-Tallas (the minister of defense), and 'Abdallah al-Ahmar (the assistant secretary general of the Ba'th).

It would be easier to dismiss these prominent Sunnis as mere tokens but for the fact that the regime and the party have not, in fact, shown any sectarian bias in their social policies. Obviously legislation in Syria does not formally award privileges on the basis of religious identity, but even covert distortions in the pattern of public expenditures are extremely rare.[7] State investment in social services, infrastructure, and the public sector has been consistently designed to promote the national economy rather than particular interests. The Ladhiqiya region, where Alawis prevail, has benefited from state programs—but only in a manner consistent with its status as the site of Syria's only ports and oil-pipe terminus.[8]

Religion is never the sole basis of a Syrian's identity, nor is it the sole medium in which he defines his interests. Loyalties to one's confessional group compete or are synthesized with other parochial bonds to family, tribe, or cult, and with more universal ties to class, party, even nation. In reconciling all these ties, deciding which interests or dimensions of one's identity take priority, Syrians may reach different conclusions according to the specific context in which they are acting. One of the best students of modern Syria has noted:

> A Syrian officer may act like an officer in a restaurant if he feels this will get him quicker service; he may be very conscious of his kin group in choosing a marriage partner; he may act as a member of a particular Alawi tribe during an intra-Alawi dispute within the armed forces; he may act as an Alawi, villager, peripheral non-Sunni or Ba'thi—or all five—during a coup d'état, as a socialist during regime economic policy formation and as a Syrian during a war with Israel.[9]

The resort to confessionalism by Ba'thists has evolved in frequency and purpose over the years. When the party first formed in the 1940s, it already drew a disproportionate share of its membership from religious minorities. Serious manipulation of confessional bonds did not begin until 1961, when the party had to be reconstructed following a three-year hiatus (activities were suspended while Syria was part of the United Arab Republic). To restore the party's depleted membership speedily, cadres recruited large numbers of their friends, relatives, and neighbors—which led to the formation of a series of cliques sharing common social, geographic, and religious identities. This set the stage for the invocation of confessional ties during the factional struggles between the pan-Arabist and regionalist wings of the party that followed. Both wings fought to extend their influence within the officer corps by appealing to cliques of minority officers.[10]

Hafez al-Assad employed his own ties to the Alawi community first to support the regionalist branch of the party and then to promote his own faction within that branch. After his 1970 coup, confessionalism remained one of the hallmarks of his rule—particularly within the military. Not only did Alawi officers enjoy unusually rapid promotions, but several new units of special forces were recruited primarily among Alawis. The largest of these was a commando brigade called *Saraya al-Difa'*, led by the president's younger brother, Rif'at. Alawis soon commanded all the military intelligence services, supervised by Muhammad al-Khawli, an Alawi general who had served in the air force with the president. The Assad brothers and other key Alawis also dominated the Presidential Security Council, which coordinates the civilian security agencies and police with their military counterparts.[11]

By concentrating his confessional allies in positions of command, Assad ensured the loyalty of the officer corps and protected his regime from the threat of military coups (which has plagued all Syrian governments since 1949). This strategy was especially useful in the security apparatus: confessional elites were less likely to feel empathy for the wider segments of the population they might be called upon to arrest, torture, or murder in the pursuit of public order. The police and the special forces became an elite, sharing a sense of "distinctiveness" that detached them from the rest of the population.[12]

This use of confessionalism did not, however, mean the regime had become sectarian. Alawis commanded the military, but *the* Alawis—as a group—did not rule Syria. The privileges enjoyed by Alawi officers had no direct parallels among civilians. The Assads were not trying to promote Alawism or the Alawi community; rather, they sought to pursue their own political programs by using the Alawis. In fact, their manipulation of confessional alliances were never restricted to Alawis. For example, a Christian clique from villages where the regime is exceptionally popular has enjoyed systematic promotion within the General Intelligence Service (*al-Mukhabarat al-Amma*).[13]

Of course, there was a danger that groups of Alawis, working together and exercising wide power over the rest of society, would eventually develop a sectarian consciousness. In other Arab states efforts to bend religious groups to political purposes have backfired: Sadat's effort to harness Islamic fundamentalist sentiments led to his own assassination.[14] How long could the troops of the *Saraya al-Difa'* dominate Sunni towns, living off the fat of the land, before they began to develop collective "Alawi" interest? As the national profile of Alawis rose and Muslim Brotherhood accusations of sectarianism abounded, all Syrians grew acutely sensitive to religious affiliations.

The growth of sectarian sentiments in Syria has been steadfastly opposed by the regime itself. This may have less to do with its ardor for secularism than with its desire to eliminate any basis for organized opposition. Even the Alawi community, if it ever became politically united, would pose a threat to the hegemony of the regime.

For example, the Assads have paid careful attention to the divisions among Alawis. Historically, the Alawis never formed a single, integrated community, but were divided into three cults (*al-Shamsiya, al-Qamariya,* and *al-Murshidiya*) and four tribes (*al-Haddadin, al-Khayyatin, al-Kalbiya,* and *al-Matawira*). Today promotions and access to political power are concentrated on the groups expected to be most loyal to the president, that is, members of his own tribe, cult, and village. Most of the members of the Presidential Security Council are from Assad's own tribe (*al-Matawira*), while others (including 'Ali Haydar) hail from his native village, Qardaha.[15] In fact, confessionalism as practiced by the Assad regime often blends into outright nepotism, which compounds the effects of other forms of favoritism in keeping the internal divisions of the Alawi community alive.

Personal relations with the president not only stratify confessional bonds, they provide access to power independent of religious identity. The three leading Sunnis in the regime, Khaddam, Tallas, and Ahmar, are old friends of Assad's who used positions they held in the 1960s to promote his rise to power. Even since, they have formed the core of *al-Jama'a* (literally, "the group"), the president's personal clique which monopolizes high office in Syria. The president's Alawi intimates are also members of this group, but so are more recent Sunni recruits such as Muhammad Halabi and General Hikmat al-Shihabi and Christians like General Yusuf Shakur.[16] Although the members of the Jama'a generally occupy high office, their formal titles rarely reflect their full powers. The Jama'a itself is essentially an informal organization. It is a patronage network, nestled atop a pyramid of similar networks, which extend deep into Syrian society.[17] Within the group, President Assad acts as the patron, conferring power and wealth in exchange for service and obedience. Outside the group, Assad's retainers sponsor their own clienteles, by the use or abuse of their official powers. Through their connections at the highest levels of the regime, these networks have access to an impressive array of powers and resources. As a result, in the Jama'a and many of its attendant networks, it is possible for "enlightened self-interest" to largely or entirely eclipse religion as the basis of fealty.

For example, Rif'at Assad derives power not only from the military units he commands but also from his clients among important economic elites. He sponsors select businessmen, granting them exemptions from normal import-export restrictions, giving them first chance to bid on state tenders, and protecting them from investigation by various regulative agencies. In return, Rif'at receives various forms of personal support as well as "a piece of the action." To take advantage of such a relationship, Rif'at's clients must have great capital and daring, so they are recruited primarily from the nouveau riche entrepreneurs of Damascus and Aleppo. The fact that these urban elites are overwhelmingly Sunni or Christian has never inhibited their relationship with Rif'at.[18]

The Ba'th had never really been innocent of patronage networks. Secular patronage had been used alongside confessionalism both during the 1961 reorganization and the factional battles that followed.[19] The Jama'a actually began as one of many contending client groups that formed in the Syrian military during this struggle. But the increasing scope and frequency of resort to patronage during the 1970s had important political consequences. For example, Assad's personal supervision of his clients in the armed forces finalized a division between the civilian and military wings of the Ba'th that had been brewing for a decade.[20] Similarly, his packing the Regional Command with members of al-Jama'a resulted in greater homogeneity and centralism than the party had known for years. But the most novel application of patronage was in an effort to tie the public to the party. Before it took power in 1963 the party had won public sympathy by championing causes such as industrial nationalization and Arab unity. Ba'thists had enjoyed a reputation for public service and personal integrity that was virtually unique among Syrian politicians. During the 1970s this image changed drastically, and the creation and control of patronage networks then became the party's major task.

For example, during the 1960s Ba'thist militants encouraged the formation of the Popular Organizations (*al-Munazzimat al-Sha'-biya*) to help mobilize key elements of the population. So-called "General Federations" were created to incorporate trade unions, peasants, craftsmen, women, sports leagues, students, youth, writers, journalists, and teachers.[21] Originally these were autonomous bodies and Ba'thist cadres had to win their support by participating in them, working on their behalf, and demonstrating their common interests. Under the new regime, the Ba'th began to exercise much tighter control over the Popular Organizations, binding their members to the party by means of patronage. The Ba'th was the only party that could legally operate on school grounds and university campuses, and its cadres soon occupied their "commanding heights." Through control of academic appointments, scholarships, and admissions, the party won a large—if jaded—following among students and teachers. Intellectuals and literati discovered that collaboration with the party increased their likelihood of publication and enhanced opportunities for foreign travel. Union members seeking higher wages or better working conditions (particularly in the public sector) found appeals to the Ba'th were generally more effective than complaints to management.

It was in the countryside, an area of traditional support for the Ba'th, that the use of patronage produced the greatest response. The party-controlled General Federation of Peasants, which included 40 percent of the rural work force, underwent the same transformation as the rest of the Popular Organizations. Moreover, the party could also woo support by influencing the allocation of loans and credits by the state Agricultural Bank or the distribution of seeds and fertilizer through the national system of agricultural cooperatives.[22] Traditional rural notables (the *shuyukh* and the *makhatir*) and newly prosperous farmers were eager to serve as representatives of the party, adding their wealth, prestige, and knowledge of local conditions to the party's arsenal. A crude indication of the scope of this development is given by the fact that by 1976 there were 3,413 agricultural cooperatives in Syria, with 256,036 members—nearly double the number that existed prior to the party reforms.[23]

Patronage has thus become the key weapon in the Ba'thist repertoire. The power of the party as a whole depends upon its skill in extending or withholding benefits from its clients. This is why the conventional perspectives on the party tell us so little. Sectarian loyalties play an insignificant role in the Ba'th, and even confessional bonds are only one among many avenues by which patronage is extended. Has the growth of clientage eroded standards of discipline and made the party more vulnerable to the cupidity of private interest? Or can patronage actually augment its powers, substituting for loyalties previously generated by ideological principle or bureaucratic procedure? To grasp the full effects of patronage of politics in Syria, we have to take a detailed look at the conditions under which such networks emerged and the way they became enmeshed with the organization of the Ba'th.

Patronage and the Integration of Elites

Patronage establishes a relationship of political subordination by a more or less explicit act of exchange: goods and services are traded for loyalty and obedience. The full diversity of political relations that can be constructed in accordance with this principle is rarely appreciated. For example, patronage is often—and falsely—disparaged as a purely traditional or even primitive form of political behavior. It is true that the power of village notables in Syria is still based partly on the tradition of *wasta:* their ability to "mediate" on behalf of relatives and neighbors who seek concessions from the national authorities. Yet today the exercise of *wasta* is also enmeshed in the system of state-directed patronage, which operates on a scale and logic with no traditional precedent, executed through offices such as the Agricultural Bank and supervised from distant Damascus. In the liberal West the frequent equation of patronage with political corruption reflects the common understanding that political and economic institutions function most efficiently when they are kept separate and distinct. Corporate boards are supposed to pursue profits, not popularity; and politicians are supposed to increase the public welfare, not their bank accounts. Patronage tends to violate this separation: it is the most "economic" of political relationships.

Many Syrians do believe the Assad regime is corrupt—but not for the same reasons a classic liberal would. Except for a handful of Western-educated intellectuals, it is the inequity and not the inefficiency of patronage that offends Syrians. If everyone had equal access to patronage, few would complain. This is not because the Syrians are venal or immoral, but because the separation of politics and economics assumed by the liberal definition of corruption does not exist in Syria. Syrians, whatever their particular ideological orientation, believe that economic activities *require* the support of state power and that economic and political processes cannot be disentangled.[24] In their historical experience, it is the effort to conduct business without political supports that has proven inefficient. In the context of Syria's state capitalist institutions, the liberal conception of corruption is virtually meaningless.

However, in a sense both the Syrian and liberal perceptions of corruption are beside the point: to gauge the consequences of patronage we need measure neither its efficiency nor its equity but its effectiveness. In politics, patronage can only be dismissed as corruption if it proves ineffective as a means of generating power. A student of Soviet politics (where liberal definitions are also inapplicable) has put this quite precisely: "*Corruption* refers to an organization's loss of its specific competence through failure to distinguish between rather than confuse [particular] member with [general] organizational interests."[25] In other words, patronage may be corrupting or not, depending upon whether its powers are harnessed to or drained from an organization.

Therefore, corruption has little to do with the precise division of spoils between patron and client (it may even be clear who is exploiting whom). Rather, it is found in the relationship between the patron and the office he occupies or the organization of which he is a part. If the patron alone benefits from the services of his clients, the organization's resources are being squandered for purely personal interests. On the other hand, if the loyalty of clients can be used to promote the wider interests of the organization, benefits personally appropriated by the patron may be tolerable as the price of increased collective power. The degree to which patronage has a corrupting effect, then, depends upon whether an organization can keep networks of clientage under collective control and ensure that patrons apply part of their influence to the service of general interest.[26]

Syrian Ba'thists developed several techniques to limit the corrupting potential of the patronage networks that proliferated in the 1970s. They were able to tap the powers latent in these networks without paying too great a price in diverted resources or corroded authority. They learned to exploit patronage rather than being exploited by it.

When Hafez al-Assad staged his 1970 coup, he acted as head of a coalition of officers, civil servants, and party functionaries united against the neo-Ba'thists (extreme-left regionalists who had ruled Syria since 1966). This coalition had formed gradually, gaining strength after the party congress of 1968, where various complaints against the regime had been aired without response. Assad's associates had various grievances, provoked by everything from military strategy to bureaucratic feuding, but they all agreed that the neo-Ba'th was representing the interests of only a segment of the population and that its policies were divorcing the government from the mass of society.

In its heyday, the neo-Ba'th had formed one of the most radical governments in the Arab world. It launched nationalization and land reform programs, wiping out the urban notables (*wujuha*) who had formerly dominated Syrian economy and politics. Its restrictions on "luxury consumption" and foreign trade offended the middle class, especially merchants, who turned to the Muslim Brotherhood to vent their grievances. The more prosperous elements of the peasantry (whom the Syrians themselves call "kulaks"), traditionally close to the Ba'th, became worried as officials at the Ministry of Agrarian Reform began to discuss plans for rural collectivization and the creation of state farms. The authority of state bureaucrats and factory managers was curtailed as party militants pressed themselves into all facets of public life. The party even began to form its own militias and advocated guerrilla warfare with Israel—thereby alienating the professional officer corps. This aggressive foreign policy, augmented by denunciations of "reactionary" Arab monarchies, led to the suspension of normal diplomatic relations with Syria's neighbors and almost total dependence on the Soviet bloc for arms and aid.[27] Between 1970 and 1973 the new Assad regime discarded or reversed most of the neo-Ba'th's more antagonizing policies. Talk of collectivization was silenced and the state farms, with the exception of a few for poultry and livestock production, were disbanded. Trade controls were gradually relaxed and programs of government loans for small businesses were inaugurated. Municipal elections were held in 1972, giving citizens their first chance to vote in eleven years, and elections to the People's Council followed a year later.[28] In 1973 four left-wing parties were invited to join with the Ba'th in forming a Progressive National Front, ending the proscription of all political organizations (except the Ba'th) that had been in effect for a decade.[29]

With respect to the mass of the population these policy changes were sufficient: the government needed only their acquiescence, not their loyalty. But there were also a number of strategic elites from which the regime required more. Officers and bureaucrats had to be induced to collaborate, not merely comply. Unless the intellectuals, students, and kulaks were appeased, the regime could never dream of popular support. This was no simple matter. Each elite demanded a different form of concession; yet too many concessions could drain and even undermine the regime. If democratization, liberalization, and political reform were pushed too fast, these elites might find it easier to replace the regime than to support it.

As a first step toward the formation of an elite coalition the regime had to bring the Ba'th itself under control. Civil servants could hardly be expected to behave professionally, nor would kulaks and entrepreneurs invest much so long as they continued to be countermanded and harassed by party militants. Thus the internal structure of the party was overhauled in 1972, centralizing decision making and strengthening the Regional Command at the expense of the party congresses.[30] The party's ideology was deliberately vulgarized to stress the "common denominators" among several discrete traditions of Ba'thism, thereby sanctioning a kind of pluralism.[31]

The new regime had to devise supplementary techniques for asserting discipline within the party and control over those elites who remained outside it. As it happened, patronage could perform both these functions. Patronage networks spread spontaneously and piecemeal, growing in those areas where the interests of the regime and the elites overlapped. Members of the Jama'a had always supported increasing the role of private enterprise, but their overtures to the business community were redoubled after the October 1973 war. Israeli air strikes had gutted Syria's economic infrastructure, destroying $4.5 billion in capital goods. To expedite reconstruction, the regime declared an *infiraj* (relaxation) of economic controls and a general liberalization of trade.[32] Private entrepreneurs were encouraged to help rebuild the economy by establishing small firms, often acting as subcontractors (especially in construction) or agents (in negotiating foreign tenders or public requisitions) of the government.

Economically, this procedure was a success: the coordination of private energies with the state apparatus and an influx of foreign aid allowed the erection of a new infrastructure within three years. But political changes attended this process. Initially, the designation of private agents by the state was a purely administrative procedure, with contracts awarded to those firms with greatest assets or lowest bids. However, speed was important to reconstruction, and these procedures were increasingly overlooked. Businessmen began to ensure their tenders by splitting their commissions with bureaucrats or regime figures (this was when Rif'at Assad's networks began to grow). Management in the public and private sectors became cronies, pooling their influence for mutual profit. In 1976 Muhammad Haydar, the deputy prime minister for economic affairs, noted that this process was giving rise to a "new bourgeoisie" through a merger of entrepreneurs and officials. (Ironically, Haydar lost his own post the same year, accused of graft.)[33]

Even more important, though less visible, was the evolution of the regime's relations with rural elites. The land reform program launched in 1963 was not discarded, just arrested. To please the experts at the Ministry of Agriculture who were worried about productivity, new sequestrations were halted and already-confiscated lands were leased (or sometimes sold) to those who could prove that they would make efficient use of them, rather than being redistributed to the landless.[34] The major beneficiaries of these changes (aside from a small group of urban investors) were the kulaks and the village notables who could pay the state-levied rents. The new policies aggravated conditions of land scarcity, forcing small landholders and landless peasants to seek seasonal or permanent work outside their own plots. This benefited the rising class of farmers in a second way: between 1970 and 1975, real wages in agriculture declined, while capital accumulation rose to a level unmatched since the inception of land reform.[35]

As this process unfolded, the "rural middle class" became even more thoroughly tied to the Assad regime than the urban business elite. Purges of neo-Ba'th radicals created many vacancies in rural party branches, peasant federations, and agricultural cooperatives (where that faction of the party had been especially well entrenched). The kulaks were eager to occupy these posts, both for the powers they accorded and to ensure they would not again fall into the hands of radicals. The government was happy to tolerate this movement both because the cooperation of the kulaks enhanced the authority of the regime and because of important social ties with this group: many senior Ba'thists were themselves the sons of kulaks. Since the 1950s the university, the army, and the party had provided the major avenues of social mobility for ambitious children of the countryside and smaller towns. This process was now renewed: a new generation of Ba'thists emerged in the 1970s as the kulaks grew more prosperous, sent their sons on for higher education, and encouraged them to develop ties with the party.[36]

Of course patronage percolated into the Ba'th bureaucracy, and the military as well. The regime was particularly anxious to secure the loyalty of the military. Privileges extended directly to important officers included promotions, housing, and pay increases—and, after 1976, the opportunity to engage in business or outright pillage in Lebanon.[37] Special units, such as the *Saraya al-Difa'*, were formed both to provide plum posts for loyal officers and as a reserve against coups by the conventional military.

The most obvious threat was that patronage networks would provide strategic elites (or even members of the regime other than Assad himself) with autonomous centers of power, allowing them to act independently of the regime. Most networks were accordingly restricted to single institutions or social groups. The military was carefully insulated from linkage to civilian networks. Lower-echelon networks were often attached and subordinated to others under direct control of members of the Jama'a. In particular, Rif'at al-Assad, Tallas, and Ahmar personally supervised, and profited from, the direction of patronage.

This attempt to engineer the working of patronage networks clearly enhanced the regime's influence—but at a price. Among those groups who had not associated themselves with an influential network, principled or self-interested resentment began to build. Some professionals, especially doctors, lawyers, and engineers, were offended by those of their colleagues who built careers on connections rather than merit. Many Sunnis were appalled by the blatant use of confessionalism in the military, and fears of sectarianism were aggravated. These fears were not reduced by the spectacle of the president's brother, whose use of power was anything but subtle: Rif'at's profiteering was legendary; he "married" any girl who took his fancy; and often he used his troops to secure "reservations" at Damascus nightclubs. Perhaps most seriously, a large section of urbanites felt injured by the growing influence of the kulaks. The balance of power between the city and the countryside was being reversed: the kulaks extended credit that had once been proffered by the *bawayiki* (merchant-peddlers); they competed with local retailers and moved into the suburbs.[38]

If such resentments had arisen in a period of general prosperity and progress, they might have been shrugged off and ignored. But by 1976 conditions in Syria were beginning to sour rapidly. As Syria became more involved in the Lebanese civil war, its foreign sponsors reduced or suspended their aid.[39] This halted the boom of post-1973 reconstruction spending, without eliminating the 25 percent inflation rate that had accompanied it. In June the regime sent troops into Lebanon to defend the Maronite right against the Palestinians and the Lebanese left. This appalled most Syrians, who clearly felt their country was supporting the wrong side. What popularity the regime had achieved through its earlier reforms and victories was quickly dissipated.

This decline was almost immediately manifested in renewed activism by the Muslim Brotherhood and its offshoots.[40] The brotherhood recruited heavily from precisely those groups who were now threatened by the regime's use of patronage: professionals and urban merchants.[41] It was buoyed by the same currents that were fueling a resurgence of politicized Islam internationally: the flow of funds from the Gulf states, disenchantment with the failure of nationalist parties, and the continuing peril of the traditional "petty bourgeoisie."[42] Moreover, the leadership of the brotherhood had recently passed from traditional religious scholars to a new generation who were younger, more militant in their demands, and more eager to sacrifice themselves for an Islamic state. In November 1976 brotherhood commandos inaugurated a tactic that would grow more popular over the next few years: the assassination of prominent Alawis. This strategy not only liquidated the apparent enemies of the Islamic movements, it had the advantage of highlighting for the public just how many Alawis had moved into senior offices.

Many of the most vocal critics of the abuse of patronage and the rise of the "new class" were themselves Ba'thists. The party's organ, *Al-Ba'th*, took the lead in denouncing corruption in the summer of 1976, and other state-directed papers soon followed suit. At first the regime sought to accommodate demands for reform, and in August a new cabinet charged with eliminating corruption was formed under General Khulayfawi, whose personal integrity was unquestioned.

The Khulayfawi cabinet was not able to accomplish much until late in 1977, when two concrete strategies were adopted to ameliorate public grievances. First, efforts were made to revive the democratization process, which had languished somewhat since 1973. New elections for the People's Council were slated for August 1977, but opposition groups called a boycott and the voter turnout was shockingly small.[43] This prodded the regime into taking more dramatic action. A number of exiled political leaders, including Salah al-Bitar (head of the ousted pan-Arabist wing of the Ba'th) and Ma'ruf al-Dawalibi (former chief of the Muslim Brotherhood) were allowed to return to the country for the first time since 1966. When Hafez al-Assad was reelected to the presidency in February 1978, his inaugural address hinted that the Progressive National Front would soon be expanded to include "independents." This was widely interpreted, even in the upper echelons of the party, as meaning that figures like Bitar and Dawalibi might be invited to participate in the government if they dropped their ties to the underground opposition.[44]

Second, and even more important, on August 8, 1977, the president himself denounced corruption in a speech before the People's Council. He announced the creation of special security courts in each province to examine charges of malfeasance, and a week later the Committee for the Investigation of Illegal Profits, with special judicial powers, was created to coordinate this campaign. The committee returned its first indictments in September, arresting thirty-two leading businessmen and public-sector managers.

No doubt many Ba'thists, including the president himself, sincerely hoped these reforms would raise the regime's popularity and reduce support for the brotherhood. However, the path of accommodation soon revealed a variety of shortcomings. The excitement following the return of exiled politicians suggested that if they were allowed to participate in elections, the Ba'th might suffer a major humiliation. The Committee on Illegal Profits found that it could not press its investigation very far without implicating senior party figures, particularly Rif'at. The brotherhood's assassination campaign began to cut deep, souring the prospects for further "appeasement": among those killed in the winter of 1977–78 were Dr. Ibrahim Nu'ama and Dr. Ali 'Abid al-Ali, both relatives of the president. Most seriously, several problems combined to fuel divisions within the regime and party. Factions sympathetic to the pan-Arabist wing and neo-Ba'th had been reactivated (both by domestic democratization and instigation from neighboring Iraq) and the rapid rise of new cadres through patronage networks provoked a series of intraparty power squabbles.

In March 1978 the campaign against corruption was dropped. No official announcement was made; in fact, newspaper investigations of individual abuses continued to appear. But the editors of the three leading dailies (including *Al-Ba'th*) were sacked, and corruption was no longer discussed as a general social problem. Kulayfawi's cabinet resigned and was replaced by one headed by the loyal, but tainted, Muhammad Ali Halabi. Naji Jamail, commander of the air force and an old friend of the president, was dismissed from the Regional Command and placed under house arrest. The precise details of his falling out with the regime are unknown, but he is widely reputed to have opposed the growing power of Rif'at al-Assad and to have supported the work of the Committee on Illegal Profits.[45]

This sharp end to the strategy of appeasement made civil war in Syria virtually inevitable. Brotherhood assassinations increased steadily; in June 1979 the commandos passed over into urban guerrilla warfare with an attack on a military school in which over sixty Ba'thist officer cadets were killed. Through the fall and winter of 1979–80 the government and the brotherhood exchanged attacks and reprisals: there were a few major battles, a constant stream of midnight murders, machine-gun duels, and apartment block assaults. Although the final round did not come until the February

1982 Hama insurrection, the regime's triumph was actually assured once it weathered the uprising of March 1980. In that month massive demonstrations broke out in Aleppo, Hama, and Hums, where citizens *not* affiliated with brotherhood took to the streets to protest the ongoing cycle of violence, the suspension of civil liberties, and the receding prospects for democratization. If demonstrations on this scale had continued, the regime could not have lasted long.

Yet the demonstrations lost momentum—or were suppressed—in less than a week. Doubtless Assad's regime "won" the civil war primarily because of its simple military superiority: Muslim Brotherhood cells were hunted down and liquidated, and other dissidents were cowed by the sheer ruthlessness of the government's campaign. But it should not be forgotten that even during the March 1980 demonstrations the regime retained the support of large segments of the Syrian population. Of course many people simply stood on the sidelines, unenthusiastic about both the government and the prospect of an Islamic state. But beyond this, the regime exercised genuine influence among precisely those groups that counted politically: the strategic elites linked to it by patronage. In the heat of the civil war, the regime risked the crassest abuses of patronage in an effort to improve its security. The March demonstrations were partly provoked by a freeze on consumer prices—which pleased organized labor but offended merchants. The budget for education was increased, civil service salaries were raised, and a massive program to extend electricity, medicine, and other services to the countryside was launched.[46] Rif'at and the president's other brothers formed highly subsidized fraternities for students, intellectuals, and Alawis under their personal command.[47]

This massive resurgence of patronage was not equally effective in all areas: despite inducements to silence, the Lawyer's Association protested the imposition of martial law and had to be suspended.[48] The business elite and the city of Damascus simply kept quiet. The Federation of Trade Unions and the Revolutionary Youth Brigades (*kata'ib shabibat al-thawra*) were very vocal in support of the regime, organizing demonstrations and parades, although neither played a major military role. The most fervent commitment came from the rural population, who genuinely supported the regime.

The Halabi cabinet was disbanded and a new one, consisting of technocrats under the leadership of 'Abd al-Ra'uf al-Kassim, was formed. A new Control and Inspection Committee was created to supervise the behavior of party cadres, and a Central Committee (of seventy-five members) was created to maintain a tighter linkage between the Regional Command and the rank and file. Measures were taken to reduce the role of patronage within the state bureaucracy and in connection to the "new class," but there was no change in the party's relation to the kulaks or in the use of confessionalism within the army. In effect, the use of patronage was streamlined, not eliminated. The majority of Ba'thists appear to have found this compromise acceptable, but during the next two years many Ba'thist intellectuals—those who lacked the stomach for the massacres ahead—requested, and were granted, sabbaticals or furloughs abroad.[49]

Patronage and Political Development

Many Ba'thists who had joined the party before 1970 found the party's later transformation disconcerting or degrading. They had believed that the party was the best hope for a revolutionary transformation of Arab society, and they had struggled for years to bring it to power. The realities of the 1970s were severe disappointment. The prospects for immediate, radical change receded. The solidarity that had knitted party members together decayed.

The Ba'th does not actually rule Syria today. That "honor" was appropriated by the Assad regime (comprised of the Jama'a and its agents in key institutions). As a power elite, these men are concerned foremost with preserving and enhancing their own authority. Yet, their enchantment with pure power and occasional willingness to promote themselves at public expense has never entirely effaced their loyalty to a concept of collective, national interests. President Assad in particular has often put his personal power at risk to press for his vision of Syria's future. This vision is still Ba'thist in inspiration. The peregrinations of realpolitik have not completely eclipsed Ba'thist hostility toward sectarianism, feudalism, and imperialism—the traditional enemies of the "Arab renaissance." Efforts to build up Syria's national economy and military are still linked to the pursuit of comprehensive Arab unity.[50]

The influence of Ba'thism is not limited to sentiments surviving within the regime. Alongside the military and the bureaucracy, the party itself is one of the three pillars on which the authority of the regime rests—and it has great influence over the other two. It is this institutional presence that guarantees the vitality of Ba'thism.

The weakest of these pillars is the state bureaucracy.[51] An early objective of the Assad regime was to arrest the growing breach between the party and the civil service. Bureaucrats were given greater power to implement policy and even attained a certain respect as sources of advice in technical matters. But their control over the direction and objectives of policy remained extremely limited: they were concerned with means, not ends. In fact, when the regime sought consultation on the wider objectives of economic policy, it was more likely to turn to the party than to the bureaucracy. During the economic crisis of 1976–77, when the existing draft of the fourth five-year plan had to be scrapped, a special session of party cadres was convened to discuss the parameters of the new plan.[52] Similarly, when military expenditures and civil war forced the adoption of an austerity program in 1980, it was the delegates to the eighth party congress who decided where the cuts should be made and who would shoulder them.[53]

The second pillar of the regime, the military, is far more potent. The armed forces have been the regime's most decisive supporters, implementing its foreign policy, ensuring its domestic security, and lending a touch of steel to its pronouncements. Yet, despite the intimacy of this relationship, the Assad government is not actually a military regime. The Jama'a does not "represent" the military any more than it represents the Alawis—and for similar reasons.[54]

The regime, aware that the enormous power at the disposal of the military also makes it a serious potential rival, has taken a series of measures contrived to reduce the likelihood of coups. In addition to trying to purchase the loyalty of the officer corps by largess and patronage, it has also been careful to restrict the ability of the corps to organize politically. Divisions within the military, between combat and security units, between Ba'thist and non-Ba'thist officers, are carefully exacerbated and exploited.[55] Fraternization between officers and civilian elites, which might lay the groundwork for a coup, are carefully policed by the Ba'th's Political Bureau. Syria's three military intelligence bureaus spend as much or more energy supervising the behavior of the officer corps than they do on conventional espionage. Real political influence is thereby confined to a select group of officers who have proven their loyalty to the regime.

These arrangements have not depoliticized the military, nor do they provide an absolute guarantee against coups—several dozen air force cadets were arrested in January 1982 for conspiring to bomb the president's residence. They do make the execution of a coup more laborious and complex, increasing the regime's opportunities to expose and prevent them. Only a tiny group of officers have the kind of influence necessary to contemplate a coup, and even they have to worry about the possibility of counter-coups by other units. Any officers seeking to take power (as opposed to just murdering the president and letting authority fall where it may) would have to recruit supporters among civilian elites, especially party members. This leads to an interesting situation where those officers who are most capable of making coups and their most probable civilian confederates are all Ba'thists. Even among officers who do not aspire to make coups, linkages to the party are crucial measures of influence. Work within the party's military wing is one of the surest ways to secure promotions; and any officer hoping to have a say in policies at the national level had better learn to work with the civilian Ba'th.

Recently the influence of the party over the other two pillars of the regime was formalized and enhanced by a change in the structure of government. When President Assad suffered a heart attack in November 1983, Rif'at moved his troops and followers to key positions in a bid to secure the succession for himself. These movements were opposed by other members of al-Jama'a and the military, culminating in an armed clash in February 1984 between Rif'at's *Saraya* and elements of the Third Armored Division led by General Shafiq Fa'iz. After Hafez al-Assad recuperated, he took measures to prevent future succession crises by creating a triumvirate of vice-presidencies. Khaddam became vice-president for state affairs and first in line to succeed Assad; Rif'at became vice-president for defense; and Zuhayr Musharqa became vice-president for party affairs.[56]

Through three salient effects this restructuring blunted the power of the military and enhanced the authority of the party. First, it encouraged powerful figures in the regime to try to act as representatives of institutions—the army, the party, and the bureaucracy—rather than as leaders of personal factions. Secondly, it placed these institutions on a more equal footing: any one of them trying to impose its candidate during a succession crisis would encourage the other two to unite in resistance. Most important, these arrangements separated Rif'at from his power base in the *Saraya* and forced him to seek the cooperation of other army officers. But the only thing all military factions agreed upon was their contempt for Rif'at, who was—with general applause from the party leadership—driven into exile in June 1984.[57]

The web of patronage that branches out from the offices of the Ba'th party is distinct from networks affiliated with other institutions in two ways. First, individual party networks—unlike those of the military or Jama'a—involve small commitment of resources, with few political risks. Deciding whether or not to allow a village notable control over local distribution of insecticides is a far more casual, flexible process than deciding whether a Damascus entrepreneur should be allowed to make an illegal commission on an arms deal. With less at stake, the party can afford greater give-and-take than other patrons can. This works to the advantage of its clients, who can almost "shop" among the party's functionaries, looking for the one who will accept the least commitment in exchange for the fullest patronage. An extremely diverse body of potential clients are thereby attracted to the party, where access is so much easier than among upper-echelon networks. This leads directly to the second trait of the Ba'thist networks: their sheer extent and size. In terms of numbers alone, the party manages the largest networks in the country. The cross section of society participating in these networks—students, peasants, unionists, intellectuals—is also far wider than that associated with any other institution.

Indeed, the party's networks are the most important link between the government and society. If the regime ever hopes to build mass support, it will have to work from this foundation. Despite the way it tarnishes the party's reputation, patronage has offered the party its first chance to institutionalize a mass following. Neither the charismatic leaders of the original, pan-Arabist wing nor the populist radicals of the neo-Ba'th tied so many people, so thoroughly, to the party apparatus.

The fact that the party is developing a mass following does not mean that it is popular. Clients find the party's patronage useful, not necessarily admirable. Patronage does not engender the kind of enthusiasm that can be expected to survive harsh winters—either the party continues to deliver the goods or people will defect. Yet, this apparent vulnerability may also be a source of concealed strength. If the party's associates and fellow travelers are more fickle than in the past, they are also more involved and predictable.

Ideologically rigorous parties may be thoroughly unresponsive to changes in public moods and pressures; but parties based on patronage have to be more accommodating. Crudely, the Ba'th networks function like a market: people address their demands to the local cadre, who determines whether a deal can be struck, and on what terms. Patronage networks expand, contract, and offer different services according to changes in social circumstances. Curiously, this is analogous to the way parties are supposed to function in a modern democracy, where they broker the exchange of political influence and popular demands. Indeed, it should be noted that in the United Kingdom and the United States the system of representative parties evolved out of an earlier order based on patronage.[58]

Of course, Syria today is anything but a democracy; people can press demands through the party, but only on local issues—the regime's monopoly over coercion and national policy making remains undiminished. Nor is Syria clearly on a path that will lead to democracy: even under otherwise favorable circumstances, patronage must be embedded in certain rules of exchange that guarantee autonomy for all participants before it can contribute to democratization.[59] But Syria possesses at least one of the conditions that potentially promote democracy.

For the future, two factors that threaten the Ba'thist system of patronage are likely to supersede any debate about democracy. The first challenge to the system arises from the same resentments that helped fuel the civil war at the end of the 1970s. The Muslim Brotherhood, which once gave voice to this resentment, has been silenced (for now); but the malaise remains and will soon find another vehicle for its expression. Strangely, the most probable such vehicle is the Ba'th itself. Idealists dedicated to ending the party's decadence might well dismantle the patronage networks in an effort to restore the party's "ideological purity." Militants who chafe at the "corruption" within the party also have resources to do something about it. In recent years the most likely source of a coup in Syria has been from younger officers and cadres seeking to save the party from Rif'at al-Assad and his cronies.

The patronage system is also challenged from precisely the opposite direction—by its main beneficiaries. Thus far, the regime has been able to squeeze power from patronage because it has kept all networks carefully under control. But there is a constant tendency for clients to seek greater advantages, to press for greater concessions or reduce their own costs of participation in a network. The regime's increased reliance on certain groups, particularly the kulaks, since the civil war, has enhanced the power of these groups to demand greater benefits in exchange for loyalty. Unless the regime can continually reinforce the mechanisms of control—the material and ideological incentives that keep personal avarice bent to the service of the entire organization—the system of patronage will tend to consume itself: clients will devour more resources than they contribute. If this happens, patronage would become corrupt in a political, rather than just a moral, sense.

For the Ba'th and the Assad regime, patronage is too important as a source of power to be simply discarded. Yet patronage must be used in a way that neither ignites a revolt by idealists nor enflames the venality of existing clients. Over the next few years the greatest domestic task for Syrian government will be to straddle the horns of this dilemma. There are signs that the regime is already rising to this challenge. It has begun to prune the tree of patronage, eliminating those networks that are most open to misuse while preserving useful ones. The most important step in this streamlining was the elimination of Rif'at al-Assad in 1984, when the president approved his brother's exile to Geneva. Rif'at had come to symbolize the worst abuses of public office and was the focus of popular hatred. His removal lent a ring of credibility, previously lacking, to the regime's other efforts to contain the corruption of patronage.

Other anticorruption measures quickly followed. Most dramatic was the crackdown on smuggling between Syria and Lebanon—which had been supplying 70 percent of Syria's nonmilitary imports. Most of this contraband trade was supervised by the Syrian army, so restricting the trade meant dismantling a number of key patronage networks and shuffling the chain of command in the responsible units. This redirected the flow of patronage back to officially tolerated, especially confessional, channels.[60]

It is too soon, of course, to judge whether actions of this kind will be successful. The regime will probably have an easier time asserting its control over the well-defined patronage networks of the military than over the countless local networks—particularly in rural areas—managed by the party. Still, the history of the patronage system in Syria suggests that the regime will not shy away from taking whatever measures prove necessary. Many members of the Jama'a suffer from cupidity, but few are stupid enough to let avarice erode the foundations of their authority.

IRAQ

Its Revolutionary Experience under the Ba'th

■

Phebe Marr

The Ba'th party regime in Iraq has been notable among Arab states, even among Third World states, for the degree of stability it has been able to achieve amid ongoing socioeconomic change. Among its accomplishments have been a high degree of institutionalization both at state and party levels, rapid economic and social change in favor of the previously underprivileged classes, continuity at top levels of leadership permitting the accumulation of experience, and the relative insulation of the military from political decisionmaking.

In many respects the Ba'th, which has ruled Iraq since 1968, is the epitome of the secular nationalist revolutions that swept the Arab world in the 1950s and 1960s. These varied in content and style, but they shared a number of characteristics. First, they drew on vaguely defined sentiments of Arab nationalism and a desire for Arab unity. Second, they were largely secular, with heavy emphasis on state-building and national loyalty. Third, they were progressive, desiring rapid economic development and a redistribution of wealth and social benefits to the lower classes. Fourth, they borrowed heavily from Western (especially Marxist) ideologies and models of development. Fifth, they began as military coups executed by small groups of people who then went on to create au-

The views expressed in this article are those of the author and do not reflect the official policy or position of the Department of Defense or the U.S. Government.

thoritarian systems and state-controlled bureaucratic structures that they used to engineer change from the top down.

The Iranian revolution has now challenged almost all of the assumptions and achievements of the Ba'thist regime. First, the Islamic Republic stakes its legitimacy on an indigenous, rather than an imported, ideology—Islam. Second, it has relied on a mass-based popular movement to carry out its revolutionary aims. Third, its anti-imperialist zeal, demanding cultural as well as political and economic independence from the West, has far outstripped that of the Ba'thists. Last, in its removal of the Western-educated middle and upper classes and its reliance on the support of the underprivileged classes, the Iranian revolution has been more thoroughgoing than the Ba'th. These issues have contributed to and are at the core of the long and bitter war between the two countries that erupted in 1980, a war that has tested the validity of both revolutionary regimes.

More than the Iraqi regime is at stake in this confrontation. The Iranian experience is a challenge to the legitimacy of the previous radical, secular, nationalist revolutions in the Arab world. The significance of the Iran-Iraq conflict lies in the fact that Iraq is one of the strongest of these revolutionary regimes, while the challenge from Iran is massive and direct. How well Iraq meets the challenge is likely to determine trends in the area for some time to come.

For both social scientists and policymakers, the Iraqi experience raises a number of questions. How has the Ba'th institutionalized its revolution, and how effective has it been in mobilizing the population behind its aims? What sort of leadership has the Ba'th brought to power, and how have the backgrounds and outlook of these leaders affected the revolution? What has been the direction of Iraq's social and economic policies, and how effective have they been in changing Iraqi society? And most important of all, how much legitimacy has the Ba'th achieved through its ideology and its programs?

Institutionalization

No revolution can succeed without a high degree of institutionalization. The Ba'th has learned this lesson well; one of the chief strengths of the Ba'th regime has been its party organization and discipline. The Ba'th has been characterized by a higher degree of institutionalization than any regime since the mandate. Previous governments have all relied to a much greater extent on personal and kinship ties, patronage networks, and shifting coalitions involving tribal, military, sectarian, and ethnic groups as well as various unorganized constituencies.

The Ba'th is not entirely free from these features. As is well known, a network of "Tikritis"—near and distant relatives of President Saddam Hussein, who all originate in the northern Tigris town of Tikrit—man the security and intelligence services and are disproportionately represented in key military positions. Nevertheless, the regime has maintained control over the country, not through this Tikrit network, but mainly through an elaborate party organization reaching down to local levels. An important feature of this organization has been considerable overlap of personnel in the three top bodies, the Revolutionary Command Council (RCC), the Regional Command of the party, and key ministries, as well as increased Ba'thization of bureaucratic and military structures.

The party hierarchy has been described frequently.[1] At its base is the *halaqah* (circle or cell) composed of three to seven active members, which functions at the neighborhood level. The cell, originally organized for clandestine action, could function as the nucleus of an underground movement if the need should arise. The next unit in the hierarchy is the *firqah* (section) composed of three to seven cells that operates in an area the size of a small urban quarter or village. It plays the critical role in recruitment of new members and links the lower and upper party echelons. The party relies on the firqah for execution of policy made at higher levels. It also relies on appointed party units, located in offices, factories, schools, and other bureaucratic structures, for the execution of party policy. Above the firqah is the *shu'bah* (division), composed of two to five firqahs and headed by an elected command. The *shu'bah* generally encompasses a major section of a city or a large rural district. Above the shu'bah is the *far'* (branch), formed of at least two shu'bahs, also with an elected command. The branch encompasses a governorate or, in the case of Baghdad, a major subsection of the city. Over the branches are five *tanzims* (area commands), one each for Baghdad, the Euphrates, and the Central, Southern, and Northern areas. At the pinnacle comes the Regional Command, with control over party policy at the national level.[2]

Functioning parallel to this party organization are the professional unions that have mushroomed since 1968. They mobilize the population along broad occupational lines. Some of these, such as the Lawyers' Union, were established in the days of the monarchy. Others, such as the General Federation of Farmers' Unions, sprang up after the revolution of 1958. All, including special associations for women and youth, have expanded under the Ba'th, which has used them as a means to extend its reach over large segments of the population, as well as to allow a limited measure of citizen participation in public affairs. While these associations are theoretically autonomous, the Ba'th controls their activities through election of Ba'thists to positions in their hierarchies.

The latest addition to the political structure erected by the Ba'th is the National Assembly, which provides a measure of controlled participation in government to the general populace. It contains 250 members and has the legal authority to propose laws; to legislate (a function it shares, at least theoretically, with the RCC); to confirm the budget; and to debate questions of internal and external policy. It can also question ministers about their decisions, although RCC members may not be questioned about their deliberations, which are secret. Although the National Assembly is an attempt to give non-Ba'thists some say in government, in practice its functions are limited. Candidates are screened, and only those who believe in the principles and aims of the Ba'th revolution may run for election. Members of the previous landholding and mercantile classes are likewise proscribed. A third restriction is imposed on those whose parents were not born in Iraq or who are married to foreigners, features designed to eliminate those with foreign (and especially Persian) ties.[3] Since the bulk of the assembly is Ba'thist, its proceedings are under party control.

These political institutions, designed to formulate policy and translate ideology into programs, are largely innovations in Iraq. Two other institutions, the military and the bureaucracy, which predate the regime and even the monarchy, have been greatly expanded by the Ba'th and brought under the regime's control. The most important of these is the military. Although little is known about the officer corps, all evidence indicates that it has been thoroughly Ba'thized. The doctrine of the party holds that the military will neither be kept separate from the political sphere, as is the case in Western liberal democracies, nor be allowed to dominate the political process, as in military regimes. Rather, the military is to be an arm of the party. Its leaders will be party members first and military specialists second.[4] Party discipline is thus relied on to keep the military from intervening directly in politics. In fact, the regime has had marked success in keeping the military out of the policymaking process, except in areas concerning defense and security. The officer corps is formally indoctrinated with Ba'th ideology in classes given at various levels. Party functionaries are assigned to units to assure compliance with party directives. Ba'th membership is a virtual prerequisite for promotion, and only Ba'th party members are allowed into the military academy. No other party is allowed to recruit in the army.[5]

Nevertheless, the military remains an area where the regime's control may be weak. Like most professionals, officers tend to put the interests of the service over that of the party. The resignation in 1979 and subsequent death of former President Ahmad Hasan al-Bakr, an officer whose ties with the military were extensive and deep, have left a gap that neither Saddam, now commander-in-chief of the armed forces, nor his cousin, Adnan Khair Allah Talfah, the minister of defense, has filled as yet. The war has strengthened the role of the military and greatly expanded its size. Recurrent purges and dismissals, due mainly to reversals in the war, have raised in acute form the perennial conflict over which comes first—party loyalty or military competence. Saddam's active role as commander during the war is an attempt, thus far successful, to keep the military subservient to civilians, but reports of conflicts between the civilian and military leadership over the conduct of the war have surfaced. On several occasions Saddam may have been obliged to reduce his detailed management of the war. Despite these tensions and the enormous pressures of war, the Ba'th's success in keeping the military subordinate to civilian leadership must be counted one of its major achievements.

Along with the military the intelligence service has grown under the Ba'th. Little is known about its staffing and operations other than the fact that several intelligence organizations function parallel to one another. Reorganized in 1973 after an abortive coup by the chief of intelligence, the party intelligence service has kept its top posts in the hands of those personally loyal to Saddam. Whatever its actual effectiveness, the security apparatus is widely believed to be ubiquitous, spreading an atmosphere of apprehension and fear that in itself fulfills some of the security service's goals. Much of the regime's stability rests on the security apparatus and the leadership's willingness to use it. Saddam's ruthless purges and selective executions indicate that he will not take chances on loyalty even among close associates and relatives. While the security system has been generally effective, it has its weaknesses. One is in the field of foreign intelligence, as indicated by the failure to accurately assess Iran's ability to respond to Iraq's invasion. Moreover, in several critical areas—for instance, among the Kurds—intelligence may be weak at local levels. Nor has it prevented a number of assassination attempts on Saddam. Meanwhile, the tight security system and the absence of open political dissent alienates important segments of the educated population.

While party organization and discipline have been emphasized by the regime, bureaucratic structures have also been greatly expanded and brought under Ba'th control. In accordance with the Ba'th socialist ideology, government control has been expanded to all large and medium-sized industry, all international trade and most domestic trade, much of the transportation and construction sectors, and about 30 percent of the agricultural sector.[6] All educational establishments as well as the press, radio, and TV are in government hands, directly or indirectly. This has not only centralized decisionmaking and strengthened state institutions, but it has put a substantial percentage of the work force, possibly one-fourth to one-third exclusive of the military, in government employ.[7] By 1987 there was a shift in emphasis from the public to the private sector as the war revealed the former's inefficiencies, but not sufficient to loosen the commanding grip of the state over the economy.

The care and attention devoted to building state and party mechanisms, and the ability of the government to mobilize large segments of the country's human and material resources, must be considered one of the Ba'th's current strengths. Nevertheless, there are several potential weaknesses in this institutional structure. One is the blurring of party loyalty by the presence of Tikiritis at top levels of the political structure. (In 1987 about one-third of both the RCC and the Regional Command were Tikritis.) While no Tikritis reach the top without a party commitment, their presence undermines party discipline while compelling the president to balance the interests of family against those of state and party.

Closely allied to this weakness is another: the growing personal power of Saddam (discussed below) and his use of state—rather than party—institutions to execute his will.

A third weakness relates to the unfinished business of the revolution. The Ba'th with its highly centralized structures is probably reaching only the modernized sectors of the state. Among traditional groups, such as the urban lower class, and the bulk of the rural population, only marginally touched by modernization, the party may have little relevance and less reach. Workers in factories have complained of a lack of services and of meaningful contact with state institutions that can serve their needs.[8] It is significant that the working class has been a source of support for the Communist party in the past. Rural migrants are another group the regime may not be reaching.[9] In recent years an influx of villagers from the Shiite south have crowded into government-built housing in Baghdad. One such area, al-Thawrah City (renamed Saddam City), contains over a million inhabitants. Meanwhile, among the general populace and especially the educated middle class, there is resentment at the monopoly of power held by a small group of party officials.

The Political Elite

The Ba'th, with its secular Arab nationalist ideology, its strong emphasis on egalitarianism and the redistribution of wealth, and its long history of clandestine opposition activity prior to 1968, has appealed disproportionately to certain groups within the population and brought certain kinds of men to the fore.

As is abundantly clear, the key figure in the leadership structure is Saddam Hussein, and the main trend in the structure's evolution has been the increased concentration of power in his hands. Nevertheless, the portrayal of Saddam as the strongman of Iraq, however justified, has obscured the complexity of forces within which he has had to operate and the group on which he must rely for support. A chief feature of this group has been its homogeneity.

The Top Level

In 1987 the Regional Command consisted of seventeen members.[10] Nine also sat on the RCC. Of the fifteen-member RCC originally instituted in 1969, only three members remained.

What kinds of men have risen to the top and what significant background factors do they share? From the first, the group has been wholly Arab, with one exception. In 1982 one Kurd was placed on the RCC, although not in the Regional Command of the party. The same Kurd is vice-president of the republic, but his position is largely cosmetic, and he would not succeed the president in case of a crisis. The virtual absence of Kurds in the chief national policymaking bodies is offset only marginally by the fact that the Kurds have their own autonomous decisionmaking body to handle local affairs in the north. Moreover, Kurds are represented in the Council of Ministers and in the National Assembly.

Until 1977 the leadership structure was overwhelmingly, although not exclusively, Arab Sunni in composition with a small but varying number of Shiites over time. Following Shiite disturbances in 1977, the first Shiites were brought into the RCC, and in the Regional Command their number rose to a third. In June 1982 a new Regional Command was elected, and the balance was strikingly shifted in favor of the Shiites. Of the seven new Regional Command members, the majority were Shiite, giving the Shiites parity with the Sunnis for the first time since the inception of the regime, although their number has subsequently been slightly reduced. Meanwhile, the RCC has also become more balanced; in 1987 it had four Arab Sunnis, three Arab Shiites, one Christian, and one Kurd (largely symbolic). Thus the party has met the Iranian challenge in part by broadening Shiite representation at the top of the party and state structure. Traditional Sunni dominance within the Ba'th leadership, it should be noted, has *not* been based on a sectarian policy but is related to the fact that the core of the original leadership elite originated in the central area of the country where Arab Sunnis predominate.

A third feature of the group is its narrow geographic base. Almost two-thirds of its members come from the northern towns of the Mosul-Anah-Baghdad triangle, and of these, five originate in Tikrit. This has varied over time; for much of the early 1980s, for example, there were only three Tikritis, including Saddam, and about one-third of the Regional Command came from the Shiite south. By any standards, however, the populous southern provinces have been underrepresented, while Kurds are almost absent at top levels. It is noteworthy that the overwhelming majority of these leaders, whether from the north or the south, were born in provincial towns. A distinct minority come from Baghdad and Mosul. The absence in this group (and in all of its predecessors stretching back to the 1920s) of representatives from Basra is striking.

Family ties remain important but not dominant. One of Saddam's maternal cousins is minister of defense (as well as a member of the RCC and the Regional Command). An uncle on his father's side was promoted to the Regional Command in 1986. Marriage to his daughters has also been used to cement ties with the political and military elite. Nevertheless, Saddam has not hesitated to discipline and dismiss relatives on occasion. His half brothers were removed from critical security positions in 1984 for reasons never clearly explained.

Most, although not all, Regional Command members come from poor or lower-middle-class families and had to struggle to achieve their middle-class status. Most have college degrees or diplomas from higher institutions, often acquired late in life. Only one has a doctorate. In general, advanced degrees are confined to the ministers, and even among these the number of doctorates is declining.

The overwhelming majority of this group are in their late forties or early fifties. The average age of the group in 1986 was fifty-two. This fact alone indicates that the group represents a distinct generation that has shared common experiences, above all the underground party struggle of the 1960s. The great majority of the Regional Command members joined the party either before or during 1958. An overwhelming majority have spent time in jail. All have passed the critical test of loyalty to the party in the difficult years following the party's 1963 fall from power after only nine months in office, a bond they share. Only one has studied or lived outside an Arab country for any length of time prior to holding high office, although some have acquired limited foreign experience through trips abroad. While genuine knowledge of foreign cultures has been missing at the top levels of the Ba'th leadership, this insularity has been partly overcome by the presence of foreign-educated (mainly

Western) Ba'this in the cabinet, although here, too, foreign exposure has been drastically reduced since the 1970s.

Owing to the regime's longevity, members of the Regional Command have a high degree of political and administrative experience, which helps make up for other weaknesses. In 1987 over 40 percent had served five years or more, while the top three figures, Saddam himself, Izzat Ibrahim, and Taha Ramadhan, have been in the Regional Command since the inception of the regime. All the members have had long party and public service. The same is true at the ministerial level, where turnover is greater.

Recruitment: The Second Stratum

As should be clear, the only vehicle of elite recruitment in Iraq today is the Ba'th party. Nonparty channels, including the military, the professional organizations, other progressive parties, or technical expertise, will not assure access to real decisionmaking status without party credentials.

As indicated previously, kinship ties with Saddam and a Tikrit connection are the major exception to this rule. However, even among Tikritis, the key figures are also long-standing party members of proven loyalty. Relatives with low party standing are not in top positions. Nevertheless, it cannot be said that these individuals owe their positions solely to a climb through party ranks.

The recruitment and training process for party members is rigorous. There are several levels of membership, starting from *mu'ayyad* (supporter), the first step inside the party, to *rafiq* (comrade), a full member. At each step the candidate is given greater responsibility and scrutiny. Achieving full membership may take anywhere from five to ten years.[11]

Little hard evidence exists on the size of the party cadre, and estimates vary. Before the war Saddam Hussein claimed a million supporters, but this may have included "friends" of the party not formally in the structure. A more recent estimate from official sources claims 1.5 million.[12] Full party members, estimated at 10,000 in 1976,[13] were said to number about 25,000 to 30,000 in 1984.[14]

A study of representatives elected to the National Assembly in 1980, 75 percent of whom were party members, gives a rough profile of the party cadre at the middle and upper middle levels.[15] In most respects, their backgrounds were remarkably similar to those of the top leadership. Some 80 percent of those studied had a high school education; 64 percent had gone beyond high school; and half had college degrees. Almost none of this education had been acquired outside the country. Thus, exposure to a non-Iraqi environment among the Ba'th's second stratum is as limited as it is at its top leadership levels. Occupational backgrounds are similar as well. The largest group in the study had experience in government and party service; the second largest in the educational field. About 15 percent had been technocrats, 10 percent professionals, and another 10 percent farmers. There were few workers and few military men. In this Assembly a large Shiite contingent (at least 40 percent) existed, indicating a substantial Shiite presence in the party. Although Kurds were represented in the assembly, few were party members.

A follow-up study of the second assembly elected in 1984 indicated a similar profile, but this body revealed significant trends in two directions. The Shiite contingent increased, while the age of the delegates decreased. In this assembly a substantial minority of the party membership (17 percent) was born after 1945,[16] which means that they probably joined the party after its advent to power in 1968. This indicates that since the war began, and under Saddam's leadership, the party has rapidly made room for two key groups that could cause problems if left out of the leadership structure—the Shiites and the post-1968 generation of party members.

Several conclusions can be drawn from these background factors. Homogeneity of background, and especially the age, education, and experience of the group, has given it a high degree of cohesion and unity of outlook. This cohesion, despite internal and external threats to the regime, has played a major role in its longevity. The lesson learned by the Ba'th is that cohesiveness and discipline among the cohort group count more than broad-based representation in holding on to power. However, the latter has not been totally neglected. Meanwhile, the limited foreign exposure of the group and its roots in Iraqi soil, and particularly in small town provincial environments, help account for the leadership's intense nationalism and its wariness of foreign connections.

Saddam Hussein

Whatever the collective outlook of the Iraqi leadership, there is little doubt that one individual, Saddam Hussein, has done more to shape it than all others combined. Born in 1937 to an Arab Sunni peasant family in a village north of Tikrit, Saddam had a difficult childhood.[17] His father died before his birth, and although his mother remarried, he was raised in Tikrit by his maternal uncle, Khair Allah Talfah, a former army officer retired in 1941 for his participation in the anti-British Rashid Ali movement, who instilled anti-imperialist and Arab nationalist sentiments into Saddam at an early age. It was during these years with his uncle in Tikrit that Saddam's ties to the Talfah clan, later augmented by his marriage to Khair Allah's daughter, Sajidah, were cemented.

Saddam completed his secondary school education in Baghdad, where he also plunged in the mid-1950s into anti-British and antimonarchical politics, participating in demonstrations, joining the Ba'th party in 1957, and undergoing a brief term in jail. He was selected as a member of the infamous Ba'th hit squad assigned to assassinate Abdul Karim Qasim in 1959 and was wounded in the attempt. His removal of the bullet lodged in his leg during his escape without the aid of a doctor, and his adventure-filled flight from Iraq to Syria and Egypt, have been memorialized in an Iraqi film. This episode marked him as a man of daring and cool courage, willing to use any means to achieve his ends.

Once in Egypt, Saddam finished high school and enrolled in law college, while continuing his Ba'thist activities. After the 1963 coup in Iraq he returned to his country, but he held only minor party posts during the party's short tenure in office that year. More important was his climb up the ladder during the party's underground period from November 1963 to July 1968. During this time he linked his fortune to that of Ahmad Hasan al-Bakr and the party's moderates. He also assumed more and more responsibility for the civilian wing of the party, playing a key role in its organization, including the suppression of opposition within the party. He played an important, though not dominant, role in the first coup of July 1968, which brought the Ba'th back to power in collusion with a group within the military, and an even more important role in the second one, two weeks later, which resulted in total Ba'th domination of the government.

Three factors help account for Saddam's rise to his present pre-eminent position since 1968. First, his capacity and willingness to shelter behind President Bakr, the man who had the more visible position in the regime until the mid-1970s. Second, his astute understanding of, and ability to manipulate, domestic politics. Third, his ability to take the lead in matters of state, even when they involved risk. By 1979, when Saddam's exercise of real power had become apparent to all, he obliged Ahmad Hasan al-Bakr to step down as president, leaving himself in a position of paramount power within Iraq. Even before this shift, however, the way had been prepared by the development of a full-blown personality cult through media exposure, posters, and personal appearances, which not only made it clear that Saddam was Iraq's leader but blurred and diminished the role of the party and its hierarchy. The war has increased this trend.

This record illustrates several features of Saddam's personality that should be taken into account when considering the current ideological struggle with Iran. Saddam has shown patience and a tenacious perseverance in the pursuit of long-range goals, the will and capacity to exercise power and to take calculated risks, and a willingness to be ruthless when necessary, but also an ability to be flexible when the situation demands it.

Like his colleagues in the party leadership, Saddam has been deeply affected by his twelve years of largely underground political activity before 1968.[18] The experience has given him a deeply ingrained suspicion of conspiracy. Although this aspect of his personality has receded somewhat in recent years, it is never very far from the surface, as repeated arrests and executions demonstrate. It has also made Saddam a tough and calculating politician with little use for romantic revolutionaries. He has indicated that he has learned much from Lenin, and in its organization and discipline the Ba'th party in Iraq resembles nothing so much as the Communist party of the Soviet Union. Above all, Saddam's outlook has been influenced by the failure of the Ba'th in 1963, from which he has drawn three lessons: first, that serious splits within the leadership must be avoided at all costs; second, that real power must be vested exclusively within the party; and third, that the party must capture and securely hold the organs of state.

To avoid the fate of the Ba'th in 1963, Saddam has used a variety of tactics. The first and most important of these has been the purge. Purges, often ruthless, have taken place periodically since 1968, the most severe of them as a result of contraventions of loyalty. Second, Saddam has taken care to prevent members of the RCC or others from developing independent constituencies. Third, he has attempted to establish countervailing centers of power within bureaucratic structures to act as checks and balances in cases of need. (For example, the party militia has been used as a balance to the military; the National Assembly as a balance to the party.) However, these have *not* been allowed to undercut the centralism of the state and party. In fact, the system may be plagued with too much centrism. The ubiquitous presence of party officials in the bureaucracy and the need to refer decisions to higher and higher levels have led to much inefficiency, most notably in the industrial and military sectors.

Recently Saddam has invoked a fourth tactic: going over the heads of the RCC and the party leadership to the people, playing the role of statesman and father of his people rather than mere party politician. It is this new role and the reduction of checks and balances within the leadership of Saddam's judgment that account for some of the miscalculations that resulted in the war with Iran and some subsequent military mistakes, like "Mehran," resulting from his orders. On the other hand, his emphasis on state, as well as party, institutions does give him the flexibility to appeal to nonparty groups when necessary.

Diversity Among the Leadership

Despite Saddam's dominant political position within the party and country, his rule is not entirely monolithic. Complexity, diversity, and sometimes even divisiveness exist at top party levels, as the frequent purges suggest. Little is known about the individual political opinions of RCC members, and even less about potential opposition to Saddam, but some current differences within the elite can be inferred on the basis of past evidence. Many of these have been buried in the common war effort, but they will surface again when the conflict subsides or if Iran clearly identifies Saddam's removal alone as the price for peace.

While some differences crystallize around personal issues, for example, resentment of the power and influence of the Tikritis, others revolve around policy issues and the nature and direction of the

Ba'th revolution. Although the traditional categories of right and left are only marginally accurate here, we may use these terms as shorthand. On the left are those whose commitment to ideological purity and organizational discipline are deepest. They have always been more suspicious of the West, and specifically of the United States; they have desired closer cooperation with the Soviet Union and are more resistant to the growing cooperation with the conservative, pro-Western monarchies of the Gulf. It is difficult to identify members of the current leadership who might harbor these views, but several who did may have been among those executed in 1979. Since the war, and Iraq's overwhelming financial and logistical dependence on the Gulf oil states, this group has suffered a political setback.

On the right are those in the political elite traditionally identified with a pan-Arab orientation, particularly in the Fertile Crescent. They have desired less Soviet and communist influence in Iraq. They see Israel as the main foreign enemy and want concentration on this problem, rather than a continued embroglio with Iran. Some may still have an orientation toward Syria, despite bitter relations between the two regimes. The war with Iran has also weakened this group because of the need to focus on Iran, rather than Israel, and because of Syria's alliance with the Islamic Republic.

Saddam has tried to steer a middle course, leaning heavily on pragmatism and flexibility, but his policy does not rely merely on avoiding extremes. Since the war a new point of view has emerged—an emphasis on Iraq as a sovereign state and nation and its role as a model of national development for other countries of the Arab and Third Worlds. To buttress this position, Saddam has relied heavily on economic and social development at home and international support abroad. The war is also hastening an emphasis on Iraq as a nation-state.

Economic and Social Policies

Any assessment of the revolutionary experience in Iraq under the Ba'th must give consideration to the regime's economic and social programs and the impact they have had on the country's socioeconomic structure. Although the war has curtailed much economic and social development, their effects can nevertheless be assessed.

Three areas are especially significant: social policies, economic policies, and the process of secularization.

Social Policies

One of the regime's most important social aims has been the reordering of Iraq's class structure, particularly the elimination of the old upper and middle classes of landlords and merchants and the prevention of the rise of a new capitalist middle class. The Ba'th has gone further than the previous revolutionary regimes in its egalitarian policy.[19] A 1970 modification of the previous land reform law reduced the amount of land allowed to individual landowners, undercutting the growth of a new landed class. To service the farmers, cooperative societies have spread widely; in 1982, they totaled 1,959 with 393,900 members. Since the late 1970s the regime has leaned toward the private sector to develop agriculture.

In the commercial sector independent fortunes gained through trade have been eliminated through state control over banking, finance, international trade, and large retail trading outlets. Development projects awarded on a turnkey basis, rather than as joint ventures, have prevented oil wealth from accruing to private companies and individuals. A strict agent's law has curtailed the profits made by Iraqi agents for foreign firms. Most important of all, the government has undercut the private sector by absorbing most of the emerging middle class into its own employ, where it can control its income through wages and salaries. By 1978 the state was the largest single employer in the country, with well over 600,000 working directly for the government. Nevertheless, the regime has not been able to prevent private wealth from being accumulated by certain groups still operating in the private sector. Among these are private professionals (doctors, engineers, and technocrats) and, above all, contractors, the new affluent class.[20] By 1987 the trend toward increased government control over the economy had been reversed. Government jobs had been reduced and some economic functions turned over to the private sector.

The regime has also attempted to distribute the benefits of economic development as widely as possible, particularly among the lower and lower-middle classes, its political base. Until the war, rent and price controls kept food, housing, and everyday necessities within a comfortable range for the lower classes. The war, however, and Iraq's supply difficulties have changed this, and by the mid-1980s inflation had become a serious problem in Baghdad. Persistence of this inflationary cycle could undercut the gains made by the salaried middle class and worsen the conditions of the poor with obvious consequences for Ba'th political support.

Since 1968 consumption of food per capita has risen,[21] and free public health and education up to and including the university level are universally available. These advantages, while benefiting all Iraqis, have been disproportionately advantageous to the lower classes. Nevertheless, despite these changes, inequalities still remain, especially between rural and urban areas; between the highly endowed central provinces, with Baghdad at their center, and the poorer northern and southern areas, and even within urban areas themselves.[22] It is in these northern and southern provinces that the greatest potential for discontent exists.

The most important social efforts of the regime have gone into education and the eradication of illiteracy. Here results have been striking. Between 1968 and 1983, elementary school attendance more than doubled, from 1 million to 2.6 million; intermediate and secondary school attendance almost quadrupled, from 250,000 to almost 1 million; and university enrollment more than tripled, from 37,000 to 122,700.[23] In 1978 the Ba'th passed a law making it compulsory for all illiterate adults, male and female, to complete two years of instruction in government-sponsored literacy centers.[24] By the 1980s statistics indicated that almost 10 percent of the work force may have had a high school education, while almost 4 percent may have been college-educated.[25]

There have also been other dramatic social consequences of the regime's policies. The most striking of these has been massive migration to the cities. Between 1958 and 1978 Iraq was transformed from a predominantly rural into a predominantly urban country. In 1957, 63 percent of the population was rural; by 1977 the same percentage was urban.[26] Even more startling, the percentage of the population engaged in agriculture, according to recent statistics, dropped from about 50 percent in the 1960s to a figure possibly as low as 30 percent in 1977.[27] Economic figures show that only a small portion of the new urbanites have been absorbed into modern industry; more have gone into construction. A number of unemployed or underemployed exist in the traditional urban economic sector consisting of shopkeepers, street vendors, and the like. The war has found use for much of the excess manpower, but the structural problem remains and will have to be faced in acute form after the war when thousands of soldiers are demobilized.

The rapid growth of an educated middle class has also created problems for the regime. While some of the professionals and technocrats have been absorbed into the party structure, others have not been and are potentially alienated. These highly trained people have tended to be dissatisfied with the tight controls exercised by the party on intellectual and professional life and with their own inability to play a larger role in the political life of the country. While this group is not openly hostile, its passive resistance and lack of motivation have tended to adversely affect economic progress and efficiency.

Economic Development

The first priority in the regime's development plans has been industry.[28] Prior to the war the government invested in capital-intensive heavy industries such as iron, steel, aluminum, and petrochemicals (much of it concentrated in the Basra area). A small investment went into intermediate industries, some of them distributed throughout the south; little went into consumer goods industries with higher levels of employment.[29] This has produced industrial growth, but it has been insufficient to bring about a structural change in the economy. In the 1960s industry employed between 6 and 7 percent of the labor force; by the end of the 1970s it employed 9 percent.[30] Meanwhile, the agricultural sector has declined in employment, possibly by 20 percent. Clearly, industry has been unable to absorb the surplus agricultural labor. Instead, much of this labor has gone into the construction sector (as mentioned above), which increased from 2 to 10 percent of the employed population before the war. One study has indicated that much of the new urban migration was employed in small-scale, traditional industries on which little government money or attention was spent.[31] Even before the war foreign labor had to be imported, much of it in agriculture, and since 1980 this has been extended to the bureaucracy as well. Estimates of the foreign labor force in Iraq vary.

In 1982 it was placed as high as 1 million,[32] but the economic difficulties of the war have forced cutbacks. Meanwhile, much of the heavy industry in the Basra area has been rendered inoperable due to fighting in the area.

Economists have also questioned the productivity of the new industries in terms of the capital invested. Despite heavy inputs of machinery, output has not increased proportionately. Two areas of weakness are unskilled labor and ineffective management.[33] While an unemployed or underemployed class of unskilled laborers crowds into the cities, the technical and professional middle class is mired in bureaucracy and political control. Prior to the war both groups had been propitiated by pay raises, increased standards of living, and the potential for rapid social mobility; but the war has put their mobility on hold. A continuance of the conflict, which prevents development, can only worsen their situation. A further weakness in Iraq's economic development lies in the fact that the country has not yet made substantial gains in diversifying its economy. It is more dependent on oil for revenue now than it was before 1973.

The regime has taken only sporadic interest in agriculture, the Achilles' heel of the economy. Figures are notoriously unreliable, but most economists agree that agricultural production either stagnated or grew only marginally during the 1970s, depending on the crop under consideration. Agricultural imports increased from 14 percent of the food supply in 1964–66 to 33 percent in 1975–77, and they continued to climb at least up to 1980.[34] Just before the war the regime devoted more attention to agriculture, channeling funds into large-scale irrigation projects, but little attention has been devoted to smaller schemes and extension services.[35] One result of this relative neglect has been the rural exodus described above.

The service sector, mainly public administration, has had the fastest growth, rising uninterruptedly until its share of GDP was over 40 percent in 1976.[36] With the war it has increased further, although there has been an effort to turn some segments of the economy, such as agriculture and health care, over to the private sector in order to free the government to concentrate on the war. As these and other figures suggest, it is the state, rather than the productive sectors, that has been the major source of employment for the new urbanites, a factor that will need correction after the war.

The war situation has, of course, intensified the regime's short-term economic problems. For the first year and a half of the war, consumer imports were increased and the economy expanded in an effort to shore up public support. At the same time mobilization for the war effort withdrew a large supply of workers from the labor force, which slowed down the economy and increased inflation. In 1982, when it became apparent that the war would continue for some time, this policy was supplanted by an austerity program, which brought expenditures into line with revenues to some extent.

There have also been some war-related benefits. The closure of Iraq's Gulf ports early in the war resulted in an ambitious pipeline program. By 1987 Iraq had expanded its pipeline capacity through Turkey to the Mediterranean and through Saudi Arabia to the Red Sea, raising Iraq's export capacity to over 2 million barrels per day. An additional planned pipeline through Saudi Arabia will, when completed, bring Iraq's export capacity above prewar levels and give Iraq considerable flexibility in exporting its oil. The war has also put a priority on efficiency and spurred local production in areas that will provide peacetime benefits.

The Policy of Secularism

All Iraqi regimes since 1920 have been based on a policy of secular nationalism, some more pronouncedly than others. This has been dictated partly by the religious diversity within Iraq, but in the Ba'th case it is also a matter of ideology. While not attacking Islam overtly, Ba'th programs have tended to downplay Islam in favor of the secular state. A number of policies already mentioned give evidence of this, in particular the growth of state institutions and welfare programs at the expense of private and religious institutions, and the spread of secular education. However, it is probably only since the 1970s that the majority of the school-age population at the primary level in rural areas has been attending schools.[37] Hence, residual traditionalism remains among a considerable portion of the older and rural population.

By its nature, secularism is difficult to measure. But one gauge of the relative weakness of religious institutions in Iraq is the small number of clergy relative to the size of the population, as pointed out by Batatu in his study of the Shiites in Iraq.[38]

One good example of the regime's secular policy is its position on women. A paramount aim of the Ba'th is "the liberation of the Arab woman and her release from her antiquated economic, social, and legal bonds," which it deems are in conflict with Iraq's Arab and Islamic heritage.[39] The regime has passed legislation giving women equal pay for equal work, outlawing job discrimination on the basis of sex, and establishing day care centers for working women. Although the regime has been slow to tamper with the traditional religious preserve of family law, even here the Ba'th has consciously moved in the direction of strengthening the nuclear family and the woman's position within it.[40] An amendment to the personal status law passed in 1978 imposed stiff penalties for forced marriages, allowed a *qadi* (religious judge) to overrule a guardian's refusal to allow a woman not a minor to marry the man of her choice, made polygamy more difficult, and expanded the situations under which a woman can ask for a divorce.[41] However, Saddam has refused to move faster than he feels public opinion will accept.[42]

It must be pointed out that the regime has not relied wholly on positive measures to enforce its ideological position. The exile of Khomeini from Iraq in 1978; the suppression of al-Da'wah and other secret Shiite opposition movements; the execution of Baqr al-Sadr, the leading Iraqi Shiite *mujtahid*, and his sister; the closing of the frontier to Shiite pilgrims; and the expulsion of thousands of Iraqis of Persian origin represent the negative side of the regime's secularizing policies. As a result of the war and the Iranian challenge, there has also been a shift in Ba'th ideology in favor of Islam and an increase in the construction of mosques, but it is an Islam clearly seen as subordinate to Arab nationalism as a focus of loyalty.

Meanwhile, the war effort has been accompanied by an intense propaganda campaign in favor of secular nationalism and an Arab identity in an attempt to maintain the loyalty of the Arab, and especially the Arab Shiite, majority. All evidence suggests that it has been successful among the younger generation, the educated, and the growing middle class, the backbone of the regime's support. Among the rural Shiites, the older population, and possibly the uprooted elements in the city, it may be less effective. However, although there were Shiite riots in Karbala and al-Najaf in 1974 and 1977, there have been no large-scale defections among the Shiites since the war, and feelings of patriotism in the face of the Iranian threat have, by most reports, intensified.

The Role of Ideology

In the view of the regime itself it is its ideology that gives it legitimacy. The Ba'th considers itself a revolutionary party aiming at nothing less than the fundamental revitalization of Arab society among modern, progressive, secular lines, a concept embodied in the party's name, Ba'th, or Renaissance. The three foundations of party ideology are well known and are summarized in the party slogan, "Unity, Freedom, Socialism."

By unity the party means the eventual political union of all Arab-speaking states, temporarily divided into regions (countries) by the Western powers after World War I. While the ideological zeal for unity has receded in a divided Arab world, among the Iraqi Ba'th Arab unity is still tacitly accepted as a distant goal, and Arabism is the constant theme of government pronouncements. Until the war this had some practical effects in the shape of measures such as those allowing Arabs from other countries to live and work in Iraq without visas and to own land and businesses on the same terms as Iraqis, but these have been curtailed because of the war. Nonetheless, the war has allowed Iraq to pose as the defender of the eastern gate of the Arab world and has strengthened feelings of Arab identity among much of the Iraqi population, exclusive of the Kurds.

The concept of freedom generally embodies not only the idea of collective freedom of a nation from foreign control and influence, but also presumes the participation of individual citizens in the nation's social and political life. In Ba'th Iraq emphasis has clearly been placed on the first part of this definition. Few regimes in the Arab world have been as intensely concerned with political and economic independence as Iraq. As for domestic political freedom, it has long since been submerged in loyalty to the state. Real political participation by any but Ba'thists is severely limited. Saddam has rejected Western-style parliamentary democracy in favor of a consultative process, seen as more in keeping with Arab traditions: "If you ask me whether Western democracy is suitable for the Arab nation, my answer is no. Let us go back in history to the time of the early Arab Muslims. Their democracy never followed a Western pattern, and they relied on consultation rather than a parliament. That is why our own understanding of democracy should be based on the particular characteristics of our nation, as well as of our party."[43]

While other political parties, including the Communists and various Kurdish parties loyal to the state, have been permitted in the past, they have not been allowed to compete for real power. The Ba'th, as the vanguard of the revolution, dominates the political process, and this is clearly spelled out in numerous documents.

Socialism, the third element of the Ba'th party slogan, in the Iraqi definition means government ownership of the commanding heights of the economy—all large-scale industry, international trade and finance, and some retail trade. But the Ba'th allows for some private enterprise in agriculture and commerce. There has been evidence of more pragmatism in the economy since the late 1970s. In agriculture, for example, most collective farms have been phased out, while encouragement has been offered to small and medium-sized private businesses. Ba'thists reject the class struggle as the engine of social change in favor of Arab nationalism.

While these principles form the basis of Ba'th ideology, under Saddam they have undergone a number of shifts. These have become more decisive as the war has been drawn out. With the increase of oil wealth in the mid-1970s, stress was increasingly put on economic development and social change and the emphasis changed to what may be termed "Ba'thism in one country." Ba'thism would become synonymous with Iraq, its bastion, and then spread to the rest of the Arab world under Iraq's leadership.[44]

Meanwhile, the meaning of Arabism has been more broadly defined to include the Kurds. Arabs are considered those who are Arab in language, feeling, or heritage; Salah al-Din, a Kurd by birth, has been frequently mentioned as an example. Iraq's ancient history is now stressed and made part of the broader Arab heritage. The origins of the Arabic language are traced back to Aramaic, and the earlier Semitic civilizations of Mesopotamia have been defined as Arab.[45] This theme has gone hand in hand with an emphasis on Iraqi patriotism, which is, nonetheless, Arab in spirit and identity. These motifs have been echoed and encouraged in literature and art as well in an attempt to tie Iraq's unique past to its present, and both to its Arab heritage.[46]

The Iranian revolution, with its religious ideology, has challenged this worldview, root and branch. In order to counter the challenge the Ba'th has recently placed more emphasis on Islam, but not as the focal point of its ideology. On the contrary, Islam is still kept firmly subservient to Arab nationalism. It is considered a part, but not the dominant part, of the Arab heritage. Moreover, religion is, to a certain extent, separated from the state. "Although we may be inspired by religion," Saddam Hussein has stated, "we do not deal with life by following a religious path. Today, after 1,400 years, religion has taken many new paths, new meanings, new conduct, new schools of thought. We do not believe in dealing with life through religion because it would not serve the Arab nation."[47]

Indeed, Islam's contributions to Arab history are consciously compared to those of the Ba'th. Muhammad is said to have united the Arabs and to have brought a social and intellectual revolution—precisely the modern Ba'th goals. Saddam has made increasing references to Iraqis' Shiite heritage and his sympathy with it. His speeches have been laced with references to Ali as a model for emulation, while Mu'awiyyah, his historic enemy, has been impugned. "Mu'awiyyah did not triumph over Imam Ali. He won the earth . . . and lost the heavenly values." On one occasion Saddam told his Iraqi audience, "We have the right to say today—and we will not be fabricating history—that we are the grandsons of Imam Hussein."[48]

Up until the Iranian revolution the traditional Ba'thist ideology had served the regime well. It managed to link the two poles of thought that had caught the imagination of the younger generation of Arabs in the 1960s and 1970s—Arab nationalism and socialism. Politicians in Baghdad could shift emphasis from one aspect to the other as the situation demanded, while both could be held up as ultimate ideals, even if they could not be realized immediately. Now the regime is faced with a challenge of a different order, one entirely outside the Ba'th framework, no matter how flexibly defined. The Iranian revolution is calling the regime's legitimacy into question on grounds of religion or rather lack of it, on its borrowing of a foreign ideology (socialism), and on undemocratic leadership.

Despite some severe setbacks, the Ba'th regime has thus far met the challenge. It has modified its ideology to take account of both Islam and indigenous Iraqi patriotism, and it has rapidly integrated more Shiites into the party hierarchy. It has defended its country against numerous Iranian attacks, although hard-pressed at the front. But the regime is still vulnerable on several counts. It has not yet solved the perennial Kurdish problem; rapid social change has still left rural portions of the population marginally modernized; and the Ba'th has been too exclusive, both with regard to the participation it allows in the political system and in its definition of Iraq's aims and goals. Notwithstanding these caveats, the changes wrought by the Ba'th in state-building and in the transformation of social structures are profound and likely to remain. Iraq in the 1980s is a very different country from what it was in the 1960s.

STATE-BUILDING AND POLITICAL CONSTRUCTION IN THE YEMEN ARAB REPUBLIC, 1962–1977

■

Robert Burrowes

Modern state-building and political construction came late to North Yemen. On the eve of the 1962 revolution, Yemen was one of the last extant examples of a relatively complex, large-scale traditional social system. A conservative Islamic society, it was little changed in the 1950s from the Yemen of two or even several centuries earlier. At mid-century it was virtually devoid of piped water, motor vehicles and engines, electricity, telephones or radios, much less the modern ideas and institutions that go with these things.

The persistence of traditional Yemen was largely the result of a conscious effort, during the first half of the twentieth century, to preserve it. At a time when the world's few remaining traditional societies were crumbling under the impact of modernity, two remarkable imams revived and reinvigorated the historic order of Yemen, simultaneously insulating it almost completely from the outside world. Imam Yahya contained the effects of the new ideas and practices that had come with the second Ottoman occupation in the latter half of the nineteenth century. He and his son and successor, Imam Ahmad, were also able to limit the impact on Yemen of the rising tide of modernism and nationalism that engulfed the Arab world in the decades after World War I and the breakup of the Ottoman Empire. Between them, they occupied the imamate and guarded Yemen's gates from 1904 to 1962.

Imams Yahya and Ahmad were aided in their task by Yemen's

geographic isolation. Despite its proximity to Aden Colony and the major sea lane to Asia, North Yemen remained a backwater, outside the mainstream of events during the last decades of the age of imperialism and colonialism. The imams were aided further by the fact that Yemen's traditional economic system was to a high degree self-contained and self-sufficient. Based upon subsistence agriculture, the economy produced most of the things the Yemenis consumed; exports of small amounts of coffee and hides were sufficient to permit import of the small number of necessities and luxuries not locally produced. The Yemen of the imams remained intact largely because it and the modern world had little need for or interest in each other.

The imamate of Yemen was the political expression of the Zaydi sect, the branch of Shiite Islam to which most of the people of the Yemeni highlands adhere. The Zaydi imamate fit comfortably into Max Weber's category of patrimonial traditional political systems. It was sacred—that is, theocratic—and it was ruled according to custom and tradition by a small ruling caste. According to Zaydi political thought, the imam was the secular and religious leader of the community of the faithful and could be elected only from those males who had, among other attributes, direct descent from Ali, the cousin and son-in-law of the Prophet.

In the absence of any ministerial structure, the imamate was truly the imam's government, one over which he exercised direct personal control. The highest administrative officials were immediate subordinates of the imam, usually personal confidants and often located in the imam's household; indeed, most top positions in the imamate in the 1930s and 1940s were occupied by the several sons of Imam Yahya. In addition to a corps of clerks and scribes, there was a specialized, but relatively undifferentiated, officialdom for the implementation of laws and decisions. Structurally, the imamate state was only slightly differentiated from the larger society. For example, the standing army was small and for the most part nonprofessional, forcing the imam to rely for defense on the levy of tribal irregulars. Consequently, the capacity of the imam to penetrate his society, to regulate behavior in it, to draw resources from it, and to use those resources as he saw fit was quite limited.

Imams Yahya and Ahmad tried with some success to centralize and extend the imamate during the first six decades of the twentieth century. The small army and provincial administration were improved with turn-of-the-century Ottoman organization and procedures. Nevertheless, the strengthening of the imamate during this period was primarily the result of the forceful personalities, dedication, and energy of these two men. They achieved what they did largely within the limits of tradition and without the help of the ideas and techniques of modern statecraft. As late as the end of the 1950s, the most important tool of the imamate was the telegraph, a device that the imams controlled directly, and they used military campaigns, the hostage system, subsidies, and factional manipulation to consolidate their power at the center and to extend their domain somewhat on the periphery at the expense of the largely autonomous tribes. They were also successful in establishing firm Zaydi rule over the southern uplands and the Red Sea coast, areas populated by adherents of the Shafi school of Sunni Islam.

Politics under the imamate was the preserve of a tiny minority at the top of a largely closed system, was organized into loose factions, and was conducted on a personal, face-to-face basis. The beginnings of modern politics came to Yemen in the 1940s in the form of growing opposition to the imamate. Although preceded by a few years by two small, clandestine groups, the first major opposition organization was founded in Aden in 1944. This organization, the Free Yemenis, played an important role in the failed effort to remove the ruling family from the imamate in 1948. Although it existed as an organization for only a few years, the Free Yemenis led directly to the formation of other opposition groups in the 1950s, among them the Yemeni Unionists. Far from being radical modernists, the leaders of the Free Yemenis were the mid-twentieth-century equivalents of the Turkish reformers of the Ottoman Empire during the Tanzimat period in the mid-nineteenth century. They evolved only slowly from favoring a constitutional imamate to favoring a republic, and their conception of republicanism was decidedly old-fashioned.

By the early 1950s, however, many of the small number of young Yemenis studying abroad and a few of the far larger number working abroad had been drawn to other, more modern politics by way of the culturally congenial Muslim Brotherhood; although a few stayed with the brotherhood, most of them later migrated from it to secular political movements. Based and nurtured in Aden or the political capitals of the Arab world, Yemeni branches of the Communist party and such pan-Arab entities as the Arab Nationalist Movement and the Ba'th party were founded and began to attract a Yemeni following. More important, by the late 1950s, a large number of Yemenis had come under the spell of Gamal Abdal Nasser and his evolving blend of nationalism and socialism in Egypt.

The al-Sallal Era

The Yemen Arab Republic was created after a coup by young army officers under the nominal leadership of colonel Abdullah al-Sallal on September 26, 1962, a week after Imam Ahmad died. His successor's escape and rallying of tribal support resulted in a bitter, costly civil war. Substantial Egyptian and Saudi Arabian support for the republicans and the royalists, respectively, served to broaden the conflict and to extend it until the end of the decade. Things done or left undone during this period brought changes and released forces that made the further modernization of Yemeni society and government inescapable. The imamate itself was replaced by a secular president. A host of Egyptian advisers supervised the wholesale replacement of the imam's household government with a council of ministers and some two dozen ministries and other government agencies. A number of mixed public-private economic enterprises were also created.

This initial effort at modern state-building was largely ill-conceived and hastily executed, and the changes were often more formal than substantive. Egypt tried to make the YAR over in its own image, and most of the new institutions were pale carbon copies of those in Cairo in the early 1960s; as such, they were often ill-suited to conditions in Yemen and to the Yemenis for whom they were intended. Some remained inoperative paper organizations—"ghost," as some Yemenis have called them—and others were hastily staffed by a few holdovers from the imamate who knew nothing about modern government and by young republicans who lacked prior experience with any form of governance. Most of these institutions were closely controlled by Egypt, either directly through its own advisers or indirectly through Yemenis beholden to the Egyptians. Many of the mixed enterprises were partly owned by Egypt and linked to their Egyptian counterparts.

Egypt did not allow the YAR to create large, modern armed

forces during its involvement in the civil war. Edgar O'Ballance claims that in 1965 "the Yemen army was still less than 6,000 men in strength, and was made up of a jumble of small infantry units scattered about the country, some of which were either incorporated into the [Egyptian] formations or in some other way under [Egyptian] command."[1]

Conditions during the first years after the 1962 revolution did not permit Yemeni republicans to take politics into their own hands and to reorder political life in the YAR. Egypt became more deeply involved in the country's internal affairs as the civil war dragged on, and Egyptian conduct of the war and control over much of the civil administration left little room for Yemeni politics and politicians. As Fred Halliday notes: "It was only in 1965—three years after the Imam was ousted—that the first political organization, the Popular Revolutionary Organization, was set up"; an empty shell, it held its only Congress in January 1967.[2] Indeed, Yemeni politics was run out of Cairo as much as out of Sanaa by the middle of the 1960s. At one point President al-Sallal, by then President Nasser's puppet, was detained in Egypt in order to let another group of Yemenis have a go at leading the republic. When the results proved unsatisfactory, al-Sallal was returned to office in Sanaa and many from the other group were put under house arrest in Egypt.

As frustration with the civil war and the Egyptian presence deepened, the political energies of many Yemenis were diverted into small, ephemeral political groupings that were in favor of some form of negotiated settlement with the royalists and were to varying degrees anti-Sallal and anti-Egyptian. At the same time the Yemeni branches of the pan-Arab parties that had surfaced after the revolution found the political climate increasingly inhospitable. The fate of the Arab Nationalist Movement (ANM), the strongest of these groups, is illustrative. Shortly after the revolution, the ANM opened a cultural center, assumed operation of the fledgling republic's only radio station, and expanded its previously clandestine trade union activities. Suspicions that President Nasser was ready to abandon the republic and make peace with Saudi Arabia led the Yemeni branch of the ANM to break with Egypt and with ANM headquarters in Beirut in late 1964. The honeymoon over, the Egyptian-backed al-Sallal regime soon closed down ANM activities and purged ANM members from posts in the republic administration. Protest demonstrations sponsored by the ANM led to further repression, and many ANM members and sympathizers fled south to Aden.

The al-Iryani Era

The al-Sallal regime was ousted by a broad coalition under the titular leadership of Qadi Abd al-Rahman al-Iryani in November 1967, only a month after the departure of the last of the Egyptian forces. Egypt's withdrawal was forced by its defeat by Israel in the Six-Day War; it was facilitated by the Khartoum Agreement, which ended the confrontation between Egypt and Saudi Arabia in Yemen. Despite the lessened foreign involvement after 1967, the civil war between Yemeni republicans and royalists dragged on for more than two years.

The lag in political construction relative to state-building and modernization, already evident by the end of the al-Sallal era, increased considerably during the six and one-half years of President al-Iryani's rule.[3] To understand the political constraints operating on all three of these processes—and especially on political construction—it is necessary to recognize that, despite the effects of five years of rapid change, Yemen in 1968 remained an essentially traditional society. Moreover, beneath a surface of anti-Egyptian feelings, the movement that replaced al-Sallal contained a strong restorative undercurrent. In addition to seeking to return control over the destiny of Yemen to Yemeni hands, it sought to restore certain traditional Yemeni values and practices that had been challenged by Arab socialism and other modern ideas during the Egyptian interlude. In sum, the mood and movement that brought al-Iryani to power were nationalist and conservative. The sociopolitical composition of the regime headed by President al-Iryani reflected this mood and the continued vitality of tradition and traditional groups in Yemen. As Robert Stookey points out, it rested upon "a coalition between sheikhs of the tribes, large and small, and the community of Zaydis educated in the traditional legal and theological disciplines."[4] This conservative base was strengthened by the purge of secular progressives in 1968 and by the restoration of moderate royalist elements in the national reconciliation that finally signaled the end of the civil war in 1970.

Special mention must be made of the new power and position of the tribal sheikhs. In the course of consolidating the Zaydi state in the twentieth century, Imams Yahya and Ahmad had tipped the historic balance of power between the state and the tribes—between the center and the periphery—in favor of the former. The long civil war that followed the 1962 revolution reversed this trend and led to the reassertion of tribal power and autonomy. The territory subject to the authority of the republican state shrank and the "land of insolence" in which the tribes were free of any higher authority, including that of the royalists, expanded. During the darker days of the conflict, the republic had sway loosely over little more—and sometimes much less—than the territory within the southwestern triangle formed by the roads connecting Sanaa, Taiz, and al-Hudayda. In addition, in their effort to compete with the royalists and the Saudis for tribal support, the regime and its Egyptian patrons had renewed the old practice of granting subsidies to the tribes. Sheikhs who were thought to be leaning toward the republic were granted pensions as recruiters and commanders of auxiliary "popular forces." Other sheikhs drew subsidies from the royalists and their Saudi patrons, and a few managed to collect from both sides in the conflict. Consequently, many previously impecunious and weak sheikhs found themselves quite affluent and in command of large, well-armed forces. Finally, a number of "republican tribalists"[5] had through their early and more or less continuous support of the republic established strong claims on the new political system. Their solid republican credentials legitimated future assertions of power and autonomy by their tribes.

Events immediately after the ouster of President al-Sallal served to strengthen further the position of the sheikhs. Whatever their performance, President al-Iryani and his colleagues were in no position in 1968 to curtain the power of the tribes. The withdrawal of Egyptian forces in late 1967 had made the nontribal republicans all the more dependent upon the arms of their tribal allies for defense against the royalists in the continuing civil war. No less important, tribal elements played a key military role in the successful attempt by the conservative republicans to beat back a challenge by the resurgent ANM and other progressive forces in 1968.

The power of the sheikhs did not merely increase during and after the civil war; it assumed new forms and acquired new bases.

Important sheikhs were given key consultative and executive positions in the growing central government for the first time,[6] which probably contributed more than any other factor to the expansion and consolidation of their power. No longer merely a volatile and potentially rebellious part of the environment of the Yemeni state, the tribal sheikhs were now full-fledged participants in an enlarged bargaining system that was still new and unfamiliar to all the players. In the relatively open and uncrystallized al-Iryani regime, they learned quickly how to pyramid their power and influence. In addition to acquiring top positions for themselves, they used their influence to place clients in office, and those so placed in turn enhanced the influence of their patrons. The sheikhs' new opportunities for enrichment and patronage at the center provided them with the resources needed to consolidate their traditional power base on the tribal periphery. In turn, the strengthening of this power base, and the credibility it gave to threats of political conflict, if not armed rebellion, gave the sheikhs a further claim on benefits at the center, which could be ignored by the state only at great risk.

Members of the tribal families were governors in six of the YAR's ten provinces in 1973. Given the weakness of the central government outside the three main cities, the governorships were particularly important elements of tribal power. By far the most important of these governors was Sinan abu Luhum, longtime governor of al-Hudayda province and a leader of the Nahm tribe in the Bakil tribal confederation. Sinan's relatives held key army commands, and his brother-in-law Muhsin al-Aini was the leading modernist politician during the al-Iryani era. Sinan was perhaps the shrewdest and most successful tribal politician during this period, and he moved with skill and ease between modern and traditional politics, between the center and the periphery; he was reputed by many to have become the chief broker of Yemeni politics, making and unmaking governments almost at will. In an obvious reference to Sinan, a United Nations' report described with surprising candor the multibased power of the tribal governors: "Several Governors remain powerful because of their tribal leadership, maintain almost complete independence from the central administration and report directly to [President al-Iryani]. Their power and influence not only dominate the life of the people of their tribe, which administratively belongs to a different province, but also of those in the province over which they have administrative authority."[7]

The possibility that statist, antitribal politicians might one day attempt to curtail the power of the sheikhs by force was lessened by the "tribalization" of the armed forces. Tribal units were incorporated into the small, unreformed regular army, and tribal leaders were placed in command of some of its key units. For example, four of Sinan's relatives—two brothers, a cousin, and a son—held command positions. As a consequence, the armed forces became less an instrument through which the fledgling state could extend its authority over the tribes than an instrument through which the tribes could defend their power and authority against the state. Indeed, the tribalized army was the linchpin of the system of tribal power during the al-Iryani era. By blocking reform of the army—and thereby keeping it weak, divided, and partially under their control—the tribal leaders were able to minimize the likelihood of the army's becoming an autonomous center of power or an effective instrument of state power. Furthermore, given the weakness of the state's armed forces, the existence of subsidized tribal irregulars outside the army both kept alive the historic fears of tribal rebellion and made it possible for the tribal leaders to deny the state access to, much less control over, large areas of the north and east.

Finally, the position of the sheikhs was buttressed further from outside by Saudi Arabia. In choosing to take a chance and accept the republic in 1970, Saudi Arabia hedged its bet by continuing to pay subsidies to the tribes—former tribal foes as well as friends—and by presenting itself as the patron and protector of tribal interests. This arrangement both gave the Saudis a foothold in the Yemeni political system and gave the tribal leaders an external political staging area.

The al-Iryani coalition and the decentralized system of power and political brokerage within which it operated placed severe limits upon efforts at state-building and modernization. These efforts were even more tightly constrained early in the al-Iryani era by the civil war and a severe financial crisis, which included growing external debts and soaring deficits in the government budget and the balance of payments. Another immediate concern was a long drought and the acute famine it caused. Of necessity, these matters of defense and economic survival took precedence over other concerns during this desperate time, and the efforts of the al-Iryani regime until the early 1970s were focused on the here and now. As one participant in these events proclaimed: "State-building! What state-building? We were trying to save, not build, the state in those days."[8]

Nevertheless, the YAR did make modest progress in the course of al-Iryani's rule. Early on, a small group of young, Western-educated modernists was able to diagnose the YAR's economic problems and to prescribe some remedies, as well as to design several of the necessary government institutions. A central bank made possible the creation of a commercial banking system in 1972, and the new Finance Ministry began to subject government expenditures to elementary budgetary procedures in 1974. The Central Planning Organization (CPO), created in 1972, quickly established itself as the government's chief locus for the formulation of development policies and for contact with the growing number of foreign-aid donors and contractors.

A number of important development projects were also begun during the al-Iryani era. Major improvements in the transportation and communications systems were the most important accomplishments. The international airport at Sanaa was constructed, and telephone links among the major cities were established; work continued on the Sanaa-Saada highway, the Sanaa-Taiz highway was paved, and a number of other road projects were planned. Construction of many schools, mosques, medical facilities, and government buildings was begun in the cities and major towns, and the electrical and water systems of the three major cities were extended and improved somewhat. The Tihama Development Authority was established and the first of its projects to expand irrigated farming was brought to the implementation stage. Preliminary planning also began on a number of other large agricultural schemes.

The regime made no serious attempt at popular organization, and it dealt sternly with efforts of this sort by others. Its leading figures often publicly expressed the view that in the Yemeni context political parties were bad, unnecessary, or both. The regime early banned all parties, and the ban remained in effect during its tenure; on two occasions—1968 and 1972–73—it took sternly repressive measures against parties and partisan activity.

The flurry of leftist activity at the outset of the al-Iryani era served to reinforce the instincts of the regime to view partisan activity with suspicion. The Arab Nationalist Movement had re-emerged at that time and was helping to defend the republic against the royalist offensive that followed the withdrawal of Egyptian forces in late 1967. The ANM was aided in these efforts by the National Liberation Front (NLF), which had just wrested power from the British in Aden; the NLF, an outgrowth of the old ANM, gave what little support it could to the YAR during these turbulent months because it feared that a royalist victory in the north might threaten its precarious position in Aden. The ANM in Sanaa manned and armed part of the Popular Resistance Forces (PRF), the citizens' militia created to defend the capital against the royalists during the siege of Sanaa in early 1968. At about the same time, it took the lead in organizing units of the PRF in Taiz, al-Hudayda, and the large towns. Seeking to radicalize as well as defend the republic, the ANM also organized a number of peasant leagues in the countryside. Although most of them demanded modest reforms, in a couple of areas the leagues arrested landlords and declared an end to the power of the local sheikhs.

The first of two confrontations between the al-Iryani regime and the partisans occurred after the siege of Sanaa was broken in February 1968. The main burden of defending Sanaa had fallen on young Shafi officers and troops, many of whom had been influenced by the progressive ideas of the ANM and of the NLF regime in Aden. Heady with their recent victory, the more militant of the defenders of Sanaa began openly to express their desire to move the republic into the mainstream of revolutionary Arab nationalism. Opposed to both the royalists and the republican tribalists, they rejected Arab efforts to secure a compromise settlement of the civil war, called for a strengthening of the professional army and of the PRF, and demanded Shafi equality with the Zaydis in the government. For their part, the conservative and traditional elements in the al-Iryani regime became increasingly alarmed by these ideas and more determined than ever to eliminate the partisans from the political arena. The arrival of a shipload of Soviet arms at al-Hudayda in March 1968 was the occasion for an initial test of strength, each side being intent on preventing the arms from falling into the hands of the other. In the brief armed skirmish that ensued, forces loyal to the regime prevailed over ANM-inspired elements of the PRF. Throughout the spring and summer of 1968, the lines were more sharply drawn between the two sides, and each worked to prepare itself for the expected showdown. The left tried to regroup, and in June ANM elements created a new political party, the Revolutionary Democratic party. On their side, conservative politicians and tribal leaders met in July and adopted a plan to purge the left and leftist ideas from the YAR. Earlier, concerned about the influence of the NLF in the southeastern border area of the YAR, the government had given the Front for the Liberation of Occupied South Yemen (FLOSY) permission to conduct anti-NLF activities from Taiz. The FLOSY had just lost out to the NLF in the struggle to be the political heir to Britain in Aden. The government's replacement of a handful of young Shafi commanders provided the spark that ignited the Sanaa mutiny, a bloody three-day battle in August 1968 in which army and tribal elements loyal to the regime smashed the challenge from the left. In the next several months the regime consolidated its position by purging the armed forces, banning the trade unions and the new Revolutionary Democratic party, and dissolving the peasant leagues and the PRF. Hundreds of militants were arrested, exiled, or forced to flee to Aden. With the left driven underground or abroad, the center of gravity of the al-Iryani regime shifted in an even more conservative and traditional direction.

The second confrontation between the regime and the partisans was the domestic political correlate of conflict in 1972 and 1973 between Saudi Arabia, the YAR, and the NLF regime in Aden. Relations between the YAR and its southern neighbor, renamed in 1970 the People's Democratic Republic of Yemen (PDRY), became increasingly strained after 1969. Fanned by the revolutionary fervor of the NLF and especially by Saudi-backed efforts to raise a rebellion and overthrow the regime in the PDRY, the smoldering conflict between the two Yemens rose to a serious level early in 1972; it erupted in a brief border war in September of that year, and flared up again in the spring of 1973. The banned Revolutionary Democratic party reemerged in the YAR, and engaged in a program of underground political organizing and agitation in rural areas close to the border with the PDRY. The Organization of Yemeni Resisters, a group formed of ANM elements purged from the YAR army in 1968, made its first appearance at this time. The political activities of these two groups were accompanied by numerous acts of sabotage and violence by PDRY-supported guerrillas in the border area. In 1973, in response, the al-Iryani regime unleashed the harshest campaign of repression—arrests, imprisonments, and public executions—to occur during its tenure.

Despite its bias against the expansion of politics, the al-Iryani regime did make two attempts at political construction in the early 1970s. One was the creation of an official political organization, the ban of parties notwithstanding. Established in early 1973, the National Yemeni Union was proclaimed the political body for all Yemenis; its political bureau, topped by President al-Iryani, read as a "who's who" of YAR politics. Nevertheless, although accorded ample funds and high priority, the National Yemeni Union failed to develop to the point of having any lasting political impact. It never launched an organizing and indoctrination campaign among the people; indeed, it was not opened for membership until the spring of 1974, fifteen months after its creation. In retrospect the union was less an expression of a new commitment to political organization than a hastily designed attempt by the regime to preempt the political arena during the period of uncertainty following the agreement in late 1972 by the two Yemens to end their border war through political unification. As the prospect for unification receded, the leaders of the regime seemed quickly to lose interest in the party, and no one appeared to mourn its passing when it was abolished in 1974.

The other, far more important act of political construction in this period was the creation of the Consultative Council. The YAR's first permanent constitution, proclaimed by President al-Iryani in December 1970, provided for a 179-member legislature, with 159 members elected indirectly and the remainder appointed by the president. National elections, another first for the YAR, were held in March 1971, and the Consultative Council was convened for its initial session in the following month.

The Consultative Council was a council of notables, not unlike early English parliaments. In the absence of explicit party organization and ideology, the members were grouped in shifting factions and only tenuously linked to one another and to their constituents. As a result of some fraud and a districting system skewed toward rural and tribal areas, the majority of the members were tribal sheikhs or other local notables with conservative orientations or connections. While not a sovereign law-making body in the Western parliamentary sense, the Consultative Council nonetheless did have real powers, among them the powers to withdraw confidence from the government and to refuse to give its assent to proposed legislation and the budget. As governance under the new constitutional system settled into a more regularized pattern, the council asserted its prerogatives and became an increasingly powerful institution. Its members soon learned to use their votes to secure for themselves material benefits, influence, and deference. As a consequence, the council had by 1973 become the chief symbol and a key instrument of the power of the tribal sheikhs on the national level.

The rising influence of the council and its members was not unrelated to the fact that since its inception its speaker was Abdullah ibn Hussein al-Ahmar, paramount sheikh of the Hashid confederation, the most powerful tribal grouping in Yemen. A tribal aristocrat and sure of his prerogatives, Sheikh al-Ahmar moved easily between his tribal and government positions, and derived symbolic and tangible benefits from each. The acknowledged national spokesman for the tribalists, he shared in the inner deliberations of the al-Iryani regime. An additional source of his influence in government circles was his close patron-client relationship with Saudi Arabia, a relationship both he and the Saudis valued highly and took care to maintain.

The Undoing of the al-Iryani Regime

The seeds of the collapse of the al-Iryani regime lay in the fundamental contradiction between its traditionalist foundations and the need for—and the growing possibility of—additional state-building and modernization. The domestic political constraints on these processes became more apparent and significant after 1972, as remittances from Yemenis working abroad, budget subsidies from Saudi Arabia, and foreign economic assistance combined to resolve the YAR's immediate financial crisis.

The resolution of the contradiction between the tribalized political system and the requirements of progress might have been deferred or achieved less dramatically had it not been for the 1972–73 conflict between the two Yemens. Although that conflict diverted attention from development and placed new strains on the

YAR's limited resources, these considerations were secondary in importance to the way in which it exposed the underlying defects of the Yemeni state and political system. What stood out most clearly was the utter powerlessness of the state to prevent the tribal periphery, with Saudi Arabia's encouragement and assistance, from dragging the YAR into armed conflict with the PDRY. Unable to defend the borders and to control events inside those borders, the central government and the armed forces were for the most part helpless bystanders in a conflict in which Saudi Arabia used Yemeni tribalists as its surrogates in peninsular politics.

Although discredited by the PDRY's rout of their irregular forces in the fall of 1972, the tribal leaders reached the apogee of their power in 1973–74. In part this was because the state and the armed forces had in their impotence discredited themselves to an even greater degree. More important than this was the sharp decline in the prestige and influence of President al-Iryani, a crucial development in light of the vital role he had played as the bridge between various groups—modernists and traditionalists, republicans and ex-royalists, civilian politicians and army officers. People of all political persuasions in the YAR began to question both the efficacy of his remaining in office and the viability of the political formula and system associated with his rule. The tribalists came to think that they could better protect their recent gains without him, and many modernists came to think that modernity could not be advanced with him. An important cause of President al-Iryani's growing powerlessness was Saudi Arabia's loss of confidence in him and its decision to place greater reliance on its tribal clients in Yemen, especially on Sheikh al-Ahmar. The withdrawal of Saudi and domestic support for the Yemeni head of state ushered in a period of political stalemate and drift. Uncertainties about the future, unbridled pursuit of self-interest, and a growing cynicism and lack of norms in public life gave Yemen an end-of-an-era flavor. By early 1974 many leading Yemenis sensed that the end was in fact near, and that a change was coming.

The al-Hamdi Era

President al-Iryani was sent gracefully into exile following a bloodless coup on June 13, 1974. The Command Council, composed of army officials and under the chairmanship of Colonel Ibrahim al-Hamdi, was created and assumed all legislative and executive powers. The council immediately suspended the 1970 constitution and the Consultative Council and dissolved outright the moribund National Yemeni Union. A new government was appointed several days later with the modernist politician Muhsin al-Aini as prime minister and foreign minister. It included several other modernists and several members of the preceding government.

Ibrahim al-Hamdi was in his mid-thirties at the time of the 1974 coup. The son of a respected judge, he had studied for and begun a traditional legal-administrative career only to switch to one in the military shortly after the 1962 revolution. A young man of known abilities and ambition, al-Hamdi rose quickly to public prominence in the last years of al-Iryani's rule. He served as deputy prime minister in 1972, and held the post of deputy commander in chief of the armed forces from 1973 until the time of the coup. He was also a leader in the growing cooperative movement, and as such became the first president of the Confederation of Yemeni Development Associations in 1973.

The June 13 Correction Movement, as the new regime was called, had most of the familiar earmarks of a protest against civilian misrule by young reform-minded officers. On the day of the coup, President al-Hamdi[9] explained that the military had assumed power both to end "exhaustive feuds" between President al-Iryani and the Consultative Council and to deal with the "collapse in the internal political situation, administrative slackness, and corruption in the bureaucracy."[10]

However, the nature and dynamics of the coup were far more complex than this. It had been promoted, if not engineered, by tribal and other conservative leaders who viewed the overthrow of the faltering al-Iryani regime as an opportunity to shore up the system from which they had derived so many benefits in recent years. At the center of this cluster of conspirators were Sinan abu Luhum and the major tribal sheikhs of the north, including Abdullah ibn Hussein al-Ahmar and Ali Ahmad al-Matari. In addition, the promoters of the coup had the blessings of Saudi Arabia.

The first eighteen months of the al-Hamdi era were dominated by a protracted and convoluted struggle for power. Behind the rhetoric and politicking lay important policy differences over relations with Saudi Arabia, sources of military aid, and restoration of the 1970 constitution and civilian rule; and behind these differences lurked the fundamental, unresolved issue of the relationship between President al-Hamdi and the politicians who initially backed his assumption of power. The struggle intensified as al-Hamdi became more assertive and made clear his intention to be more than an interim ruler or puppet, a development that did not fit the agendas of Muhsin al-Aini, Sinan abu Luhum, and Sheikh al-Ahmar.

President al-Hamdi's hold on power during the early months was extremely tenuous, and depended primarily upon key figures in the fragmented armed forces, most notably his brother, Abdullah al-Hamdi, commander of an elite brigade; Ahmad Hussein al-Ghashmi, the chief of staff; and Abdullah Abd al-Alim, commander of the paratroops and commandos. Although President al-Hamdi's personal popularity with the people grew quickly, this was not readily convertible into a political resource. For their part, the civilian modernists had little power to bring to bear on the struggle and, in any case, were divided in their assessment of the new regime. Some were suspicious of either or both the military and the involvement of the tribalists and the Saudis in the coup. Many of those who knew al-Hamdi well, and realized that he was a true nationalist with modernist views, thought that he would not dare to act against his promoters, and, if he did, would be swept from office.

The sequence of dramatic political events in 1975, beginning with the dismissal of Prime Minister al-Aini in January and ending with the final adjournment of the Consultative Council in October, ranks with the 1962 revolution and the overthrow of the al-Sallal regime as a major turning point in the modern history of Yemen. In a series of swift, deft moves, President al-Hamdi sharply curtailed the national political power of the most prominent tribal leaders. In so doing, he fundamentally changed the configuration of forces in Yemeni politics and altered the sociopolitical bases of the Yemeni state. At the time, many Yemenis who understood and approved of what the young president was doing followed his actions with awe and disbelief.

President al-Hamdi followed a divide-and-conquer strategy in his attempt to consolidate his power in 1975. The several months of political maneuvering between him and Prime Minister al-Aini ended with the abrupt replacement of the latter by Abd al-Aziz Abd al-Ghani in January. The move was widely interpreted at the time as a victory for Saudi Arabia and conservative elements in the YAR, and it is true that Saudi leaders were wary of al-Aini's Ba'th party ties, and that Sheikh al-Ahmar backed his dismissal. Nevertheless, President al-Hamdi acted primarily on his own initiative and for the purpose of eliminating from the scene a powerful competitor whom many Yemenis had given a better-than-even chance of outmaneuvering him after the coup.

In the early spring of 1975, and again with Sheikh al-Ahmar looking on benignly, President al-Hamdi acted to curtail the influence of Sinan abu Luhum and his power clan. In this instance, he probably played on traditional tribal enmities, and convinced al-Ahmar that Sinan, whose tribe is of the confederation that is the historic enemy of the Hashid confederation, had become powerful enough to pose a threat to his position as Yemen's leading tribalist.

Later in the spring Sheikh Ali Ahmad al-Matari, the leader whose tribal lands straddle the vital highway between Sanaa and al-Hudayda, tried to alert al-Ahmar and the other sheikhs to the necessity of closing ranks against al-Hamdi. Aware of these political activities, al-Hamdi moved quickly and seized the weapons caches of tribalists loyal to Sheikh al-Matari. Despite the vigorous opposition of the non-alarmed Sheikh al-Ahmar, he also removed Lieutenant Colonel Mujahid abu Shuwarib from an imposing array of key military and political posts, including those of deputy commander in chief, member of the Command Council, and governor of Hajja province. Majahid, a Hashid tribalist and brother-in-law of al-Ahmar, made his way secretly to Hajja, where he attempted to use the threat of a tribal uprising to regain his offices. Al-Hamdi stood his ground, and Mujahid was forced to back down after a month when the army garrison and other elements in Hajja refused to support him. Lieutenant Colonel Yahya al-Mutawakkal, who had opposed the dismissal of Mujahid, was in turn dismissed from the Command Council and from his post as interior minister in July.

The ouster of Mujahid abu Shuwarib in the spring of 1975 brought relations between President al-Hamdi and Sheikh al-Ahmar close to the breaking point and ushered in several months of muted political conflict. While al-Ahmar tried to rally the support of the tribes and other conservatives, President al-Hamdi sought both to strengthen his position in the armed forces and to convince the lesser sheikhs that his dispute was with the big sheikhs and not with the tribal system as such. Both antagonists sought support from Saudi Arabia in their struggle. Publicly, their differences centered on the issue of a return to constitutional government and elections for a new Consultative Council, Sheikh al-Ahmar's power base in the central government during the previous regime. Reversing a decision taken by the Command Council a month earlier, President al-Hamdi announced in May that the 1970 constitution would not be restored on the first anniversary of the June 13 coup; Sheikh al-Ahmar responded by pressing still harder for the early holding of the promised elections. The controversy was brought to a head in October 1975 with a bit of political theater on both sides. President al-Hamdi staged demonstrations against the old Consultative Council and its tribal members; and then, bowing to these expressions of the popular, he permanently adjourned the council and deferred the elections to an unspecified time in the future. At this point, al-Ahmar held a tribal convocation at which he publicly broke with al-Hamdi, deounced the regime as illegitimate, and called upon the tribes to unite behind him in open rebellion.

Sheikh al-Ahmar failed to gain the initiative, for many of the tribes were unresponsive to his call. Consequently, a long "no war, no peace" standoff began between the state and those tribes that exercise control over large areas of the north and east of Yemen. Saudi Arabia worked to stabilize the stalemate by providing each side with aid on condition that it not act to eliminate the other by force of arms. Nevertheless, time seemed to be on President al-Hamdi's side throughout 1976 and early 1977. He refused to allow the armed forces to be drawn into a major military campaign that would be hard to win and that could serve to unite the other tribes against him. His strategy was to isolate and to ignore the quasi-rebellion, and to devote the resources of the state to the development of those areas of the country that were under his control and recognized his authority. He anticipated that with time tribesmen in the "land of insolence" would come to see the relationship between their future well-being and allegiance to the state, and would either depose their present sheikhs or force them to end the rebellion and come to terms with the state. On occasion, al-Hamdi used small incidents as "carrot-and-stick" object lessons. When tribal elements in the Arab area challenged the state in the spring of 1976, the regime unleashed a strong military assault on the guilty parties. President al-Hamdi insisted that the responsible local sheikhs come before him in Sanaa to pledge allegiance to the state and to present the grievances of their followers; he then accepted their pledge and ordered the government to act quickly on the grievances. Some Yemenis began to refer to the "Arab model" in discussing al-Hamdi's strategy toward the rebellious tribes.

After a year of relative calm, the largely cold war between the tribes and the state heated up noticeably during the first half of 1977. Apparently at the instigation of Sinan abu Luhum, a group of tribal leaders met in the north in early January in order to mount a renewed effort to organize opposition to the al-Hamdi regime. The tribalists denounced the regime as "communist and atheist," threatened it with "holy war," drew up a list of demands and grievances, and established an "information and mobilization council" to advance their cause. In February an attempt by Saudi Arabia to reconcile the differences between President al-Hamdi and Sheikh al-Ahmar failed when the former refused to accede to some of the latter's demands for the restoration of tribal leaders to prominent positions in the central government. Thereafter, acts of harassment and defiance by tribalists against the armed forces and other agencies of the state increased in number and severity. By the spring of 1977 Sanaa was full of ominous rumors about the growing threat of tribal rebellion and about the likelihood that an impatient President al-Hamdi would soon take vigorous action against the tribalists. These predictions seemed to be coming to pass in the early summer when the regime responded to provocations in the northern towns of Saada and Khamr—Sheikh al-Ahmar's home—by mobilizing armored units and sending planes against targets in the north. Tensions eased suddenly in July, probably because of Saudi intervention, and the stalemate between the tribes and the state appeared reestablished.

At the other end of the political spectrum, relations of the al-Hamdi regime with the partisans and the progressive parties during the three years following the 1974 coup were more ambiguous and less dramatic than those with the tribalists. The official ban on political parties remained in effect, and the regime often warned the partisans against open activity and occasionally—for example, in the summer of 1976—subjected them to harassment and arrest. Moreover, the paratroop and commando forces under Lieutenant Colonel Abd al-Alim carried out a successful program of pacification and local development in order to lessen the influence of the partisans in the countryside near the border with the PDRY. In balance, however, the al-Hamdi regime did not deal harshly with the progressive parties. Al-Hamdi maintained personal contact with some of the partisan leaders and turned a blind eye to most of their barely clandestine activities.

On their side, most of the partisans respected President al-Hamdi for his nationalism and his commitment to national strength and development, and they warmly applauded his actions against the tribalists. Many of the younger partisans were won over to the regime by al-Hamdi's offer of important positions in the national effort. The leaders of the progressive parties hoped and campaigned for a formal partnership with President al-Hamdi as a way back into the political system from which they had been expelled in 1968. In part with this in mind, six of the parties announced in mid-1976 the formation of the National Democratic Front. The six parties—the Revolutionary Democratic party, the Organization of Yemeni Resisters, the Labor party, the Popular Democratic Union, and the two wings of the Yemeni Ba'th party—declared their desire to collaborate with President al-Hamdi and issued a moderate program calling for more planning, a stronger state, and greater independence for the YAR.

State-Building and Modernization under al-Hamdi

The surgical operations performed by President al-Hamdi on the political system in 1975 were designed primarily to strengthen his precarious position. A secondary effect, perhaps unintended, was the relaxation of some of the domestic political constraints that had served to thwart or distort efforts at state-building and modernization during the al-Iryani era. As one minister said with satisfaction in 1976: "A small group of us—ten to fifteen in number—are free for the first time to make and act on decisions affecting development. We are having an impact."[11]

Prime Minister Abd al-Ghani and his fellow technocrats did not have an independent political base, individually or collectively. They depended for their positions and decision-making freedom upon President al-Hamdi and his military colleagues. Despite the predictable irritations between the two groups, however, each respected and realized its need for the other. Both regarded state-building as the primary task of the current phase of the YAR's development and both recognized the need to strengthen the state at the center and to increase its capabilities to reach and have an impact on the periphery. Their strategy was to increase the capacity of the state to deliver services and then to exchange those services for allegiance to the state, a quid pro quo designed both to advance modernization and to strengthen the state.

Potentially the most far-reaching act of state-building during the al-Hamdi era involved steps toward the modernization of the armed forces. President al-Hamdi was aware that he depended for his position largely upon the more professional elements in the armed forces, and that their continued support depended upon his satisfying their desires for a stronger, more modern military establishment.

Throughout the al-Iryani era, attempts to reequip and to reorganize the military had been blocked or delayed for a variety of political reasons, most often because of the understandable reluctance of the tribal leaders. Thereafter, a modest armed forces modernization plan prepared near the end of the al-Iryani era had to wait for implementation until President al-Hamdi ousted Prime Minister al-Aini and purged the tribal officers in early 1975. This done, the Abu Dhabi-financed program to use Jordanian military advisers to introduce modern methods of management, administration, and communications proceeded apace through 1976. Although important, this effort to make the army more efficient and businesslike did not attack its main organizational defect: the fact that the army, even after the purge of tribal officers, consisted of a large number of relatively self-contained fighting units—little armies within the army. Despite shakeups in command, some of these units continued to have parochial loyalties and to serve as power centers for contending factions. In short, the army remained something other than a unified instrument of state power. To correct this situation, the Command Council adopted a major plan in 1976 that envisaged the reorganization of the army into a smaller number of more interdependent units. Implementation of this plan was delayed because of its great sensitivity; it had real power implications, both inside and outside the army, and promised at the very least to affect the careers of many senior officers. Moreover, President al-Hamdi's efforts to end the fragmentation and competition within the army through reorganization were complicated by the fact that he had gained power through the support of some of the units whose power the new plan would curtail, including the brigade led by his brother.

The military assistance agreement between the United States and the YAR, approved in the summer of 1976, provided President al-Hamdi with some of the leverage he needed to effect the reorganization of the army. The agreement, financed by Saudi Arabia and valued at $139 million, provided for the rearming and general reequipment of a number of infantry battalions. Although the agreement was modest in scope, official U.S. sources indicated that it was only the first of a number of military aid agreements foreseen for the two countries; indeed, negotiations were already under way in 1977 on a second triangular deal that would involve F-5E planes and other heavy weapons. Most observers in 1977 felt that the reorganization and reequipment of the armed forces, if carried through as expected, would both strengthen President al-Hamdi's links with those forces and tilt the balance of military power between the state and the tribes decidedly in favor of the former.

The armed forces were not the al-Hamdi regime's only target of reform. Prime Minister Abd al-Ghani made a major effort to develop and modernize the courts and the legal system. A plan to reorganize the hierarchy of courts and to revise the procedures for selecting and disciplining judges, prepared before the al-Hamdi coup, was revived in 1975 and put into effect by decree in the spring of 1976. In a more important effort at legal reform, the government adopted the YAR's first commercial law code in mid-1975; a team of Sudanese judges arrived in 1976 to set up and initially operate the new commercial courts.

The Abd al-Ghani government was working in 1976 on a number of fronts to increase the administrative capabilities of the largely unreformed and archaic state bureaucracy. As early as 1973 leading modernists had concluded that advances in public finance and planning would come to naught as long as the ministries and other government agencies in Sanaa and the provinces lacked the skills required to implement programs and make efficient use of revenues. At about the same time, the Central Planning Organization and the United Nations Development Program put together a package of institutional support projects designed to introduce teams of foreign experts into selected government agencies.

In late 1975 the Abd al-Ghani government initiated an effort to increase the ability of the state to extract taxes and other revenues. To begin to remedy a situation in which taxes amounted to less than 10 percent of Gross Domestic Product, the government reorganized the Tax Office and the Customs Office and replaced many of the old functionaries in these two offices with new graduates. In another move a team of tax experts from the International Monetary Fund (IMF) was attached to the new Ministry of Finance, which only two years earlier had begun to subject government expenditures to formal budgetary procedures.

Favorable economic conditions joined with the political changes to make possible modest gains in modernization during the three years after al-Hamdi came to power. The financial constraints on development activities eased considerably as a result of an increase in the Saudi budget subsidy, the dramatic rise in external development aid, and the massive inflow of remittances of Yemenis working in Saudi Arabia and elsewhere. Remittances alone more than doubled from $225 million in 1974–75, to $525 million in 1975–76, and were estimated to be growing at an even faster rate in 1976–77. This torrent of money made it possible for the YAR to build up a sizable balance-of-payments surplus over this period, despite negligible exports and a fourfold increase in imports. By mid-1977 the increasing supply of imported consumer goods and the boom in commercial and residential construction were everywhere evident in the cities and even in places in the countryside.

As in the last years of President al-Iryani's tenure, government development activities during the al-Hamdi era focused primarily upon basic infrastructure. Considerable emphasis was also, however, placed upon providing health, education, and other basic services. Sanaa University, created in 1970, underwent rapid expansion. Light industry and most commercial activity, largely left to the private sector, thrived and grew apace.

Political Construction under al-Hamdi

Al-Hamdi's behavior after the 1974 coup provides an unclear index of his concern for political construction. Elections to a new legislature were not held, and the 1970 constitution was not reinstated, amended, or replaced. The Command Council, declared at the time of the coup to be an interim body during a transitional phase, remained the sole repository of legislative and executive authority; and even the council existed only in a formal sense by 1976, its membership reduced by political attrition to only al-Hamdi and three others. More and more, the regime revolved around al-Hamdi, in fact as well as in the popular imagination.

Al-Hamdi's wariness of politics was especially evident in his dealing with the National Democratic Front (NDF) created by the progressive parties in 1976. As a young army officer he had been associated with the Yemeni wing of the Arab Nationalist Movement before it was forced underground following its confrontation with the conservative republicans in 1968; he had kept his personal ties with many of the partisan leaders after he went his separate political way, and he continued to do so after he assumed power in 1974. When apprised by partisans in 1976 of their intentions to launch the NDF, he reportedly did not discourage them; indeed, some say he gave them encouragement. In the year after the formation of the NDF, however, he did not acknowledge its existence, much less endorse it in public. In his wooing and warning of the partisans, al-Hamdi seems to have been trying to keep them at once powerless and unalienated, until such time as he could decide what role—if any—they might safely be allowed to play in the political system. Perhaps he hoped with time to win over the partisans individually, rather than deal with them as a group with its own political organization and agenda. In any case, there is no evidence to suggest that he seriously considered the reincorporation of the progressive parties as such into the political system of the YAR.

The political implications of al-Hamdi's deep involvement in both the Confederation of Yemeni Development Associations (CYDA) and the Correction Movement are also ambiguous. The Local Development Association (LDA) movement began with the founding of a cooperative in al-Hudayda just before the 1962 revolution and a second one in Taiz in the mid-1960s. The movement, rooted in a Yemeni tradition of local self-help and funded by local taxes and foreign gifts, spread rapidly by example throughout the southern provinces of the YAR in the early 1970s. Ibrahim al-Hamdi was an early convert to the LDA movement and established the first LDA in the rural north of the country in the middle of the al-Iryani era.

When the spread of the movement led to talk of a national organization, it was Colonel al-Hamdi who seized the initiative from others and orchestrated the creation of CYDA in 1973; he was elected its first president late that year and retained that post after the 1974 coup.

The Correction Movement, a subsequent initiative, was viewed by some Yemenis as primarily a device to generate a new political structure. The movement was launched in June 1975, on the first anniversary of the al-Hamdi coup, and marked a return to the regime's initial theme of combatting administrative inefficiency and corruption. The higher Correction Committee was set up and charged with the task of forcing the public and mixed public-private bureaucracies to end their isolation from the people and to meet popular needs and desires, and correction committees were established for this purpose in each of the provinces.

The histories of CYDA and the Correction Movement raise as many questions as they answer with regard to al-Hamdi's involvement in political construction. Yemeni observers noted a waxing and waning of his commitment and attention to these major organizational efforts. It has been suggested that the results of the local development board elections in 1975 dampened his enthusiasm for the LDA movement and caused him to rethink the prudence and efficacy of using it as the basis of a grass-roots political organization. Although conservative local notables lost control of many of the development boards, a result desired by al-Hamdi, the victors in some instances were leftist partisans who were not identified with the al-Hamdi regime; indeed, in a few cases, candidates who were explicitly pro-regime were defeated by the partisans linked to the Revolutionary Democratic party. Whether or not these election results did cause him to have second thoughts, President al-Hamdi was less publicly involved in the LDA movement after 1975 than previously. Moreover, he felt compelled in the summer of 1976 to lecture CYDA and the local development boards on the need to focus on development and to stay out of politics.

The fact that the Correction Movement was promoted heavily by the regime for the first time in the fall of 1975, only several weeks after the mixed results of the LDA elections were in, has been interpreted by some Yemenis as evidence of a decision by President al-Hamdi to build his political base on that movement instead of on the LDAS. Even here, however, his initial enthusiasm was not followed by sustained attention and promotion during the several months before and after the first national Correction Movement conference in mid-1976. Even allowing for the many other demands on him, President al-Hamdi's sporadic, if not halfhearted, involvement in CYDA and the Correction Movement in 1976 and 1977 suggests either that he did not place high priority on political construction at that time or that he questioned the appropriateness of these organizations' means to this end.

In early 1977 al-Hamdi announced plans to convene a General People's Congress in al-Hudayda in the summer of that year. According to official statements, the congress was to bring together several thousand delegates selected by the LDAS, the Correction Movement, and other Yemeni organizations. The declared purpose of the congress would be to review the experience of the YAR since the 1962 revolution and chart the future course of the republic. Some Yemenis interpreted this to mean that the congress would propose the drafting of a new constitution. It also suggested that the results of the congress would be used as the basis of a nationwide political education campaign, and that this would be followed in turn by a national plebiscite and national elections. Skeptics, however, found significance in the fact that the congress was soon postponed from the summer until sometime later in the year.

The Demise of the al-Hamdi Regime

Sanaa was infused with optimism around the time of the September 26 Revolution Day celebrations in 1977. Most observers agreed that the YAR's current economic situation and longer-term development prospects were bright: workers' remittances were flowing in like a torrent, and the YAR's public and private sectors seemed increasingly able to take advantage of this new bounty. Political prospects were also judged to be relatively bright. It was widely rumored that the on-again-off-again reconciliation between the state and the tribes—between President al-Hamdi and Sheikh al-Ahmar—was imminent, and that it would be effected on terms favorable to al-Hamdi and with the blessings of Saudi Arabia. The YAR's relations with its Yemeni brothers in the PDRY were regarded as cordial and improving.

The mood changed swiftly to one of profound uncertainty when on the evening of October 11 President al-Hamdi and his brother, Abdullah, were cut down by assassins. The conflicting and often bizarre accounts of the event gave way over following weeks to a widely held belief that the assassination was the work of a small group of senior army officers acting with the prior knowledge and probable encouragement of persons high in the Saudi regime who had become uneasy over al-Hamdi's increasing independence and moves to improve ties with the PDRY. Although this is probably true, it is likely that the officers acted less on behalf of Saudi patrons than out of the belief that they had better get al-Hamdi before he got them in the course of this effort to reform and secure the loyalty of the armed forces. It seems that fear and suspicion had come to pervade the highest reaches of the regime, with a corrosive effect on the network of personal relations upon which al-Hamdi's position depended.

Deputy Commander in Chief and Chief of Staff Ahmad al-Ghashmi promptly assumed the post of chairman of the Command Council, called upon the nation for calm, and pledged to continue the course of the June 13 Correction Movement. Despite minor mutinies by al-Hamdi supporters, and their subsequent purge or flight, the political system of the YAR was marked by a relative calm during the months following the assassination. Nevertheless, fear persisted that the YAR was in store for turmoil and instability, and that this would shatter the fragile prosperity and development gains of the previous few years. These fears were not allayed by the assassination of President al-Ghashmi in June 1978, after only eight months in office, and by the assumption of the presidency by a young and little-known army officer, Ali Abdullah Salih. The killing of al-Ghashmi apparently was the work of a faction in the PDRY regime and had less to do with the domestic politics of the YAR or the relations between the two Yemens than with a fierce internal power struggle in the PDRY. Nevertheless, it did not bode well for politics within the YAR or between the two Yemens.

Conclusion

During his short tenure, the dynamic and charismatic al-Hamdi fostered a political environment—an ethos and set of power relationships—that sustained and accelerated the prosperity and development activity begun during the al-Iryani era. He tilted the political balance in favor of the modernists and the modern sector, and he came to personify national strength and development in the minds of many Yemenis.

However, like his two predecessors, al-Hamdi left to the future the task of political construction in the YAR. His personalist regime was not institutionalized at the top and had very shallow and amorphous political underpinnings. He failed to foster a strong leadership structure and to generate a political organization capable of reaching down into the society. In short, he ran what was increasingly a one-man show. Al-Hamdi's greatest state building accomplishment remains his effort to expel from the state and hold at bay the leading tribalists. Although many of the tribalists were gradually reincorporated into the regime in the early 1980s, they were not readmitted to the same degree or on the same terms as during the tenure of al-Iryani—nor is it likely that they will be in the future. Nevertheless, al-Hamdi's considerable political achievement was of an essentially negative sort. His change in the political equation was more an act of destruction than of construction: while he eliminated powerful enemies, he did not aggregate and organize powerful supporters. As a result, he created a political vacuum, or, as a Britisher close to Yemeni politics observed, he "hollowed out" the political system.[12] It is to the remedy of this situation that the regime of Ali Abdullah Salih has addressed itself with some success in the 1980s.[13]

PART 3

Marxist Movements and Governments

■

THE NON-COMMUNIST LEFT IN IRAN

The Case of the Mujahidin

■

Sepehr Zabih

In the violent struggle to determine the nature of the Iranian political system since the beginning of the present century, three ideological orientations have been dominant: in the 1905–11 constitutional movement, nationalism with a heavy emphasis on Western-oriented secularism was at once challenged by—and mixed with—political Shiism. The rise of communism and the Bolshevik Revolution introduced a third ideology. These competing, and occasionally complementary, ideologies have twice given rise to revolutionary upheavals: once in the early 1950s, when Dr. Muhammad Musaddeq seized power as a representative of secular Anglophobic nationalism (initially in league with the politicized Shiite clergy and subsequently in opposition to them),[1] and again in 1978–79, when the three ideologies joined to overthrow the Pahlavi dynasty.

There are many accounts of the genesis of the People's Mujahidin, a movement that integrates radical Shiism with elements drawn from Marxism. These accounts usually fall into one of four categories. Some are written by sympathetic Iranian scholars who have done little or no field work in the country either before or since the revolution. Others are basically self-appraisals by the organization, written for purposes of propaganda and public relations. Still others are by opponents of the Mujahidin who have an almost paranoid fear of the group, seeing it as a synthesis of the worst of communism with the most evil features of Shiite fundamentalism. A fourth source of information about the party is the records of the trials of its leaders under the shah and, more frequent and revealing, under Khomeini.[2]

Sorting out fact from fiction is extremely difficult, especially for the 1981–82 period, when the organization was locked into a life-and-death battle with the Khomeini theocracy, but the following facts are largely indisputable. Prior to and immediately after the June 1963 religious uprising, which was easily crushed by the government, the idea of forming a new and more effective antigovernment political organization began to take shape among groups known for their nationalistic, liberal, and religiously progressive ideas. These groups had been haunted by the shah's security forces since the fall of the National Front government in 1953. They resurfaced briefly in the early 1960s, when American pressure convinced the shah to form a less repressive government under Dr. Ali Amini, which was subsequently to preside over some major land and other social reforms. All of the opposition groups took advantage of the relative thaw, among them the National Front and its more radical and less secular offshoot, Nehzate Azadiye Iran (Iran's Liberation Movement), led by Mehdi Bazargan (the post-shah provisional head of government).

The June 1963 religious uprising and the severity of government reprisals against the basically fundamentalist Shiite insurgents and their followers among the lower middle classes and the bazaaris quickly put an end to the resurgence of legitimate opposition. In defeat, however, the opposition forces arrived at several important conclusions. The uprising made them realize that (1) with even minimum planning, Shiism's martyrdom philosophy was ripe for exploitation for revolutionary ends, as witnessed by thousands of chanting religious zealots who had literally rushed toward firing machine-guns and laid their bodies in front of the advancing tanks of the shah's army; (2) secular opposition groups such as the National Front and the by then discredited pro-Soviet Tudeh party could not be trusted to do battle against the well-armed security forces; (3) the ease with which these forces were able to crush the uprising stemmed from the opposition's inexperience in armed struggle and the absence of a sufficient number of trained cadres.

The first to draw logical conclusions from the above premises were Saeed Muhsen, Muhammad Hanifnejad, and Aliasghar Badizadegan, all three affiliated with the Center for Islamic Propaganda, an organization founded in the early 1960s by a group of politically active Iranians in the holy city of Mashhad. On September 6, 1965, they founded the Mujahidin. Soon thereafter the founding members swelled from three to twelve, including Masud Rajavi, the Rezai brothers, and at least two young women.

They were convinced that neither nationalism as a broad ideology, nor communism as a pro-Soviet doctrine, was sufficient to evoke sustained response among politically articulate Iranians. They also believed, in view of the severe repression to which dissidents were then subjected, that it was suicidal to wage another mass protest against the shah. What was needed was a clandestine organization with a front such as the Center for Islamic Propaganda for protection. It could also not be simply an affiliate of the existing opposition groups because more often than not they had manifested their ineffectiveness. The National Front had been discredited in the early sixties, while the Tudeh or the Fedayeen Islam were marked as pawns of one or another foreign power.

Additionally, it was decided that the new organization had to appeal to two important political sentiments—radical Shiism and non-Soviet Marxism. The first, because past experience showed that radical Shiism could be used to generate extremely effective political actions, ranging from a shutdown of the entire bazaar to mass hunger strikes, and ultimately to acts of violence. The second, because politically articulate Iranians, especially of the lower middle class or even of the lower echelons of the upper class, had shown consistent susceptibility to leftist radicalism. Even though pro-Soviet communism was discredited, many educated Iranians seemed to respond positively to some variety of Marxism.[3]

Thus the founders of the Mujahidin convinced themselves that a Marxist-Islamic ideology would fill the political vacuum that had existed in Iran for nearly ten years. It is important to note that the original leaders of the group never publicly acknowledged that such was the group's ideology. For tactical reasons they always deemphasized, even denied, the Marxist strand, until several trials forced some of them to take a public stand on the issue.

The organization attracted followers throughout the country almost immediately after its formation. From the outset it acquired considerable support in Mashhad, and then spread its activity to Tehran, Tabriz, Shiraz, Isfahan, and Adadan. Between 1965 and 1978 the Mujahidin were implicated in at least 374 violent political acts. The Savak (Persian acronym for State Security and Intelligence Organization) had a mixed record in coping with this new and potentially threatening underground movement. Frequently, when Mujahidin cadres had been gunned down in street battles or executed after a trial before a military tribunal, the Savak would announce the total eradication of the group. Just as frequently the Mujahidin would make a comeback with spectacular acts of political terrorism against government officials and, often, U.S. military advisers to the Iranian army.

Two factors compounded the usual problems of intelligence and counterintelligence for the Savak. One was the Mujahidin's cover of religious education and Shiite theological training. In the late 1960s and early 1970s many local mosques throughout Iran had become the headquarters for Husseiniyeh Ershad (Shiite term for enlightenment in Imam Hussein's teachings). After Friday prayer, scholars and often ordinary people such as students, teachers, and even government employees, would participate in lecture-format seminars designed to teach the "overall" significance of Imam Hussein's martyrdom. The seminars' real purpose was to convince the faithful that Islam, especially its Shiite denomination, was an all-inclusive ideology with answers and solutions, including political actions, to all aspects of man's life. These forums, which were tolerated by the government for a few years, became the main vehicle of the Mujahidin's propaganda and mobilization efforts.

Dr. Ali Shariati, one of the early ideologues of the Mujahidin, led one such Husseiniyeh Ershad in Tehran. It was closed down when Savak agents realized the effectiveness of this mobilization of fairly representative cross sections of the urban population through a local mosque.[4] When that vehicle was denied them, the Mujahidin concentrated on infiltrating the bazaar and major universities and colleges, even high schools.

The second factor causing special problems for the Savak was the transnational dimension of the Mujahidin organization, which in the late 1960s and early 1970s began to establish close links to radical opposition groups in the Arab Middle East, among them the PLO. After the 1979 revolution the Mujahidin not only acknowledged these links, which included training in guerrilla camps and receiving supplies of weapons and explosives, but boasted of participation on the side of the PLO in the Black September War against the Jordanian army in 1970.[5] It was not until 1975, when an Iran-Iraq rapprochement was affected, that Iraq terminated its long-standing policy of aiding and abetting the shah's enemies, above all the Mujahidin. The PLO and radical Shiite groups in Lebanon such as the Amal persisted in their support for these organizations to the end of the shah's rule.

Ideological and Organizational Problems

The Mujahidin did not succeed in maintaining ideological uniformity during their struggle against the shah. Both the Marxist and the Islamic "progressive" components of the movement's ideology were the subjects of considerable disagreement, which the Savak skillfully exploited for its own purposes. Some Mujahidin cadres believed that espousing even non-Soviet Marxism in a country adjacent to the USSR, with its long tradition of support for Moscow-directed groups such as the Tudeh party, was simply not acceptable. Furthermore, if Marxism had to be embraced, why not join the People's Fedayeen (then not supported by the USSR), which in many ways, and above all in its acceptance of armed struggle, was similar to their own organization? Mujahidin cadres with more pronounced Islamic sentiments thought the espousal of even the most watered-down brand of Marxism would make it impossible for the group to make sufficient inroads in the bazaar and in other traditionally religious lower-middle-class groups.

These ideological divisions do not appear to have seriously impeded the Mujahidin's ability to plan and carry out acts of violent resistance. Data that became available after the 1979 revolution show that between 1966 and 1978, either alone or in conjunction with the Fedayeen, they conducted 1,153 violent acts, ranging from sabotage and kidnapping to ambush killings of U.S. military advisers and military judges, disarming of isolated military and gendarmerie outposts, and blowing up bridges and oil and gas pump stations. During this period at least fifty-seven Mujahidin died, either in the course of armed struggles with Savak agents or as a result of trial and execution by military tribunals.

Scrutiny of Mujahidin casualties indicates that about 65 percent of them were university students or recent graduates in such fields as engineering, medicine, business, and accounting, while the rest were employees of government and private enterprises and small traders; 15 percent were young women ranging from eighteen to twenty-four years of age.[6]

In 1975, partly as a result of skillful Savak exploitation and partly owing to the inherent conflicts mentioned earlier, those who could no longer accept the Islamic components of Mujahidin ideology broke away to form a Trotskyite group named the Organization for the Struggle to Liberate Workers, often simply known as Peykar, or Struggle. The group was basically secular and, at least in its initial years—prior to 1978—it rejected violent struggle in favor of propaganda and mobilization efforts. It considered itself a genuine Marxist-Leninist organization, rejecting the Soviet-supported Tudeh party and another Marxist group known as Ranjbaran, or Toilers, with a pronounced Maoist orientation.[7]

Through the turbulent year 1978, the Mujahidin was one of the most radical organizations, with proven ability in guerrilla warfare. Thus Khomeini and his entourage both inside and outside Iran had no difficulty identifying with and supporting it. In the final stage of the revolutionary struggle a number of respected clerics recently released from prison also supported the Mujahidin. Among them was Mahmud Taleghani, a prominent secular and nationalist ayatollah with close ties to the late Dr. Musaddeq (his relations with Khomeini after the latter assumed supreme theocratic authority deteriorated to the point where his untimely death in September 1979 became suspect of foul play).

On January 4, 1979, the Mujahidin issued an eighteen-point declaration called the Minimum Expectation Program (MEP).[8] A comparison of the movement's later statements with the MEP shows a gradual de-Islamization stemming from the enmity of Khomeini and his fundamentalist associates toward the Mujahidin, as well as from the Islamic Republic's loss of credibility among many politicized Iranians. Such comparison also shows that once the Mujahidin declared war on Khomeini in June 1981, the group reversed its course and began to deemphasize the Marxist components of its action program. They did this because they wished to appeal to the better-educated Muslim Iranians, as well as to the non-leftist and nationalist groups whose support they needed for staging a massive popular uprising against the Islamic Republic.

The MEP did not specifically address the nature of the political system that the Mujahidin envisaged for Iran, but in supplementary editorials and commentaries the organization has advocated a "People's government of elected councils." Since the Persian term for council—Shora—is similar to the Russian term, soviet, many critics have charged the Mujahidin with espousal of a barely disguised communist system. While disavowing any admiration for the present Soviet system, the Mujahidin have in fact voiced support for a federative Marxist system akin to the Yugoslav model, even though their political literature is invariably imbued with Koranic and "truly" Islamic concepts and rhetoric.

In the economic field, the MEP demanded three specific measures:

1. All comprador investments must be appropriated. Foreign-owned colonialist banks that had plundered the nation must be closed down. Foreign-owned and comprador businesses, plants, and affiliated agricultural enterprises must be expropriated and handed over to the people, and the management of these operations handled by a staff council (comprising workers, clerical personnel, and a representative of the government).

2. National control must be established over all of the nation's natural resources, including petroleum. All colonialist agreements in this field must be terminated.

3. Large-scale investment enterprises whereby luxury industrial conglomerates were allowed to expand at the expense of moderately scaled and small industries must be avoided. Preference should be given to agriculture over industry, or healthy economic development and ideological channeling of technocrats and bureaucrats would be impossible.[9]

The Mujahidin program also included a strong pronouncement against a paper tiger army top-heavy with the latest weaponry. Using precious resources to build up an unwieldy facade of an army, it observed, was as unbalanced and misguided as allowing haphazard economic and social growth. Reviewing the main characteristics of a popular army, the MEP proposed that there be no undue distinctions of privileges within its ranks between enlisted men, NCOS, and commanders; and that there be a close structural relationship with the masses. The prototype for this kind of army, according to the MEP, was the model army of the early days of Islam, which was composed of soldiers and officers whose sole motivation was service to God and the people.

On the question of political freedoms and the rights of women and ethnic minorities, the Mujahidin stated that complete freedom of the press, the activity of political parties, and the holding of political rallies, irrespective of belief or ideological principles, would be granted:

> It is our firm Islamic belief that as long as different ideologies and viewpoints are founded on truth and in direct proportion to their sincerity in seeking justice and equity, they have no fear of their ideology being the object of debate. Of course, it should be made crystal clear that there are distinct demarcations between revolutionary freedom and democracy and the approach of liberalism and irresponsible capitalism, distinctions which cannot be ignored in any revolutionary system. As the Koran expresses it, "Do not follow that of which you have no knowledge or penetrating understanding." (Sura 17, Al-Isra', 36)

According to the Mujahidin, an examination of the lives of the Prophet and Imam Ali reveals no instances of either of them ever suppressing the viewpoints of any of their opponents. Imam Ali always stressed that he would never be the first to draw his sword or launch a conflict to counter the views of someone else, no matter how hostile the manner in which the opponents might present their views. Imam Ja'far Sadeq, the sixth imam of the Shiite sect, sat for hours while his ideological and philosophical opponents ranted and harangued him, never losing his patience and dignity or behaving in any way disrespectfully to them. If we believe that Islam is the highest path, say the Mujahidin, why should we feel threatened by other ideas and opinions?

On women's rights the MEP vowed absolute equality and total prohibition of exploitation and discrimination. This position, it was asserted, is part and parcel of the uncompromising *Tawhidi* (divine integration) worldview of Islam. Equal wages for equal work—in addition to special concessions for worker sisters in consideration of their particular needs—is the primary and fundamental principle in the Islamic defense of the rights of working women.

In another cardinal principle of their social program, the Mujahidin stated that peoples of different regions must be provided with full political rights to enjoy their own cultures within the framework of the overall unity, solidarity, and sovereignty of the country. They emphasized the fundamental tie between the "revolutionary and progressive national spirit of the Kurds and the national spirit of the heroic people of Iran as a whole." "If, however, Kurdish ethnic and regional interest is allowed to come in conflict with the national, anti-imperialist struggle of the country as a whole, the imperialists and the enemies of the Revolution will benefit. Therefore, the genuine Kurdish participants in the struggle should be conscious of accompanying their aspirations to assert the Kurdish identity with an emphatic condemnation of any tendency towards separatism or secessionism."

The Mujahidin's elaborate program for workers and peasants was spelled out in detail in the MEP. All antilabor regulations and legislation must be done away with, and new labor laws must be enacted based on the views of the workers. Housing must be provided for all workers, and the management of the Workers' Welfare Bank and other labor banks and funds must be turned over to the workers themselves. The administration of factories should be carried out by a council of representatives of the employer.

Like the workers, the oppressed Iranian peasants must not be forced to bear the debts incurred by governmental agencies of the Pahlavi regime. The lands that were usurped from the peasants by the institutions of that regime should be returned to the peasant owners. Basic technology and interest-free agricultural loans must be provided and a concerted effort must be made to encourage and provide the necessary conditions for the establishment of people's cooperatives.

The MEP outlined the following goals in foreign affairs:

1. A complete political and economic boycott of the racist governments of Israel and South Africa should be instituted. By the same token, assistance must be provided to liberation movements around the world.

2. Iran should withdraw from all humiliating imperialist agreements, open or secret, political or military, and join the United Nations's bloc of nonaligned nations.

The Mujahidin could not ascertain the degree of popular support for its program because it was denied the opportunity of free participation in elections or grass-roots activity between April 1979 and April 1981. Not only did it boycott the referendum on the Islamic Republic Constitution in December 1979, but Masud Rajavi, one of its prominent leaders, was forced to withdraw as a presidential candidate the following January. Nor was the organization able to elect a single member of its own slate in the elections to the majlis in March and May 1980. But as late as March 1981 it still avoided attacking Khomeini directly. Instead, the brunt of the Mujahidin attack was on the pro-Khomeini Islamic Republican party, whose overthrow was editorialized in the communications organ of the movement, the *Mujahid*, as the only road to salvation.

However, between April and June 1981, the Mujahidin moved rapidly toward an open struggle with Khomeini. The high point was the bloody street riots of June 20 protesting Banisadr's impeachment as president. A month later Masud Rajavi masterminded the spectacular flight to Paris of Banisadr, himself, and several air force officers. Rajavi, who survived Savak repression, explained that the decision to flee was reached when it became clear, with the bloody events of June 20, that the Khomeini regime had now started its own reign of terror against the Mujahidin organization. It was in the course of this incident that about twenty young girls protecting their fellow Mujahidin marchers were arrested and promptly executed. The Mujahidin had thought that, as during the anti-shah rallies and demonstrations, the security forces would be reluctant to fire on or otherwise mistreat a protective line of young, female Mujahids. The brutal treatment of the arrested females convinced them that the Pasdaran—the Revolutionary Guards—would show no mercy to Khomeini's opponents.[10]

Organization

In the course of over sixteen years of urban guerrilla warfare against first the shah's regime and then the Islamic Republic, the Mujahidin had been organized into two distinct networks of cells. The larger organization, now numbering perhaps several hundred thousand followers and sympathizers, is led by well-known public personalities. Apart from that network there is a shadow structure of secret leaders, each reportedly in charge of twelve-member action committees whose membership is a highly guarded secret and whose leadership rotates regularly.

This shadow organization made two significant decisions at the beginning of Khomeini's revolutionary regime. One was to refuse to give up their arms, the quantity of which had increased substantially as a result of the two-day street battle in Tehran on February 9–11, 1972. The other was to keep its shadow structure secret and acknowledge only the larger, public organization. The leaders of this second group, like Rajavi, Saadati, Muqaddam, and Khiyabani, surfaced as legitimate politicians when released from the shah's prisons, and for a time tried to secure some representation in the new regime's institutions.[11] When war was declared on the Islamic Republic in May 1981, after the Mujahidin rejected Khomeini's demand that they disarm, the organization returned to its practice of guerrilla warfare, except this time they had a larger following and much more experience in urban guerrilla warfare. Their following, according to Rajavi, extends to every walk of Iranian life, as demonstrated by the involvement of some air force officers in preparing the flight of Banisadr and Rajavi from Iran.

How directly and exclusively responsible the Mujahidin's secret cells were for the two devastating bomb blasts of June and August 1981 (which killed both President Rajai and Premier Bahonar) has not been ascertained. In the wake of the June blast at the IRP headquarters, Rajavi, still in hiding in Iran, refused to claim credit, although many knowledgeable observers were convinced that Mujahidin infiltrators were responsible.

What must be noted is the Mujahidin self-confidence in the justice of their cause and the inevitability of their ultimate success. In early September Banisadr claimed that he had ordered the Mujahidin not to assassinate Khomeini, for he did not wish to make a martyr of him. Indeed, why attempts to eliminate Khomeini have not been undertaken has been a puzzle to those who have been duly impressed by the Mujahidin's ability to plant their dedicated agents in the inner sanctum of the fundamentalist regime. Some reports have suggested that several such attempts were made in the summer of 1981. But the fact that Khomeini, unlike the assassinated Behesti, Rajai, and Bahonar, never leaves his residence in Jamaran in northern Tehran makes access to him more difficult.

The Mujahidin have been careful to demonstrate their reluctance to resort to violence. Violence as a means, according to Rajavi, was imposed on the organization only when Khomeini denied it every legitimate means of political activity. "Violence, bombing, and terror could not resolve Iran's problems, but it is Khomeini's terrorism that has pushed our people to armed resistance."

Since the ouster of Banisadr, the Mujahidin have been a bit more forthcoming about their political ideology. In early August 1981 Rajavi told the foreign press that the Covenant of Freedom and Independence signed with Banisadr incorporates the fundamental objectives of his organization.[12]

"First, we want freedom for all political parties. We reject both political prisoners and political executions. In the true spirit of Islam, we advocate freedom, fraternity, and an end to all repression, censorship, and injustices." As to Khomeini's claim of representing the totality, or even the majority of the Shiite clergy, the Mujahidin, who had withdrawn their recognition of Khomeini as the deputy of the hidden imam, seriously questioned it. "The bloodsucking clique following Khomeini is a small minority. The Iranian clergy throughout our history has sided with the masses of deprived people and never turned against them with clubs and bayonets. We have close contact with the genuine clergy, many of whose members are in prison or under house arrest."

The Mujahidin are presently concentrating on the recruitment of army officers. Rajavi seemed to be convinced that as long as Khomeini is alive, the Pasdaran will remain loyal to him because they owe him their very existence. The army, on the other hand, has very little reason to display irreversible loyalty to the Imam, even though after every major act of violence against the government, it issues the by now familiar declaration of allegiance "to the Imam of the Shiite Ummat." Because the army reflects the Iranian community as a whole, it is likely that the Mujahidin have gained similar support among its members as they have within the community at large. It is evident that in the ultimate battle between the Mujahidin and the Pasdaran, the support of even some members of the armed forces could tip the balance in favor of the Mujahidin.

Even though the Mujahidin together with the followers of Banisadr and secular forces may now constitute a majority of politically articulate Iranians, as long as Khomeini remains in power and is backed by the Pasdaran a peaceful transfer of power to the above coalition seems unlikely. It may be that the Mujahidin are well aware of this fact, for a concerted effort is underway to discredit Khomeini as a leader. The Mujahidin are bent on depicting themselves as the true martyrs of the new revolution of freedom and independence, and Khomeini's harsh punishment plays well into the hand of the Mujahidin's propaganda.

They now picture Khomeini as worse than Hitler, with Rajavi claiming that compared with Khomeini, the shah was a noble and innocent man. "Khomeini has killed as many people so far as the shah did throughout his reign. Nearly 10,000 of the Mujahidin are in jail. In the worst days of the shah, the number of political prisoners was never more than four to five thousand," said Rajavi in mid-August of 1981.[13] The bloody campaign to destroy all opposition forces, which began in earnest after the August 1981 bomb blast, has been indeed costly for the Mujahidin. Though claims and counterclaims by both sides often tend to be vastly exaggerated, independent sources confirm that between June 1981 and April 1982 approximately 3,500 of the Mujahidin were either executed or fell in numerous street battles with the Pasdaran and armed groups of various revolutionary committees throughout the country. About five thousand arrested Mujahidin have repented of their "sins" and are being reeducated in camps very similar to those set up by the Vietnamese after the fall of South Vietnam, or in Cambodia under the Khmer Rouge. Another eight to ten thousand have been spending time in prisons for lesser offenses, such as the possession of copies of the clandestine *Mujahid* newspaper and similar acts of defiance.

In March 1982 the Mujahidin organization in Paris called attention to an especially cruel turn in Khomeini's campaign to reeducate the repentant members. To show their complete change of heart, they have allegedly been ordered to join the firing squads in charge of executing their former comrades in arms. Whether or not this is an accurate account, there is little doubt that the organization has borne the brunt of the ferocious reprisal of the Islamic regime. It is further indisputable that of the nearly one thousand officials of the Khomeini regime killed in the same period, ranging from president to chief justice to plain Pasdar, the Mujahidin were responsible for up to 65 percent of the killings. Other evidence of their predominance in the armed struggle against the regime lies in the fact that for every three members of the other three guerrilla groups killed in action or executed by the Islamic revolutionary tribunals, approximately ten members of the Mujahidin have perished in the same fashion.

These heavy losses have affected Mujahidin strategy. After a major encounter with the Pasdaran in February 1982 in which Musa Khiyabani—the Mujahidin field commander—along with his wife, Rajavi's wife, and a half dozen of their adjutants were ambushed and killed, the organization decided to avoid public confrontation with the Pasdaran. Instead of announcing the identity of its new field commander, Rajavi declared in Paris that henceforth the acts of "legitimate resistance" will be conducted clandestinely, without disclosure of the identities of the participants and the locations of these operations.[14]

While the killings of its members have deeply troubled the Mujahidin, they have not signaled the end of their violent movement. From mid-February 1982, after the ambush killing of Khiyabani and others, to the present, the Mujahidin have conducted an average of sixty operations per week. Some of these have resulted in the assassinations of important clerics who served as Khomeini's deputies. Others were less spectacular, but nonetheless showed that the end of their violent struggle was nowhere in sight.

The Mujahidin have shown a remarkable adaptive capacity. Just as during their struggle against the shah, they seem to alternate between clandestine operations and infiltration and occasional frontal assaults on the security forces. However, they suffer from a number of liabilities that must be overcome before they can aspire to the violent overthrow of Khomeini, or succeed him once he is gone.

One liability relates to their ideological ambivalence. After they had joined the followers of Banisadr to organize the National Resistance Council (NRC), they appealed to all opposition groups within and outside Iran to do the same. Except for the Kurdish Democratic party, few of any significance have done so. Their reservations invariably stem from the Mujahidin's ideological orientation. Secular forces of the anti-Soviet left insist that the goal of establishing an Islamic Democratic People's Republic is both unattainable and a contradiction in terms. If anything, they believe, Khomeini's regime has showed that an Islamic government will be basically fundamentalist and hence antidemocratic. Thus, they cannot join the NRC so long as the Mujahidin retain the Islamic component of their ideology in their political platform.

But Rajavi himself has repeatedly rejected the notion of the incompatibility of the Shiite religion with pluralistic democracy. He would never abandon the "true" Islam that has guided the Mujahidin since its inception in the mid-1960s. Although not saying so in so many words, he believes that the common denominator of Shiite radicalism should be emphasized if the movement wishes to retain its ties to the masses.

On the other hand, the more traditional groups, like the bazaaris, have equally strong reservations about the Marxist emphasis of the Mujahidin. Although at the beginning of June 1981 a number of bazaar merchants helped the Mujahidin organization quite generously, the execution of several of them for doing so, plus the continuous, unchanging reiteration of the Mujahidin's political program, has disenchanted many of them.

Finally, it is important to note that the Mujahidin, alone or in conjunction with other guerrilla groups, have not as yet been able to provoke a massive popular uprising against the present regime similar to that of 1978–79. While their heroism and many acts of suicidal devotion to their cause have certainly created for them an aura of martyrdom and hero worship, all evidence points to the absence of the kind of massive support the anti-shah forces mustered in a similar phase of the 1979 revolution.

Since 1983 several critical issues have dramatically changed the Mujahidin's fortunes. In that year a number of their coalition partners left them. Some, like the Kurdish Democratic party, went beyond a friendly parting of ways and turned against Mujahidin guerrillas in Kurdish regions of Iran and Iraq. Others, like Banisadr's followers, denounced their former cohorts in newspaper articles and other written materials. A contributing factor to the apparent disarray in the leadership was Rajavi's divorce of his second wife—the daughter of Banisadr—and marriage to Maryam Abrishami, the wife of a leading member of the Mujahidin leadership cadre. This rather bizarre episode was presented as an "act of supreme sacrifice designed to promote collective leadership and appeal to the female half of the Iranian populace."

More traumatic events occurred in the spring of 1986 when,

upon constituting a new government in France, Prime Minister Jacques Chirac eased the Mujahidin leadership out of France as an integral part of a short-lived accommodation with the Islamic Republic. Rajavi and his aides were warmly received by the Iraqi government and a large number of Mujahidin guerrillas, estimated at five to ten thousand, began to filter back to western Iran, notably in Kurdistan in the proximity of Sardasht and Mahabad. "Iran Liberation" since this time almost exclusively represents the Mujahidin, who in June 1987 renamed their military force the National Liberation Army of Iran, with full backing of the Baghdad regime.

To the surprise of many, including some of the more recent defectors, this force has been in continuous operation, sometimes at battalion strength, against the Iranian military, notably the Pasdaran. Two anti-Mujahidin military operations, code-named *Nasr* one and two (Arabic for victory), launched in winter and spring of 1986–87 failed to eradicate the guerrilla bases along the Iran-Iraq Kurdish borders. Simultaneously the political and public relations efforts of the group have endeavored, with some success, to depict it as the only active militant opposition to the Tehran regime.[15]

Mujahidin publications in Persian, English, and Arabic enjoy a wide circulation in countries with Iranian communities. With the flight to Paris of Rajavi at the end of 1981 and the intensification of the armed struggle, members of those communities abroad began to publicize their views through student associations, media participation, street rallies, and other forms of public manifestation. Additionally, Radio Mujahid, broadcasting from inside Iranian Kurdistan, is used as a central voice by the organization's headquarters in Paris and is monitored and its messages circulated widely by its membership around the world. Rajavi himself issued daily communiqués from Paris and subsequently from Baghdad on events in Iran and, more significantly, on the identities of Mujahidin executed or killed in action.[16]

From all these sources it is impossible to reconstruct a fairly accurate picture of the composition of the cadres and their socioeconomic background. When the data on the prerevolutionary period are combined with those of the post-1979 era, the following general conclusions emerge. First, the Mujahidin have a basically urban social background. Second, the group has shown a remarkable appeal to young women in urban centers in and around Tehran, Mashhad, Tabriz, Isfahan, Shiraz, and Abadan. Nearly

27 percent of its members appear to be female. A typical female Mujahid is in her late teens or early twenties, a university student or factory office employee from a fairly extended family in which a male member has earlier joined the Mujahidin. She is well-versed in the Koran, a bit ambivalent about socialism and Marxism, but highly dedicated to the cause. Third, economically a majority of Mujahidin belong to the lower middle class, but a quite significant minority, particularly among students abroad, hail from either the newly rich traders and businessmen who prospered during the final oil-generated boom under the shah, or, occasionally, even from better-off upper-middle-class families. Fourth, the Mujahidin's appeal, generally speaking, is most evident among two groups in terms of level of education: First, traditionally educated children of bazaaris and/or urban lower-middle-class groups who have also acquired a basically secular education at state-sponsored schools. Both of these are Islamic in their educational outlook, and indeed have often challenged the meager state-sponsored curriculum in religious education by demonstrating their mastery of Shiite theology to embarrassed, semieducated, state-trained teachers. And, second, secularly educated groups from nontraditional urban families who are not particularly well versed in Koranic principles and are often employed by the state. They are extremely susceptible to the appeal of the Mujahidin, which, by seeking to enhance their Islamic awareness, has also forged for them a sense of identity and even unity with the rest of the underprivileged strata of the Iranian population. It is from this second educational group that the Mujahidin have recruited their more militant cadres.

The difficulty of accurately depicting the ethnic composition of the cadres is enormous. This is particularly true in view of the very close ties between the Kurdish Democratic party and the Mujahidin prior to 1984. Since June 1981 the two have integrated their operations and propaganda so closely that this type of investigation has become quite risky.The Kurdish factor aside, the ethnic composition of the group represents a slightly disproportionate dominance of Persian-speaking Iranians, most in such cities as Tehran, Mashhad, Isfahan, and Shiraz. Azerbaijanis are the largest linguistic group in that northwestern province as well as in the capital city and elsewhere. The Mujahidin are also quite strong in the Caspian provinces of Gilan and Mazanderan.

Significant strata of Iranian society in the recent past have proven susceptible to the appeal of idealistic and radical movements, and the People's Mujahidin probably will persist as a violence-prone organization. If, on the other hand, the politics of reconciliation and accommodation should become firmly established, the appeal of the Mujahidin and similar groups will doubtless erode. But nothing in contemporary Iranian politics suggests that such a development is contemplated by political groups in or out of power.[17]

IDEOLOGY VERSUS PRAGMATISM IN SOUTH YEMEN, 1968–1986

■

Manfred Wenner

The protected, deepwater port of Aden was considered vital to the trade and political interests of the British Empire, which took control of it in 1839. Under British administration Aden became one of the busiest ports in the world, especially after the opening of the Suez Canal made whoever controlled Aden an automatic "player" in the contest for influence and ascendancy in the Red Sea and Horn of Africa regions. Such influence stems partly from Aden's possession of two strategically located islands: Socotra, about 120 miles southeast of Aden, and in theory capable of controlling access from the Indian Ocean to the straits known as Bab al-Mandab; and Perim, located in the middle of the straits. Bab al-Mandab derives its significance from the fact that it is the southern access point to the Red Sea, and therefore a potential "choke point" for Red Sea traffic.[1] Essentially, this means that one could, by controlling Bab al-Mandab, control access to the Suez Canal and affect traffic to Israel, Saudi Arabia, Egypt, the Sudan, North Yemen, and Ethiopia.[2]

Until 1967 Great Britain exercised the predominant influence in the region (with the tacit cooperation of the French, whose presence in the former colony of Djibouti long after their departure from other colonies helped to make clear the general Western interest in this region). In late 1967, however, after an unsuccessful attempt to create a political structure amenable to their continued presence and influence, the British departed, and the People's Republic of South Yemen was established. In November 1970, in line with ideological changes, the state changed its name officially to the People's Democratic Republic of Yemen (PDRY). Because of the PDRY's tendency to associate itself with the USSR in the international arena, it has generally been accorded the status of Soviet "satellite" since the late 1960s.

Historical Background

In the past two centuries, two powers have been of particular importance to Aden: Great Britain, whose interest in Aden stemmed directly from its concern over the trade routes to Asia (and India in particular); and the Ottoman Empire, whose reemergence as a Red Sea power was directly related to the opening of the Suez Canal. With the opening of the canal the Turks revived their interest in southwestern Arabia and reoccupied North Yemen after a hiatus of many years. This in turn brought a British reaction: the decision to establish a tentative presence in the Adeni hinterland, which at the time (the late nineteenth century) was a complex set of principalities, sheikhdoms, naqibdoms, and other statelets of various sizes, powers, and orientations, most often with a tribal affiliation.

This decision eventually required Britain to play an ever-increasing role in these territories—as a provider of subsidies to tribal leaders (thus altering, or in other instances making permanent, existing political relationships), as an arbiter of local disputes, as an ally and provider of money and weapons when the imams of North Yemen sought to expand their influence toward the south (in an attempt to regain what they perceived as their traditional patrimony), and, eventually, as a motivator and organizer of new forms of political association.

In order to facilitate their administration of the hinterland, which continued to grow in scope, the British created two distinct administrative subdivisions, which roughly accorded with the geographical and economic divisions of the area: the Eastern Aden Protectorate (EAP), and the Western Aden Protectorate (WAP). In general, those nearer Aden (in the WAP) were more affected by British administration and policies, and were to play a more important role in events after independence.

All the while, the economic importance of the port continued to grow. The result was an immense cultural, economic, social, and political gap between the city of Aden (which was governed separately as a crown colony after 1937), with its cosmopolitan and diverse population of about 150,000, and the sparsely settled, essentially tribal population of about 500,000 spread over a vast, largely inhospitable land and governed indirectly through subsidies and by traditional leaders.

In the 1950s, in an effort to retain control of Aden for as long as possible, the British sought to amalgamate these two disparate entities into one unified whole, to be named the South Arabian Federation. This proposal brought about the growth of a multitude of organizations that sought to resist British plans, especially those calling for the incorporation of the "world-city" of Aden into the traditional hinterland. The leaders of these organizations came from the labor unions and political parties that had grown up in the cosmopolitan atmosphere of the port. Significant also was the fact that a substantial part of Aden's population was of *North* Yemeni origin. Aden, with its relative political freedom, unmatched anywhere else in the region at the time, became the focal point for extensive political organizing by these North Yemenis, as well as by others from nearby countries, such as Haile Selassie's Ethiopia.

The outbreak of revolution in North Yemen in 1962 provided an important impetus to events in the south: it was now possible to conceive of (1) a reunification of the two parts of "historic" Yeman, a unity that in fact had not existed for more than 150 years, and (2) a revolution in the south (i.e., Aden and its hinterland) as well. By 1967 the cost of the pacification efforts in southern Arabia, combined with the decision to retreat from "east of Suez," led the British to withdraw from Aden completely. The dominant group in the constellation of anti-British organizations, the National Liberation Front (NLF), eventually took over the reins of government in what was to become the People's Democratic Republic of Yemen.[3]

The NLF and Independence

The total withdrawal of the British was an economic blow to the new state. Not only were British subsidy payments eliminated, there was also the loss of the indirect income from the British-operated military and maritime facilities. And, as if that were not enough, the Suez Canal was closed as a result of the Arab-Israeli dispute and the aftermath of the 1967 war. As a consequence, Aden experienced a significant reduction in the number of ships calling, which in turn affected the tourist and transit trade that had made the city so prosperous.

The United States, which had earlier indirectly aided groups and individuals that had opposed the NLF, decided that it was not interested in providing the latter with assistance. Moreover, it seems to have effectively communicated its lack of interest (opposition?) to other potential Western suppliers of economic and development assistance. The result was that a political party that was already less than enthusiastic about Great Britain, the United States, and their allies and friends now began to move in a decidedly opposite ideological direction, with all that that would come to imply for the social, economic, and political characteristics and orientations of South Yemeni society.[4]

The first two years of South Yemen's independence were characterized by the political ascendancy of Qahtan al-Shaabi and Faysal Abd al-Latif, relative moderates who were evidently prepared to allow the new state to retain the economic patterns and associations of the preindependence period, so long as essential reform measures to transform South Yemen into a more modern state were not abandoned or fatally watered down.[5] In general it is fair to characterize these reforms as no more "socialist" than some of the patterns of nationalization and state control in Great Britain, France, and Italy.

Despite al-Shaabi's and Abd al-Latif's control of much of the NLF's machinery, a party congress held at Zinjibar in 1968 adopted a program of nationalization, collectivization, state initiatives, and control of both old and new sectors of the economy, as well as a series of radical social and economic goals. Al-Shaabi and Abd al-Latif were forced to resign, and a so-called hard core of left-wing ideologues assumed control of the party machinery and the state's policy-making organs. Salim Ruba'i Ali and Abd al-Fatah Isma'il, both originally from North Yemen, were the dominant figures.

The two new leaders soon diverged in their views of foreign policy: on South Yemen's relations with North Yemen (where the civil war had now ended), as well as on its relations with other

Arab states of the region. They also disagreed on the extent to which South Yemen ought to be associated with major world powers outside the Middle East that were either capable of or interested in giving economic and/or military assistance—both of which were, by this time, desperately needed. Salim Ruba'i Ali tended to associate himself more closely with a clique favoring closer relations with the People's Republic of China; Isma'il, on the other hand, tended to associate himself with, and promoted the development of, a faction favoring the Soviet Union. (In South Yemeni terms, this made Isma'il the moderate.)

Under the leadership of 'Ali and Isma'il, the government undertook a number of determined policies: (1) the elimination of the supporters of the previous government, which drove literally thousands of South Yemenis into exile (primarily in North Yemen); (2) the radical transformation of society; and (3) aggressive "anti-imperalism" on the foreign front, including support with men and material of a number of revolutionary movements, notably the Dhofar Liberation Front in neighboring Oman, which later became the Popular Front for the Liberation of the Occupied Arab Gulf (PFLOAG) and still later the Popular Front for the Liberation of Oman (PFLO).

Social changes were to include various agrarian reform programs, nationalization of all industrial enterprises (with the important exception of the British Petroleum refinery and its ancillary properties, which were not nationalized until 1977), and the promotion of collectivization schemes among peasants, fishermen, and just about every occupation in the social structure, as well as the nationalization of all land and dwellings. It has been said that the NLF program of domestic reform went further than any similar program in the People's Republic of China and the USSR. The result was that the economic situation deteriorated even further, making it less likely than ever that Western sources would be found to assist in economic development programs, or fund, much less operate, any significant technical assistance. While agricultural productivity sank, additional elements of the population elected to leave, especially the remnants of the middle class; the entrepreneurs of Aden; many of those with technical or industrial skills that could now be easily and profitably marketed in North Yemen; and even some agriculturalists. In fact, it has been widely reported that in the mid-1970s the total population of the PDRY fell below what it had been more than twenty years earlier. Perhaps as many as a half million of its inhabitants left the country—either temporarily or permanently.

Despite these developments, the fact that major members of the PDRY's elite were of North Yemeni origin, while many former South Yemenis exercised major political responsibilities in North Yemeni governments (for example, Abdullah al-Asnaj), made it possible to undertake at least preliminary discussion of terms for some form of political association (if not outright union) between the two Yemens. These discussions appear to have led to the next major change in the PDRY.

In late 1977, the day before he was to go to South Yemen to participate in a round of union talks, the North Yemeni president, Ibrahim al-Hamdi, was assassinated, apparently by agents of the Saudi Arabian government, which feared any real movement in the direction of union between the Yemens. Al-Hamdi's successor was Ahmad Hussein al-Ghashmi, who, it was believed by Salim Rubai Ali, had at least tacitly approved of the assassination. Rubai Ali appears to have decided to have al-Ghashmi assassinated in turn, which occurred in mid-1978.

Instead of bolstering Rubai Ali's position, this led other members of the NLF to turn on him, and he was executed after a brief trial. His replacement as president was Abd al-Fatah Isma'il, whose accession led to a pronounced turn toward the USSR. There was little if any attendant change in domestic policies. Under President Isma'il, himself of North Yemeni origins, a new and more active campaign to bring about change in the relationship between the two Yemens was instituted. Furthermore, a still more rigorous program for the collectivization of all aspects of South Yemeni economy and society was adopted; in fact, it would be accurate to say that with the formation of the Yemeni Socialist party (YSP) and the decisive demotion of the supporters of Rubai Ali, a far more dogmatic and rigidly leftist regime had taken over. Furthermore, the increasingly Marxist-Leninist orientation of the regime in the south only tended to aggravate the relationship with North Yemen.

Isma'il appeared to believe that active support of the major opposition force in North Yemen, the National Democratic Front (a diverse group of individuals and cliques with economic and social grievances of varying degrees of seriousness), as well as some judicious inciting of certain tribal groupings with related grievances in the southern areas of North Yemen, would produce sufficient leverage to bring about a change in the policy orientation of the new North Yemeni leader, Colonel Ali Abdullah Salih.

Once again, the results were not quite what had been desired: the minor skirmishes that took place in the southern areas of North Yemen and the increase in NDF activities were suddenly and unexpectedly escalated into a major confrontation, over which the local participants soon had little or no control. Other states, both regional and extraregional, saw far more important and wider issues involved, and used the confrontation for their own purposes. Among these were

1. Saudi Arabia, with at least two distinct interests: (a) to "punish" South Yemen for its intransigence and opposition to Saudi interests and objectives (despite the resumption of relations between the two in 1977); and (b) to make certain that North Yemen remained a pliable and dependent neighbor, rather than deciding to cooperate more extensively with South Yemen.

2. The United States, also with at least two distinct interests: (a) to have the Carter administration appear able to stand up to what was being depicted as another Soviet threat and cope effectively with developments in the Middle East; and (b) to enable the United States to move additional military material into the Arabian Peninsula without having to have the transfer approved through the normal (and often contentious) congressional process. These military supplies were to be delivered to North Yemen via Saudi Arabia, which essentially made them a joint Saudi-American lever on North Yemen.

3. The Soviet Union, which in the event of any PDRY reversals would presumably be called upon for assistance for any loss of hardware; this, in turn, would enable the USSR to consolidate its position and expand its influence in the area.

4. The North Yemeni government of Ali Abdullah Salih, who expected to obtain more than $300 million in modern military equipment that he probably could not have obtained otherwise, and who hoped that these supplies, and the assistance of the United States, would make it possible for him to loosen the close reins that the Saudis insisted upon.

In the event, some military hardware was delivered, and the policy objectives of the Saudis and the Americans were largely achieved.[6] In South Yemen, after many months of internal disputes (which in some areas bordered on civil war), Ali Nasir Muhammad (al-Hasani), who was prime minister under Isma'il, succeeded in deposing the latter in April of 1980. Allegedly he had the assistance of another individual who has played a significant role in many of the changes since independence, Ali Ahmad Nasir Antar (al-Bishi). There appears to have been, within days, a tangible relaxation of the tight, almost totalitarian controls over nearly all aspects of South Yemeni society, including, for example, the prohibition of all conversations between South Yemenis and any "foreigner," which term included other Arabs.

Although the PDRY made gestures designed to reassure the Soviet Union and other providers of assistance, the new president just as clearly undertook policies that suggested that avenues to the West were now open, and that some of the more radical of the PDRY's regional policies were going to be abandoned. Specifically, Ali Nasir (a) acted to develop a rapprochement with North Yemen; (b) appeared eager to regularize relations with Saudi Arabia and other Gulf states, probably with an eye to receiving some financial assistance; (c) publicly opposed the training of members of radical groups such as the PLO in the PDRY; (d) decreased the level of military and other aid provided by the PDRY to the Marxist government of Mengistu Haile Mariam in Ethiopia; and (e) seemed intent upon regularizing relations with neighboring Oman.[7]

The willingness of the regime to provide the most intimate details of its domestic and financial conditions for the World Bank Report of March 1979 shows that there were elements within the government even before the fall of Isma'il who were interested in promoting less rigid, less dogmatic, less ideological, and less radical policies.[8]

Following the devastating floods of the spring of 1982, conservative Arab states responded with emergency aid, and additional support was provided by Western governments and financial institutions. It appeared that the Eastern bloc states were incapable of providing adequate relief on short notice, much less in the amount required. Spare parts and other equipment, needed immediately in order to cope with the disaster, were either long in arriving or never arrived at all. The subjective and long-term effects of this difference in response should not be minimized. It is likely that in the fluid matrix of leadership politics in the PDRY the flood provided support for those favoring better relations with the conservative Arab states and the West.[9] Nevertheless, no irrevocable "tilt" to the West had taken place in the PDRY. Many of the issues that have concerned the Western states over the years continued to be important: for example, continuing close relations with the USSR and many of its closest allies; diplomatic support for many Soviet actions and positions, including the invasion of Afghanistan; continued (though diminished) support for various "progressive" and "revolutionary" movements in various parts of the globe; and, last but not least, continued influence of the more radical elements of the party in significant leadership positions.

In January 1986 Ali Nasir appears to have decided to eliminate his major opponents at the highest levels of the state and the party, and most especially in the YSP's Political Bureau. Allegedly on the advice of Ali Ahmad Muhammad, the governor of Abyan Province, an attempt was made to assassinate six major members of the Political Bureau, as well as a significant number of the cadres loyal to them. Although evidently planned some time in advance, the assassination scheme was not wholly successful. Three of the intended victims were able to escape and organize their own cadres and militias in an effort to crush the forces of Ali Nasir Muhammad. The result was a short civil war, primarily fought in the Aden area, between the two most obvious factions. The violence was so widespread, fierce, and protracted that Europeans from both East and West desperately sought to leave Aden. Estimates of the total number of casualties soon exceeded ten thousand, although most likely no objective and completely accurate figure will ever be available.

In early 1986 it was not yet clear precisely what had precipitated the conflict, but it was possible to draw some general conclusions based upon the preliminary reports. First, Ali Nasir Muhammad was forced to flee the country. Second, Abd al-Fatah Isma'il, who had returned from five years' exile in the USSR, died of his wounds, but the forces allied with him seem to have improved their relative position within the political elite. Although the new president, Haydar Abu Bakr al-Attas, had served with Ali Nasir Muhammad and publicly committed himself to the previous policy of good relations with neighboring and conservative states, he was thought to have received important support from the Isma'il faction. Third, although the new leadership had not yet clearly defined itself, it seemed from the early reports that the ideological and tribal alliances that were going to characterize the state in the next period might be quite different from those of the period 1980–86.

Politics in the PDRY

In the PDRY, politics is a complex and continually changing combination of the following elements:

1. Personal origin. This particular variable is essentially an either/or characteristic: birth and socialization in North or in South Yemen.

2. Tribal affiliation. Although in theory the number of possible affiliations is in the dozens, in reality there are only about six that have been politically relevant during the past twenty-five years.[10]

3. Ideological orientation. In today's PDRY this variable runs the gamut from expressed sympathy with some of the more radical strains of Marxist thought (i.e., 1940s Maoism; Trotskyist ideas concerning the desirability or necessity of "continuing revolution") through the more standard version of Marxism-Leninism as promulgated by the USSR, to the still acceptable "right," or moderate socialism in the incarnation common in such contemporary Western European countries as Sweden.

4. Personalism. The politics of personality has definitely not been eradicated in the PDRY. This variable includes the links created by the patrimonial system that characterizes nearly all of the Middle Eastern polities; the bonds created by previous association (for example, during the campaigns for independence or for control of the various political organizations that have developed over the years); the ability to control resources that can influence policy (patronage, coercive opportunities); the ability to establish and exploit personal links with foreign leaders; and, finally, charisma, insofar as it exists in the PDRY.

5. Opportunism, or simple taking advantage of opportunities for personal advancement, as well as (perhaps) advancement of the interests of one's social or political group or organization.

6. The many links between North and South Yemen, as shown

most clearly in the ease with which individuals from either side of the frontier have been able to serve in the highest levels of government of the other (depending, of course, on ideological position and on the prevailing state of relations between the two countries). It should be added, however, that with the passage of time, this is not as true as it was earlier, and indeed in the South today one is almost required to demonstrate one's southern origins and orientation.

7. The influence of outside participants on domestic and foreign policy parameters.

8. The straightforward economic interests of groups in the PDRY—for example, the Adeni business community, the rapidly growing fishing industry, or elements within the government itself who see growth as dependent upon expansion of some sector of the economy with which they are involved.

9. Regional players, such as Ethiopia under the current regime, Libya's Colonel Muammar Qaddafi, and the various liberation fronts that have at one time or another sought, received, or been considered for assistance (Eritrea, PFLAOG, Dhofar Liberation Front, etc.).

The point, of course, is that it is a dangerous simplification of reality to attribute the various actions and policies of the PDRY since independence solely to its relationship with the USSR.

Soviet Objectives

The motivations ascribed to the Soviet Union in various locations around the world would seem to be a function of one's preexisting notions of what objectives the Soviet Union happens to be pursuing—either in the short or the long term. For example, among the least militant and aggressive ideas of what the USSR is seeking in the Red Sea region, one might include (but not necessarily be limited to) the following. (1) Developing "leverage" that could be used in the future, especially in negotiations or discussions with political opponents (e.g., the United States) with respect to the future status of the region, and Soviet rights of access to it. Many analysts suggest that what the USSR really wants is recognition on the part of the United States and the West in general that it is entitled to participate in the making of regional policy in an area that abuts its southern flank. (2) Actively seeking to decrease the influence and prestige of the United States and its regional friends. (3) Obtaining a long-term lease or control over a "warm-water port" from which naval operations and trade relations could be more effectively undertaken (whether for purely economic or broader politico-military *and* economic reasons).

An individual holding the above views of Soviet objectives would be able to support them by pointing to the example of Soviet assistance of South Yemen since 1970 and suggesting that the level of this assistance was quite minimal in comparison with the potential (or even real) gains. Furthermore, he or she might suggest that the low level of Soviet support for the PFLOAG (and later the PFLO) indicated quite clearly that the USSR was unwilling to be dragged into any protracted peninsular conflict. In fact, this is not the only evidence that could be adduced to support this viewpoint, but for the moment it is sufficient.

On the other hand, one could posit a considerably more provocative list of reasons for Soviet involvement in the Red Sea region. Recent Soviet policy maneuvers may be seen as designed to: (1) enable the USSR to disrupt, and then eventually control, regional trade; (2) enable the USSR to control all Middle Eastern oil and gas fields; (3) enable the USSR, should it choose to do so, to take over the Middle East in its entirety, incorporating it into the Soviet sphere. This would obviously present a major threat to adjacent areas, such as East Africa, North Africa, and Turkey.

An individual with this more gloomy view of Soviet objectives would be able to support it by noting the Soviet attempt to obtain the United Nations Trusteeship for Eritrea in the post–World War II era (not to mention the similar request for Libya); the willingness of the USSR to provide not just "adequate" supplies of military equipment, but even the troops and trainers of a dependent state (Cuba); and the willingness of the USSR to invest substantial amounts of money and material in regimes of doubtful longevity if their locations appear to be of strategic importance (e.g., Ethiopia, South Yemen).

Conclusions

Some analysts will insist that the ideological predilections of the NLF set it on the path of subservience to the ideology and policy objectives of the USSR (not to mention its methods of policy implementation) from the outset. The PDRY has been willing to sign and implement military and assistance agreements of the type usually associated with states closely tied to the USSR (e.g., twenty-year treaties of alliance and friendship of the type signed with Afghanistan). And, the PDRY has been a reliable supporter of Soviet policy initiatives in a number of instances (e.g., the invasion of Afghanistan) when no other Middle Eastern country would publicly say anything positive about the USSR.

The PDRY's government's view and orientations have undergone a number of marked changes since independence in 1967. Many of them were clearly associated with a change in the leadership; some of them, in addition, were the result of events in the region over which the PDRY may not have had any measure of control or influence. Examples of this latter category would include the war in the Ogaden, the existence of (legitimate) discontent in the Dhofar region with the policies of Sultan Said; the ebb and flow of tribal and regional politics in North Yemen, and the motives, policies, and behavior of various other Arab states and leaders in the continuing Arab-Israeli conflict. The recent decision of the government to encourage foreign investment (by permitting repatriation of hard currency earnings), the acceptance of Western firms as participants in infrastructural development programs, the outright wooing of Western oil exploration and development firms, and the decision to end support for the PFLO in Dhofar and to participate in a number of Arab organization and policy initiatives all make it difficult *not* to believe that there has been a pronounced shift in the direction and emphasis of South Yemeni government policy.[11]

I cannot detect an unambiguous and deliberate policy on the part of the Soviet Union to achieve specific objectives in the Red Sea region. This is not to say that the Soviet Union does not have a policy; it is only to suggest that there does not appear to be sufficient evidence to warrant the conclusion that it has a long-range goal toward which it is inexorably moving.

The primary reason for this conclusion is that the Soviet Union appears to have embarked upon a set of bilateral arrangements with the countries of the area. There is little evidence of a coordinated multilateral program, despite the (superficially significant) tripartite agreement between the PDRY, Ethiopia, and Libya. It would appear that the USSR has skillfully managed to exploit grievances based upon past misgovernance, incompetence, and injustices, not to mention poverty, ignorance, disease, an uncaring administration, and all the other ills of less-developed societies. But—and this is precisely the point—each of the affected governments, at least in the Red Sea region, tends to judge the success or failure of its association with the Soviet Union and its friends precisely on the basis of its own limited resources, interests, and objectives, and *not* in terms of some global program to alleviate social ills, modify reactionary social systems, or restructure the world economic system (despite occasional rhetoric in that direction). And, if we may use other Middle Eastern states such as Egypt, Somalia, and Iraq as indicators, when the bilateral arrangement with the USSR is no longer satisfactory to the local "partner," it is either modified, or occasionally even completely severed.

Afghanistan clearly represents a different case. For one thing, it borders on the Soviet Union (and so would probably have been subject to the "Brezhnev Doctrine" regardless of circumstances).[12] For another, it has been directly occupied by Soviet troops, who attempt to guarantee that Soviet policy objectives are implemented. Neither of these conditions applies in the case of either Ethiopia or the PDRY. Furthermore, neither of these two states is important to the development of the Soviet economy. Neither of them is a potential channel for subversive ideas of ethnic separatism, Islamic fundamentalism, or similar anti-Soviet ideologies across a proximate frontier. And, last but not least, neither of them has presented the USSR with a direct threat of Western expansion into what was seen as essentially neutral territory (at least by the Soviets).

Based on the above analysis, it seems that American policy in the Red Sea region has often been short-sighted. Perhaps the best single instance of this is the 1979 decision to accept the Saudi version of events in southwestern Arabia, and therefore argue to the press and the Congress that events there demonstrated that an "aggressive Communist-inspired South Yemen was attempting to expand militarily." Such acceptance of the Saudi interpretation may be understandable in light of Saudi Arabia's relations with the PDRY, its vast oil reserves, its moderate policy within OPEC, and its size and influence in the Islamic world and in the Middle East region as a whole, but it does not excuse the lack of independent analysis.

There do appear to have been some efforts made on both the PDRY and the U.S. sides to improve relations. The fact that the Reagan administration was willing to lift restrictions on the sale of aircraft parts to the PDRY (in 1982) and that the PDRY has been willing to deal more closely with countries and international bodies in which the United States often plays a determining role are two recent indicators of a desire to downplay some of the old antagonisms. In both countries, however, there are also those elements that do not look with favor upon such a resumption of relations, much less any relaxation of tensions. And it is also likely that in both there are those whose careers may be seriously jeopardized by an obvious accommodation between the two states—either in terms of their position on domestic affairs, or in their foreign policy stance.

How, then, do we finally assess the interplay between the demands of ideology and pragmatism in the contemporary PDRY? One cannot, of course, ignore its marked inclination to Marxist-Leninist analyses of current events, nor the YSP's evident commitment to certain Soviet models for its domestic economic and political policies. At the same time, it is necessary to recognize the effectiveness with which the government has kept control of domestic policy making, and how on more than one occasion foreign and domestic policies have clearly not accorded with Soviet interests and objectives. The events of early 1986 also make clear that the ruling elites, no matter how divided, do not inform the Soviets of their internal operations, disputes, or even goals.

It would appear, then, that in the PDRY we have a country whose political and economic past has clearly influenced its perceptions of the exterior world, but whose political elite has also shown a pragmatic approach to ameliorating the considerable array of problems with which it must cope. While the events of 1986 show that the internal ideological and policy disputes are quite deep and held with a predilection for violence which many thought unlikely, it is not a time when the West should abandon the possibility that the outcome of the tension between ideology and pragmatism may develop in a fashion which is acceptable to both South Yemen, its regional cohorts, and the Western world.

THE PDPA REGIME IN AFGHANISTAN

A Soviet Model for the Future of the Middle East

■

Ralph H. Magnus

The central political issue in modern Afghan history has been the struggle to establish a stable relationship between the competing claims to political legitimacy posed by traditional tribal structures, nationalism, and Islam. The major outlines of this struggle became apparent during the reign of Amir Abdur Rahman (1880–1901), when the role of the balancing wheel in this configuration of forces was played by the institution of the Afghan monarchy.[1] Afghanistan's experience of repelling two British invasions was in all probability the central factor in shaping these varied elements into a complex compound that might be called a kind of "traditional nationalism":

> The fact that it was the urban centers of eastern Afghanistan rather than the Afghan tribes that were most severely damaged by these wars is of great historical significance. Because of the weakened position of the urban sectors, the nationalist, anti-British struggle was led primarily by the Afghan tribes and the religious establishment, and became a religious war as well as a nationalist one. Islam became a potent national force . . . used by the Afghan rulers to mobilize popular opinion and enlist the support of the masses in their struggle against the Sikhs and against British imperialism.[2]

Under the strong and ruthless leadership of the "Iron Amir," Abdur Rahman, the monarchy established itself in the last two decades of the nineteenth century in a historically unprecedented position of dominance, suppressing both tribal independence and the traditional autonomy of Islamic institutions. In the process, it began the creation of a modern nationalist elite attached to the royal court in Kabul. With the more humane and relaxed atmosphere of Amir Habibullah's reign (1901–19), the Kabuli governmental elite took on a more independent, self-conscious, and self-assured style, developing into a modernist, nationalist, anti-imperialist and, potentially at least, anti-monarchical party—"The Young Afghans," under the philosophical influence of Mahmud Beg Tarzi, himself a member of the royal family and the editor of the court newspaper, *Siraj al-Akhbar Afghaniyah* (The Lamp of the News of Afghanistan).[3]

Amir Habibullah's adherence to his pledge to the British to maintain Afghanistan's neutrality during World War I resulted in an alliance of convenience against him. Both of the opposition groups were led by members of the royal family: the modern nationalists by the amir's third son, Amanullah Khan (who was strongly under the influence of his father-in-law, Mahmud Beg Tarzi), and the traditionalist-religious elements by the amir's brother, Nasrullah Khan. In 1919 the amir was assassinated, and Amanullah seized the throne. He immediately arrested his uncle Nasrullah (who had claimed the throne as well) and placated both the modernists and the traditionalists by proclaiming Afghanistan's complete independence from British influence and attacking British frontier posts. It proved to be a brilliant strategy, both internationally and internally. Weary of four years of war, facing Muslim and Hindu unrest in India, and no longer worried about the Russian menace, the British did not attempt to maintain the informal protectorate they had established forty years earlier with the Afghan monarchy. They recognized Afghan independence. With the prestige gained by this victory, Amanullah moved with his allies in the modernist elite to transform Afghanistan along modernist, nationalist, and, in reality, secularist lines, in imitation of the reforms of Kemal Atatürk in Turkey and Reza Shah Pahlavi in Iran.[4]

The Amanullah experiment remains to this day highly controversial. Whether his overthrow in 1929 was a conservative religious and tribal reaction to this reform or a matter of rival forces taking advantage of a weakened ruler to reassert their independence is still unclear. Also unclear is the involvement, or lack of involvement, of foreign forces. It is the firm belief of a number of Afghans, including both Marxists and some mujahidin groups, that he was overthrown by the British because they feared his friendship toward the Soviet Union.

Tribal and religious elements gained the upper hand, temporarily replacing the Pushtun ruler (the Pushtuns have been Afghanistan's largest ethnic group for centuries, and once ruled an empire stretching to the Indus and beyond) with a Tajik ex-bandit who took the name of Amir Habibullah II Ghazi. However, motivated by Pushtun ethnic chauvinism, as well as by the prospect of looting the capital, many of the Pushtun tribes and some of the religious leaders shifted their support to another prominent member of the extended royal family, and the Muhammadzai dynasty was shortly reestablished under King Muhammad Nadir (r. 1929–33).

It was a severely weakened monarchy in many respects. The Pushtun tribes and prominent religious leaders had demonstrated their power as king-breakers and king-makers. During the following decades, the monarchy under Nadir Shah and his son Zahir Shah (r. 1933–73) was forced to act with great caution. Following the assassination of Nadir Shah in 1933, the royal family gradually succeeded in rebuilding, and eventually in surpassing, the power of the central government attained by Amanullah, but the alliance with the modern nationalist elite was never reestablished with the closeness of the earlier period. Some elements continued to support the exiled King Amanullah, and wider elements were dissatisfied with the slow pace of reform.

In 1948, under Sardar (Prince) Shah Mahmud Khan Ghazi's premiership, the monarchy attempted to bring the modern nationalist elite back into wholehearted cooperation with the government on the basis of free elections, a free press, and freedom of political association. However, criticism of the royal family in the press and Parliament became too strong to be tolerated. In 1952 the authorities cracked down with the banning of newspapers and groups, and a number of arrests. The following year a new strong man, Sardar Muhammad Da'ud Khan, the king's cousin and the nephew of Prime Minister Sardar Shah Mahmud Khan, took over effective control in a "family coup." Da'ud undertook a program of rapid socioeconomic development, which was attractive to the nationalist elite, but in practice involved only their expertise, not their political participation. Prime Minister Da'ud Khan realized that such a program could not be instituted in Afghanistan without a strong military basis of power. But this, in turn, could be accomplished only with large-scale foreign aid (as in fact was the case with the development of the projects he had in mind). Given the circumstances of geography and of Afghanistan's advocacy of "Pushtunistan" (the claim of Afghans and of some ethnic Pushtuns in Pakistan that the referendum held before the British departure from India should have involved a choice of independence for the Northwest Frontier Province, Pushtun princely states, and tribally administered areas), military aid could be sought only from the Soviet Union, although economic aid was sought and secured from both the East and the West.[5]

The "Decade of Da'ud" (1953–63) thus seemingly reestablished the alliance between the monarchy and the nationalist-modernist elites at the expense of the tribal and religious leadership. The modernists soon became alienated by Da'ud's autocratic methods, however, even though they agreed with his goals, and in 1963 King Muhammad Zahir, who had reigned, but not ruled, for thirty years, saw the opportunity to forge a new alliance with both traditionalists and nationalists. The traditional democracy of the Afghan tribal system would be transferred to the national level. The new era was symbolized by the appointment of a Tajik, Dr. Muhammad Yusuf (who had been a minister in Da'ud's cabinet), as prime minister—the first non-Pushtun to hold that position in Afghan history.[6]

Sadly, the era of cooperation proved to be all too brief. The first meeting of the newly elected legislature in October 1965 broke up in chaos and rioting, incited, if not completely controlled, by the communists under Babrak Karmal, who had been elected from a Kabul constituency. Uncertain of royal support, Dr. Yusuf resigned. It was an inauspicious beginning, and the system of constitutional monarchy did not regain its momentum until its final months.

Sincere in his desire to turn over the responsibility for political leadership to the modern elite and to reign as a constitutional monarch, but beset by conflicting and often self-interested advice, the king hesitated either to intervene openly or to allow a freely competitive political party system to establish itself. Many in the royal family had supported the constitutional monarchy only as a temporary expedient in order to get rid of Da'ud as prime minister; for his part, Da'ud's pride was injured at having been rejected by his cousin and most of those who had supported him in his modernization programs. He thus refused to give the new system his support, although he did not at first openly oppose it.[7]

Although the king was personally respected, it was widely felt that government officials were in general arrogant, incompetent, cruel, unjust, and corrupt. No section of the urban elite emerged to provide leadership for the new political system, although there was more widespread support for economic development and an active central government than most observers felt would be possible.[8] The traditionalists who dominated the legislature were loyal to the monarch and Islam, but had no common political program. The modernists were now divided into a number of factions, none of them capable of providing a national leadership.

As the principal drafter of the constitution of 1964 and educated in both shari'a and Western law (at al-Azhar University in Cairo and at Columbia), Muhammad Musa Shafiq seemed ideally suited to provide leadership for the constitutional system, but it was not until the last year of the monarchy that the king moved from behind the scenes to appoint him prime minister and provide the royal support he had hesitated to give the four earlier prime ministers under the liberal constitution of 1964.

During the 1960s, however, new movements had surfaced among both the Islamic and nationalist elites. On January 1, 1965, the People's Democratic party of Afghanistan (PDPA) was founded, to be followed by other Marxist organizations. Although they publicly stated their loyalty to the constitutional monarchy and their belief that the changes they desired could be accomplished by peaceful means, their ultimate aim was revolution, and they had no illusions that it could be accomplished by anything less than violence. They endeavored, with some success, to attract a broad spectrum of political and social malcontents. In Afghanistan's traditional system, non-Pushtuns and even Pushtuns who were not part of the ruling tribe and clan, the Muhammadzai Durranis, suffered from discrimination. It was these tribal and ethnic groups, particularly the rural youths who were the first generation to be exposed to the Western-style educational system, who formed a common pool for both the Marxist and Islamic political parties.

The leaders of the new Islamic movements were neither the traditional mullahs nor the Sufi *pirs*, such as those who had participated in the ouster of King Amanullah in 1929. Rather, they were faculty members from the shari'a (Islamic law) faculty of Kabul University, including Abdur Rahim Niazi, Burhanuddin Rabbani, and Abdul Rasul Sayyaf.[9] The shari'a faculty had formal educational ties with al-Azahar University in Cairo, and in Egypt many Afghan scholars came under the influence of the ideas of the Muslim Brotherhood. Rabbani translated the works of Seyed Qutb, the Muslim Brotherhood Supreme Guide executed by Nasser in 1966, into Afghan Dari.

There is blame enough (or credit, depending on one's point of view) to go around for the fall of the Afghan monarchy in the coup of July 1973. King Muhammad Zahir had vacillated too long before deciding to attempt to recover the dynamism and sense of direction lost with the fall of the Yusuf cabinet in October 1965. His backing of Shafiq was too little and too late; the idea that a constitutional monarchy would solve Afghanistan's fundamental problems had been discredited. For their part, the traditionalists had too narrow an outlook. They were finally unable to overcome their traditional viewpoint that the central government was either their natural enemy or a source of immediate favors. But the greatest failure, undoubtedly, was that of the liberal nationalist elite. They were best able to understand the opportunities they had and the dangers they faced if they failed, yet they proved to be as divided and narrow-minded as the traditionalists. The failure of the monarch, the traditionalist elite, and the modernist, liberal elite thus cleared the way for two elements who hated the new system: Sardar Da'ud and the communists. Da'ud was undoubtedly motivated in part by personal animosity toward his cousin, the king, but he felt as well that he had given the constitutional system a fair trial and it had failed the nation. The communists had always wanted a revolution and power for themselves and they felt that Da'ud would be the perfect transitional figure to bridge the gap between the monarchy and the true revolution. The alliance between the two was forged with the direct participation of the Soviet Union.[10]

The First Afghan Republic (1973–78) was a truly transitional regime. Continuity was provided by President Muhammad Da'ud Khan, the most able *sardar* (prince) of his generation of the royal family that had ruled Afghanistan since 1747. By becoming president instead of king, he formally repudiated the traditional role of Afghan monarchy as the symbol of national unity and political legitimacy. Nonetheless, traditionalists, both tribal and Islamic, looked upon Da'ud as a strong, effective monarch rather than a revolutionary leader. Da'ud soon confirmed their belief by moving against his erstwhile communist allies, in violation of the agreements he had made under Soviet sponsorship. Soviet president Nikolai Podgorny was hastily sent to Kabul in November 1975 to protest, but to no avail.[11] Da'ud felt that his reputation with the nationalist elite as a whole, the bulk of whom were not Marxists, was strong enough for him to ignore his original allies. Eventually, in the Loya Jirgah (the general assembly, convened on important issues and representing the supreme constitutional authority) of January 1977, Da'ud attempted to repeat his royal cousin's 1964 constitutional experiment and serve as the balance wheel between the modern nationalists and the traditionalists. But the new Islamic ideological movements refused to accept Da'ud, even without his communist allies. Indeed, they viewed even the traditional Afghan monarchy as un-Islamic. In the end, Da'ud was even less successful than King Zahir; his constitution lasted fifteen months instead of ten years.

Da'ud's fatal mistake was in foreign rather than domestic policy. He gambled that he could shift away from dependence on the Soviet Union in foreign policy and development and establish a truly nonaligned (although certainly not anti-Soviet) policy with the support of the newly rich oil states of Iran and the Arabian Peninsula. These conservative monarchies required that he cease his anti-Pakistani policies, which had included support for armed Baluch separatist movements as well as his traditional advocacy of "Pushtunistan." This was more than the Soviet leadership could tolerate. They feared that, should Da'ud succeed in this reorientation, their twenty-five years of investment in establishing their predominant influence in this strategic area would go to waste. Seeing very little danger of a counter action by the United States and the West (which had just allowed the fall of Vietnam and the establishment of Soviet-influenced regimes and bases in Angola, the Horn of Africa, and Aden), they moved in the summer of 1977 to bring about the reunification of the PDPA factions and prepare for the coup of April 1978.[12]

The standard ideological appeal under the PDPA is to the "national democratic revolution," whose institutional form is the National Fatherland Front (NFF), formally established in 1981. Despite its importance as the broad organization designed to capture all possible elements of support, it took a year and a half from the time of the Soviet invasion to organize the NFF. At first there were even more urgent tasks, such as attempting to reconcile the *Khalqi* and *Parchami* wings of the PDPA. This complicated the task of organizing the necessary "front" organizations of workers, intellectuals, students, and so forth in the urban areas (essentially, in Kabul) under reliable party control. Even more difficult was the task of trying to persuade some tribal leaders to participate, since the countryside was estimated to be 80 percent mujahidin-controlled.

The constitution of the NFF, adopted at its founding congress on June 15, 1981, made a deliberate effort to establish its continuity with past manifestations of Afghan nationalism. The PDPA, "the guiding force of the National Fatherland Front and of the whole of the society of Afghanistan," is the first of the twelve groups listed as the NFF's organizational members (most, if not all of these groups date from after the 1978 coup, and many were created only after the Soviet invasion). These groups include farmers, workers, youth, women, journalists, artists, businessmen, religious figures, and tribal representatives. Membership in the NFF was open on an individual basis as well, upon written application. The congress was the supreme body, and was to meet at least every five years (as of July 1985, it had not met again since its founding). A national committee of ninety-seven was named, with the actual administration of the front to be in the hands of a twenty-three-member executive committee, chaired by Politburo member Saleh Muhammed Ziray, with Suleiman Layeq, the minister of tribes and nationalities (and a member of the Mojadidi religious family, whose relatives head one of the mujahidin organizations), as vice-chairman. A further linkage to the past was made by naming Abdul Hadi Dawi to the national committee. Dawi had been a protégé of Mahmud Beg Tarzi's, and Tarzi had turned over the editorship of *Siraj al-Akhbar* to him in 1919. Under Dawi's editorship the paper had changed its name to *Aman-i Afghan* (Afghan Peace) and become the unofficial court newspaper.

Reflecting the importance of newspapers in the development of modern Afghan nationalism, *Anis*, founded in 1927 as a private paper and resurrected during the 1930s as the mouthpiece of the Kabuli nationalist elite, was reestablished as the newspaper of the NFF.

However, the problems facing the NFF have thus far proved to be insurmountable. An early indication was given by the assassination of some of those who had been delegates to the founding congress, including a religious figure and a retired general. In 1981 the mujahidin reportedly had a target list of thirty front members.[13]

Organizational difficulties continued to plague the front; it was not until more than four months after the founding congress that the formation of a NFF provincial committee was announced for Kabul province.[14] All indications are that it remains a paper organization, holding periodic meetings and sending delegations and messages, but of little value as a propaganda group and even less as an adjunct of the government administration. Programs, reports, correspondence, and even the collection of dues were all lacking two years after its founding, and a year and a half later the list of unfinished and incompetently performed tasks had grown even longer. Even more important: "Required propaganda has not been carried out to attract people to the Armed Forces and to train the people in the spirit of serving the Armed Forces."[15]

Ethnic and Tribal Appeals

If the PDPA regime's appeal to the concept of a single, unified Afghan nation represents its desire to establish continuity with the predominant political idea of twentieth-century Afghan governments, its separate appeals to the numerous ethnic, linguistic, and tribal groups in the country establish its connections with another Afghan tradition: the policy of "divide and rule" often exercised in practice by governments in Kabul. In its propaganda the PDPA regime claims that its official policy of nondiscrimination and of the participation of all ethnic groups, tribes, and sects in political life is unprecedented in Afghan history, and represents an entirely new order: no more special privileges for the Pushtuns in general, and for the Muhammadzai royal clan in particular.[16]

Although there is no doubt of the reality of discrimination under the old regime, it is also true that the monarchy was moving in the direction of genuine change, particularly in its last decade, under the 1964 constitution. Indeed, it could be said that in this final period the country's traditional elites had succeeded in capturing (by legal political means and electoral politics) a good deal of the actual power of the central government. Unfortunately, they were still too divided among themselves and lacking in national leadership to do very much with it. A good deal of the relative popularity of the monarchy's overthrow in the coup of July 1973 stemmed from the fact that the urban, educated elite, including both communists and the much more numerous noncommunists, feared that the traditional elites now had too much power, and would attempt to undo the reforms achieved over the past decades by the modernizing central governments.[17]

The PDPA regime's appeal to ethnic and tribal groups are partially inspired by the successful Soviet policy used against Central Asian Muslims in the 1920s and 1930s and partly by the sheer military necessity of securing some allies, however unreliable, to help reestablish some kind of government presence in the vast areas of the Afghan countryside lost to mujahidin control.[18]

The policy of appealing to individual ethnic groups would seem to promise significant long-term benefits as well, should it succeed in its short-term aim of defeating the mujahidin. The ethnic composition of Afghanistan is such that virtually every major ethnic group (and several of the minor ones too) have significant cross-border coethnics in Afghanistan's four neighbors, Pakistan, Iran, China, and the USSR. If Afghan ethnics establish links to fellow Uzbeks, Tajiks, and Turkmen in the USSR, they might become reconciled to communist rule, and see Soviet actions in Afghanistan and Soviet rule in general in a more positive light. This is especially so because they had good reason to feel oppressed politically and culturally by previous Pushtun-dominated Kabul governments. It was not until Da'ud's presidency that a small amount of radio broadcasting was allowed in Uzbeki Turkic, but publications were exclusively in the two national languages, Dari (or as it was known before the 1964 constitution, Kabuli Farsi) and Pushtu (the language of the dominant ethnic group and hence officially promoted by Afghan governments, even though the educated Pushtun elites in Kabul and the government itself had, over the years, become linguistically and culturally "Persianized").

Efforts to establish ties between Soviet Central Asian ethnics and their Afghan brethren began in the first days of the communist regime. In July 1978 the Uzbek-language weekly *Yulduz* (Star) appeared in Kabul, soon to be followed by Turkman and Baluchi weeklies.[19]

Members of Central Asian nationalities living in the Soviet Union are widely employed in propaganda in Afghanistan. Having had the "benefit" of over a century of Russian and a half century of communist rule, they are considered the senior partners in the development of their more "backward" fellow ethnics.[20]

In the past the special status of the Pushtun tribes of the frontier with Pakistan was acknowledged by the existence of a separate autonomous department of "Frontier and Tribal Affairs," whose president had cabinet rank. The person holding this title after the return of Babrak Karmal was Faiz Muhammad, one of the original Parchami officers who had carried out the coup of 1973. As the mujahidin were strongest in the Pushtun tribal areas, where they had easy access to Pakistan, Karmal instituted an active policy of meeting with tribal leaders, even with those of the Safi tribe, which had been among the first to rise against the regime after the 1978 coup. He insisted that all was forgiven, and that he understood that the loyal tribes had been justified in opposing Amin's tyranny. Faiz Muhammad was very active in the traditional task of his ministry, i.e., buying off tribal *khans* to gain support for the government. However, in September 1980 he was drawn into a mujahidin ambush and killed.[21]

In May 1981, just before the constituent congress of the National Fatherland Front was to meet, the Ministry of Frontier and Tribal Affairs was renamed the Ministry of Tribes and Nationalities, and a "high tribal *jirgah*" (assembly) was announced under its jurisdiction. Two weeks later this jirgah was listed as one of the founding organizational members of the National Fatherland front.

It has been proven impossible, in practice, to do away with all of the privileges of the Pushtun tribes. One of the few demonstrations of popular opinion to have successfully forced a modification of a policy of the PDPA regime occurred when the Pushtuns of Paktia Province, who had been granted exemption from military conscription by Nadir Shah in 1929 as a reward for their aid in his gaining the throne of Kabul, came to Kabul and openly protested against the regime's conscription decrees.[22]

In fact, as the regime's attempts to strengthen the regular military forces continued to be frustrated, despite great efforts, an increasing emphasis was placed on the creation of tribal militias, paid by the government and given certain arms, but serving only in their own tribal territory.

In only a few cases, however, have these tactics proven to be useful to the Soviet/PDPA forces. In general, the tribes extract what money, food, arms, and other support they can get from Kabul, and continue to cooperate with the mujahidin in secret. The heavy fighting in 1983 in the Paktia and Paktika provinces, areas where this policy had been applied extensively, gave clear evidence of its failure. Even when some tribal khans tried to support the Soviet/Kabul forces, they had no authority once a tribal jirgah had decided to join the mujahidin in fighting with the *jihad*. They turned their government-supplied weapons against their donors. Similarly, in 1984 the 3,000-strong tribal militia of Hassan Khan Karokhel (Ahmadzai), occupying the strategic hill country east of Kabul and thus guarding the main electric power transmission lines to the capital, defected en masse to the mujahidin. (They had, in fact, been cooperating with the mujahidin for years, as their territory was the best route to the Panjshir Valley.) As a result, the pylons carrying power to the capital were destroyed, and the regular troops sent out to rebuild them were crushed.[23]

In the area where the nationalities policy would seem to have the greatest chance of success—the non-Pushtun north, where Turkic and Tajik peoples had been deliberately "colonized" (Pushtunized) by Afghan governments—its influence is diminished by the fact that many of the peoples are descended from refugees who fled the establishment of Soviet power in Central Asia a generation of two before.[24] On the other hand, in the Pushtun areas, where the tribal system is the strongest and where past governments have operated on a very similar system of buying off tribal leaders, the tribal democracy of the jirgah and the fact that most of the mujahidin and refugees in Pakistan are themselves Pushtuns works against the PDPA regime.

For the most traditional villagers, regardless of their ethnic background, the call of the Islamic jihad has far more appeal than that of urban Kabulis—particularly when those Kabulis are communists. Increasingly, the resistance cuts across the traditional tribal and ethnic divisions of Afghan society. Successful regional commanders of the mujahidin are able to extend their influence and gain support beyond their native areas, and in cases where the mujahidin have been divided along ideological grounds, local traditional elites have forced the rival commanders to cooperate if they wished to maintain the crucial support of the local people.[25]

Islam under the PDPA Regime

In the traditional social and political system, the Islam of Afghanistan was in practice a preliterate folk Islam taught by self-educated village mullahs and Sufi pirs—the Islam of shrines and amulets rather than that of learned disputations on the fine points of the shari'a. Legalistic and formal Islam was under government control, but it was undoubtedly the lesser part of Afghanistan's Islamic heritage. As in most Muslim traditional states, it was manipulated by the political authorities for their own purposes, basically to strengthen the power of the central government against both domestic and foreign rivals and enemies. It was necessary that the mass of the population, who had little or no idea of a nation-state, be given some kind of Islamic legitimation to justify the rule of a particular lineage of a particular Pushtun tribe over peoples of different tribes, languages, and racial compositions.[26] In this still overwhelmingly traditional, tribal, and preliterate society, in which over 99 percent of the population were Muslims, the Afghan rulers thus had no special claim to Islamic legitimacy as had the Ottoman sultans, the Iranian shahs, the Saudis, or the Hashemites. It was true that in 1747, at the founding of the Durrani Empire, the special reputation for piety of the minor Saddozai clan helped the claim of Ahmad Khan Abdali to the throne. But in the early nineteenth century the Saddozais had been ousted by the more powerful Barakzais, various branches of which ruled Afghanistan until 1978. The king of Afghanistan *was* a religious figure, but only because he was first of all a political leader—and in the traditional order it was impossible to separate religion from politics.[27]

Aside from the traditional Islam of the villages and the state-sponsored Islam of the elites and official *ulama*, there were powerful independent centers of Islam in the Sufi orders: the Naqsbandiya, the Qadiriya, and the Chishtiya, each of which had its origins outside of Afghanistan. The traditional hereditary leaders of the Naqsbandiya and Qadiriya, the Mojadidi and Gailani families, were powerful religious and political figures in Afghanistan and their present heads are leaders of two of the mujahidin political organizations.

In the last decade or so of the monarchy and during the first republic of Muhammad Da'ud Khan, a new type of militant, revolutionary Islam emerged from the Faculty of Theology of Kabul University, largely from professors who were influenced by the ideas of the Muslim Brotherhood during their studies at al-Azhar in Cairo.[28] The liberal policies of the 1964 constitution allowed these ideas to spread rapidly to the student population of the capital, and by 1969 there were street demonstrations against government policies. By 1975, during Da'ud's republic, there was an attempt at an Islamic revolution in the Panjshir Valley and neighboring areas, led by Ahmad Shah Mas'ud (today the legendary mujahidin leader of the Panjshir Valley), a former engineering student and member of the *Jam'iyyat-e Islami* ("Islamic Society"). Despite covert Pakistani support, this challenge was handled with relative ease by President Da'ud. The Islamic revolutionary parties were young and inexperienced, to be sure, but they also had to contend with the fact that Da'ud was still viewed as the legitimate Islamic ruler of Kabul by the ordinary citizen.

In the period after the coup of April 27, 1978, there was an effort to promote the party's chief, Nur Muhammad Taraki, as a kind of traditionally Islamic Kabul ruler, a kindly white-haired father figure (he was sixty-one). This clashed, however, with political reality. With a combination of boundless optimism that the masses would welcome their "reforms," even though these stemmed from Marx instead of Muhammad, and a nagging fear that the religious leaders and masses (together with the foreigners) would join to oust them as they had King Amanullah in 1929, the Khalqi regime moved to assert a new revolutionary legitimacy throughout the country. Taraki expressed this clearly: "We are strong enough to keep all antidemocratic and international forces, who could turn against our revolution in the name of religion or because they are paid by a foreign power, under control. We shall defeat them and silence them. The people will follow us out of conviction or out of fear of punishment."[29]

The PDPA regime moved with vigor against all opposition, or

anticipated opposition, with arrests, executions, and military action. The new literacy programs, instead of starting with ABCs, literally began with the initials of the PDPA.[30] The Hazrat Sahib of the Shor Bazaar, the head of the Mojadidi family and the Naqshbandiaya Sufi order, along with most of his extended family, were arrested and eventually executed.[31] In a move of startling stupidity, the national flag was changed from its traditional black, red, and green tricolor (which Da'ud had changed from vertical to horizontal) to an all-red flag with a small gold party emblem. In a few ill-chosen actions, the Khalqi regime undid its own attempts to present an Islamic face to the population, and thus aroused the nationwide mujahidin movement. This movement, in turn, in less than two years had so undermined the regime's power that it could only be preserved through the direct intervention of the Soviet Union.

It is probable that the Karmal wing of the PDPA, the Parchamis, had they been in power after the April coup, would have been clever enough, as well as subservient enough to the advice of their Soviet masters, to have avoided some of the stupidities of the Taraki-Amin policy on religion. Whether this would have made any long-term difference, it is difficult to say, for their fundamental policy is no different from that of the Khalqis. Their official policy follows closely the example of the Soviets in Central Asia in attempts to co-opt the official ulama into the state structure (as, indeed, they have been incorporated under the Afghan monarchy as well) and to proclaim the freedom of religious ceremonies and beliefs, while in practice attempting to replace the Islamic basis of society first with ethnic nationalism and later with socialism.[32]

The regime purports to respect "the fundamental principles" of Islam and freedom to practice Islamic rituals. It actively fosters Islam through support for scholars, clergy, and believers with subsidies, the building of mosques and shrines, and support for the *hajj*. The speeches, public appearances, and ceremonies of the leaders of the PDPA and DRA are full of formal observance of Islamic ritual and customs. The regime claims that it is the mujahidin and their foreign masters, "Western imperialists, Chinese hegemonists, and regional reaction," who are destroying the welfare of the Muslim people of Afghanistan and attacking mosques, schools, and clergy.

The regime's efforts to receive Islamic legitimacy are reflected organizationally in its instituting a "supreme council of religious scholars and clergy" in April 1982 under the authority of the department of Islamic affairs of the DRA, whose president had been raised to cabinet rank.[33] Through this council, religious scholars participate as one of the groups within the National Fatherland Front, as well as in local units established in the provinces.

The ulama have been courted by exemptions from conscription laws and by the return of lands (both religious endowments and personal lands) previously taken under the regime's Land Reform Decree No. 8. The government has made allowances of "cash and goods" to the clergy and allotted ever-increasing funds for the construction, maintenance, and heating of mosques and religious shrines.

The policies of the PDPA regime vis-à-vis Islam are thus not all too different from those of previous Afghan central governments' attempting to promote nationalism and modernization. They create and co-opt an official ulama; they identify the aims of the state in development with Islamic precepts; they seek to identify the defense of the nation with the defense of Islam; and they conform to Islamic behavioral norms, at least in public. However, in the past these policies, although they might have contained more than a small measure of self-interest, were not cynical. They were the policies of Muslim believers, modernists to be sure, but believers nonetheless. Today they are policies instituted by an avowed Marxist party that is aiding a Soviet-conducted war against its own people. As a result, these policies are actively repudiated and resisted by the people. Ulama officially associated with the regime are special targets for the mujahidin.[34] Even the ulama in Kabul itself have had to be removed from their mosques for antiregime preaching.[35] And Afghans sent on the hajj defect, including even the government-appointed leaders of the Afghan *hajjis* themselves.

One of the most spectacular of the mujahidin actions against religious collaborators took place on Afghan New Year's Day (March 21), 1984. An explosion in the mosque of the Polytechnic Institute of Kabul University killed four and wounded seven of the regime's supporters, who had been gathered for the purpose of denouncing the mujahidin and President Reagan for his declaration of "Afghanistan Day."[37]

As might be suspected, the Iranian Islamic revolution poses a special problem for the PDPA regime. At its inception, the Taraki-Amin regime praised the Iranian revolution's anti-imperialist character, but was soon forced to denounce its call for an Islamic jihad against the Kabul regime.[38] On coming to power, Babrak Karmal attempted once again to appeal to friendship with Iran, particularly when speaking to Shiite audiences.[39] Following the open split between the Iranian government and the USSR in 1983, after the arrest and trial of Tudeh party leaders, however, Karmal changed his tune and denounced the entire "reactionary ruling circles" of Iran.[40]

Still, the PDPA regime is clearly sensitive to its isolation from the Islamic community as a whole and from its neighbors in particular. It has decried its exclusion from the Organization of the Islamic Conference as "illegal," and called its own foreign policy of instituting direct talks with Pakistani and Iranian neighbors "on the situation around Afghanistan" an example of the Islamic principle of the peaceful resolution of disputes between Muslims.[41]

Organization and Ideology

The PDPA arose from a very small segment of Kabul's intellectual elite, which was itself but a minute fraction of the country's population.[42] Louis Dupree notes that estimates of party membership in April 1978 varied from 10,000 to 50,000, but also observes that in Afghanistan it is well to lop off the last zero from such statistics. Deep divisions within the Kabul elite, dividing this group from society, made it into something of a tribe in itself—the tribe of the educated, governmental elite.[43] In the first cabinet of the DRA, for instance, of the twenty-two members, ten had had higher education in the United States, two in Egypt, one each in France and West Germany, four exclusively in Afghanistan, and four (all military officers) in the USSR.[44] The bitter legacy of internal conflict within the PDPA hangs over the regime, even after five years. According to an interview with Babrak Karmal in the West German magazine *Der Spiegel*, up to 4,500 members of the PDPA were killed after torture and 8,000 jailed under Amin's terror: "The regime was a hundred times more cruel than Pol Pot was in Cambodia."[45] It took the invasion of 80,000 Soviet troops and the execution of Amin at their hands to bring back Karmal from his exile and restore the Parcham faction to power in the second, "corrective," phase of the Sawr Revolution.

Although the Russian "Great Socialist Revolution of October" was highly praised in the program of the PDPA, Marxism-Leninism was nowhere mentioned in the program for national democratic reform. In its current phase, the PDPA advocates "a method other than capitalism" for Afghanistan, and it is not until the final concluding paragraph of the party's platform that it states, "We will never relinquish our aim to realize a complete society, which can be accomplished only through socialism."[46] In the party's constitution, adopted more than fifteen months before the manifesto in *Khalq,* its Marxism-Leninism was asserted somewhat more clearly and forcefully—but this was not a public document.[47]

Although there is hardly any concealment that the party is Marxist-Leninist, this aspect is still played down to general audiences. It is stressed only to selected groups, especially cadres and state employees in the military and security branches, and to foreign communist audiences. Thus, in his speech on the twentieth anniversary of the PDPA in January 1985, Babrak Karmal held out the ultimate goal of socialism, but the policy cited for the current phase is still the "Action Program" of March 1982, as adopted by the PDPA conference on March 15. This document exclusively uses "national democratic" phraseology; there is not a single mention of the party's ultimate goal of socialism; nor is Marxism-Leninism anywhere to be found.[48]

The PDPA regime claims major numerical and "qualitative" gains for the party. At the beginning of 1985, Babrak Karmal claimed a membership of 120,000 (permanent and candidate).[49] It was said that this represented a gain of 32,000 in a single year. The quality of the party is also said to have been improved by the fact that some seven thousand members (as of July 1984) had received "serious theoretical training" in the USSR, socialist countries, and in the Social Sciences Institute of the PDPA Central Committee.[50]

What these numbers of course cannot reveal (even given the somewhat dubious assumption that they bear much relation to reality) are the motivations and loyalties of party members. Clearly, party membership includes important privileges and monetary rewards. For example, any house abandoned by its owners, who are assumed to have fled the country, can be occupied without ceremony by party members. Significant opportunities for corruption are also the traditional prerogative of government officials and party members. These economic advantages, ironically, become all the more valuable with the increasingly effective efforts of the mujahidin to interdict the supply routes to the cities, especially Kabul. Moreover, many of the defectors from the regime, including very senior bureaucrats and military-police officers, report that they were secretly working for the mujahidin, who ordered them to maintain their jobs and party positions for the purpose of intelligence and subversion. One foreign reporter who visited Kabul as the guest of the mujahidin reported that most of the mujahidin underground members he met were government bureaucrats and army officers.[51]

In fact, one does not have to rely on antiregime sources to discover the weaknesses of the PDPA; they are acknowledged in surprisingly frank terms by regime spokesmen themselves, and surfaced in public in the only national congress of the party to be held since the Soviet invasion. This congress, held in March 1982 after a nationwide series of local party meetings in the hopes of ending the intraparty feuds, was intended to be a spectacular demonstration of party unity. It turned out to be just the opposite. The extent of the conflict was revealed by the fact that Interior Minister Sayed Muhammad Gulabzoy, the senior official of the Khalq faction in the regime, openly challenged Karmal to identify the alleged traitors in the party, and he received widespread support among the delegates.[52]

The practical consequences of these splits are many, especially in the military and security services. There are numerous instances where mutinies have occurred when Khalqi officers, who are particularly strong in the military, have been replaced by Parchami appointees. In 1983 the deputy defense minister, Major General Khalilullah, a Khalqi, personally assaulted and injured his superior, Lieutenant General Abdul Qader, a Parchami who was a leader of the coups of both 1973 and 1978.[53] In December 1984 Abdul Qader was removed from the defense ministry and given a party position. His replacement, the chief of staff Nazar Muhammad, happened to be a Khalqi (at least originally). Although the motivation for this move might well have been the dismal performance of the military in fighting in 1984, at least part of this dismal performance stems from the hatred of the Khalqi officer corps for their Parchami leaders. According to mujahidin sources, the KGB took over direct interrogation of prisoners in 1984, since they could no longer trust the reliability of the reports provided by the faction-ridden Afghan security services.[54]

It appears that Moscow has only limited hopes for the present generation of Afghan communists. Its long-term strategy for Afghanistan envisages the building up of a new generation of military and civilian cadres, trained in Russian and in Marxism-Leninism in the USSR. Estimates are that between 15,000 and 20,000 young people have been sent to the USSR since 1978, and they are now beginning to return at the rate of 3,000 per year.[55] This would seem to conform to the second stage of the Sovietization of Central Asia, when the original cadres of the revolutionary period, who were infected with local nationalism, even if it was a communist variety of nationalism, were replaced after Stalin's purges with Russianized cadres.

The prospects for the success of such a strategy in Afghanistan are not yet clear, but two powerful factors would indicate that it might be considerably more difficult in Afghanistan than it was in Central Asia. A number of scholars have, moreover, questioned the durability of the strategy of Russianization in Central Asia itself. In Afghanistan such a generational ideological change would be taking place in a country that is by no means pacified, as was Central Asia. The Soviets in the 1920s and 1930s were effectively able to isolate Central Asia from the outside, particularly from the Islamic world. This has not happened to Afghanistan as yet, although it is clearly a part of the USSR's current strategy. Afghanistan's long and proud history of resistance to foreign aggression and its recognized international status as an independent, nonaligned, and Islamic state tie the Afghan jihad firmly to the international situation of the region and the world. If this international support can exhibit but a fraction of the solidarity and heroism shown by the Afghan people in their resistance thus far, it is by no means inconceivable that the leaders of the Soviet Union might conclude that the political and security costs of maintaining their current policy in Afghanistan are against their own long-term interests.

The Era of Glasnost in Kabul

In 1986–87 the Soviet Union under Gorbachev's leadership attempted to redeem its failed Afghan policy. Babrak Karmal, who never had been able to overcome the fact of having arrived along with the Soviet tanks in December 1979, was replaced at the head of the PDPA regime by Dr. Najibullah, the head of the KHAD secret police since the Soviet invasion. In that the Soviets were still wary of the intraparty chaos that had accompanied past changes of leadership, this action was accompanied by massive Soviet troop deployments in the center of Kabul—something that had been avoided as an obvious contradiction of their position that the PDPA regime was an independent government.

The significance of the regime change was twofold. On the one hand, KHAD had proven itself to be the most efficient organization of the regime. Simultaneously, though scarcely backward in the application of coercion, its major successes were more political than military. Through the infiltration of resistance organizations, payments to local leaders, and the exploitation of ancient rivalries, it had scored some notable local successes despite the fact that the mujahidin as a whole had increased in strength and effectiveness from year to year.

In the winter of 1986–87 the political strategy of the Soviets moved into high gear. A unilateral cease-fire was declared, along with unilateral withdrawals of Soviet troops, and the mujahidin was invited to take part in a process of "national reconciliation." Mikhail Gorbachev even went so far as to speak of the acceptability of former King Muhammad Zahir's having a role in this reconciliation.

Some observers have seen these moves as a breakthrough in Soviet policy, signifying a willingness to accept a noncommunist and nonaligned Afghanistan. To date, however, the mujahidin and their supporters have been highly skeptical. They have refused to accept a unilateral cease-fire or token troop withdrawals as anything more than an effort to apply the old formula of a "national-democratic revolution" under the leadership of the PDPA. Although unlikely to succeed on any large scale with the mujahidin, such a policy does offer the possibility of attracting some of the war-weary elements within the country and exile communities. Perhaps even more important, it would tend to put the onus of the conflict on the mujahidin and thus reduce their international support.

Regardless of its intent, this policy is indeed a signal that the Soviet Union is not at all pleased with the failure of its chosen instrument, the PDPA, to gain any domestic or international legitimacy or credibility. The military escalations of the Soviets have been countered by the growing mujahidin military effectiveness and the increased support from their friends, particularly the deployment of U.S.-made "Stinger" antiaircraft missiles. A long-term policy of gradual "Sovietization" through changes in the educational system and the training of new cadres in the USSR has proven impossible to carry out without a prior military victory and the international isolation of the resistance. Thus the commitments and sacrifices of the Soviet Union in Afghanistan appear to be increasingly burdensome (and open-ended), both domestically and internationally, and in sharp contrast to the efforts of the new Soviet leadership to present a fresh and dynamic image. As this realization sinks in, they may well conclude that the best solution for their own long-term interests is not the continuation of a "bleeding wound" but rather the acceptance of an independent, noncommunist and nonaligned Afghanistan, whose status would be guaranteed by international agreements.

PART 4

Challenge to Democratic Practices and Principles

■

ISRAEL

The Politics of the Second Generation

■

Emanuel Gutmann

One of the conspicuous features of Israel's polity is the combination of the basic parameters of an open society and of constitutional democracy with the characteristics of an "open civilian fortress" society with "a strong military and security ethos."[1] It is a besieged society under intermittent external threat and with permanent internal stress as well. The sociological and psychological implications of this situation have only recently been systematically explored.

As a state created by Zionists, Israel was intended to be the vehicle of the Jews' control of their own political destiny, which after the Holocaust clearly also meant individual physical survival. For some Jews the founding of Israel was the vindication of two thousand years of survival in adversity; for others, the Jews' proper integration into the family of nations. Some saw it as marking the dawn of redemption or as presaging the approaching messiah; others, as signifying Jewish reentry into history. Only a few did not see, or purposely averted their eyes from seeing, the heavy personal and communal price paid for statehood, both by Jews and by others. But considering all the historical and contemporary alternatives, this price was considered by almost all Jews as more than worth paying.

Mastery of their own fate did not mean only, or primarily, independence from the will and control of others. It also meant a strong belief in the possibilities and legitimacy of self-determination in the basic sense of this term: the exercise of leadership and the activation of what one can very loosely call human engineering for the creation of a better world, composed of free nations, a more just society, and perhaps even nobler men. One of the most attractive features of this social movement was that it combined these ideological and idealistic, almost utopian, elements with down-to-earth realism and a sense of the feasible. Some have criticized such an account of Zionist pre-independence history as lopsided or as overly idealized,[2] but the role of the ideological dimension in the sense of the grand vision of a new and better world cannot be gainsaid in connection with Israeli independence. At the same time, this is not to deny the preeminence of the power-political elements that made the independence of Israel possible and continue to be instrumental in its existence.

In retrospect, what are some of the salient structural, institutional, and ideological factors in Israel that have been undergoing substantial change during the past four decades, and how have these affected policy in recent years? The focus of this chapter will be mainly on domestic developments, with some remarks on their external interconnections.

Quite a number of rather dramatic changes have taken place in the composition of Israel's population (I am here especially concerned with the political and social implications of these changes). Basically, there are three kinds of demographic factors at issue: the composition of the Jewish majority; the relative size of the Jewish and Arab populations of the country; and, less directly pertinent, the relationship between the Israeli (Jewish) population and the diaspora.

The population of Israel has grown very rapidly since independence, but rather unevenly, inasmuch as this exceptional growth is primarily the result of the Jewish immigration into the country. In 1948 about 800,000 people lived in the territory that had become Israel; of these, some 650,000 were Jews (80 percent of the total population). By 1967, in less than twenty years, the total population had grown almost fourfold to about 2.8 million, of whom 2.4 million (about 85 percent) were Jews. By 1985, eighteen years later, the population had grown by another 65 percent, to 4.3 million, and the Jewish part of it was down slightly, to 83 percent. If, however, one takes into account not only Israel in its almost unchanged pre-1967 borders, that is, the area over which it claims sovereignty, but that area plus the territories under its control on the West Bank and the Gaza Strip, then in 1967 the population was 3.75 million, of which the Jews constituted about 68 percent, and by 1985 this had grown to almost 5.6 million, of which the Jews were about 65 percent.

During these years over 1.7 million immigrated into the country, but the distribution of immigrants over the years has been very unequal. Almost 1.3 million arrived before 1967, of whom more than 750,000 arrived during the first three years after independence, more than doubling the population by 1951; since 1967 fewer than 400,000 have immigrated. The crucial feature of this immigration was its composition from the point of view of the country or continent of origin (which is what "ethnic factor" is understood to mean in Israel), and its impact on the composition of Israel's population as a whole. In spite of repeated protests against the oversimplification and the misleading connotations of the statistical classification of Jews into Ashkenazim (i.e., European, with very few exceptions) and Orientals (also called Sephardim, mainly from present-day or formerly Islamic countries), it is still widely used by the population at large, as well as by the statisticians. At independence there was an 80 : 20 ratio between Ashkenazim and Orientals, and the percentage of Ashkenazim immigrants during the British Mandate (1920–47) reached 90. Then the ratio shifted, and between 1948 and 1967 it stood at 56 : 44. As a result of this development, by 1967 the Oriental population (measured to be the immigrants from these countries as well as their Israeli-born children) almost achieved parity with the Ashkenazim. From 1967 until 1985, with the highly reduced rate of immigration, the percentage of Oriental immigrants sharply declined again, inasmuch as the major sources of this immigration had been depleted. Nevertheless, as a result of the natural increase in the Israeli population during this period, by the mid-eighties the Orientals have come to make up roughly 55 percent of the Jewish population, with most of them by now second- and third-generation natives. One of the more recent developments is that the birthrate of second- and third-generation Israeli-born Jews of both groups is approaching parity. Another factor affecting this bifurcation of the Jewish population is that in the past two decades over 20 percent of all Jewish marriages were mixed in this ethnic sense. Although among the Israeli-born generation of whatever origin there is a growing concern about the perpetuation of this ethnic division, ideological or moral condemnation by itself will not end the problem, and it continues to confront Israeli society with some agonizing conflicts and difficult prospects.

By the end of the 1960s, then, the main contours of present-day Israeli society from the point of view of its ethnic composition had been established, with a rough numerical equality between the two Jewish ethnicities. However, in comparing these two segments of social groups it was and is evident that far-reaching disparities exist between them in almost all respects: political effectiveness, social status, socioeconomic rating, and in all of these (and in others) to the obvious advantage of the Ashkenazim. Moreover, in spite of, or perhaps even because of, quite vigorously pursued policies of integration into the receiving society, it had become apparent by the 1960s that a total homogenization of Israeli Jewish society would not and could not take place, and perhaps should neither be anticipated nor cherished.

Until the late 1960s, by which time only a decade or a little more had elapsed since the years of the biggest mass immigration in the early and mid-1950s, the predominant leadership role of Ashkenazim in all facets of public life, including the political, had not been seriously challenged, nor could it have been. Perhaps the single most significant development of domestic politics, starting in the 1970s, was the growing social, cultural, and, above all, political assertiveness of Orientals, which may or may not have reached its peak of vehemence in the early 1980s. The firmest indicator of this change can be seen in the 1977 election results, in which a substantial switch of political allegiance of Orientals to the Herut party and the Likkud parliamentary bloc headed by Menachem Begin contributed significantly to that party's great electoral victory, which in turn brought about the first change of the party in power in thirty years. Even today debate continues as to the precise dimension of this electoral shift of 1977, which continued through 1984.[3] The motivations for this massive vote for Herut/Likkud (between 65 and 70 percent of Orientals in each of the last three elections) are of course manifold, and include such factors as personal support for Begin (and in 1984 for Sharon and Levi), the identification with a populist party, and support for hawkish policies, Greater Israel, and military aggressiveness. But clearly it was also a protest vote by the Orientals against the old Labour party regime and all it stood for in their eyes.

The second major demographic change has to do with the Jewish-Arab relationship in Israel and in the Israeli-ruled areas. With the creation of the state of Israel, a demographic volte-face took place. Within its borders the Arabs became a rather small minority, whereas the Jews, who had before been a minority, emerged as the massive majority. Israel's military victory in 1967 brought more than one million Arabs under Israeli military rule, however, and as a result, although Israeli Arabs constituted 15 percent of Israel's population, that figure jumped to about 36 percent when one counted the total population of Israel and the territories under its control. By the mid-1980s the Israeli Arabs had risen to 18 percent of the population, and all Arabs under Israeli control to almost 38 percent.

The third, somewhat different, factor is Israel's relationship with the Jewish diaspora. Of the approximately 15 million Jews in the world in the early 1980s, fewer than 4 million live in Israel. The United States, with over 5.5 million Jews, has about 50 percent more Jews than Israel, which makes it, not Israel, the world Jewish demographic center.[4] Evidently on this score Zionism, with its original hope for the return of all (or most) Jews to Palestine/Israel and for the end of their diaspora existence, has thus far been less than fully successful. Nor does it seem likely at this point that this goal is going to be achieved in the future.

Notwithstanding this demographic situation, or possibly in spite of it, Israel in a number of ways plays a central, perhaps the central, role in the existence of contemporary Jewry. Before independence world Jewry was intimately involved in the diplomatic and public opinion struggle to establish the state of Israel, and some segments of the diaspora offered material and personal assistance during the War of Independence. This high degree of concern did not cease thereafter, but it subsided quite considerably in the 1950s and early 1960s, to be brought to a new pitch in 1967, at which level it has remained ever since, with only minor fluctuations. This concern for Israel in the diaspora during the last twenty years has not, however, generated much immigration to Israel.[5] Close personal and family relations persist, economic connections continue to fluctuate between higher and lower reciprocal involvements, and there is an increasing flow of Israeli emigration to the major centers of the Jewish diaspora. Not least important has been the nexus based on the political activities of Israel for harassed and persecuted Jewish communities abroad, as well as the active involvement of the strong Jewish communities, primarily in the United States, in support of the Israeli state.

The Palestinian diaspora resulting from the 1948 and 1967 wars is the Arab counterpart of the Jewish diaspora. In this case also the diaspora is numerically stronger than the remnant who stayed on their native soil, although most of the diaspora is concentrated in adjacent lands. There is considerable tension between the center and periphery as to political leadership and the determination of national policy, but hegemony seems to rest with the diaspora, at least for the time being. Also, between 1948 and 1967, the Palestinians in general and their diaspora in particular remained comparatively inactive politically, and it was only as a result of the 1967 war and its territorial consequences that Palestinians became fully mobilized and their diaspora exerted claims to leadership, not disputed by West Bankers and people of the Gaza Strip. Even in this state of affairs, however, an invisible partitioning line, following the pre-1967 "Green Line" demarcating Israel from its neighbors, continues to separate Israeli Arabs from the Palestinians who live on the other side of this line in the so-called "territories."

Another factor that has contributed to the transformation of Israeli society during the past twenty years should briefly be mentioned. This is the generational factor, which in the framework of our concern here is usually presented by distinguishing between the generation of the founding fathers—that is to say, the ruling elite at independence and the early decades thereafter—and the second, successor generation, which attained positions of power in the seventies, specifically with the government formed by Yitzhak Rabin in 1974. The leadership of the second generation has been criticized for a lack of both "independent world views" and the necessary acumen of rulership, as a result of which its government has been called "weak, incohesive and lacking in authority." One analyst calls the members of this government an "abortive generation."[6] This may be an unduly harsh judgment. More likely, this is a typical case of postrevolutionary leadership.

Whether the Israeli public at large is less ideologically motivated than the leadership is rather doubtful.[7] Ideology has both a consensus-forming and a divisive effect, and both are at work in Israel, as elsewhere. It has become customary to speak of the "Zionist consensus" as an ideologically all-embracing umbrella, the existence of which is usually attributed to at least two factors: the tragic common history, especially of recent years (the Holocaust), and the common enemy across the Israel's borders. The overwhelming majority of Israeli Jews would consider themselves to be partners in this consensus,[8] which serves as the ideological underpinning of what is usually presented as Israel's consociational or quasi-consociational political regime.[9] This regime permitted the Israel Labour party, the dominant (but not majority) party, to run the government quite efficiently and essentially democratically for almost three decades in spite of a highly fractionalized party system.[10] During this period an almost fully consociational regime existed for only three years (1967–1970), during and after the Six-Day War, when the main center-right-wing opposition group, then called Gahal (later the Likkud), headed by Begin, joined the government in the first cabinet of national unity. The breakup of this cabinet in 1970 was indicative of the limits of consensus politics; at issue was Israel's policy toward the territories taken in the war, with Gahal rejecting (at that time) any notion of withdrawal from any of them, while the Labour party did not rule out the possibility of a repartitioning of Palestine west of the Jordan.

This breakup seems to signify the beginning of the end of consensus politics in Israel; later events such as the Yom Kippur War and the Lebanon war of 1982–83 have finally brought consensus to an end. Meanwhile, the Labour party has lost its dominant position, and what amounts to a quasi-two-party system has emerged, with the Labour party and the Likkud holding each other in some sort of parliamentary balance. With a much more volatile electorate on the one hand and a steady decline in policy options open to the government on the other, genuine consensus politics no longer have a place, in spite of the fact that some of the basic conditions for consociationalism continue to exist. The second cabinet of national unity (1984) is not a repeat of the first and cannot therefore be seen as based on consensus politics, in any event as far as the crucial problem of the future of the territories is involved. The cabinet is based, nevertheless, on a common economic policy, on a common antiterrorist strategy, and a basically agreed-upon border dispute approach; it also agreed on the move to extricate Israel from Lebanon, the intrusion into which had been the main reason for the final breakdown of consensus politics. The discontinuation of consensus politics is most evident in that the cabinet of national unity has agreed to disagree over long-range West Bank politics, which has meant in practice an enforced status quo on the Israeli side. To the extent that this cabinet has worked, and has had important achievements to its credit, it signifies the triumph of parliamentary constraints and pragmatisms over ideological politics.

Some observers of the Israeli scene have seen in such developments an indication of a secular process of forgoing ideology, with the concomitant emergence of a basically materialist, hedonistic orientation, of welfarism and of individualistic values overshadowing the social, even collectivist, values that had characterized the public spirit of the earlier generation. Some, however, claim on the contrary to have found in Israel, quite in accord with similar developments in the West, and perhaps not only in the West, signs of the so-called postmaterialistic culture.[11] These two trends can and do flourish conterminously, in Israel as elsewhere, inasmuch as they are reactions to each other. Whatever the extent of these phenomena elsewhere, and leaving aside here the question to what extent this approach permits a correct reading of the ideological map, it seems that as far as Israel is concerned, one should not overrate the scope of the materialist tendency nor of the postmaterialist one. Whatever the dimensions of these contradictory tendencies among the young generation, and bearing in mind that such developments usually have a lengthy gestation period, there seems to be ample evidence to claim that they became discernible and acquired some social and political significance in the 1970s and later.

It has been customary to subsume the wide range of the ideologies of Jewish Israel under three main headings, usually called "camps"—namely, the Labour (or socialist, or left) camp, the civic (or center, or right) camp, and the religious camp.[12] To thesc should be added the Arab sector.

The single most salient change in the socioeconomic basis of the major political camps during the past two decades is that both the Labour party and the Likkud have become "ethnic" parties (or party blocs). In the present context this means that between 60 and 70 percent of their supporters come from one ethnic group: at least 65 percent of Ashkenazim support Labour, and about 70 percent of Orientals vote for the Likkud. Before the 1970s there may also have been a slightly uneven ethnic support, but certainly not to the degree since then. The Oriental support for the Likkud gradually grew from election to election until 1981, when it may have reached its climax; but among the young Oriental voters support for the Likkud continues to be overwhelmingly high. Not all this support can be seen as strictly ideological, whatever the exact meaning of this term. For many Oriental Jews such a vote is primarily a repudiation of the Labour party, the one-time perennial ruling party, during whose time in office most of Orientals (or their parents) immigrated to Israel, and which many hold responsible for what they consider to have been discrimination against them. In part, the growing vote for the Likkud is also a major symptom of the rightward tendency, of which more below. Be that as it may, there is little doubt that the electoral move to the Likkud is viewed by many of the people concerned as one of political maturity, self-confidence, and assertion. Given the more recent volatility of Israeli voters and the preference of many, but by no means most, of them for personalities or short-range policy issues over parties, however, present-day loyalties and support cannot be taken for granted. As indicated, those who switched to Likkud and who have Oriental backgrounds (but others as well) have come from the Labour camp; but the same is true of former supporters of religious parties, and particularly of the National Religious party, who now support the Likkud and other parties with an extreme nationalistic outlook.

The second ideological trend noticeable in the past two decades is the pronounced move of the electorate as a whole to the right. As has been noticed, this is not a uniquely Israeli phenomenon, but it does seem to have some special Israeli traits.[13] In the first

Knesset elections in 1949, just about one-half of Israelis voted for left-wing parties, at that time committed in varying degrees to socialism. That figure has since declined to between one-third and two-fifths of the electorate. But more significantly, perhaps, the left-wing commitment of those who stayed within the Labour camp has considerably weakened. By the same token, the domestic economic and social policies pursued by the Labour party when it is in power, although including attempts to preserve some of the achievements of the past, are now reconciled to middle-of-the-road measures. The other side of this coin is the sociological phenomenon that most working-class people have defected from the Labour camp, and this basically not because of that camp's relinquishment of a socialist message or its nonegalitarian policies, but perhaps in spite of it. Workers have moved to the right in large numbers, and the people involved are mainly of Oriental background.[14]

But perhaps the most striking ideological transformation of the past twenty years is the radicalization of Israeli politics, but again only in a very special way. What had characterized the first generation after independence was a discernible tendency toward moderation in all political camps. Always allowing for a few significant exceptions, the Labour camp became less left-oriented, the right-wing less hawkish, and even the mainline religious representatives became at times more accommodating. This overall tendency was one aspect of the aforementioned consensus, but it also had to do with the necessities of coalition government and more generally with coming to terms with statehood.

By and large this moderating tendency has been reversed, beginning in the early 1970s, in the right-wing and religious camps, and to a much lesser degree, if at all, in the Labour camp. This undoubtedly is a facet of the move to the right. This radicalization has directly affected only comparatively small numbers of people; however, because of the visibility of the activities of some of them and the public relations adroitness of others, at times they receive a disproportionately large amount of attention and perhaps also of influence.

The radical right is made up of a growing number of groups and organizations of all sorts. Among these are military and political hawks, some of the West Bank settler groups, vigilante organizations, and so forth. There are secular people among them as well as religious ones, but the simple common denominator of all of them is their determination to hold on to the West Bank, open it up to further Jewish settlement, and incorporate it into Israel at an opportune time. The motivations of these groups are quite diversified, but at least some members, above all the settler Gush Emunim organization, claim to be the genuine revivalists of Zionist pioneering. Some are willing, perhaps even eager, to come into collision with the authorities in the pursuit of their political goals; but they also know that they have quite widespread support among numerous segments of the population. And as political action groups they have been partly successful in having their viewpoints and policies adopted by the various governments since the mid-1970s. Their successes, and their public struggles, even if unsuccessful, have impressed parts of the Israeli population by their spiritedness and dedication.

On the other hand, radicals of the most extreme kind, like Rabbi Kahane, who use Scripture to promote racist motives and denigrate democracy any time it clashes in their view with religion or nationalism, have little chance of public support other than from minute groups of disciples. The main cause for the appearance of such ideas is the exasperation of these people at the continued threat to Israel and to Israelis from the Arabs and the impatience resulting from their disbelief that a peaceful settlement of the Arab-Israeli conflict is possible on terms acceptable to Israelis.

Kahane is driven, so it seems, by an atavistic, tribal kind of xenophobia with a supposedly religious fanaticism. He comes closest to recent fundamentalist phenomena in the Muslim world. Gush Emunim is a much more complex and sophisticated phenomenon. To the extent that religious persuasions or faith genuinely play a role in their motivation, theirs is a living messianic fervor imbued with a belief in man's duty to do God's will, perhaps even to anticipate it.[15] Together with mainstream religious Zionism, they regard the state of Israel as the dawn of messianic redemption; the Six-Day War was a sign of divine intervention in order to complete the territorial redemption of the Holy Land by the liberation of those areas of Eretz Israel that contain the holiest shrines of Judaism and where the main scenes of its history in its formative periods and in antiquity took place. The redemption of the land was, of course, one of the main principles of Zionism right from the beginning, but Gush Emunim gave it a very special, messianic, quasi-mystical connotation, while at the same time engaging in very down-to-earth and shrewd practices in order to implement their political goals in respect to this land.[16]

Distinct from organizations and groups that are involved with general political issues yet are religiously motivated, extremism by religious bodies in matters regarded as of direct and genuine religious relevance—such as sabbath observance, marriage laws, autopsies and transplantations, and public display of materials they consider to be pornographic—is also rising. Most of the ultraorthodox communities from which the activists of these extreme protest groups are recruited and that provide them with popular support are outside the Zionist consensus and outside the political system by their own choice. In recent years some of these sects have seen fit to participate in the political power game, while others have remained in their self-imposed social and political isolation, and continue at least formally to deny the legitimacy of a secular Jewish state. The first group wants to use the machinery of the state to impose a religious way of life on the public at large, while the second is unwilling to be coerced by anybody, including of course the government, to do or not do anything unacceptable. In recent years some of these groups have become more aggressive, in particular in areas of their dense concentration in Jerusalem, with a growing readiness to stage mass demonstrations and even to give way to violence, mainly arson and other kinds of damage. The overall picture is one of growing extremism, both in terms of demands and the means employed. Needless to say, the majority of the orthodox sector abhors this religious radicalization and tries to distance itself from these groups on both scores.[17]

As compared to the first two decades or so of independence, the Israeli Arabs have undergone tremendous social changes, and they have become no less radicalized politically than any other sector. Clearly this had to do with at least four quite independent factors, which together converged on this population. One was the quite dramatic change of the economic and social status of Israeli Arabs—the rise of their standard of living, the changes in their kinship and family structure, the marked improvement in their educational standards and legal situation—accompanied by only slight advancements in political life. A second factor was the virtual disappearance in 1967 of the Green Line, which had earlier, since 1948, cut them off from their kinspeople on the then Jordanian West Bank. With its disappearance, for all practical purposes all Arab countries were open to them. This led to, among other things, the possibility of more intimate relations with the Palestinian national movement, which in the form of the PLO had about that time begun a new stage of development. Third, Israeli Arabs were exposed to the tremendous transformations in the Arab world at large, including the multifarious political and religious, extremist, radical, and fundamentalist movements. And, finally, Israeli Arabs have also been affected by processes among the Israeli Jews, including the political developments in their own home country.

Politically, the Israeli Arabs were early on under the tutelage of a small number of notables of the traditional type who collaborated with the Israeli authorities; more recently most of them have sought an outlet for their national feelings by supporting a communist-led Arab populist party, while others prefer an attachment to a Jewish party. Whether these existing options satisfy the national aspirations of all Israeli Arabs is hard to ascertain, but their radically changed political outlook is a certainty.[18]

Toward the end of the fourth decade of its independence, Israel has preserved intact its parliamentary democratic system of government, which has shown both originality and continuing innovation.[19] Its latest achievement was the cabinet of national unity which rotated the post of prime minister in mid-term between the heads of the two coalescing, but adversary, parties with equal strength in the cabinet. But toward the end of its four-year term of office it has become clear that the coalition's blessings are limited in a deeply cleaved society with rampant political distrust. A governmental arrangement of this kind may achieve certain specific policy objectives but beyond these becomes a prescription for policy stalemate and political incapacity.

The Israeli public is as politicized as ever and hardly less ideologically motivated than earlier. Nevertheless, politics nowadays appears to revolve around personalities more than parties or policies. A major charge has been the inaccessibility of party leadership positions to Oriental Jews. There is now no group seriously outside the political system other than the Israeli Arabs. They have full political equality, of course, and they make full use of their political rights. Nevertheless, although genuine access to the levers of power is by no means closed to them, it is still limited as far as they are concerned. Other groups are also underrepresented, such as women and some underprivileged social strata, but by and large, government is quite open. Also, it would seem that the threat of a forthcoming struggle of some elements of the Oriental community for full civil and social equality and unreserved access to, and participation in, the policy-making process, which had looked rather ominous, has subsided, and the peak of this conflict has passed.

On the other hand, all the indications are that the quite different conflict over the role of religion in Israel's public life will henceforth escalate and result in a real confrontation. This is indeed a cardinal issue for the future of Israeli society, inasmuch as the nature of the Jewish state will be up for discussion, and it is not a matter only of internal concern to the Jews of Israel; it will also affect Israel's non-Jewish population and Israel's relation with the diaspora.

TURKEY

Democratic Framework and Military Control

■

Jacob M. Landau

The history of the Turkish republic—beginning with the institution of a multiparty system in 1946—may be viewed as a continuous struggle between a new state and the forces attempting to undermine it. These counterforces have varied in strength and nature and, fortunately for the future of democracy in Turkey,[1] have never joined. Still, each singly was powerful enough to at least endanger the survival of democracy. Over a twenty-year period, between 1960 and 1980, the military intervened three times in Turkish politics and imposed temporary control. The antiestablishment groups challenging the democratic regime had to reckon with the military forces, which gradually changed from behind-the-scene actors in politics before 1960 to active participants.[2] This essay will attempt to outline and analyze the interplay between democratic government, antiestablishment groups, and the military, as manifested from the end of World War II to the present.[3]

Before the war dissident groups existed, but their activities were held in check by the forceful personality of Mustafa Kemal Atatürk and by his immense prestige;[4] during the war order was maintained by the resolute leadership of İsmet İnönü and the martial law he imposed. Consequently, this discussion will start with the era following the end of World War II. The time span under consideration may be divided into four periods, extending over fourteen, eleven, nine, and five years respectively, punctuated by the three military interventions.

The first period commences with the 1946 elections, which inaugurated the multiparty era, and ends with the first military intervention, in 1960. Competitive politics unavoidably foster politicization, and Turkey was no exception. During the first four years of this period, until 1950, Turkey continued to be governed by the Republican People's party (founded in 1923), and during the subsequent decade by the Democratic party (set up in 1946), which in 1950 won popular support largely as a result of a backlash of discontent with the single-party rule of the Republican People's party. There were other political parties after 1946, but until 1960 these two were the only mass parties in Turkey. By deciding to allow the transfer to a multiparty system, the Republican People's party asserted its commitment to democracy in Turkey. The Democratic party, on the other hand, while paying lip service to democracy, betrayed an increasing determination from the mid-1950s on to continue in power at any cost, taking steps to control the press (by new legislation), politicize the military (by appointing officers they trusted to key positions), and muzzle the opposition (by harassing other parties).[5]

They seriously underestimated, however, the military's commitment to a democratic Turkey. One of Atatürk's achievements had been to isolate the military from day-to-day politics, which may explain why they refrained from intervening for so long. But they had also been educated to consider themselves guardians of the republic. By 1960 not a few military officers interpreted the moves of the Democratic party as signs of an authoritarianism that ran counter to the fundamental values of the republic and endangered the democracy that had evolved there. On May 17, 1960, they took over the government.

The second phase of Turkey's postwar history spans the years between May 17, 1960,[6] and March 12, 1971, when the military intervened again. The officers who had seized power in 1960 had voluntarily relinquished it to a civilian government following the October 1961 general elections. The new constitution of 1961[7] and a modified party law that facilitated the formation of new political parties, along with the virtual abolition of press censorship, heralded a liberal decade in modern Turkish political history. The general elections of 1961 were largely based on proportional representation, and the Constituent Assembly sought to prevent reestablishment of an authoritarian regime by setting up a constitutional court intended to curtail possible abuse of power by the government.

Democracy flourished, but so did dissident groups, many of which were extra-parliamentary. Their adherents and supporters had gathered strength since the early 1960s because of the broadening scope of the media and an increase in literacy (to about 60 percent). A spate of publications, both original Turkish works and translations of foreign materials, proliferated in this liberal climate;[8] ideologies that could not be advocated previously were now freely preached and discussed. The most prominent among them was Marxism, although Pan-Turkism and Islamism also found partisans.[9] During the late 1960s these tiny but dedicated groups resorted increasingly to violence. With elected politicians seemingly unable to restore law and order, the military decided to step in once again.

The third chapter in the history of the post–World War II Turkish republic begins with the coup of March 12, 1971. This time the military retained power for two and a half years. It delivered an ultimatum to the then-ruling Justice party[10] and its leader, Prime Minister Süleyman Demirel, demanding the immediate restoration of law and order. Demirel resigned, and the military supervised affairs through governments made up of technocrats (rather than politicians). Terrorists were hunted down and censorship was tightened. But the tide of sharp political debate, which had moved into the open in the sixties, could no longer be turned back. (Such openness, part and parcel of any democratic system, led in Turkey to the deterioration of this very system.) And history to some extent repeated itself. Soon after the October 1973 elections, when elected civilians again took over the government, violence resurfaced. By the late 1970s it had become a constant fact of life in Turkey, particularly in urban areas. Political assassinations numbered as many as twenty-five to thirty daily; university studies were disrupted; the economy suffered; journalists and politicians were intimidated; parliament was rendered unable to legislate. Those responsible were chiefly Marxist-inspired leftist groups and extreme nationalist rightist ones.[11] Radical Islamic fundamentalists, although not actively involved in acts of terrorism, contributed to the general atmosphere with their own brand of extremist propaganda.[12] It appeared, in short, that the Turkish state and society were falling apart.[13]

On September 12, 1980, the military intervened for a third time, marking the start of the fourth period of postwar Turkish history, which continues up to the time of this writing. With the ultimate failure of the two earlier interventions to improve the political system and to crush the dissident forces, so clearly visible and operating more or less freely, the military now opted for radical treatment. Numerous people suspected of terrorist acts were hunted down relentlessly and brought to justice, with the remnants of their groups driven deep underground.[14] Under the banner of a return to Kemalism (by which term the totality of ideals and measures advocated by, or attributed to, Mustafa Kemal Atatürk is generally understood), far-reaching institutional reforms were carried out before free general elections were held again on November 6, 1983.[15]

Now that we have witnessed three military interventions in Turkey within a single generation, we may attempt to evaluate their overall objectives, the factors for and against which intervention took place, the military's methods of seizing power, the return to civilian government, and, finally, the issues addressed and the relative successes and failures of each intervention.

The 1960, 1971, and 1980 military interventions in Turkey were drastically different from most twentieth-century military coups, wherein military strongmen who have seized power have retained it for extensive periods. In the Turkish republic, on the other hand, as threefold experience has demonstrated, military interventions in politics were aimed at restoring civilian rule, expressed in a freely elected civilian government, and a multiparty system. The spokesmen for all three interventions proclaimed their ultimate intention to reinstate democracy "in the Kemalist sense of the term."

Variations in the precise interpretations of democracy from one intervention to another were owing not only to differences in time among the three, but also to the fact that the Kemalist government proper had never been an ideal democracy in the strict sense of the term; rather, it held democracy in high esteem but adapted its tenets to various constraints, for immediate practical purposes. The 1960 intervention resulted in a "neo-Kemalism," expressed in a regime more liberal than any other in twentieth-century Turkey, with some attention being paid to Turkey's socioeconomic problems. The 1971 coup, on the other hand, with its emphasis on law and order, sought to tighten political rule. And the takeover of 1980 set out to accomplish nothing short of altering the system—overhauling the existing political power structure and instituting what amounted to a presidential regime. These differences of objective may be better understood in light of the general situation prevailing in Turkey at the time of the respective military interventions, as well as in light of the forces against which each intervention was directed.

By 1960 the Democratic party had been governing for ten years, with a comfortable majority in parliament and substantial—although gradually diminishing—support within the country. Its authoritarian moves, referred to above, exasperated people who would have preferred institutional change via democratic avenues. As the Democratic party had been using patronage very extensively, and had succeeded in penetrating many (perhaps most) public bodies, the military establishment remained the only national organization cohesive and powerful enough to unseat the Democrats from the dominant position they refused to relinquish. When it did so, the army prorogued parliament, banned the Democratic party, arrested its leaders, and brought them to trial. The alternative regime instituted by the officers included provisions that were supposed to prevent a return to the Democratic party's patterns of government—built-in guarantees, the military hoped, of a stable and liberal system.

By 1971 civilian government had been ruling Turkey for ten years, in a more liberal atmosphere than had prevailed during the pre-1960 era. However, it was precisely this relatively relaxed atmosphere that led to instability and a lapse of law and order, most visible in the growing violence between rival ideological groups of armed youths. Their actions were inspired by the heady wine of extreme political literature and triggered by what appeared to them to be successful student uprisings in the United States and Europe. Small groups with rival Marxist interpretations attacked one another, but also increasingly directed a part of their violent activities against the political establishment. Rightist youths, in the universities and elsewhere, calling themselves Grey Wolves (an ancient Turkish symbol for free steppe life), counterattacked the left. As the civilian government proved increasingly unable to curb violence, the military stepped in once again. This time, however, their intervention, while expressing criticism of the cabinet and the politicians, indicated that these were not really perceived as purposefully undermining the democratic system (as the Democratic party had done before 1960); rather, the intervention was aimed at the violent groups and those suspected of aiding and abetting them. Since the Turkish police were clearly unable to cope with the situation, the martial-law powers granted to the security forces enabled them to pursue, arrest, and indict the terrorists. Once this appeared to have been satisfactorily accomplished, civilian government took over again without any changes in the system.

The situation in the country in 1980 was radically different from and even more menacing to the democratic system than the conditions that had preceded the interventions of 1960 and of 1971. Antagonistic forces reared their heads both among certain official political groupings (as among the Democratic party in 1960) and within armed illegal organizations (as in 1971).

Looking first at the latter, there was a marked rise in ideologically motivated physical violence, which grew more frequent and aggressive, spreading from Istanbul and Ankara, where most of it had been focused in the 1960s, to smaller towns and villages. No less alarming was the fact that some leftist groups espoused the cause of the Kurdish minority in Turkey and opened their ranks to young Kurds; Turkish central authorities have always regarded anything smacking of Kurdish nationalism as separatist anathema. Public debate became increasingly sharp everywhere, reaching the level of verbal violence; it penetrated even the trade unions, which in an attempt to be catch-all organizations and prevent breakaways had previously struggled against excessive politicization.

Antidemocratic pressures from within the official political structure were exerted during the 1970s by groups that had recently emerged from the political wilderness and were being increasingly represented in parliament. The Islamic fundamentalists, whose ultimate goal was the establishment of a theocracy in Turkey, had had their activities sharply circumscribed since the 1920s by the secularization drive of the Kemalists. Their attempts at mass organization hovered for many years on the border of legality, not infrequently moving underground. The relatively liberal conditions of the 1960s enabled them to work more openly, however, and by 1970 they had set up a political grouping, the Party for National Order. This was banned a year later (for introducing religion into politics, which is illegal in the Turkish republic), but reestablished in 1972 as the National Salvation party, which came to have the third largest representation in the 1973 and 1977 parliaments, even sharing in coalition cabinets between 1974 and 1977. Also profiting from the liberal sixties, the right-wing nationalists succeeded in 1965 in taking over a medium-sized party called the Republican Peasants and Nation party by managing to have their leader, Alparslan Türkeş, elected as the party's president. In 1969 this was renamed the Nationalist Action party. It was led by a group of retired military officers with marked chauvinistic and antileftist views whose constant (although unavowed) goal was the establishment of an authoritarian regime in Turkey. Although at first the Nationalist Action party enjoyed only a small following (some of it from pan-Turk circles), by 1977 it was the fourth largest in the parliament, and it shared in coalition cabinets even earlier, between 1975 and 1977. Meanwhile the left, increasingly fragmented and extra-parliamentary, deteriorated into armed illegal organizations, engaging ever more frequently, as did various right-wing youth groups, in terrorist acts.[16]

Furthermore, not only was the democratic multiparty system assailed from without and from within, but, for the first time, there was also a tangible connection—even cooperation—between the forces practicing terrorist violence and those scheming within the political framework: namely, the Nationalist Action party's sponsorship and instigation of armed activities brought by right-wing youth movements. The military's concern over the possible outcome of this double menace is evident not merely from their declarations after seizing power in September 1980, but also from their severe treatment of both suspected terrorists and political party leaders (all of whom were arrested and several of whom were tried). In particular, the leaders and hundreds of activists of extreme left groups and of the Nationalist Action party were accused, in lengthy public trials, of caching arms and ammunition with subversive intent. All political parties were closed down and their leaders banned from political activities. Terrorists were arrested and public order reestablished.

The situation immediately preceding each intervention and the forces against which each was aimed also largely dictated the military's moves, their use of power, and the style of restoring civilian rule. In both 1960 and 1980, the coups resulted in the military's assuming direct control and overhauling the political system. The officers who took over the government declared themselves rulers in the politicians' stead, governing first by decree and gradually preparing for a subsequent transfer of power back to civilians, with new constitutions and different institutional bases. In 1971, on the other hand, they resorted largely to behind-the-scenes manipulation, chiefly through the intermediacy of trusted civilians, most of whom were uncommitted politically (such as Nihat Erim, who had resigned from the Republican People's party in order to serve as an independent). For the military's main intention in 1971 was not to reform the system but to crush terrorism and restore law and order. Despite these differences, however, transfer of power to civilians took place in an essentially identical manner in all three cases—via the parliamentary elections of 1961, 1973, and 1983, respectively.[17]

The crucial differences between the three military interventions evidently pertain to the issues to which each addressed itself, the steps the military took, and the consequences thereof. In 1960–61 the military banned the Democratic party, opening the way for another pattern of the multiparty system. A constitution was drawn up that instituted a bicameral parliament for the first time in Turkey's history. It was to be elected in a manner that guaranteed more equitable proportional representation, ensuring the participation and possible success of smaller parties. However, this also ultimately led to fragmentation, which was at least partly responsible for the absence, in the 1960s, of absolute majorities in several parliaments, and the consequent need for coalition cabinets. The resulting instability was one of the causes of occasional parliamentary paralysis and of the escalation of verbal and subsequently physical violence. Perhaps sensing the danger of this development, those who had engineered the 1960 coup—middle-ranking officers well aware that they could not really expect the top military command to continue to implement their policies—took measures they hoped would ensure stability and the reputation of their reforms. In 1961, after quarreling among themselves, twenty-two of the thirty-eight officers responsible for the coup became senators for life. But this proved ineffective in stemming the tide of violence that was a major sign of the deterioration of public security and the erosion of democracy in Turkey, since the officer-senators disagreed among themselves on many important issues.

The officers responsible for the intervention of 1971, unlike those involved in 1960–61, constituted the top military command. Hence they expected that their proximity to the center of government (e.g., on the National Security Council) would ensure law and order, as well as enable them to retain a measure of control over public affairs. They proved to be as wrong as their predecessors of a decade earlier. The ensuing civilian government failed to cope effectively with public clashes and disturbances, which soon deteriorated into armed terrorism despite warnings by the top military command.

The leaders of the 1980 coup—who were the very top officers, including the chief of staff and the commanders of the air force and navy—were aware more keenly than the military had ever been before of the need for long-term answers to Turkey's political dilemmas. The problems were far more complex than ever before, and the military deemed it necessary to reexamine and redefine the entire concept of democracy, as understood by Atatürk and elaborated into a more liberal framework during the multiparty era. Before transferring power back to civilians in the 1983 elections, General Kenan Evren, the leader of the intervention, and his collaborators set out to mold a system that would ensure the future of democracy in Turkey while substantially limiting options for forces that might seek to undermine it: a system that would restrict dissident elements while encouraging everyone else to compete and participate in the political process within the prescribed—mostly democratic—rules of the regime. Their methods merit more than passing mention, as they will probably affect politics in Turkey for some time to come.

The most striking characteristic of the measures carried out by the military following the 1980 intervention was their unprecedented scope. Suspected terrorists and the leaders of the political parties active in 1980 and the two extremist trade union organizations, one comprising extreme left elements, the other extreme right ones connected with the Nationalist Action party, were arrested and put on trial. (Many were sentenced by the courts to prison terms, others to internal banishment, i.e., forced residence in a specified part of Turkey.) A Consultative Assembly,[18] selected by the ruling military command in late 1981, drew up new legislation, which, although actively debated, ultimately had to conform to the overall wishes of the military. The most important results of the assembly's deliberations were the constitution that was approved by popular referendum on November 7, 1982, the Party Law of April 24, 1983, the Trade Union Law of May 7, 1983, and the Election Law of June 13, 1983. The 1982 constitution introduced a presidential regime in Turkey. The president of Turkey is now not only symbolically impressive but also serves as an umpire in many important issues and possesses extensive executive and other powers: he appoints the chief of staff and the premier, and he presides over cabinet meetings and the National Security Council (the latter's powers were enlarged, too); he may call for new elections if parliament refuses the premier a vote of confidence. Furthermore, he nominates numerous officials to the judiciary, the Higher Education Council, and several other official bodies. Guarantees were built into the new constitution preventing the old political parties and extremely politicized trade unions from participating in politics, and recent laws ban their leaders and activists from involvement for five to ten years. The bureaucracy was purged of thousands of suspected political extremists. Some were dismissed, others transferred to less influential positions (e.g., they were removed from radio and television services). Through the newly established Higher Education Council, the military removed or transferred a sizable number of university teachers suspected of radical political views, appointing new rectors, deans, and department chairmen, and restructuring the curriculum in sensitive subjects (such as political science).

Moreover, new parties had to be officially approved (most were blacklisted) and their founders and candidates confirmed (several were vetoed). The obvious aim of this was to prevent fragmentation (by licensing only a very few parties expected to attract a large following) and extremism (by insisting on moderate platforms and nonradical leaders).

However, even after all these precautions, several surprises awaited Evren (who was elected president of Turkey by popular referendum in November 1982) and his colleagues. Three parties obtained the green light to compete in the November 6, 1983, parliamentary elections: the somewhat right-of-center National Democratic party, led by retired general Turgut Sunalp; the somewhat left-of-center People's party, headed by Necdet Calp, formerly state secretary in the premier's office; and the moderately right-of-center Motherland party, formed and led by Turgut Özal, a noted economist and previously a vice-premier, who had been dismissed from office by Evren several months earlier. The entire military leadership backed the first two, in a well-orchestrated campaign among the electorate. Evren even appeared on radio and television to attack Özal. Nonetheless, the electorate gave Özal and his Motherland party about 45 percent of the total vote and an absolute majority of 211 in a parliament of 400—perhaps a signal that it was still committed to the continuation of democracy in Turkey: the people had fearlessly elected whom they wished, despite the strong recommendations of the military leadership. However, the fears expressed in some quarters that Evren would dismiss Özal proved groundless; his greeting of Özal upon his electoral success and his allowing the new premier to form a government in December 1983 augur well for the future of democracy in Turkey.

The same may be deduced from the results of the countrywide local elections of March 25, 1984, which were generally seen as politically significant. While in rounded figures the Motherland party was first, again, with almost 44 percent of the total vote, the second and third places were won by two political parties banned from participating in the November 6, 1983, parliamentary elections: the left-of-center Social Democracy party obtained about 23 percent of the vote, and the right-of-center True Path party more than 13 percent. At the same time, the favorite parties of the former military regime achieved strikingly modest results: the Peoples' party and the National Democratic party received, respectively, just about 8.5 percent and 7 percent (a sixth party, also new, received approximately 4.5 percent). This puts the support given to the three new parties at about 40 percent—which comes close to censuring the ban imposed upon these parties some four and a half months earlier and to being an adverse vote for the parties favored by the former military regime.[19]

The explicit aim of the coup of 1980 was to perpetuate stability by incorporating certain checks and balances in the political system, the most important of which was the granting of vast political powers to the president (Evren's term of office, significantly, is six years). In theory, such measures may bring about greater stability in Turkey by ensuring the smooth functioning of the political machine, based on concepts of law and order. The true test, of course, lies in their effectiveness in actual practice, under the complicated conditions of Turkish society. It is this practical test that will determine the future and main characteristics of democracy in Turkey.[20] A presidential regime per se need not curtail democracy, as the examples of the United States and France indicate. Obviously, both these countries enjoy strong popular support for a democratic regime. Turkey does too.

LEBANON

The Role of External Forces in Confessional Pluralism

■

Edward Azar

Until the late 1970s Lebanon was a relatively tangential issue for both the United States government and U.S. scholars. (There is an oversimplified "establishment" view among government analysts and academics in the United States that the core Middle East problem is the Palestinian-Israeli conflict, and that the other three dozen conflicts in the region are peripheral and will wither away.)[1] For the United States, and probably for the Soviet establishment as well, a problem becomes significant or worthy of attention only when it spills over into East-West relations. Politicians and scholars ignored the problems of Lebanon until its complexities were revealed when U.S. Marines failed to carry out what was said to be a mission of conflict containment.

The central dilemma in Lebanon is the inability of the several religious communities that make up the country to develop an analytical consensus about the structures and processes that would satisfy their identity needs and interests. In Lebanon, as in other multicommunity societies, political and economic competition leads to fears (real and imagined) of communal marginalization, extinction, or absorption. Threatened identities motivate powerful resistance against present and potential threats of discrimination because identity needs are basic human needs. And they are not *only* psychological needs—they reflect concrete social, political, economic, and existential concerns and interests of individuals, groups, communities, and non-states.

Unfortunately for those who suffer from them, identity-driven conflicts are obstinate and do not lend themselves to traditional forms of settlement. Furthermore, contemporary international institutions and the world system are not tailored to deal with such conflicts. The United Nations, for example, like most regional organizations patterned after it, clearly limits its jurisdiction to interstate conflicts. Article 2, ch. 7 of the UN Charter states that "nothing contained in the present Charter shall authorize the United Nations to intervene in matters which are essentially within the domestic jurisdiction of any state."

In Lebanon commitment to the conflict has become the sine qua non of loyalty to the community—an absorbing, full-time concern, overshadowing many other societal, communal, and individual interests. It has frustrated intracommunal alliances and destroyed repeated attempts at promoting intercommunal consensus-building. This situation is likely to continue for the foreseeable future, despite the goodwill of many Lebanese.

Confessionalism and Intercommunal Threats in Lebanon

Lebanon is a former French mandate. The boundaries of the contemporary state of Lebanon were demarcated by the League of Nations after World War I, and the country's independence was granted by France following World War II. France holds sole responsibility for Lebanon's modern boundaries, for it was the French who unilaterally enlarged Lebanese territory to twice its previous area and French determination that ultimately reconciled the Muslim population in the newly added territory to accept their Lebanese status. While France takes the credit for Lebanon's borders, the United Kingdom and the United States played the key role in the achievement of Lebanese independence when they jointly compelled France to give up its mandate over Lebanon and allow free elections in 1943. The United States has intervened militarily in Lebanon in 1958 and 1982 in order to augment the Lebanese government in power. A dozen or so regional and international states have intervened in Lebanon in the past forty years without being able to help Lebanon bring about the desired peace.

During the past four decades the Lebanese ruling and communal elites have tried to establish a workable formula for intercommunal cooperation, albeit with mixed results. They succeeded for a short while, but the consensus fell apart in the late 1960s and left behind it a burning country from 1975 to the present.

Why did the system fall apart the way it did? The reasons are varied and complex. However, the legacy of colonialism, the inability and unwillingness of the ruling elites to satisfy the basic identity needs of some of Lebanon's communities, and the extensive external intervention (both solicited by Lebanese and imposed on them by outsiders) have worked to create Lebanon's protracted social conflict and its destructive consequences.

The French established the state machinery in Lebanon during their mandate over the country between World War I and World War II. However, the people of Lebanon needed time to develop a national consciousness. The Lebanese political system needed time to address the concerns of the various religious and ethnic groups and create the conditions for security, pluralism, and intercommunal trust. After all, colony and protectorate status were Lebanon's lot for four centuries before independence in 1944. Unfortunately for Lebanon, that time had served them poorly. The series of internal and regional crises between 1944 and 1987 have prevented the Lebanese from establishing a national identity.

At the time of independence a basic split prevailed in the population over the essence of the future state. Lebanese Sunni Muslims tended to favor a merger with Syria and pro-Arab policies. The Lebanese Christians wanted an independent, sovereign state with some distance from regional Arab conflicts and political alliances. The compromise struck in 1943 between leaders of the Maronites and Sunnis, known as the National Pact, established a political formula which, despite its inherent weaknesses and the fact that today all of Lebanon's confessional communities insist on altering it, has remained a basis for intercommunal coexistence and power sharing since independence.

The leaders who concluded this pact, realizing that Lebanon is small, communally diverse, naturally poor, and militarily weak, established a compromise which they thought would ensure domestic peace and regional goodwill. They accepted Lebanon's unique character and Arab identity and advocated power sharing and international neutrality. They established a confessional system which provided the institutionalization of allocating political power along the lines of Lebanon's most basic power groups, the major religious communities.

Whereas several scholars have argued that Lebanon's political system was ingenious, others have thought it to be unfair in that it kept the Shiite Muslims and other Christian groups virtually powerless. Some have thought it to be a hindrance to the evolution of a just, modern, and secular state in which national identity, rather than confessional identity, can flourish. In any case, there is one observation that most analysts of Lebanon's political and demographic environment can make, namely that Lebanon's political compromise of 1943 has provided the perfect justification for external intervention whether invited or imposed.

Fear and Dependence on External Actors in the Lebanon Conflict

Protracted social conflicts are rooted in fear and foreign dependence. When they occur in countries like Lebanon, which are made up of minorities and where no single community is able to dominate the others or is willing to be absorbed or to melt away, fear leads to dependence on external forces. This phenomenon of dependence on external support represents a community's approach to strengthening itself, avoiding liquidation, or establishing hegemony over others.[2] Unfortunately, external support becomes an addiction that perpetuates the conflict.

After many years of jockeying for the attention and support of would-be backers, the Lebanese have collectively exhausted the options. Every community has tried a marriage of convenience with external and internal groups. Without exception, every Lebanese group has been disappointed with the outcome. Groups, communities, and countries have come to help Lebanon, but on their own terms and with their own agendas. Crisis and abandonment have been experienced without exception by every Lebanese community.

The cycle of fear and dependence manifests itself as a complex web of psychological components between groups in general, and also in their relationships to the conflict itself. This web locks the groups into the conflict, which, in turn, begins to have functional significance for the groups. Henry Tajfel[3] indicates that a protracted conflict becomes part of the culture, and the fact that it is protracted becomes part of that society's mythology.[4] The conflict becomes seemingly insoluble. With the passage of time, its complexities increase, as do the functions it has for each of the groups' identities.

Fear manifests itself most strongly as a fear of marginalization, of isolating oneself or one's group and thereby risking assimilation or destruction of that group. When marginalized members and groups are isolated from the conflict, they become stereotyped, possibly scapegoated or victimized. Isolated groups in such a precarious situation find it very hard to be party to the management and resolution of conflict for fear of losing whatever minimal gains they may have made. Negative signals received from out-groups are exaggerated, and even positive signals are seen in a negative light in order to protect one's group identity. Muzafer Sherif's experiments[5] show that group identity, the desire to be distinct from other groups, enhances competition among peer groups. Isolation from the "other" enhances one's group identity.[6]

Helplessness and the Disincentives for Conflict Management

Protracted social conflicts feed on the paralysis and sense of helplessness that all participants acquire. They provide the environment for self-entrapment[7] and block creative, peaceful change. Individuals and communities become so frustrated and depressed that they conclude that all attempts at change are doomed to failure. The state of affairs encourages dependence on external forces rather than on one's own abilities and resources. In protracted conflicts dependence on external parties and allies is a constant. As a group's identity becomes locked into the conflict, the group becomes dependent on the conflict. It becomes a drug.

Comparisons between political and personal problems must be drawn cautiously; it is far too easy to see a society as being psychologically disabled through its involvement in a conflict. Rather than being confronted, the issue is assimilated into the myth of the conflict. Such comparisons do, however, illuminate some of the psychological processes that can slow down the resolution of protracted social conflicts, as illustrated by Lebanon's communal and national dependency relationships with three major countries: Syria, Israel, and the United States.

Dependence on Syria

Between 1967 and 1975 Lebanon witnessed an influx of illegally armed Palestinians. Encouraged by its own interpretation of an agreement reached with the Lebanese government in 1969 (the Cairo Accord), the PLO began to wage war on Israel from Lebanese territory. In conducting its war against Israel, the PLO sought support for its goals and actions from sympathetic Lebanese, who tended to be Muslims. By 1973 the Lebanese Christian community, which had hitherto been slightly supportive of the Palestinians in their quarrel with Israel, turned against the PLO. Led by the Maronite Christians, the majority of the Lebanese Christian community (and part of the Muslim Shiite community in south Lebanon) took up arms against the PLO and its allies, arguing that the behavior of the PLO in Lebanon had become intolerable, dividing the nation and destroying the state.[8]

The PLO war against Israel invited deadly retaliation against the Palestinians and Lebanese in south Lebanon, the Beirut area, and elsewhere. It created complex problems for everyone—internal refugees, civilian insecurity, housing shortages, and other social and economic disruptions. The Lebanese army split along religious-communal lines, and the PLO became a state within a state, thus doing away with Lebanon's national sovereignty.

By 1976 it appeared that the PLO and its Lebanese allies were on the verge of defeating the Christian community and transforming Lebanon into a confrontation state in the war against Israel. At this juncture, the Lebanese Christian leadership turned to Syria for help. Although Syria had been a supporter of the PLO and its Lebanese allies, it had its own long-term objectives in Lebanon and the region. These were broader than those of the PLO and their Lebanese allies. There were, of course, other regional and international events and dynamics that dictated the choice of Syria. The Lebanese, desperate for Syria's support, overlooked Syria's manipulation of Lebanon, the country's internal structural weaknesses, and the regional view of the Assad regime. This rather myopic dismissal of crucial realities resulted in Syrian military and political control of Lebanon.

The Syrian intervention achieved its short-term goal: prevention of an imminent defeat of the Lebanese Christian community. Syria obliged not out of concern for a desire to preserve Lebanon's political system as such, however, but because for a fleeting moment Syria's interests matched those of the Lebanese nationalists' leadership: prevention of a radical takeover.

Fundamentally, the Syrian strategy in Lebanon was to preserve the political, social, and economic status quo under Syria's hegemony. Ever since the 1920 demarcation of present-day Lebanon, the Syrians have advocated "Greater Syria." Perhaps Syria today no longer consider physically annexing Lebanon, but it is determined to control events there at any cost.

Syria is vulnerable. Demographically, the country's population growth rate outpaces its resources growth and its ability to provide for the fast-increasing needs of the Syrian people. It desperately needs capable management of the urban problems, including housing, water, productive jobs, and educational and medical facilities, before further alienation and disintegration of the state start to set in. Syria's needs for an internal political integration of its Shiite, Druze, Christian, and other marginalized religious and cultural communities is also acute. In regional terms Syria is relatively strong militarily, but weak technologically and vulnerable politically. Syrian attention is fixated on territory coveted or lost. The Golan presents the greatest challenge of all. It is these issues that determine Syrian behavior in Lebanon—not the health and survival of any Lebanese group or community, or even the defeat of any group or community.

Dependence on Israel

To counter the Syrian menace that they had helped create in 1975–76, the Christians of Lebanon attempted to solicit Israeli help, believing that in such an alliance the Israelis would see Lebanon as separate from the Arabs, and even as separate from Islam. They naively convinced themselves that Israel must understand the vital strategic importance for the Middle East of Lebanese democracy and economic strength, and that, as a persecuted minority, the Jews must innately understand the predicament of another religious minority that did not want to have its voice in the region silenced forever. So-called similarities between political structures, it was thought, would translate into common goals, necessitating the maintenance of only limited "strategic" contacts with a few Israeli leaders.[9]

However, the Lebanese who had predicted Israel's overt and coordinated partnership based on their knowledge of the extent of Israeli covert assistance were wrong. Lebanese-Israeli relations required the establishment of a deep bond in order for the Lebanese to be sure of Israeli support against Syria or any other country. This could not happen between Israel and Lebanon, or between the Jews and Christians of the region. Secret political and military deals did not change fundamental attitudes. The one goal that Israel and Lebanon shared—namely, the reduction of the Palestinian influence in Lebanon and, more specifically, the elimination of the military presence of the PLO—made it possible to attempt a partnership. But one common goal does not make an alliance. Once it had been more or less achieved, Israel and Lebanon diverged.

However, neither Israel nor Lebanese nationalists seem to have appreciated how difficult it is to cut Lebanon off from the web of regional interdependence. The Israeli claim that "Lebanon will be the second state in the region to sign a peace treaty with Israel" implies that only weak, vulnerable, capitulating states will ever agree to a full peace with Israel. Such a sad assumption produces only a negative and unrewarding connection, if any at all. Regional peace is essential to the long-term survival of the nations of the region. But a peace based on vulnerability, asymmetry, and dependence cannot be serious and lasting. Even the weakest regional parties have ways of countering this approach, or any unilaterally dictated approach.

Israel did not fight a war in 1982 for the purpose of liberating the Lebanese per se. This was a secondary objective on the part of a few Israeli leaders.[10] The primary reason for the invasion—and indeed for prior Israeli actions in Lebanon—was control of the Palestinians and the limitation or elimination of their military and organizational capability. Israel was determined to deal with the Palestinians on its own terms. This meant dispersing the PLO's centralized command, emasculating its military capability, nipping any independence movement in the bud, and physically scattering its men and officers to the far corners of the region. Israel sees the Arabs, regardless of the differences among them, as hostile, threatening, and desiring its destruction. In this respect Lebanon was not much different from other Arab League members—perhaps a shade more Westernized, but so what! Israel saw it as untrustworthy and willing to permit the use of its territory as the launching pad for terrorist attacks against Israeli civilians.

The Lebanese (primarily the Christians), for their part, sought Israeli aid without fully appreciating Israel's accomplishments or psyche. They failed to foresee the inevitable outcome of a partnership short of open recognition and normalization. That a peace treaty was Israel's minimum, nonnegotiable price for the invasion of 1982 should have been clear from the beginning.

Dependence on the United States

Like most of their counterparts in the Middle East, the Lebanese political elites possessed only the most superficial understanding of American political institutions and behavior. They assumed that because they had visited, lived, or studied in the United States, they knew how the system worked. It is difficult for Lebanese officials to believe that the United States is a giant with severe constraints on what it can and cannot do in world affairs.

In 1975–76, the Lebanese felt bitterly betrayed by the West, particularly by the United States. Somehow, they assumed that the presence of American companies in Lebanon, Lebanese democracy, its Westernized culture, and its mediating capacity in the Middle East would bring the United States to Lebanon's rescue. This exaggerated Lebanese view of America's power to shape events in the region, and of American willingness to employ such power on behalf of Lebanon, has limited the ability of the Lebanese elites to look for alternatives. Lebanese elites, like many in the Middle East, have not understood what has happened in America since Vietnam. The Lebanese assumed that they were somehow the targets of a complex plot, rather than the incidental victims of an American world-weariness and failure to project power through the effective championing of peace and development simultaneously. Thus every negative incident was seen as a part of "the conspiracy," and every positive development was reinterpreted negatively.

In the late 1970s there were a few Lebanese and Americans who appear to have felt differently about U.S.-Lebanese relations. The

Christian anti-PLO nationalists argued that the United States would come to see their point of view if they found ways to communicate it to the American political, religious, and popular elites. The group organized, and after 1978 started to show results. They were more successful than they imagined. Under President Ronald Reagan, the United States began to focus on Lebanon. Even though the U.S. approach turned out to be controversial, unworkable, and finally a failure, the fact that it was pursued so vigorously should not be dismissed. For years the Lebanese tried to attract a solid American commitment. Once it had been obtained in 1982, they assumed that their interests were assured: the United States would stand by them until the country had been reconstructed, the army rebuilt, and all foreign forces withdrawn.

But then events moved rapidly and unfavorably. The Lebanese government did not fully grasp the monumental differences between 1958 and 1983. It urgently advocated the dispatch of a weighty Marine presence without fully appreciating the potential cost of its introduction on the scene. The U.S. internal squabble over the scope and form of a U.S. projection of might in Lebanon and the Middle East broke the back of the U.S. mission before it took hold. Ultimately, the White House (where most of the support for the U.S. policy toward Lebanon resided) would be constrained by Congress and by public opinion. Hard-won U.S. support for Lebanon was thus withdrawn before it had been able to take root and bloom.

Once American support had been obtained, the Lebanese government did not move rapidly (within the roughly six-months time frame allocated to it by the U.S. government) to resolve or at least address the country's internal problems, or to devise constructive initiatives capitalizing on the American "pragmatic" agenda of rapid solutions. In a sense, the Lebanese elites got carried away by their own arguments. In fact, the Lebanese convinced themselves that the country was a "vital strategic asset" for the United States. That Lebanon was able to convince the administration for a few weeks did not, however, transform the shattered country into a viable partner, let alone a vital interest, and reality inevitably caught up with wishful thinking. Lebanon is no more vital to the United States than Vietnam was, and the lessons of the latter have not yet been forgotten by Americans.

For its part, the United States misjudged the Lebanese government by assuming that it could make the decisions and act authoritatively. The Lebanese leadership's hands were tied in a dozen different ways. At the same time that the Lebanese overestimated American capabilities, the United States underestimated Lebanese helplessness and overlooked the role of the Lebanese political culture in its decision-making process. The United States did not really appreciate the extent of Syrian penetration in Lebanon and was in no mood to take serious action to alter the situation.

The United States assumed that Lebanon was ripe for quick, pragmatic solutions and accordingly applied short-term remedies, such as sending the Marines with a fuzzy and dubious (from the Lebanese point of view) mission. The United States then grew impatient with the complicated decision-making and reconciliation processes in Lebanon and abandoned the effort altogether.

The U.S. foreign policy establishment shares a common perspective regarding countries and regions. Intellectually, the United States is attracted to global and macro-regional policy approaches, yet in reality it ends up dealing with almost all issues on a bilateral basis. As a result of this tension in foreign policy conceptualization and operation, the United States often appears inept or insincere. President Reagan announced his Middle East peace plan before he began to tackle the goals he had set for himself in Lebanon. This approach, understandable from the U.S. regional policy point of view, precipitated a blow to the president's initiative and to his Lebanon policy.

Conclusion

Protracted social conflicts immobilize and reinforce dependency. They do not wither away but spill over and escalate to more destructive levels. A long-term conflict resolution approach to the protracted Lebanese conflict involves a two-pronged strategy and requires time and patience. Complex problems are not going to yield solutions overnight. Lebanon, like other countries, may experience further fragmentation before an acceptable political structure emerges and normal life returns.

The Lebanese need a theory to guide their political and socioeconomic organization and relations. The 1943 format failed because it was based on the myth of a unitary political society and culture. The Lebanese know by now that their political relationships are driven by their religious affiliation more than by any other single variable. The various religious communities in Lebanon diverge in their aspirations and ideas about the nature of governance, communal autonomy, cultural heritage, and images of the future. Perhaps greater decentralization, increased local autonomy, more communal representation in state institutions, and other shifts in power sharing are called for. In any case a thorough, broad-based discussion of the institutional, economic, and social implications of such a shift is needed. Lebanon's relations with all its neighbors must be based on mutual appreciation for the psyches and vulnerabilities of these states. Some would argue that it is difficult to pursue this goal openly and honestly at present, given the intractability of the Arab-Israeli conflict, but that implies continued paralysis and insecurity for decades to come.

PART 5

Islamic Fundamentalism

■

EX ORIENTE NEBULA

An Inquiry into the Nature of Khomeini's Ideology

■

Roger Savory

Two adjectives commonly used to describe the Ayatollah Khomeini's brand of Islamic ideology, and that of the Islamic Republican party in Iran, are "radical" and "fundamentalist." Some have identified other elements in this ideology. For example, Nikki R. Keddie writes:

> Many Iranians had become disillusioned with Western governmental forms and with similarly "Western" Marxism and nationalism. At a minimum these did not have the appeal of Khomeini's radical Islam, which in fact incorporated many features of parliamentarism, nationalism, socialism, and a "Third Worldist" reaction against the West as the great exploiter of oppressed peoples, while at the same time retaining the Islamic identity that was still crucial to most Iranians. It is perhaps this radical and unacknowledged syncretic mixture of traditional and revolutionary ideas, more than the "fundamentalism" that is so often attributed to the Khomeini school, which accounts in large part for Khomeini's great success with masses of Iranians.[1]

The purpose of this chapter is to inquire into the nature of Khomeini's ideology and, in particular, to discuss whether it may properly be called "fundamentalist" and in what sense it deserves to be called "radical" or "revolutionary."

What Is Meant by "Fundamentalism"?

Fundamentalism is a neologism. The word is not to be found in the main body of the *Oxford English Dictionary*, but is listed in the *Supplement* to that work, which contains new words coined during the course of the compilation of the dictionary (that is, between 1884 and 1928). The definition of *fundamentalism* given in the *Supplement* is as follows: "A religious movement which became active among various Protestant bodies in the United States after the war of 1914–18, based on strict adherence to traditional orthodox tenets (e.g., the literal inerrancy of Scripture) held to be fundamental to the Christian faith; opposed to *liberalism* and *modernism*." *The Shorter Oxford English Dictionary* gives the date of the first occurrence of the word *fundamentalism* as 1923, and repeats verbatim the definition of the *Oxford English Dictionary* from "strict adherence" onward, but omits the historical preamble of the latter from "A religious movement" down to "based on."

In view of this definition, it is not surprising that the term *fundamentalism* has from the beginning been fraught with ambiguity and has been liable to misinterpretation; nor is it surprising that it has acquired a pejorative significance among those who do not subscribe to such beliefs. When the fundamentalist movement began in the United States after World War I, there were those who thought that a fundamentalist was the same as a "conservative" Protestant. Such people regarded fundamentalism as merely a reaction against the "liberalizing tendencies of modern thought" and considered that its "teaching was identical with that of classical Protestant orthodoxy."[2] In other words, for such people fundamentalism meant nothing more than a return to the fundamentals of the Christian faith. If fundamentalism signified nothing more than a "strict adherence to orthodox tenets," it would appear to be synonymous with orthodoxy; at most, it would seem to connote a return to orthodoxy.

However, the example of a "traditional orthodox tenet" given by the *Oxford English Dictionary*, namely, "the literal inerrancy of Scripture," gives one pause. It suggests that in the Christian tradition fundamentalism is *not* synonymous with orthodoxy or a return to orthodoxy, if by orthodoxy is meant belief in the teachings of the catholic and apostolic Church on matters of doctrine. The literal inerrancy of the Bible is a doctrine that has been held from time to time by various Christian sects, but has never formed part of the mainstream of Christian doctrine. For Christians, then, there seems to have been some confusion between "orthodoxy" and "fundamentalism."

For Muslims, on the other hand, the literal inerrancy of their sacred text, the Koran, has always been a dogma and consequently has never been a matter for dispute. The Koran, in Muslim belief, is the literal word of God revealed to His messenger, Muhammad, through an intermediary, the archangel Gabriel, and communicated to man through the mouth of Muhammad. As S. H. Nasr has put it, "Not only the content and meaning come from God but also the container and form which are thus an integral part of the revelation."[3] To believe in scriptural inerrancy, therefore, a Muslim does not need to be a fundamentalist, but merely an orthodox Muslim.

The second half of the *Oxford English Dictionary* definition quoted above is more germane to our purpose. Fundamentalism, it says, "is opposed to *liberalism* and *modernism*." Thus, it seems, fundamentalism is also synonymous with "traditionalism" and "revivalism." In this sense, there *are* parallels with the Muslim experience. In the eighteenth century Islamic fundamentalism or revivalism arose as part of the Muslim response to Ottoman Turkish and subsequently Western domination of the central lands of Islam. On the political level, Islamic revivalism gave rise to nationalist movements in many parts of the Islamic world; on the religious level, it manifested itself in the Wahhabi movement in Arabia, a puritanical and fundamentalist movement that aimed at purifying Islam from within. Because of the indivisibility of religion and politics in the Muslim tradition, however, even on the political level what the late Sir Hamilton Gibb called the "revolutionary theocratic aspect" of the Wahhabi movement "came to the fore, and the initial thrust of its attack on what it perceived as a lax and corrupt Muslim state was transformed by the Muslim movements which adopted Wahhabi ideas in India, North Africa, the Sudan, and even as far away as Nigeria and Sumatra, into general opposition to Western powers in those areas and to Muslim governments which either failed to resist the growing influence of those powers or which actively collaborated with them."[4] Khomeini's Islamic ideology includes both these elements: puritanism and a pathological hatred of Western ideas. Since both these elements are common to most, if not all, the eighteenth- and nineteenth-century Islamic fundamentalist or revivalist movements, these aspects of Khomeini's ideology may legitimately be called "fundamentalist" and not dissimilar from those of the earlier movements.

The Millenarian Element in Fundamentalism

The ideology of the twentieth-century American fundamentalist movement contains an all-important element that is *not* mentioned in the *Oxford English Dictionary* definition of fundamentalism quoted above: millenarianism ("The belief and practices of those who seek, by way of a religious and/or political movement, to secure a comprehensive, salvationary solution for social, personal, and political predicaments," according to *The Fontana Dictionary of Modern Thought*).[5] Millenarianism is found in greater or lesser degree, together with the doctrine of the literal inerrancy of the Bible, in the ideology of many Protestant Christian movements during the sixteenth and seventeenth centuries. Although movements holding such views waned for a while in the eighteenth century, they reemerged during the nineteenth century, both in Great Britain and the United States. These movements were the forerunners of the American fundamentalist movement of the 1920s. Millenarianism is also an all-important element in the Ithna 'Ashari Shiite ideology of Khomeini and the ruling Islamic Republican party in Iran today. It seems, therefore, that a utopian eschatology of the millennium may also be considered to be an ingredient of fundamentalism, and a comparison with the Christian experience may be instructive.

Millenarianism has proved to be an extremely effective weapon in Khomeini's armory because the masses, in times of social upheaval, have always tended to turn to a messiah.

> Journeymen and unskilled workers, peasants without land or with too little land to support them, beggars and vagabonds, the unemployed and those threatened with unemployment, the many who for one reason or another could find no assured and recognized place—such people, living in a state of chronic frustration

> and anxiety, formed the most impulsive and unstable elements in medieval society. Any disturbing, frightening or exciting event—any kind of revolt or revolution, a summons to a crusade, an interregnum, a plague or a famine, anything in fact which interrupted the normal routine of social life—acted on these people with peculiar sharpness and called forth reactions of peculiar violence. And one way in which they attempted to deal with their common plight was to form a salvationist group under a messianic leader.[6]

Although Norman Cohn was writing about medieval Christendom, his words have equal relevance to the Islamic Revolution in Iran. The structure of Iranian society in the early twentieth century had changed little since medieval times. In the cities, the wealthier people maintained "a reasonably good life behind secure walls while the majority lived in poverty, disease, illiteracy, and slum conditions."[7] Most of the population eked out a bare existence in the villages. The foundations of social development in Iran were not laid until after the accession to power of Reza Khan (later Reza Shah) in 1921. The reforms effected by Reza Shah in the fields of education, in the legal system, and in public health, and his policy of industrialization, hastened the development of the Iranian middle class. In particular, they created a new professional, bureaucratic intelligentsia and an industrial working class. As the pace of industrialization and modernization increased under Muhammad Reza Shah (1941–79), a new class of highly trained technocrats was produced, and at the same time a sweeping program of agrarian reform was instituted that abolished the old, quasifeudal tenurial system. Changes in traditional modes of behavior and moral attitudes did not keep pace with economic change, a fact that produced feelings of psychological stress and insecurity at many levels of society. The land reform program was initially instituted as an act of simple social justice, and the first phase of the program achieved its objective of breaking the power of the major landlords. The later phases of the program displaced many unskilled farm laborers from the land. The latter flocked in large numbers to the cities, where they created a largely unemployed and dissatisfied lumpenproletariat.

Such periods of rapid social change and disruption have, on a number of occasions in history, been a godsend for the messianic leader. The messianic leader would impose himself on the people

> not simply as a holy man but as a prophet and saviour or even as a living god. On the strength of inspirations or revelations for which he claimed divine origin, this leader would decree for his followers a communal mission of vast dimensions and world-shaking importance. The conviction of having such a mission, of being divinely appointed to carry out a prodigious task, provided the disoriented and the frustrated with new bearings and new hope. It gave them not simply a place in the world but a unique and resplendent place.[8]

Such messianic uprisings usually

> occurred under similar circumstances—when population was increasing, industrialization was getting under way, traditional social bonds were being weakened or shattered and the gap between rich and poor was becoming a chasm . . . a collective sense of impotence and anxiety and envy suddenly discharged itself in a frantic urge to smite the ungodly—and by doing so bring into being, out of suffering inflicted and suffering endured, that final Kingdom where the Saints, clustered around the great sheltering figure of their Messiah, were to enjoy ease and riches, security and power for all eternity.[9]

Millenarian expectations continued to flourish in the second half of the nineteenth century in Britain, the United States, and Canada. "The basis on which the Millennial edifice rested was the belief in a literal interpretation of the Bible; without such a belief, millenarians could not make a case for their faith in the personal reign of Christ." The whole future of millenarianism was tied to "the maintenance of an inerrant and infallible text."[10] In Ithna 'Ashari Shiism, millennial beliefs are based not on infallible scriptural texts, but on the tradition of the infallible Ithna 'Ashari Shiite *imams* and the teachings of the (in the popular mind) equally infallible *fuqaha*, or interpreters of the religious law. According to Ibn Babuya, a celebrated tenth-century Ithna 'Ashari *faqih* (jurisprudent), the Mahdi is the *khalifa* (vicegerent) of God and the Living Proof of God on earth. Ithna 'Ashari Shiites believe that the Mahdi will return to earth to fill it "with justice and equity, just as now it is full of oppression and wrong."[11] Regarding the authority of the imams, Ibn Babuya says:

> Our belief regarding them is that they are in authority (*ulu'l-amr*). It is to them that Allah has ordained obedience, they are the witnesses for the people and they are the gates of Allah (*abwab*) and the road (*sabil*) to Him and the guides (*dalil*, pl. *adilla*) thereto, and the repositories of His knowledge and the interpreters of His revelations and the pillars of His unicity (*tawhid*). They are immune from sins (*khata'*) and errors (*zalal*); they are those from whom "Allah has removed all impurity and made them absolutely pure" [33:33]; they are possessed of the power of miracles and of [irrefutable] arguments (*dala'il*).[12]

In the twentieth century chiliastic beliefs continue to form a central part of the ideology of Protestant fundamentalist groups in the United States. "Times of historical peril or seismic change bring with them spiritual scenarios of proportionate dimensions," Gabriel Fackre has pointed out. Instead of drawing people apart from the world to prepare them for the end, however, the substitution of apocalyptic revelation for eschatology transfers to the plane of absolutes of good and evil. "One's political opponent becomes the Antichrist and the beast, which means that measures appropriate to the conflict can be legitimized by the legions of decency arrayed against the troops of the blasphemer."[13]

This is precisely the use that has been made of the Ithna 'Asahri apocalyptic ideas by Khomeini. For example, with respect to the hostage crisis, Khomeini declared: "This is not a struggle between the United States and Iran, it is a struggle between Islam and blasphemy."[14] The United States has become the "Great Satan," and President Saddam Hussein of Iraq is the "Satan of the Great Satan." A reign of terror has been instituted against the alleged supporters of these and other "forces of evil," and this reign of terror has been justified in part within the framework of an apocalyptic vision of a cosmic struggle between good and evil. It seems clear, then, that both in Christian and in Khomeini's fundamentalism, millenarian ideas assume an important role, and in the case of Khomeini they have a direct impact in the political arena. On the Iranian domestic scene, the transference of moral absolutes to the political level has meant that anyone who voices a criticism of the regime is an "enemy of the people" and therefore also an enemy of God. Khomeini and his fellow religious leaders send innocent people before firing squads without a moral qualm, in much the same way that the leaders of the Inquisition sent people to the stake secure in the knowledge that they were thereby saving their immortal souls. Of course the religious leaders of Iran are not concerned with the saving of the immortal souls of their victims, but only with the destruction of their bodies.

What Does "Radical" Mean?

Nikki R. Keddie, in the passage quoted at the beginning of this paper, refers to Khomeini's "radical Islam," and suggests that it is "this radical and unacknowledged syncretic mixture of traditional and revolutionary ideas . . . which accounts in large part for Khomeini's great success with masses of Iranians."

Semantically, the words *radical* and *fundamental* were, in their pristine innocence, not so far apart. The *Oxford English Dictionary* defines *radical* as: "going to the root or origin; touching or acting upon what is essential or fundamental." Its definition of *fundamental* is: "of or pertaining to the foundation or groundwork; going to the root of the matter." Yet the term *fundamentalism*, as defined in the preceding section, and the term *radical*, as commonly used today, seem to be poles apart.

Historically, radicalism had its origins in the opposition that arose in Britain in the 1760s to the "royal system" of George III. It was fueled by the French Revolution, in which the young poets Wordsworth, Coleridge, and Southey saw "rainbow visions of a new age which would restore righteousness to the earth."[15] As the Revolution pursued its destructive course, however, disillusionment set in, and radicalism was viewed more soberly in the nineteenth century. A "radical reformer" then meant one who held advanced views of political reform along democratic lines. How one regarded such "radical reformers" depended on one's political views. One could talk disparagingly about the "radical mob at Oxford," or one could, with Carlyle, characterize radicals as "friends of the people." In any event, it seems that two important elements of radicalism are utopianism and populism.

The utopianism of the fundamentalist, as has been noted, has its roots in chiliastic beliefs, based on a literal interpretation of Scripture in the Christian tradition and, in the Ithna 'Ashari Muslim tradition, upon the authority of infallible imams possessed of esoteric knowledge transmitted to them by the Prophet, and thus ultimately from God. The utopianism of the radical, however, is based on a belief in the inevitable progress of society toward an era of perfect justice as a consequence of the natural goodness of man. It may thus be seen as the secular counterpart of the salvationist utopianism of Khomeini.

Populism, the second important element of radicalism, identifies the "will of the people" with morality and justice. The masses, because of their poverty, are seen as morally incorrupt; by contrast, the bourgeoisie and the upper classes, because of their wealth and property, are ipso facto considered to be corrupt.

Populism in Khomeini's Ideology

The populist idea of the "will of the people," or the "general will," has been espoused with enthusiasm by Khomeini as a guiding principle of government. Predictably, it has undergone a transformation that calls to mind the fate of similar populist ideas in both the French and the Bolshevik revolutions. In the French instance, Robespierre's "republic of virtue" was metamorphosed into the Reign of Terror. In the Soviet Union, the theoretical "dictatorship of the proletariat" became the reality of the dictatorship of the Communist party. In Khomeini's Iran, the "general will" by which the Islamic Republican party professes to be guided has proved in practice to be synonymous with the "Imam's line." If the "will of the people" in the Islamic Republic of Iran has conflicted with the "Imam's line," the people have had to be reminded that the "will of the people" cannot be set against the "will of God," and that Khomeini and his fellow religious leaders are the only interpreters of God's will. For Robespierre, the "natural order" was the sovereignty of the common people. In the Islamic Republic of Iran, sovereignty belongs not to the people, but to God; this is one of the two fundamental principles of an Islamic state. If the rulers of a state based on this principle are Islamic jurists who claim to be the sole interpreters of God's will, such a state is ipso facto bound to be a totalitarian state. As Khomeini himself has stated so succinctly: "There is no place for opinions and whims in the government of Islam. The Prophet, Imams and the people obey God's will and the *shari'a*";[16] and the interpretation both of God's will and of the shari'a is in the hands of the *mujtahids*, the high-ranking jurists who at the moment dominate the government of Iran. The dominant group in the Central Council of the Islamic Republican party in Iran believes "that the greatest danger to the current revolution is a . . . betrayal by secularists" and it advocates "extirpation of any secularist dissent."[17] One is led to the inescapable conclusion that those Iranians who imagined that the overthrow of the shah would be followed by some form of secular government were totally deceived by the smokescreen of the "general will" emitted by Khomeini. Robespierre had a simple moral equation: rich = bad; poor = good. In peacetime, virtue, "the natural quality of the people," would, he thought, be a sufficient guarantee of good government.[18] If the natural *vertu* proved lacking, "virtue by intimidation" must be induced. He consoled himself with the thought that "intimidation is merely justice prompt, severe and inflexible. It is therefore an emanation of virtue."[19]

A mind capable of such perverted logic, unable to see the circular nature of such arguments, could move easily and imperceptibly into an acceptance of the use of terror. "The inconsistency between an almost Christian ideal of society, and a program of political terrorism, had ceased to be apparent to Robespierre."[20] He persuaded himself "that it was reasonable to put to death, with slight concessions to legal appearances, hundreds of fellow-countrymen. Moral scruples . . . should not be allowed to obscure a moral principle."[21] In his more lucid moments, he realized that the virtue had gone out of the Revolution.

The fatal flaw in Robespierre's concept of the "general will," which he had inherited from Rousseau, was that he did not foresee that the "general will," writ large, might acquire a demonic power of its own. If he did have premonitions that "the subtler and more formidable tyranny of the autonomous General Will" might replace "the tyranny of an imposed government," he thought this would be only a transitory problem.[22]

In Iran the transition from the loudly proclaimed "will of the people" to the "will of God," which, as interpreted by Khomeini, is called "the Imam's line," has been traumatic for Iranian liberals of the National Front, who naively believed that, once the shah was overthrown, a utopian era of constitutional democracy would automatically be ushered in. The transition has also dealt a severe blow to the hopes of left-wing groups: the mujahidin (*Mojahedin*) ("Islamic Marxists"); the *Fida'iyyin* (*Fedayeen*) (Marxist-Leninists); and the Tudeh party (the official communist party of Iran). None of these groups, of course, was interested in establishing liberal democracy in the Western sense of the term, but none intended to establish a theocracy. The loss of individual rights has been accompanied by a suspension of all objective moral judgment on the part of the regime, which has enabled it to conduct a reign of terror against non-Shiite Muslim minorities, against non-Muslim minorities, and against anyone accused by *fasad fil-ard* ("causing corruption in the land"); in short, against anyone whose views deviate from "the Imam's line."

"Salvationist utopianism has always been connected with intolerance and has therefore tended to express itself in tyrannical political practice."[23] The end product of a populist regime, in which the "will of the people" is manipulated by power-seeking demagogues, is the same. Radical theories, with their strong components of utopianism and populism, are merely the secular counterpart of the soteriological and millennial theories of Khomeini's ideology. As Robespierre began to doubt whether the innate goodness and purity of the masses would usher in his "republic of virtue," he adopted the position that it would be necessary to instill "virtue by intimidation." All those who rejected his ideal were by definition "corrupt," and "a bad man, a bad citizen, and a corrupter of morals" were "all counter-revolutionists."[24] This is the language Khomeini would understand, and he would endorse the conclusion to which Robespierre came, that "it was easier to bribe or coerce the crowd than to educate it."[25] Khomeini employs both bribery and coercion: bribery in the form of social welfare handouts to those who find themselves unemployed because of the fact that the industrial sector is operating at only a fraction of its capacity; coercion in the form of the summary execution of those found guilty of "causing corruption in the land." In its Koranic usage, *fasad fill-ard* is often simply equated with *kufr*, "unbelief." In its wider sense, it means "doing evil" in general, and is contrasted with *ihsan* "doing good." In other words, it is a general ethical principle, not a legal charge as understood in Western law. The great advantage of such a charge, from the point of view of the regime, is that it may be interpreted in whatever way the prosecutor chooses, and consequently no defense against this charge is possible. The whole process, of course, is "a betrayal of true Islamic principles—the responsibility of the individual before God, the brotherhood of man, humanity and compassion, tolerance and open-mindedness."[26]

Is Khomeini's Ideology Revolutionary?

It will be necessary to divide this section into two parts, the first dealing with the internal aspect of Khomeini's ideology and the second with its external aspect. This division is made necessary by the fact that the "export model" of Khomeini's Islamic revolutionary movement is quite different in character from the one designed for internal consumption. The latter is designed to destroy initiative on the part of the masses; the former seeks to mobilize the revolutionary fervor of the masses, particularly in countries that possess significant Ithna 'Ashari populations, in order to attempt to overthrow the existing governments of those countries and to establish in them Islamic republics analogous to that in Iran.

This dichotomy between the internal and external policies of a revolutionary regime is noticeable to some degree in the case of the French Revolution, but is much more clearly apparent in the case of the Bolshevik Revolution. In Russia the revolution was soon stabilized on the basis of totalitarian rule by the dominant Bolshevik party. "The freedom of speech and press for which generations of Russian revolutionaries had fought since the days of the Decembrists was completely destroyed within a matter of months."[27] By 1918 the Bolsheviks had set up a Department of International Propaganda for Eastern Peoples in order to foment agitation in the countries of Asia. In 1919, at the Second Congress of Muslim Communists, the decision was taken to support local nationalist movements as a means of overthrowing Western imperialism in Asia. This congress decided that Iran was the country most ripe for the application of the new communist Asian policies. A local nationalist movement in the Iranian province of Gilan was taken over by the Bolsheviks with the object of transforming it into a "liberation" movement involving the whole country. The analogy with the way in which the Islamic Revolution in Iran has developed is a close one.

Khomeini's Revolutionary Ideology: "Export Model"

The overthrow of the shah was initially hailed by many Muslims, both in the Middle East and elsewhere, as a "victory for Islam" over a ruler who had aligned himself with the West.[28] This initial jubilation soon subsided, however, when Iran's neighbors in the Persian gulf area began to reailze that Khomeini saw himself as the leader of an Islamic revolutionary movement closely allied to the goals of Arab "revolutionary" states such as Syria and Libya. Initially, too, there was a strong rapport between Khomeini and the Palestine Liberation Organization, because the PLO had contributed to the overthrow of the shah. Relations between Khomeini and the PLO deteriorated, however, when Khomeini began to realize that the Palestinian state sought by the PLO was a *secular* state, and Khomeini transferred his support in Lebanon to Shiite groups such as *al-Amal*, and, more recently, the even more revolutionary *al-Jihad al-Islami* and the "Islamic *Amal*" factions.

The ideological bases of the export version of Khomeini's Islamic revolutionary movement are two: first, the claim that Khomeini is the leader, not merely of the 100 milllion Ithna 'Ashari Shiites in the world (Khomeini puts the figure at 200 million), but of *all* Muslims, numbering at least 800 million; second, to return again to my initial quotation from Keddie, "a 'Third Worldist' reaction against the West as the great exploiter of oppressed peoples." Khomeini's claim to lead the whole Muslim world is not a figment of the imagination. It is actually written into the Constitution of the Islamic Republic of Iran. Article 10 reads: "All Muslims form a single nation, and the government of the Islamic Republic has the duty of formulating its general policies with a view to the merging and union of all Muslim peoples, and it must constantly strive to bring about the political, economic and cultural unity of the Islamic world."[29] For Sunni Muslims everywhere, the unthinkable has happened. For the first time in nearly 1,400 years of

Islamic history, Ithna 'Ashari Shiism, the minority and, in medieval times, not infrequently persecuted sect of Islam, had acquired sufficient political power to challenge the status quo of Sunni predominance in the Islamic world.

In a number of Persian Gulf states there is a substantial population of Shiites (Kuwait, 30 to 40 percent; Dubai, 30 percent; Qatar, 20 percent). In Oman, Sunnis and Shiites are roughly equal in number. In two states Shiites are actually in the majority (Iraq, 56 percent; Bahrain, 75 percent), and Shiites now constitute perhaps 45 percent of the population of Lebanon. In the heady days of the 1979 revolution, Khomeini clearly hoped that he could rapidly mobilize these Shiites against their own governments, in which Sunnis in every case held power. Even before he returned from Paris to Iran, Khomeini called on the five million Shiites in Iraq to demand autonomy for themselves. On the first anniversary of the 1979 revolution, Khomeini issued the call "O Muslim nations of the world who are oppressed, arise!"[30] In the spring of 1980 Iran's foreign minister, Sadiq Qutbzada (Ghotbzadeh), went on a "goodwill tour" to a number of Arab states, in the course of which he claimed, with a fine disregard for history, that all the Persian Gulf states had originally been Iranian. An attempt was made on his life, and he returned to Iran.

These rebuffs to his early attempts to extend the Islamic Revolution by subverting the governments of neighboring Arab states angered Khomeini. Muslim leaders who refused to accept his claim to supreme leadership of the Muslim world were denounced in scathing terms. President Zia al-Haqq of Pakistan, who claimed to be "intensely Islamic," had in fact instituted a rule that "was the exact antithesis of Islam," it was asserted. Indeed, he "could much more readily be likened to the ex-shah."[31] Not only were Muslim heads of state who rejected Khomeini's leadership, considered anti-Islamic, they were the agents of imperialism. Increasingly, President Saddam Hussein of Iraq became the target of virulent attacks in the propaganda war, because he refused to "understand the revolution in Iran" and to realize that it was only natural for the Muslim masses in Iraq to see it as the symbol of their own liberation.[32] Saddam Hussein hit back by reminding Iranians that "the Qur'an was written in Arabic, and God had destined the Arabs, not the Persians, to play a vanguard role in Islam." He challenged Khomeini's claim to speak for all Muslims, and dismissed Khomeini's revolution as "non-Islamic."[33]

In Khomeini's demonology, Saddam Hussein now became "the Satan of the Great Satan." There was an escalation of mutual vituperation, and on September 7, 1980, the Iraqis invaded Iran in what was probably intended as a preemptive strike. Since Islamic juridical theory frowns on warfare between fellow-Muslims, each side denounced the other as *kuffar* ("infidels"), thus legitimizing the process.

Despite his preoccupation with the Iran-Iraq war, which is still in progress seven years later, Khomeini has not abandoned his hopes of propagating his brand of Islamic revolution on foreign soil. The president of the Islamic Republic of Iran, Sayyid 'Ali Khamana'i, has declared that "the revolution, like the gentle spring breeze, does not recognize gates and walls, distance, barriers, or frontiers."[34] In March 1981 the Arab states of the Persian Gulf took the threat seriously enough to form the Gulf Cooperation Council with the object of coordinating their mutual defense policies through a collective security pact. The six signatories of this pact were Saudi Arabia, Bahrain, Oman, Kuwait, Qatar, and the United Arab Emirates.

The situation in Lebanon affords Khomeini the most fruitful ground for extending his influence. As early as December 1979 thousands of Shiite volunteers went to Lebanon to fight alongside the forces of the PLO against the Israelis and their Maronite Christian allies. After the Israeli invasion of Lebanon in the summer of 1982, more Iranian volunteers arrived in Syria, and established themselves at Baalbek in the Bekaa Valley in northeast Lebanon. Not only have the Iranians set up a military training center there, but a radio transmitter broadcasts the "Voice of the Iranian Revolution" for eight hours daily. Revolutionary seminars are held and films about the Iran-Iraq war shown. A Beirut newspaper, an organ of the Falange party, has accused the Iranians of preparing to proclaim an "Islamic state" in Baalbek. Such a development is not beyond the bounds of possibility, because indigenous Shiite groups such as *al-Amal*, and the new Shiite terrorist groups calling themselves *al-Jihad al-Islami* and the "Islamic *Amal*" have been increasingly active in Lebanon. The "Islamic Jihad" group claimed responsibility for blowing up the U.S. Embassy in Beirut on April 17,

1983, with the loss of some sixty lives. The attack, said the group, was "part of the Iranian Revolution's campaign against the imperialist presence throughout the world." Since that date, there have been numerous terrorist attacks on both American and French targets in Lebanon for which Shiite groups have claimed responsibility.

The strident anti-Western rhetoric, directed in particular against the United States and "that corrupt germ" Israel, to use Khomeini's phrase, reached a crescendo during the American hostage crisis in Tehran, and has been moderated only slightly as a result of a gradually dawning realization that a modicum of ideological purity may have to be sacrificed in the interest of purchasing food and other necessities from the West. It is ironic that Great Britain, the archimperialist in Dr. Musaddeq's rhetoric in the 1950s, has benefited from the assumption of that role by the United States and has greatly increased its trade with Iran. Trade between Iran and Canada, which earned much abuse from the Khomeini regime for its "immoral" behavior in helping some of the American diplomatic hostages to escape from Tehran, has also increased.

The USSR, which had confidently expected to be welcomed as a natural ally by Khomeini, has, much to its irritation, not only found itself placed in the same category of infidels as the rest of the Western world but, largely as a result of its occupation of Afghanistan, has itself been branded as an imperialist power (in Marxist dialectic, of course, a socialist country by definition cannot be "imperialist"). Moscow has discovered to its chagrin that Khomeini, unlike Western liberals, is not prepared to excuse and condone its action in Afghanistan.

Khomeini's Revolutionary Ideology: Domestic Model

The similarity between the course of the Bolshevik Revolution and that of the Islamic Revolution in Iran becomes even more striking when one looks at Khomeini's domestic policies. The Islamic Republic of Iran is, by virtue of its own internal dynamics, a totalitarian state. The key Koranic text on the subject of government (4:59) is: "O ye who believe! Obey God, and obey His Messenger, and those who are in authority among you." In Khomeini's Iran the religious leaders have declared themselves to be "those who are in authority among you." They are the guardians and only authorized interpreters of the religious law, which has the force of divine authority. They are endowed with personal and doctrinal infallibility (*'ismat*) as the representatives on earth of the Mahdi, the Ithna 'Ashari messiah. Their authority is therefore absolute. It may be expressed in the formula: obedience to the *faqih* equals obedience to the Hidden Imam equals obedience to God. Conversely, disobedience to the *faqih* equals disobedience to the Hidden Imam and hence disobedience to God. Disobedience to the *faqih* therefore constitutes not only a crime against the state but a sin against God, and capital punishment is the normal punishment for such disobedience.

Since the 1979 revolution, the *fuqaha* ("jurisprudents") have used their absolute power to stifle civil rights and to deny human rights in Iran. Spokesmen of the regime have reacted to criticism of its human rights record by suggesting that the whole concept of human rights is of Western provenance and therefore by definition un-Islamic.

> The clergy have done everything to curb any development of independent mass activity. Working class militants opposing the prevailing policies on even the most elementary trade union or economic issues have been jailed or sacked. Corporate consultative committees have been set up to replace any remnants of the independent workers' committees formed during the struggle against the Shah. Strikes are declared acts of treachery. Austerity measures, justified by reference to the fight against the U.S. and now Iraq, have reduced even further the level of employment. . . . *Politically and ideologically, the clergy has consistently campaigned for (and implemented) a system of government beyond popular control: they* are the ones who know what is best for the Moslem community. Their success in this is a factor in reducing the self-confidence and willingness of the masses to undertake independent activity. [Some emphasis added][35]

On the domestic front, therefore, the course of the Islamic Revolution in Iran closely parallels that of the Bolshevik Revolution. Undeniably, it has effected a revolution, in the sense of overturning the existing political and social order, a revolution succinctly expressed in the slogan *shah raft imam amad* ("the shah has gone;

the imam has come"). But, just as Lenin's long-term goal was to establish the dictatorship of the Communist party, so Khomeini's long-term goal is the establishment of a totalitarian state deriving its authority from the will of God as interpreted by the religious leaders (the doctrine of *vilayat-i faqih*), and paying lip-service only to the concept of the will of the people.

Other Elements in Khomeini's Ideology: Parliamentarism, Nationalism, and Socialism

The three remaining elements in Khomeini's "syncretic mixture of traditional and revolutionary ideas" identified by Nikki R. Keddie, parliamentarism, nationalism, and socialism, can be touched on only briefly. The few outward appearances of constitutional procedures on the part of the Islamic Republic were hailed with joy by Western journalists who, like many naive liberals in Iran, saw the 1979 revolution as the dawn of constitutional democracy in that country. A reporter for the *Economist*, surveying the Gulf scene in June 1981, wrote ecstatically: "It is the nearest thing Iran has ever had to democracy." Banisadr was referred to as "the People's President" because he obtained 70 percent of the vote in the presidential election of January 1980. Clearly the reporter, typical of many who routinely characterized elections during the shah's time as "rigged," had not inquired too closely into the manner of Bani-Sadr's election. And the "nearest thing Iran had ever had to democracy" turned out to be nothing more than a front for the secret Revolutionary Council, which made the real decisions. After the "People's President" had barely succeeded in escaping from Iran with his life in June 1981 (some of those who helped him to escape were not so fortunate), the fiction of parliamentarism could no longer be sustained by even the most optimistic observers of the Persian scene.

When Khomeini was planning the final stages of the Islamic Revolution, he was fond of saying that he regarded himself as "a Muslim first, and an Iranian second." Since the Revolution, there have been many signs of a concerted attack on all aspects of Iranian culture that antedate Islam. An attempt was made to abolish the great pre-Islamic Iranian national festival of Nowruz, but this failed. The name of Firdawsi, the author of Iran's national epic (celebrating ancient, pre-Islamic Iran), was removed from universities and streets. Young revolutionaries assumed "Islamic" rather than the specifically Iranian names commemorating ancient Persian kings such as Cyrus and Darius, Ardashir, Shahpur, and Bahram, and heroes such as Kaveh and Rustam, names by which they had earlier been known as a matter of course. There was a sudden interest in the learning of Arabic, the sacred language of Islam, a knowledge of which was previously confined to the religious classes and some university professors. However, after Iraq launched its invasion of Iran in September 1980, Khomeini found it expedient to make use of Iranian nationalist sentiment. Although initially perceived as a Shiite-Sunni conflict, the war rapidly assumed the more traditional character of an Arab-Iranian struggle, and the rhetoric of both parties reflected this.

In 1984 the universities reopened their doors after having been closed since June 1980. The decision to reopen the universities demonstrates the confidence of the authorities that dissent has been effectively suppressed. They had been closed in 1980 as the result of criticism by Khomeini that they had failed to provide students with "an Islamic education." The universities, he said, "must change fundamentally. They must be reconstructed in such a way that our young people will receive a correct Islamic education side-by-side with their acquisition of formal learning, not a Western education."[36] In other words, the universities are to be an agency of the state, and the curriculum is to be approved by the political party in power, the Islamic Republican party. The iron fist of the state apparatus is clearly visible within the velvet glove: "I request that all our young people not resist or try to sabotage the reform of the universities; if any of them do so, I will instruct the nation as to how to respond."[37]

During the cultural revolution that took place between 1980 and 1984, many members of the teaching staff of universities were fired. All faculty hired since 1984 have had to pass an ideological examination, and applications for university teaching positions have to be accompanied by four references, preferably from members of the Shiite clergy. All students admitted to universities since 1984 have been subjected to a rigorous ideological interrogation and examination of their family background, and once admitted, students have to obtain twenty-five credits in "Islamic ideology" before graduation, regardless of the course of study followed.

This mandatory "Islamic ideology" requirement is part of a general trend toward the deemphasizing of the Persian language, Persian history (particularly the history of pre-Islamic Iran), and other branches of culture traditionally frowned upon by the religious establishment, such as art, music, and philosophy. Archaeology was an early casualty of this process, because, prior to the Revolution, most archaeological research in Iran had been directed toward the reconstruction of Iran's ancient, pre-Islamic past. There have been some signs recently of a slight relaxation of this attitude. It is significant that 'Ali Shari'ati, an ideologue of the Islamic Revolution who enjoyed immense popularity among university students, made little reference to Islamic history in his writings. Indeed, he "admits that in his studies he disliked history."[38]

Socialistic ideas are to be seen most clearly, perhaps, in the emphasis placed by the regime on catering to the needs of the *mustaz'afin*, the "needy" or "weak" members of society. The regime has displayed great skill in perverting Islamic terms to give them a socialist, or even Marxist, flavor, thereby rendering them more palatable to those who like to combine their Islam with Marxist ideology. *Mustaz'af*, the tenth form of the Arabic root *z'f*, occurs only five times in the Koran (4:75, 4:99, 4:100, 4:126, and 8:26). It is rendered by Arberry as "abased," by Palmer as "weak," and by Pickthall and Dawood as "oppressed" or "feeble." Of the five occurrences, three are obviously of specific, rather than general, application: 4:75 refers to the *al-mustaz'afin* among the men, women, and children of Mecca who were crying out for deliverance before the capture of Mecca by the Muslims; 8:26 reminds Muslims of the time when they were few in number, weak (*mustaz'afun*), and in fear of being snatched away by their enemies; 4:126 refers to the "weak among children" (*al-mustaz'afin min al-wildan*), and is used in a context dealing with orphans. Finally, 4:99 and 4:100 are closely linked contextually with 4:97, which distinguishes sharply between "those who strive in the way of God and risk losing their lives and property" and "those who sit still at home"; 4:98 specifically states that these two categories of persons are not of equal rank in the eyes of God. Pickthall renders 4:99 as follows: "Lo! as for those whom the angels take (in death) while they wrong themselves, (the angels) will ask: In what were ye engaged? They will say: We were oppressed in the land. (The angels) will say: Was not Allah's earth spacious that ye could have migrated therein? As for such, their habitation will be hell, an evil journey's end." In other words, the excuse offered by those who failed to strive in the way of God but sat idly at home—namely, that they were "oppressed," or "weak" (*mustaz'afin*) in the land—is not accepted by the angels, and they are consigned to hell; 4:100 mitigates the harshness of this judgment by excepting the "weak" (*al-mustaz'afin*) among men, women, and children who were unable to devise a plan and were not shown a way (presumably to migrate elsewhere, as recommended in 4:99). Thus in none of the five instances in which the tenth form of the root *z'f* appears in the Koran is the word *mustaz'afin* used in the way it is now used by the Khomeini regime—namely, as a generic term for the members of a socially or economically deprived or disadvantaged class of society, the "oppressed masses" of Marxist terminology. The idea of the *mustaz'afin* as the "oppressed masses" has also been extended by the Khomeini regime to embrace the Muslim *umma* as a whole.

Socialist ideas were also present in the thought of Bani-Sadr, president of the Islamic Republic of Iran until his quarrel with Khomeini and dismissal on June 22, 1981. Bani-Sadr advocated total control of the economy by the state—the state acting, of course, in the best interests of the people. Was there not a danger in concentrating so much power in the hands of the state? Bani-Sadr tended to think not, because a state operating on Islamic principles could not become tyrannical. "Since Islam is a religion that rests on universal laws and one nature, and which envisages liberation from the traps of these perpetual realities, it is not possible for it to become the opiate of the masses. . . . In an Islamic government, belief must not be an instrument of government, but the government must be an instrument of Islamic belief."[39] In other words, Bani-Sadr's form of utopianism was based not so much on a belief in the sinlessness of the masses as on that of the immaculate nature of a state based on Islam. There was, however, an anarchistic streak in Bani-Sadr's ideology. Ultimately, he believed, all power emanating from men was to be condemned, even if the rulers claimed to be acting in accordance with the will of God.[40] This, surely, was the rock on which his alliance with Khomeini foundered.

Conclusion

It would thus seem that all the elements of the "syncretic mixture of traditional and revolutionary ideas" identified by Nikki R. Keddie (in the quotation with which this chapter opened) were at one time or another made use of by Khomeini in the formulation of his revolutionary ideology. Part of the secret of Khomeini's success undoubtedly lay in his ability to dupe the many groups of Iranian intellectuals who supported him before, during, and, for a period, after the Revolution. Many of these have now expressed their unhappiness with the course of events, but at the time they had allowed themselves to be deceived by their own delusions, and ignored what Khomeini himself said about his intentions. Another secret of his success has been his populist propaganda, which has made him immensely popular with the masses because it identifies the "will of the people" with notions of morality and justice. In extending the idea of the innate morality of the Iranian masses to embrace the "oppressed masses" of the Third World in general, Khomeini has made extensive use of what V. S. Naipaul has called "the lie"—namely, the notion that only Western society and Western governments are corrupt, Third World society and Third World governments being by definition pure.[41] "The lie," assiduously fed to the Third World by Western liberals, has been absorbed with alacrity by the Third World, which is now feeding it back to the West.

Khomeini was successful in creating an ideological fog in which large numbers of Iranian intellectuals and members of the bourgeoisie lost their sense of direction. He was successful in persuading the masses that they, by virtue of the theoretical ascendancy of the "will of the people," would actually have a say in the government of the country. It is doubtful, however, whether he would have succeeded in overthrowing the shah, and even more doubtful whether he could have maintained himself in power without the assistance of the fundamentalist, millenarian ideology of Ithna ʿAshari Shiism. It is this millenarian ideology alone that enables the *mujtahids* to claim infallibility as the representatives on earth of the Hidden Imam, and to claim to be the only possible form of legitimate goverenment in Iran until his return to earth.

Cui bono? Who benefited from the Islamic Revolution? Important groups that initially supported Khomeini, such as the *Mujahidin* and *Fidaʿiyyin,* have been severely purged and many of the surviving leaders of the groups are in exile. Other groups, such as the formerly powerful National Front and the National Liberation

Movement, have been outmaneuvered and effectively neutralized as political forces. The foremost beneficiaries of the Revolution are, of course, the religious leaders and their auxiliaries, the theological students in the *madrasas*, or religious seminaries. At the time of the Revolution it was calculated that there were 180,000 *'ulama* (members of the religious classes in general) in Iran—that is, one for every two hundred people—a not insignificant force. Some elements of the population (for example, industrial workers) have obtained short-term benefits in the form of exorbitant wage increases, and the traditional Islamic milieu of the bazaar continues, by and large, to support Khomeini. However, for many people in Iran: for Muslims who are not Ithna 'Ashari Muslims (Kurds, Turcomans, etc.); for Iranians who are not Muslims (Christians, Jews, Baha'is, Zoroastrians); for educated, emancipated Iranian women who hoped to secure a larger role for women in society and for all those middle-class Iranians of whatever ethnic or religious background who supported the 1979 revolution because their goal was a secular, constitutional democratic government, the results of the Revolution have not been progressive, but retrogressive and reactionary.

There is a reluctance to admit that the ulama in Iran, as a collectivity, have never supported progressive, much less revolutionary, social goals for domestic consumption. Ayatollah Burujirdi, the sole marja'-i taqlid[42] in 1960, denounced the shah's land reform program as un-Islamic; even if the Land Reform Act were passed, he said, it would be illegal.[43] Similarly, the enfranchisement of women and civil rights for women, designed to enhance the status of women in Iranian society, were also declared to be contrary to Islam.[44] Because the ulama, from the beginning of the nineteenth century, when Western political and social ideas increasingly made an impact on Iran, came forward as populist leaders against the encroachment of these ideas and against the governments that promoted or at least condoned them, the inference has been drawn by some that the ulama were revolutionary in character. This is a false deduction. The opposite is true. The ulama were and are reactionary, in the sense that they were and are opposed to change, and favored and still favor a return to traditional values and the traditional social order. At no time have the ulama agitated for a structural change in society. In short, the domestic model of Khomeini's revolutionary ideology is not revolutionary in character, but reactionary, and is solely designed, like Lenin's, to consolidate the power of the governing party.

Messianic considerations apart, it is possible to see the Islamic Revolution in Iran as possibly the first revolution in modern times with negative and retrogressive goals. The slogan of the French Revolution was "liberté, égalité, fraternité." In Khomeini's Iran, freedom exists only as freedom within the context of Islam, as interpreted by the religious leaders. Equality between believers and nonbelievers is an alien, un-Islamic concept. Whatever the Constitution of the Islamic Republic may say on the subject, there is in practice no equality between Shiite and Sunni Muslims, between Muslims and non-Muslims, or between men and women. Few Shiite mujtahids have ever been prepared to accept the principle of the equality of all citizens before the law, a fundamental principle of constitutional democracies.

I will close with two propositions: (1) Because of the ethnic and religious diversity of Iran, I believe that, in the long term, consensus regarding its polity can be achieved *only* by a secular form of government. (2) Just as the Reign of Terror during the French Revolution made inevitable the reaction that brought Napoleon Bonaparte to power, it is probable that Khomeini's reign of terror will, in due course, bring about a reaction in Iran in favor of secular government. As Maxime Rodinson has put it so trenchantly: "Good moral intentions, whether or not guaranteed by divinity, are of insufficient weight to shape the policies of nations."[45] In times of stress men retreat within the shelter of divine certainty, whether based (as in the case of Christian fundamentalists) on the literal inerrancy of the Scriptures or (as in the case of Ithna 'Ashari Shiite) on the infallibility of an imam in indefinitely prolonged occultation and of his self-appointed representatives on earth. After the death of Khomeini, however, whether he be currently regarded as the Hidden Imam in person, or as the vicegerent of the Hidden Imam, or simply as the forerunner of the Hidden Imam, I venture to predict that other voices will make themselves heard in Iran.

PART 6

Liberation Movements

■

THE PLO

Millennium and Organization

■

John Amos

Max Weber saw history as the interplay of modes of power that he characterized as the charismatic and the routinized.[1] Charismatic power is leadership exercised on the basis of personal attributes. It is legitimate because of the gift of grace. Routinized power is exercised through systematic organization. It is legitimate because it is rational.

The themes of charisma and routinization dominate contemporary Middle Eastern politics. The charismatic impulse is now manifest in the Islamic trend, a movement that asserts the primacy of religion in human affairs. Routinization is manifest in the increasing importation of Western organization, with its twin emphases on empiricism and rationality. The interplay between these themes forms the backdrop for Middle Eastern politics in general, and for PLO politics in particular.

Since its inception in 1964 the Palestine Liberation Organization has had an anomalous history. On the one hand, it appears to be the embodiment of the national aspirations of large numbers of Palestinians; on the other, it appears to be fraught with division and to be incapable of coordinated or consistent political action. At one level of analysis, this anomaly can be understood as the result of a number of factors: the organization makeup of the PLO, a composite of a number of independent Palestinian organizations operating in a very uneasy coalition; the vagaries of Palestinian political ideologies, with their emphasis on continued struggle; and the linkages between the PLO and its member organizations and the surrounding Arab governments. Taken together, these factors combine to produce a "PLO politics" that is extremely complex and fluid and, in many respects, is a microcosm of the politics of the region.

At another level of analysis, however, the PLO can be seen as an example of the larger themes of charisma and routinization. The charismatic theme is manifest in PLO ideologies, which are millennial in the sense that they look forward to some eschatological solution to the Palestine conflict. They have as their major thesis the notion of protracted conflict until the end of time, and as their minor thesis an overwhelming expression of despair and alienation. The routinization theme is manifest in the attempts of PLO leaders to create an organization capable of transferring the allegiance of Palestinians from the largely destroyed traditional social institutions to a political framework structured along pragmatic Western political patterns—an organization capable of governing an earthly Palestinian community.

The ebb and flow of PLO history reflects the interactive dynamics of these two themes. The organized PLO failed to garner any widespread political support because it was too pragmatic. Its leadership was replaced by that of dynamic young men with a collective charisma. This new leadership rapidly became absorbed in attempts to create a systematized power structure. After 1970 those leaders in turn were challenged by even younger militants on the grounds that they had become "professional revolutionaries" and "armchair guerrillas." This challenge initially was beaten back but reemerged in the wake of the 1982 Israeli invasion of Lebanon.

History, Fragmentation, and Alienation: The Setting of Despair

The context of PLO politics and ideology is the Palestinian diaspora. From 1948 onward, Palestinian populations were scattered throughout the Arab world. The largest of these populations is now located in Jordan, followed in size by populations in Syria and Lebanon, with even smaller communities in the Gaza Strip, Kuwait, Egypt, the Gulf states, Iraq, and Saudi Arabia. Other Palestinian enclaves are distributed throughout Europe, Latin America, and the United States.[2]

Between 1948 and 1967 Palestinian communities on the borders of Israel were exposed to constant war. During and immediately after the 1967 war a second wave of refugees moved outward from the West Bank, in the face of Israeli occupation, to the East Bank of the Jordan River and beyond. A smaller group moved away from the Golan Heights as that area was occupied. The group in Jordan had just begun to settle in when it was exposed to the violence of the 1970–71 Palestinian-Jordanian war. As a result, Palestinians in Jordan moved northward into Lebanon and Syria.[3] Violence in Lebanon, which escalated into the Lebanese civil war of the 1970s, caused Palestinians to move from Lebanon into the Gulf states, a movement accelerated by the 1982 Israeli invasion.

The original pre-1948 Palestinian community was a network of clans and tribes, indistinguishable in its outlines from other traditional Arab social orders. The trauma of continuous geographical movement completely unhinged this community. A study of West Bank camps describes the situation: "The refugees then are not organized by descent groups or by village of origin. There is no inter-camp organization of this kind, and not even the co-villagers living together in the same refugee camp form such groups. Instead, relationships with former co-villagers take the form of personal networks, tying together relatives and people of the same area of origin."[4]

These camps and other Palestinian enclaves functioned as psychological pressure cookers that produced successive generations of angry and alienated young men and women.[5] The Palestinian self-image that emerged from this experience was that of an individual living a transitory existence outside of all normal bounds of society.[6] The theme of permanent alienation runs through Palestinian writings: "As we began to wander away, there was however a rejection, a self-hating phase of alienation from reality as a people without a homeland, of alienation from the Arab world, alienation from our father's generation, alienation from the code of ethics and ideology that governed our affairs and the affairs of other people around us, alienation from our Palestinianness and refugeeism."[7]

This sense of alienation was compounded by the ambiguous legal situations of Palestinians in Arab states. When the mandate ended in 1948, Palestinians were left without citizenship or other identifiable legal status. They eventually acquired a melange of legal statuses in a number of Arab countries: Jordan granted its Palestinian population, including those in the Gaza Strip, citizenship after 1950. Other Arab states granted a combination of full or partial citizenship on a selective basis.[8] Elsewhere, Palestinians had the status of resident aliens.

Their legal position in Arab states was that of an outside (and often discriminated against) minority. Politically, their status rested at bottom upon their economic utility to the regime in question. For example, Palestinians were employed in large numbers in the Gulf states at a time when these states were undergoing economic development and lacked sufficient indigenous skilled manpower. However, as the Gulf states' own nationals acquired skills formerly supplied by Palestinians, the demand for Palestinian employees declined and the Gulf states began systematically to reduce their expatriate Palestinian labor forces.[9] As their economic value to regimes declined Palestinian populations in the Gulf were subject to other policies aimed at reducing a potential political threat.[10] After terrorist attacks in a number of Gulf countries, Palestinians (many of them holding Syrian documents) were deported.[11]

As a consequence of such circumstances, Palestinians have remained a floating community throughout much of the Arab world. Because Palestinians lacked a definable political identity from the outset, they were psychologically vulnerable to the ideological and intellectual currents prevalent in their countries of residence. In the early sixties the Palestinian community in the Gaza Strip was permeated by Egyptian political orientations of either the Nasserist or Muslim Brotherhood variety. Gaza-based Palestinian militants in turn formed the cadres that founded two major Palestinian organizations, Fatah and the Popular Front for the Liberation of Palestine (PFLP).[12] In Lebanon and parts of the Gulf, Palestinians were influenced by the Arab Nationalist movement (ANM) and also joined Fatah, the PFLP, and the Popular Democratic Front (PDF), among others. In Syria and Iraq, Palestinians adopted Ba'thist ideology. Palestinians in Syria and Iraq were recruited into al-Sa'iqa and the Arab Liberation Front (ALF), respectively.

Because of Palestinian vulnerability to the emotional appeal of competing Arab-based ideologies, political divisions within Palestinian communities reflected the larger political divisions within the

Arab world itself. From the beginning, however, Palestinian leaders had expressed a sense of Palestinian separateness: in the 1920s Palestinian congresses adopted resolutions distinguishing Palestinian national aspirations from those of the rest of the Arab world.[13] After the 1967 war this sense of difference was increasingly worked into Palestinian political thought and action.

Millennialism and Protracted Conflict

Two of the three groups that ultimately formed the PFLP called themselves Heroes of the Return and Vengeance Youth. Although heroism and revenge are both traditional Arab themes, the implication of these names is that extraordinary action will totally alter an unacceptable situation. Similarly, the acronym for Fatah (HaTaF) could be read aloud to mean "death," with its implication of self-sacrifice for a cause.[14]

Aside from the names of guerrilla groups, millennial themes are articulated in Palestinian ideological statements, particularly where these deal with conceptions of the Palestinian conflict. Fatah's conception of the "Palestinian revolution," for example, is a blend of Fanonist theories of the psychological necessity of violence and Islamic millennialism; the millennial theme implicit in Fatah's conception of the Palestinian revolution was carried to its ultimate end with the statements of Black September. The "will" of Munich guerrillas, terrorists who murdered Israeli Olympic team personnel in September 1972, articulate an apocalyptic vision of endless violence and bloodshed:

> We are an integral part of the armed Palestinian revolution which is a part of the Arab Liberation movement. Therefore, we urge that Palestinian rifles should not be laid down, regardless of conspiracies, impressions, and difficulties of the past. We also urge the Arab nation to activate its guns and activate its men. . . . For the land will not be liberated, without fighting, and fighting alone; without death, and death alone; without blood, and blood alone.[15]

Black September's words were echoed a decade later by an unnamed leader of the Abu Nidal group, Fatah, the Revolutionary Council, in 1982:

> Where what is called terrorism is concerned, we believe that there is no other means of combating Zionism than armed struggle. We believe that it is an objective necessity to punish the traitors. Is that terrorism? We are not concerned about terminology. The imperialists practice mass killing and exploitation of the people. They do not want the exploited to use violence and they want the masses to accept the law of the jungle so as to safeguard imperialist interests . . . we will persevere in our struggle and destroy the Zionist imperialist alliance in our country.[16]

Millennial themes are also present in the statements of the PFLP and PDF. These organizations, as well as their offshoots, utilize the language of Marxism, and their vision of the return is embodied in the concept of the revolution. Although language used by the popular fronts is less chiliastic in its overtones than that used by some of the Fatah offshoots, it contains the same insistence on a total transformation of the Palestinian condition. No compromise solution is to be accepted:

> The schemes of the enemy forces hostile to our revolution run along the following lines in the present phase: the attempt to contain the revolution politically, prior to aborting it, by means of inviting it to participate in the bargaining at Geneva. The Palestinian state plan is nothing but an imperialist plan to give the defeatist leadership 20 percent of the land of Palestine in return for the legitimate recognition of Israel and insuring the security of its borders.[17]

The PFLP conceived the scope of revolutionary violence in the broadest possible terms:

> We are determined to make the law of revolution the law of the world, even if this would lead to the destruction of the system invented by the capitalist world over the bodies of the exploited. . . . The PFLP has a revolutionary vanguard, has blown up the standards and concepts imposed by imperialist capitalist ideology on the white western man and the underdeveloped human.[18]

With their mystique of millennial violence, these ideologues functioned to provide some common ground of appeal to Palestinians who were fragmented both geographically and sociologically. They legitimated resistance leadership and provided a rationale for resistance organizational cohesion. However, the very dynamism implicit in millennial action was antithetical to any form of organization (or policy) aimed at creating a stable and predictable human environment. While millennial calls to action may have solved the problem of motivating apathetic and psychologically depressed Palestinians, it was dysfunctional in terms of organizational stability.

Political Organization: Integration and Clique

The practical problem confronting Palestinian leadership was not only to motivate an apathetic community that seemed to have lost control of its destiny, but also to channel Palestinian energies into an organizational structure capable of providing centralized political control and engendering the permanent loyalty and cooperation of its members.[19] This organizational structure, along the lines proposed by Western organization theory, required at least three elements: (1) control over the behavior of its members; (2) a defined focus of authority; and (3) the ability to motivate its members.[20] In Max Weber's terminology, such an organization is dominated by virtue of a defined distribution of command. The powers of command, in turn, were accepted because they were embodied in a system of consciously made rational rules.[21]

Palestinian politics since the days of the Arab Higher Committee have, however, been characterized by coalitions and networks of relationships that are based on the clique as a unit of action.[22] A clique is defined as a group of individuals tied together by a variety of shared attributes: personal friendship, descent, and/or reciprocal political, economic, or social interests. It is characterized by a rough equality among its members and by a lack of any formal organizational relationship.[23]

Organizational decentralization and factionalism were institutionalized in the PLO structure: PLO offices in Arab countries, for example, were dependent upon host countries and operated independently of one another. The PLO military arm, the Palestine Liberation Army (PLA), was organized as an integral part of existing military establishments and also operated as a series of decentralized cadres of officers. As a consequence, the early PLO was unable either to formulate consistent and effective policy or to engender any claim to legitimacy. Because it has no organizational links, it was easily taken over, following the 1967 war, by young militants, principally those drawn from Fatah.

Even though the leadership of the PLO is now in the hands of Palestinian Resistance leaders, its structure reflects divisions within the Palestinian community. Its politics were (and are) the politics of the clique, now based on the guerrilla organizational format (Fatah was formed by a small circle of men who had known one another for some time). The formal PLO decision-making apparatus consists of the National Council (PNC), the Central Council, and the Executive Committee. There is no clear line of authority among these institutions. Theoretically, the PNC is the supreme authority for PLO policies and programs. It is scheduled to meet every two years, or earlier upon request of the Executive Committee. Membership in the PNC has varied, however, and its scheduled sessions have been irregular. At its first session, in May 1964, some 160 delegates attended. At the 1968 and 1969 sessions, following the June 1967 war, the delegate count dropped to eighty-four. In the early 1970s the number of delegates attending PNC sessions increased to 115; this number grew gradually to 151, and then to 175 by January 1973. By March 1977 (concurrent with a move to establish a Palestinian state in any liberated part of Palestine), the number of PNC delegates increased to 290.

This gradual expansion is attributable, on the one hand, to Chairman Arafat's policy of co-opting as many groups as possible into the PLO structure. On the other hand, it reflects the pattern of factionalism that resulted in the emergence of successive waves of guerrilla and other Palestinian groups. The size and the representation of different groups have been major sources of conflict within and among Palestinian commando organizations.

The other two institutions of PLO are equally fraught with conflict. In 1970, following an agreement on the number of commando organizations to take part in the PNC itself, the Central Council was formed to act as a coordinating body. The Central Council was to consist of twelve members of the commando organizations, the speaker of the PNC, the commander of the PLA, and three independents. Originally its membership was fifteen seats, but in the next several years this was expanded to forty-one seats. It had increased to fifty-five seats by 1980.

The Executive Committee, elected in 1969 (chaired then and now by Yasser Arafat), originally had eleven members: four from Fatah, two from al-Sa'iqa, and five independents. By the end of its first year in existence the committee had been expanded to include the PFLP. By March 1977 its membership consisted of seventeen seats, some of which were occupied by "independents" from the West Bank. The function of the committee was (and is) to act as the PLO's executive and control its armed forces and its several administrative departments. Here again the continual expansion in numbers is the result of a strategy of bringing in all possible groups.

In 1971 Yasser Arafat promoted a bureaucratic model that called for the complete unity of all commando groups within the framework of the PLO. This was opposed by a PFLP plan that called for an organization in which each group would maintain its separate ideological and organizational identity. Neither plan was acceptable. As a consequence, the organization evolved as an uneasy symbiosis, in which the PLO decision-making structure serves as an umbrella within which individual groups maintain their separate identities.[24]

Within this symbiosis the kaleidoscopic nature of Palestinian politics is accentuated: organizations, and even factions within organizations, retain their identity over extended periods of time. For example, the Popular Struggle Front (PSF) of Samir Ghosha, which was founded in 1969 and absorbed by Fatah in 1971, reemerged in 1974 to join the then Rejection Front. In 1976 the PSF allied with the PFLP and ALF in opposing Syrian and Christian forces in Lebanon. But by 1985 the PSF had joined the National Salvation Front, a Syrian-sponsored anti-Arafat coalition.[25] Conversely, the Action Group Liberation of Palestine (AGLP), headed by the late Dr. Isham Sartawi, broke away from Fatah in 1969. In 1971, however, it rejoined Fatah, and Sartawi ultimately became one of Arafat's top aides.[26] The Heroes of the Return, one of the groups that combined to form the PFLP in 1967, reemerged. In 1984 the Heroes opposed PFLP leader George Habash's proposal to join the NSF.

Millennialism: Generation and Organizational Dynamics

The use of millennial ideologies as a technique for producing political identification and organizational cohesion was by its nature self-limiting: millennial emphasis on ultimate solutions exacerbated rather than diminished existing conflict. Conflicts within the PLO structure, basically conflicts within and among factions or cliques, were not solved. Nor was any organizationally institutionalized mode of conflict management created to resolve these conflicts.

The existence of these conflicts was tolerable as long as there was an outside threat of sufficient magnitude to require Palestinian unity of action. When a peace settlement became a possibility after the 1973 war, however, this fragile cohesion rapidly broke down.

In February 1974 the PLO Executive Council split over the issue of whether to modify military strategy to discontinue international terrorism so that it would be possible for the PLO to engage in peace negotiations. Chairman Arafat and the majority of the PLO decided on a policy of stopping international terrorism in order to reserve a viable diplomatic option. This strategy was vigorously opposed by the PFLP and the General Command. In the end, Arafat and the Centrists prevailed, but they did so at the cost of splitting the PLO.

The PPLP, GC, Popular Struggle Front (PSF), along with some splinter groups from Fatah (notably the Abu Nidal group), formed their own organization, the Rejection Front, following the twelfth PNC meeting in Cairo in 1974. The Rejection Front rapidly acquired the support of a number of Arab states, notably Syria and Libya,[27] and itself gradually took on an organizational format in response to Egyptian peace efforts. At a "Summit of Resistance" in Tripoli, Libya, a number of anti-Egyptian Rejection Front states formed a loose organization consisting of a joint political and military command. A series of other summits followed, including one in Baghdad in November 1978, at which the coalition, consisting of the Rejection Front, Syria, Iraq, Algeria, Libya, and South Yemen, and now calling itself the Rejection and Steadfastness Front, declared its opposition to any peace formula.

While the rejectionist movement originally grew out of splits within the Resistance, its major impetus came from Arab states that wanted to block a peace settlement. In the years immediately following the 1973 war, these states' energies were focused on isolating Egypt and preventing the Egyptians from becoming (what was widely perceived as) an American outpost in the Arab world. After the 1982 Israeli invasion of Lebanon, the Rejectionists' goal was to force the Israelis out of Lebanon and to prevent any Jordanian negotiations with Israel.

Although the overall goals of the Rejectionists were similar, there were conflicts within the movement. The Libyans, for example, wanted to use the Rejectionist movement as a springboard for their drive to replace the Egyptians as leaders of the Arab world and to promote their own brand of anti-Americanism. The Syrians wanted to transform the Rejectionist movement into a coalition capable of blocking Iraqi policies. The Iraqis wanted to use the movement to promote Iraqi influence in the Arab world.

The complexity and intensity of conflicts within the Rejectionist movement, and between the movement and other Arab states, was in turn reflected within the Resistance itself. As various Arab states maneuvered for their own ends, they sought support from factions within the PLO. As a consequence, PLO factional patterns tended to conform to the larger alliance patterns in the Arab world.

This environmentally augmented factionalism within the PLO was in turn woven into the pattern of generational conflict that had characterized the PLO from the beginning. After the "historic" leaders took over the PLO in the late 1960s, a younger opposition almost immediately surfaced. In 1971 a group calling itself the Free Officers of al-'Asifah surfaced within Fatah. The Free Officers eventually became the nucleus of Black September and were linked to left-wing factions within Fatah and elsewhere in the PLO. Black September was suppressed in 1971 as a consequence of a PLO policy change favoring negotiations and concomitantly downplaying international terrorism. The young militants did not disappear, however, but rather split off into other groups, principally Abu Nidal's Black June and its offshoots. This younger generation had links to Iraq, Syria, and Libya. Again, this generation of militants was motivated by millennial ideologies.[28]

By 1980 the combination of factionalism, inter-Arab connections, and generational conflict had combined to produce a three-way split within the PLO, and more particularly within Fatah. One group, headed by Khalia al-Wazir, was identified with the historic leadership of the PLO and Fatah and opted for a strategy of rapprochement with Jordan, with the aim of creating some form of Palestinian state linked with Jordan. This faction was originally backed by Iraq and Saudi Arabia. A second group, also with connections to the Fatah leadership, was set up by Sala Khalaf and opposed any union with Jordan. This group demanded an independent Palestinian state and received some initial Egyptian support. The late group was led by Nimr Salih, connected with the Rejectionists, and opposed any negotiations. In turn, Nimr Salih and his followers were backed by Syria, Libya, Algeria, and (within the Resistance) by al-Sa'iqa, the PFLP, PDF, and GC.[29]

In the wake of the 1982 Israeli invasion of Lebanon these embryonic divisions were the foci of full-scale splits. In May 1983 Colonel Sa'id Musa Maragha (Abu Musa) led a rebellion against Arafat and PLO conservatives. At the end of that year he was joined by Nimr Salih of Fatah. Styling their joint effort the Fatah "uprising," the GC, the PSF, and al-Sa'iqa executed a series of attacks on Arafat and his followers in Tripoli, Lebanon.[30] As a result of this fighting, Arafat was forced to evacuate Lebanon.

Following an attempt by the PLO leadership to isolate its opponents at the Aden meeting in June 1984,[31] and the subsequent PNC session in Amman in November,[32] the "Uprising," GC, al-Sa'iqa, and PSF met in Damascus to create the National Salvation Front. NSF, in turn, had extensive Syrian backing and some links to Iran through the Lebanese Shiite Hizbullah.[33]

The NSF spokesmen were quite clear in their goals. According to them, the chief goal of the NSF was to take over the PLO structure by ousting what they considered to be the passive leadership of Arafat and his supporters. NSF ideologues accused Arafat of giving up the military option, of failing to continue the armed struggle. In accordance with this ideological orientation the NSF and its members acted to block any movement toward a negotiated settlement. The Tripoli war, for example, was in part designed to block any agreement between Arafat and King Hussein of Jordan. PLO leaders who were identified with any kind of negotiations—for example, Isham Sartawi—were targeted for assassination. Apparently most of these attacks were launched by Abu Nidal's Black June group.

In addition, the Rejectionists launched a series of attacks designed to prevent any peace negotiations whatsoever. Again, most of these attacks were carried out by Black June and its offshoots and were in support of an articulated strategy designed to "punish" all those regimes that had backed Egypt's return into the Arab fold and the union plans between Jordan and the PLO.[34] In these attacks Rejectionists operated in concert with Shiite militants, who also were motivated by millennial considerations. In the summer of 1985 NSF leaders visited Iran to conclude an agreement coordinating the activities of NSF and Iranian-sponsored organizations in conducting terrorist attacks against the Gulf states. According to NSF spokesmen, this agreement was "to punish" Gulf states for attending the Arab summit in Casablanca. The bomb attacks on the Saudi and Moroccan embassies in Beirut can be seen as the opening volley in this campaign, which may also be directed against Arafat supporters.[35]

Millennialism, Organization, and Political Development in the Middle East

Organizational development in the West is a process of increasing institutionalization of formalized structures of roles or positions, pragmatic definitions of the scope and relationship of power and authority attached to these roles, and patterns of symbols and motivational values that stress rational problem-solving behavior. In Weber's terminology, this is the classic process of routinization. A formal organization in the Western sense, then, is a structure of precisely defined relationships in a culture whose behavioral values reinforce this structure.

In the Middle East, however, this process of routinization is discontinuous. Peculiarly Western notions of rationality and organization are neither the only nor the predominantly accepted modes of thought or action. The charismatic theme, with its attendant millennial, philosophical, and political expressions, remains a powerful ideational force in the Middle East. In the case of the Palestinian Resistance, specifically the PLO, these themes interact with traditional forms of political organization to produce a politics of great complexity. Use of millennial appeals to motivate a Palestinian community in the throes of despair succeeded. But it did so increasingly at the cost of organizational development and stability. Indeed, each succeeding generation of young Palestinians appears to be more susceptible to millennial appeals. Until, or unless, this pattern is altered, it will be difficult for any Palestinian Resistance leadership either to negotiate or, once having negotiated, to enforce any sort of peace settlement.

KURDISH NATIONALISM

■

Arthur Campbell Turner

The topic of any nation unfree but striving to be free evokes somber reflections. The present age is supposed, with some justice, to be the age of nationalism, but to be in harmony with a general historical current does not guarantee success. Imperial regimes have everywhere crumbled, giving way to successor states that are frequently despotic and sometimes scarcely viable. The sanctity of existing boundaries, whatever they may be, is defended against nationalist or subnationalist threats to them by no one more strenuously than the rulers of these nations. As Rupert Emerson has wryly noted, "the newly established states cannot tolerate having their rule challenged by disaffected minorities or regions, no matter how good the claim of the latter to separate national existence may be. . . . *My* right to self-determination against those who oppress me is obviously unimpeachable, but *your* claim to exercise such a right against me is wholly inadmissable."[1]

Such considerations are very relevant to the case of the Kurds. Here we have a genuinely distinct, numerous people, recognizable and recognized as such for aeons past, who are to be found in more or less contiguous areas under the rule of five different states. All these states are more or less hostile to the aspirations of the Kurds, though not equally so. Two of the states did not exist at all as political entities before the early 1920s, and their independence dates from considerably later; another (Turkey) is basically different in structure from what it was earlier.

The Kurds are to be found chiefly in Turkey, Iran, and Iraq, with much smaller numbers in Syria and the Soviet Union. Exactly how many Kurds there are in all, or in any of these countries, it is impossible to say. Estimates vary astonishingly widely. The uncertainty is particularly great in regard to Turkey, and not accidentally. The official pretense of republican Turkey has tended to be that the Kurdish problem does not exist because the Kurds do not exist. Tortuous terminology has been used to this end. For example, the problem of the Kurdish areas of Turkey has been referred to as the "eastern question," and the Kurds themselves as "Mountain Turks who have forgotten their mother tongue." Nationalist Kurdish activity, or even a public insistence by individuals that they do belong to that group can lead, and has led for thousands, to arrest and detention. But even in the case of the other four countries, there is an obvious official motivation to downplay the question by putting the number of Kurds as low as possible.

For Turkey the highest estimate, doubtless implausible, is that of Yosef Gotlieb, who estimated that 8.5 million Kurds live in Turkey and constitute "at least a quarter" of that country's total population. He speaks of the Kurds as being "a nation of 18 million people."[2] At the other end of the scale, Derk Kinnane firmly declared some two decades ago that "well-informed estimates . . . agree" that there are about 2.5 million Kurds in Turkey, 1.4 million in Iran, 1.2 million in Iraq, plus a quarter of a million in Syria and between sixty thousand and a hundred thousand in the Soviet Caucasus: a total of between 5 and 6 million.[3] This is almost certainly too low, especially allowing for some natural population growth in the interval. Dr. Nikki Keddie, a level-headed observer, puts the number of Iranian Kurds at about four million.[4] The most generous estimates of the size of the Kurdish population are sometimes boosted, as was that of the contemporary Kurdish nationalist leader Jalal Talabani, by adding into the total the Lurs of southwestern Iran and the Yazidis of northwestern Iraq, and by discovering pockets of Kurds in Lebanon, the Caucasus, and Afghanistan. These are farfetched claims. It is difficult to see the relevance of claiming for a national cause scattered groups who have shown no awareness of or support for that cause.

Stephen Pelletiere, in a recent and very well-informed study of the Kurds, estimates that there are at least 3 million in Turkey, over

2 million in Iran, and close to that number in Iraq, with very small colonies in Syria and the USSR: a total of between 7 and 7.5 million.[5] Perhaps this is too conservative, but it is certainly not too large.

Some general statements about demographic and political significance can be made with considerable confidence. Proportions are reasonably clear, even if absolute numbers are not. The largest number of Kurds—and by a considerable margin—live in Turkey. A smaller number are in Iran, followed closely by Iraq. The numbers of Kurds in Syria and the Soviet Union, though not negligible, are much smaller and not politically significant. In Iraq and in Turkey the Kurds are easily the largest minority group, second in size only to the Arabs in Iraq and the Turks in Turkey. Their existence poses a unique problem for each state. In Turkey the Kurds amount to perhaps 10 percent of the population, but that part of the traditional Kurdish homeland that lies within the Turkish borders constitutes between a quarter and a fifth of the country's total area. In Iraq, if one posits a Kurdish population of between 2 and 2.5 million, it amounts to between one-fifth and one-sixth of the total Iraqi population; the Kurdish lands occupy between one-quarter and one-fifth of Iraqi territory.

In Iran the situation is different. The Kurds, though numerous and amounting to perhaps 7 percent of the whole population, are only one of a number of important minority groups who together make up slightly more than half the population; native Persian speakers, the core people of the state, probably amount only to some 45 percent of the total.[6]

If, in some historical eventuality difficult to imagine (and indeed improbable), the Kurds were to achieve their own separate sovereign state, one including within its borders all the principal Kurdish-inhabited areas, it would—whichever of the varying estimates of population one accepts—have an area and population greater than those enjoyed by more than half the member states of the United Nations. Thus the questions raised by their historic fate and present condition are not trivial ones. Moreover, it would be a state that, unlike so many, would be substantially monolingual. The Kurdish claim to nationhood is underpinned by their possession of their own language, Kurdish, an Indo-European language related to Persian but with its own grammar and vocabulary. Kurdish is spoken in two principal versions, divided roughly into a northern and a southern branch.

Their religion separates them from some of their neighbors, but not from others. Nearly all Kurds are Muslims of the Sunni persuasion; that is, they belong to the mainstream of Islam. But the same fact sets them sharply apart in Iran, where Shiism is the state religion.

Kurds are also set apart from other ethnic groups in the several countries in which they live by their culture, their style of dress, their way of life, their own historical consciousness, and a general attitude toward them on the part of other peoples of dislike mixed with apprehension. The mutual antipathy between Arab and Kurd is summarized in two proverbial sayings: the Kurdish proverb, "A camel is not an animal, an Arab is not a human being," and its Arabic counterpart, "There are three plagues in the world, the Kurd, the rat, and the locust."[7]

Extreme personal bravery, pride, quarrelsomeness, martial ardor, and a passionate attachment to independence—such are the characteristics invariably ascribed to the Kurds by all observers. Most Kurds are also poor and illiterate.

Kurdistan—the name has been in use for about a thousand years—is an extensive area definable in terms of present-day frontiers as being in southeastern Turkey, northeastern Iraq, and northwestern Iran, spilling over slightly into northern Syria and the southern edge of the Soviet Union. Kurdistan is roughly crescent-shaped, with one tip in northern Syria, broadening to a width of several hundred miles as it curves east and then south, terminating somewhere near Kermanshah in Iran. It is an area of plentiful rainfall. The important river systems include much of the upper courses of the Tigris and the Euphrates, and all of the Great and Little Zab rivers. Kirkuk and Mosul in Iraq mark the southwestern edge of the area. Much of Kurdistan consists of extremely high mountains, especially at its core, which is the point where the frontiers of Turkey, Iraq, and Iran meet. Kurdistan is difficult of access, and communications are bad, features that have contributed to the character of its people and to the success with which it has been defended in innumerable wars and skirmishes.

The Kurds were once mostly nomadic or seminomadic, but this began to change in the nineteenth century. Tribal organization has also weakened, although there are areas in the remoter parts of Kurdistan where the tribe is still the all-important social group. The settled Kurds are farmers growing a variety of crops. Many Kurds today have moved out of the ethnic homeland to earn a living. Large numbers of them subsist in the slums of Turkish cities. The foothills and plains area on the Mosul-Kirkuk line in Iraq is mixed in population—half Arab and half Kurd. Since it is also one of the country's two great oil-producing centers, it is not accidental that control of it has been one of the great bones of contention since the early twentieth century. A further demographic complication was the forcible resettlement in the 1970s by the Iraqi government of many Kurds in the south of the country.

The Kurds have inhabited their mountain fastness throughout recorded history. Just as certain group characteristics such as those mentioned above have been consistently observable, there is also a rather sad consistency to their history: resolute in frustrating attempts to dominate them, they have equally shown a conspicuous failure to unite for their common good. Intertribal rivalries have often been a more important motivation than combining to defeat the non-Kurd. There have been great Kurdish leaders and Kurdish rulers, but there has never been anything that could properly be called a national state. The most eminent Kurds known to history have tended—a little, perhaps, like émigré Scotsmen—to make their careers and shape their aims in an environment other than that of their limiting natal or ancestral soil. The greatest of all Kurds, Saladin (Salah al-din, c. 1138–93), was the ruler of a vast Muslim empire whose main power base was Egypt. Of twentieth-century Kurds, İsmet İnönü was a leader of republican Turkey second only in importance to the great Atatürk, and Abdul Karim Qasim was a charismatic and erratic ruler of Iraq.

The failure of Kurds to unite or even to cooperate with one another has been a negative, debilitating factor. As Derk Kinnane has written:

> Leaders again and again fought valiantly against imperial powers to preserve the rule of Kurds over their own people. When the foreign government was weak, the Kurdish princes and chieftains rejoiced in independent action. When the empire was strong, those Kurds who enjoyed its favor gladly fought those Kurds who

> did not. It was easier for a Kurdish prince to be vassal to a foreign overlord than give up his struggle with a rival Kurd.[8]

To the ordinary mountain Kurd even today, the locality he lives in, the authority of the *agha* or the sheikh, and his own extended family are the realities. The Kurdish nation is a distant concept, only vaguely perceived; the authority of the state he happens to live in is even more so. And, as another observer has recently written: "their *aghas* . . . are always ready for a confrontation with authority. But they . . . will associate themselves with a movement just long enough to realize some personal gain—then they decamp with their followers."[9]

That the Kurds are an ancient people is beyond doubt; precisely how ancient is a debated ethnological question with which we need not concern ourselves deeply here. Perhaps they are the same as the *Karduchoi* mentioned by Xenophon in the *Anabasia*, the wild people whom the Ten Thousand encountered as they passed through the Zagros Mountains. It may be that they are the descendants of the Medes, as Kurdish tradition perfervidly maintains.

The Kurds were converted to Islam (probably from Zoroastrianism) in the course of the great Arab conquests of the early seventh century. In the medieval period a number of local rulers in Kurdistan established some degree of local power and at different times suffered various vicissitudes, attacked by Timur in 1400 and harassed by the Turkoman Bayandur dynasty.

In the sixteenth and seventeenth centuries, owing to a process of renewal and consolidation in both Turkey and Persia, the regional configuration of power attained a certain stability, which was in the reign of Shah Abbas the Great (Abbas I, 1587–1629), a revived Persia under the Safavid dynasty confronted the Ottoman Empire. The territory of what is today Iraq became a frontier zone, disputed between the two great empires, with the boundary between them shifting from time to time. The Treaty of Erzerum of 1639 established the frontier more or less as it remained until the twentieth century. About three-quarters of Kurdistan was in the Ottoman dominions, and about one-quarter in Persia. The importance of the Treaty of Erzerum for the Kurds was that it fixed a boundary between Turkish Kurdistan and Persian Kurdistan that substantially persists to the present day and inevitably has some role in dividing not merely the land but also the Kurdish people themselves. Most Kurds tended to support the Ottomans, since the Turks, like the majority of Kurds, were Sunni, while the Persians were Shiite. But each empire used Kurdish chiefs and their followers as border bulwarks against the other power.

Since neither the Ottoman nor the Persian rulers were particularly interested in imposing their rule on a local basis in the Kurdish areas, it might seem that this situation of regional rivalry would have enabled the Kurds, in their pivotal position, to secure some degree of autonomy for themselves. So it did, but only for individual Kurdish rulers, not for the people as a whole. Rivalries kept the Kurds disunited and, in any larger political sense, ineffective.

Nevertheless, local dynasts of some note did arise and, for a time, flourish, for the pashas of Mosul and Kirkuk did not aspire to govern directly more than the open plains near the cities. The rest of Kurdistan was ruled, nominally as sanjaks, by local Kurdish leaders, the Dere Beg, or valley lords. There were numbers of such, of varying importance. At remote and defensible Amadiyah the Bahdinan family ruled in virtual independence until reduced to vassalage by Ahmad Pasha around 1730. The region between the Great and Little Zab rivers was the principality of the Soran family. However, the main Kurdish power was that of the Baban house, which arose in the eighteenth century and was responsible for the building in 1781 of the town of Sulaimaniya, which became and has remained the focus and shrine of Kurdish national feelings, so far as such a thing can be said to exist.

The greatest of the Babans was Sulaiman Pasha (1750–64), who extended his dominion considerably, as did his successor. The Babans and their disciplined Kurdish troops were a regional military force of importance for many decades and the chief support of their Mamluk overlords. With time, however, the Baban dynasty fell more and more under Persian influence and was weakened by fratricidal rivalries, but it was not replaced by direct Turkish administration until 1850 (one instance of a general trend in that direction).

Thus, for a period of approximately two centuries, very roughly from the early seventeenth century until the early nineteenth, the area between Georgia and the southern Zagros was a broad band of autonomous Kurdish states, where the chieftains ruled their tribes without any control by central authorities. The situation was much the same, whether on the Turkish or Persian side of the border established in 1639. Intrigues by the central authorities, especially with a view to keeping the tribes divided and ineffective, abounded, and there was no lack of occasional violence, but in essentials the situation remained stable. The Kurdish rulers were treated, if not as equals, at any rate as feudal tenants of their territories, provided that they managed in their own way to maintain order there. But this had nothing to do with either an official recognition of Kurdish nationality or a subjective awareness of such an idea by the Kurds themselves. These concepts were to emerge only much later. Even when the eighteenth century briefly producd a Kurdish shah of Persia, Karim Khan Zand, the curious event evoked no Kurdish national feelings.

Change came for Kurdistan, and the old near stability came to an end, as a consequence of the strenuous reforming efforts of Sultan Mahmud II (1808–39), who aimed at restoring the decaying Ottoman Empire. One part of these reforms was the attempt to reestablish direct imperial administrative control over areas in practice lost to local rulers. The attempt failed against Muhammad Ali in Egypt; in Kurdistan, in the long run, it succeeded. It had substantially done so by the middle of the century. The last Mamluk pasha of Baghdad, Daud Effendi, was forcibly deposed by Mahmud II in 1830, but the centrally appointed governors (twelve between 1831 and 1969) who succeeded him were venal and largely incompetent. A striking exception was Midhat Pasha (1869–72), who in his few years in Baghdad reorganized the administration in all departments. Midhat put into effect in Iraq the Tanzimat reforms promulgated by Sultan Abdul Majid in 1840. Regional administration was based on the new *vilayet* system. Each vilayet, or province, was divided into a number of *sanjaks*, and was under a *vali*, or governor, responsible directly to Istanbul. By 1880, in the region controlled hitherto from Baghdad, after some experimentation, administration was organized in terms of three vilayets: from north to south, those of Mosul, Baghdad, and Basra, and remained in this form until the end of the Ottoman Empire. The vilayet of Mosul, which included the Kurdish area, had Kirkuk and Sulaimaniya as sanjaks. The system had some modest successes, especially in the two southern vilayets. Municipal self-government was encouraged in the towns, and some progress was made in education, sanitation, and communications.

But in the mountainous Kurdish areas the trend toward direct rule by Turkish officials in place of the former indirect rule and the emphasis on the Turkish language and Turkish ways gave offense. Also disturbing was the administrative attempt to push the private ownership of land in place of the traditional tribal or communal ownership. Kurdish leaders were accustomed to being treated as lesser partners in a feudal relationship. The new Turkish valis treated all tribesmen as *fallahin,* and by force of arms aimed at, if they did not always achieve, uniform acceptance of two anathemas: regular taxation and conscription.

The almost inevitable consequence was a series of rebellions. The most important nineteenth-century revolts in Turkish Kurdistan, which sometimes spilled over into and affected Persian Kurdistan, were those of the Baban (1806–8), of Mir Muhammad (1883–36), of Badr Khan (1843–47), and of Sheikh Ubaidalla (1878–81), the last directed against the Persians. These were essentially revolts of traditional rulers who resented increasing encroachments on their authority. Still, a first hint of a broader idea gradually appeared. Both Badr Khan and Sheikh Ubaidalla tried to find allies and to create a wide autonomous area. And there is certainly a new note in the letter said to have been written by Ubaidalla (there is some uncertainty in the attribution) to a British consul in 1878: "The Kurdish nation is a people apart. Their religion is different and their laws and customs are distinct. . . . The chiefs and rulers of Kurdistan, whether Turkish or Persian subjects, and the inhabitants of Kurdistan one and all are united and agreed that matters cannot be carried on in this way with two governments."[10]

Nationalism similar to that which developed in Europe and was later exported to other parts of the world was very slow to develop among the Kurds, however, and indeed has still not fully developed. Perhaps it never will. Even in the beginning it lagged well behind the dawning perception of national identity among the Arabs, the Persians, and the Turks.

The Young Turk Revolution of 1908 in Turkey, which brought to power a group that intended to refashion the Ottoman Empire into a unified nation-state based on secular Western models, jarred loose all existing political and ethnic relationships in the empire. The first signs of nationalist agitation among a new Kurdish intelligentsia occurred between 1908 and 1914. Kurdish political clubs were established in Istanbul, Mosul, and Baghdad, among other cities, as well as among groups of exiles in France and Switzerland. Newspapers and journals to propagate the Kurdish cause were founded. However, there was very little unity among these groups, who on occasion even betrayed one another to the Turkish authorities. And it was all very small-scale: an affair of students, lawyers, and journalists, with little or no connection with the traditional leaders of Kurdish tribal or semitribal populations in the mountains. Moreover, the Young Turks, who had at first proclaimed liberal sentiments recognizing the equality before the law of all the peoples of the multinational empire rapidly became hostile.

An oppressed people held in subjugation by more than one alien oppressor has to endure the fact that, at critical moments, the oppressor states will perceive a common interest in cooperating to maintain their oppression. A people thus oppressed can hope for liberation only if, through some unlikely stroke of luck, its oppressors are simultaneously rendered impotent to continue in that role.

The Kurds were never this fortunate, although the possibility appeared briefly at the end of World War I. Perhaps a more sophisticated people, further along in the process of national development, could have made more of the occasion. For centuries the two oppressors of the Kurds had been the Ottoman Empire and the Persian Empire. By 1918 both were in a condition of virtual impotence. The Turkish Empire had suffered total military defeat, and the Arab areas were in revolt. The Persian Empire, though undefeated because it had been technically neutral during the war (although in practice under joint British-Russian domination), was in disarray, passing through the last dreary years of the Qajar dynasty, a phase that lasted until the installation of 1925 of Reza Shah of the Pahlavi dynasty. There was briefly a possibility that an autonomous Kurdistan might be constituted out of the Kurdish areas of the defeated Ottoman Empire. This abortive project came about as a kind of by-product of concern in the West for the fate of the Armenians, whose homeland lies immediately north of the Kurdish one, to some extent overlapping with it.

As Christians, the Armenians had been sporadically persecuted by the Turks in the decades before World War I. In this the Kurds, as fellow Muslims, had sometimes assisted the Turks. The persecution of the Armenians reached its climax during the war in large-scale massacres and enforced migrations. Sympathy for the Armenians—who had for a long time been emigrating in considerable numbers to Western Europe and the United States, and were therefore not voiceless—was great, if ineffective. When the demise of Turkey in its existing form became first imminent, then an accomplished fact, it was indeed "a heady and hopeful time"[11] for the non-Turkish peoples of the empire. Their ambitions received a further stimulus from President Wilson's proclaimed enthusiasm for the ideas of self-determination.

The project of an independent Armenia, however, or one under American mandate (one of the ideas of the time that fell by the wayside), necessarily involved large-scale migrations of peoples. By the end of World War I there were very few Armenians in Armenia. The people would have had to be reassembled from other parts of the defunct Turkish Empire, and from Russia, Persia, and elsewhere in the Middle East. Worse, the Turks and the Kurds living in the area proposed for the Armenian political entity, an overwhelming majority, would have to be persuaded or coerced into leaving. To purchase the (unlikely) acquiescence of the Kurds, their national claims would also have to be recognized. Indeed, there had for some time been British travelers and political officers, even politicians, who were well disposed toward the Kurds. Also, the Kurdish cause was ably represented at the peace conference in Paris by what would now be called a lobbyist in the person of General Sharif Pasha, a former Turkish diplomat of Kurdish extraction, who had been resident in France throughout the war and was the spokesman of the Kurdish Committee of Progress and Development (created in 1909, when it separated from the Young Turks' Committee of Union and Progress).[12] Still, it is unlikely that even in the aftermath of World War I, with its immense upheavals in the Middle East, the idea of Kurdish autonomy would have gained serious consideration on its own merit. The Armenian issue was the catalyst.

The abortive Treaty of Sèvres (August 10, 1920) between the Allies and defeated Turkey did envisage the creation of an independent Kurdistan comprising the Kurdish areas of present-day Turkey and Iraq (although not of Persia),[13] but in practice this was worth little or nothing. The revival of Turkey under the directing energy of Mustafa Kemal (1881–1938), as a state much reduced in area and therefore ethnically much closer to homogeneity, produced in a short span of years an astonishing bouleversement in Turkey's position. The Greeks were driven from the western fingers of Ionia, which they had inhabited for millennia. The brief existence of independent Armenia (1918–20) was forcibly terminated. The Treaty of Sèvres was never ratified, far less enforced. It was replaced in 1923 by the Treaty of Lausanne, which was much more favorable to Turkey and made no mention of Armenia or Kurdistan.

For the Kurds, the total result of the whole period of upheaval and opportunity represented by World War I and its aftermath was simply that when it was over they were a people ruled not by two states but three—Turkey, Persia, and Iraq (or, counting Syria and Russia, five). These were not old, ramshackle empires: they were new states anxious to assert or create a national identity—conditions not favorable to minorities within them. It was then, however, that the situation crystallized into its present shape. The uncertainty turned on the future of the Mosul vilayet of the former Turkish Empire.

British interest in establishing imperial strongpoints in the Middle East, and British military activity in the area during the war, had made it likely that some sort of British presence there would be maintained after the war. Before the opening of the Suez Canal (1869), the fastest route to India was the overland one via Mesopotamia, and British interest in the area was not new.[14]

The San Remo Conference of April 1920 was assigned a mandate for Iraq to Britain, and in 1921 the British government installed King Faysal I (who had just been expelled by the French from Syria), a member of the Hashemite family from the Hijaz, as ruler of the new political entity. The name suggested correctly that the essential core of the kingdom was the river and its delta lands (*Al Iraq* means the "cliff" or "shore"), comprising the former vilayets of Baghdad and Basra, and that its essential ethnic character was Arab. The present-day state also includes much of the *Jazira* (the "island"), that is, the region between the two rivers and north of the delta, as well as part of the Kurdish mountains, neither region being part of *Al Iraq* as the term was earlier used.

The limits of the new state to the north were at first undecided. The Mosul vilayet had been assigned to France in the Sykes-Picot agreement of 1916, and France did not waive its claim until 1920. The Turks, resigned to the loss of the Arab lands, had no intention of losing, if they could avoid it, the Mosul vilayet, with its Kurdish majority, its Turkoman minority, and its probable oil. Military action by Mustafa Kemal actually forced the British to evacuate part of the area in 1922.

British policy showed some degree of fumbling and uncertainty. They had no wish to hand over the Mosul vilayet to the Turks, but they were at first uncertain whether or not to attach it to the new Arab state of Iraq. Their initial move was to try to find a Kurdish leader who would assume responsibility for an autonomous regime in the vilayet. Sheikh Mahmud Barzinja was chosen for the role and installed as governor in Sulaimaniya in 1918; but his ambitions for genuine independence and territory expansion, combined with administrative incapacity, proved inconvenient. He was removed in 1920, reinstalled in 1922, and removed once again in 1923. In the summer of 1923 the Kurdish area of Mosul was incorporated by fiat in the new Iraqi state, and in March 1924 the Kurds elected their share of delegates to the Constituent Assembly. The Iraqi government had accompanied incorporation of the area with promises that Kurds would be appointed to official posts in the Kurdish areas, and that the Kurdish language would be used there—the first in a long series of such promises, seldom totally disregarded, but seldom scrupulously observed. Since the Treaty of Lausanne had replaced the Treaty of Sèvres, and there was no prospect of an independent Kurdistan to be achieved by great power action, the Iraqi Kurds as a whole, earlier hostile to the idea of incorporation into an Arab kingdom, began after 1923 to cooperate with the mandatory government. By 1925 Kurdish notables were regularly elected to the new parliament, and there were Kurds in both the cabinet and the senate. Kurdish was, in fact, being used in the schools in Kurdish areas and for local official correspondence; the majority of officials employed in Kurdish districts were Kurds.

The international status of the Mosul area was, however, still unclear. The Treaty of Lausanne had evaded the issue by providing that the frontier between Turkey and Iraq should be fixed by "friendly arrangement" within nine months, and that, failing this, the dispute should be referred to the council of the League of Nations. It was so referred in 1924, and the Turks sought, and the British consented to, a reopening of the whole issue. A commission of inquiry was sent by the league to Iraq in 1925. The commission sensibly soon abandoned its first impractical idea of holding a plebiscite in Kurdistan. The commission's report came down in favor of the union of the three vilayets (Mosul, Baghdad, and Basra) on historical and economic grounds: they had an economic unity based on the rivers, and the Mosul vilayet had historically been administered from Baghdad. The commission's report was adopted by the league council, whose decision was influenced by the barbarous measures of repression Turkey was using against its own Kurds in 1925. The Treaty of Ankara (1926), signed by Britain, Iraq, and Turkey, settled the frontier on a line that corresponded closely to that of the old Mosul vilayet.

The award of the Mosul vilayet to Iraq had been made conditional by the league on the protection by the British of the local rights and usages of the Kurds, and on the prolongation of the mandate for twenty-five years. The mandate, however, lasted only another five. Britain, yielding to anti-British nationalist agitation in Iraq, which had never completely ceased since the beginning of the relationship in 1918, proposed to the league in 1931 that it be allowed to relinquish its mandatory role, though there was much head-shaking in Geneva and a flood of Kurdish petitions against the proposal. Britain's withdrawal was accepted by the league. In 1932 Iraq became independent. Under the Iraqi-British treaty of 1930, which replaced the mandatory link, Britain retained military bases in Iraq, there was a defense agreement, and Britain retained a "special relationship." This endured through various vicissitudes until the Iraqi revolution of 1958. However, Britain was no longer in a position to control the policy of the Baghdad government toward its Kurdish subjects.

However little the Kurds may have advanced generally in terms of a developed national feeling and political sophistication, there is no doubt that the Kurds of Iraq are more advanced than their ethnic brethren in other states. A substantial number of Kurds have participated in politics in Baghdad at all levels throughout the history of modern Iraq. Even before Iraq was founded, their area was more politically active and experienced than the adjacent areas. Sulaimaniya was always regarded as the center of Kurdish nationalism and culture—the virtual spiritual capital of the Kurds. And even if there are fewer Kurds in Iraq than in the other two states, it is in Iraq that they constitute the highest proportion of the total population.

In Iraq, too, there has simply been more change, more action, more experimentation in matters relating to Kurdish nationalism than elsewhere. If the history of Arab-Kurdish relations in Iraq has often been an unhappy one, at least there has been a recognition that the problem exists; it has been more or less realistically faced, and some attempt has been made to solve it. Neither Turkey nor Iran has explicitly recognized, in the way that Iraqi governments have done time and again, that the Kurds exist, and that their cooperation and participation are essential to the success of the state and to the nation-building process.

The story of the Kurds in republican Turkey is an unhappy one. Soon after coming to power in 1920 the government of Mustafa Kemal (later Atatürk) began to adopt a policy of Turkification and assimilation. Turkey was the poorest of the three countries that had large Kurdish minorities. Unlike Iraq and Iran, it had no oil. With very limited resources, the government tended to channel its funds for aid and development into the more westerly provinces. Turkish Kurdistan was given short shrift, and the economic situation of the Turkish Kurds deteriorated. But if Turkey had little wealth, it had an army that had made an excellent showing in some theaters during the war and was more than adequately competent in putting down rebellions.

There were three major Kurdish rebellions in Turkey in the period before World War II. The first was led by Sheikh Said of Palu, and occurred in a broad band of territory stretching from Lake Van west to the Euphrates. The precipitating factor was the abolition of the caliphate in 1924. In February 1925 Sheikh Said, much respected as a religious leader, proclaimed a jihad, or holy war, against the "godless" Turkish administration, and sought "an independent Kurdistan under the protection of the Sultan Caliph." Though it spread considerably, the revolt had been put down by the early summer. Sheikh Said and nine of his companions were tried, condemned to death, and hanged, while others were sentenced to imprisonment. Later, several of the affected tribes were moved to the southwest into Turkish-speaking regions—the start of a policy often followed later in Turkey as well as Iraq, and one that began in Turkey the process of detribalization, already under way in Iraq. The brutal manner in which the rebellion was put down had its effects: as mentioned above, it influenced the verdict of the League of Nations in the matter of the Mosul vilayet; and the example of what had happened in Turkey to their fellow Kurds helped to reconcile Iraqi Kurds to living in the Iraqi state.

The next revolt took place in 1930 among Kurds of the Jelali tribe living on both sides of the Turko-Iranian frontier, in the vicinity of Mount Ararat. It largely took the form of a siege by Turkish troops of Mount Ararat, where the Kurds had taken refuge. The Kurds were ably led, having among them several former officers of the Turkish army, but the government troops had the advantage of numbers, discipline, and an air force. Even so, putting down of the revolt, and the subsequent customary punishments and deportations, took several months. There are a number of interesting features about the rebellion of 1930–31. It seems to have been largely organized by a nationalist organization calling itself *khoybun* ("being oneself"), which came into existence in Lebanon in 1927 as an amalgamation of various Kurdish patriotic societies formed in Cairo, Istanbul, Beirut, and Damascus. *Khoybun* carried on an active propaganda campaign, addressed appeals to the great powers and the League of Nations on behalf of Kurdistan, and called on Kurds in other states to assist their oppressed brethren in Turkey. In July 1930 the rebels issued a manifesto beginning: "Brother Kurds, you must be worthy to become a great nation. . . . Unite in the struggle we have started."[15]

In fact, the 1930–31 rebellion did evoke some cross-border cooperation among Kurds, although not enough to make a serious difference to the outcome. In August 1930 Kurdish chiefs in Syria (a French mandate) organized a force of two hundred men, who crossed the Turkish border and occupied a nearby area, remote from the seat of the revolt. Turkish troops attacked and the force recrossed back into Syria. The French authorities were mildly sympathetic to the Kurds, but they yielded to diplomatic pressure from

Turkey, put the Kurdish chiefs involved under surveillance, and removed some of them from the frontier area. Similarly, an Iraqi Kurdish chief, Sheikh Ahmad of Barzan, made a raid into Turkish territory with five hundred horsemen and was repulsed by the Turks. The inevitable executions and other punishments, including enforced deportations, followed, continuing over several years. There is no agreement among the authorities as to the exact scale of these reprisals, nor on the precise number of Kurdish casualties. They were, however, certainly considerable. The reprisals were accompanied by a policy of breaking up the Kurdish tribes and advancing permanent Turkish army posts into Kurdish territory. A border readjustment with Iran, agreed upon in 1932 and involving a minor exchange of territory, made it easier for the Turkish army to control the Ararat area.

The third Kurdish rising in the period before World War II was that of June 1937. It was led by a local chief, Sayyid Reza of Dersim, and was occasioned by the establishment of Turkish gendarmerie posts in the Dersim area, hitherto unaffected by central authority. Sayyid Reza gathered to his cause between one and two thousand tribesmen and for a number of months succeeded in excluding Turkish troops from the entire Dersim district. An unsuccessful attempt was made by some Syrian Kurds to come to his assistance, and in Baghdad newspapers Iraqi Kurds called for foreign investigation of the situation. But by November the Turks had won. Sheikh Sayyid Reza, his two sons, and a number of other chiefs were tried, condemned to death, and executed. The Turkish government decreed the deportation to other vilayets of all the tribes involved in the affair, to the number of some fifty thousand.

In 1937 a four-power pact, the Treaty of Saadabad, was concluded among Turkey, Iraq, Persia, and Afghanistan. No doubt a precipitating factor was the Italian conquest of Abyssinia in 1935–36, which created a sense of vulnerability among lesser powers in the Middle East.[16] The four states agreed in the Treaty of Saadabad to cooperate in the event of an external threat, and for the prevention of foreign intrigues within their borders. Article F addressed itself to opposing "the formation and activity of associations, organizations, or armed bands seeking to overthrow established institutions."[17] Kurds supposed, with some justice, that this was aimed at them.

For some three decades after the late 1930s there was little in the way of overt demonstrations of Kurdish discontent in the eastern Turkish provinces. The reasons were manifold. The price of rebellion had been demonstrated to be high; the process of enforced breakup of the tribal structures was gathering steam; railways and roads were built that connected the remote eastern vilayets of Anatolia to the metropolitan centers farther west, and enabled government troops to be moved eastward more easily.

After Atatürk's death in 1938, Turkish policy toward the Kurds was slightly relaxed, although in essence it remained the same. In the early 1960s, in sympathy with the struggle beginning in Iraq, there was some recrudescence of Kurdish activity in Turkey. Cultural associations sprang up in the major cities. Arms were smuggled across the border to assist the Iraqi Kurds.[18] The government reacted by arresting fifty Kurdish intellectuals. Official policy wavered back and forth between conciliation and oppression as Turkey's central government went through a series of convulsive changes. Bilingual Kurdish-Turkish journals were allowed to appear in the mid-1960s, but were prohibited by the Demirel government in 1967. In response, a series of mass demonstrations by Kurdish students took place in cities in the Kurdish area, including one by 25,000 in Diyarbaki—an unprecedented event. More oppression, with more rumblings of discontent, followed.

The new military government established in Ankara in September 1980 by General Evren did much to end the disorder in the country, endemic for twenty years. The establishment of strong government, however, works against the Kurds, themselves among the prime creators of disorder. In Turkish Kurdistan sporadic disorder continues to occur.[19]

The relations between the Kurds of Iran and the Iranian central government, whatever its character, and the general population are determined by factors the converse of those in Turkey and Iraq. In the latter two countries Kurds are a group apart because of race, not religion. In Iran, the Kurds are also set apart ethnically, but they are only one among a number of such minorities. The difference that matters is the Kurds' adherence to Sunni Islam while the state religion of Iran and the religion of the great majority of its population is Shiite.

Until the revolution of 1979, the Iranian Kurds had perhaps been the least unfavorably treated of their people (though there was not a great deal to choose between their experience and that of their fellow Kurds in Iraq). The existence of so many minorities in Iran was doubtless an inhibiting factor. The attack on Kurdish culture in Iran was never so thoroughgoing as in Turkey. Nevertheless, the ruler of Persia between 1925 and 1941, Reza Shah—like Kemal Atatürk, whom he in many ways resembled—was trying to create a unified, orderly, secular state. In addition to building roads, schools, and hospitals in the most remote areas, his administration dealt directly with the Kurdish population, and not, as previously, through the tribal chiefs, and made considerable progress in disarming the tribes. These policies naturally bred resentment and led to two small revolts in the 1920s, led by Ismail Simko of the Shikak tribe. Simko, who was mainly motivated by personal ambition, was ambushed and killed by government forces in 1930.

World War II for a time changed everything in Iranian Kurdistan. The Anglo-Russian invasion of Iran in August 1941, regarded as necessary in order to maintain a secure supply line from the Indian Ocean to the Soviet Union, involved the abrupt deposition of Reza Shah, whose policies had been pro-German, and his replacement by his inexperienced twenty-two-year-old son, Muhammad Reza. In northwestern Iran government authority disintegrated. The Russians occupied Azerbaijan province, the southern part of which has a Kurdish population, and prohibited any deployment of Iranian forces in their area. Farther south, but still in Kurdistan, the British occupied Kermanshah. The British allowed the Iranian army to operate in their area. As the disintegrating Iranian troops retreated from Azerbaijan, rifles and ammunition fell into the hands of the Kurdish tribes, while "those restless chiefs whom Reza Shah had maintained in exile were permitted to return to their homes where they quickly regained local dominion."[20]

Events throughout the entire area of Iraqi and Iranian Kurdistan between 1941 and 1946 were of an extraordinary complexity and fluidity, with alignments and intrigues among Kurdish parties and groups, as well as between the Kurds, the Russians, and the British, forming and reforming in bewildering patterns. The most important outcome of all this, however, was the brief existence of the Mahadad Republic.[21]

Soviet policy toward the Kurds lacked a clear-cut character for some two years after the joint Anglo-Soviet invasion of Iran. Perhaps the same can be said of Soviet policy toward the Kurds in general. No doubt there were (and are) conflicting views in Moscow. On the one hand, a dissident minority in three nations, two of which (Turkey and Iran) have a common border with the Soviet Union, appears to offer delicious opportunities for fishing in troubled waters. On the other hand, an autonomous Kurdistan dominated, as it probably would be, by traditional and tribalist figures, might well be too independent and too little inclined to further the purposes of the Soviet Union. Since the 1920s, and especially in the 1950s and 1960s, there have been many Kurds calling themselves communists or sympathizers with the Soviet Union, but these have not formed any real part of the fighting strength of the Kurds.

Shortly after the Soviet invasion of northern Iran in 1941, the Soviet authorities took a number of tribal chiefs and other notables by train to Baku, where they met Baghirov, prime minister of the Azerbaijanian Soviet Socialist Republic. Although the Soviet Union had bound itself by treaty with Britain and Iran not to intervene in Iranian internal affairs, and to withdraw its troops six months after the end of the war, it is likely that some assurances were given of Soviet support for Kurds who wanted to throw off the Persian yoke. This tied in with local developments in Mahadad (formerly Sauj Bulaq), the chief town in the Kurdish part of Azerbaijan, lying south of Lake Urmia and about twenty miles from the Iraqi border.

Because the Russians did not maintain a garrison as far south as Mahabad for long after the invasion, the area had become a kind of no-man's-land where political innovation was possible. In September 1942 a group of Mahabad Kurdish citizens organized what was later to prove the origin of the most important Kurdish nationalist group to date. The new organization was known as the *Komala* (or *Komula*), short for *'komala-i-Zhian-i-Kordestan,* i.e., the Committee for the Regeneration of Kurdistan. The Komala gained rapidly in membership and popularity, attracting attention throughout the Middle East.[22] Little by little, power in Mahabad shifted from the "purely nominal" provincial governor, appointed in Tehran, into the hands of the Komala. Qazi Muhammad, an authoritative figure from a family of Sunni religious leaders in Mahabad, became the effective head of the group. The administration of the region comprising Mahabad and some twenty to forty miles in every direction around it was substantially in the hands of this group from roughly 1943 on; that is, some two years before the Mahabad Republic formally came into existence. C. J. Edmonds, possibly with some measure of flattery, says it administered the district "with commendable efficiency and success."[23] The excellent local tobacco crop made it financially solvent.

In 1945 Soviet policy became bolder. Apparently there was some notion of attaching northwest Iran to the Soviet Union. The Tudeh party, the communist front in Iran, was instructed to change its coat and became "the Democratic Party of Azerbaijan," and began to use Azerbaijani Turkish as its language. In September, Kurdish notables, including Qazi Muhammad, were shunted to Tabriz and then to Baku for a second meeting with Baghirov. The Russians apparently hoped that the Kurds would join the new party and also the puppet Azerbaijan Republic that they were in the process of creating on Iranian territory. However, on his return Qazi Muhammad announced the creation of the Democratic Party of Kurdistan, with a program of objectives calling for autonomy within the Iranian state, and the use of Kurdish in education and administration. The Komala was dissolved, or rather subsumed in the new party. This was the beginning of the Kurdish Democratic party, the main vehicle (though much bedeviled by internal divisions) of Kurdish agitation and political effort in subsequent decades.

The Iranian garrison of Tabriz surrendered to the Soviet-backed Azerbaijanians in December 1945, and two puppet republics emerged under Soviet auspices in Azerbaijan province—one Azerbaijanian and one Kurdish, the latter at Mahabad, which had enjoyed real, though not formal, independence for several years, being under less direct Soviet control. Qazi Muhammad became president of the Mahabad Republic, and a mini-parliament of thirteen members was formed. There was a brief, exuberant flowering of Kurdish nationalism in all its aspects, including the use of the distinctive national costume and language. Mulla Mustafa Barzan, the greatest Kurdish leader of the twentieth century and a tireless and resourceful guerrilla fighter, was driven out of Iraq, arrived with supporting forces, was made a general, and became the military mainstay of the Mahabad Republic.

The demonstration of Kurdish autonomy in action was stimulating and has never been forgotten. But as a phenomenon it was brief and ambiguous. If the Russian aim in supporting it was to apply pressure on Iran to gain an oil concession, these fumbling moves in Azerbaijan had little relevance. If it was annexation of the region, the Soviet Union had dubious allies. As Stephen Pelletiere asks, "What did the Russians want from the Kurds and what did the Kurds think they were getting away with? . . . All in all it can be argued that the Kurds had done precisely what the Russians did not want them to do."[24] Kurds would not long cooperate with Turkish-speaking Azerbaijanis, and neither group was likely to prove biddable in the long run. If the Mahabad Republic attracted widespread Kurdish interest and support, that boded little good for the Russians: most of Iranian Kurdistan was in the British zone.

In any event, successful diplomatic pressure from the new shah and from the Great Powers persuaded the Soviet Union tardily to fulfill its treaty obligations with Britain and Iran. Its troops were withdrawn from Azerbaijan province in May 1946. In December Iranian government troops recaptured Tabriz, and the two puppet republics collapsed. Qazi Muhammad surrendered and was tried for treason and hanged, together with his closest collaborators. Mulla Mustafa Barzani, however—not an Iranian subject, and therefore not open to a charge of treason—made a curious visit to Tehran, during which he vainly tried to secure from the British Legation guarantees of personal security if he returned to Iraq, and also dickered with the Iranian authorities about a project whereby his tribe, disarmed, would be settled in Iran. He subsequently returned north and, after a period of uneasy truce had broken down, the majority of his followers went back across the border into Iraq. Mulla Mustafa himself, however, with a few hundred of his crack mountaineer followers, fought or evaded all would-be interceptors—Iranian, Iraqi, and Turkish—and by June 1947 had made his way north into Soviet Armenia. He remained in exile in the Soviet Union for the next eleven years.

The little republic was not only betrayed from without, in that it did not receive the armed support it had some reason to expect; it was also, like all Kurdish national striving, weakened by internal division. It rested on the support of enlightened townspeople, but did not enjoy the solid support of the tribes. "During 1946 the

Kurdish tribes, naturally opposed to government control, felt as restive under Qazi Muhammed as they had under the Central Government, even though he was of their own race. . . . The tribes almost all sided with the Iranian army."[25]

After the fall of the Mahabad Republic there was little significant Kurdish activity in Iran for more than a decade, or indeed even until the fall of the monarchy in 1979. The Kurdish nationalist movement went underground. The Iranian government prohibited the Kurdish language and the Kurds' printing presses were destroyed. The Iranian KDP, meeting in secret, adopted a leftist program in 1956.

Until the revolution in 1958 there was a degree of cooperation between Iraq and Iran in keeping the Kurds in check. When the Iraqi revolution broke out and Mulla Mustafa Barzani returned to Iraq, however, there were some contacts between the Iranian KDP and its counterpart in Iraq. Stirrings in Iran were met by increased government surveillance and harassment, and many of the leaders of the Iranian KDP were arrested. At the same time, Barzani's influence contributed to the emergence in it of a more conservative leadership. Barzani frowned upon a futile move to begin guerrilla activity in Iranian Kurdistan. The shah had little liking for the new revolutionary regime in Baghdad, and was giving Barzani financial support as a way of embarrassing Iraq.[26] Conversely, Iraq allowed the Iranian KDP to open an office in Baghdad and provided the movement with limited amounts of arms and money. During the prolonged, though intermittent armed struggle of the Iraqi Kurds against the Iraqi government, from 1961 to 1975, the shah's substantial and steadily increasing support in arms and money and in providing sanctuary was essential.

During the 1960s and 1970s something of a divergence developed between the Iranian and Iraqi Kurdish nationalist movements, though there was no overt break. The Iranian KDP party conferences of the early 1970s showed that party to be falling increasingly under the dominance of leftist intellectuals, some of whom—like so many of the Iranian opposition—had studied abroad. The party congress of 1973 called for armed struggle in cooperation with all revolutionary Iranian parties. With the collapse of the shah's regime, the situation was ripe for the assertion of an active Kurdish movement in Iran.

The government of Iraq cannot be said to have been unaware of the difficulty of the task it faced in regard to the Kurds. In a cabinet memorandum of the early 1930s, King Faysal wrote, "The government rules over a Kurdish group most of which is ignorant and which includes persons with personal ambitions who call upon this group to abandon the government because it is not of their race."[27]

The Kurdish situation in Iraq has developed in the context of two limiting conditions, which have defined the ground of debate and conflict for both parties over six decades. The Kurds have conceded that their future lies within the Iraqi state, and for its part the Iraqi state has recognized that there is such a thing as the Kurdish nation, which is entitled to some degree of special treatment. This is what has given the Kurdish-Iraqi relationship its flexibility, its interest, and its hope, never entirely lost, of the achievement of a resolution satisfactory to both sides.[28]

The activities of Sheikh Mahmud Barzinja in the early mandatory period have already been mentioned. His repeated uprisings were put down, as customary in such affairs in the 1920s, 1930s, and 1940s, by cooperative actions involving Iraqi troops and Royal Air Force bombings (announced in advance) of insurgent Kurdish villages. (The RAF maintained a base at Habbaniya, near Baghdad, until 1958.) Toward the end of the mandate, as a tactic to persuade the League of Nations to accept Iraqi independence, British pressure moved the Baghdad government to assure the Kurds of the national rights that have been the standard in such negotiations ever since: namely, education in the Kurdish areas to be conducted in Kurdish; local officials who are Kurdish or at least speak Kurdish; and some kind of administrative autonomy short of independence. In 1931 a Local Language Law was promulgated. There has never been much doubt about what the Iraqi Kurds want. Debate and acrimony have arisen over details such as the limits of the Kurdish area and over the sincerity with which the government is carrying out its promises.

In the 1930s leadership of the Kurdish nationalist cause in Iraq was taken over by the Barzanis, and particularly by Mulla Mustafa Barzani. The Barzanis were tribal leaders whose territory centered on Barzan, in the remotest northeast corner of Iraq, almost the only area where detribalization had not yet undermined the old ways. Mulla Mustafa, born about 1904, was the youngest brother of Sheikh Ahmad Barzani,[29] the hereditary head of a religious order that in the nineteenth century had developed into a tribe, a possible occurrence in Kurdistan. The tribe steadily grew in strength and territory, numbering some nine thousand by the 1940s.[30] Mulla Mustafa always deferred in public to his elder brother, but it was he who became famous as a national leader—the preeminent Kurd of the twentieth century.

Mulla Mustafa was the outstanding champion of Kurdish rights for some forty years. In origins and character he was a tribal leader; but, though he never personally liked the intellectuals of his cause, he recognized the necessity of working with them, and he bridged the gap between the two halves of the movement as no one else had been able to do. In the end came defeat and death in exile in 1979, but his achievements nevertheless had been truly formidable.

In 1931, fighting on behalf of his brother, Mulla Mustafa had his first serious brush with the authorities. At first the two Barzanis defeated the Iraqi troops sent against them; eventually, however, they were forced over the border into Turkey. Handed back to Iraq by the Turks, they were sent into exile for a decade, first in southern Iraq, then in Sulaimaniya.

In the absence of the Barzanis, the 1930s in Iraq Kurdistan were fairly uneventful: "A not very effective presence of government organs was offset by not very effective risings of Kurdish tribes."[31] Some developments of the period are, however, worth noting. The creation of an Iraqi national army afforded a legal outlet for the martial enthusiasm and ability of individual Kurds, with many becoming officers. (In the later troubles, some Kurdish Iraqi officers always deserted to the rebel cause: most, however, quite happily fought their fellow Kurds.) There also emerged in this period an increasing number of Kurdish intellectuals who became active in politics. Every Iraqi cabinet since the 1920s has had its Kurdish members, the proportion varying. Their personal attitudes and policies have also varied, some being timeservers—careerists indifferent to the Kurdish cause—while others have done what they could to advance Kurdish interests within the inescapable reality of an Iraqi state.

The upheavals of the war years enabled Mulla Mustafa to escape from Sulaimaniya and return to Barzan in 1943. Prime Minister Nuri es-Said, the astute, pro-Western stalwart of the Hashemite monarchy who played so large a part in Iraqi politics between 1930 and 1958, conducted some obscure negotiations with Mulla Mustafa in 1943–44 through Majid Mustafa, a Kurdish cabinet member loyal to Baghdad. It is possible that these parleys had been suggested by the British. Nuri showed himself ready to make considerable concessions, but the episode led nowhere since he was forced out of office in June 1944. In the summer of 1945 government troops attacked Baranzi in his homeland and he was forced over the border into Iran, where he was to play a signal part in the story of the Mahabad Republic. It was during this brief period in Iraq, between 1943 and 1945, that Barzani established links with the young Kurdish intellectuals—lawyers, teachers, journalists—of the recently founded party called Heva ("Hope"), and so blossomed into something more than merely a tribal leader.

There are three great landmarks in Iraqi-Kurdish relations between the later 1950s and the present: the revolution of 1958, the coming to power of the present Iraqi regime in 1968, and the collapse of Kurdish resistance in 1975; with, perhaps, a fourth such event being the outbreak of the Iraq-Iran war in 1980.[32]

The July 1958 revolution in Iraq, which resulted in the murder of the royal family and of Nuri es-Said, and the replacement of the monarchy by a radical republican regime, was at first greeted (like the Iranian revolution almost exactly twenty years later) with foolish cries of joy by every group and political party—including the Kurds—that had been opposed to the fallen regime. At first there seemed some reason for this. Barzani was welcomed back to Iraq by Brigadier Abdul Karim Qasim, the charismatic but eccentric figure who was now dictator of Iraq. Barzani followers were allowed to return north (although Mulla Mustafa himself was held in Baghdad). The provisional constitution issued two weeks after the revolution said that the Iraqi people (*sha'b*) was a partnership of two nations (*qawn*). This recognition of Kurdish status, never made before with such emphasis and never subsequently retracted, is a kind of benchmark in all subsequent Kurdish-Iraqi affairs. The KDP was licensed as a "patriotic party" in February 1960.

The honeymoon ended in 1961. It had become increasingly clear to Barzani that the unstable Qasim had no intention of allowing any substantial administrative and cultural autonomy for Kurdistan. Barzani was merely being used. Still, the three peaceful years of more or less favorable official treatment had enabled the

KDP (whose president Barzani had somewhat reluctantly become) to consolidate and expand to an unprecedented degree. In 1961 Mulla Mustafa and the KDP drew up a six-point program of demands asking for wide autonomy inside Iraq.[33] Qasim responded that the proposals were a threat to the territorial and political integrity of Iraq and took some measures against the Kurds. Anti-Kurdish riots occurred in Baghdad. Disorder broke out in the north; it was not instigated by the Barzanis, but suspicions were deepening on both sides. In September 1961, in a fit of pique, Quasim ordered the bombardment of Barzan, Mulla Mustafa's home village. The latter, who had already withdrawn to the northern hills, was thus edged into leading a rising with which he had at first not sympathized. After some hesitations on both sides a war began that lasted, with intermissions, for fourteen years. No other Kurdish leader had ever maintained such a struggle against a central government for so long a period—an achievement all the more remarkable in that the Kurds were not solidly united behind Barzani. He had to face the opposition of local enemies as well as of government troops and planes. Nor did he enjoy the solid support of the KDP. The KDP joined in the struggle in December 1961, but Mulla Mustafa kept the areas of Kurdistan under their control operationally distinct from those defended by Barzani forces.

From this point until the debacle of 1975 there existed, within fluctuating borders, a Kurdish-run territory in which the writ of the central government did not run. It constituted a mountainous crescent in Iraq running along the frontiers of Iran and Turkey, some three hundred miles long and thirty to seventy miles wide. Columns of government troops penetrated the redoubt from time to time; they would be surrounded and cut off. Air strikes were ruthlessly employed by the government, but their effectiveness is a subject of controversy.

The frightful winters in Kurdistan usually, though not always, interrupted military operations for several months each year. And each time there was a change of regime in Baghdad—and there were several in the 1960s—there was a pause for negotiation. In February 1963 Qasim was overthrown and executed by a temporary alliance of officers belonging to the Arab Socialist (Ba'th) party and Arab nationalists, but this regime lasted only half a year. The Ba'thists were ousted from power by the army, and al-Salem Aref became president. From 1963 to 1966 there was a virtual cessation of hostilities between the government and the Kurds. In June 1966 a promising Kurdish peace plan, the Twelve Point Program of Premier al-Bazzaz, was put forward, but quickly became nugatory when Bazzaz lost power after President Aref was killed in an air crash. Aref was succeeded by his brother, who remained in power until 1968. Meanwhile, a split had formed within the Kurdish movement, essentially between leftist and rightist factions, which has persisted to the present. The leaders of the radical faction were Ibrahim Ahmad, secretary-general of the KDP, and the young lawyer Jalal Talabani, who had been active in the Kurdish underground before 1958. Barzani, who had majority support among the Kurds, opposed them and succeeded in expelling them from the party and from Iraq (they took refuge in Iran in August 1964).[34]

After exactly a decade of upheaval, the coming to power of the (second) Iraqi Ba'th regime in July 1968 brought into being, under the leadership of Ahmad Hassan al-Bakr and later Saddam Hussein Takriti, a stable and successful government that has combined, in proportions appropriate for Iraq, ideological zeal, pragmatism in policy, ruthlessness, and adroitness.

The new Ba'th administration made no bones about the fact that they regarded the Kurdish problem as the most serious one confronting Iraq. After a series of negotiations with the Kurds, the government issued the manifesto (a unilateral fiat, not a treaty) of March 11, 1970, which was, or seemed, extraordinarily generous in its concessions to Kurdish nationalism—more so than any previous offer from Baghdad. The document began by declaring that the Kurds of Iraq were part of the divided Kurdish people and that the Kurdish national movement in Iraq was part of the general Iraqi national movement. The government promised to put into operation within four years an autonomy plan that would fully recognize Kurdish rights. The Kurdish language was given official status as the primary language in the Kurdish areas and the secondary language elsewhere in Iraq. There were to be a Kurdish vice-president in the central government and five Kurdish cabinet members. The *pesh marga* (the armed force of the Kurds) was to be partly integrated into the Iraqi army and paid by the government. Unresolved was the question of the oil-rich Kirkuk area, with its mixed population. Its future was to be determined by a plebiscite—which, however, was never held.

A four-year cessation of hostilities followed. The eighth congress of the KDP, meeting legally in Iraqi Kurdistan under official patronage in July 1970, marked the high-water mark of the movement. As time passed, Barzani became convinced, rightly or wrongly, of the government's bad faith. Also, he was being pushed by external factors, albeit reluctantly—he was entering his seventies—into resuming the war. The shah of Iran, who disliked the revolutionary regime next door, did not wish to see it solving its problems and growing stronger. He offered to substantially increase the assistance he had given Barzani in years past. Also, aid seems to have been forthcoming from Israel, always ready to help handicap a militant Arab state, and from the United States through the CIA, whose motivation was the fact that in the early 1970s Iraq seemed to be falling more and more into the position of a Russian satellite, as evidenced by the Soviet-Iraqi treaty of 1972.

The Iraqi government's Autonomy Law for the Region of Kurdistan was announced and put into effect on March 11, 1974, exactly four years after the 1970 manifesto. It was somewhat less favorable than the 1970 proposals. Irbil (halfway between Kirkuk and Mosul) was designated the regional capital instead of the historic, and less accessible, Sulaimaniya. Moreover, the limits of the region were to be decided by a census, thus suggesting (correctly, as the event proved) that they would be drawn as narrowly as possible, and that Kirkuk would certainly not be within them. Nevertheless, the law did provide for a degree of autonomy for the Kurdish region, with an elected regional legislature and an executive drawn from it, and with devolution of some government functions to the regional entity. Some observers consider that it was a mistake for Barzani and the KDP to decide to renew the war, but it cannot now be known how sincerely the proposals would have been implemented by the government.

The last phase of the war, 1974–75, was fought more fiercely and on a larger scale than any earlier one. Barzani possessed ample supplies of heavy weapons supplied by Iran, and a thousand or so Iranian troops actually crossed the frontier to support him. The Kurds to some extent abandoned their traditional guerrilla hit-and-run tactics for main-force confrontations (with some success).

The end came abruptly and disastrously when the shah and Saddam Hussein Takriti, meeting in Algiers at an OPEC summit in March 1975, brought to a conclusion a series of tentative negotiations that had been conducted over several months, swallowing their ideological dislike of each other's regimes in order to gain concrete mutual advantages. It was a textbook example of how lesser states (and peoples) will be sacrificed by larger states for the sake of their own interests. Iran gained an improved riverline frontier on the Shatt al-Arab—the international border was agreed to be on the *thalweg*, the center line of the deepest channel, instead of, as hitherto, on the left, or eastern, bank. In return, all Iranian support was withdrawn from the Kurds. The key clause of the joint declaration of March 6, 1975, repeated almost verbatim in the treaty of June 13, is sufficiently explicit without mentioning the Kurds. The two parties undertook to exercise "a strict and effective control over their common boundaries with a view to putting a definitive end to all acts of infiltration of a subversive character no matter where they originate from."[35]

As George Lenczowski said, in an apt analogy, "that agreement was a sort of Yalta for the Kurdish Nationalists."[36] The Kurdish resistance collapsed in a few days. Barzani, in Tehran, had the new situation spelled out to him by the shah. For a few weeks Iraqi Kurds were to be permitted, if they chose, to move into Iran. Somewhere between fifty and a hundred thousand did so, but were not allowed to settle in Iranian Kurdistan, where they might have constituted a new menace. They were instead dispersed in other areas. Barzani lived for a time in Tehran before moving to the United States. He died in Georgetown University Hospital on March 1, 1979.

"Within a month of the Algiers meeting the Baghdad government ruled in Kurdistan as no outside government probably ruled since the dawn of history."[27] By May 1975 all armed resistance in Iraqi Kurdistan had come to an end. The Iraqi army moved in unresisted, and a long-term program of road-building and the establishment of army posts in the area was put into effect. The government's main strategy for preventing future outbreaks seems to have been the compulsory relocation, continued over several years, of large numbers of the Kurdish population. At least one to two hundred thousand Kurds were affected. Some were settled in the uncongenial, hot delta lands of the south (later some of these were allowed back), others in the northern plains, in mixed-population areas.

Yet Baghdad has never abandoned, only modified in detail, the

1974 program for Kurdish autonomy. In 1980 a new electoral law was promulgated that also provided for an elected fifty-member regional council for the Kurds. The first elections for the council were held in 1980, and it has been functioning since 1981. As in dealing with other problem groups (e.g., the Shiite Arab majority), the government has combined firmness or ruthlessness with economic concessions designed to win support. A very substantial amount of the budget for the Kurdish areas has gone into industrial projects, schools, hospitals, dams, and agrarian improvements.

The internal politics of Kurdish nationalism since 1975 might be summarized as "factionalism and frustration." The area has not been without sporadic violence, the murder of foreign technicians in particular having occurred on several occasions, but the possibility of any large-scale armed resistance to the central Iraqi government is clearly over. The power of the traditional leaders has been scotched, though not destroyed. Fifteen years of fighting produced in the end only defeat and suffering. Violence did, however, increase again in the early 1980s, until a cease-fire in December 1983.

After the defeat the Iraqi Kurds split decisively into their two factions. Talabini, the leader of the leftist faction, shuttled about between Syria and Turkey, organizing opposition to Barzani. In November 1975 he created a new Kurdish political organization, the Kurdistan Patriotic Union (KPU, also written PUK), as a replacement for the KDP. The Barzani faction, led after Barzani by his two sons, refurbished the KDP as the "KDP Provisional Leadership." Talabini, at first a supporter of the Ayatollah Khomeini's regime, by 1984 had made his peace with the Baghdad government. The Barzani brothers intrigued with the Iranian government and launched an abortive cross-border attack in November 1983.

In Iran an intermittent and indecisive war has been conducted by the new regime against Kurdish insurgents in their home area since 1979. This insurrection has never posed any serious threat to the central government and will in all probability be dealt with decisively when the distraction of the war with Iraq is over.

The outbreak of that war in September 1980 has led, on the whole, to surprisingly little change in the situation of the Kurds. It might seem to offer opportunities for the traditional game of inciting one's enemy's minorities to rise; but this, while attempted, has met with very little success. As I have written elsewhere, one of the noteworthy lessons of the Iraq-Iran war has been the remarkable extent to which existing state structures have stood up to the strain, even in ethnically nonhomogeneous countries like Iran and Iraq.[38] There has, indeed, been some stirring of Kurdish activity in Turkey, leading to an agreement in October 1984 between Iraq and Turkey on coordination against guerrilla activity.

Diplomatic circles in 1984–85 were rife with reports of a final, definitive settlement between Saddam Hussein's government and the Kurds that would concede a good deal more to them than any previous offer, including control of the Kirkuk area, and thus would purchase real and lasting peace in Iraqi Kurdistan. Such a possibility exists, but it would have implications for the other two states with large Kurdish minorities. Neither Turkey nor Iran wants to see Iraqi Kurds given a substantial autonomy, which would set a "bad" example for Turkish and Iranian Kurds, as well as perhaps setting free the energies of the Iraqi Kurds—no longer fighting their own government—to stir up trouble across the borders. Turkey, through whose territory a pipeline now takes the greater part of Iraq's oil to world markets (because of the closure of Iraq's gulf ports), has the means by which to exert pressure if it wishes. And Iran in turn can put pressure on Turkey, if not on Iraq, because an agreement of January 1985 envisages that another pipeline may carry Iranian oil across Turkish soil, with needed transit dues going to Turkey.

The Kurdish situation is unlikely to change substantially in the foreseeable future, although concessions to the Iraqi Kurds and a more favorable situation for them are, indeed, possible or even likely. But anything beyond that—union, independence—is, it must be said with some regret, simply not in the cards. The Kurds are, and will remain, pawns in the hands of greater forces. The Kurds possess a genuine national culture, and it has many admirable aspects. One, surprisingly enough, is its restraint. No Kurdish emissaries blow up or shoot Turkish, Iranian, or Iraqi diplomats in the streets of foreign capitals. And, despite their reputation for violence, the Kurds have fought only in self-defense. They have not sought to rule other peoples. Their fate in the near future is the status quo or something closely resembling it. Yet, at the same time, no efforts to crush them have succeeded, or are likely to succeed, in extinguishing the undying flame of their proud identity.

PART 7

Problems in Strategy and Security

■

THE PERSIAN GULF

Stability, Access to Oil, and Security

■

John Duke Anthony

When the Iran-Iraq conflict degenerated into open warfare in September 1980, following months of desultory Iranian shelling across the border, harassment of Iraqi diplomats, attempted assassination of Iraqi leaders, and other tensions, officials in Washington worried about the impact on oil supplies.[1] In the years since then, each country has lashed out at the other's oil facilities, with Iran mounting attacks against Kuwait and with Iraq threatening Iran's loading terminals at Kharg Island. In reaction to the massive mobilization of Iranian troops along its borders, in 1983 Iraq decided to break the deadlock. Its means since then have been twofold, each signaling Baghdad's desperation and determination to bring the war to an end: the use of chemical weapons in land operations and the employment of French-made Super Etendard aircraft and Exocet missiles to strike at ships entering or leaving an Iraqi-proscribed combat zone inside Iranian waters. Tehran's response has been to increase terrorist activity in several Arab countries and to send human waves into battle against Iraq's superior artillery, sacrificing thousands of teenage youths with virtually no military training or cover other than an *Allahu Akbar* ("God is great").

One American analyst, aware of his fellow citizens' short attention span with respect to international affairs in general, has gone so far as to call the conflict "the forgotten war."[2] The truth is that the war has never been forgotten, just ignored most of the time. The intermittent fears about threats to the West's and America's oil lifeline have continued to grab headlines, but even this form of attention has quickly receded whenever the threats have proved or appeared groundless. For most Americans, including a substantial proportion of elected officials, the war has simply seemed too distant from, and largely irrelevant to, the United States.

To many, the war has been, and remains, essentially a conflict between two anti-American regimes. Victory by either of these seemingly inscrutable countries has hardly seemed an attractive prospect to most Americans. In this light, some have wondered, only partly in jest, whether it is not possible for both to lose. History has been answering in the affirmative, but without a smile: it *is* possible for both to lose. But if either side loses—*really* loses, as opposed to being worn down to capitulation—there seems little doubt that Japan and most of the West, including the United States, also stand to lose. Such a loss could come in the form of a severe curtailment, if not the complete loss for an extended period, of the oil supply from an area that boasts 60 percent of the world's proven reserves.[3]

What began in 1980 as a typical military conflict between two states with a legacy of personal, political, economic, and social rivalries subsequently degenerated—in part because of its protracted length and in part because of the juggernaut nature of the Iranian revolution and the rigid fervor of its leaders.[4] The war has seen not only the introduction of chemical weapons by Iraq, but preparations by Iran as well to engage in chemical warfare. The Iranian Islamic revolutionary government has employed and continues to use school-age children at the front. As if conscripting students as soldiers were not inhumane enough, large numbers have been sent without weapons to be killed either by detonating mines or by absorbing intensive defensive fire. (However, results of the human wave on the battlefield have as yet proved inconclusive for Iran.)[5] The war's casualties have been staggering: nearly half a million killed (100,000 Iraqis and about 300,000 Iranians); about one million wounded, many suffering amputation of legs blown off by minefields; 50,000 Iraqi and 8,000 Iranian prisoners of war. Add to this the devastation of Iranian cities such as Ahwaz, Dezful, and Masjid Sulaiman in the south; capture by Iran of Iraq's former oil exporting terminal at Fao, and major destruction in one of Iraq's largest cities—Basra—as well as in the Iraqi Kurdistan towns of Penjwin and Garmak. Quite apart from the impact of the "oil glut" in the mid-1980s, Iraqi attacks on the major Iranian oil terminals such as Kharg Island and Bandar Khomeini, the capping of Iranian wells at the Nowrez and Ardeshir fields, and Syria's closure of its oil line from Iraq have on their own account brought about a substantial decline in Gulf oil production.

American economic interests in the region, diverse as they are, have one essential feature in common: the need to secure Gulf oil.[6] This has been and remains the raison d'être of the numerous U.S. efforts to foster Gulf security, the prime reason for refinements and variations upon the Rapid Deployment Force (RDF), the "Bright Star," "Jade Tiger," and "Accuracy" military exercises, and the establishment in January 1983 of the unified U.S. Central Command (CENTCOM).[7] The need to keep the region's oil lanes open and secure has prompted everything from reflagging Kuwaiti vessels and deployment of U.S. naval vessels in the Gulf to worse-case scenarios for American—or, as argued by some, even Israeli—armed intervention to deter threats to Gulf security.[8]

The United States has attempted to secure its economic interests in the Gulf by fostering the already strong financial and commercial interdependence between it and the region.[9] This interdependence is evidenced by U.S. investments, the repatriation of U.S. oil companies' profits and dividends, and U.S. exports of goods and services to Arab states.[10] Of additional importance is the advantage that (by the U.S. government's own reckoning that every $1 billion in exports pays for 40,000 full-time jobs), the more than $5 billion exported annually from the United States to the Arab Gulf states in the mid-1980s provided several hundred thousand jobs for American workers and the principal source of livelihood for many thousands more dependents and spouses. Still more weight is given to U.S.-Gulf interdependence by the fact that close to 50,000 U.S. citizens live and work in the Gulf region.[11] There are several hundred U.S. firms doing business in Saudi Arabia alone.[12]

Arabs, for their part, are concerned that revenues from oil be spent on investments in the United States that will continue to produce income in the event that future oil income drops.[13] Even as the West continues to need Gulf oil, these states need to ensure revenues with which to purchase Western goods and technology. It is, moreover, at least as much in the interest of Western countries to encourage industrialization of the Gulf states, which guarantees that the Gulf will need huge inflows of cash to pay for imports and expertise. This in turn guarantees the Gulf countries' interest in maintaining reasonable levels of oil and production and export.

Some Americans have observed that the United States could lessen its involvement in the Gulf, inasmuch as (1) there is a global oil glut; (2) in the mid-1980s the United States imported less than 5 percent of its oil from the area, as a result of decreased demand worldwide for petroleum in general and a combination of successful conservation measures and switches to alternative energy sources at home; and (3) Europe and Japan, more than the United States, stand to be affected most by an oil slowdown.[14] The reality, however, is that a "glut" exists only so long as oil flows out of the Gulf and into the international market. Even if it were true that only Europe and Japan would be affected by a cutoff, the blow that would be dealt to the Western economic structure by European and Japanese distress—European and Japanese dependency ratios on Gulf oil being 40 and 60 percent respectively—would be tremendous.[15]

A short-term interruption in, or minimal reduction of, the quantity of oil exported through the Strait of Hormuz could be accommodated by temporary alterations in supply patterns, thanks to surplus production capacity. However, a total cutoff of Gulf oil could not be accommodated at or near the consumption levels of the mid-1980s. Such an interruption would produce a devastating combination of worldwide inflation and recession, a financial crisis, and concomitant high levels of unemployment.[16]

"The energy crisis did not vanish; it became so bad that it helped force the industrialized states into the worst recession in the postwar era and many Third World oil importing states into a full-scale depression. We traded gas lines for unemployment lines, and a capital crisis over recycling oil costs for a capital over economies unable to pay for previous oil imports," Anthony H. Cordesman has observed.[17] The reason a worse oil crisis did not follow the shah's fall in 1979 and the Iran-Iraq war in 1980 was because Saudi Arabia raised its production levels. In 1980 this meant producing two to three million barrels per day (bpd) more than the kingdom's development plan required. Although in the first half of 1983—at the recession's height—the kingdom's production had slipped to one-third of its 1980 production level, it still produced 7 percent of the world total, 10 percent of the noncommunist total, and 23 percent of the OPEC total.

The U.S. Department of Energy reported in 1983 that, regardless of conservation measures and the employment of alternative energy supplies, the noncommunist oil nations will begin a slow but steady rise in oil imports by 1990. In 1986 a Masters' Report produced by the U.S. Geological Survey concluded in unequivocal terms that by the mid-1990s the Middle East not only will have regained its central role in global energy supplies, but that Saudi Arabia, as a leading petroleum producer, will have resumed its preeminent role within the region.[18] The United States, however, more than any other industrialized nation in the world, has fallen short of its goals over the past decade to increase domestic or alternative energy supplies. The development of nuclear power, the production of synthetic fuels, and the mining of coal have all lagged behind projected needs. In the mid-1980s the U.S. Strategic Petroleum Reserve was capable of guaranteeing operation in the United States for ninety days. A slowdown in Gulf oil shipments, let alone a cutoff, could change these figures rather abruptly, placing extraordinary strains on the reserve, with the ultimate prospect of draining it completely.

In spite of an impressive array of statistics demonstrating extensive U.S.-Gulf economic interdependence, and in spite of the millions spent on U.S. programs to increase exports and facilitate trade, the nature of U.S. bureaucracy is such that while one part of the federal government has worked to increase trade with the Gulf, another part has worked to hinder it. Barriers to facilitating U.S.-Gulf relations have been set up in the form of antiboycott legislation, stiff U.S. licensing requirements, and the predictably public, frequently hostile, congressional scrutiny that arises over most, if not all, proposed arms sales to any Arab state.[19]

With regard to Arab investments in the United States, the furor that arose in the 1970s and continued into the 1980s has largely died down except for isolated complaints. Investment from Saudi Arabia alone, mainly in U.S. government securities, has been estimated at $70 billion.[20] The American capital market, however, has proved large enough to convince most people that it would be very difficult for any foreign group of investors to control any significant level of U.S. open-market operations, even if this were their objective. It is clearly in the United States' interest to strengthen the financial links that benefit not only Arab investors looking for a stable market in which to invest, but also the American companies that benefit from this injection of capital, thereby helping the overall U.S. balance of payments position. Theoretically, greater potential exists to garner favor and dependence on the part of Arab investors who seek out the United States as a "favorite" financial haven.

Military Dimensions

In his State of the Union address in January 1980, four weeks after the Soviet invasion of Afghanistan, President Carter enunciated what in effect was the first expansion of the Monroe Doctrine in 150 years and, to some, a unilateral extension of the NATO alliance to cover the Gulf. Carter said: "Any attempt by an outside force to gain control of the Persian Gulf region will be regarded as an assault on the vital interests of the United States of America, and an assault will be repelled by any means necessary, including military force." To Carter's credit, he explained that the "grave threat" to Gulf security had to be met by "collective efforts" and "consultation and close cooperation with countries of the region." But just what would constitute an assault and how extensively the United States might be prepared to pursue diplomacy before resorting to military force, not to mention what kind of military force might be used, have all been the subject of keen debate at the highest levels of the U.S. government and throughout the foreign policy and national security establishment.[21] A major flaw, many felt, was Carter's failure to address a far more likely scenario—that control or curtailment of oil supplies might be effected, not by an outsider, but rather by a belligerent insider, such as revolutionary Iran.[22]

Overextension, awkwardness of supply lines, and difficulty in securing base rights in a region both dependent on and distrusting of the United States have hindered the major instruments created to render the Carter Doctrine credible: CENTCOM and its predecessor, the Rapid Deployment Force (RDF). Soviet aircraft from Aden and Socotra in South Yemen, Baku in the USSR, or Afghanistan are two to three hours' flying time away. By contrast, American planes would need between fourteen and seventeen hours' flight time to arrive from the U.S. mainland.

No Arab state, Egypt included, was inclined to accede to a U.S. request for bases, but much fervor was generated by the Carter Doctrine. For example, at a Senate Foreign Relations Committee hearing on February 6 and 7, 1980, on the issue of U.S. bases in the region, Richard Foster of the Center for Strategic and International Studies declared, "The process of disintegration of the Arab tribal states in the Persian Gulf is well advanced: the Saudi Arabian government may have only a few months of life left unless we make serious moves to shore it up."[23] The regime in Riyadh did not oblige Mr. Foster. Half a decade later, Saudi Arabia was arguably stronger than before, as a result not of American rapid deployment forces coming to its rescue, but of the kingdom's own successful defensive operation, using U.S.-supplied fighter planes, against Iran.

From the outset, the realities the RDF faced made it—so the pundits said—neither rapid, nor deployed, nor a force. According to CENTCOM leaders, a fighter squadron, plus 800 paratroopers and a limited number of B-52 bombers, could be in action in the Gulf within forty-eight hours (with another three thousand troops to follow by the end of the week). Impressive as this may seem, critics stress that any sustained action beyond that point would most likely be severely circumscribed, owing to geographic and political considerations. To transport an infantry division to the Gulf could easily require an entire month.[24]

In mid-1980 the American military owned 271 C-141s and 77 C-5As to transport troops and services all over the world. According to mobilization and power projection authorities at that time, it could take as many as 823 C-141s to airlift a division to the Middle East, an impossibility given the situation. Of related concern, all agreed that the dispatching of C-141s and C-5As to handle contingencies in the Gulf would risk leaving other strategic areas, most notably Europe, unprotected. (A new transport plane, the CX, capable of carrying the XM-1, the new American battle tank, several thousand miles nonstop, did become available for use in Gulf security in 1985, but its production costs exceeded by 500 percent the estimated $81 million.)

In addition, a variety of difficulties confront the U.S. Navy in the Middle East: (1) The Suez Canal can be closed in a few hours, but it might take up to a year or longer to open. (2) Although it took seventy days to sail to Vietnam from the U.S. West Coast, the operative conditions for ships making the journey were relatively benign—no naval or air threats were encountered. This might not be the case in the Middle East. (3) The U.S. aircraft carrier fleet has declined from twenty-four to twelve since Vietnam. (4) The Soviet Union has five times the logistics-based potential and five times the number of battleships in its "surge force" stationed in the Black Sea.[25]

As for the effort to secure bases, the results have been minimal. Kenya, thus far the closest collaborator in such contingency planning, although located furthest from the Gulf, offered the U.S. Navy use of Mombasa as a regular port of call. The Somali government, however, demanded too high a price for American access to facilities at Berbera. Oman, the one Gulf state to have participated thus far in joint maneuvers, agreed to permit only limited use of an airfield, and conditional access to three other air bases.[26]

In view of these difficulties, a joint Arab force made up of Egyptian, Jordanian, or Saudi Arabian troops has been suggested as a short-range alternative to the RDF and CENTCOM. Though the forces entailed, especially if combined, would be formidable, prior agreement on politically thorny issues would have to be reached, not the least of which is Egypt's continued expulsion from the Arab League. As a result of the Camp David agreements, Egypt's military is politically hamstrung in the face of threats to Arab states that have little or nothing to do with Israel (i.e., Iranian counterinvasions of Iraq, Iranian air forays into Saudi Arabian territory, Iranian-inspired coup attempts (e.g, in Bahrain in December 1981), and periodic Iranian threats to close the Strait of Hormuz).[27]

Among suggestions put forward by naval specialists for improving CENTCOM's capabilities are the following: (1) Provide it with assigned troops (rather than designating forces that are also earmarked for other contingencies). (2) Restructure the Marine Corps so that it has no role other than that of supporting CENTCOM.

(3) Design strategic airlift solely on the basis of moving troops and not equipment (CENTCOM's tanks should be prepositioned in the region and resupply carried out by fast SL-7 ships). (4) Provide a marine amphibious unit to be available for landing in a benign environment. (5) Upgrade mining countermeasures (to be able to resist more effectively any regional or other powers or groups that might seek to threaten navigation in the Strait of Hormuz).[28] One reassuring realization about the Strait has been the near impossibility of anyone being able to block it by mining, because of currents and width of passage.[29] Instead, Iran has attempted air strikes on ships moving toward Kuwait, Saudi Arabia, and Iraq; and Iraq has sought to block Iranian exports and imports by attacking tankers in the northern Gulf.

Apart from the inherently flawed attempts at building a capacity for direct intervention in the Gulf via the RDF and CENTCOM, U.S. military projections into the region have taken the form of arms sales and, since the Iran-Iraq war began, the dispatch of AWACS radar planes to Saudi Arabia. Many analysts, however, have voiced concern that the Reagan administration's emphasis on the military dimension of Gulf security has been overplayed and that far more attention should have been given to the political dimension.[30]

Political Dimensions

American approaches to Gulf security have taken several forms, each covering a number of concerns and all influenced by the Iran-Iraq war. The most basic of these concerns to to reduce the vulnerability of the oil fields and the production facilities themselves, and their links via pipeline and shipping to markets in the West.[31] U.S. political responses have included increased economic and security assistance to key states, attempts to engage countries in the region in a "strategic consensus" along the lines of the ill-fated Baghdad Pact in order to "face off" the Soviet Union, and an international energy-sharing agreement such as that which led to the establishment of the International Energy Agency (IEA), an effort to ensure adequate oil supplies in the event of a halt in Gulf oil shipments.[32] These all bear some examination.

The transfer of control of energy resources vital to the industrialized states to a group of countries in the cradle of civilization, and their use of the influence implicit in such a shift, would have been impossible to imagine during the colonial era, at a time when resort to military force was considerably less problematic and more "legitimate" than it has come to be today.[33] In effect, U.S. foreign policy formulation and execution has become constrained and conditioned by the need to weigh more heavily than ever before the interests of the oil producing countries. No less important, the needs of U.S. allies for adequate energy supplies have also ranked high among the factors determining U.S. foreign policy objectives and activities.[34]

The specter of another Arab oil embargo on the scale of the 1973 embargo cannot be entirely discounted. However, the response of the Gulf states, and indeed all Arab states, during Israel's invasion of Lebanon in 1982 was largely one of "non-performance." In addition, many U.S. policy makers have concluded that the infrastructure of mutual need between Arab investors and American markets has become so tight, if not binding, that attempts to implement another embargo for political reasons would likely have as savage an effect on producers as on buyers. Revolutionary upheaval in the oil-producing states, however, is a catalyst for change that the United States has seemed chronically unable to foresee, understand, or accommodate. Much of this has to do with America's isolationist tendencies and its general unfamiliarity with the inner dynamics of the Islamic world and the needs and concerns of its policy makers.

Revolutionary Iran's declared intention has been to hasten the overthrow of the conservative Gulf states and a number of other countries. The process of fomenting internal unrest has rapidly become one of the most destabilizing factors in the region. It exploits the expectations aroused in the development process, the frustrations of unfulfilled wants, and the negative reaction of some conservative elements to modernization, as well as the revolutionary and radical elements existing in all societies.[35] Terrorist attacks and support for insurrection in Lebanon and Syria have had their Iranian component, as have bombings in Kuwait and the repeated disruptions by Iranian pilgrims in Mecca and Medina.[36] The toppling of the Saddam Hussein regime in Iraq and its replacement by a government more compatible with the regime in Tehran would almost certainly produce a major shift in the regional balance of power at the head of the Gulf, the Arab world's eastern border, leaving the Arab states of the lower Gulf perilously exposed.

Some American analysts perceived a Soviet master plan, a kind of pincer movement, aimed at Iran and Saudi Arabia from Soviet positions of influence in Afghanistan, Ethiopia, and South Yemen. Unless the United States mounts a counteroffensive, many contend, it will have no one to blame but itself if further Soviet inroads are made at American expense.[37] Only a distinct and consistently overruled minority has argued that while concern with Soviet interest, growing involvement, and possible intentions has been and remains fully warranted, attention nonetheless ought to be given to the view that the United States itself may have had something to do with Afghanistan, Ethiopia, and South Yemen moving away from the Western sphere; that the reason these "losses" occurred might be partly owing to possible Soviet and local perceptions of a U.S. lack of will to contest Soviet advances, or a general U.S. indifference to the importance of the three countries in terms of the overall calculus of American national interests.[38]

In the midst of the debate over what the nature and orientation of America's Gulf security policies should be, former U.S. ambassador to Egypt and Saudi Arabia, Hermann F. Eilts, wrote:

> While I do not share the view that the Soviet bear is about to implant himself on the shores of the Persian Gulf, neither is complacency in order. United States' efforts to strengthen the security posture of the Gulf area need to be pursued. A primary requirement for success is . . . *refurbishing American political credibility in the Gulf area and re-establishing a political climate in which some measure of confidence in American willingness to pursue evenhanded area-wide policies is restored.* Simply ringing military alarm claxons will not persuade most Gulf leaders. They want constructive American political actions on bilateral and area-wide problems (emphasis added).[39]

With the exception of Afghanistan, from 1979 onward none of the proponents of the "Soviet behemoth" school could point to actual Soviet thrusts into the Gulf—although many regularly came close to implying as much.[40] To the globalists, however, it required little to sustain the analogy that what had happened to Europe at the end of World War II could as easily happen again in the Gulf if the West did not wake up in time to see and ready itself to oppose the threat. They advocated the need for a rapid build-up of conventional forces capable of protecting American and allied interests.

In the aftermath of the 1973 oil embargo, the International Energy Agency (IEA) was set up in Paris to deal with both the short-term and the long-term vulnerability of American, European, and Japanese energy import dependence. The diversity of the interests involved remain so numerous and problematic as to raise serious questions about the IEA being truly able to assist in rendering Gulf security a reality. Even so, in the formation of the agency, U.S. interests appear to have prevailed, in the sense of the IEA being viewed by many as a counterforce to OPEC. Certainly, a major objective was and continues to be the avoidance of cut-throat competition, which could easily occur among countries seeking to outbid one another for scarce oil supplies.

To reduce vulnerability, the agreement provides for the creation and maintenance of an emergency sharing mechanism for the Western countries and Japan. All IEA participants have pledged themselves to the creation of a strategic petroleum reserve equal to sixty days' oil imports. The objective of combining this build-up of energy stocks with the securing of an agreement on a sharing formula was to deter future use of "the oil weapon" by warning producing countries that future supply disruptions would cost them far more than at the time of the 1973 embargo. Should deterrence fail, the hope was that the scheme of drawing on stocks and administering the sharing mechanism could provide just the right amount of cushion to allow time for more effective consultation, negotiation, and, possibly, political settlement. The Iran-Iraq war has tested the latter aspect of the sharing arrangements' assumptions severely, however, since the United States has no diplomatic relations with Iran, which has in any case refused to negotiate an end to the conflict. At the same time, U.S. relations with Syria, which has been aligned mainly with Iran, plummeted following the U.S. bombing of Syrian artillery positions in December 1983.[42]

The IEA, on balance, appears best geared to deal with possible short-term emergency situations. At one point in 1984, as a parallel measure undertaken almost in tacit admission of uncertainties about the efficacy of the IEA approach, Saudi Arabia floated its own reserves, estimated to be in the range of sixty million barrels. From the U.S. perspective, the IEA centerpiece is clearly its sharing mechanism. In this regard, the IEA reflects the American preoccupation with a possible repeat of the 1973 embargo, in which, most concede, neither Europe nor Japan but the United States would be the primary target. To the degree that stocks plus sharing do in fact deter, most agree that this is all well and good. But deterrence may fail, and it is difficult to overlook the fact that, since the IEA was established, there has never been Allied support for pursuing a confrontational approach on questions related to Gulf security, whether on the matter of oil supply or on any other issue.[43]

Considering the pitfalls of direct U.S. military involvement in the Gulf, the defense of Gulf states threatened by aggression seems best served by bolstering their self-defense capabilities. But as anyone who witnessed the spectacle of the 1981 AWACS debate knows, getting even radar planes to aid the Arab Gulf states through an American Congress determined to avoid giving offense to Israel has brought into question whether the judicious sale of a range of U.S. defensive equipment to the Gulf states is politically feasible.

Successive U.S. administrations have had to acknowledge that there is no ultimate guarantee that military equipment sold to one state will not end up at some point being transferred to another. Sales of U.S. military equipment to Israel are perhaps the most obvious cases in point. Wholesale illegal transfers of American weaponry by Tel Aviv to other countries—including revolutionary Iran, even at the time when Iran held U.S. diplomats hostage—have been widely reported in the media. For the most part, however, the serious constraints in U.S. foreign military sales procedures have been of some help. Certainly, nothing to date has shown that any of the Arab Gulf states, in contrast to Israel, has ever been anything but scrupulous with respect to U.S. wishes in this regard.

In sum, a consistently crippling factor that has diminished the effectiveness of several U.S. approaches to Gulf security has been Congress's persistent inclination to view proposals to assist the Gulf states militarily solely in terms of the Arab-Israeli conflict. At the very least, this view has been myopic; more often it has been inapplicable. It takes no expert to acknowledge what the Arab Gulf states have been saying for years—that the principal threat to them, certainly in the 1980s, comes from Iran, not the Soviet Union, and that in the unlikely event of an Israeli-Gulf confrontation, it is the Gulf that would require protection, not Israel. America's pursuit of its own interests and those of its allies in assuring Western access to the Gulf's energy supplies has, therefore, been rendered exceptionally difficult owing to third parties bent on intimidating U.S. elected officials with the threat of defeat at the polls unless they conform to Israel's foreign policy objectives.[44]

Most Americans are unaware that U.S. ties with the Gulf states, begun in the 1930s, developed after World War II into a broadly based relationship that included a military aspect from the beginning,[45] although it was not until the mid-1960s that Saudi Arabia turned to the United States for modern air defense equipment. In 1974, at Saudi Arabia's request, the U.S. Department of Defense carried out a survey of the kingdom's needs for the next ten years. What was involved in this ten-year plan were relatively small and limited forces, not nearly the size of those of the other states in the area, such as Israel, Syria, Iraq, Iran, and Jordan. Not until 1978 did the amounts or the kinds of defensive equipment involved begin to cause serious strains in the U.S.-Saudi and U.S.-Gulf security relationships, strains introduced primarily by the Israeli lobby in the United States. In that year, the U.S. Congress approved, after a bitter fight, the tripartite sale of advanced fighter planes to Israel, Egypt, and Saudi Arabia. The sale was bitterly contested by Israel and its lobby, which wanted the long-range fighters to themselves.[46]

Never before had U.S. aid of any kind to Israel been tied to that which was simultaneously being extended to Arab countries; Israel feared the loss of its "preferential status." The Israelis nevertheless received $480 million to buy fifteen F-15s, added to the twenty-five previously ordered, and seventy-five F-16s. Saudi Arabia bought sixty F-15s for $2.5 billion and Egypt paid $400 million for fifty F-5ES. In order to mollify the opposition of the Israeli lobby, extraordinary restrictions were placed on the equipment for the Saudi F-15S.[47]

A similar fight ensued in Congress over the AWACS radar planes, with the U.S. Senate Foreign Relations Committee asserting that the AWACS were an essential element in achieving "strategic consensus" in the region. It also analyzed various scenarios in which AWACS could be used in confrontation with Israel, noting technical and political problems with each scenario.

If there was any question of the effcacy of these sales to Saudi

Arabia, it was dispelled by the crucial utilization of one of those F-15s in 1984—three years after the sale—by Saudi Arabia in repelling an imminent attack by Iranian jet fighters. And AWACS monitored the defensive action undertaken at that time by the kingdom's armed forces. Many have opined that this one action stopped the long-predicted Iranian massive assault on Iraq that was to have come in the summer of 1984. A fact overlooked by many as the event unfolded, however, was that nothing in the action was in the least bit threatening to Israel.

Tangible U.S. security assistance to the Baghdad regime has also been blocked by the strident opposition of the Israeli lobby. The United States has thus had little choice but to extend tacit approval for the French shipment of Super Etendards to Iraq.[48]

Barring direct aid to Iraq, whose five hundred operational combat aircraft of Soviet and French manufacture far outweigh Iran's depleted capabilities of some sixty operational fighter-bombers, the U.S. interest in promoting stability, security, and access to the Gulf's petroleum supplies is best served by support for the self-defense actions of the newest of all Arab regional organizations: the Gulf Cooperation Council (GCC).

The GCC and Its Individual Member States

On May 25, 1981, as a response to the threat of the Iran-Iraq war, six Gulf countries—Saudi Arabia, Kuwait, Bahrain, Oman, Qatar, and the United Arab Emirates (UAE)—formed a confederation to address their economic and security needs, the Gulf Cooperation Council.[49] One of the key factors in the initial success and promise of the GCC is certainly the stability of its individual member states and their commitment to the organization's goals. A strong case can be made that the six GCC states are among the most politically stable societies not only in the Middle East but anywhere in the developing world. In terms of abrupt regime change, the area encompassed by the six GCC countries (and Iraq, too) has witnessed less upheaval in the past two decades than any other Third World region. In the few instances of forced change of leadership, the change has merely led to a perpetuation and rejuvenation of the existing system of rule by substituting a more effective leader of the same family for one whose legitimacy had waned.[50]

The impressive degree of continuity with respect to regimes and governmental systems within the GCC has permitted outsiders and insiders to predict with considerable accuracy these states' policies, actions, and reactions to particular events. This predictability—a trait closely aligned to, if not synonymous with, stability—is largely owing to the longevity and resilience of the top leadership in the area. Moreover, although many of the heads of state lack extensive formal educations, the range and depth of their on-the-job practical experience would match or exceed that of many of their counterparts elsewhere, including the West. The longstanding internal and intraregional stability of the six GCC states thus provides a sound basis for Western access to Gulf oil.[51]

Two GCC countries, Oman and Bahrain, have been key to the success of U.S. military operations in the region. One of Oman's islands, Masirah, was used to launch the unsuccessful hostage rescue attempt. The sultanate has played other crucial roles as well. Since shortly after the Iran-Iraq war began, 100 percent of the maritime traffic through the Hormuz Strait has avoided Iranian maritime channels, using Oman's territorial waters instead. The special relationship linking the United States and the West with Oman has been critical to assuring the free flow of oil and has contributed as much as any other factor to the deterrence of aggression by Iran, the sole Gulf country that has frequently, at various points during the war, signaled an intent to "close" the strait.[52]

Bahrain's strategic role is based on the fact that its location permits early surveillance of all shipping en route to Iraq, Iran, Kuwait, and Saudi Arabia in the Upper Gulf. For years Bahrain has permitted a small U.S. fleet to dock at its port on a half-yearly rotating basis. Other factors adding to the archipelago's strategic importance are its refineries, terminals, storage facilities, and the underwater pipeline to the Arabian Peninsula through which Saudi Arabia provides 85 percent of the oil that Bahrain refines for export.[53]

Added to the Omani and Bahraini efforts have been official statements to the effect that all six of the GCC states would welcome international aid in maintaining freedom of navigation in the Gulf. These statements of policy bear considerable weight in light of the fact that it is the GCC countries, and not Iran or Iraq, that produce the bulk of the Gulf's oil available for export.[54]

The principal arms recipient in the region, as is well known, has been Saudi Arabia.[55] Since 1980, the kingdom has contracted to purchase more than $14 billion in U.S. military goods and services. Despite that total, the great bulk of which has consisted of construction work (e.g., barracks, schools, clinics, etc.) and services, not weaponry, the kingdom remains vulnerable to regional threats and is in need not only of additional amounts of U.S. equipment already in its inventory, but of newer, more advanced defensive weaponry.[56]

In contrast to the long-standing security relationship with Saudi Arabia, U.S. arms transfers to and military training agreements with the remaining five GCC states are newer and, to date, have been relatively insignificant. Oman and Bahrain have been permitted to purchase a limited amount of advanced weaponry from the United States, while Kuwait, the United Arab Emirates, and Qatar have been permitted only marginal access to U.S. military inventories. Owing largely to the increasing success of the Israeli lobby in thwarting most arms transfers from the United States to the Arab world, the United States lags far behind what the British and French are willing to supply, especially with regard to aircraft and air defense systems, some of which are more advanced than what the U.S. government had considered offering. The most notable example is Saudi Arabia's 1985 agreement with Great Britain to purchase $7 billion worth of Tornados and other advanced aircraft.[57]

The GCC and the Iran-Iraq War

The GCC's Ministerial Council has met on numerous occasions. With the Iran-Iraq conflict raging only twenty minutes away by air from Arabia's borders, the foreign ministers of Saudi Arabia, Kuwait, Qatar, Bahrain, the UAE, and Oman have been constantly weighing what steps they might take on their own to enhance the prospects for regional security cooperation. In the absence of a credible collective security arrangement, the GCC has been hopeful that two particular measures taken by Saudi Arabia might continue to serve as deterrents. These remain the utilization of (a) the kingdom's U.S.-supplied AWACS to monitor the Gulf's airspace, and (b) U.S.-supplied F-15 fighter planes to resist violations of Saudi Arabian territory.

A continuing GCC agenda has been to (1) find a nonmilitary,

preferably diplomatic, way to end the bloody Iran-Iraq war, which has already cost a quarter of a million lives and over $45 billion in GCC aid to Iraq; (2) maintain freedom of navigation in the Gulf; and (3) strengthen security within the GCC.

Foremost on the GCC agenda since its establishment has been the need to deter a military attack by Iranian forces or any widening of the Gulf war that could lead to U.S. or other outside intervention. As a first step, the GCC conducted a series of joint military maneuvers in 1983 and 1984. To be sure, the number of combat-ready troops involved—fewer than 30,000—was minuscule by U.S. standards. Yet they represented the first joint maneuvers ever held between Arab states. Rather than seeking to make a show of force, the purpose of the exercises was to test the coordination of the six states' Western equipment and command systems, especially in air defense, radar, and communications.

In the event that local defenses fail to deter aggression from Iran, and intervention by U.S. forces becomes more popular, it is important to recognize the limit of these forces.[58] In the event of a crisis in the Gulf requiring prolonged U.S. intervention, American soldiers would have to be borrowed from locations scattered around the world, with the attendant risk of bringing troop strengths in Europe and elsewhere to unacceptably low levels.[59]

The costs, moreover, would not be limited to American manpower. Top U.S. military and civilian officials admit that creating a capacity for effective American intervention in the Gulf would require tens of billions of dollars for improved sea and airlift capabilities and new light-armored divisions. Yet whether taxpayer expenditures of this magnitude would be possible or, more important, would really be necessary has hardly been the subject of serious discussion and debate within the Congress. All of which has been puzzling, especially as the states in question are among the world's very few that are able and willing to pay their own defense bills and to do so in cash.

Strengthening the GCC states, in short, would cost the U.S. taxpayer nothing. More important, such assistance would lessen substantially the likelihood that American (or Israeli or some other country's) soldiers might one day have to intervene to defend U.S. or other Western interests in the region.

The inclination of many in the Reagan administration to downplay local initiatives in international crisis areas, and to use armed intervention when U.S. interests have appeared indirectly or potentially threatened, does not bode well for what is at stake with regard to long-term American interests in the Gulf. The efforts of the GCC have deserved far more U.S. and other Western support and encouragement than, in light of the record, they have actually received. Neither the process nor the outcome—enhanced potential for self-defense—has posed or does pose the slightest threat to Israel, Iraq, Iran, or anyone else. This is clearly in keeping with Western interests.

Since the advent of the Iranian revolution, there has been an extraordinary new challenge to U.S. foreign policy: terrorist attacks against military installations and even attempts to blow up Congress and the Washington Monument. Attacks against U.S. embassies in Pakistan, Libya, Kuwait, and Lebanon have also occurred. The most spectacular to date was the suicide truck-bomb by pro-Iran terrorists which plunged into the U.S. Marine compound in Beirut on October 23, 1983, killing 241 Marines, while another bomb across town rained death on their French counterparts. The incident did as much as anything else to effect the ignominious withdrawal of the U.S. peacekeeping forces from Lebanon. The attacks were carried out by members of an Iranian-backed group operating from Syrian-held territory in Lebanon's Bekaa Valley. Khomeini-backed forces have made no secret of their goal: total U.S. withdrawal from the Middle East and the defeat of the "Great Satan."[60]

Although some of the attacks in Libya and Pakistan were indigenous responses to Israeli policies, none prior to the *Achille Lauro* incident in 1985 were carried out by Palestinians, the bogeymen most targeted by the U.S. government's Office to Combat Terrorism (OCT). Iran, not the PLO or any other Palestinian group, was responsible for the attacks in Beirut and Kuwait. Yet many in the OCT have continued to concentrate on the PLO and its affiliates, accepting Israel's charges against all evidence to the contrary.[61]

The great fear that the defeat of Yasir Arafat in Lebanon would lead to greater Palestinian radicalization and terrorism has, as yet, not been founded on any reality.[62] However, if the United States is to be regarded as serious about warding off the potential desperation that might lead to Palestinian terrorism in the Gulf, it will have to deal seriously with the question of Palestinian disenfranchisement, which occurred for the fourth time in the devastating Israeli invasion of Lebanon in 1982 and the subsequent eviction by Syrian forces of still more Palestinians from Tripoli in the months that followed.[63] One need only be reminded of the several hundred thousand Palestinian workers in the Gulf to know that the potential for unanswered grievances to explode in sabotage and other acts of violence there cannot be discounted.[64]

The ineffectiveness of U.S. political and diplomatic approaches to an issue of such region-wide volatility and concern has been and continues to be directly correlated with destablization in a host of locales throughout the Middle East. The case can be made, for example, that the split in the PLO occurred in large measure because the dissidents felt that the United States had not responded positively to several major policy concessions and diplomatic overtures undertaken by Arafat—concessions and overtures that coincided with a period of suspension of the PLO's armed struggle with Israel. Washington appears unable or unwilling to find public ways of encouraging Arafat in his pursuit of diplomatic, rather than military, means to achieve Palestinian goals. In short, there must be a hopeful alternative to acts of political extremism for Palestinians if the Middle East as a whole, and the Gulf in particular, is to remain in a primarily Western sphere of influence.[65]

Alongside Palestinian nationalism, religious extremism is another factor that has motivated acts of political violence, of which the bombings in Kuwait and the attack in Mecca were but two examples.[66] If nothing else, U.S. policy could benefit by displaying greater sensitivity to the religious sensibilities of the people of the region, and of the Gulf particularly, in view of Saudi Arabia's role as protector of Islam and its holiest places.[67] The debate over moving the U.S. embassy in Israel from Tel Aviv to Jerusalem is a case in point. Not only are the move's proponents ignoring the strong feelings of some 160 million Arabs, who find the serious consideration being given in the United States to the proposed move deeply offensive, but they are also ignoring and incensing nearly one billion Muslims, two-thirds of whom live outside the Middle East.

THE DIMENSIONS OF AMERICAN FOREIGN POLICY IN THE MIDDLE EAST

■

Robert J. Pranger

Prior to America's entry to the Middle East at the end of World War II, the region was, in L. Carl Brown's words, the "most penetrated political system" in the world in terms of outside intervention. An elaborate "game" was played in the Middle East by insiders and outsiders, which to some extent continues to the present day.[1] America's alliance with Great Britain against Hitler in North Africa and its partnership with the Soviet Union, which required that supplies be shipped through the Persian Gulf, placed American Middle East policy in the familiar category of outside intervention by a great power. With the end of the war and the onset of Soviet-American competition, U.S. involvement escalated in pursuit of a grand strategy of containment of the Soviet Union.[2] The Truman administration developed a plan for containment directed first against the Soviet forces in northern Iran and then against communist designs in Greece and Turkey, a plan also implemented in Europe and the Far East. Every American administration since Truman has, in one way or another, built on this containment policy, although sometimes with differing degrees of ambition and dedication.[3]

At the same time, however, postwar American foreign policy in the Middle East has been dominated by two issues of special national interest to the United States where regional and domestic, rather than international, questions have been paramount: Israel and the Arabs. The making of American policy toward Israel has been influenced within the legislative and executive branches of the U.S. government by the pressures of domestic political interests. As for the Arabs, there are two American policies, one determined by the greater considerations of international politics (including, of course, the politics of oil), and the other dictated by, and intertwined with, the special relationship Israel enjoys with the United States. Having two policies toward the Arab world rather than one has created a schizophrenia in overall American policy that has made this policy very difficult to manage. Only by understanding these inconsistencies in the U.S. approach toward the Arabs is it possible to appreciate the tortured relationship between the United States and the Arab world since the end of World War II.

It is important, therefore, in analyzing U.S. foreign policy in the Middle East, to see it as at once international, regional, and domestic in orientation, with the three dimensions in some ways asymmetrical and unsynchronized with one another. American policy in the Middle East is three policies, not one. We shall examine each of these dimensions and then see how—or if—they relate to one another. Before this three-dimensional analysis, however, it is necessary to review briefly the European legacy to U.S. foreign policy in the Middle East.

The European Legacy

American foreign policy in the Middle East has found itself ensnared in a politics not of its own making: the conflict between Israel and the Arabs. While America's strong backing for Israel's independence was evident in both U.S. support for the partition of Palestine in 1947 and for recognition in 1948, the historical fact remains that all other major powers of the day, including the Soviet Union, did likewise. Yet in a fundamental way the most commanding issue of the contemporary Middle East and of American policy in the region, the Arab-Israeli struggle, owes its origins to nineteenth- (and early twentieth-) century European politics. Both in terms of power and ideology, the basic tenets of the conflict between Israel and the Arabs are, in large measure, alien to the United States. And no matter how powerful a nation may be, there are limits to what its foreign policy can do with a history it has not created.

At the same time, however, the European powers, diminished in their potency and reoriented in their diplomacy, no longer have much capacity to resolve the conflict. In a sense, the Arabs and Israel must rely on themselves to square their differences, but what capabilities they have are circumscribed by European imperialistic and anti-Semitic legacies that cannot be exorcised from the region unless there is peace but, paradoxically, prevent this peace because they cannot be eliminated. What is this European legacy and how has it hampered American foreign policy in the Middle East?

The Middle East's European inheritance with which American foreign policy must contend is fourfold, representing some of the saddest chapters in modern history: (1) anti-Semitism, (2) imperialism, (3) nationalism, and (4) totalitarianism. Since each has also given rise to its own mythology, it is necessary to examine briefly certain issues relating to political knowledge, ideology, and symbolization.

Probably nowhere in U.S. policy is the poetical, subjective impulse as strong as on the subject of the Middle East. The origins of the Arab-Israeli conflict encourage what has been called the "poetics of space," a quasi-fictional, even mysterious, understanding of the region.[4] Yet there is also a noticeably strong preference for empirical, positivistic knowledge in the modern social sciences and historical studies that concentrate on the Middle East. At the very least, therefore, a dichotomy exists between policy and understanding, or, perhaps more accurately, understanding itself is affected by tricks in a language that appears empirical but is more imaginative.[5]

Especially important in the history of the modern Middle East has been the expansion of Western ideas and movements that were born in Europe of mythic origins—anti-Semitism, imperialism, nationalism, and the cult of authority that is at the base of totalitarianism. The Middle East has been penetrated both by these ideas and by reactions to them. Their initial relevance to the late Ottoman Empire was obscure, but given the empire's weakness, they achieved a specious relevancy by virtue of the power of the Western nations. Here was an instance of imposed cogency that quite literally superimposed a new Middle East map on indigenous cultures. An Arab living in Jerusalem before the British mandate in Palestine was no more involved with the rise of nations in Europe than was an Eskimo living near the North Pole, and yet within a few short years after World War I, Jerusalem would become a composite reflection of some of the saddest chapters in modern European history. It is little wonder that to this day Arabs living on the West Bank lament a fate that they did not create for themselves, and which they see as about as relevant to their historical identity as the modernization of Communist China. What many Arabs see in their contemporary history is an alien presence to be endured until they can come to some kind of peace not so much with this painful reality as with themselves. Israel is a symbol of Arab alienation.

Behind imposed meanings and self-alienation in the Middle East lies the power of political symbolization to transform what is genuinely alien into something approaching, but not quite achieving, cultural validity. What Susanne Langer has called "symbolic transformation," whereby individuals and groups actively appropriate environmental stimuli even when these stimuli may be somewhat uncharacteristic, operates to create a complex pattern of identities in the Middle East, part endogenous, part exogenous.[6] As Dan Segre has noted of Israeli identity, some decisions will have to be made about just who an Israeli is: such a person cannot be both Moses and Spartacus.[7] Similar observations about national confusions have been made of contemporary Arab thought and politics.[8] In other words, people can live with personalities at once authentic and inauthentic, but their behavior is likely to reflect anomalies and tensions that produce alienative results when they become manifest in political action.

The International Dimension of U.S. Foreign Policy in the Middle East

Any policy for the Middle East must be based on an understanding of the role of the Middle East in world affairs since the late seventeenth century. In George Lenczowski's *The Middle East in World Affairs* the real story begins with the 1699 Treaty of Carlowicz between the Habsburgs and Ottoman sultan after the battle for Vienna, as a result of which the Turks ceased to be a formidable enemy threatening Western Christendom; on the contrary, Europe would now threaten the integrity of the Ottoman Empire. Lenczowski then continues the story of Western expansion and Middle Eastern response with an examination of the role of outside powers, of the Middle Eastern states, and of the problems of war and peace, with special attention to American policy in the Middle East since the end of World War II. Strategy and oil were both involved in America's ascendancy.[9]

Underlying the idea of a Middle East prominent in world affairs is the view that this region was gradually brought into international relations from the eighteenth century onward by an expanding Western imperialism. William McNeill, in his *The Rise of the West*, draws a magisterial picture of "the human community" since the dawn of civilization in the "ecumene" made up of four great civilizations—the European Far West, the Middle East, India, and the Far East. In this ecumene McNeill traces the rise of the European Far West to dominate world history in three stages: (1) 1500–1700, the challenge to other civilizations; (2) 1700–1850, domination of the others; and (3) 1850–1950, the emergence of global cosmopolitanism.[10] Through this expansion, the Middle East, India, and the Far East were brought into an international system largely defined by the great European powers. After the end of World War II, with the decline of these same European powers, the United States came to dominate this system and to be challenged by the Soviet Union in this domination.

Definition of America's global status did not take the explicit course of European imperialism in the nineteenth and early twentieth centuries (except for the relentless pursuit of oil), but focused on containment of the Soviet Union, although Soviet perception of American ascendancy argues a more classical imperialistic expansion of U.S. interests.[11] Two contending strategies of containment, one limited to "strongpoints" and the other ambitiously extended to an entire "perimeter" of defense, vied with one another, as John Lewis Gaddis has observed in his *Strategies of Containment*.[12] What is important, however, is that the Middle East could fit into both these strategies, with every administration since Truman somehow involved with situating the region in the context of a broader international strategy. The Truman, Eisenhower, and Carter doctrines all had their origins in the Middle East and all were explicitly related to perceived threats to U.S. interests in the region from the Soviet Union.[13] President Nixon's response to the imperatives of Vietnam withdrawal, the Nixon Doctrine, quickly found some of its most notable applications in the Middle East.[14] And early in the Reagan administration the idea of a revived global strategy against Soviet foreign policy was applied to events in the Middle East.[15] It became clear in the 1973 Middle East war, however, that not all the troubles for American foreign policy in the region could be traced to the Soviet Union, as Washington learned in the painful lessons of economic interdependence during the Arab oil embargo.

Stanley Hoffmann's *Primacy or World Order* details the new realities of American foreign policy in an age of interdependence where certain issues are no longer simply matters of a grand global strategy against the Soviet Union. Now the rules of the "diplomatic-strategic" chessboard must be combined with new "games of interdependence."[16] For the Middle East this would suggest that its power, as a region, is growing in directions of greater independence from the rules of superpower rivalry. In other words, the "world affairs" in which the Middle East finds itself are increasingly defined by Middle Easterners, as well as outside powers.[17]

American policy toward the Middle East reflects a long history of international politics in the region, of which the U.S. involvement is but one chapter.[18] This is particularly true of the major crises confronting the United States in the Middle East since Israel's independence: 1948–49, Arab rejection of Israel's statehood; 1956, the last gasp of British rule in Egypt; 1967, Israel's rise as the premier power in the Middle East; 1973, Arab resurgence in the balance of power; 1979, the collapse of the Persian Gulf security system; and 1982, the triumph of sectarian fragmentation over cosmopolitan unity in the Arab world. In none save the last of these crises has the Palestinian question been central, but it remains on the agenda of policy difficulties for the United States. Since 1967 and events in Jordan during 1970, related to the 1967 war, the problem of the Palestinians has proved fundamental to the formation of a relevant American policy in the Middle East.

Israel's victories in the 1948–49 war of independence did not win Israel recognition from the defeated Arab states. Quite the contrary: from the late 1940s onward, American policy has been troubled by the single most important crisis in U.S. relations with the Middle East, the question of Israel's national status in Arab eyes. The general rejectionist stance of the Arabs, except for Egypt, which finally made peace with Israel in 1979, has led to the single most important dilemma of American relations with the Arab states as regional powers—namely, that despite official Arab rejection, there is the undeniable presence of Israel as a third power in the most sensitive areas of Arab-American interaction. Israel's role in U.S. policy will be analyzed more fully below, but it is important to note that this actually arose from (a) the international crisis accompanying the end of the British mandate in Palestine; (b) the partition of Palestine by the United Nations and Arab refusal to accept this; (c) Israel's independence; and (d) the first Arab-Israeli war. Arab rejection of Israel is no isolated regional problem, but illustrates instead the essentially international character of the Middle East in world affairs.

The 1956 Suez crisis further plunged the Middle East into the postwar international environment by bringing both the United States and the Soviet Union into the picture as key players in the Arab-Israeli struggle.[19] In his personal intervention to force British, French, and Israeli forces out of Suez and the Sinai, President Eisenhower applied the idea of U.S. national interest directly to a crisis at once regional and international. Egypt's President Nasser, in turn, had already enlisted the support of Eastern bloc nations in 1955, and turned to the Soviet Union for support against what he perceived to be Western imperialist intervention.

June 1967 marked the ascendancy of Israel as the Middle East's paramount military power, but the war creating this ascendancy became an international crisis of great proportions and marked a watershed in postwar Middle Eastern politics.[20] The results of this war occasioned serious international concern, including both superpowers, thereby leading to the most important United Nations action in the Middle East since the partition of Palestine, the passage of Security Council Resolution 242.

The October 1973 war—a kind of "revenge match" for the disasters that befell Arab powers in 1967—brought the superpowers to the brink of military confrontation.[21] Again, regional conflict and international affairs were closely intertwined in the Middle East, this time ending in Security Council resolutions 338 and 339 and the establishment of an international conference in Geneva. Subsequent events in the region, especially Sadat's remarkable trip to Jerusalem, suggested that the two premier regional powers, Egypt and Israel, might settle their long-standing animosity directly and by themselves, but in reality it took American mediation at Camp David to realize a peace treaty. Even direct negotiations between Egyptians and Israelis required international intervention.

The Soviet invasion of Afghanistan and the fall of the shah of Iran in 1979 illustrated once again the close relationship between regional and international issues in the Middle East. During the nineteenth and early twentieth centuries the expansion of Europe's Great Power rivalries into the Middle East was mainly a game of thrust and parry between England and Russia, the northern approaches to Persia and India being the main focal points.[22] Soviet political meddling and then armed intervention in Afghanistan, with consequent encirclement of Iran and Pakistan, is a prime example of the revival of the "Eastern question" in the Middle East.

Almost simultaneously with the 1978 unrest in Afghanistan and the 1979 Soviet military invasion came instability and revolution in Iran. Some have explained the Iranian Revolution primarily in terms of regional issues—the shah's domestic policies, the spread of Islamic fundamentalism, the age-old struggle between Shiite and Sunni Islam, and so forth—but, yet again, the Middle East's conflicts proved of great significance to world affairs, creating an "arc of crisis" that threatened global stability.[23]

Israel's invasion of Lebanon in 1982 precipitated the fifth major international crisis in the Middle East since Israel's independence in 1948. If the creation of Israel sparked the first Arab war against the new state and marked the beginning of Arab rejection as the centerpiece of American relations with the Arab world, then Israel's war in Lebanon completed the circle, with Israel, for the first time, attacking an Arab nation not out of self-defense but as a deliberate policy of military power projection to weaken and fragment the Arab world through decimation of the PLO. And again the bitter struggle among Middle Eastern powers expanded into an international crisis in which the United States, France, Great Britain, and Italy intervened, first to protect withdrawal of PLO forces from Beirut and then, unsuccessfully, to support Lebanese efforts at national reconciliation. Meanwhile the Soviet Union buttressed Syria's strength, thereby ensuring Syrian hegemony in Lebanese affairs once Israel began to withdraw its forces from Beirut and subsequently from southern Lebanon.

Following Israel's invasion of Lebanon, American intervention in the Middle East escalated in both military and political terms. Militarily, U.S. efforts were confined to Lebanon, but soon this military support for Lebanese unity proved inadequate to the task at hand at the levels of involvement permitted by American opinion (and even the approved levels no longer commanded any national consensus). At the same time, however, the 1982–84 period of direct U.S. military involvement in Lebanon brought with it strenuous American diplomatic efforts. There was the largely unsuccessful attempt to secure the withdrawal of both Israeli and Syrian forces from Lebanese territory—something only partially accomplished by unilateral Israeli decisions—and also American and Arab initiatives toward a more comprehensive Middle East peace, beginning with the Reagan plan of September 1982 and continuing in 1985 under the aegis of a Hussein-Arafat action plan with Egyptian, Saudi, and hesitant American support.

Regional Policy: The Israeli Factor

Without Israel's creation in 1948, the United States might have emerged from World War II as a great power in the Middle East, but it is impossible now to imagine American foreign policy in this region without Israel as the focus of a "special relationship" with the United States and without the Arab-Israeli conflict as the great constant in this policy.[24] Ironically, the end of the imperialistic outreach of the great European powers, caused by the trauma of World War II, brought with it the bequest to the Middle East of two other European legacies that had horrible consequences in the same conflict, anti-Semitism and totalitarianism.

British imperialism never sought to colonize the Middle East but, quite the contrary, sought both to rule and to maintain distance.[25] The destruction of European Jewry by Nazi Germany made Israel an urgent necessity in the mind of President Harry S. Truman, however, thereby transferring the plight of Europe's Jews, in the president's mind, physically and morally to the Middle East.[26] Truman's position made Israel a third partner at the center of Arab-American relations.[27]

For every Arab leader after 1948 the United States became both an external and an internal actor in the Middle East, on the one hand a superpower in the postwar period, and on the other, at the same time, an internal force through its support of Israel. In both cases the United States was seen in Arab eyes as an alien element despite long-standing friendship in cultural and economic fields. Oil alone could not ensure Arab-American amity.

Ironically for U.S. foreign policy in the Middle East, it is not only an American policy for the Arab world that is problematic—the question of whether it is possible for the United States to have an "Arab policy" in the way, for example, the French do—but also whether there can be an American "Arab policy" separate from the question of Israel. America's common bond with the Arab world is less a set of well-defined "national interests" specific to the region than the common interest shared by both Arabs and Americans, for very different reasons, in Israel. One cannot explain U.S. Middle East policy, in its essence, without reference to Israel, and one cannot explain Arab policy toward the United States, in any critical respect—at least until Khomeini's Iran—without reference to Israel.

Every bilateral relationship of any consequence between the United States and Arab countries, or in a multilateral sense with the "Arab world," has a third-party factor: Israel. In a bitter historical irony, without any imperial involvement in the classic "Eastern question," the United States has nonetheless become the imperial power par excellence in the Middle East because of the Israeli factor.

In a very profound sense, then, from the standpoint of most Arab leaders, there is no such thing as a "U.S. foreign policy in the Middle East," only variations on an Israeli policy. The same thing might be said about American policy toward the Arab world: Washington grades various Arab states, consciously and unconsciously, in terms of how "radical" or "moderate" they are on the Israeli question. It can even be argued that it is through Israel that the Middle East becomes comprehensible to American presidents; their "understanding" is based on specious familiarity with Westernized Israel rather than with the unfamiliar Arab and Islamic worlds.[28]

The role of Arabists in the shaping of American foreign policy toward the Middle East is largely symbolic rather than real. They provide a kind of direct access to the Arab world, within the older Orientalist tradition, ostensibly separate from the Israeli factor. Resident Orientalists in the U.S. government seem outwardly to be partisans of a definition of American national interests where Israel is one among several major priorities, rather than the ubiquitous factor it actually is; their impact on the long-term development of U.S. foreign policy in the Middle East is to give Washington's "Arab policy" a less imperialistic cast than some may think it should have. Yet even though the Arabists have a more symbolic than concrete function, they have often posed a real threat to Israeli interests, insofar as Jerusalem aims at all times for the maximization, not minimization, of the Israeli factor in American Middle East policy.[29]

If this focus on Israel in U.S. Middle East policy is palpably consistent in all matters of importance not only to Israel but to the Arab world, then Israel itself becomes an exceedingly powerful actor in the Middle East—the aim of Israeli foreign policy. It often appears in Washington and Arab capitals, as well as in Jerusalem, that the United States is forced, by a propulsion of its own making, to bend its own policy interests to that of its client. This is also the principal objective of Israel's policy, though the United States would prefer not to be seen this way in the Arab world. However, understanding Israeli goals, the Arabs most often treat American policy as if it were made not in Washington but in Jerusalem. Officially, the United States terms such Arab views fanciful (and they do reach mythical proportions), but there is frequently unease in Washington about Arab perceptions of Israeli dominance in American policy.

The problem for Israel with the Israeli factor in American policy, so carefully cultivated by Jerusalem, is that Israel's status in this policy is as determined by the Arab world as American Arab policy is by Israel's central role. Israel's status in Washington is directly related to Arab rejection of Israel, since the cardinal principle of American Israel policy is "Israel's right to exist." Where would Israel's "special relationship" with the United States be if it were not for the embattled image it cultivates?[30] Presumably, if every Arab state and the Palestinians were to suddenly recognize Israel as a sovereign state and negotiate peace treaties with it, the Arabs and Israelis would quickly achieve parity in American policy. A case in point here—indeed, the only case—is Egypt's treaty with Israel. Overnight, Egypt gained a position in U.S. foreign policy in the Middle East qualitatively different from that of any other Arab state; and equally sudden, Egypt attained a pariah status in the eyes of the other Arab states roughly comparable to that held by Israel. While some change has occurred in Egypt's status in the Middle East since Sadat's assassination, the bitterness of Arab rejection remains a strong factor in Egypt's relations with other Arab states even as it continues to enjoy the position of Arab power par excellence in Washington.

It would be too simplistic, of course, to define U.S. foreign policy in the Middle East as strictly an "Israeli policy," since it is well recognized in Washington that there must be some semblance of "balance," however symbolic, between American interests in Israel and in the Arab states. Trilateralism of this sort makes definition of U.S. interests in the Middle East exceedingly difficult. Two recent efforts at such definition, by Harold H. Saunders and Seth Tillman, both insist that the problem for American policy is not in *defining* these interests but in *ordering* them: Israeli and Arab priorities may be in direct conflict and yet have nearly equal status for the United States from the standpoint of vital American national interests.[31] The derivation of Arab-American relations from the question of Israel's existence, and the partial dependence of this existence on the state of Arab-American relations, leads, in fact, to a foreign policy that is extraordinarily complicated and amenable to no easy explanation. This is not so much a "pro-Israel" or "anti-Arab" policy as an American-Israeli-Arab policy where the interests of each corner of the triangle are confused with those of the others.[32] It is a policy more ambiguous than some might expect and one that tends to be unclear about its objectives, electing instead to wait on events. Under these conditions, U.S. foreign policy in the Middle East, being highly reactive, is also potentially inadequate for protection of vital interests. Passivity can be dangerous, especially when coupled with a policy that is innately ambiguous; realizing this, Washington has elected, when not facing a specific crisis in the Middle East, to find a way out of this into a more productive defense of its interests, that is, to search for a peace settlement between the Arabs and Israel.

The fundamental American regional policy in the Middle East, since Israel's independence, has thus been the effort to settle the Arab-Israeli conflict. Beginning with U.S. leadership on the subject of Palestine's partition, and extending to the aftermath of the 1982 Reagan plan, there is an unmistakable American preference for seeking a permanent peace in the Middle East as the only way to protect U.S. interests in both Israel and the Arab world without confusing these interests. Often these peace efforts come only in the wake of a major crisis, thus demonstrating the dangerously passive tendencies of American policy in the trilateral tangle of interests. At the same time, however, since the historic turning point of the June 1967 war, every American administration has placed Middle East peace high on its foreign policy agenda, and the process of seeking such peace has been more or less continuous.[33]

The primary objective of this policy is better management of American interests in the Middle East, but the very necessity of improved methods involves the United States to a greater degree in Middle Eastern affairs. And with American involvement of any kind has come increased Soviet interest in the Middle East, quite separate from Moscow's historic aims in the region. But the existence of an American peace policy in the Middle East allows the United States some latitude as a "mediator" (though not necessarily an unbiased one) standing between Israel and the Arabs, and identifying its interests as somehow separate from those of the warring parties.[34]

Peacemaking turns out to be the best policy available for protecting U.S. interests in the Middle East. Nevertheless, any move by the United States to free its interests from those of Israel, even in the name of peace, brings inevitable strains not only in relations with Israel itself but within American domestic politics, where Israel's interests are forcefully represented. If there is an Israeli factor in United States relations with the Arab world in the Middle East region, it derives from the strong presence of this same factor in the American domestic political process.

Domestic Policy: Foreign Policy as Public Policy

Foreign policy is "foreign" for those for whom it is intended rather than for those who formulate and apply it. In the United States, where Middle East policy is often engulfed in debate, this policy becomes "public policy."[35] A great outside power such as the United States may be more "foreign" in its foreign policy in the Middle East than other powers, not only because it is physically located outside the region but because its political culture produces foreign policy in a manner quite alien to the way other powers may develop theirs. In fact, among world powers only the United States places such a premium on the division of opinion in the making of foreign policy, as contrasted with strong central government control either by parliamentary majorities or by some form of consensus. It is true that both majority rule and consensus are highly valued in the making of American foreign policy, more often in the breach than in actual practice. Yet despite the arguments of some that the so-called "special relationship" between Israel and the United States invariably dictates a pro-Israeli policy stance, every American administration will be divided on Middle East policy at certain points, and, even when in agreement, may find itself on a collision course with Congress and even with public opinion. In U.S. Middle East policy, the president's pivotal role cannot be ignored in any confrontation.[36]

Division among the domestic sources of Middle East policy—government, parties, interest groups, and public opinion—will most likely create a policy of considerable complexity, even more complex than if it were determined merely by the complicated international and regional factors already noted. As a result, U.S. foreign policy in the Middle East is a richly variegated, three-dimensional mosaic, and not a pro-Israeli monolith at all. The problem, of course, is that any foreign policy, in communications with other nations, must sometimes be definite and unambiguous in its meanings, whereas American Middle East policy most often appears highly ambiguous in its basic intentions.

The great weakness of American foreign policy worldwide is its failure to communicate U.S. interests in unambiguous language, strategy, and action, and nowhere is this more the case than in the Middle East. Ambiguity and irrelevance are promoted by the domestication of foreign policy messages resulting from a failure to translate a parochial idiom into a more universal one. America's use of abstractions specific to its domestic experience and considered self-evident to an international audience—catch words such as "freedom"—sometimes gives others the sense that this ethnocentrism is not so much unintended as ill-intended. When Arabs in the Middle East look closely at American policy, they see intentional obfuscation, not unintentional ethnocentrism.

This Arab view is not entirely incorrect. There is a sense in which one might call U.S. foreign policy in the Middle East a kind of illusory disingenuousness, where a language of equivocation persists along with a strategy based on incompatible interests and a mode of action strongly influenced by domestic factors that produce inconsistent policies. American Middle East policy, in terms of language, strategy, and action, is not an unintended ethnocentrism but an intended one, a deliberate policy of ethnocentric behavior in the context of a regional policy highly influenced by international factors, thus enabling the U.S. policy to be at once international, regional, and domestic. This is hardly a formula for unrivaled success, since the policy's three dimensions are never compatible. But, such a policy, difficult as it is, has been practiced by the United States in the Middle East since 1948, and more by necessity than by choice. Every president who becomes entangled in Middle East policy must confront its basically asymmetrical three-dimensional nature.

The *language* of U.S. foreign policy in the Middle East is that of equivocation. Support is announced for both Israeli and Arab objectives in the region, even though these may be fundamentally incompatible: the two sides are in a state of war with each other (except in the case of Israel and Egypt). One is reminded here of the late Tennessee Senator C. Estes Kefauver, appearing before a Berkeley audience during the 1956 presidential election campaign as Adlai Stevenson's vice-presidential running mate and announcing that some of his favorite constituents were Arabs and Israelis! At the highest levels of U.S. policy making, this "evenhandedness" is often practiced, even though the Arabs are convinced American policy is basically pro-Israeli, and the Israelis are always suspicious that balanced rhetoric in Washington hints at something more sinister in the way of concrete policy to press Arab claims on Israel. Such equivocation is often rationalized in Washington as the best of all possible worlds, since it allows the United States to be the only great power with open channels to the two warring sides. Yet more often than not this same equivocation provides U.S. interests with little protection from sniping on all sides: American policy is frequently sabotaged by both Israel and hostile Arab states simultaneously, as presidents and secretaries of state have found, much to their sorrow, when embarking on yet another peace initiative in the Middle East.

This language of equivocation also expresses an American *strat-*

egy of pursuing incompatible interests in the Middle East. As already noted, two recent studies of U.S. interests in the Middle East both conclude that the problem is not one of defining interests in this region, but of ordering them. For example, are oil and Israel equal priorities? If they are not equal in some abstract and general sense, what happens when events, as in 1973–74, make them equal? Yet this "equality" involves two strongly incompatible strategies that can only be made provisionally compatible by the most adroit diplomacy, as was the case in Kissinger's negotiating strategy after October 1973. But only a major crisis forced this kind of diplomatic undertaking, and the costs to the United States were significant, much more so than the costs to the warring parties. Furthermore, the Israeli and Arab sides of this diplomatic strategy both shared only the United States as a common bond, at least until the Camp David peace of 1978–79, thereby placing American policy in an extremely vulnerable position as far as its interests were concerned.

Indeed, Camp David, though successful in achieving an Israeli-Egyptian peace, illustrates the dangers to U.S. interests in the Middle East from pursuing a strategy of incompatible interests. So important to the United States was the prospect of achieving an agreement between Israel and Egypt that wider American interests in the Arab world were ignored, particularly on the Palestinian question. As a result, the president most sympathetic to Palestinian self-determination, and thus perhaps the president in the most advantageous position to achieve a comprehensive Middle East settlement, Jimmy Carter, sacrificed his advantages for the sake of a more limited achievement of terminating at least part of the American strategy of incompatible interest.[37]

Of course, for the United States, the outcome of a bilateral peace between Israel and Egypt was a further accentuation of its incompatible interests in the Middle East, rather than any solution to them. Whereas peace was achieved between Cairo and Jerusalem, Arab rejection of Camp David only made more dramatic the gulf between Israeli and Arab interests in American policy. Carter had succumbed to the strong temptation on the part of all American presidents to appease powerful domestic constituencies in foreign as well as domestic policy, something he had already signaled in his quick retreat from the joint U.S.-Soviet communiqué on the Middle East in October 1977.[38]

Action in U.S. Middle East foreign policy is strongly influenced by domestic factors, thereby reinforcing the language of equivocation and the strategy of incompatible interests already present in this policy. In short, the interactions between language, strategy, and action in politics are made all the stronger by powerful domestic interests. These domestic dimensions of American Middle East policy are found in bureaucratic politics within the executive branch, in relations between agencies—especially Congress—and interest groups, in the electoral process and the two major political parties, and in both attentive and more general public opinion. In no area of U.S. foreign policy are all these domestic factors, interacting with one another, as powerful as in Middle East policy.

In a recent book on American policy in the Middle East Steven L. Spiegel terms the divisions within the executive branch "the other Arab-Israeli conflict."[39] Surely the importance of Middle East policy generally dictates exceedingly high-level decision making in Washington, bringing into play the major agencies in the National Security Council—State, Defense, CIA, and the White House. Students of "bureaucratic politics" see these agencies as inevitably seeking aggrandizement of their own interests. Nonetheless, the important central role of the presidency in the Middle East policy is clear.[40]

Congress, too, is an active player. Not only is Capitol Hill a major focus for intense lobbying by Israel's supporters and groups favorable to the Arab side, but special powers held by Congress or arrogated by Congress to itself, such as the legislative veto, give this institution considerable influence on foreign policy issues of great public sensitivity, such as Israel.[41] Perhaps more in reference to Congress than to the executive branch it is accurate to say that "foreign policy is public policy," for domestic interests truly interact there with international and regional priorities, thereby giving rise to a foreign policy that is not always consistent or easy for outsiders to understand.[42]

Congressional actions on sensitive foreign issues inevitably lead to friction with the executive branch. Of special importance in recent years have been frictions between the executive and legislative branches over military assistance programs for Arab powers still technically in a state of belligerency with Israel, most notably Jordan and Saudi Arabia. Congress reacted negatively to the prospect of an American-supplied Arab capability, and in the case of Jordan this has led to initiatives by Amman to the Soviet Union for a badly needed air defense system. Saudi Arabia has not yet turned to the Soviet Union, but after the serious difficulties it confronted in obtaining F-15 fighter aircraft and AWACS surveillance assistance (because of extraordinary congressional debates, finally decided in Rayadh's favor only by a narrow margin of votes), the Saudis have turned to the French and British for a new surface-to-air missile defense system and new fighter bombers, with the idea of diversifying their suppliers.[43]

Allegedly, Congress is more sensitive to short-term domestic considerations in foreign affairs, while the president is said to take a longer-term internationalist perspective on Middle East problems. This generalization, however, can be rather misleading, especially as far as the executive branch is concerned. For those who have worked on Middle East policy within the National Security system, nothing is more evident than the fact that presidents seldom enter office with strong internationalist tendencies.[44] In the postwar period only Eisenhower and Nixon have been exceptions to this rule, and at one point they were president and vice-president together. Of the two, only Eisenhower consistently preferred to look at the Middle East from international and regional perspectives rather than through the lens of domestic considerations, with his policy reaching its strongest expression in his adamant opposition to the British-French-Israeli attack on Nasser's Egypt in Suez during 1956. Nixon affected an "even-handed" approach on taking office in 1969 but constantly wavered in his resolution until the 1972 election, when, by his own admission, he became the most pro-Israeli of postwar presidents, a matter of some historical dispute but an interesting self-perception from someone whose secretary of state, four years earlier, was determined to move Israel out of the territories it had occupied in the June 1967 war.[45]

Power and Ideology in U.S. Middle East Policy

The asymmetrical interaction of international, regional, and domestic dimensions in American Middle East policy has significant repercussions for any discussion of "power and ideology" in the Middle East. U.S. foreign policy in the Middle East is driven by no less than three ideologies, corresponding to the policy's three dimensions: international, regional, and domestic. In a sense, all three ideologies are only partially relevant to the Middle East and, therefore, sometimes have little relevance for U.S. national interests in the region.

Containment of the Soviet Union, the American international policy for the Middle East, has both ideological and geopolitical bases, the ideological being the least relevant for the Middle East. The truly dynamic ideologies in the Middle East—religious fundamentalism of various kinds—are more anticommunist than is American policy, and yet they threaten American interests more than Soviet ones. In fact, the Soviet Union finds it relatively easy to accept the harsh criticism it receives from the ayatollahs, knowing full well that their chief target is the United States. And, of course, attempting to rally allies against fundamentalist regimes in the name of anticommunism would be silly in the extreme. In other words, an American ideologically oriented anticommunist policy may not achieve the political goal of preventing the expansion of the Soviet Union.

At the regional level American ideology tends to embrace gradual change under capitalist economies, or the regime closest to this evolutionist model—the doctrines of stability and moderation. U.S. interest in this type of change under the influence of private markets is both ideological and practical: for example, Americans make more money in countries with oil-rich regimes dedicated to capitalism than they do elsewhere in the Middle East. At least on a regional level ideology and tangible interests seem to match—or do they? The problem for any regional policy that depends on a gradual change under the influence of private market economics is that change in the Middle East is usually spasmodic rather than steady, and not necessarily in the progressive, secularist direction so necessary to modern capitalism.[46] In ideological terms, therefore, what is "private" in the Middle East may bear little resemblance to what that term stands for in the West, and the idea of capitalism may be more metaphorical there than real. True enough, Middle East businessmen participate extensively in financial and futures markets outside the Middle East. But that is precisely the point: the centers of Middle East capitalism lie largely outside the region, not within it. Hence, capitalism itself is another foreign import, an exogenous variable, not an endogenous one. Time and again, reliance on Western capitalism as an evolutionary ideology has been shown to be irrelevant—or explosive—in the Middle East, yet this remains central to the American ideology of "stability" and "moderation" in the region. The fact is that, ideologically speaking, there is no typical Middle East pattern of development, just as there is no generally valid outside pattern for the region.

From the perspective of American domestic politics, wherein Israel has the favored status, the key value for the Middle East region is seen to be "freedom." Often it is said that Israel is "the only democracy in the Middle East," and that the continuing special relationship between Israel and the United States rests on compatible political systems. Arab rejection could be interpreted, under these circumstances, as reflecting fear that the Israeli system might appear attractive to Arab populations under authoritarian rule. Because of shared democratic values, the United States and Israel may be seen as allies on something of the same plane as the NATO partnership and, indeed, some have even suggested that Israel join NATO. Of course this has also led some to the idea that Israel might be considered a "strategic" as well as an "ideological" partner for American foreign policy in the Middle East.[47]

Aside from questions of its relevance, the problem with such a strongly domestic ideology for U.S. policy in the Middle East is obvious: the Arabs cannot believe that Washington is serious about an Arab policy when it holds important such a deliberately ethnocentric standard of values for its "allies" in the Middle East. How, for example, does the United States justify a close, if not special, relationship with Saudi Arabia? If only one country in the region is eligible for the kind of ideological support the United States reserves for Western Europe and Japan, then one might legitimately doubt the depth of American commitment to friendly Arab countries. Under these circumstances, an Arab power is not so much penalized for being Arab—American policy is not overtly racist, as was British policy before World War II—but for being non-Israeli. Some Arabs have wondered, given America's fervent ideological support for Israel, whether future relations between the United States and the Arab world will not more and more be governed by American misperceptions of Arab policies based on invidious comparison with Israel, even among Americans sensitive, if not sympathetic, to Arab claims and interests.[48]

The manifestations of American power in the Middle East correspond to the international, regional, and domestic dimensions of American Middle East policy, and are also distinct from one another. From an international viewpoint, American power in the Middle East is exercised in ways to achieve strategic political-military balance with the Soviet Union, and the containment of Soviet power. The results have been the introduction of Turkey into the NATO alliance, the building of CENTO, the development of security-assistance policies in the region, and most recently the organization of a new U.S. military presence in Southwest Asia under the Carter Doctrine and the defense measures that followed in the wake of the Soviet invasion of Afghanistan and the fall of the shah of Iran. All of these measures involve a deliberate political-military intervention by the United States, a projection of American power into the Middle East for purposes of containing Soviet advances in a region judged strategically vital for American global interests.

The exercise of American power within the Middle East itself, however, has been focused more on economic than on military relations with indigenous powers. In fact, American policy has been quite careful not to push too strongly the containment of the Soviet Union as the main basis for friendship with nations in the region. It has been necessary to make this distinction between the Middle East as an international problem and as a regional problem not only because of the importance of American economic relations with Arab countries, but also because the United States and these countries do not necessarily share the same strategic outlook when it comes to threats to security. Whereas the United States may judge the chief security threat to its interests to be the Soviet Union, the Arab powers have generally seen Israel as the main security issue for themselves.

When one approaches the Middle East from the standpoint of American domestic ideologies, in which Israel enjoys a special relationship with the United States, then one sees a third dimension of American power, a moral one. Despite the attraction this holds for many Americans, within the Middle East itself this dimension of American power, as it relates to Israel, is a source of friction between the United States and the Arab states, and therefore has limited application. The irrelevance attributed to this moral dimension by the Arab states strengthens its value in American politics in that it translates into the Arab rejection of Israel's status as an independent state. The Arabs must confront the fact of this moral dimension of American power, therefore, with a view toward either accommodating or rejecting American insistence that all Arab states and the Palestinians recognize Israel's existence.

The course of a peace policy may at times be associated with appeasement or well-meaning naiveté, but Middle East peace and the diplomatic means of achieving it are of supreme national interest to the United States. This fact once again highlights the importance of the Middle East in world affairs, not only in political-military terms, as a rich strategic prize in the competition among great powers, but as laboratory for diplomatic innovations that may have application beyond this region itself. In no area of American postwar foreign policy has there been such a premium placed on the art of diplomacy, and despite numerous frustrations, no region has been more important for the development of a creative American diplomatic style to accompany a strong military capability.

NOTES

■

Introduction: Ideology and Power in the Middle East

1 J. L. Talmon, *The Rise of Totalitarian Democracy* (Boston: Beacon Press, 1952), pt. 2, "The Jacobin Improvisation."
2 Karl Mannheim, *Ideology and Utopia: An Introduction to the Sociology of Knowledge*, trans. Louis Wirth and Edward Shils (New York: Harcourt, Brace–Harvest Books, 1936), chap. 2.
3 Ibid., pp. 73–74.
4 Pierre-Joseph Proudhon, *Carnets*, 2 vols. (Paris: Librairie Marcel Rivière, 1960), vol. 1, p. 176.
5 Karl Loewenstein, *Political Power and the Governmental Process* (Chicago: University of Chicago Press, Phoenix Books, 1965), p. 9.
6 M. Graeme Bannerman, "Lebanon," in David E. Long and Bernard Reich, eds., *The Government and Politics of the Middle East and North Africa*, 2d ed. (Boulder: Westview Press, 1986), p. 196; also Elie Adib Salem, *Modernization without Revolution: Lebanon's Experience* (Bloomington: Indiana University Press, 1973).
7 Kenneth Burke, *A Grammar of Motives* (1945), in *A Grammar of Motives and A Rhetoric of Motives* (Cleveland and New York: Meridian Books, 1962), p. 123.
8 See Robert J. Pranger, *Action, Symbolism, and Order: The Existential Dimensions of Modern Citizenship* (Nashville: Vanderbilt University Press, 1968), pp. 183–95.
9 Ernst Cassirer, *The Myth of the State* (New Haven, Conn.: Yale University Press, 1946), pt. 1.
10 William Butler Yeats, "The Circus Animals' Desertion," in *The Collected Poems of W. B. Yeats* (New York: Macmillan, 1959), p. 336.

11 Albert Camus, *The Rebel*, trans. Anthony Bower (New York: Vintage Books, 1956), pts. 3–4.
12 Talmon, *The Rise of Totalitarian Democracy*, pp. 1–13.
13 William McNeill notes the intensity and scope of "European warlikeness, when compared with the attitudes of other major civilizations of the earth," in his *The Rise of the West: The History of the Human Community* (Chicago: University of Chicago Press, 1963), p. 570.
14 C. J. Jung, "The Phenomenology of the Spirit in Fairy Tales," in *Psyche and Symbol*, ed. Violet S. de Lazlo (Garden City, N.Y.: Doubleday Anchor Books, 1958), pp. 61–112. The application of the "magic world of the hunter" to Nazism.
15 Thomas Mann, *Doctor Faustus* (1948).
16 Robert J. Pranger, *The Eclipse of Citizenship: Power and Participation in Contemporary Politics* (New York: Holt, Rinehart and Winston, 1968), chaps. 2–3.
17 Walter Lippmann, *Public Opinion* (1922); reprint, New York: Macmillan, 1961), pp. 16–17.
18 Susanne K. Langer, *Philosophy in a New Key* (New York: Mentor Books, 1958), p. 46.
19 Maurice Merleau-Ponty, *Phénoménologie de la perception* (Paris: Gallimard, 1945), pp. 64–77, "Le champ phénoménal."
20 See Erich Fromm on *Ersatzgemeinschaft* in *Escape from Freedom* (New York: W. W. Norton, 1941).
21 Harold Isaacs, *Scratches on Our Minds: American Images of China and India* (Westport, Conn.: Greenwood Press, 1973), p. 38.
22 See Pranger, *Action, Symbolism, and Order*, pp. 200–201.
23 See Pranger, *The Eclipse of Citizenship*, pp. 10–17.
24 See Michael Oakeshott, "Rationalism in Politics," in *Rationalism in Politics and Other Essays* (New York: Basic Books, 1962), pp. 1–36.
25 Edward W. Said, *Orientalism* (New York: Vintage Books, 1979), pp. 31–49.
26 Ibid., pp. 54–55.

Iran: The Nature of the Pahlavi Monarchy

1 Donald N. Wilber, *Reza Shah Pahlavi: The Resurrection and Reconstruction of Iran, 1878–1944* (Hicksville, N.Y.: Exposition Press, 1974), chap. 2.
2 *Ibid.* See also Abrahamian Ervand, *Iran between Two Revolutions* (Princeton: Princeton University Press, 1982), chap. 3; General Hassan Arfa, *Under Five Shahs* (London: John Murray, 1964); Amin Banani, *The Modernization of Iran, 1921–1941* (Stanford, Calif.: Stanford University Press, 1961); L. P. Elwell-Sutton, "Reza Shah the Great: Founder of the Pahlavi Dynasty," in George Lenczowski, ed., *Iran under the Pahlavis* (Stanford, Calif.: Hoover Institution Press, 1978), chap. 1; William S. Haas, *Iran* (New York: Columbia University Press, 1946);

George Lenczowski, *Russia and the West in Iran, 1918–1948* (Ithaca, N.Y.: Cornell University Press, 1949); A. C. Millspaugh, *The American Task in Persia* (New York: Century, 1925); Mohammed Reza Shah Pahlavi, *Mission for My Country* (London: McGraw-Hill, 1961).

3 See Abrahamian, *Iran between Two Revolutions*, chaps. 4, 5; Leonard Binder, *Iran: Political Development in a Changing Society* (Berkeley and Los Angeles: University of California Press, 1962); E. A. Bayne, *Persian Kingship in Transition* (New York: American University Field Staff, 1968); Richard W. Cottam, *Nationalism in Iran* (Pittsburgh: University of Pittsburgh Press, 1978), chap. 15; L. P. Elwell-Sutton, "Political Parties in Iran: 1941–1948," *Middle East Journal* 3, no. 1 (January 1949); Nikki R. Keddie, "The Iranian Power Structure and Social Change, 1800–1969," *International Journal of Middle East Studies* 2, no. 1 (January 1971); George Lenczowski, "The Communist Movement in Iran," *Middle East Journal* 1, no. 1 (January 1947); Rouhollah K. Ramazani, *Iran's Foreign Policy, 1941–1973* (Charlottesville: University Press of Virginia, 1975), pts. 1 and 2; Sepehr Zabih, *The Communist Movement in Iran* (Berkeley and Los Angeles: University of California Press, 1966); Sepehr Zabih, *The Mossadegh Era: Roots of Iranian Revolution* (Chicago: Lakeview Press, 1982).

4 See annual reports, Agricultural Cooperative Bank of Iran, Tehran, 1349 (1970/71) to 1356 (1977/78); also, Karim Goodarzy, *Iran Land Reform: A Decade of Progress* (Tehran: Land Reform Training Institute, 1970); A. K. S. Lambton, *Landlord and Peasant in Persia*, 2d ed. (London: Oxford University Press, 1969); A. K. S. Lambton, *The Persian Land Reform, 1962–1966* (London: Oxford University Press, 1969); Mohammad Reza Shah Pahlavi, *The White Revolution* (Tehran: Imperial Pahlavi Library, 1967); A. A. Valian, "Land Reform Program in Iran," paper read at the meeting of the International Academy of Comparative Law, Pescara, Italy, September 1970.

5 Principles 4 and 13. For general policy orientation see Kokab Moarefi, *The Iranian Symbol and Structure of Social Development and Welfare Services* (Tehran: Ministry of Social Welfare, July 1975); Shahpour Rassekh, "Planning for Social Change," in Ehsan Yarshater, ed., *Iran Faces the Seventies* (New York: Praeger, 1971), pp. 143–65.

6 See *Karnameh-ye-Sazman-e Zanan-e Iran* (The Balance Sheet of the Women's Organization of Iran) (Tehran: 2536 Esfand 1977).

7 Jahangir Amuzegar, *Iran: An Economic Profile* (Washington, D.C.: Middle East Institute, 1977), p. x.

8 Ibid., p. ix.

9 Reza Shah Pahlavi, *Safarnameh-ye Mazandaran* (The Mazandaran Memoirs) (Tehran, 1976), also quoted in part in *Iran Nameh* 2, no. 2 (Winter 1984), pp. 347–66.

10 Wilbur, *Reza Shah Pahlavi*.

11 Muhammad Reza Shah Pahlavi, *Besu-ye Tamaddon-e Bozorg* (Toward the Great Civilization) (Tehran).

12 Shanrokh Meskoob, *Sug-e Siavash* (Tehran, 1972).

13 Pio Fillipano-Ranconi, "Tradition of Sacred Kingship," in Lenczowski, ed., *Iran under the Pahlavis*, p. 60.
14 Roger Savory, *Iran under the Safavids* (Cambridge: Cambridge University Press, 1980), chap. 2.
15 Edward G. Browne, A *Literary History of Persia* (Cambridge: Cambridge University Press, 1929), vol. 1, p. 135.
16 For a clear statement of Shiite creed, see Allamah Sayyid Muhammad Husayn Tabataba'i, *Shiite Islam*, trans. and ed. Seyyed Hossein Nasr (Albany: State University of New York Press, 1975).
17 Abrahamian, *Iran between Two Revolutions*, pp. 118–35; Wilbur, *Reza Shah Pahlavi*, pp. 78–80.
18 Jalal Matini, "Rustam: Qahraman-e Hamaseh-ye Melli-ye Iran," *Journal of the College of Literature and Humanities*. Collection of Speeches, first and second Ferdowsi weeks. Ferdowsi University (Mashhad, n.d.), pp. 69–103.
19 See Ahmad Kasravi, *Tarikh-e Mashruteh-ye Iran* (A History of Iranian Constitution) (Tehran: Amir Kabir, 1961).
20 Supplement to the Basic Law, 1907.
21 The most succinct statement of this point is found in Ayatollah Khomeini's concept of "Islamic Government." See *Islam and Revolution: Writings and Declarations of Imam Khomeini*, trans. and annotated by Hamid Algar (Berkeley: Mizan Press, 1981), pp. 27–150.
22 Article 35, Supplementary to Basic Law.
23 Kasravi, *Tarikh-e Mashruteh-ye Iran*.
24 Malek al-Shoara Bahar, *Tarikhe-e Mokhtasar-e Ahzab-e Siyasi-e Iran* (A Short History of the Iranian Political Parties) (Tehran: Rangin Press, 1944).
25 Abrahamian, *Iran between Two Revolutions*, p. 281; Zabih, *The Communist Movement in Iran*.
26 See Bahar, *Tarikhe-e Mokhtasar-e Ahzab-e Siyasi-e Iran*.
27 For the accomplishments of Muhammad Reza Shah period see Amuzegar, *Iran: An Economic Profile;* Julian Bharier, *Economic Development in Iran, 1900–1970* (London and New York: Oxford University Press, 1971); Lenczowski, ed., *Iran under the Pahlavis*.
28 See Gholam R. Afkhami, *The Iranian Revolution: Thanatos on a National Scale* (Washington, D.C.: Middle East Institute, 1985).
29 Banani, *The Modernization of Iran*, chap. 3.
30 Abrahamian, *Iran between Two Revolutions*, pt. 2; Cottam, *Nationalism in Iran*.
31 See concepts of negative equilibrium and positive nationalism in Ramazani, *Iran's Foreign Policy*, pts. 2, 3, and 4.
32 For background information, see N. S. Fatemi, *Oil Diplomacy* (New York: Whittier Books, 1954); Fereidun Fesharaki, *Development of Iranian Oil Industry* (New York: Praeger, 1976); George Lenczowski, *Middle East Oil in a Revolutionary Age* (Washington, D.C.: American Enterprise Institute, 1975); and *Oil and State in the Middle East*

(Ithaca, N.Y.: Cornell University Press, 1960); Fuad Rouhani, A *History of OPEC* (New York: Praeger, 1971); Anthony Sampson, *The Seven Sisters* (New York: Viking Press, 1975); Robert B. Stobaugh, "The Evolution of Iranian Oil Policy, 1925–1975," in Lenczowski, ed., *Iran under the Pahlavis*, pp. 201–53.

33 For a discussion of problems of party politics in Iran, see Afkhami, *The Iranian Revolution*, chap. 2.

34 S. H. Udy, Jr., "The Comparative Analysis of Organizations," in James G. March, ed., *Handbook of Organizations* (Chicago: Rand McNally, 1965), pp. 688–91.

35 Bank-e Markazi Iran, *Annual Reports*, 1974/75, 1975/76, 1976/77.

36 Afkhami, *The Iranian Revolution*, chap. 3.

Saudi Arabia: Traditionalism versus Modernism— A Royal Dilemma?

1 There are some eighteen identifiable such "sibling clusters," some with multiple male members, others with only one.

2 "Sitting" with the king was the custom used by Faisal and his predecessors of having the king's counselors present in his office while he worked on state matters. He could thus immediately solicit their views when desired, and royal counselors, alert to the monarch's moods, could initiate ideas for royal consideration. Faisal never demanded that these senior counselors spend what sometimes turned out to be several hours each day with him, but it was generally believed he rather expected them to attend. Those who did not were sometimes indirectly chastised with intimations of alleged lack of interest. Fahd, from all accounts, has not made as much use of the practice as did his predecessors.

3 In Saudi Arabia the term *progressive* must be understood in a relative rather than absolute sense.

4 Known as *tawhid* in Saudi Arabia. Its adherents call themselves *muwahhidun*. Critics of this Hanbali school of Sunni Islam have scoffingly dubbed its adherents *wahhabis*, a term that has pejorative connotations.

5 The late King Faisal would always give pride of place to his uncle, Prince 'Abd 'Allah ibn 'Abd al-Rahman, when the prince entered the room, even though the latter had no official position. Faisal would insist that Prince 'Abd 'Allah take his chair and would usually seat himself on a plain wooden chair. Nevertheless, when it seemed likely that 'Abd 'Allah might suddenly appear, Faisal would ask his official visitors in advance not to discuss sensitive political matters in his uncle's presence and shift the conversation to banalities. Many a time this happened with the American ambassador.

6 For an English translation of Qusaybi's poem, see the *Wall Street Journal*, April 25, 1984, p. 34. Also the *Financial Times* (London), April 25, 1984, p. 1. Although Fahd is not mentioned by name in the poem, the

implication of who was intended is clear. Once the poem was published, Fahd had little choice but to meet the minister's public challenge by dismissing him. Qusaybi's departure is a loss, but some hoped that the king might take the point of Qusaybi's poetic criticism. He did not.

7 The *ikhwan*, literally brotherhood, were the unitarian tribal zealots, who had assisted 'Abd al-'Aziz in founding the third Saudi state and were settled by him in *hijar*, or paramilitary religious settlements; who later intolerantly excoriated their non-unitarian Muslim neighbors as unbelievers and waged war against them; and who finally challenged 'Abd al-'Aziz's rule as not in conformity with their concept of true Islam and suffered defeat at his hands.

8 It is curious to recall that in 1948 a U.S. Treasury expert, sent to Saudi Arabia to study monetary reform, seriously considered recommending that the kingdom adopt American dollar notes as currency. He was dissuaded from doing so on the grounds of Saudi national sovereignty sensitivities and the public's alleged insistence on specie.

9 The sixty-year-old Saud was deposed because of profligacy and incompetence and died in exile in 1969. His "image" is being rehabilitated in present-day Saudi Arabia.

10 The collateral Jiluwi branch of the royal family had governed the Eastern Province since shortly after the reestablishment of the Saudi state in 1902. Upon the death of his powerful elder brother, Amir Saud, in 1968, Amir 'Abd al-Mushin ibn 'Abd Allah al-Jiluwi was designated by the late King Faisal to be governor of the Eastern Province and he held that position until 1985. In the previous decade national cabinet officials, especially from the technical ministries and from special royal commissions, had quietly circumvented the executive functions of Amir 'Abd al-Mushin, leaving him with largely ceremonial functions. The governorship of the oil-rich Eastern Province is regarded as a plum. For years senior princes of Al Saud without high positions have coveted it. To avoid having to designate one from among them, and thereby incurring the ire of other princely gubernatorial aspirants, Saudi monarchs had generally been content to keep the position in the Jiluwi branch of the family, arguing historic precedent. The new appointment of King Fahd's son to the position was cleverly executed, but has caused some grumbling among various of the monarch's half brothers. Muhammad ibn Fahd was initially appointed acting governor while 'Abd al-Mushin al-Jiluwi was undergoing medical treatment, and he was then suddenly and unexpectedly formalized as full governor by royal decree. It was a fait accompli before other princely aspirants could argue their claims. While it is too early to judge, it seems that Muhammad ibn Fahd is introducing more businesslike procedures into the Eastern Province administration.

11 The daily public *majlis* system in Saudi Arabia, which is utilized by the king and all provincial governors, is an effective means of keeping the senior members of the royal family in direct touch with public grievances. Any citizen may appear and submit to the king or governor either a written or verbal petition or appeal on any subject. While not grass-roots de-

mocracy, as some Saudis claim, in the hands of responsible and sensitive leaders, it disposes of minor litigation with commendable fairness and dispatch.

12 When the third Saudi state was founded by 'Abd al-'Aziz in 1902, he assumed secular leadership and vested religious leadership in his father, 'Abd al-Rahman, who bore the title of *imam*. In 1920 'Abd al-'Aziz, who had generally been referred to as *hakim* or *shaykh al-shuyukh* by his tribal followers, adopted the secular title of sultan of Najd and its dependencies, adding Hijaz to this territorial designation after his conquest in 1924–25 of that area. In 1927 he elevated his secular title to king of these areas, and in 1932 he redesignated the state as the kingdom of Saudi Arabia.

Following 'Abd al-Rahman's death in 1928, 'Abd al-'Aziz could formally add the religious title of *imam* to his appellations, but rarely used this. The issue of the relative priority of secular and religious titles again briefly assumed prominence during the protracted Saudi-Yemeni negotiations, leading to the Treaty of Tayif in 1934. Imam Yahya of Yemen, even though bested in combat, sought to upstage his victorious fellow monarch, and perhaps embarrass him, by insisting upon protocol precedence for the religious title of *imam* over that of king. 'Abd al-'Aziz, not to be outdone, utilized the personal designation of *imam* along with the royal secular title and insisted that Yahya, on his part, also agree to use both titles. A titular balance between religious and secular designations could be struck without giving preeminence to one or the other.

Jordan: Balancing Pluralism and Authoritarianism

1 These figures are estimates based on data in microstudies.
2 This concept and other perspective analysis appear in Paul A. Jureidini and R. D. McLaurin, *Jordan: The Impact of Social Change on the Role of the Tribes* (New York: Praeger, 1984).
3 Peter Gubser, *Jordan: Crossroads of Middle Eastern Events* (Boulder, Colo.: Westview Press, 1983), pp. 112–13.
4 Hassan Bin Talal, crown prince of Jordan, *Search for Peace* (New York: St. Martin's Press, 1984).
5 These points, as well as some others in this chapter, are derived from Gubser, *Jordan: Crossroads of Middle Eastern Events*, pp. 89–91.
6 Ibid., p. 104.
7 Hassan, *Search for Peace*, pp. 85–95.

Labor Politics, Economic Change, and the Modernization of Autocracy in Contemporary Bahrain

1 George Lenczowski, "Political Institutions," in Ruth N. Anshen, ed., *Mid-East: World-Center* (New York: Harper, 1956), p. 135.

2 Ibid., pp. 130–34.
3 See George Lenczowski, ed., *United States Interests in the Middle East* (Washington, D.C.: American Enterprise Institute, 1968), p. 70.
4 See George Lenczowski, *Oil and State in the Middle East* (Ithaca, N.Y.: Cornell University Press, 1960).
5 See, for example, Muhammad Sadik and William Snavely, *Bahrain, Qatar, and the United Arab Emirates* (Lexington, Mass.: D. C. Heath, 1972); Ali Khalifa Al-Kuwari, *Oil Revenues in the Gulf Emirates* (Boulder, Colo.: Westview Press, 1978), chap. 4; A. S. Gerakis and O. Roncesvalles, "Bahrain's Offshore Banking Center," *Economic Development and Cultural Change* (January 31, 1983); Emile Nakhleh, *Bahrain* (Lexington, Mass.: D. C. Heath, 1976); Emile Nakhleh, "Labor Markets and Citizenship in Bahrayn and Qatar," *Middle East Journal* 31 (Spring 1977); Emile Nakhleh, "Political Participation and the Constitutional Experiments in the Arab Gulf: Bahrain and Qatar," in Tim Niblock, ed., *Social and Economic Development in the Arab Gulf* (New York: St. Martin's Press, 1980); John Townsend, "Problems Confronting the Establishment of a Heavy Industrial Base in the Arab Gulf," in Niblock, *Social and Economic Development;* Henry T. Azzam, "The Labour Market Performance in Some Arab Gulf States," in May Ziwar-Daftari, ed., *Issues in Development: The Arab Gulf States* (London: MD Research and Services, 1980); H. Bowen-Jones, "Agriculture in Bahrain, Kuwait, Qatar, and UAE," in Ziwar-Daftari, *Issues in Development;* and Michael E. Bonine, "The Urbanization of the Persian Gulf Nations," in Alvin J. Cottrell, ed., *The Persian Gulf States* (Baltimore: Johns Hopkins University Press, 1980).
6 Sadik and Snavely, *Bahrain, Qatar, and the United Arab Emirates,* p. 145.
7 See Lenczowski, "Political Institutions," p. 120.
8 Nakhleh, *Bahrain,* pp. 78–80.
9 Sadik and Snavely, *Bahrain, Qatar, and the United Arab Emirates,* pp. 128–29.
10 Ibid., p. 156.
11 Nakhleh, *Bahrain,* pp. 78–80, and 43–47.
12 Fuad I. Khuri, *Tribe and State in Bahrain* (Chicago: University of Chicago Press, 1980), p. 216; Nakhleh, *Bahrain,* p. 78.
13 Nakhleh, *Bahrain,* pp. 136–37.
14 Ibid., pp. 68–70.
15 *Arab Report and Record* (ARR), March 16–31, 1968.
16 ARR, January 1–15, 1969.
17 Sadik and Snavely, *Bahrain, Qatar, and the United Arab Emirates,* pp. 129–31.
18 The Economist Intelligence Unit, *Quarterly Economic Review of Bahrain,* first quarter 1979.
19 Nakhleh, *Bahrain,* pp. 82–83.
20 ARR, August 1–15, 1974.
21 ARR, September 16–30, 1974.

22 *ARR*, May 16–31, 1975.
23 *ARR*, June 1–15, 1975.
24 *ARR*, January 16–31, 1976.
25 *ARR*, February 15–29, and March 16–31, 1976.
26 *ARR*, June 16–30, 1977.
27 Nakhleh, "Labor Markets and Citizenship," pp. 147–48.
28 *ARR*, August 16–31, 1975.
29 *ARR*, December 16–31, 1975.
30 *ARR*, December 1–15, 1976.
31 *ARR*, September 1–15, 1977.
32 *ARR*, March 16–31, 1978.
33 *ARR*, February 28, 1979.
34 Sadik and Snavely, *Bahrain, Qatar, and the United Arab Emirates*, p. 59.
35 *ARR*, March 16–31, November 1–15, and December 1–15, 1967.
36 *ARR*, January 16–31, 1968.
37 *ARR*, February 1–15, 1968.
38 *ARR*, October 1–15, 1968.
39 *ARR*, January 1–15 and 16–31, 1969.
40 Sadik and Snavely, *Bahrain, Qatar, and the United Arab Emirates*, p. 60.
41 *ARR*, March 1–15, 1972.
42 *ARR*, October 1–15, October 16–31, and November 16–30, 1974.
43 *ARR*, April 1–15, and May 1–15, 1975.
44 Gerakis and Roncesvalles, "Bahrain's Offshore Banking Center," p. 271; *ARR*, November 16–30, 1975.
45 *ARR*, June 1–15, 1975.
46 *ARR*, June 16–30, 1977.
47 *Middle East Annual Review* 1978 (London: Macmillan, 1977), p. 163.
48 *ARR*, February 15–28, and September 1–15, 1978.
49 *Middle East Annual Review* 1980 (London: Macmillan, 1979), p. 183.
50 Khuri, *Tribe and State in Bahrain*, pp. 194–95.
51 Ibid., p. 196.
52 Ibid., p. 202; Nakhleh, *Bahrain*, p. 78.
53 Khuri, *Tribe and State in Bahrain*, pp. 203–14.
54 Ibid., p. 195.
55 Nakhleh, *Bahrain*, p. 79.
56 Ibid., pp. 79–80.
57 Ibid., p. 80.
58 Ibid., pp. 81–82.
59 *ARR*, June 15–30, 1974.
60 *ARR*, April 16–30, 1976.
61 *ARR*, May 16–31, 1976.
62 J. S. Birks and C. A. Sinclair, "Preparations for Income after Oil: Bahrain's Example," *Bulletin of the British Society for Middle East Studies* 6 (1979): 39. See also Avi Plascov, "Modernization, Political Development, and Stability," in Shahram Chubin, Robert Litwak, and Avi Plascov, eds., *Security in the Gulf* (London: Gower, 1981), p. 120.

63 Michael Field, "Economic Problems of Arabian Peninsula Oil States," in Chubin, Litwak, and Plascov, *Security in the Gulf*, pp. 41–42.
64 Gerakis and Roncevalles, "Bahrain's Offshore Banking Center," pp. 287–88.
65 See Bob Jessop, *The Capitalist State* (New York: New York University Press, 1982), chap. 3.
66 Arnold Hottinger, "Political Institutions in Saudi Arabia, Kuwait, and Bahrain," in Chubin, Litwak, and Plascov, eds., *Security in the Gulf*, p. 7.
67 Plascov, "Modernization," p. 141.
68 Ibid., p. 133.
69 Jessop, *Capitalist State*, p. 160.
70 Nakhleh, *Bahrain*, p. 84; Birks and Sinclair, "Preparations for Income," p. 47; Rodney Wilson, "The Evolution of the Saudi Banking System and Its Relationship with Bahrain," in Niblock, ed., *State, Society, and Economy in Saudi Arabia* (New York: St. Martin's Press, 1982).
71 See Arthur Stinchcombe, *Constructing Social Theories* (New York: Harcourt, Brace and World, 1968), chap. 2.
72 Field, "Economic Problems," p. 43.
73 *ARR*, November 1–15, 1976.
74 Keith McLachlan, "Oil and the Persian Gulf," in Cottrell, *Persian Gulf States*, pp. 217 and 213.
75 Nakhleh, "Labor Markets and Citizenship."
76 Azzam, "The Labour Market Performance," p. 29; Nakhleh, "Labor Markets and Citizenship," p. 153.
77 Field, "Economic Problems," p. 42.
78 J. S. Birks and L. A. Sinclair, "Economic and Social Implications of Current Development in the Arab Gulf: The Oriental Connection," in Niblock, *Social and Economic Development*, p. 154.
79 Gerakis and Roncesvalles, "Bahrain's Offshore Banking Center," pp. 286–87.
80 Ibid.
81 Scott Lash and John Urry, "The New Marxism of Collective Action: A Critical Analysis," *Sociology* 18 (February 1984): 43.
82 Khuri, *Tribe and State in Bahrain*, pp. 53–56 and 94–95.
83 International Labor Office, *Yearbook of Labor Statistics* (Geneva: ILO, 1972, 1982).
84 For an important attempt to formulate a parallel approach to the one suggested here, see Niblock, "Social Structure and the Development of the Saudi Arabian Political System," in Niblock, *State, Society, and Economy in Saudi Arabia*.
85 Lenczowski, "Some Reflections on the Study of Elites," in Lenczowski, ed., *Political Elites in the Middle East* (Washington, D.C.: American Enterprise Institute, 1975), p. 2.

Approaches to the Understanding of Egypt

1 David Hirst and Irene Beeson, *Sadat* (London: Faber and Faber, 1981).
2 Mohammed Heikal, *Autumn of Fury: The Assassination of Sadat* (London: Andre Deutsch, 1983).
3 See, for example, Amos Perlmutter, *Egypt: The Praetorian State* (New Brunswick: Transaction Books, 1974), and Anour Abdel-Malek, *Egypt: Military Society* (New York: Random House, Vintage Books, 1968).
4 Fouad Ajami, "The Struggle for Egypt's Soul," *Foreign Policy* 35 (Summer 1979): 3–30.
5 Jacques Berque, *Egypt: Imperialism and Revolution* (New York: Praeger, 1972), pp. 24–25.
6 For a current exposition of this view, see Galal Ahamed Amin, "External Factors in the Reorientation of Egypt's Economic Policy," in Malcolm H. Kerr and El Sayed Yassin, *Rich and Poor States in the Middle East: Egypt and the New Arab Order* (Boulder, Colo.: Westview Press, 1982), pp. 285–315.
7 See, in particular, Mahmoud Hussein, *Class Conflict in Egypt, 1945–1970* (New York: Monthly Review Press, 1973), and Abdel-Malek, *Egypt: Military Society*.
8 See, for example, Hassan Riad, *L'Egypt Nasserienne* (Paris: Les Editions des Minuit, 1964).
9 See, for example, Nadime Lachine, "Class Roots of the Sadat Regime," *MERIP Report* 56 (April 1977): 3–7. For a discussion of the new class and emergence of the public sector, see John Waterbury, *The Egypt of Nasser and Sadat: The Political Economy of Two Regimes* (Princeton, N.J.: Princeton University Press, 1983), pp. 17–20, 57–82, 247, 260.
10 Leonard Binder, *In a Moment of Enthusiasm: Political Power and the Second Stratum in Egypt* (Chicago: University of Chicago Press, 1978), p. 26.
11 Clement Henry Moore, *Images of Development: Egyptian Engineers in Search of Industry* (Cambridge, Mass.: MIT Press, 1980), p. 165.
12 Donald M. Reid, *Lawyers and Politics in the Arab World, 1880–1960* (Minneapolis: Bibliotheca Islamica, 1981), pp. 149–75.
13 For the most recent critique, see Waterbury, *Egypt of Nasser and Sadat*, pp. 247–60.
14 Manfred Halpern, *The Politics of Social Change in the Middle East and North Africa* (Princeton, N.J.: Princeton University Press, 1963).
15 Perlmutter, *Egypt: The Praetorian State*.
16 For various interpretations of class relations in the countryside, see Mahmoud Abdel-Fadil, *Development, Income Distribution, and Social Change in Rural Egypt, 1952–1970: A Study in the Political Economy of Agrarian Transition* (Cambridge: Cambridge University Press, 1975), pp. 41–50; Mahmoud Hussein, *Class Conflict in Egypt*, pp. 15–61; and Abdel-Malek, *Egypt*, pp. 57–61.
17 Robert Springborg, *Family, Power, and Politics in Egypt: Sayed Bey*

Marei—His Clan, Clients, and Cohorts (Philadelphia: University of Pennsylvania Press, 1982).

18 Partial accounts of some functional areas of policy making can be found in Raymond Baker, *Egypt's Uncertain Revolution under Nasser and Sadat* (Cambridge, Mass.: Harvard University Press, 1978), pp. 197–234; and James Mayfield, *Rural Politics in Nasser's Egypt* (Austin: University of Texas Press, 1971), pp. 230–52.

19 Binder, *In a Moment of Enthusiasm*, p. 156; Waterbury, *Egypt of Nasser and Sadat*, pp. 272–73.

20 See Waterbury, *Egypt of Nasser and Sadat*, p. 281.

21 Springborg, *Family, Power, and Politics*, pp. 89–105.

22 Waterbury, *Egypt of Nasser and Sadat*, p. 17.

23 Ibid., pp. 241–50; Nazih N. M. Ayubi, *Bureaucracy and Politics in Contemporary Egypt* (London: Ithaca Press, 1980), pp. 339–69; Moore, *Images of Development*, pp. 117–18.

24 Ayubi, *Bureaucracy and Politics*, pp. 360–70; Moore, *Images of Development*, pp. 109–30.

25 Clement Henry Moore, "Professional Syndicates in Egypt," *American Journal of Arabic Studies* 3 (1975): 60–82.

26 Saad Eddin Irahim, "Anatomy of Egypt's Militant Islamic Groups: Methodological Note and Preliminary Findings," *International Journal of Middle East Studies* 12, no. 4 (December 1980): 423–53.

27 Heikal, *Autumn of Fury*, pp. 242–55.

28 Halpern, *Politics of Social Change*, pp. 251–80; Riad, *L'Egypt Nasserienne*, p. 77.

29 Abdel-Malek, *Egypt: Military Society*, pp. 3–52.

30 Eliezer Be'eri, *Army Officers in Arab Politics and Society* (Jerusalem: Israel Universities Press, 1969), pp. 279–85.

31 See, for example, P. J. Vatikiotis, *The Egyptian Army in Politics* (Bloomington: Indiana University Press, 1961).

32 Mark N. Cooper, "The Demilitarization of the Egyptian Cabinet," *International Journal of Middle East Studies* 14, no. 2 (May 1982): 203–25.

33 Ayubi, *Bureaucracy and Politics*, pp. 345–53.

34 Shahrough Akhavi, "Egypt: Diffused Elite in a Bureaucratic Society," in I. William Zartman et al., *Political Elites in Arab North Africa* (New York: Longman, 1982), p. 243.

35 For a review of this literature, see Ayubi, *Bureaucracy and Politics*, pp. 77–156.

36 Karl A. Wittfogel, *Oriental Despotism* (New Haven, Conn.: Yale University Press, 1957).

37 James Heaphy, "The Organization of Egypt: Inadequacies of a Non-Political Model for Nation-Building," *World Politics* 18 (1966): 177–93.

38 Ayubi, *Bureaucracy and Politics*.

39 See, for example, Iliya Harik, "Mobilization Policy and Political Change in Rural Egypt," in Richard Antoun and Iliya Harik, *Rural Politics and*

Social Change in the Middle East (Bloomington: Indiana University Press, 1972), pp. 287–314.

40 Ayubi, *Bureaucracy and Politics*, p. 87.

41 Moore, *Images of Development.*

42 Richard Critchfield, *Shahhat: An Egyptian* (Syracuse, N.Y.: Syracuse University Press, 1978).

43 See, for example, Nicholas S. Hopkins, "Notes on the Political Economy of an Upper Egyptian Village" (paper delivered at the annual conference of the Middle East Studies Association, Washington, D.C., 1980); and Andrea B. Rugh, "Coping with Poverty in a Cairo Community," *Cairo Papers in Social Science* 2, no. 1 (January 1979).

44 On "Sultanic Socialism," see Moore, *Images of Development*, pp. 54–61.

45 John Waterbury, "Corruption, Political Stability, and Development: Comparative Evidence from Egypt and Morocco," *Government and Opposition* 11, no. 4 (Autumn 1976): 426–45.

46 Mark N. Cooper, *The Transformation of Egypt* (Baltimore: Johns Hopkins University Press, 1982), pp. 218–21; Springborg, *Family, Power, and Politics*, pp. 230–31.

47 For a firsthand account of that repression, see Mustapha Amin, *The First Years of Prison* (Cairo: Modern Egyptian Library, 1974), in Arabic, and *The Second Year in Prison* (Cairo: Modern Egyptian Library, 1975), in Arabic.

48 Ahmad Shukri Mustapha, for example, founder of the *Takfir wal Hijra*, was an agronomist and one-time government employee. Hassan al Banna, founder of the Muslim Brotherhood, was a teacher.

49 R. Hrair Dekmejian, "The UAR National Assembly: A Pioneering Experiment," *Middle Eastern Studies* 4 (July 1968): 361–75.

50 See, for example, Iliya F. Harik, *The Political Mobilization of Peasants: A Study of an Egyptian Community* (Bloomington: Indiana University Press, 1974).

51 Anthony Nutting, *Nasser* (London: Constable, 1972).

52 Malcolm H. Kerr, "The Political Outlook in the Local Arena," in Abraham S. Becker, Bent Hansen, and Malcolm H. Kerr, *The Economics and Politics of the Middle East* (New York: American Elsevier, 1975), pp. 41–54.

53 Cooper, *Transformation of Egypt*, pp. 35–38.

54 See various chapters in Kerr and Yassin, *Rich and Poor States.*

55 Cooper, *Transformation of Egypt*, pp. 175–77, 200–203.

56 Hirst and Beeson, *Sadat*; Heikal, *Autumn of Fury.*

57 This, for example, is the thrust of the argument in Saad Eddin Ibrahim, *The New Arab Social Order: A Study of the Social Impact of Oil Wealth* (Boulder, Colo.: Westview Press, 1982), pp. 161–74.

58 Cooper, *Transformation of Egypt*, pp. 162–68.

59 Moore, *Images of Development*, pp. 175–78.

60 For such an analysis, see Ayubi, *Bureaucracy and Politics*, pp. 85–87, 157–270.

61 Vatikiotis, *Nasser and His Generation* (London: Croom Helm, 1978).
62 Faud Ajami, *The Arab Predicament: Arab Political Thought and Practice since 1967* (Cambridge: Cambridge University Press, 1981), pp. 77–136.
63 Gabriel Baer, *Studies in the Social History of Modern Egypt* (Chicago: University of Chicago Press, 1969), pp. 93–108; *Fellah and Townsman in the Middle East* (London: Frank Cass, 1982), pp. 228–323.
64 For an overview of the application of Weberian concepts to Middle Eastern political systems, see James A. Bill and Carl Leiden, *Middle East Politics* (Boston: Little, Brown, 1979).
65 Springborg, *Family, Power, and Politics*, pp. 71–114.
66 Heikal, *Autumn of Fury*, pp. 242–55; Moore, *Images of Development*, pp. 166–204.
67 Hanna Batatu, *The Old Social Classes and Revolutionary Movements in Iraq* (Princeton, N.J.: Princeton University Press, 1978); and Baer, *Studies*.
68 Nazih Ayubi, "Implementation Capability and Political Feasibility of the Open Door Policy in Egypt," in Kerr and Yassin, *Rich and Poor States*, p. 405.

Ba'thist Ethics and the Spirit of State Capitalism: Patronage and the Party in Contemporary Syria

1 For the most important sources of such criticism, see Sami al-Jundi, *Al-Ba'th* (Beirut: Dar al-Hahar, 1969); Munif al-Razzaz, *Al-Tajriba al-Murra* (Beirut, 1967); and Muhammad Umran, *Tajribati fil-Thawra* (Beirut, 1970).
2 Raymond Hinnebusch, "Political Recruitment and Socialization in Syria: The Case of the Revolutionary Youth Federation," *International Journal of Middle East Studies* 11 (1980): 143–74; another study in this tradition is Adeed Dawisha, "Syria under Assad, 1970–1978: The Centers of Power," *Government and Opposition* 13 (Summer 1978): 341–54.
3 For an example of this sort of perspective, see Abbas Kelidar, "Religion and State in Syria," *Asian Affairs* 61 (February 1974): 16–22. This kind of approach is in keeping with the traditional assumption in Middle Eastern studies that "primordial loyalties" continue to prevail over all others. For persuasive dissent from this thesis, focused on the case of Syria, see Nikolaos Van Dam, "The Struggle for Power in Syria and the Ba'th Party (1958–1966)," *Orient* (March 1973): 10–20; and Michael Van Dusen, "Syria: Downfall of a Traditional Elite," in Frank Tachau, ed., *Political Elites and Political Modernization in the Middle East* (New York: John Wiley and Sons, 1975), pp. 115–55.
4 Nikolaos Van Dam provides an excellent account of this debate, reproducing a series of internal party circulars on the question of confessionalism (*ta'ifiya*), in *The Struggle for Power in Syria* (New York: St. Martin's Press, 1979). For an example of how such criticism persists, see Salah al-

Din al-Bitar, "Afwak Shab Suriya al-Azim," *Al-Ihya al-Arabi*, July 25, 1980.

5 For an exquisite example of this, see Jabir Rizq, *Al-Ikhwan al-Muslimun waal-Mu'amira 'ala Suriya* (Cairo: Dar al-Itisam, 1980). For a more systematic account of the evolution of the brotherhood's program, see Umar Abd-allah, *The Islamic Struggle in Syria* (Berkeley: Mizan Press, 1982).

6 For the role of Alawis in the Regional Company, see Alasdair Drysdale, "The Syrian Political Elite, 1966–1976: A Spatial and Social Analysis," *Middle Eastern Studies* 17 (January 1981): 3–30; and for their role in the military, see Moshe Ma'oz, "Alawi Officers in Syrian Politics, 1966–1974," in H. Z. Schriffrin, ed., *The Military and the State in Modern Asia* (New Brunswick, N.J.: Transaction Books, 1976), pp. 227–97.

7 The one exception is the requirement in the 1973 national constitution that the head of state be a Muslim. However, when the regime first drafted the constitution there had been no such stipulation–it was added only under the pressure of massive protests by the Muslim Brotherhood. See John Donahue, "La Nouvelle constitution syrienne et ses detracteurs," *Traveaux et Jours* (April–June 1973): 93–111.

8 See Alasdair Drysdale, "The Regional Equalization of Health Care and Education in Syria since the Ba'thi Revolution," *International Journal of Middle East Studies* 13 (1981): 93–111.

9 Alasdair Drysdale, "Ethnicity in the Syrian Officer Corps," *Civilisations* 29 (1979): 359–74.

10 Itamar Rabinovich, *Syria under the Ba'th* (New York: Halsted Press, 1972); idem, "The Compact of Minorities and the Syrian State, 1918–45," *Journal of Contemporary History* 14 (1979): 693–712; and Van Dam, *Struggle for Power in Syria*.

11 For the structure of these organizations, see *Report from Amnesty International to the Government of the Syrian Arab Republic* (London: Amnesty International, 1983), pp. 12–14.

12 The sense of distinctiveness makes the use of ethnic minorities as soldiers popular throughout the Third World; see Cynthia Enloe, *Police, Military, and Ethnicity: Foundations of State Power* (New Brunswick, N.J.: Transaction Books, 1980), pp. 127–40.

13 During a 1982 visit to Syria the author met members of this clique both guarding the border with Jordan and guarding the president's residence. In general, Syria's Christian communities have had excellent relations with the Assad regime.

14 Mohamed Heikal, *Autumn of Fury* (New York: Random House, 1983), pp. 128–38.

15 These connections are thoroughly documented in Hanna Batatu, "Some Observations on the Social Roots of Syria's Ruling Military Group and the Causes for Its Dominance," *Middle East Journal* 35 (Summer 1982): 331–44.

16 For a brief description of the *Jama'a* and its operation, see Moshe Maoz,

"Hafiz al-Assad: A Political Profile," *Jerusalem Quarterly* 8 (Summer 1978): 16–31.

17 The term *patronage* is used here with some reluctance. There is a vast literature on this concept, with rather contradictory associations. A good introduction is Steffen Schmidt et al., eds., *Friends, Followers, and Factions* (Berkeley and Los Angeles: University of California Press, 1977). For example, some scholars treat "patronage" as a comprehensive political culture, transcending or indeed effacing the claims of group or class membership. Others treat it as a political technique, one among many that can be employed by individuals, groups, or classes. (The former perspective can be found in Robert Springborg, "Patterns of Association in the Egyptian Political Elite," in George Lenczowski, ed., *Political Elites in the Middle East* (Washington, D.C.: American Enterprise Institute, 1975), pp. 83–108; the latter in Michael Gilsenan, "Against Patron-Client Relations," in Ernest Gellner and John Waterbury, eds., *Patrons and Clients in Mediterranean Societies* (London: Duckworth, 1977), pp. 167–84. The case of Syria tends to sustain the latter tradition: patronage appears as a technique, which can be turned to the service of classes, elites, or any other social body. For a definition of patronage, see below; and for additional qualifications of that definition, notes 28 and 29.

18 For an overview of these networks, see Stanley Reed, "Dateline Syria: Fin de Regime?" *Foreign Policy* 39 (Summer 1980): 176–90. For additional details, arising from the work of the Committee for the Investigation of Illegal Profits, see *Tishrin*, October 8, 1977.

19 The Ba'th party had grown up out of *halaqat*, or circles of disciples around a key proselyte; see Michael Van Dusen, "Political Integration and Regionalism in Syria," *Middle East Journal* 26 (1972): 123–36.

20 For the growth of this division, see Eliezer Be'ri, *Army Officers in Arab Politics and Society* (New York: Praeger, 1970); and Rabinovich, *Syria under the Ba'th*.

21 Dr. Adil Zabub et al., eds., *Suriya fi Ammiha al-Thalith Ashr* (Damascus: Wizarat al-I'lam, 1976), pp. 245–89.

22 Jean Honoyer, "Le Monde rural avant les reformes," in Andre Raymond, ed., *La Syrie d'aujourd'hui* (Paris: Centre National de la Recherche Scientifique, 1980), pp. 273–96; and Jean Metral and Paul Sanlaville, "L'eau, la terre, et les hommes dans les campagne syrienne," *Revue de Geographie de Lyon* 3 (1979): 229–37.

23 Al-Maktab al-Markazi Lil-Ihsa, *Al-Majmu'a al-Ihsa'iya al-Sanawiya* (Damascus: Wizarat al-Takhatit, 1977), p. 224.

24 Yahya Sadowski, "Political Power and Economic Organization in Syria" (Ph.D. diss., University of California, Los Angeles, 1984), pp. 31–44.

25 Ken Jowitt, "Soviet Neotraditionalism: The Political Corruption of a Leninist Regime," *Soviet Studies* 35 (July 1983): 275.

26 For effective use of "corruption" in the modern Middle East, see John Waterbury, "Corruption, Political Stability, and Development: Com-

parative Evidence from Egypt to Morocco," *Government and Opposition* 11 (1976): 426–45.

27 For a description of the party and its activities in this period, see Avraham Ben-Tzur, "The Neo-Ba'th Party in Syria," *Journal of Contemporary History* 3 (1968): 161–89.

28 Elisabeth Picard, "Syria Returns to Democracy: The May 1973 Legislative Elections," in G. Hermet, *Elections without Choice* (New York: Macmillan, 1978), pp. 129–44.

29 For an overview of this period, see Malcolm Kerr, "Hafiz Assad and the Changing Patterns of Syrian Politics," *International Journal* 28 (Autumn 1973): 689–706; and Moshe Ma'oz, *Syria under Hafiz al-Assad: New Domestic and Foreign Policies* (Jerusalem: Hebrew University, 1975).

30 Raymond Hinnebusch, "Political Organization in Syria: A Case of Mobilization Politics" (Ph.D. diss., University of Pittsburgh, 1975), pp. 237–40.

31 The "mainstream" tradition of Ba'thism, derived from the works of Mishil Aflaq, was partly reinstated, as were a variety of tendencies from the Neo-Ba'th period. But the works of other seminal figures, especially Zaki al-Arsuzi, which had been neglected, received increasing prominence. An interesting indications of these trends are the changes in the documents included in brief histories of the party, such as *Nidl Hizb al-Ba'th al-Arabi al-Ishtiraki, 1943–1975: Dirasa Tarikhiya Tahiiliya Muwajjaza* (Damascus: al-Qiyada al-Qawmiya, 1978).

32 The political causes and consequences of the *infiraj* are analyzed in detail in Yahya Sadowski, "The Knife's Edge: The Failure of Economic Liberalization in Syria" (unpublished, 1978).

33 Haydar is quoted in Elisabeth Longuenesse, "The Class Nature of the State in Syria," *MERIP Reports*, no. 77 (May 1979): 9.

34 The best overall account of this process to date is Bu'ali Yasin, *Hikayat al-Ard wal-Fallah al-Suri, 1945–1975* (Beirut: Dar al-Hawa'iq, n.d.). For a briefer description, see Bichara Khader, "Propriete agricole et reforme agraire en Syrie," *Civilisation* 25 (1975): 62–83.

35 'Abd al-Mu'min Muhammad Alabi, ed., *Anmat Tawzi al-Dakhl wal-Ujur fil-Qutr al-Arabi al-Suri, 1960–1975* (Kuwait: al-Ma'had al-Arabi lil-Takhtit, 1979), vol. 1, p. 66.

36 A remarkable account of this is Kamil Ismail, *Die sozialokonomischen Verhaltnisse der bauerlichen Bevolkerung im Kustengebirge der Syrischen Arabischen Republik* (Berlin: Akademie Verlag, 1975). For the social background of the Ba'thists, see R. R. MacIntyre, "The Arab Ba'th Socialist Party: Ideology, Politics, Sociology, and Organization" (Ph.D. diss., Australian National University, 1969).

37 The officer with the most extensive business operations in Lebanon, not surprisingly, turned out to be Rif'at al-Assad. He was reputed to have a hand in everything from East Beirut cement plants to the hashish trade of the Biqa' Valley. In 1977–78 he formed his own Lebanese militia to protect these investments: a group called *Rursan al-Arab*, which fused a

smattering of Ba'thist ideology with the toughest thugs who could be bought away from other militias.

38 In Hama urban-rural tensions were especially virulent, and there was a long history of tension between the kulaks and the urban notables. See Jean Gaulmier, "Notes sur la propriete fonciere dans la Syrie centrale," *L'Asie française* (1933): 56–84.

39 Adeed Dawisha, *Syria and the Lebanese Crisis* (New York: St. Martin's Press, 1980); and Itamar Rabinovich, *The War for Lebanon, 1970–1983* (Ithaca, N.Y.: Cornell University Press, 1984).

40 The Muslim Brotherhood was the backbone of resistance to the Assad regime, but it was supported by a series of smaller, and often more radical, Islamic movements. The best account of these movements available in English is Umar F. Abd-allah, *The Islamic Struggle in Syria* (Berkeley: Mizan Press, 1983).

41 Hanna Batatu, "Syria's Muslim Brethren," *MERIP Reports*, no. 110 (November 1982): 12–20.

42 Michael Fischer, "Islam and the Revolt of the Petite Bourgeoisie," *Daedalus* 111 (Winter 1982): 101–25.

43 "Syrie: La Democratisation difficile," *Maghreb-Machrek* 77 (November 1977): 14–18. However, the presidential election of February 1978 produced a high voters turnout for Assad—largely thanks to public reaction against the Sadat initiative.

44 Dina Kehat, "Syria," in Colin Legum, ed., *Middle East Contemporary Survey, 1977–78* (New York: Holmes and Maier, 1979), pp. 723–30.

45 Jamail's mysterious fall was the first major change in the structure of *al Jama'a* and it excited many rumors. He was a Sunni and many blamed his ostracism on an Alawi conspiracy. Others claimed he favored stronger Syrian ties to Saudi Arabia, even at the expense of relations with the Soviet Union. Whether any or all of these stories are true, Jamail's rivalry with Rif'at is well attested to.

46 *Middle East Economic Digest*, special report (March 1980): 31–39.

47 Rif'at formed an association of intellectual clients called *al-Rabita*. His brother Jamail established a group called the Imam Murtad League, which recruited in the villages behind Ladhiqiya. Both of these bodies were almost exclusively Alawi, and were the most nearly sectarian bodies the regime had ever tolerated (*New York Times*, December 20, 1983). For the fate of these bodies, see below.

48 The suspension of the Lawyers' Association attracted attention across the Apa' World. See *The Tribune* (bulletin published by the Committee for Defense of Freedoms and Political Prisoners in Syria), no. 10 (December 1983): 10–32.

49 *Middle East Economic Digest*, January 11, 1980, and January 18, 1980.

50 During the 1983 Syrian drive to pressure the U.S. Marines out of Lebanon, it became popular to claim that Assad was actually a "pan-Syrianist," sympathetic to the *gawmiyyuh suriyun*, who seek to integrate Syria and Lebanon. Not only did such claims misrepresent Syrian interests in Leba-

non, they also ignored the history of Ba'thist hostility to the idea of "Greater Syria" and their attacks on the *gawmiyyun* in Syria during the 1950s.

51 The bureaucracy is primarily responsible for economic policy, since both foreign and military affairs are monopolized by the office of the president. See Samir 'Abduh, *Dirasa fil-Biruqratiya al-Suriya* (Damascus, 1972), pp. 15–45.

52 Rizqalla Hilan, *Al-Thaqafa wal-Tanmiya al-Iqtisadiya fi Suriya wal-Buldan al-Mukhallifa* (Damascus: Dar al-'ilm, 1980), p. 173.

53 *Middle East Economic Digest*, February 1, 1980.

54 For some observations on the decline of military influence in Syria, see Gabriel Ben-Dor, "Civilianization of Military Regimes in the Arab World," in Henry Bienen and David Marell, eds., *Political Participation under Military Regimes* (Beverly Hills, Calif.: Sage, 1976), pp. 39–49.

55 Alasdair Drysdale, "The Syrian Armed Forces in National Politics: The Role of the Geographic and Ethnic Periphery," in Roman Kolkowicz and Andrejz Korbonski, eds., *Soldiers, Peasants, and Bureaucrats* (London: George Allen and Unwin, 1982), pp. 52–76.

56 *New York Times*, March 7, 1984, and March 12, 1984.

57 *New York Times*, September 12, 1984.

58 James Scott, *Comparative Political Corruption* (Englewood Cliffs, N.J.: Prentice-Hall, 1972), pp. 93–112 and 145–57, makes this argument in detail. For additional insights on the contribution of patronage to democracy, see Max Weber's classic, "Politics as a Vocation," in Hans Gerth and C. W. Mills, eds., *From Max Weber* (New York: Oxford University Press, 1946), pp. 77–128.

59 For details on the conditions under which patronage may evolve into democratic exchange, see Martin Shefter, "Party and Patronage: Germany, England, and Italy," *Politics and Society* 7 (1977): 403–52; and John Brewer, *Party Ideology and Popular Politics at the Succession of George III* (Cambridge: Cambridge University Press, 1976).

60 *The Middle East* (September 1984): 43–44.

Iraq: Its Revolutionary Experience under the Ba'th

1 See Hanna Batatu, *The Old Social Classes and the Revolutionary Movements in Iraq* (Princeton: Princeton University Press, 1978), pp. 744–45; Majid Khadduri, *Socialist Iraq* (Washington, D.C.: Middle East Institute, 1978), pp. 38–40; and Christine Moss Helms, *Iraq: Eastern Flank of the Arab World* (Washington, D.C.: Brookings Institution, 1984), pp. 83–86.

2 Above the Regional Command comes the National Command, composed of Ba'thists from other Arab countries as well as Iraq, supposedly with jurisdiction over Ba'thist contingents in these countries. For a description of this hierarchy, see Khadduri, *Socialist Iraq*, and Helms, *Iraq: Eastern Flank*, fig. 4.1, p. 84.

3 Iraq News Agency (INA) (Baghdad), 16 March 1980; Foreign Broadcast Information Service (FBIS), 19 March 1980, E 1-3.
4 Republic of Iraq, Ministry of Information, *Political Work in the Armed Forces* (Baghdad: al-Hurriyyah Printing House, 1978).
5 In 1978 a number of Iraq Communist party members were executed. Among other things, they were accused of recruiting members in the army.
6 Republic of Iraq, Ministry of Planning, *Man: The Object of Revolution* (Baghdad: Government Press, 1979), p. 34.
7 Republic of Iraq, Ministry of Planning, *Annual Abstract of Statistics 1978* (Baghdad: Government Press, 1979), pp. 38–39.
8 Eric Davis, "State Policy, Ideology and Labor Mobilization in Contemporary Iraq," unpublished paper, symposium, University of Exeter, July 1981.
9 Hanna Batatu, "Iraq's Underground Shi'a Movements," *Middle East Journal* 35, no. 4 (Autumn 1981): 582–83.
10 These were Saddam Hussein, Izzat Ibrahim, Taha Ramadhan, Tariq Aziz, Adnan Khair Allah Talfah, Hassan Ali al-Amiri, Sa'dun Shakir, Muhammad Hanzah al-Zubaidi, Abd al-Ghani Abd al-Ghafur, Mahmud Abd al-Wahhab al-Shaikhli, Abd al-Hassan Rahi Firawn, Sa'di Mahdi Salih, Mazban Khadr Hadi, Sa'dun Hammadi, Kamil Rasin Rashid, Ali Hasan al-Majid, and Latif Nusayyif Jasim.
11 For a description of the process involved in climbing the party ranks, see Batatu, *Old Social Classes*, p. 1010, and Helms, *Iraq: Eastern Flank*, p. 87.
12 For the first estimate, see Fuad Matar, *Saddam Hussein: The Man, the Cause and the Future* (Beirut: Express International Printing, 1981), p. 230; for the second, Helms, *Iraq: Eastern Flank*, p. 87.
13 Batatu, *Old Social Classes*, p. 1078.
14 These figures were supplied by an official representative of the Iraqi government.
15 Amatzia Baram, "The June 1980 Elections to the National Assembly in Iraq," *Orient* 3 (September 1981): 391–412. Unless otherwise specified, the following material is drawn from this article.
16 Amatzia Baram, "The Ruling Political Elite in Ba'thi Iraq 1968–1986: The Changing Features of a Collective Profile," unpublished article, 1987, pp. 59, 61, 63–64.
17 Amir Iskandar, *Saddam Husain: Munadilan, Mufakkiran wa Insanan* (Saddam Husain: The Fighter, the Thinker and the Man) (n.p.: Hachette, 1980), pp. 17–25. Unless otherwise specified, the material on Saddam's career comes from this source.
18 For these activities, see ibid., pp. 37–93; Matar, *Saddam Husain.*, pp. 31–48.
19 Much of the following information has been taken from Phebe Marr, *The Modern History of Iraq* (Boulder, Colo.: Westview Press, 1985), pp. 240–42, 278. See also "Iraq: The Agrarian Reform," *Arab World File* 288 (28 May 1975): 14–15.

20 Affluence and corruption have crept into the Ba'th party itself. Saddam has taken stern measures to stop its spread. In February 1978 a number of lawyers, including some party members, were executed for using their official positions for their own personal benefit.
21 The World Bank, *World Tables: Social Data*, 3d ed. (Baltimore: Johns Hopkins University Press, 1983), p. 45.
22 Shakir Moosa Issa, "Distribution of Income in Iraq, 1971" (Ph.D. thesis, University of London, 1978), p. 11.
23 *Statistical Pocketbook*, 1982, pp. 56, 57, 59, 60. See also John Kimball, *The Arabs*, 1983 (Washington, D.C.: American Educational Trust, 1983), p. 28.
24 Alya Sousa, "The Eradication of Illiteracy in Iraq," in Tim Niblock, ed., *Iraq: The Contemporary State* (New York: St. Martin's Press, 1982), p. 103.
25 *Annual Abstract of Statistics*, 1978, p. 38.
26 Republic of Iraq, *Statistical Abstract*, 1958 (Baghdad: Zahra Press, 1959), p. 12; *Annual Abstract of Statistics*, 1978, p. 27.
27 *Annual Abstract of Statistics*, 1978, p. 38. The World Bank put the percentage of the population engaged in agriculture higher, at 42 percent in 1980. World Bank, *World Development Report*, 1983 (New York: Oxford University Press, 1983), p. 189.
28 In the 1960s investment in industry averaged 23 percent of development budgets; in the 1975–80 Ba'th plan it rose to 32 percent.
29 Zeki Fattah, "Production, Capital Stock, Productivity and Growth in the Industrial Sector of an Oil Economy: Iraq 1960–1970" (Ph.D. thesis, Oxford University, 1976), p. 38.
30 *Annual Abstract of Statistics*, 1978, p. 38.
31 J. S. Birks and S. Sinclair, "The Challenge of Human Resources Development in Iraq," in Niblock, *Iraq*, p. 248.
32 U.S. Interest Section, "Foreign Economic Trends Report: Iraq" (Baghdad: United States Interest Section, 1984), p. 8.
33 See, for example, Edith Penrose, "Industrial Policy and Performance in Iraq," in Abbas Kelidar, *The Integration of Modern Iraq* (New York: St. Martin's Press, 1979). The situation was recognized by the government in a series of well-publicized seminars on productivity led by Saddam Hussein and reported in *al-Thawrah* in September 1976.
34 United Nations, Economic Council for West Asia (ECWA), "Industrial Development in Iraq—Problems and Prospects" (Beirut: EWA/UNIDO, 1979), p. 28.
35 Keith McLachlan, "Iraq: Problems of Regional Development," in Kelidar, *Integration of Modern Iraq*, pp. 145–47.
36 ECWA, "Industrial Development in Iraq," p. 16.
37 Kozo Ueda, "Preliminary Report on the Estimation of Population at School Ages by Sex and Group of Liwas for 1957–1980 in Iraq" (Beirut: ECWA, n.d.), pp. 10, 14; *Annual Abstract of Statistics*, 1973, p. 508; and *Annual Abstract of Statistics*, 1958, p. 77. These figures show that in the three most urbanized provinces in Iraq, in 1957, 46.5 percent of

the school-age population was in elementary school; in 1972, 71.7 percent. In the six least urbanized provinces the figures were 28.4 percent for 1957, and 50 percent for 1972. Since that time schools have spread more rapidly in rural areas.

38 Batatu, "Iraq's Underground Shi'a Movements."

39 Arab Ba'th Socialist Party, *Revolutionary Iraq, 1968–1973* (Baghdad: Arab Ba'th Socialist Party, 1974), p. 184.

40 Marr, *Modern History of Iraq*, p. 272.

41 Amal Rassam, "Revolution within the Revolution? Women and the State in Iraq," in Niblock, *Iraq*, pp. 94–95.

42 Matar, *Saddam Hussein*, p. 260.

43 Ibid., p. 271.

44 Ibid., pp. 238–40.

45 Ibid., p. 235. See also Pierre Rossi, *Iraq: The Land of the New River* (Paris: Les Editions J.A., 1980), p. 35. The latter is a public relations book sponsored by the Iraqi government and obviously reflecting its view. It is interesting to note that these ideas were spread in the school system in the 1930s and early 1940s, before the second British occupation. They reflect the thinking and policy of Iraq's leading educators Sati'-l-Husri and Fadhil al-Jamali. For a textbook espousing these ideas, see Darwish al-Miqdadi, *Ta'rikh al-Ummah-l-Arabiyyah* (History of the Arab Nation) (Baghdad: Matbaat al-Maariq, 1936).

46 See Amatzia Baram, "Mesopotamian Identity in Ba'thi Iraq," *Middle Eastern Studies* 19 (October 1983), and Amatzia Baram, "Culture in the Service of Wataniyya: The Treatment of Mesopotamian-Inspired Art in Ba'thi Iraq," *Asian and African Studies* 17 (November 1983).

47 Matar, *Saddam Hussein*, p. 278.

48 Speech by Saddam Hussein, Baghdad, 8 August 1979, FBIS, 9 August 1979, p. E-4.

State-Building and Political Construction in the Yemen Arab Republic, 1962–1977

I wish to thank the Hagop Kevorkian Center for Near Eastern Studies at New York University for support and encouragement of my research during the period 1982–86. My thanks also to the Joint Committee on the Near and Middle East of the Social Science Research Council and the American Council of Learned Societies for funds for research in the YAR in 1978.

1 Edgar O'Ballance, *The War in the Yemen* (Hamdan, Conn.: Archon Books, 1971), p. 145.

2 Fred Halliday, *Arabia without Sultans* (New York: Random House, 1975), p. 128.

3 Although his proper title was chairman of the Republic Council, Qadi al-Iryani was usually referred to in English as President al-Iryani.

4 Robert Stookey, "Social Structure and Politics in the Yemen Arab Republic," *Middle East Journal* 28, no. 3 (1974): 251.

5 This apt label is used by Halliday (*Arabia without Sultans*, p. 126). Halliday cites Sheikh Naji bin Ali al-Gadr as an example of a sheikh who received money and arms from both the Egyptians and the allies of the royalists. In the course of only three years he went from being a minor sheikh with 120 armed men at his disposal to being the paramount sheikh of the Bakil tribal confederation with thousands of men under his command (ibid., p. 117).
6 According to Stookey, a pattern of shared authority between the tribal sheikhs and the imamate's religious and civil officials had been firmly established in Zaydi areas at the local level before the 1962 revolution. "The basic innovation of the . . . al-Iryani regime consists in generalizing this collaboration to the national level, and recruiting the sheikhs, who rarely if ever held office under the Imams, into the formal ruling establishment" ("Social Structure and Politics," p. 252).
7 United Nations Development Program, "Background Paper for a County Programme for the Yemen Arab Republic" (Sanaa, March 1973, mimeographed), p. 13.
8 Conversation with Hussein al-Hubayshi, Sanaa, 1978.
9 Yemenis and others commonly referred to al-Hamdi in English as president despite the fact that the position entitling him to act as head of state was that of chairman of the Command Council.
10 *Arab Report and Record*, June 1974.
11 Conversation with Dr. Abd al-Karin al-Iryani, Sanaa, 1976.
12 Interview with a subject who prefers to remain unidentified, Sanaa, 1978.
13 For an analysis of the Ali Abdullah Salif era, and a more detailed account of the period covered in this article, see Robert Burrowes, *The Yemen Arab Republic: The Politics of Development*, 1962–1986 (Boulder, Colo.: Westview Press, 1987).

The Non-Communist Left in Iran: The Case of the Mujahidin

1 See Sepehr Zabih, *The Mossadegh Era: Roots of Iranian Revolution* (Chicago: Lake View Press, 1982).
2 Some of the Western language sources are: Ahmad Faroughy and John Loup Reverier, *L'Iran contre le chah* (Paris: Jean Claude Simeon, 1979); Ervand Abrahamian, "The Guerrilla Movement in Iran, 1963–1977," in *MERIP Reports* 86 (March–April 1980); Shahram Chubin, "Leftist Forces in Iran," *Problems of Communism* (July–August 1980); and Sepehr Zabih, *Iran's Revolutionary Upheaval: An Interpretive Essay* (San Francisco: Alchemy Books, 1979).
3 For a comprehensive study of the communist movement in Iran, see Sepehr Zabih, *The Communist Movement in Iran* (Berkeley and Los Angeles: University of California Press, 1966).
4 See "Resalate Inghelabi Ali Shariati" (The Revolutionary Mission of Ali Shariati), *Mujahid* (Tehran) (April 1980).

5 *Mujahid*, nos. 44 and 48 (Tehran) (April 1980); also, Sepehr Zabih, "Ideology and Socio-Economic Background of the People's Mujahidin of Iran," in *International Political Science World Congress* (Rio de Janeiro, 1982).
6 Sepehr Zabih, *Iran's Revolutionary Upheaval*, p. 41.
7 See *Ranjbar*, especially nos. 121–37 (April 1980). (*Ranjbar* is the official organ of the Mujahidin, published in Iran until 1981, thereafter in West Germany.)
8 *Mujahid* (London) (in English) 1, no. 5 (May 1980), pp. 25–29. Also, "Last Defense of Martyred Mojahed Ali Mihandust," *Moslem Students Society* (Long Beach, Calif., March 1981) Pro-Mujahidin in the United States.
9 *Recognition and Evolution* (Tehran, 1975). Published by the Mujahidin with a pronounced Marxist bent.
10 *Mujahid* (Tehran) (June 22, 1981); and *Keyhan* (Tehran) (June 21–25, 1981).
11 *Mujahid* (in English) 1, no. 6.
12 *Moslem Student Society* (August 12, 1981).
13 *Mujahid* (August 17, 1981) (clandestine in Persian).
14 Radio Mujahid (February 11, 1982); and *Keyhan* (Tehran) (February 12, 1982).
15 See *Iran Liberation*. News bulletin of the People's Mujahidin of Iran (Washington, D.C., and London) nos. 30–49 (May–July 1987).
16 Based on daily communiqués issued by Rajavi's office in Paris, broadcast by the Mujahidin Telephone News Service in Western Europe and the United States between July 12, 1981, and February 28, 1982; *Jomhuriye Islami* (organ of the ruling Islamic Republican party); *Ettelaat* (June 23, 1981); and *Keyhan* (Tehran) (March 20, 1982).
17 For more recent studies of the subject, see Ervand Abrahamian, *Iran between Two Revolutions* (Princeton, N.J.: Princeton University Press, 1982), pp. 480–96; and Sepehr Zabih, *Iran since the Revolution* (Baltimore: Johns Hopkins University Press, 1982), pp. 97–107; and *The Left in Contemporary Iran: Ideology, Organization and the Soviet Connection* (Stanford, Calif.: Hoover Institution Press, 1985).

Ideology versus Pragmatism in South Yemen, 1968–1986

1 The first press reports alleging Soviet military installations on the Red Sea appeared in the 1950s (concerning North Yemen). In fact, no such fortifications existed. In the past few years, similar installations are alleged to have been built on Perim as well as on Socotra; indeed, the latter has been said to be the site of a major Soviet military base that includes submarine "pens." I have been unable to locate acceptable evidence for these allegations. The best description of Bab al-Mandab and its importance is John Duke Anthony, *The Red Sea: Control of the*

Southern Approach (Washington, D.C.: Middle East Institute, 1980).

2 Most of these states participated in the Taiz Conference of March 1977 to signal outside powers that they were prepared to act to prevent foreign control of the Red Sea. See, among others, Ferdinand Hurni, "Counter-Movement on the Red Sea," *Swiss Review of World Affairs*, May 1977, p. 7.

3 The development of the British presence in southern Arabia has been covered in an extensive literature. The following works may be profitably consulted for brief summaries and bibliographies: Robert W. Stookey, *South Yemen: A Marxist Republic in Arabia* (Boulder, Colo.: Westview Press, 1982); Fred Halliday, *Arabia without Sultans* (New York: Random House, Vintage Books, 1975); and M. W. Wenner, "The People's Republic of South Yemen," in Tareq Ismael, ed., *Governments and Politics of the Contemporary Middle East* (Homewood, Ill.: Dorsey Press, 1970), pp. 412–29.

4 John Duke Anthony, "Relations between the United States and the PDRY: Problems and Prospects," in *Diego Garcia, 1975: The Debate over the Base and the Island's Former Inhabitants* (Washington, D.C.: U.S. Government Printing Office, 1976), p. 86.

5 The summary and the immediately following précis of events and developments between 1967 and the mid-1980s draws primarily from the following sources: Wenner, "The People's Republic of South Yemen"; Halliday, *Arabia without Sultans*; Stookey, *South Yemen*; as well as: Richard F. Nyrop et al., *Area Handbook for the Yemens* (Washington, D.C.: U.S. Government Printing Office, 1977); Fred Halliday, "Yemen's Unfinished Revolution: Socialism in South," *MERIP Reports* 81 (October 1979): 3–20; J. E. Peterson, *Conflict in the Yemens and Superpower Involvement* (Washington, D.C.: Georgetown University Press, 1981; and Aryeh Y. Yodfat, *The Soviet Union and the Arabian Peninsula* (London: Croom Helm, 1983).

6 See *Proposed Arms Transfers to the Yemen Arab Republic* (Washington, D.C.: U.S. Government Printing Office, 1979); *U.S. Interests in, and Policies toward, the Persian Gulf* 1980 (Washington, D.C.: U.S. Government Printing Office, 1980); Laurie Mylroie, *Politics and the Soviet Presence in the PDRY: Internal Vulnerabilities and Regional Challenges* (Santa Monica, Calif.: Rand, 1983), and Halliday, "Yemen's Unfinished Revolution."

7 On the changes after 1980, see the articles by David Shirreff in the *Middle East Economic Digest* and Chris Kutschera in *The Middle East*. *New York Times*, June 15 and 22, 1980, also carried articles on the changes.

8 World Bank, *People's Democratic Republic of Yemen: A Review of Economic and Social Development* (Washington, D.C., 1979).

9 *The Middle East*, July 1982.

10 Information on the tribal affiliation of major leaders is now difficult to obtain. For the significance of tribal affiliations in the past (i.e., under

British rule), see Wenner, "The People's Republic of South Yemen." Among recent writers on this factor, see Halliday, "Yemen's Unfinished Revolution"; M. Abir, *Oil, Power, and Politics* (London: Frank Cass, 1974); Mylroie, *Politics and the Soviet Presence;* and Ursula Braun, *Nord-und Suedjemen im Spannungfeld Interner, Regionaler und Globaler Gegensaetze* (Bonn: Europa-Union-Verlag, 1981). As of this writing, all major ministers and figures in the YSP are of South Yemeni origin.

11 There is at least the distinct possibility that the PDRY will join the list of oil producing states in the near future, though precisely how significant the deposits are is not yet known. After what the South Yemenis believed to be inexcusably long delays and lack of real exploratory efforts on the part of the Soviet Union, they decided to permit some Western countries to explore in limited areas (notably the Italian AGIP concern). In the spring of 1982 the media carried the first reports of strikes of modest fields (*Financial Times* [London], April 2, 1982). Since that time, the reports on the economy of the PDRY that have not featured the disastrous floods have been on the scramble by Western firms for concessions. See, for example, the two articles by Nigel Harvey in *Middle East Economic Digest:* "South Yemen Sets the Bait for Foreign Oil Firms" (July 22, 1983) and "South Yemen's Oil Excites Western Interest" (April 6, 1984). It is of some interest that the PDRY leadership has made it quite plain that it wants *Western* firms to undertake the exploration and exploitation of the oil, and it would not seem unreasonable to speculate on the long-term impact of this on economic relations with the West.

12 The Brezhnev Doctrine was apparently first formulated by S. Kovalev and is understood to cover such matters as "damage to the fundamental interests of other socialist countries," "damage to socialism," threats to the defense capabilities of the Soviet Union and related matters. See *Current Digest of the Soviet Press* 20 (October 16, 1968): 10–12.

The PDPA Regime in Afghanistan: A Soviet Model for the Future of the Middle East

The views, opinions, and findings of this study are those of the author and should not be construed as an official Department of the Navy position, policy, or decision.

1 Amir Abdur Rehman's use of religion to create national unity (and increase his own power) is detailed in Hasan Kawun Kakar, *Government and Society in Afghanistan: The Reign of Amir 'Abd al-Rahman Khan* (Austin: University of Texas Press, 1979); see especially pp. 147–61 and 176–79.

2 Vartan Gregorinan, *The Emergence of Modern Afghanistan: Politics of Reform and Modernization, 1880–1946* (Stanford, Calif.: Stanford University Press, 1969), p. 126.

3 Amir Habibullah's third son, Amanullah, became the son-in-law of

Mahmud Beg Tarzi and belonged to a secret Mashruta (constitutional) group that met to discuss ways and means of modernizing the country. See Louis Dupree, *Afghanistan* (Princeton, N.J.: Princeton University Press, 1978), p. 437, n. 4.

4 For the Amunullah period, see Dupree, *Afghanistan*, pp. 441–57; Gregorian, *Emergence of Modern Afghanistan*, pp. 227–74; Leon B. Poullada, *Reform and Rebellion in Afghanistan: King Amanullah's Failure to Modernize a Traditional Society* (Ithaca, N.Y.: Cornell University Press, 1973); and M. Mobin Shorish, "The Impact of the Kemalist 'Revolution' on Afghanistan," *Journal of South Asian and Middle Eastern Studies* 8, no. 3 (Spring 1983): 33–45.

5 Dupree, *Afghanistan*, pp. 499–558, is the best source for this period of Afghan history, and it is he who coined the phrase "the decade of Da'ud."

6 Dr. Muhammad Yusuf, personal interview, May 1970 (Kabul).

7 Ralph H. Magnus, "Muhammad Zahir Khan, Former King of Afghanistan," *Middle East Journal* 30, no. 1 (Winter 1976): 78.

8 Charges that government-sponsored development was unfairly concentrated in the capital were widely publicized in the debates on the confirmation of the Etemadi government in 1967, which were broadcast live over Radio Kabul. See *Vote of Confidence Debates*, November 11–13, 1967, tape 5 (American embassy translation).

9 The shari'a faculty was not established at Kabul University until 1952, even though the faculty of medicine (the first of the university's departments) was founded in 1932. Kabul University, *General Catalog*, vol. 1 (1968), pp. 1 and 133.

10 Sajjad Hyder, lecture (Islamabad), April 1983; confirmed in interviews with Ambassador Hyder (the Pakistani envoy to Moscow, 1975–80).

11 Ibid.

12 This is developed more fully in my chapter "Afghanistan and Gulf Security: A Continuing Relationship," in Robert G. Darius, John W. Amos II, and Ralph H. Magnus, eds., *Gulf Security into the 1980s: Perceptual and Strategic Dimensions* (Stanford, Calif.: Hoover Institution Press, 1984), pp. 7–30.

13 Eliza Van Hollen, *Afghanistan: 18 Months of Occupation* (U.S. Department of State, Special Report No. 86, August 1981), p. 2.

14 Eliza Van Hollen, *Afghanistan: 2 Years of Occupation* (U.S. Department of State, Special Report No. 91, December 1981), p. 3.

15 "National Fatherland Front 5th Plenum Resolution," *Foreign Broadcast Information Service, South Asia* (henceforth cited as *FBIS*), p. C3, citing a Kabul broadcast of June 15, 1983.

16 This is asserted in the "Basic Principles of the DRA," proclaimed by the Revolutionary Council in April 1980 as an interim constitution until the Loya Jirgah (the traditional supreme council of the nation) can be elected to ratify a permanent constitution.

17 There are numerous descriptions of the traditional system of authority in Afghanistan; one of the best of these, which relates this order to the

changes of the 1964 constitution and to the effects of communist rule, is that of Pierre Centilivres and Micheline Centlivres-Dumont, "Village in Afghanistan," *Commentaire* (Paris) (Winter 1981–82): 514–25, as translated in "Political Sociology of Traditional Hierarchy Studied," *JPRS* L/10329 (February 17, 1982): 2–13.

18 The analogies between the Soviet wars against the Central Asian *basmachi* have been made by a number of scholars, and by the Soviets themselves. See, especially, Alexandre Bennigsen, "The Soviet Union and Muslim Guerrilla Wars, 1920–1981: Lessons for Afghanistan," *Conflict* 4, nos. 2/3/4 (1983): 301–24. It is also addressed in a monograph by Mark C. Storella, *The Central Asia Analogy and the Soviet Union's War in Afghanistan* (New York: Afghanistan Forum, 1984).

19 Eden Naby, "The Ethnic Factor in Soviet-Afghan Relations," *Asian Survey* 20, no. 3 (March 1980): 248.

20 Marie Broxup, "The Soviets' Education Policy: Crushing the Muslim Community," *Les Nouvelles d'Afghanistan* (Paris), nos. 19–20 (October–November 1984): 10–12; translated as "Education System Assessed under Soviet Occupation," *JPRS*, NEA 84–187 (December 28, 1984): 34.

21 "AFP: Government Trying to Win Over Frontier Tribes," *FBIS* (December 12, 1980): C4, from an AFP dispatch datelined Islamabad, December 11, 1980.

22 Louis Dupree, "Afghanistan in 1982: Still No Solution," *Asian Survey* 22, no. 2 (1983): 133.

23 Sayd B. Majrooh, "Afghan Militia Force, a New Failure of Kabul-Soviet Authorities," *Afghan Information Centre, Monthly Bulletin* 42 (September 1984): 2–3.

24 Audrey Shalinsky, *Central Asian Refugees in Afghanistan: Problems of Religious and Ethnic Identity*, Afghanistan Council of the Asia Society, Occasional Paper no. 19 (New York, December 1979).

25 Anders Fange, a Swedish journalist, relates an instance of such local pressures, which he observed in northern Afghanistan. The local *shura* (council) of village elders forced two rival mujahidin groups to cooperate, since one had a captured artillery piece and the other a former Afghan army officer who knew how to use it. Private interview, April 1983 (Peshawar).

26 See Louis Dupree, "Afghanistan," *The Muslim World* 56, no. 4 (1966): 269–76, and Dupree, "The Political Uses of Religion: Afghanistan," in Kalman H. Silvert, ed., *Churches and States: The Religious Institution and Modernization* (New York: American Universities Field Staff, 1967), pp. 195–212. See also Akbar S. Ahmed, "Religious Presence and Symbolism in Pukhtun Society," in Akbar S. Ahmed and David M. Hard, eds., *Islam in Tribal Societies, from the Atlas to the Indus* (London: Routledge and Kegan Paul, 1984), pp. 310–30; and Richard Tapper, ed., *The Conflict of Tribe and State in Iran and Afghanistan* (London and New York: Croom Helm, St. Martin's Press, 1983).

27 The Afghan constitution of 1964 specified that the king must be a Hanafi Muslim and that official rites be conducted according to Hanafi law. The

1932 constitution of Nadir Shah specified that Hanafi Islam was the state religion of Afghanistan.

28 Eden Naby, "The Afghan Resistance Movement," in Ralph H. Magnus, ed., *Afghan Alternatives: Issues, Options, and Policies*" (New Brunswick, N.J.: Transaction Books, 1985), pp. 59–81.

29 *FBIS* (June 4, 1978): S5.

30 Nancy Hatch Dupree, *Revolutionary Rhetoric and Afghan Women*, Afghanistan Council of the Asia Society, Occasional Paper no. 23 (New York, January 1981), p. 9.

31 Louis Dupree, "Red Flag over the Hindu Kush, Part IV: Repressions, or Security through Terror Purges IV–VI," *American Universities Field Staff Reports, Asia*, no. 29 (1980), pp. 8–9.

32 See the works of Alexandre Bennigsen and Eden Naby, cited in notes 18 and 19 above, as well as Bennigsen's, "Mullahs, Mujahidin, and Soviet Muslims," *Problems of Communism* 33, no. 6 (1984): 28–44. An opposing view is that of Martha Brill Olcott, "Soviet Islam and World Revolution," *World Politics* 34, no. 4 (1982): 487–504.

33 "Interrelation of Sawr Government and Islam Clarified," *Haqiqat-e Engelab-e Sawr* (Kabul), February 22, 1983, p. 2, as translated by *JPRS* 93216 (April 7, 1983): 109–10.

34 "Religious, Political Figure 'Martyred,'" *FBIS* (November 26, 1982), reporting a Kabul broadcast of November 22, 1982.

35 "Presidential Palace Hit; Defense Minister Replaced," *Tehran Times* (December 5, 1984), p. 1, as reprinted in *JPRS* NEA 85–005: 63.

36 "Defector Comments on Police Desertion," *FBIS* (November 26, 1982): C1, from a report on Karachi Domestic Service in English of November 20, 1982. The defector, Police Brigadier M. Aiyub Mangal, was deputy leader of the Afghan hajj delegation. The leader also defected.

37 "4 Die, 7 Injured in Kabul Mosque Explosion," *FBIS* (March 23, 1984): C1, from a Kabul broadcast of March 22, 1984.

38 Editorial, "Are They Declaring Jihad Against Us?" *Kabul New Times*, June 28, 1979, p. 2.

39 "Karmal Addresses Representatives of Bamian Province, Defends Soviet Role," *FBIS* (December 23, 1980): C2, a translation of a Kabul broadcast of December 21, 1980.

40 "Karmal Addresses Hazara Nationality Jirga," *FBIS* (December 26, 1984): C1. See also, "Refugee Rescue Body Condemns Iran Registration Move," *FBIS* (July 13, 1984): C1.

41 "Kabul Cites Koran on Peaceful Resolution of Differences," *FBIS* (May 22, 1980): C2, a translation of a Kabul International Service broadcast in Arabic of May 21, 1981.

42 Louis Dupree, "Afghanistan under the *Khalq*," *Problems of Communism* 28, no. 4 (1979): 40. An example of the loose handling of figures can be seen in two speeches by Babrak Karmal, six months apart, in which he gives the party membership in mid-1984 as 150,000 and in January 1985 as 120,000.

43 This is developed further in Ralph H. Magnus, "Tribal Marxism: The Soviet Encounter with Afghanistan," *Conflict* 4, nos. 2/3/4 (1983): 339–68.

44 Dupree, "Afghanistan under the Khalq."

45 "Barbrak Karmal Interviewed on USSR Invasion," *FBIS* (April 2, 1980): C2, a translation of an interview published in *Der Spiegel* (Hamburg) of March 31, 1980, pp. 139–46.

46 "Platform of the People's Democratic Party of Afghanistan," in Arnold, Appendix A, p. 148. This is a translation prepared for the American embassy in Kabul of the program published in the first issue of *Khalq*, nos. 1 and 2 (April 11, 1966).

47 "Constitution of the People's Democratic Party of Afghanistan (the Party of the Working Class of Afghanistan)," in Arnold, Appendix B, p. 149. This translation was prepared by the British and American embassies in Kabul.

48 This program was published in the *Kabul New Times* on April 21, 22, 24, 25, and 26, 1982; it is reproduced as "PDPA Publishes Its Program of Action," by *JPRS* 80860 (May 20, 1982): 15–26.

49 "Karmal Speaks on 20th Anniversary of PDPA," *FBIS* (January 14, 1985): p. C3, a report of a Kabul broadcast of January 10, 1985.

50 "Afghan Party Secretary Nur Depicts Country's Progress," *FBIS Annex* (July 12, 1984): 3; a translation of an article in *Partiynayazhizn* (Moscow), no. 12, June 1984, pp. 75–77.

51 Aernout van Lynden, "With the Resistance in Kabul," *The Observer* (London), August 16, 1981, p. 10. Sayd Alem, a resistance commander of the *Jam'iy at-e-Islami* in Kabul, describes his underground organization as composed of Kabul university students, civil administrators, officers, and businessmen. "The Future of Afghanistan Viewed by a Resistance Commander," *Afghan Information Centre Monthly Bulletin* 36 (March 1984): 8.

52 "Golabzoy Interrupts Karmal at PDPA Congress," *FBIS* (March 25, 1982): C1, from an AFP dispatch from Islamabad of March 23, 1982.

53 "General Reportedly Placed under House Arrest," *FBIS* (June 22, 1983): C1, from Karachi overseas broadcast in Urdu of June 22, 1983.

54 "Karachi: Soviet Intelligene Interrogation of Mujahidin," *FBIS* (August 31, 1984): C1; see also the interview with Seyd Gharib Gharibnawaz, the former chief justice of the Kabul civil court, who defected in April 1984, as reported in "Situation in Kabul, Interview with a Chief Justice," *Afghan Information Centre, Monthly Bulletin* 38 (May 1984): 10–11.

55 "Times Reports on Moscow-Trained Afghans," *FBIS* (March 29, 1984): F2, from a report in the *Pakistan Times* (Rawalpindi, in English), March 16, 1984, p. 6; on the other hand, not all Russian-trained Afghans became supporters of the regime; see "Afghan Students in the Soviet Union" (two interviews), *Afghan Information Centre Monthly Bulletin* 46 (January 1985): 3–6.

Israel: The Politics of the Second Generation

1 S. N. Eisenstadt, "The Israeli Political System and the Transformation of Israeli Society," in *Politics and Society in Israel: Studies in Israeli Society*, vol. 3, ed. Ernest Krausz and David Glanz (New Brunswick, N.J., and Oxford: Transaction Books, 1985), p. 416.

2 Dan Horowitz and Moshe Lissak, *The Origins of the Israeli Polity* (Chicago: University of Chicago Press, 1978), p. 120.

3 Dan Caspi, Avraham Diskin, and Emanuel Gutmann, eds., *The Roots of Begin's Success* (London: Croom Helm, 1983).

4 Calvin Goldscheider and Alan S. Zuckerman, *The Transformation of the Jews* (Chicago: University of Chicago Press, 1984), p. 174.

5 Ibid., p. 204.

6 Jonathan Shapiro, "Generational Units and Intergeneration Relations in Israeli Politics," in Krausz and Glanz, eds., *Politics and Society in Israel*, vol. 3.

7 Asher Arian, *Politics in Israel* (Chatham, N.J.: Chatham House, 1985), p. 8.

8 Itzhak Galnoor, *Steering the Polity* (Beverly Hills: Sage, 1982), pp. 76–77, 78–110.

9 K. Z. Paltiel, "The Israeli Coalition System," *Government and Opposition* 10 (1975): 397–414.

10 Emanuel Gutmann, "Political Parties and Groups: Stability and Change," in *The Israeli Political System*, ed. M. Lissak and E. Gutmann (Tel Aviv: Am Oved, 1977), pp. 122–70 (in Hebrew).

11 Avi Gottlieb and Ephraim Yuchtman-Yaar, "Materialism, Postmaterialism, and Public Views on Socioeconomics Policy: The Case of Israel," *Comparative Political Studies* 16, no. 3 (October 1983): 307–35; reprinted in Krausz and Glanz, eds., *Politics and Society in Israel*, vol. 3.

12 Rael J. Isaac, *Party and Politics in Israel: Three Visions of a Jewish State* (New York: Praeger, 1982); Daniel J. Elazar, "Israel's Compound Polity," in *Israel at the Polls: The Knesset Elections of 1977*, ed. Howard R. Penniman (Washington, D.C.: American Enterprise Institute, 1979), pp. 1–38; reprinted in Krausz and Glanz, eds., *Politics and Society in Israel*, vol. 3.

13 Yael Yishai, "Israel's Right-Wing Jewish Proletariat," *Jewish Journal of Sociology* 24, no. 2 (1982): 87–97; reprinted in Krausz and Glanz, eds., *Politics and Society in Israel*, vol. 3.

14 Ibid. See also Asher Arian and Michal Shamir, "The Primarily Political Functions of the Left-Right Continuum," *Comparative Politics* 15, no. 2 (1983): 139–58; reprinted in Krausz and Glanz, eds., *Politics and Society in Israel*, vol. 3.

15 David Newman, ed., *The Impact of Gush Emunim* (London: Croom Helm, 1985).

16 Baruch Kimmerling, *Zionism and Territory: The Socio-Territorial Di-*

mensions of Zionist Politics (Berkeley: Institute of International Studies, University of California, 1982).

17 Eliezer Don-Yehiya, "Jewish Orthodoxy, Zionism, and the State of Israel," *Jerusalem Quarterly* 31 (1984): 10–30; S. Cohen and E. Don-Yehiya, eds., *Comparative Jewish Politics*, vol. 2, *Conflict and Consensus in Jewish Political Life* (Ramat-Gan: Bar-Ilan University Press, 1984).

18 Ofira Seliktar, "National Integration of a Minority in an Acute Conflict Situation: The Case of Israel Arabs," *Plural Societies* 12 (1981): 25–40; Jacob M. Landau, "The Arab Vote," in Caspi, Diskin, and Gutmann, eds., *Roots of Begin's Success;* Ian Lustick, "Israel's Arab Minority in the Begin Era," in *Israel in the Begin Era*, ed. R. O. Freedman (New York: Praeger, 1982), pp. 121–50.

19 Daniel Shimshoni, *Israeli Democracy* (New York: Free Press, 1982).

Turkey: Democratic Framework and Military Control

This essay is the text (with a few changes) of a lecture delivered at the annual meeting of the British Society for Middle Eastern Studies in Oxford, July 1984.

1 See C. H. Dodd, *The Crisis of Turkish Democracy* (Hull: Eothen Press, 1983).

2 There is a large literature on the Turkish military and politics, such as G. S. Harris, "The Role of the Military in Turkish Politics," *Middle East Journal* 19 (Winter–Spring 1965):54–66, 169–76; and E. Özbudun's *The Role of the Military in Recent Turkish Politics* (Cambridge, Mass.: Harvard University Center for International Affairs, 1966). More recent publications are K. H. Karpat's "The Military and Its Relation to the State and Democracy," in Forschungsinstitut der Friedrich Ebert Stiftung, *Die türkische Krise* (Bonn: Friederich Ebert Stiftung, 1981), pp. 107–21; F. Tachau and M. Heper, "The State, Politics, and the Military in Turkey," *Comparative Politics* 16, no. 1 (October 1983): 17–33; and J. H. McFadden, "Civil-Military Relations in the Third Turkish Republic," *Middle East Journal* 39 (Winter 1985): 69–85.

3 For those years, see F. Ahmad, *The Turkish Experiment in Democracy, 1950–1975* (London: Hurst, 1977), and W. F. Weiker, *The Modernization of Turkey from Atatürk to the Present Day* (New York: Holmes and Meier, 1981).

4 See J. M. Landau, "New Works about Atatürk," *Wiener Zeitschrift für Kunde des Morgenlandes* 75 (1983): 183–92.

5 On the Democratic party see Cem Eroğul, *Demokrat Parti* (*tarihi ve ideolojisi*) (Ankara: Siyasal Bilgiler Fakültesi, 1970).

6 W. F. Weiker, *The Turkish Revolution, 1960–61* (Washington, D.C.: Brookings Institution, 1963). For the following years of this second period, see Nadir Nadi, *27 mayıs'tan 12 marta* (Istanbul: Sinan, 1971).

7 For the texts of Turkish constitutions, including the 1961 and 1982 ones, see A. Yalçın, ed., *Türkiye Cumhuriyeti anayasaları* (Istanbul, 1982).

8 Metin Toker, *Solda ve sağda vuruşanlar* (Ankara: Akis, 1971); J. M. Landau, *Radical Politics in Modern Turkey* (Leiden: Brill, 1974).
9 D. Barchard, "The Intellectual Background to Radical Protest in Turkey," in W. M. Hale, ed., *Aspects of Modern Turkey* (New York: Bowker, 1976), pp. 21–37; J. M. Landau, "Images of the Turkish Left," *Problems of Communism* 35, no. 2 (September–October 1983): 72–74; J. M. Landau, *Pan-Turkism in Turkey: A Study of Irredentism* (London: Hurst, 1981); J. M. Landau, "Islamism and Secularism: The Turkish Case," in Sh. Morag, ed., *Studies in Judaism and Islam Presented to Shlomo Dov Goitein on the Occasion of His Eightieth Birthday* (Jerusalem: Magnes Press, 1981), pp. 361–82.
10 Successor, in a large measure, to the banned Democratic party.
11 J. M. Landau, "The Nationalist Action Party in Turkey," *Journal of Contemporary History* 17, no. 4 (October 1982): 587–606.
12 J. M. Landau, *Politics and Islam: The National Salvation Party in Turkey* (Salt Lake City: University of Utah Press, 1976).
13 Doğu Ergil, *Türkiye'de terör ve şiddet* (Ankara, 1980).
14 General Secretariat of the National Security Council, *12 September in Turkey: Before and After* (Ankara, 1982).
15 K. H. Karpat, "Turkish Democracy at Impasse: Ideology, Party Politics, and the Third Military Intervention," *International Journal of Turkish Studies* 2, no. 1 (Spring–Summer 1981): 1–43; H. Kramer, *Das neue politische System der Türkei* (Stiftung Wissenschaft und Politik–Forschungsinstitut für Internationale Politick und Sicherheit, Ebenhausen, 1983, mimeographed).
16 U. Steinbach, "Die Türkei im Umbruch," *Orient* (Hamburg) 20, no. 2 (June 1979): 42–63; J. M. Landau, "Radicalism in Turkish Domestic Politics," in Stiftung, *Die türkische Krise*, pp. 97–106; O. Oehring, *Die Türkei im Spannungfeld extremer Ideologien, 1973–1980* (Berlin: Klaus Schwarz Verlag, 1984).
17 J. M. Landau, E. Özbudun, and F. Tachau, eds., *Electoral Politics in the Middle East: Issues, Voters, and Elites* (London: Croom Helm; Stanford, Calif.: Hoover Institution Press, 1980).
18 Details in O. Oehring, "Der Verfassunggebende Versammlung in der Türkei," *Orient* 22, no. 4 (1981): 614–43.
19 Turkish press of March and April 1984. See also Bülent Ecevit, "Turkey: A Social Democrat's Reading," *International Herald Tribune*, April 7–8, 1984, p. 4; M. Ali Birand, *12 Eylül saat 04.00* (Istanbul: Karacan, 1984); L. W. Pevsner, *Turkey's Political Crisis: Background, Perspectives, Prospects* (New York: Praeger, 1984), especially, pp. 84ff. Also, a special issue on Turkey of *Les Temps modernes* (Paris), July–August 1984, 456–57; and *Inshallah: A Survey of Turkey*, supplement to *The Economist*, London, November 3, 1984.
20 For various interpretations of democracy in Turkey, past, present, and future, see N. Abadan-Unat, "Patterns of Political Modernization and Turkish Democracy," *The Turkish Yearbook of International Relations*, vol. 18 (1979; published in 1983), pp. 1–26; and U. Ergüder, "Democ-

racy in Turkey: Achievements and Prospects," in M. Heper, ed., *Turkey: Past Development and Future Prospects* (Ankara, 1983), pp. 11–18.

Lebanon: The Role of External Forces in Confessional Pluralism

In writing this chapter, I have benefited from the assistance of John W. Burton, Robert F. Haddad, Lyna Maslanka, and Chung-In Moon.

1 The Lebanon conflict, for example, was constantly seen as a distraction from the greater issue of the Palestinian question. Despite the fact that it claimed the lives of close to 100,000 people, the complexity of the Lebanese war had made it less worthy of attention as a separate conflict in the minds of policy makers.

2 The hegemonic tendencies of the Lebanese communities have been clearly documented. On Christian hegemony, see for example Jonathan Randal, *Going All the Way: Christian Warlords, Israeli Adventurers, and the War in Lebanon* (New York: Viking Press, 1983); Itamar Rabinovich, *The War for Lebanon* (Ithaca, N.Y.: Cornell University Press, 1984); Ze'ef Schiff and Ehud Ya'ari, *Israel's Lebanon War* (New York: Simon and Schuster, 1984). On Muslim and Druze hegemony, see, for example, Jean Ghanem, *Liban: Guerre ou genocide?* (Sherbrooke, 1978); Jean-Paul Peroncel-Hugoz, *Le Radeau de Mahomet* (Paris: Lieu commun, 1983); Perconcel-Hugoz, *Une Croix sur le Liban* (Paris: Lieu commun, 1984).

3 Henry Tajfel, *Human Groups and Social Categories: Studies in Social Psychology* (New York: Cambridge University Press, 1981).

4 Edward E. Azar and Stephen P. Cohen, "Peace as Crisis and War as Status-Quo: The Arab-Israel Conflict Environment," *International Interactions* 6, no. 2 (1979): 159–84.

5 Muzafer Sherif et al., *Intergroup Conflict and Cooperation: The Robbers Cave Experiment* (Norman: University of Oklahoma Press, 1961).

6 See Walker Connor, "Nation-Building or Nation Destroying?" *World Politics* 24, no. 3 (April 1972): 319–55.

7 Azar and Cohen, "Peace as Crisis," and Azar and Chung-In Moon, "Third World National Security: Toward a New Conceptual Framework," *International Interactions* 11, no. 1 (1984): 103–35.

8 See Kamal S. Salibi, *Cross Roads to Civil War: Lebanon, 1955–1976* (Delmar, N.Y.: Caravan, 1976).

9 Avner Yaniv, *Dilemmas of Security: Politics, Strategy, and the Israeli Experience in Lebanon* (Oxford: Oxford University Press, 1987).

10 See Schiff and Ya'ari, *Israel's Lebanon War.*

Ex Oriente Nebula: An Inquiry into the Nature of Khomeini's Ideology

1 Nikki R. Keddie and Eric Hooglund, eds., *The Iranian Revolution and the Islamic Republic,* Proceedings of a conference held at the Woodrow

Wilson International Center for Scholars (Washington, D.C.: Middle East Institute, 1982), pp. 9–10. [Hereinafter cited as *IR*.]

2 Ernest R. Sandeen, *The Roots of Fundamentalism: British and American Millenarianism, 1800–1930* (Chicago: University of Chicago Press, 1970).

3 Seyed Hossein Nasr, *Ideals and Realities in Islam* (Boston: Beacon Press, 1972), p. 42.

4 R. M. Savory, "The Religious Environment in the Middle East," in Robert A. Kilmarx and Yonah Alexander, eds., *Business and the Middle East: Threats and Prospects* (New York: Pergamon Press, 1982), p. 19. See also H. A. R. Gibb, *Modern Trends in Islam* (Chicago: University of Chicago Press, 1947), p. 27.

5 *Fontana Dictionary of Modern Thought*, ed. Alan Bullock and Oliver Stallbrass (London: Fontana, 1977), s.v. "millenarianism."

6 Norman Cohn, *The Pursuit of the Millennium: Revolutionary Millenarians and Mystical Anarchists of the Middle Ages* (1957; rev. ed., New York: Oxford University Press, 1977), pp. 59–60.

7 Charles S. Prigmore, *Social Work in Iran since the White Revolution* (University: University of Alabama Press, 1976), p. 19.

8 Cohn, *Pursuit of the Millennium*, p. 60.

9 Ibid.

10 Sandeen, *Roots of Fundamentalism*, pp. 107–8.

11 Asaf A. A. Fyzee, *A Shi'ite Creed* (Oxford: Oxford University Press, 1942), p. 98.

12 Ibid., p. 96.

13 Gabriel Fackre, *The Religious Right and Christian Faith* (Grand Rapids, Mich.: Eerdmans, 1982), pp. 87, 96.

14 R. K. Ramazani, *Khumayni's Islam in Iran's Foreign Policy*, in *Islam in Foreign Policy*, ed. Adeed Dawisha (Cambridge: Cambridge University Press, 1983), p. 15.

15 Keith Feiling, *A History of England from the Coming of the English to 1938* (London, 1950), p. 740.

16 Ayatollah Ruhollah Khomeyni, *Islamic Government*, Translations on Near East and North Africa, no. 1897 (Arlington, Va.: Joint Publications Research Center, 1979), p. 18 [JPRS–72663].

17 Gregory Rose, "Factional Alignments in the Central Council of the Islamic Republican Party of Iran: A Preliminary Taxonomy," in *IR*, p. 46.

18 J. M. Thompson, *Robespierre* (Oxford: Blackwell, 1935), vol. 2, p. 140.

19 Ibid.

20 Ibid., p. 143.

21 Ibid., p. 209.

22 Ibid., p. 51.

23 *Fontana Dictionary of Modern Thought*, ed. Bullock and Stallybrass, s.v. "socialism."

24 Thompson, *Robespierre*, vol. 2, p. 140.

25 Ibid., p. 230.

26 L. P. Elwell-Sutton, "Fundamentalism in Flood," *Times Literary Supplement*, August 28, 1981, p. 987.
27 David Shub, *Lenin: A Biography* (New York: Pelican Books, 1966), p. 313.
28 See Roger M. Savory, "Khumayni's Islamic Revolutionary Movement," in Robert A. Spencer, ed., *Iran-Iraq and the Gulf War* (Toronto: Centre for International Studies, University of Toronto, 1982), pp. 32–54.
29 *Constitution of the Islamic Republic of Iran*, trans. Hamid Algar (Berkeley: Mizan Press, 1980), p. 31.
30 *IranVoice*, March 3, 1980, p. 7.
31 *IranVoice*, January 21, 1980, p. 2.
32 Ibid.
33 Savory, "Khumayni's Islamic Revolutionary Movement," pp. 48–49.
34 *Toronto Globe and Mail*, November 2, 1981.
35 Azar Tabrizi, "Mystifications of the Past and Illusions of the Future," in *IR*, p. 112.
36 *Islam and Revolution: Writings and Declarations of Imam Khomeini*, trans. and annotated by Hamid Algar (Berkeley: Mizan Press, 1981), p. 297.
37 Ibid., p. 298.
38 Nikki R. Keddie (with a section by Yann Richard), *Roots of Revolution* (New Haven, Conn.: Yale University Press, 1981), p. 224.
39 Ibid., p. 228.
40 Ibid., p. 227.
41 This is not a novel idea. In the early 1950s Prime Minister Muhammad Musaddeq asserted that "whatever corruption took place in Iran was the result of the AIOC [Anglo-Iranian Oil Company]." Rouhollah K. Ramazani, *Iran's Foreign Policy, 1941–1973* (Charlottesville: University Press of Virginia, 1975), p. 190.
42 *Marja'-i taqlid:* primus inter pares among the mujtahids, the highest legal authority to which a person may have recourse on a matter of religious law.
43 Willem M. Floor, "The Revolutionary Character of the Iranian 'Ulama: Wishful Thinking or Reality?" *International Journal of Middle East Studies* 12 (1980): 504.
44 Ibid., p. 509.
45 Maxime Rodinson, "Islam's Growing Political Power," reprinted from *Le Monde* in *Atlas World Press Review*, March 1971, p. 21.

The PLO: Millennium and Organization

1 Max Weber, *On Law in Economy and Society*, trans. Edward Shils and Max Rheinstein (New York: Simon and Schuster, 1967), pp. 334–37.
2 On the geographical distribution of Palestinians, see Rony E. Gabbay, A *Political Study of the Arab-Jewish Conflict* (Geneva: Librarie E. Droz,

1959), pp. 169ff; *Arab Press Service*, 16 September 1985; 18 June 1984; 2 September 1985; 16 November 1983. For more general treatments of how the distribution came about, see Don Peretz, "The Arab-Israeli War: Israel's Administration and the Arab Refugees," *Foreign Affairs* 46, no. 2 (January 1968): 336–46; Peter Dodd and Halim Barakat, "Palestinian Refugees of 1967: A Sociological Study," *Muslim World* 60, no. 1 (April 1970): 123–42; Cheryl Rubenberg, *The Palestine Liberation Organization: Its Institutional Infrastructure*, Palestine Studies no. 1 (Belmont, Mass.: Institute of Arab Studies, 1983), pp. 8–9.

3 On the Jordan Civil War itself, see *The Times* (London), 23 September 1970; *Time*, 21 September 1970, p. 18; *Newsweek*, 21 September 1970, p. 20. The movement itself was also part of a PLO strategy to move its bases of operations farther away from the front lines with Israel. See Arafat interview in *al-Watan al-'Arabi*, 25–31 October 1979, pp. 28–31.

4 Yoram Ben-Porath and Emanuel Marx, *Some Sociological and Economic Aspects of Refugee Camps* (Santa Monica, Calif.: Rand, 1971), pp. 16–20.

5 On the emotional attitudes of these Palestinians, see Jabra I. Jabra, "The Palestinian Exile as a Writer," *Journal of Palestine Studies* 8, no. 2 (Winter 1979): 77–87.

6 See Sulafa Hijjawi, trans., *Poetry of Resistance in Occupied Palestine* (Baghdad: al-Jumhuriya Printing House, 1968).

7 Fawaz Turki, "To Be a Palestinian," *Journal of Palestine Studies* 3, no. 3 (Spring 1974): 12.

8 Gabbay, *A Political Study of the Arab-Jewish Conflict*, pp. 202–19.

9 Ibid.

10 *Arab Press Service*, 18 June 1984, 16 September 1985.

11 *Arab Press Service*, 7 May 1984, 18 June 1984, 9/16 November 1984.

12 See Malcolm Kerr, *The Arab Cold War*, 1958–1967, 3d ed. (New York: Oxford University Press, 1971); William S. Quandt, Fuad Jabber, and Ann Mosley Lesch, *The Politics of Palestinian Nationalism* (Berkeley and Los Angeles: University of California Press, 1973), pp. 186–98.

13 Y. Porath, *The Emergence of the Palestinian-Arab National Movement, 1918–1929* (London: Frank Cass, 1974); Sami Hadawi, *Bitter Harvest: Palestine Between 1914 and 1967* (New York: New World Press, 1967).

14 See Abu Nidal interview with Fulvio Grimaldi, *L'expresso*, 21 May 1978.

15 The "will" of the Munich guerrillas in *Wafa*, 11 September 1972.

16 Quoted in *Liberation* (Paris), 25 April 1983.

17 Excerpted in *Arab World Weekly*, 1 February 1969.

18 George Habash, *May Day Speech*, excerpted in *Arab World Weeky*, 10 May 1975.

19 See the comments of Ghassan Tuwayni, "Arafat and the PLO," in *an-Nahar Arab Report*, 2 December 1974.

20 These organizational elements are set forth in some detail in Amatai Etzioni, *Political Unification: A Comparative Study of Leaders and Forces* (New York: Holt, Rinehart and Winston, 1965), pp. 3–13.

21 Weber, *On Law in Economy and Society*, p. 334.
22 On early Palestinian politics, see Porath, *The Emergence of the Palestinian-Arab National Movement*.
23 This definition is abstracted from the work of Steffen W. Schmidt, Laura Gausti, Carl H. Lande, and James C. Scott, *Friends, Followers, and Factions: A Reader in Political Clientelism* (Berkeley and Los Angeles: University of California Press, 1977).
24 For an exhaustive analysis of the development of PLO organizational structure, see Rubenberg, *The Palestine Liberation Organization;* Helena Cobban, *The Palestinian Liberation Organization: People, Power and Politics* (Cambridge: Cambridge University Press, 1984), pp. 245ff.
25 See *Arab World*, 28 November 1969; *an-Nahar Arab Report*, 14 July 1975; *Arab Press Service*, 19 August 1985.
26 *al-Anwar*, 10 January 1971; Quandt et al., *The Politics of Palestinian Nationalism*, p. 129.
27 On the Rejection Front and Syrian domination of that front, see *Arab World Daily*, 12 June 1970; *Arab World Daily*, 19 October 1971; *Arab World Weekly*, 20 January 1978; *Arab Press Service*, 16/23 January 1984; and Abu Nidal interview, *L'espresso*, 21 May 1978.
28 *Middle East Intelligence Service*, 16–30 April 1978; *Arab Report and Record*, 16–30 April 1978; *Los Angeles Times*, 25 April 1978; *al-Siyasa*, 30 April 1979.
29 *Arab Press Service*, 13 February 1984.
30 Barry Rubin, "Yasser Arafat's Tightrope in Arab Politics," in Shireen Hunter, ed., *The PLO After Tripoli* (Washington, D.C.: Center for Strategic and International Studies, 1984), pp. 11–17.
31 *Arab Press Service*, 19 August 1985.
32 Ibid.
33 Ibid.
34 *Arab Press Service*, 16/23 January 1984, 29 July 1985.
35 Ibid.

Kurdish Nationalism

1 Rupert Emerson, *Self-Determination Revisited in the Era of Decolonization* (Cambridge, Mass.: Center for International Affairs, Harvard University, 1964), p. 11.
2 Yosef Gotlieb, *Self-Determination in the Middle East* (New York: Praeger, 1982), p. 72.
3 Derk Kinnane, *The Kurds and Kurdistan* (London: Oxford University Press, 1964), p. 2.
4 Nikki R. Keddie, "The Minorities Question in Iran," in Shirin Tahir-Kheli and Shaheen Ayubi, eds., *The Iran-Iraq War* (New York: Praeger, 1983), p. 91.
5 Stephen C. Pelletiere, *The Kurds: An Unstable Element in the Gulf* (Boulder, Colo.: Westview Press, 1984), p. 16.
6 Keddie, "Minorities Question," p. 91.

7 Great Britain, Naval Intelligence Division, *Iraq and the Persian Gulf* (1944), p. 325.
8 Kinnane, *Kurds and Kurdistan*, p. 22.
9 Pelletiere, *Unstable Element*, p. 26.
10 Slightly differing versions of this are given in Pelletiere, ibid., p. 51, and Kinnane, *Kurds and Kurdistan*, p. 24.
11 William Eagleton, Jr., *The Kurdish Republic of 1946* (London: Oxford University Press, 1963), p. 10.
12 Sa'ad Jawad, *Iraq & the Kurdish Question, 1958–1970* (London: Ithaca Press, 1981), pp. 5–6; Hassan Arfa, *The Kurds: An Historical and Political Study* (London: Oxford University Press, 1966), pp. 29–32.
13 J. C. Hurevitz, *Diplomacy in the Near and Middle East: A Documentary Record, 1914–1956* (Princeton, N.J.: Princeton University Press, 1956), 2: 82.
14 A well-informed, if hostile, account, based on archival material of British dealings with the Arabs before, during, and after the war, is to be found in H. V. F. Winstone, *The Illicit Adventure. The Story of Political and Military Intelligence in the Middle East from 1898 to 1926* (London: Jonathan Cape, 1982). Winstone, however, is silent on the subject of the Kurds.
15 Arfa, *The Kurds*, p. 21.
16 Turkey had lost the Dodecanese Islands and Tripoli to Italy in 1912, and some wartime Allied agreements had envisaged also giving Smyrna to Italy.
17 Pelletiere, *Unstable Element*, p. 93.
18 Edmund Ghareeb, *The Kurdish Question in Iraq* (Syracuse, N.Y.: Syracuse University Press, 1981), pp. 8–11.
19 See Ghareeb, *Kurdish Question*, pp. 9–11.
20 Eagleton, *Kurdish Republic*, p. 14.
21 There are two very good sources on the Mahabad Republic: Eagleton, *Kurdish Republic*, and Archie Roosevelt, Jr., "The Kurdish Republic of Mahabad," *Middle East Journal* 1, no. 3 (July 1947): 247–69. Roosevelt's article is reprinted in Gerard Chaliand, ed., *People without a Country: The Kurds and Kurdistan* (London: Zed Press, 1980), pp. 135–52, where it is rather *hors serie*, having been written more than thirty years before the other material in the book. Arfa also has a fascinating personal account in *The Kurds*, pp. 70–102.
22 Arfa, *The Kurds*, p. 72.
23 C. J. Edmunds, "Kurdish Nationalism," *Journal of Contemporary History* 6, no. 1 (1971): 97.
24 Pelletiere, *Unstable Element*, p. 106.
25 Roosevelt, "Kurdish Republic," p. 268.
26 Ghareeb, *Kurdish Question*, pp. 12–13.
27 Ibid., pp. 1–2.
28 See Uriel Dann: "The Kurdish National Movement in Iraq," *Jerusalem Quarterly*, no. 9 (Fall 1978): 131–44.
29 "Mulla" was a personal name in this case, not a religious title. Sheikh

Ahmad was a religious eccentric with a remarkable talent for remaining "above the battle." He was always regarded by the authorities, Iraqi or British, as more of a moderate than his impetuous brother. He died in 1969.

30 Pelletiere, *Unstable Element*, p. 97.

31 Dann, "Kurdish National Movement," p. 135.

32 A detailed history of relations in these years may be found in Pelletiere, *Unstable Element*, pp. 115–92.

33 Text in Arfa, *The Kurds*, p. 134.

34 A detailed retelling of different versions from the different parties of what happened is in Pelletiere, *Unstable Element*, pp. 139–57.

35 Tereq Y. Ismael, *Iraq and Iran: Roots of Conflict* (Syracuse, N.Y.: Syracuse University Press, 1982), pp. 61–63.

36 George Lenczowski, *The Middle East in World Affairs*, 4th ed. (Ithaca, N.Y.: Cornell University Press, 1980), p. 220.

37 Dann, "Kurdish National Movement," p. 143.

38 See Arthur Campbell Turner, "Nationalism and Religion: Iran and Iraq at War," in James Brown and William P. Snyder, eds., *The Regionalization of Warfare* (New Brunswick, N.J., and Oxford: Transaction Books, 1985), pp. 144–63.

The Persian Gulf: Stability, Access to Oil, and Security

1 See John Duke Anthony, "The Iran-Iraq War: Regional and International Implications," in M. S. El-Azhary, ed., *The Iran-Iraq War: An Historical, Economic, and Political Analysis* (London: Croom Helm), pp. 105–25.

2 Edmund Ghareeb, "The Forgotten War," *American-Arab Affairs* 5 (Summer 1983): 59–75. See also Anthony H. Cordesman, "The Iraq-Iran War: Attrition Now, Chaos Later," *Armed Forces Journal International* 120, no. 10 (May 1983): 36, 38, 40–41, 116–17; "The Iran-Iraq War in 1984: An Escalating Threat to the Gulf and the West," *Armed Forces Journal International* 121 (March 1984): 22–24, 27, 30, 75; and "The Gulf Crisis and Strategic Interests: A Military Analysis," *American-Arab Affairs* 9 (Summer 1984): 8–15.

3 See John Duke Anthony, *The Gulf Cooperation Council and America's National Interests*, National Council Reports Series, no. 3 (Washington, D.C.: National Council on U.S.-Arab Relations, 1985).

4 See Richard Cottam, "The Iran-Iraq War," *Current History* 83, no. 489 (January 1984): 9–12, 40–41; Adeed Dawisha, "Iraq and the Arab World: The Gulf War and After," *The World Today* 37, no. 5 (May 1981): 188–94; Stephen R. Grummon, *The Iran-Iraq War: Islam Embattled*, Washington Papers, no. 92 (New York: Praeger, for the Georgetown University Center for Strategic and International Studies, 1982); and Christine Moss Helms, *Iraq: Eastern Flank of the Arab World* (Washington, D.C.: Brookings Institution, 1984).

5 "Politics and Dissent," in John Christie, ed., *Gulf States Newsletter* 287 (May 19, 1986): 2.
6 The single best annotated bibliography on the subject is J. E. Peterson, *Security in the Arabian Peninsula and the Gulf States, 1973–1984*, Occasional Papers Series, no. 7 (Washington, D.C.: National Council on U.S.-Arab Relations, 1985). See also id., *The Politics of Middle Eastern Oil* (Washington, D.C.: Middle East Institute, 1984) and "Defending Arabia: Evolution of Responsibility," *Orbis* 28 (Fall 1984): 465–88.
7 See the excellent survey article by Thomas L. McNaugher, "Arms and Allies on the Arabian Peninsula," *Orbis* 28, no. 2 (Fall 1984): 489–526.
8 See, for example, Miles Ignotus, "Seizing Arab Oil," *Harper's* 250, no. 1498 (March 1975): 45–62; and Joseph Churba, Edward Friedland, and Aaron Wildavsky, *The Great Détente: Oil and the Decline of American Foreign Policy* (New York: Basic Books, 1974). During 1987 armed U.S. intervention moved from scenario to engagement with Iranian forces.
9 See Ronald G. Wolfe, ed., *The United States, Arabia, and the Gulf* (Washington, D.C.: Georgetown University Center for Contemporary Arab Studies, 1980).
10 See Joseph Story, *U.S.-Arab Relations: The Economic Dimension* (Washington, D.C.: Georgetown University Center for Contemporary Arab Studies, 1980).
11 See John G. Sarpa, *U.S.-Arab Relations: The Commercial Dimension* (Washington, D.C.: National Council on U.S.-Arab Relations, 1983).
12 See ibid., and Story, *Economic Dimension;* also *U.S.-Arab Trade Investment and Technology Transfer: A Time of Transition*, National Council Report Series, no. 4 (Washington, D.C.: National Council on U.S.-Arab Relations, 1985).
13 Odeh Aburdene, "U.S. Economic and Financial Relations with Saudi Arabia, Kuwait, and the United Arab Emirates," *American-Arab Affairs* no. 7 (Winter 1983–84): 76–84.
14 See Anthony, *Gulf Cooperation Council and America's National Interests.*
15 Ibid.
16 See John Duke Anthony, *The Iran-Iraq War and the Gulf Cooperation Council*, National Council Reports Series, no. 2 (Washington, D.C.: National Council on U.S.-Arab Relations, 1984).
17 Anthony H. Cordesman, "The Oil Glut and the Strategic Importance of the Gulf States," *Armed Forces Journal International* 121, no. 3 (October 1983): 30–47.
19 See Robert G. Lawrence, "Arab Perceptions of U.S. Security Policy in Southwest Asia," *American-Arab Affairs* 5 (1983): 27–38; also Sarpa, *Commercial Dimension*, and *Trade, Investment, and Technology Transfer.*
20 Story, *Economic Dimension.*
21 See Peterson, *Security in the Arabian Peninsula*, pp. 49–71.
22 See Shirin Tahir-Kheli and Shaheen Ayubi, eds., *The Iran-Iraq War: New Weapons, Old Conflicts* (New York: Praeger, for the Foreign Policy Institute, 1983); also James A. Bill, "The Arab World and the

Challenge of Iran," *Journal of Arab Affairs* 2, no. 2 (Spring 1983): 155–71; Shahram Chubin, "The Iran-Iraq War and Persian Gulf Security," *International Defense Review* 17, no. 6 (1984): 705–12, and R. K. Ramazani, "Iran's Islamic Revolution and the Persian Gulf," *Current History* 84, no. 498 (January 1985): 5–8, 40–41.

23 U.S. Congress, Senate, Committee on Foreign Relations. Subcommittee on Near Eastern and South Asian Affairs, *U.S. Security Interests and Politics in Southwest Asia*, Hearings, February 6, 7, 20, 27, and March 4 and 18, 1980 (Washington, D.C.: U.S. Government Printing Office, 1980).

24 Robert P. Haffa, Jr., *The Half War: Planning U.S. Rapid Deployment Forces to Meet a Limited Contingency, 1960–1983* (Boulder, Colo.: Westview Press, 1984); Richard Halloran, "Poised for the Persian Gulf," *New York Times Magazine*, April 1, 1984, pp. 38–40, 61.

25 U.S. Congress, Senate, *U.S. Security Interests and Policies in Southwest Asia* (cited in note 23 above).

26 John Duke Anthony, "Strategic Oman," *Journal of Defense and Diplomacy* (January 1985): 12–14.

27 See John Duke Anthony, "The Arab States of the Gulf," in *U.S. National Security Policies for the 1980s* (Washington, D.C.: National War College, 1980).

28 Martin L. Cover, "FMF (Fleet Marine Force) for the RDF," *U.S. Naval Institute Proceedings* 108, no. 6 (June 1982): 51–55.

29 Marshall L. Miller, "Will Iran or Iraq Close the Straits of Hormuz?" *Armed Forces Journal International* 121, no. 5 (December 1983): 24–26. See also Thomas M. Johnson and Raymond T. Barrett, "Mining the Strait of Hormuz," *U.S. Naval Institute Proceedings* 107, no. 12 (December 1981): 83–85. A more extended discussion of the strait can be found in Rouhollah K. Ramazani, *The Persian Gulf and the Strait of Hormuz* (Alphen aan den Rijn: Sijthoff and Nordhoff, 1979).

30 See, for example, Christopher Van Hollen, "Don't Engulf the Gulf," *Foreign Affairs* 59, no. 5 (1981): 1064–78, and I. William Zartman, "The Power of American Purposes," *Middle East Journal* 35, no. 2 (Spring 1981): 163–77.

31 U.S. Congress, House of Representatives, Committee on Foreign Affairs, Subcommittee on Europe and the Middle East, *U.S. Interests in, and Policies toward, the Persian Gulf*, 1980, Hearings, March 24, April 2, May 5, July 1 and 28, and September 3, 1980.

32 One of the best overall accounts of events during this period is James H. Noyes, *The Clouded Lens: Persian Gulf Security and U.S. Policy*, 2d ed. (Stanford, Calif.: Hoover Institution Press, 1982).

33 The most unabashed advocate of turning back the clock in terms of the relationship between imperial powers and the Arabian Peninsula is J. B. Kelly, *Arabia, the Gulf, and the West: A Critical View of the Arabs and Their Oil Policy* (London: Weidenfeld and Nicolson, 1980). Kelly, a New Zealander popular among American far-right strategists associated with the Heritage Foundation, was prominent in the 1981 efforts by the

Israeli lobby to defeat President Reagan's proposal to sell Airborne Warning and Control Systems (AWACS) to Saudi Arabia.

34 Jonathan Alford, "Les Occidentaux et la securite de Golfe," *Politique Etrangere* 46, no. 3 (September 1981): 667–90. See also Valerie Yorke, "Oil, the Middle East, and Japan's Search for Security," *International Affairs* (London) 57, no. 3 (1981): 428–48, and the essays by Neville Brown and Makoto Momoi on European and Japanese concerns respectively in Abbas Amirie, ed., *The Persian Gulf and Indian Ocean in International Politics* (Tehran: Institute for International Political and Economic Studies, 1975).

35 See James A. Bill, "The Challenge of the Iranian Revolution and the Iran-Iraq War to Stability in the Gulf," in Philip H. Stoddard, ed., *The Middle East in the 1980s: Problems and Prospects* (Washington, D.C.: Middle East Institute, 1983), pp. 122–29.

36 Mazheer Hameed, *Arabia Imperiled: The Security Imperatives of the Arab Gulf States* (Washington, D.C.: Middle East Assessments Group, 1986).

37 See, for example, Faisal Al-Salem, "The U.S. and the Gulf: What Do the Arabs Want?" *Journal of South Asian and Middle Eastern Studies* 6, no. 1 (1982): 8–32; Abdulaziz H. Al-Sowayyegh, *Arab Petropolitics* (London: Croom Helm, 1984); and Bruce R. Kuniholm, "What the Saudis Really Want: A Primer for the Reagan Administration," *Orbis* 25, no. 1 (Spring 1981): 107–21. See also Robert W. Tucker, *The Purposes of American Power: An Essay on National Security* (New York: Praeger, 1981), and "American Power and the Persian Gulf," *Commentary* 70, no. 5 (November 1980): 25–41.

38 Hermann Frederick Eilts, "Security Considerations in the Persian Gulf," *International Security* 5, no. 2 (1980): 79–113, and no. 4 (1981): 186–203; Fred Halliday, *Soviet Policy in the Arc of Crisis* (Washington, D.C.: Institute for Policy Studies, 1981). On the background to Moscow's close strategic political and military relations with Aden, see John Duke Anthony, "USSR-PDRY Relations," in *Diego Garcia: Debate over the Base*, U.S. Congress, House of Representatives, Hearings (Washington, D.C.: U.S. Government Printing Office, 1976); and "The People's Democratic Republic of Yemen," in *International Yearbook on Communist Affairs* (Stanford, Calif.: Hoover Institution, 1982, 1983, and 1984). See also Stephen Page, "Soviet Policy toward the Arabian Peninsula," in Stoddard, ed., *Middle East in the 1980s*, pp. 88–98.

39 Eilts, "Security in the Persian Gulf."

40 See, for example, James A. Phillips, *Moscow Stalks the Persian Gulf* (Washington, D.C.: Heritage Foundation, 1984), and David Lynn Price, "Moscow and the Persian Gulf," *Problems of Communism* 2 (March–April, 1979): 1–13.

41 See Brown, *U.S. Security Policy in Southwest Asia.*

42 Talcott Seelye, *U.S. Arab Relations: The Syrian Dimension* (Washington, D.C.: National Council on U.S.-Arab Relations, 1984).

43 See Eric Davis, "The Political Economy of the Arab Oil-Producing Na-

tions: Convergence with Western Interests," *Studies in Comparative International Development* 14, no. 2 (1979): 75–94.

44 One of the most consistently pro-Israel U.S. senators in recent years has been Rudy Boschwitz (R-Minn.). In May of 1986, at the time of the congressional vote on the Reagan administration's proposal to sell additional missiles to Saudi Arabia, the senator arranged for wealthy pro-Israel businessman Michael Goland, an American, to meet with key senators for the purpose of pressuring them to emulate Boschwitz's decision to oppose the president. In 1984 Goland spent $1.6 million to help defeat former Senate Foreign Relations Committee chairman Charles Percy, who, in the course of rendering consistent support for the president had taken stands on issues of importance to Israel that had been unpopular in Tel Aviv (*Washington Post*, May 5, 1986). For a more comprehensive account of the intimidating power of the Israeli lobby on issues where American national interests and those of Israel diverge, see Paul Findley, *They Dare to Speak Out: People and Institutions Confront Israel's Lobby* (Westport, Conn.: Lawrence Hill, 1985).

45 David E. Long, "U.S.-Saudi Relations: A Foundation of Mutual Needs," *American-Arab Affairs* 4 (Spring 1983): 12–22; William B. Quandt, *Saudi Arabia in the 1980s: Foreign Policy, Security, and Oil* (Washington, D.C.: Brookings Institution, 1981); Emile A. Nakhleh, *The United States and Saudi Arabia: A Policy Analysis* (Washington, D.C.: American Enterprise Institute, 1975); and John Duke Anthony, "Foreign Policy: The View from Riyadh," *Wilson Quarterly* 3, no. 1 (1979): 73–81.

46 For the background leading up to the kingdom's request for the F-15s and the context in which the Carter administration promoted the sale, see Dale R. Tahtinen, *National Security Challenges to Saudi Arabia* (Washington, D.C.: American Enterprise Institute, 1978).

47 Anthony Cordesman, *The Gulf and the Search for Strategic Stability: Saudi Arabia, the Military Balance in the Gulf, and Trends in the Arab-Israeli Military Balance* (Boulder, Colo.: Westview Press, 1984).

48 For an account of how the Israeli lobby has affected U.S. efforts to forge a stronger relationship with Iraq, see the interview of Iraqi Deputy Prime Minister Tariq Aziz by Anthony H. Cordesman in *The Iran-Iraq War and U.S.-Iraq Relations: An Iraqi Perspective*, National Council Reports Series, no. 1 (Washington, D.C.: National Council on U.S.-Arab Relations, 1983).

49 For background on the origins and early development of the GCC, see John Duke Anthony, "The Gulf Cooperation Council," *Journal of Middle Eastern and South Asian Studies* 5, no. 4 (1982): 3–18. See, too, id., "The Gulf Cooperation Council," *International Journal* 42, no. 2 (Spring 1986); Abdulla Yacoub Bishara, "The GCC: Achievements and Challenges," *American-Arab Affairs* 7 (1983–84): 40–44; *The Gulf Cooperation Council: Its Nature and Outlook*, GCC Reports Series, no. 1 (Washington, D.C.: National Council on U.S.-Arab Relations, 1986), and Abdullah El-Kuwaize, "The Gulf Cooperation Council and the Con-

cept of Economic Integration," *American-Arab Affairs* 7 (1983–84): 45–49.

50 John Duke Anthony, "The Gulf Cooperation Council," in Richard Sindelar, ed., *Swirling Currents: The Gulf in the 1980s* (Washington, D.C.: Middle East Institute, 1986); see also Rex B. Wingerter, "The Gulf Cooperation Council and American Interests in the Gulf," *American-Arab Affairs* 9 (1986): 15–26.

51 On Saudi Arabia, see A. R. Kelidar, "The Problems of Succession in Saudi Arabia," *Asian Affairs* (London) 65 (n.s. 9), pt. 1 (February 1978): 5, 23–30; Joseph Nevo, "The Saudi Royal Family: The Third Generation," *Jerusalem Quarterly* 31 (Spring 1984): 79–90; David E. Long, *Saudi Arabia* (Beverly Hills: Sage, 1976); John Duke Anthony, "Saudi Arabia's Relations with the Arab States of the Gulf," in Tim Niblock, ed., *State, Society, and Economy in Saudi Arabia* (London: Croom Helm, 1982), and "Saudi Arabia: Riding the Tiger," *Baltimore Sun* (December 31, 1978, Perspective Section, pp. 1–2); David Holden and Richard Johns, *The House of Saud: The Rise and Fall of the Most Powerful Dynasty in the Arab World* (New York: Holt, Rinehart and Winston, 1982); Robert Lacey, *The Kingdom: Arabia and the House of Saud* (New York: Harcourt Brace Jovanovich, 1982); and Amos A. Jordan, Jr., "Saudi Arabia: The Next Iran?" *Parameters: Journal of the U.S. Army War College* 9, no. 1 (March 1979): 2–8.

On Oman, see J. E. Peterson, *Oman in the Twentieth Century: Political Foundations of an Emerging State* (London: Croom Helm, 1978); John Townsend, *Oman: The Making of a Modern State* (London: Croom Helm, 1977); Dale F. Eickelman, "Kings and People: Oman's State Consultative Council," *Middle East Journal* 38, no. 1 (Winter 1984): 51–71, and J. E. Peterson, "Legitimacy and Political Change in Yemen and Oman," *Orbis* 27, no. 4 (1984): 971–98.

On the UAE, see John Duke Anthony, *Arab States of the Lower Gulf: People, Politics, Petroleum* (Washington, D.C.: Middle East Institute, 1975); "The United Arab Emirates: Transformation Amidst Tradition," in Shahram Chubin, ed., *Security in the Persian Gulf: Domestic Political Factors* (London: Gower, 1982); "The United Arab Emirates," in Richard D. Erb, ed., "The Arab Oil-Producing States of the Gulf: Political and Economic Developments," *AEI Foreign Policy and Defense Review*, 2, nos. 3–4 (1980); *The United Arab Emirates: A Political Analysis* (Philadelphia: Middle East Research Institute, 1983); and "The United Arab Emirates," in Michael Adams, ed., *The Middle East: A Handbook*, 2d ed. (London: M. Blond, 1987). See, too, Ali Mohammed Khalifa, *The United Arab Emirates: Unity in Fragmentation* (Boulder, Colo.: Westview Press, 1979); and the superb account by Malcolm C. Peck, *Venture in Unity: The United Arab Emirates* (Boulder, Colo.: Westview Press, 1986).

On Qatar, see Helga Graham, *Arabian Time Machine: Self Portrait of an Oil State* (London: Heinemann, 1978). On Kuwait, see Jacqueline S.

Ismael, *Kuwait: Social Change in Historical Perspective* (Syracuse, N.Y.: Syracuse University Press, 1982); Hassan Ali Al-Ebraheem, *Kuwait and the Gulf: Small States and the International System* (Washington, D.C.: Georgetown University, Center for Contemporary International Studies, 1984); and John Duke Anthony and John A. Hearty, "The Emirates of Eastern Arabia," in David E. Long and Bernard Reich, eds., *Governments and Politics in the Middle East and North Africa* (Boulder, Colo.: Westview Press, 1980). On Bahrain, see Emile A. Nakhleh, *Bahrain: Political Development in a Modernizing Society* (Lexington, Mass.: Lexington Books, 1976); Fuad I. Khuri, *Tribe and State in Bahrain: The Transformation of Social and Political Authority in an Arab State* (Chicago: University of Chicago Press, 1990); and John Duke Anthony, "Bahrain," in Adams, ed., *The Middle East: A Handbook*.

52 Anthony, "Strategic Oman"; see also id., *U.S.-Arab Relations: The Oman Dimension* (Washington, D.C.: National Council on U.S.-Arab Relations, 1987), and Thomas M. Johnson and Raymond T. Barrett, "Omani Navy: Operating in Troubled Waters," *U.S. Naval Institute Proceedings* 108, no. 3 (1982): 99–103.

53 Nakhleh, *Bahrain: Political Development in a Modernizing Society*.

54 Such statements were issued by GCC officials in press conferences of the GCC heads of state summits in Doha, Qatar, in 1983, in Kuwait in 1984, in Oman in 1985, and in Abu Dhabi in 1986.

55 For the historical background, see Benson Lee Grayson, *Saudi-American Relations* (Lanham, Md.: University Press of America, 1982); see also Jim Hoagland and J. P. Smith, "Saudi Arabia and the United States: Security and Interdependence," *Survival* 20, no. 2 (1978): 80–83, and Long, "U.S.-Saudi Relations."

56 See U.S. Congress, House Subcommittee on Europe and the Middle East, *Saudi Arabia and the United States: The New Context in an Evolving "Special Relationship"* (Washington, D.C.: U.S. Government Printing Office, 1981); House Committee on Foreign Affairs, Subcommittees on International and Scientific Affairs, and on Europe and the Middle East, *Proposed U.S. Arms Sales to Saudi Arabia* (Washington, D.C.: U.S. Government Printing Office, 1980); Senate Committee on Armed Services, *Military and Technical Implications of the Proposed Sale to Saudi Arabia of Airborne Warning and Control System* (AWACS) *and F-15 Enhancements* (Washington, D.C.: U.S. Government Printing Office, 1981); Senate Committee on Foreign Relations, *Arms Sale Package to Saudi Arabia*, pts. 1 and 2 (Washington, D.C.: U.S. Government Printing Office, 1981), and *The Proposed AWACS/F-15 Enhancement Sale to Saudi Arabia: Staff Report* (Washington, D.C.: U.S. Government Printing Office, 1981).

57 The consensus of most military analysts, based on the total dollar value associated with the ten-year life-span of the kingdom's "Peace Shield" air defense program (1976–86), is that the actual dollar amount of the aircraft sale that the United States forfeited to the United Kingdom in 1985

will amount to $20–21 billion. On the basis of U.S. Department of Labor figures that for each $1 billion of U.S. exports of goods and services, a minimum of 25,000 jobs are generated, the loss in terms of domestic U.S. employment opportunities can be conservatively estimated in terms of hundreds of thousands of jobs. See Thomas R. Stauffer, "Economic Implications of Lost Trade Opportunities in the Middle East, Military and Commercial," *American-Arab Affairs* 9 (1986): 9–14. Asked why he opposed Saudi Arabia purchasing additional F-15s (from McDonnell-Douglas Corporation, the manufacturer of the planes in his own district), when to do so meant forgoing an opportunity to ease the unemployment situation of his constituents, Congressman Harold Volkmer D-Mo.) responded: "Because I totally support Israel." (Thomas R. Stauffer, *Christian Science Monitor*, October 9, 1985, p. 19.)

58 The literature on the limitations of, and constraints on, the Rapid Deployment Joint Task Force and its successor, the Central Command, is extensive. See, for example, E. Asa Bates, "The Rapid Deployment Force: Fact or Fiction?" *RUSI–Journal of the Royal United Services Institute for Defense Studies* 126, no. 2 (June 1981): 23–33; Raymond E. Bell, Jr., "The Rapid Deployment Force: How Much, How Soon?" *Army* 30 (July 1980): 18–24; Michael R. Gordon, "The Rapid Deployment Force—Too Large, Too Small, or Just Right for Its Task?" *National Journal* (March 13, 1982), pp. 451–55; Joseph R. Holzbauer, "RDF—Valid and Necessary, but Some Negative Implications," *Marine Corps Gazette* 64 (August 1980): 33–38; Maxwell Orme Johnson, *The Military as an Instrument of U.S. Policy in Southwest Asia: The Rapid Deployment Joint Task Force, 1979–1982* (Boulder, Colo.: Westview Press, 1983); Thomas M. Johnson and Raymond T. Barrett, "The Rapid Deployment Joint Task Force," *U.S. Naval Institute Proceedings* 1–6, no. 11 (1980): 95–98; Robert C. Kingston, "From RDF to CENTCOM: New Challengers?" *RUSI–Journal of the Royal United Services Institute for Defense Studies* 129 (1984); and Thomas L. McNaugher, "Rapid Deployment Forces and the Persian Gulf," in *Strategic Survey, 1982–1983* (London: International Institute for Strategic Studies, 1983), pp. 133–38. The most detailed criticism of the Rapid Deployment Force is Jeffrey Record, *The Rapid Deployment Force and U.S. Military Intervention in the Persian Gulf* (Cambridge, Mass.: Institute for Foreign Policy Analysis, 1981).

59 Thomas L. McNaugher, *Arms and Oil: U.S. Military Strategists and the Persian Gulf* (Washington, D.C.: Brookings Institution, 1985).

60 Thomas M. Ricks, *The Iranian People's Revolution: Its Nature and Implications for the Gulf States* (Washington, D.C.: Georgetown University Center for Contemporary Arab Studies, 1979); see also R. K. Ramazani, "Khumayni's Islam in Iran's Foreign Policy," in Adeed Dawisha, ed., *Islam in Foreign Policy* (Cambridge: Cambridge University Press, 1983), pp. 9–32; and Fred Halliday, "The Iranian Revolution in International Affairs: Programme and Practice," *Millennium: Journal of International Studies* 9, no. 2 (1981): 108–21. For a fuller account of the

literature bearing on both the internal and external dimensions of Iran's revolution, see Peterson, *Security in the Arabian Peninsula and the Gulf States*, pp. 124–28.

61 Downplayed or overlooked by most of the American media has been the fact that, by the U.S. government's own admission, the principal organization that assumed responsibility for the security of American diplomatic personnel in the area of Beirut in which the U.S. embassy was located during the late 1970s and into the 1980s, prior to their expulsion at Israeli insistence in 1982, was the PLO.

62 In the mid-1980s, the PLO, alone among all the organizations representing Palestinians in both the occupied territories and the diaspora, continued to favor a settlement of the Palestinian dimension of the Arab-Israeli conflict based not on armed confrontation but on politics and diplomacy.

63 See Harold Saunders, *The Other Walls: The Politics of the Arab-Israeli Peace Process* (Washington, D.C.: American Enterprise Institute, 1986).

64 See John Duke Anthony, Testimony before U.S. Congress, Senate Committee on Foreign Relations, July 10, 1976, *Prospects for Middle East Peace: The Oil Factor* (Washington, D.C.: U.S. Government Printing Office, 1976); see also Leila Meo, ed., *U.S. Strategy in the Gulf: Intervention against Liberation* (Belmont, Mass.: Association of Arab-American University Graduates, 1981).

65 John Duke Anthony, "U.S.-Arab Commercial Relations: From Evangelism to Interdependence," *Middle East Economic Digest*, September 19, 1976, pp. 1–8.

66 See Jim Paul, "Insurrection at Mecca," *MERIP Reports* 91 (1980): 3–4.

67 The single best study of the inability of many U.S. government officials to project themselves into the situations confronting Arab Gulf policy makers on matters pertaining to regional security is Robert G. Lawrence, *U.S. Policy in Southwest Asia: A Failure in Perspective* (Washington, D.C.: National Defense University Press, 1984).

The Dimensions of American Foreign Policy in the Middle East

1 L. Carl Brown, *International Politics and the Middle East* (Princeton, N.J.: Princeton University Press, 1984), pp. 16–18.

2 William R. Polk, *The Arab World* (Cambridge, Mass.: Harvard University Press, 1980), pp. 317–18; George Lenczowski, *Soviet Advances in the Middle East* (Washington, D.C.: American Enterprise Institute, 1971).

3 John Lewis Gaddis, *Strategies of Containment: A Critical Appraisal of Postwar American National Security Policy* (New York: Oxford University Press, 1982), chap. 4.

4 Edward W. Said, *Orientalism* (New York: Random House, Vintage Books, 1979), pp. 54–55, from the French philosopher Gaston Bachelard.

5 Ibid., p. 55.

6 Robert J. Pranger, *Action, Symbolism, and Order: The Existential Dimensions of Modern Citizenship* (Nashville, Tenn.: Vanderbilt University Press, 1968), p. 191; see also Said, *Orientalism*, pp. 322–25.
7 Dan V. Segre, *A Crisis of Identity: Israel and Zionism* (Oxford: Oxford University Press, 1980), p. 140.
8 Fouad Ajami, *The Arab Predicament: Arab Political Thought and Practice since 1967* (Cambridge: Cambridge University Press, 1982).
9 George Lenczowski, *The Middle East in World Affairs*, 4th ed. (Ithaca, N.Y.: Cornell University Press, 1980).
10 William McNeill, *The Rise of the West* (Chicago: University of Chicago Press, 1963).
11 Compare President Truman's rationale for aid to Greece and Turkey in 1947—to create conditions of freedom against totalitarian aggression—with a Soviet view that U.S. Middle East policy is a two-pronged attack against the USSR and the Arab national-liberation movement. See Y. M. Primakov, *Anatomy of the Middle East Conflict* (Moscow: Nauka, 1979), chap. 4, who putatively connects Soviet and Arab liberation interests.
12 Gaddis, *Strategies of Containment*, chaps. 2–4, on symmetrical (perimeter) versus asymmetrical (strong point) containment.
13 The Truman Doctrine was announced on March 12, 1947, in President Truman's message to Congress recommending aid to Greece and Turkey; the Eisenhower Doctrine on January 5, 1957, in President Eisenhower's address to the Congress; and the Carter Doctrine in President Carter's state of the union message on January 23, 1980.
14 See Nixon's first annual foreign policy report to Congress, February 18, 1970, *United States Foreign Policy for the 1970s: A New Strategy for Peace* (Washington, D.C.: U.S. Government Printing Office, 1970), pt. 2, "Partnership and the Nixon Doctrine."
15 On the Reagan "strategic consensus" approach to the Middle East, see Seth P. Tillman, *The United States in the Middle East: Interests and Obstacles* (Bloomington: Indiana University Press, 1982), pp. 36–37, 266–67; Bernard Reich, *The United States and Israel: Influence in the Special Relationship* (New York: Praeger, 1984), chap. 3.
16 Stanley Hoffmann, *Primacy or World Order: American Foreign Policy since the Cold War* (New York: McGraw-Hill, 1978), pt. 2, "The Nightmare of World Order."
17 Brown, *International Politics and the Middle East*, pp. 198–233, "The Myth of the Great Power Puppeteer and Regional Puppets."
18 Ibid., pp. 175–94.
19 Chester L. Cooper, *The Lion's Last Roar: Suez 1956* (New York: Harper and Row, 1978).
20 Nadav Safran, *Israel the Embattled Ally* (Cambridge, Mass.: Harvard University Press, 1981), pp. 582–83.
21 Brown, *International Politics and the Middle East*, pp. v–vi. The 1973–74 Middle East crisis also brought with it for the first time an international economic crisis of considerable proportions, although oil had long

occupied an important place not only in regional but in world affairs. See George Lenczowski, *Oil and State in the Middle East* (Ithaca, N.Y.: Cornell University Press, 1960); *Middle East Oil in a Revolutionary Age* (Washington, D.C.: American Enterprise Institute, 1975).

22 George Lenczowski, *Russia and the West in Iran, 1918–1948: A Study in Big-Power Rivalry* (Ithaca, N.Y.: Cornell University Press, 1949).

23 See George Lenczowski, "The Arc of Crisis: Its Central Sector," *Foreign Affairs* 57, no. 4 (Spring 1979): 796–820. Also note Warren Christopher et al., *American Hostages in Iran: The Conduct of a Crisis* (New Haven, Conn.: Yale University Press, 1985); Gary Sick, *All Fall Down: America's Tragic Encounter with Iran* (New York: Random House, 1985).

24 On Israel's "special relationship" with the United States, see Peter Grose, *Israel in the Mind of America* (New York: Schocken Books, 1984); Reich, *The United States and Israel*, chap. 5; Safran, *Israel the Embattled Ally*, chap. 27.

25 See Bernard Porter, *The Lion's Share: A Short History of British Imperialism, 1850–1970* (London: Longman, 1975), p. 184, on imperial views about Indian and Egyptian capacities for "free institutions." As Said notes, Orientalism is a Western strategy of "distancing" Asia, of "Orientalizing" the Orient. See *Orientalism*, pp. 49–73.

26 Harry S. Truman, *Memoirs*, vol. 2, *Years of Trial and Hope* (Garden City, N.Y.: Doubleday, 1956), chap. 10. For the origins of the Jewish state ideal in Theodor Herzl's experience as correspondent for Vienna's *Neue Freie Presse* at the Dreyfus trial, see Carl Schorske, *Fin de Siècle Vienna: Politics and Culture* (New York: Random House, Vintage Books, 1981), pp. 149–71.

27 On State Department opposition to Truman, see Dean Acheson, *Present at the Creation: My Years in the State Department* (New York: Norton, 1969), chap. 20; Grose, *Israel in the Mind of America*, chaps. 9–12.

28 American popular and Orientalist images of the Arabs and Islam, which presumably influence presidents as well as other American political leaders, are discussed in Said, *Orientalism*, pp. 284–328.

29 On American Orientalists, see ibid., pp. 288–93, 314–20.

30 Safran, *Israel the Embattled Ally*, pp. 574–76.

31 See Harold H. Saunders, *The Middle East Problem in the 1980s* (Washington, D.C.: American Enterprise Institute, 1981), chaps. 3–4; Tillman, *The United States in the Middle East*, chap. 2. Note should also be made of the early, pioneering and influential study by George Lenczowski, ed., *United States Interests in the Middle East* (Washington, D.C.: American Enterprise Institute, 1968).

32 Brown discusses the historical continuity of "multilateralism" in the Eastern question before and after World War I in his *International Politics and the Middle East*, pp. 87–88.

33 Surely this was the case in the first Nixon administration, which entered office one and one-half years after the June war when Israeli occupation of the West Bank, Gaza, the Golan Heights, and Sinai was still very

much in a fluid state. See Robert J. Pranger, *United States Policy for Peace in the Middle East, 1969–1971: Problems of Principle, Maneuver, and Time* (Washington, D.C.: American Enterprise Institute, 1971).

34 See Saunders, *Middle East Problem in the 1980s*, chap. 4; Tillman, *United States in the Middle East*, chap. 7; Saudia Touval, *The Peace Brokers: Mediators in the Arab-Israeli Conflict, 1948–1979* (Princeton, N.J.: Princeton University Press, 1982), chaps. 1, 7, 9–11. Tillman advocates a strong American arbiter role.

35 Don C. Piper and Ronald J. Terchek, eds., *Interaction: Foreign Policy and Public Policy* (Washington, D.C.: American Enterprise Institute, 1983), chap. 3.

36 See Steven L. Spiegel, *The Other Arab-Israel Conflict: Making America's Middle East Policy, From Truman to Reagan* (Chicago: University of Chicago Press, 1985), chap. 9.

37 Tillman, *United States in the Middle East*, chap. 5.

38 Ibid., chap. 6.

39 See Spiegel, *Other Arab-Israel Conflict;* William B. Quandt, *Decade of Decisions, 1967–1976: American Policy toward the Arab-Israeli Conflict* (Berkeley and Los Angeles: University of California Press, 1977), pp. 1–36.

40 Both Spiegel and Quandt argue, however, for more concentration on presidential, as contrasted with bureaucratic, decision making.

41 Spiegel and Quandt, while never minimizing lobby activities in U.S. Middle East policy, think presidential leadership a more significant explanation for this policy. See Spiegel, *Other Arab-Israel Conflict*, pp. 390–94, and Quandt, *Decade of Decisions*, pp. 28–36. Tillman thinks presidential leadership in this policy highly desirable, but usually unattainable, given domestic pressures from Israel's supporters (*United States in the Middle East*, chap. 7).

42 The ideal of a democratically controlled foreign policy has been especially strong in American thinking since World War I. See Norman A. Graebner, "Public Opinion and Foreign Policy: A Pragmatic View," in Piper and Terchek, *Interaction*, pp. 12–14.

43 On the necessity for Saudi Arabia to maintain a position in some ways separate from U.S. foreign policy in the Middle East, see three interesting short presentations by Prince Bandar Bin Sultan: at Harvard University's John F. Kennedy School of Politics and Government, September 19, 1979; at the New York Council of Foreign Relations, January 28, 1980; and in a working paper for the Air University, U.S. Air Force, September 1979–February 1980, collected in Prince Bandar Bin Sultan, *Strategic Priorities* (published privately by Prince Bandar, 1980). The implications of this Saudi perspective for U.S. policy on the Palestine question is analyzed in Robert J. Pranger, "The Emergence of the Palestinians in American Strategy for the Middle East: Issues and Options," in Rashid Khalidi and Camille Mansour, eds., *Palestine and the Gulf* (Beirut: Institute for Palestine Studies, 1982), chap. 8.

44 Robert J. Pranger, "The President and the National Security Process," in Kenneth W. Thompson, ed., *The Virginia Papers of the Presidency*, vol. 5, White Burkett Miller Center Forums, 1981, pt. 1 (Washington, D.C.: University Press of America, 1981), pp. 1–21.

45 On the tension between Henry Kissinger and William Rogers in the first Nixon administration, see Henry A. Kissinger, *The White House Years* (Boston: Little, Brown, 1979), chap. 2. This went beyond Middle East issues to include other areas as well: See Raymond L. Garthoff, *Détente and Confrontation: American-Soviet Relations from Nixon to Reagan* (Washington, D.C.: Brookings Institution, 1985), chaps. 3, 5–9.

46 See Robert J. Pranger, "Lebanon and Its Political Change Events: The Pathology of Spasm Politics and the Challenge of Reconciliation," in Edward E. Azar et al., *The Emergence of a New Lebanon: Fantasy or Reality?* (New York: Praeger, 1984), chap. 3.

47 For a discussion of U.S. views of a strategic relationship with Israel, see Reich, *United States and Israel*, chap. 3. Also, Steven J. Rosen, *The Strategic Value of Israel*, AIPAC Papers on U.S.-Israel Relations (Washington, D.C.: American Israel Public Affairs Committee, 1982).

48 Said, *Orientalism*, pp. 288–93.

INDEX

ABOUT THE EDITORS AND CONTRIBUTORS

■

Peter J. Chelkowski has been a professor of Near Eastern Studies at New York University since 1968. He also has been director of the Hagop Kevorkian Center for Near Eastern Studies at NYU. Educated in Cracow, London, and Tehran, he has been the author, editor, or coauthor of a number of books, including *The Scholar and the Saint*, *Ta'ziyeh: Ritual and Drama in Iran*, and *Mirror of the Invisible World*.

Robert J. Pranger is currently a fellow at the University of Maryland's Center for International Development and Conflict Management. He was formerly vice president for External Affairs at the American Enterprise Institute for Public Policy Research. His books, articles, and monographs have focused on American policy for peace in the Middle East, nuclear strategy and national security, Soviet foreign policy, and in 1984 he coauthored *The Emergence of a New Lebanon*.

Gholam Reza Afkhami, a native of Iran, has been a resident scholar at the Foundation for Iranian Studies in Washington, D.C., and a visiting scholar at the Hoover Institution on War, Revolution, and Peace. Among other books, he has edited *Perceptions of Social Status in Rural Iran*, and he is the author of *The Iranian Revolution: Thanatos on a National Scale*.

John W. Amos is associate professor, Department of National Security Affairs, Naval Postgraduate School, in Monterey, California. He is the author of *Arab-Israeli Military/Political Relations: Arab Perceptions and the Politics of Escalation* and *Palestine Resistance: Organization of a Nationalist Movement*. His current research interests are Islamic fundamentalism, Islamic law, and Assyrian nationalism.

John Duke Anthony is president of the National Council on U.S.-Arab Relations and director of the council's Middle East Speakers Bureau. He was previously president of the Middle East Educational Trust, Inc. Among his more recent publications are *The Iran-Iraq War and The Gulf Cooperation Council* and *Goals in the Gulf: America's Interests and The Gulf Cooperation Council.*

Edward E. Azar is director of the Center for International Development and Conflict Management and professor of government and politics at the University of Maryland. He has coauthored two books on Lebanon: *Emergence of a New Lebanon* and *Lebanon and the World in the 1980s;* and he also has coauthored *International Conflict Resolution.* In addition, he edits the journal *International Interactions.*

Robert D. Burrowes currently is associated with the Hagop Kevorkian Center for Near Eastern Studies at New York University and is engaged in consulting and writing on political affairs. Along with publishing major articles in such journals as *World Politics,* the *Middle East Journal,* and the *Journal of Conflict Resolution,* he is the author of *The Yemen Arab Republic: The Politics of Development, 1962–1986.*

Hermann Frederick Eilts, a distinguished professor of international relations at Boston University, is the former U.S. ambassador to Saudi Arabia (1965–70) and to Egypt (1973–79). During his thirty-five years of Foreign Service experience he served as political officer in the embassy in Jidda, as director of Arabian affairs in the Department of State, and on a number of presidential missions to Saudi Arabia. He has received many professional and university honors.

Peter Gubser is the president of American Near East Refugee Aid (ANERA) in Washington, D.C. Actively involved with Middle East matters since the mid-1960s, he has written two books on Jordan: *Politics and Change in Al-Karak, Jordan* (1973) and *Jordan, Crossroads of Middle Eastern Events* (1983). He has, in addition, authored numerous articles on Syrian, Lebanese, and Jordanian subjects, and for some years has been engaged in socio-economic development projects in the region.

Emanuel Gutmann teaches politics at the Hebrew University of Jerusalem, where he was departmental chairman from 1970–75. He has been a visiting fellow and professor at Manchester University, the London School of Economics and Political Science, and Carlton University. Specializing in the politics of Israel and Western Europe, he has published on the 1981 Israeli elections and on the role of the churches in contemporary Western European politics.

Jacob M. Landau is professor of political science at the Hebrew University of Jerusalem. Among the more than a score of books he has written are *Jews in Nineteenth Century Egypt* (1969), *The Arabs in Israel: A Political Study* (1969), *Middle Eastern Themes: Papers in History and Politics* (1973), *Radical Politics in Modern Turkey* (1974), *Politics and Islam:*

The National Salvation Party in Turkey (1976), and *Tekinalp, Turkish Patriot* (1984).

Fred H. Lawson is assistant professor of government at Mills College, where he teaches international relations and Middle Eastern politics. His articles have appeared in *International Organization, The International Journal of Middle East Studies,* the *Journal of Peace Research,* and *Arab Studies Quarterly,* while his book, *Bahrain: The Modernization of Autocracy,* was published in 1986.

Ralph H. Magnus is associate professor and coordinator of Middle Eastern studies in the Department of National Security Affairs of the Naval Postgraduate School, Monterey, California. Since 1983 he has been executive director of the Americares for Afghans project of the Americares Foundation, providing medical aid to the civilian population and Mujahidin inside Afghanistan. He has edited several books, including *Gulf Security into the 1980s.*

Phebe Marr is presently a senior fellow at the National Defense University, Washington, D.C. She has written numerous articles for such scholarly publications as *Middle East Journal,* the *Journal of Developing Areas,* and the *International Journal of Middle East Studies,* as well as articles in the *Christian Science Monitor* and the *New York Times.* Her book, *The Modern History of Iraq,* appeared in 1984.

Yahya M. Sadowski in 1986 became a research associate at the Brookings Institution, where he analyzes the politics of agricultural development in Egypt, Syria, and Iraq. Since 1970 he has been studying Syria, and for the past six years he has been preparing a monograph on patterns of state formation in the Arab world. He has written for the *Middle East Journal,* the *Los Angeles Times,* and the *Miami Herald.*

Roger Savory, professor in the department of Middle East and Islamic studies at the University of Toronto, has a principal field of interest in the history of Iran from the thirteenth century to the present. He has produced a wide range of articles, reviews, encyclopedia entries, and chapters in books over the years, and his edition of *Introduction to Islamic Civilisation* first appeared in 1976 and has since been republished.

Robert Springborg is a senior lecturer in Middle East politics at Macquarie University, Sydney, Australia. He is the author of *Family, Power, and Politics in Egypt: Sayed Bey Marei—His Clan, Clients, and Cohorts.* His articles have appeared in *Middle East Journal,* the *International Journal of Middle East Studies, Middle Eastern Studies, Comparative Political Studies, Orbis,* the *Journal of Arab Affairs,* and others.

Arthur Campbell Turner, a political science educator and author for many years, published his first book, *The Post-War House of Commons* in 1942. Since then he has authored, among other works, *Bulwark of the West: Im-*

plications and *Problems of NATO, Towards European Integration, Tension Areas in World Affairs,* and *The Unique Partnership: Britain and the United States.* Since 1957 he has been a contributor to the *Encyclopedia Americana* annual.

Manfred Wenner is associate professor in the department of political science at Northern Illinois University. A specialist in the Arabian Peninsula, especially the Yemens, he has written *Modern Yemen, 1918–1966,* and coauthored *An Introduction to Yemen for Researchers and Scholars* and *Libraries and Scholarly Resources in the Yemen Arab Republic.* He also has published scholarly articles, reviews, encyclopedia entries, and chapters in books edited by others.

Sepehr Zabih is currently a research fellow at the Center for Middle Eastern Studies, Harvard University. His books include *The Communist Movement in Iran* (1966), *Iran's Revolutionary Upheaval* (1979), *The Mossadegh Era* (1981), *The Left in Contemporary Iran* (1986), and *The Iranian Army in War and Revolution* (forthcoming). He has published scholarly articles in a number of Middle East and political science journals.